DATE DUE

Workers in America

Workers in America

A Historical Encyclopedia

VOLUME 1: A–L

ROBERT E. WEIR

ABC-CLIO

Santa Barbara, California • Denver, Colorado • Oxford, England

Library of Congress Cataloging-in-Publication Data

Workers in America : a historical encyclopedia / Robert E. Weir.
    v. cm.
    Rev. ed. of: Historical encyclopedia of American labor / edited by Robert Weir and James P. Hanlan. c2004.
    Includes bibliographical references and index.
    ISBN 978–1–59884–718–5 (hbk. : alk. paper) — ISBN 978–1–59884–719–2 (ebook)
1. Labor—United States—History—Encyclopedias. 2. Working class—United States—History—Encyclopedias. 3. Labor movement—United States—History—Encyclopedias. 4. Industrial relations—United States—History—Encyclopedias. 5. Labor laws and legislation—United States—History—Encyclopedias. I. Weir, Robert E., 1952– II. Historical encyclopedia of American labor.
HD8066.H57   2013
331.0973'03—dc23   2012014153

ISBN: 978–1–59884–718–5
EISBN: 978–1–59884–719–2

17 16 15 14 13   1 2 3 4 5

This book is also available on the World Wide Web as an eBook.
Visit www.abc-clio.com for details.

ABC-CLIO, LLC
130 Cremona Drive, P.O. Box 1911
Santa Barbara, California 93116-1911

This book is printed on acid-free paper ∞

Manufactured in the United States of America

Entries appearing in these volumes are revised and expanded from Robert E. Weir and James P. Hanlan, eds., *Historical Encyclopedia of American Labor*. Westport: Greenwood Publishing Group, 2004.

Contents

Preface

As a historian, I try to avoid crystal ball gazing. My study of the past tells me that most people who have predicted the future have gotten it wrong, sometimes hysterically so and sometimes embarrassingly so. To be sure, a handful of observers manage to predict some things accurately, but I have come to believe that most of those predictions look good only if, like the famed seer Nostradamus, these futurists make their predictions so cryptic that one can read anything into them, or if we concentrate on only selected items and ignore what the prognosticators got wrong. At the end of the 19th century, for instance, Edward Bellamy foresaw the coming of radio, credit cards, and shopping malls. That seems impressive until one also recalls that he also thought that we would travel through the air in high-speed zeppelins, that women would speak and think like Victorians a hundred years into the future, and that in the year 2000 Boston would be a utopia devoid of crime, unemployment, inequality, private enterprise, racial strife, or money! And let us remember one of the most wrongheaded predictions of all time: Karl Marx predicted that the United States would be one of the first nations to abolish capitalism and move toward communism. (He also thought it unlikely Russia would do so, as it was insufficiently industrialized and lacked a strong working class.)

Having said all of this, an old axiom remains true: The best indicator of future behavior is past behavior. If one views indicators as probabilities rather than imperatives, and if one speaks of trends rather than predictions, then cautious forecasting is sometimes appropriate. (That is, if one is also prepared to be humble if proved wrong!) With this point in mind, I offer a few thoughts about current American trends on work and workers that warrant watching.

When the first edition of this work was published in 2004, labor historians such as myself engaged in vigorous debates over the future of the labor movement. Things seemed fairly bleak at the turn of the 21st century, but there were encouraging signs that, perhaps, labor unions could reverse more than two decades of erosion. And perhaps they will, but those prospects do not look nearly as hopeful as we enter the century's second decade.

One would have to be a foolish optimist to be cheered by much of what has occurred in the past few years. Put simply, organized labor is in serious trouble, and it is by no means certain that it will survive in forms now recognizable. As the revision of this encyclopedia was taking place, both Wisconsin and Ohio stripped public employees of many of their collective bargaining rights. Even Massachusetts, a state with a higher percentage of unionized workers than the national average, took steps to curtail public unions' ability to bargain over health care costs. These, mind you, are *public* unions—the very groups upon which organized labor had been placing great hope as, unlike workers in the private sector, most public employees' jobs are not subject to globalism, outsourcing, corporate downsizing, or job export to low-wage nations.

The one remaining ray of hope for unions is the fact that workers across the United States perceive corporate powerbrokers as arrogant, believe that management has too much power, and say that they would, if they could, join a labor union. Yet, as I write this preface, New Hampshire is considering adding its name to the list of right-to-work states that are making it harder for workers to organize, and an extremely conservative U.S. House of Representatives has blocked passage of the Employee Fair Choice Act, which would have allowed a union to negotiate a contract as soon as a majority of workers signed cards asking it to do so. Many members of the Republican Party make no attempt to hide either their contempt for labor unions or their desire to see the American Federation of Labor-Congress of Industrial Organizations (AFL-CIO) tossed upon the scrap heap of history. Of course, to be fair, there are quite a few labor activists who would shed few tears if the AFL-CIO ended up there.

To date, the AFL-CIO has not adapted well to political and economic trends since the mid-1970s. The most glaring cases in point have been its inability to make headway among either service-sector or white-collar workers. The AFL-CIO remains too identified with the blue-collar work whose role has been eroded in the postindustrial economy, and many of its campaigns appear to be rearguard actions designed to preserve jobs in what dispassionate observers perceive to be sunset industries.

Quite a few union supporters have called upon the AFL-CIO to rekindle the activism that marked union movements of the past. It is not at all clear that this is a good idea, either. The Change to Win Federation devotes a higher percentage of its resources to grassroots organizing, but its constituent unions have not fared any better than those inside the AFL-CIO, several have abandoned it, and the group's very survival is uncertain. Prevailing labor laws and political attitudes make old-style activism problematic. It is so easy to secure scabs these days that the prevailing belief is that any walkout that is not settled within two weeks probably cannot be won. As I was preparing the entry on the Verizon strike that took place in 2000, Verizon workers walked off their jobs again on August 6, 2011. Workers were not asking for huge wage increases, merely that a firm with billions of dollars of cash reserves not impose higher health care premiums. The strike was ended on August 22, but without a new contract. Verizon workers may yet negotiate a favorable deal, but it was deemed simply too risky to continue the strike.

The future of labor unions is in great jeopardy, though they probably will not disappear for exactly the reasons related to corporate culture that critics cite. Unions will, however, need to look very different in the future because a more basic problem today faces Americans—that is, the future of work itself is uncertain. Let us consider a past prognosticator who now seems like a prophet: Jeremy Rifkin. In 1995, Rifkin published *The End of Work*, in which he predicted that blue-collar work was a dead-end pursuit, that computers and other technological changes would displace millions of workers, that traditional market and public-sector capitalism models would become obsolete, and that millions of Americans would be forced into part-time and contingency labor. Rifkin was viewed as an alarmist, but in August of 2011, a phenomenon occurred that even thinkers during the Great Depression had seldom predicted: The percentage of unemployed Americans exceeded the percentage holding jobs in the manufacturing sector. And, yes, tens of millions have, indeed, joined the ranks of the secondary labor force of casual, part-time, and contingency workers. Economists now speak of a "natural" unemployment rate that is double that held to be the norm by their predecessors.

Whether Rifkin's gloomy assessment of the future of work comes to pass and whether it becomes necessary to make major structural adjustments to American society remain to be seen. It is, however, fair to say that the nature of work in the future is a great unknown. Great economic shifts are not unprecedented. The United States was a thoroughly agrarian nation at the time of its founding. Independent yeomen far outnumbered artisans and merchants. By the mid-19th century, the Industrial Revolution had transformed the economy of the United States and had ushered in such social changes as mass immigration and the emergence of two new social classes: the middle class and a permanent wage-earning working class.

Industrial might turned the United States into a world power. It also institutionalized capitalism and elevated from it from being contested to being the norm. By the 20th century, both the industrial system and the capitalist logic that powered it were so entrenched in the United States that the Great Depression and two world wars could shake, but not topple, them. When World War II ended, the United States was the world's unparalleled industrial leader.

The postwar boom and the outbreak of the Cold War presaged two more economic shifts: the acceleration of consumerism—often wrapped in middle-class ideology—and the development of what President Dwight Eisenhower dubbed the "military-industrial complex." The latter phenomenon funneled tens of billions of dollars into nonproductive, nonconsumer sectors of the economy such as the maintenance of a large standing military force and the creation of a massive arsenal that was largely stockpiled. The high costs associated with the Vietnam War, the recessionary trauma occasioned by soaring energy costs in the 1970s, and the end of the Cold War exposed much of the economic illogic of the military-industrial complex, but because millions of jobs had become dependent upon the perpetuation of the status quo, shifting economic resources proved politically difficult. In the interim, the American industrial system grew antiquated and uncompetitive. Deindustrialization claimed tens of millions of jobs from the late 1970s onward. Increases in the service sector offset some of the loss, although such growth has not yet provided workers with the same standard of living associated with 1950s consumer society. Family income rose beginning in the 1970s, but because more family members worked, not because jobs paid well.

By the early 1990s, many economists and labor analysts had begun to worry about the future of American work. More probably would have agreed with Rifkin had not his book hit the market at precisely the time in which the computer revolution went viral. Suddenly a new paradigm appeared that promised to drive the next big economic shift. Prognosticators once again appeared and the news was rife with stories of investment opportunities, start-up firms, independent entrepreneurs, humming Silicon Valley assembly lines, and jobs just around the bend on the Information Highway.

Some of this promise may yet come to fruition, but many of those mid-1990s stories seemed tragically quaint once the dot-com stock bubble burst in 2000. Most of the start-ups failed and billions of dollars of paper assets disappeared. More poignantly for American workers, assembly-line jobs shifted to low-wage nations overseas, and they were quickly followed by research jobs, data-entry jobs, and even ancillary service-sector work such as medical lab work, accounting, and sales. The Information Highway proved to be more like international airspace. The United States led the computer revolution, but within a single decade it was no longer the biggest player in the realm of production. The U.S. Department of Labor now projects that the information sector of the economy can expect, at best, a 4 percent increase in jobs by 2018, which will be more than offset by a projected 9 percent drop in telecommunications employment. Expectations are not good for manufacturing in any sense.

Not much that has been predicted for the postindustrial future has panned out. Free trade certainly has not done much for manual laborers; the optimistic forecasts attached to the North American Free Trade Agreement seem almost cruel in retrospect and give pause to those wishing to believe that future fast-track trade bills will fare any better. "Clean coal" remains an oxymoron, and the nuclear energy industry continues to be beset by safety problems, as even the casual observer of the 2011 Japanese tsunami or of Vermont Yankee's incident reports knows. At this writing, the future of the American economy remains tied to fossil fuels, which all but ideologues admit is unsustainable.

Most scholars agree that the workforce of the future will need greater education and "flexibility"—a loaded word that generally means workers cannot expect to stay in a particular occupation or job from hiring until retirement. At present, though, fewer than 30 percent of Americans hold a four-year college degree and the university system itself is in transition. In fact, many universities are the very models of contingent labor. By 2009, fewer than one-third of college professors were tenured or on tenure track; adjuncts now dominate the professoriate and are poorly represented by teachers' unions.

I have little desire to be the next egg-on-his-face prognosticator, so let me state that I do not know what the next American economic shift will entail. At present, both the biomedical and green technology fields hold promise, but they are ones that cannot be divorced from political debates and are not immune to outsourcing. Right now Americans are awaiting the "next big thing," and they hope that the past is a predictor that there will *be* a next big thing. Distressingly, the past also teaches us that it is the nature of empires to rise, crest, and decline. Pessimists point to the English Midlands as a likely harbinger of America's future—a postindustrial sea of unemployment, underemployment, and declining standards of living dotted with small islands of prosperity. The widening gap between rich and poor gives fuel to those predicting a two-tiered society of haves and have-nots. (Ironically, such a society would actually create the conditions that Marx predicted would have revolutionary consequences.)

In summary, the future of labor unions, work, and the American economy remains a huge unknown at present. My students often ask me what I think will happen in their lifetimes. (They are too polite to say, "When I'm as old as you.") I tell them the same thing I would advise readers of this encyclopedia: I do not know and there is no reason to think that any "expert" can tell you this. Study the past, pay attention to politics, and make up your own mind.

Acknowledgments

Thanks go to my friend and intellectual colleague Jim Hanlan of Worcester Polytechnic Institute, who was my coeditor on an earlier project of American labor, and to all the contributors of that volume. Thanks also go to my fall 2010 labor history class at the University of Massachusetts Amherst; some of the research they did made its way into this edition. In that spirit, a hearty call of appreciation goes out to Lauren Cerillo, Alex Chautin, Matt Creedon, Christoph Demers, Sean Duke, Michael Eressy, Charles Fielder, Spencer Gauvin, William Gravelle, Yusuf Hamdan, David Kamarski, Eric Lacombe, Dan Letorneau, Rob Muckle, Joshua Pitt, Camryn Roberts, and Michaela Twaroag. An extra-special "thank you" goes to Matt Maré, a graduate student in education who took my undergraduate course and helped me prepare numerous entries as his "special project" to obtain graduate credit.

Appreciation goes out to my colleagues at the University of Massachusetts Amherst for their intellectual inspiration and the forbearance of those who listened to me grumble during the days in which I was so immersed in this project that I could anticipate neither the path of the tunnel nor the light of its completion. I also appreciate the contact I have had with graduate students at UMass, many of whom offered thoughts that stuck in the back of my head and made their way into entries. A special shout-out goes to Bruce Laurie, my mentor and now an emeritus professor. I continue to be amazed by the depth of Bruce's knowledge, his critical analytical edge, and his ability to express complex ideas in plain speech.

Thanks also go to the staff and editors at ABC-CLIO, the publisher of this volume. I found them very personable, helpful in their suggestions, and willing to trust that I would deliver as promised. As an old labor advocate, I appreciated the fact that the bosses trusted the worker!

My love and deep gratitude go to my wife, Emily. She is always on the frontline of my shifting moods of the various projects I undertake, stands ready to offer suggestions, and is more organized than I could ever dream of being. She is my partner, my inspiration, and my foundation.

I dedicate this work to all of my students, past and present. Whenever one works on a research project, a tremendous amount of time is spent in solitary pursuit. Research has its rewards, but they pale in comparison with the joys of the classroom. I adore teaching and consider myself blessed to have the privilege of dealing with young people. So an extra-special "thank you" to all the students who have enriched my life at Milton High School, Community College of Vermont, Mt. Ida College, Smith College, Mount Holyoke College, the University of Massachusetts Amherst, and Westfield University.

How to Use This Work

Encyclopedias are deceptive in their surface simplicity. What could be more basic than listing topics in alphabetic order? The problem, of course, is that no single entry is discrete on its own. In the electronic age, hyperlinks can take a reader from one page to the next. In theory, these links allow readers to see the interconnectedness between people, movements, and concepts; in practice, they often induce a "surfing" mentality that fragments thought rather than unifying it. The challenge is, simply, one of showing interconnectivity in print in a way that keeps the narrative intact. This challenge presents a special dilemma for a topic such as the history of work and labor. Most entries touch upon the very *sine qua non* of social history: the troika of race, class, and gender. Moreover, there are additional factors to consider, including ethnicity, religion, regionalism, ideology, politics, and economics.

There are, in fact, so many intersections between ideas that to place a "See Also" section at the end of each entry would, in many cases, be as long as the entry itself. Instead, I have opted to use **bold type** to show the connections. Each place one encounters **bold type** is an indication that a separate entry exists for that reference, although only the first reference is so designated. This scheme is meant to encourage readers to digest the entire text and then cross-reference what is relevant to their pursuits rather than engaging in the back-and-forth surfing of hyperlink culture.

Each entry concludes with a "Suggested Reading" listing. I do not mean to imply that these works are necessarily definitive, superior, or exhaustive. In some cases, I have chosen works that are deeply familiar to me, but for the most part I have selected references because of their wide availability or because they are more readable for the target audiences for this reference work.

The target audience is, in order:

- Students taking AP (Advanced Placement) U.S. history and/or studying for the AP exam
- High school libraries
- Public libraries
- Undergraduate U.S. history students
- Generalists
- Journalists, writers, teachers, and researchers needing to familiarize themselves quickly with people, movements, and concepts

This encyclopedia is *not* a work aimed at labor historians or specialists, the bulk of whom would undoubtedly find the material insufficiently detailed and nuanced for their purposes. As in all reference works, this one aims to be the source for *first* resort, not the final word.

ACTORS AND LABOR

Although entertainment fields such as acting are not the first thing most people think of when they consider labor relations, actors are often among the first workers to be affected by technological and social changes. In the 20th and 21st centuries, the introduction of new technologies such as phonographs, radio, movies, network television, videocassettes, cable television, and the Internet have had tremendous impact on the working conditions and compensation for actors. In addition, actors have had to weather changing business practices that have altered the very definition of professionalism.

Prior to the 20th century, few actors had recourse to organized bodies to help them mediate disputes with employers. Most actors performed in theaters, music halls, and vaudeville venues in which basic standards such as determining professional status, wages, facility privileges, and working conditions were customary or individually negotiated. In practice, a few actors enjoyed fame and relative fortune, but many barely scratched out a living and the profession was viewed as tawdry by many Americans. That reputation was enhanced by the fact that actresses were sometimes forced into temporary prostitution to supplement their salaries, and actors often frequented flophouses, saloons, and cheap eateries to stretch their incomes. Theater owners (especially those owning chains), tour promoters, agents, and other managers mostly held near-dictatorial power. Two unions—the White Rats of America (formed in 1896) and the smaller Actors' National Union (formed in 1880)—had some success among vaudeville actors and led strikes in 1901, 1902, and 1916. The two organizations merged in 1910, and affiliated with the **American Federation of Labor**. Numerous smaller organizations were also established, including the Hebrew Actors Union.

Widespread success came with the launch of the Actors Equity Association (AEA), which was formed in 1913 and joined the AFL. It sought to negotiate across-the-board standards, a task that grew easier after a 1919 strike resulted in the AEA being recognized as a legitimate **collective bargaining** unit for actors. Membership soared from 3,000 to 14,000 and the AEA was able to negotiate criteria for being considered a professional, as well as standards on wages, hours, and working conditions. The AEA also represented directors and choreographers until 1959, when those groups formed their own union.

The invention of radio and improvements in motion pictures changed the way entertainment was consumed and led to new actor organizations. Movie actors often found themselves under such tight control by producers and studios that, in 1919, famed actors such as Charlie Chaplin and Mary Pickford joined forces with director

D. W. Griffith to form their own production company, United Artists. A "studio system" emerged nonetheless in which just five companies controlled much of the movie industry. As a result, actors had very little bargaining power with studios. In 1933, the Screen Actors Guild (SAG) emerged to challenge studio control. It did not gain traction until 1937, when the **National Labor Relations Act** (NLRA) led to negotiations between producers and the SAG. The SAG now negotiates such basic terms as membership rules, the way in which actors are billed in productions, compensation, **pensions**, and residuals (royalties paid on a per-view basis for performances).

The NLRA also helped the American Federation of Radio Artists, which formed in 1935, received an AFL charter in 1937, and signed its first union contract in 1938. In 1952, **jurisdiction** debates with a television actors' union led to a merger of the two organizations, and the resulting union became known as the American Federation of Television and Radio Artists (AFTRA).

Despite dire predictions from management, labor relations within the entertainment industry were mostly peaceful for a time, with the biggest controversy being AEA's opposition to Jim Crow laws and its refusal to condemn mixed-race productions. The AEA also courageously resisted the post-World War II **Red Scare**, which posed the first major challenge for the SAG since its recognition. From 1947 onward, Hollywood found itself under investigation for alleged **communist** subversion infiltration of the industry. Numerous actors, writers, and directors found their loyalty challenged, and the industry maintained a **blacklist** that endured into the 1960s and prevented many from finding gainful employment in film or television. The issue also bitterly divided SAG members: Some, including SAG President **Ronald Reagan**, cooperated with the blacklist, while others demanded resistance to it.

In 1960, the SAG engaged in its first **strike** related to a dispute with seven studios over residuals for films sold to television. Several smaller strikes took place over the next several years. The AFTRA found itself embroiled in a dispute over assignments for recently hired newsmen in 1967 and threatened a strike that was narrowly averted before the broadcast of the Academy Awards. Both it and the SAG faced numerous attempts to break their power in the 1970s. In 1974, television networks unsuccessfully attempted to overthrow the **union shop** the AFTRA maintained over news broadcasts. In 1978, both unions took part in a strike over the question of how actors would be compensated for work in commercials. (Many individuals hold dual memberships in the AFTRA and the SAG.) For its part, between 1976 and 1981, the AEA battled the National Labor Relations Board over extra fees it assessed to foreign "visitors" and other "aliens" acting on U.S. stages. The AEA mostly lost this battle, though it did negotiate a rule that visitors from Great Britain must get AEA approval.

In the 1980s, disputes arose over issues rooted in the rise of new technology. In 1980–1981, the SAG and the AFTRA negotiated over issues such as royalties for movies sold on videocassettes and salaries for made-for-television movies. The latter was settled only after a 1980 strike. The AFTRA was driven into bankruptcy when it lost a 1982 antitrust lawsuit related to its attempt to organize jingle writers. It enjoyed better success in Congress during the 1990s, when it aided in the passage of such landmark bills as the 1992 Audio Home Recording Act, the 1998 Digital

Performance Rights in Sound Recording Acts, and the 1998 Digital Millennium Copyright Acts, all of which deal (in part) with compensating actors for performances that are repackaged and sold in new formats.

The year 2000 saw a strike over commercials and payments of residuals. More than 135,000 actors struck the Association of National Advertisers and the American Association of Advertising Agencies. While the actors lost millions of dollars during their six-month strike, the greater Los Angeles area suffered losses in excess of $125 million when commercial production shifted to Canada and Europe. In the end, actors forced networks—but not cable stations—to pay residuals. Strikes also rocked the industry in 2008, which affected the Golden Globe Awards, and a 2009 job action that threatened cancellation of the Academy Awards broadcast was narrowly averted at the last minute. The latter dispute concerned disputes over control and residuals related to online content and commercials, an ongoing and unresolved issue.

In 2010, the SAG had 139,200 members and its president was the well-known actor Ken Howard. The AFTRA was headed by Roberta Reardon and had approximately 88,000 members, more than half of whom also belonged to the SAG. In March of 2012, the two unions merged, though their combined strength has dropped to around 105,000 members. The AEA has approximately 49,000 members and its president is Nick Wyman. All three unions are affiliated with the **American Federation of Labor-Congress of Industrial Organizations** (AFL-CIO), and both the SAG and the AEA also participate in the Associated Actors and Artistes of America, an AFL-CIO umbrella that emerged from the White Rats to coordinate policies in the performing arts. This organization is currently headed by Theodore Bikel. Professions such as writers, directors, camera operators, and technicians are represented by separate unions.

Suggested Reading

David Prindle, *The Politics of Glamour: Ideology and Democracy in the Screen Actors Guild*, 1988; Kerry Segrave, *Actors Organize: A History of Union Formation Efforts in America, 1880–1919*, 2007; Segrave, *Film Actors Organize: Union Formation Efforts in America, 1912–37*, 2009.

ADAIR V. THE UNITED STATES

Adair v. The United States, 208 U.S. 161 (1908), was an important U.S. Supreme Court decision during the **Progressive Era** that dealt with the legitimacy of **yellow-dog contracts**, in which workers pledged not to join **labor unions** as a condition of employment. The *Adair* ruling struck down sections of the 1898 **Erdman Act**, which forbade railroads engaged in interstate commerce from retaliation against workers who joined unions. The case involved the firing of a Louisville & Nashville Railroad worker named O. B. Coppage who was dismissed by railroad official William Adair. Coppage joined a labor union after having signed an agreement that he would not do so. By a 6–2 majority, the Supreme Court ruled that under the Fifth Amendment to the U.S. Constitution employees were free to sign yellow-dog contracts and that to uphold Coppage's suit would endanger personal liberty and property rights (the worker's labor).

A different man named Coppage was involved in the Supreme Court's 1915 decision in *Coppage v. Kansas*, 236 U.S. I., which strengthened the *Adair* decision by declaring that state laws forbidding yellow-dog contracts were also unconstitutional. In this case, the court ruled that under Fourteenth Amendment the freedom to enter into contracts was a fundamental right; thus Kansas laws against yellow-dog contracts were unconstitutional. In a vigorous dissent, Justice Oliver Wendell Holmes, Jr., argued that if workers believed that they could secure fair contracts only by joining a union, then yellow-dog contracts were violations of liberty. His logic factored into the 1932 **Norris-LaGuardia Act**, which finally banished yellow-dog contracts. The *Adair* and *Coppage* decisions stand as poignant examples of the limits of Progressive Era labor reforms. Although many important reforms were made in the early 20th century, the courts remained conservative and elected officials leery of bottom-up change.

Suggested Reading

Michael C. Harper and Samuel Joan Flynn Estreicher, *Labor Law*, 2007; Alfred H. Kelly and Winfred Harbison, *The American Constitution: Its Origin and Development*, 1976.

ADAMSON ACT

The Adamson Act (1916) established an eight-hour day for railroad workers engaged in interstate commerce, stipulated that railroads could not dock their pay to reflect the reduction in hours, and mandated that companies had to pay railroad employees time and a half for **overtime**. The act is named for Georgia Congressman William C. Adamson, who sponsored the bill. President Woodrow Wilson signed the bill largely because he feared that a planned strike by railroad brotherhoods would disrupt the defense industry, rather than for altruistic reasons. The Adamson Act nonetheless proved to be influential in the **eight-hour movement**'s long struggle to reduce the work week.

The Adamson Act also marked the first measure by Congress to regulate the hours of private workers. Although some federal employees won an eight-hour workday as early as 1868, shorter workdays were not strictly enforced, nor did the eight-hour day expand to the private sphere as quickly as activists hoped. Neither Congress nor the courts were inclined to enforce the eight-hour day; it was not until 1908 that the Supreme Court upheld the validity of various state eight-hour bills. It was no accident that the railroad industry provided a test case for the eight-hour day. Workdays were notoriously long in the railroad industry, and it was wracked by numerous bitter and dramatic strikes in the late 19th and early 20th centuries. These included the Great Labor Uprising of 1877, various strikes during the **Great Upheaval** of the 1880s, the Great Burlington strike of 1888, the New York Central strike of 1890, the Pullman boycott of 1894, and a strike against the Illinois Central that lasted from 1911 to 1914. By 1916, nearly all railroad employees worked at least nine hours per day, and many worked even more. Mandatory overtime was standard practice, and workers generally received only their standard pay for hours worked beyond their shift. Various labor organizations, including the **Knights of Labor**, the **American Railway Union**, and several railroad brotherhoods called upon the government to either seize or tightly regulate railroads. Although much rail traffic was subject to the provisions of the Interstate Commerce Act of 1887 and the Elkins Act of 1903, Congress and various presidents remained aloof from the battle until four brotherhoods threatened a strike in 1916.

The Adamson Act was hailed by most railway brotherhoods and, in 1918, the government actually seized control of the railroads for the duration of World War I. The Adamson Act was expanded in scope by the **Railway Labor Act of 1926** and amended in 1936. It was also influential in setting the precedent that the federal government could define a fair day's labor. That precedent found its fullest expression in the 1938 **Fair Labor Standards Act**, which reduced the work week to 44 hours, and a 1940 amendment that lowered it to 40 hours and thereby institutionalized the long-sought eight-hour workday.

Suggested Reading

R. Alton Lee, ed., *The Encyclopedia of the United States of America, Past and Present,* 1997; Walter Licht, *Working for the Railroad,* 1983; Frank Wilner, *Understanding the Railway Labor Act,* 2009.

AFFIRMATIVE ACTION

Affirmative action refers to programs, preferences, legal protections, and other steps that seek to compensate individuals belonging to social groups that suffered from past (or present) injustices that place them at an economic or social disadvantage. Affirmative action programs seek to reverse past patterns rooted in discriminatory distinctions made on grounds such as race, ethnicity, gender, and religious belief. More recently, affirmative action protections have been extended to categories such as sexual orientation and physical disability. In the United States, the term was first used by the National Labor Relations Board (NLRB), which complained that employers had not ceased in **unfair labor practices** banned under the **National Labor Relations Act**. Ironically, unions themselves were often guilty of discriminatory behavior; many constituent unions of the **American Federation of Labor**, for example, practiced racial discrimination.

Affirmative action is often seen as a logical extension of the equal protection clause of the Fourteenth Amendment. It first became associated with job opportunities in 1941, when President Franklin D. Roosevelt created the **Fair Employment Practices Commission** (FEPC). When former NLRB official Malcolm Ross took over as head of the FEPC in 1948, the term "affirmative action" began to appear in FEPC directives to employers that discriminated against workers because of their race, creed, color, or ethnicity. It had the effect of opening occupations such as railroad engineering to African American workers, although at the time few were clear on what affirmative action meant, what (if any) enforcement power the FEPC possessed, or whether it was even possible to stop discrimination. The FEPC's major goal was to ensure participation of minority workers in industries vital to America's participation in World War II.

Affirmative action received renewed attention with the U.S. Supreme Court's 1954 ruling in *Brown v. Board of Education of Topeka*, which desegregated public schools, but its present parameters were set largely because of actions taken in the 1960s. In 1961, President John F. Kennedy issued an executive order that required federal contractors to take affirmative action when hiring workers. Three years later, it was a centerpiece of Title VII of the Civil Rights Act. Two executive orders signed by President Lyndon Johnson in 1965 empowered the Office of Federal Contract Compliance to define affirmative action. Specific goals and timetables were adopted whose aim was to end discrimination. More controversially, targets often involved the implementation of quotas that conservatives decried as forms of "reverse discrimination" that violated color-blind provisions implied by the Constitution. Several legal challenges in the early 1970s failed, but the Supreme Court's 1978 ruling in *University of California Regents v. Bakke* greatly curtailed all quota plans, and opened the floodgates for other challenges. It also provided an opening through which ideological appointments were made to agencies monitoring affirmative action, especially the Equal Opportunity Commission and the Office of Federal Contract Compliance. Although affirmative action programs for women were given a boost by an executive order signed by President Jimmy Carter in 1979, by the 1980s many liberals complained that President Ronald Reagan had put into place officials who worked to undermine rather than enforce affirmative action. Courts, however, have more routinely curtailed affirmative action than enhanced it. The 1990 Americans with Disabilities Act remains the most recent major legislative attempt to expand affirmative action. In 1998, President Bill Clinton ordered a review of affirmative action that upheld the need for such programs but did little to strengthen them.

Organized labor has a mixed record on affirmative action. A few labor unions, such as the **United Auto Workers of America**, the **United Steelworkers of America**, the **United Farm Workers of America**, and the **Service Employees International Union**, have been strong backers of affirmative action. Others, especially building trades, police, and firefighters unions, have been more resistant. So, too, have been unions with in-place seniority systems that are vulnerable to legal challenges. Moreover, unions have struggled with rank-and-file resistance to affirmative action. Many workers continue to view affirmative action as a quota system that gives jobs to lesser qualified candidates and discriminates against white males. Others question why present-day workers must be penalized because of unfair practices that were abolished long ago. Still others complain that social class status is also worthy of affirmative action consideration, but is not taken into account. Recent revelations of how few working-class students attend elite colleges and universities gives merit to those charging class-based biases. The intense nature of the debate surrounding affirmative action suggests that it will remain a polarizing political issue for some time.

Suggested Reading

Robert P. Green and John W. Johnson, eds., *Affirmative Action*, 2009; Paul Moreno, *From Direct Action to Affirmative Action: Fair Employment Law and Policy in America, 1933–1972*, 1997; Tim J. Wise, *Affirmative Action*, 2005.

AFRICAN AMERICANS. *See* Affirmative Action; A. Philip Randolph Institute; Brotherhood of Sleeping Car Porters; Contingency Labor; Minority Labor; Slavery.

AGENCY FEE

An agency fee, also called a "fair shop fee" or an "agency shop fee," is a sum paid by employees in a **union shop** who do not want to join the union that represents the shop. That payment is usually less than the dues paid by union members. The logic behind assessing this fee is that individuals who do not join a union nonetheless reap advantages from the **collective bargaining** process. For instance, when a union contract is in place, all workers within a profession or job category are subject to the same **wage** rates and receive the same benefits.

Some employees object to dues money being used for political lobbying for causes they do not support, some fear that part of their money will be channeled into illegal activities, and some individuals are philosophically opposed to unionism. The 1977 court case *Abood v. Detroit Board of Education*, 431 U.S. 209, upheld the rights of individuals to withhold money used for political organizing—a principle extended to some private employees in the Supreme Court's 1988 ruling in *Communication Workers of America v. Beck*. Organized **right-to-work** groups, however, oppose coerced paying of union fees of any sort and argue that joining unions and paying dues should be a matter of individual choice. They often argue that agency fees violate the First and Fourteenth Amendments, though courts have disagreed with this position as long as certain stipulations are met.

Appeals to personal liberty notwithstanding, paying or withholding dues is more complicated than opponents claim. Unions claim, with some justification, that they should not have to subsidize "free riders" who benefit from services for which they have not paid. Agency fees have emerged as an attempted compromise. Employees who do not join a union pay the union what is essentially a fee for negotiating their contract. That amount charged to non-union workers usually deducts a calculated percentage of the regular dues that the union spends on matters other than directly representing workers in the workplace. Agency fees are common among public employees, as many of them are barred from specific political activity. This practice makes it easier to object to union money being spent for political purposes. In most cases, agency fees for public employees are regulated by state boards. In some cases, agency fees are considerably lower than union dues. In 2010, for example, non-union professors in the University of Massachusetts system paid $4 per week less than union members, a savings of more than $200 per year.

There is great debate over the very existence of agency fees, as well as how they are calculated. Loyal unionists argue that union membership should be a condition of employment in a union shop, but legal challenges have made this position increasingly untenable. Right-to-work states do not allow for union shops and the 1985 Supreme Court decision in *Pattern Makers v. NLRB*, 473 U.S. 95, declared that unions cannot demand full membership. At present, most agency fees conform to broad parameters set by the 1986 Supreme Court ruling in *Chicago Teachers Union, Local 1 v. Hudson*, 475 U.S. 292. Under this ruling, unions must provide a justification for the amount they assess, allow for speedy, impartial mediation of any objections to the fee, and place disputed amounts in an escrow account until resolution of the matter. In 2000, the U.S. Court of Appeals ruled in *Penrod v. the International Brotherhood of Teamsters* that the Teamsters had to reveal how much money was spent on political campaigns, and that unions had to submit to independent audits to justify their expenses.

The virulently anti-union National Right to Work Legal Defense Foundation continues to mount challenges to agency fees, but some unions have launched challenges of their own. In 2010, a case brought by the **National Education Association** on behalf of Washington State teachers made its way to the U.S. Supreme Court. The NEA contended that a 1992 state law requiring the union to obtain permission to spend money on political campaigning from each of its 80,000 bargaining unit members was overly restrictive and unconstitutional. The NEA's position got an unexpected boost by the Supreme Court's 2009 decision in *Citizens United v. Federal Election Commission No. 08-205*, which currently clouds all issues related to political spending. By striking down restrictions on how much money can be spent on political campaigns by either corporations or unions, the Supreme Court may have also undermined rules governing how much control employees or union members have over those funds. Then decision is likely to be revisited by Congress, the Supreme Court, or both.

Suggested Reading

"Fascist Soup," http://fascistsoup.com/2010/02/02/seiu-fair-share-payer-agency-fee-payer-or-non-member-union-rights/; National Right to Work, http://www.nrtw.org.

AGENCY SHOP. *See* Union Shop.

AGENT PROVOCATEUR

An agent provocateur, also called a labor spy, is a company-hired infiltrator who poses as a union member in an attempt to discredit the organization. The term can also refer to a paid saboteur who commits crimes and disguises them to look as if they were committed by union members. The latter type of agent provocateur is most likely to be used during a **strike**. Internal provocateurs seek to disrupt labor unions by intensifying factional strife within an organization, encouraging friction between labor groups, and inciting the rank-and-file to make rash statements or take violent action. Their ultimate goal is to make worker organizations liable to criminal prosecution or to discredit them before public opinion. They may also seek to create situations that lead to the arrest or public denouncement of key organizers, activists, and leaders. Tactics include writing inflammatory articles in union publications, making fiery speeches at union meetings and demonstrations that incite members to undertake foolish actions, and encouraging internal dissension. A favored tactic is spreading rumors that key union members are spies for employers or law enforcement—a ploy that helps conceal their own subterfuge. They may also engage in bombings, arson, and sabotage, but blame these activities on others.

Agent provocateurs were a common feature in labor/management disputes predating the **National Labor Relations Act** (NLRA). They were especially numerous in the mining and railroad industry, where detective agencies such as Baldwin-Felts, Thiel, and the **Pinkertons** specialized in providing undercover operatives that gathered information for clients and assisted in union-busting activities. There were so many labor spies that labor federations such as the **Knights of Labor** originally conducted their affairs in secret. One of the more famous agent provocateurs was Pinkerton agent James McParland, who allegedly infiltrated the **Molly Maguires** during the 1870s. Some historians doubt that he actually witnessed the events to which he testified, and still others think that he may have committed some of the crimes for which others were executed.

McParland was, however, merely the best-known agent provocateur. In organized labor's early days, there were very few strikes or unions in which labor spying was not an issue. An agent provocateur may have thrown the bomb that precipitated the 1886 **Haymarket** tragedy in Chicago, and they were certainly responsible for various acts of bombing mines and derailing trains. Labor spies were active in the **Colorado coal mine** struggles of the 19th and 20th centuries, the **West Virginia coal mine war** of 1919 to 1922, and the 1894 **Pullman strike**. Numerous spies infiltrated the **Industrial Workers of the World**, and industrialists such as John Rockefeller and Henry Ford kept labor spies on their payroll, with Ford continuing to do so long after the practice was made illegal.

The 1937 **La Follette Senate Committee** investigation of labor relations and civil liberties revealed widespread use of agent provocateurs. By then, the NLRA (passed in 1935) had made the use of labor spies and saboteurs illegal, but it actually did little to curtail the practice. Harry Bennett, the head of security for Ford Motor Company, retained numerous labor spies in defiance of the NLRA. Unions such as the **United Auto Workers of America** discovered, to their chagrin, that many top officials were actually labor spies. In 1957, the U.S. Senate Select Committee on Improper Activities in Labor and Management uncovered numerous incidents of illegal spying, revelations that led to the demise of the anti-union Labor Relations Associates. In more recent years, the **Detroit newspaper strike** was undermined by agent provocateurs, as was the 1990 **Pittston coal strike**. Wal-Mart has been accused of maintaining spies to ward off unionization efforts. Although the use of agent provocateurs is an **unfair labor practice**, personal testimonies reveal that the practice is widespread, investigation of allegations lax, and penalties for violation inconsequential considering that companies routinely spend millions of dollars either to break unions or to deter their formation.

Suggested Reading

Martin Jay Levitt, *Confessions of a Union Buster*, 1993; Stephen Norwood, *Strike-Breaking and Intimidation*, 2002; Robert Smith, *From Blackjacks to Briefcases: A History of Commercialized Strikebreaking and Unionbusting in the United States*, 2003.

AGRARIANISM

Agrarianism is both the practice of farming and a set of ideals that glorifies agricultural production and rural life. During the Colonial period, settlers of European descent linked farming done by yeomen who owned their own land to notions of independence and self-reliance. This ideal persisted long beyond the American Revolution. Indeed, it was not until the 20th century, long after farming was in decline, that agrarianism ceased to be the primary way in which most Americans constructed visions of the ideal life.

When Europeans established their North American colonies, most common people made their living from the land. Land holding was closely connected to wealth and vocation, so many Europeans imposed their social and religious views about property and productive labor onto unsuspecting **Native Americans**. The worldview of many European settlers in the future United States was shaped by the Protestant Reformation, particularly the idea that God gave humankind dominance over the land. Seizures of Native American lands were often justified through claims that by not making their lands "productive," Native Americans abrogated claims to them. Native Americans also found deeded land transactions baffling and often ceded land to colonists in the mistaken impression they had agreed only to mutual use of the land.

At the time of the American Revolution, farming and other rural pursuits such as hunting and trapping were the primary occupations of most whites residing in the English colonies. Even craft and trade was largely agrarian based. The new nation traded products and raw materials such as tobacco, timber, pitch, indigo, furs, and foodstuffs for finished goods. Many artisans produced goods either directly related to agriculture or in support of it. Cobblers made footwear from domestic hides, blacksmiths shoed work horses, and merchants traded in implements needed for farming. In like fashion, coopers, sawyers, and ship builders often supported the internal and external trade of agricultural products. Agrarianism was so engrained in the American psyche that intellectuals such as Benjamin Franklin and Thomas Jefferson argued that farming was the best way for most people to gain "independence," a term they interpreted in both political and economic terms. Franklin even argued that a man who did not own land could not be a trustworthy citizen, as he had no vested interest in society. In Thomas Jefferson's mind, the economic ideal was that the United States should remain an agricultural nation and rely upon European imports for what few manufactured goods Americans might need. He feared that if the **Industrial Revolution** came to America it would bring with it such widespread European social problems as poverty, slums, discontent, and environmental degradation. Indeed, although **capitalism** had begun to develop, the prevailing view into the 19th century was that working for wages should be a temporary pursuit, as it made a person dependent upon others rather than self-sufficient. In many places before and after the American Revolution, an individual had to own property to obtain the status of a "freeman" and gain the right to vote. This pattern persisted in many places until after the War of 1812 and in Rhode Island until the Dorr Rebellion of 1841–1842.

Thomas Jefferson's fears soon came to pass. Both the Napoleonic wars and the War of 1812 disrupted American trade with Europe. This had the eventual effect of encouraging domestic manufacturing, with factories emerging in New England and the Mid-Atlantic states. As early as 1830, it was apparent that some workers would toil for **wages** their entire lives, rather than using their savings to buy a farm and become yeoman farmers. The American Industrial Revolution was well under way by the 1840s, as improvements in agriculture increased yields while simultaneously reducing the need for human labor. Among the inventions that altered rural labor needs were Cyrus McCormick's mechanical reaper, introduced in 1834, and John Deere's steel plow, introduced in 1837. Despite such advances, however, most Americans were farmers on the eve of the Civil War. As late as 1890, some 9,960,000 Americans worked on farms, representing 42 percent of the nation's total workforce of 23,320,000. Even as America industrialized and urbanized, agrarianism remained the ideal for most Americans. In 1841, the Preemption Act set up provisions by which settlers (including squatters) could gain title to America's abundant public lands. It was one of numerous federal laws aimed at supporting agrarian ideals, the most famous of which was the Homestead Act of 1862, passed even as Americans fought a bloody civil war. Even post-Civil War labor organizations such as the **Knights of Labor** called for comprehensive land reforms to make farm ownership easier.

Agrarianism has been such a powerful ideal in American society that rural life and virtues have been widely romanticized. In reality, not all 19th-century farmers were Jeffersonian models of rural independence. The bulk of antebellum Southern agricultural workers were **slaves**, and the failure of **Reconstruction** after the Civil War saw the bulk of African Americans and poor whites become tenant farmers and sharecroppers rather than independent farmers. Farmers and ranchers everywhere felt the sting of economic changes that transformed their products from goods for local consumption into commodities for regional, national, and international markets. Banks, railroads, grain elevators, stockyards, and meatpackers increasingly dictated prices and production levels, often leaving farmers to struggle with high interest rates, exorbitant storage costs, and soaring freight bills. Farmers expressed collective anger by organizing reform groups such as the Grange, Farmers' Alliances, the Greenback and "free silver" movements, and the Populist Party.

These groups, especially the Populists in the 1890s, and **Progressive Era** movements such as the **Industrial Workers of the World**, the Citizens Non-Partisan League, and Minnesota's Farmer-Labor Party, helped legions of farmers, but gathering economic trends inexorably eroded agrarian ideals. First, expansion of the industrial and service sectors created a permanent wage-earning **working class** and shifted economic relations to money-based exchanges. Second, the scale of the economy favored large enterprises over small ones. Ranching was the first to give way to this trend. By the 1880s, much of the United States' meat came from large ranches employing wage-earners, not from small-scale ranchers. Nevertheless, it was not until 1920 that the number of Americans working in service occupations outnumbered those in agriculture. In that same year, the number of manufacturing jobs surpassed the number of farmers, although America was by then the world's leading industrial power.

The decline of family farms has accelerated dramatically since the late 1920s. During and after World War I, many farmers expanded their production to meet military needs and to feed war-ravaged Europe. As Europe recovered, American farmers faced sagging prices due to overproduction. The Great Depression officially began in late 1929, but many rural areas had fallen into decline years earlier. It is hard to pinpoint exactly when agrarianism ceased to be a dominant ideal for Americans, but the Great Depression's overall impact on rural America was such that agrarianism was clearly an eclipsed paradigm.

The depression ravaged rural America. Even New Deal programs such as the Agricultural Adjustment Act (AAA), which brought price subsidies for many commodities, favored large operations over small farms. Technological break-throughs such as gasoline-powered tractors, improved threshing machines, and hybrid seeds further reduced the need for agrarian labor. Although the total amount of tilled acreage increased slightly between 1930 and 1940, the number of farms and farmers actually declined. As farms were foreclosed, corporations bought and consolidated them. What came to be called "agribusiness" emerged in full force in the 1930s.

The post-World War II economic expansion did not involve resurgence in family farming. In 1930, more than 30 million Americans worked in agriculture; by 1950, barely half that number worked in the agrarian sector in any capacity, and the population devoted to small-scale agriculture plummeted. In 1950, just 15.3 percent of Americans lived off the land; by 1970, the number of independent farmers slipped to 8.7 percent. By 2010, approximately 10 percent of American workers were employed in the agricultural sector, but most farms were corporately owned and fewer than 2 percent of all farmers were independent. Despite these changes, the amount of acreage being tilled has remained relatively stable in the United States. For example, the amount of tilled acreage in 1990 was only slightly smaller than the 1930 acreage, but the average farm size was more than 300 percent larger. Between 1982 and 1997 alone, some 339,000 small farms ended up in the hands of approximately 2,600 consolidated operations. Today, producers, wholesalers, and retailers are often the same corporate entity. Firms such as Tyson and Perdue operate their own chicken ranches, just four firms control nearly three-fourths of all U.S. beef production, and corporate giants such as ConAgra, Cargill/Monsanto, Archer Daniels Midland, and AgriMark own the bulk of American farm and grazing lands. In the 1990s, there were reputedly some 100,000 family-run dairy operations, but that figure had dropped to approximately 65,000 by 2006. According to Vermont Senator Bernard Sanders, Dean Foods controls 40 percent of the entire U.S. milk market. The reality is that agrarianism has given way to agribusiness in contemporary America, and increasingly fewer Americans equate agrarianism with wealth, independence, or civic virtue.

Suggested Reading

Jane Adams, *Fighting for the Farm: Rural America Transformed*, 2002; Paul Conkin, *Revolution Down on the Farm: The Transformation of American Agriculture Since 1929*, 2009; United States Department of Agriculture, http://www.usda.gov/, accessed April 2010.

AGRICULTURAL LABOR RELATIONS ACT

The Agricultural Labor Relations Act—sometimes called the California Agricultural Labor Relations Act (ALRA)—was signed into law by California Governor Edmund Brown on June 5, 1975. The ALRA is the agricultural analog to the **National Labor Relations Act**, whose provisions excluded farm workers. The ALRA guarantees **collective bargaining** rights for farm laborers. They may openly discuss unionization, display union regalia, and engage in organizing efforts without reprisal on the part of employers. Like the NLRA, the ALRA specifies procedures by which unionization campaigns and votes take place. An Agricultural Labor Relations Board (ALRB) hears procedural complaints filed by either unions or employers and is empowered to declare an **unfair labor practice**. Its members are appointed by the governor and confirmed by the California state senate. There is also a general counsel, appointed by the governor, who investigates unfair labor practice complaints and allegations and determines whether an official complaint should be filed. The counsel also presents the case to an administrative law judge; that judge's decision may be appealed to the ALRB, which has enforcement power over decisions reached.

The ALRA specifies that employers must negotiate in good faith with workers who opt to form unions. **Wages**, working conditions, benefits, and hours of employments must be subject to collective bargaining and cannot be arbitrarily imposed. An employer cannot fire, discipline, or discriminate against any employee for joining a union. In like fashion, the ALRA protects the rights of farm workers who do not wish to join unions.

The ALRA was the by-product of years of organizing efforts by **César Chávez**, **Dolores Huerta**, and others associated with efforts to form the **United Farm Workers of America** (UFWA). It brought relative peace to California farm regions after years of bitter disputes between labor and management, as well as unsettling **jurisdiction** disputes within organized labor's own ranks. Chávez and the UFWA called for a boycott of several California grape growers in 1965 and were on the eve of settlement when the International Brotherhood of Teamsters called a strike in Salinas Valley that sandbagged UFWA negotiations. The two unions then engaged in several years of acrimonious competition that placed farm workers in the middle. The UFWA almost collapsed during its battles against the Teamsters, but it ultimately proved to have more influence in the state capital. Its greater level of influence, a successful march that dramatized continuing struggles against grape growers, and the lobbying efforts of Dolores Huerta helped secure passage of the ALRA and ensured the survival of the UFWA.

In the early years of the ALRA, the bulk of decisions went in favor of farm workers. Since 1984, however, roughly half of all unionization votes have failed and the ALRB has overseen numerous **decertification** votes. The makeup of the ALRB has become highly politicized, and its advocacy for workers often waxes and wanes depending on the political views of the sitting governor. UFWA leadership complains that the Teamsters continue to undermine the union's efforts, and growers have launched several attempts to repeal or weaken the ALRA. Although the latter efforts have been unsuccessful, the overall impact of the ALRA has not reached the potential its advocates had hoped it would. California's ALRA remains (on paper) the strongest farm labor act in the United States, although several other states have enacted their own versions of the bill and the 1992 Migrant and Seasonal Agricultural Worker Protection Act extended federal protections to many farm workers. The California act specifies that written **contracts** must be issued and regulates standards of farm and transportation safety, housing quality, and numerous other working conditions. Nevertheless, there is far less labor legislation governing farm workers overall than most other categories of workers.

Suggested Reading

Agricultural Labor Relations Act Handbook, http://are.berkeley.edu/APMP/alra/alrahandbook.pdf; Maralyn Edid, *Farm Labor Organizing: Trends and Prospects*, 1994; Susan Ferriss and Ricardo Sandoval, *The Fight in the Fields: Cesar Chavez and the Farmworkers Movement*, 1997.

AIRLINE STRIKES

In the 19th and early 20th centuries most long-distance freight and passengers were carried by railroads. After World War II, and particularly after the introduction of jet engines during the 1950s, many of the services once dominated by railroads or long-distance trucking began to shift to airlines; so, too, have some of the troubled labor/management struggles associated with earlier periods of railroading. Airline labor negotiations fall largely under the provisions of the 1926 **Railway Labor Act** (RLA). As a consequence, disputes in the industry often take a long time to resolve, because the RLA contains language requiring mandatory hearings before a Board of Mediation and **arbitration** of disputes. If either side rejects mediation or arbitration, the president of the United States can impose a 30-day "cooling off" period if a dispute threatens public interests.

Organized airline employees are generally scattered among different unions. The Air Line Pilots Association, International, represents approximately 66,000 pilots. The **International Association of Machinists and Aerospace Workers** (IAM) represents many on-ground maintenance personnel. Air traffic controllers, baggage handlers, and terminal workers usually have their own unions, although the Transport Workers Union (TWU) represents many on-ground service workers as well as some flight attendants. Other flight attendants are represented by unions affiliated with the International Brotherhood of Teamsters. In addition, numerous other smaller unions represent airline workers.

U.S. airlines have endured disputes over traditional issues such as **wages**, hours, and benefits, but also over issues more germane to transportation industries such as management-imposed **pattern bargaining**, long-haul/short-haul salary differences, the size of work crews, responsibility for maintenance f aircraft, the amount of time employees are on call, and per diem reimbursements for employees forced to be away from home. Also like railroad employees, airline employees have been greatly affected by industry consolidations and mergers. Since the airline industry was **deregulated** in 1978, major airlines have faced competition from lower-cost carriers dubbed "no-frills" airlines, as well as from various regional airlines. Deregulation has made the overall industry volatile and worsened labor relations. Since the 1980s, airline companies have aggressively sought **concessions** from their workers. Major carriers have also set up their own lower-cost regional networks, often hiring new personnel at lower wages than workers earn in their main divisions. The latter complain that these "B-scale" hires suppress wage rates for all employees. For their part, airline companies have been hurt by rising fuel costs and by lost revenues in the wake of the September 11, 2001, terrorist attacks on the United States. Increased costs for security have cut into already thin revenue streams. In the wake of these challenges, numerous airlines that were once flagship carriers have disappeared or have merged with other carriers. This list includes Braniff, Eastern, Pan American, and Trans World Airlines (TWA). By 2010, the largest U.S. airline company by volume of passengers carried was Southwest Airlines, a no-frills carrier, and—with the 2010 merger of Northwest and Delta—just four other major American carriers remained.

The first known major airline strike took place in 1932, when pilots briefly struck Century Air to resist a corporate raider's takeover attempt. Pilots struck TWA in 1946, a dispute resolved by arbitration. In 1954, American Airlines endured a short strike. The first crippling airline strike took place in 1966, when 35,400 IAM machinists acted in concert against five airlines. Their 43-day strike disrupted about 60 percent of the nation's passenger service during the height of the summer travel season. President Lyndon Johnson intervened in the dispute, which led to the industry's first multi-carrier contract.

Short strikes by Eastern Airlines pilots and National Airlines flight attendants hurt Christmas travel in 1975, but unions were thunderstruck when President **Ronald Reagan** fired 11,345 workers during the 1981 **Professional Air Traffic Controllers Strike**. This action opened the door for several particularly nasty labor/management battles. Corporate raider Frank Lorenzo, already known for engineering a takeover of National Airlines in 1978 and for manipulating TWA stock to his advantage, purchased Continental in 1981. Nineteen months of fruitless negotiations led Continental machinists to strike the airline in August 1983. Lorenzo replaced them with **scabs**. He then led Continental into bankruptcy and voided all existing union contracts. When Continental emerged from bankruptcy in 1986, most pilot salaries dropped by a third to a half of what they had been before the bankruptcy.

Striking Comair pilots walk a picket line in Hebron, Kentucky, outside the Cincinnati/Northern Kentucky Airport on March 26, 2001. (AP/Wide World Photos)

Lorenzo also headed Eastern Airlines during its worst labor troubles. Previous CEO Frank Borman had contentious relations with his unions. When he retired in 1986, Lorenzo took over. In 1988, Eastern laid off 4,000 workers and demanded concessions from the remaining employees. When the IAM and TWU struck on March 4, 1989, and pilots called a **sympathy strike**, Lorenzo repeated his Continental tactic and led Eastern Airlines into bankruptcy. This time, however, huge losses prompted him to sell the company to Donald Trump in 1989. In 1991, Trump shut down Eastern and sold it to Continental; 5,000 of Eastern's 18,000 employees lost their jobs.

In 1985, United Airlines weathered a 29-day pilots strike. Pilots charged that CEO Richard Ferris sought to break their union by attempting to replace existing wage rates with those of B-scale regional subsidiaries. Ferris was unsuccessful and United's board fired him.

President Bill Clinton imposed RLA cooling-off periods that settled a five-week dispute between American Airlines and flight attendants in 1993. In 1997, Clinton intervened in a threatened pilots' strike against American Airlines; pilots settled for less than they had hoped. He was not able to avoid a **lockout** of Northwest pilots that took place between August 28 and September 12, 1998—the nation's longest airline disruption since the Eastern troubles of 1989. Northwestern had forced more than $886 million in concessions from its workers after it declared bankruptcy in 1991. The carrier soon rebounded with record earnings, but resisted pilots' efforts to share in the prosperity their sacrifices had helped bring about. Thirty-nine months of negotiations won pilots a 3 percent salary increase, but even that required nine additional months of mediation. Pilots balked when Northwest tried to impose a salary formula pegged to its competitors' salary structures. There were also disputes over job security, pensions, retroactive raises, profit sharing, and Northwest's attempts to merge the pay scales of the parent company with that of lower-paid regional affiliates. Federal mediation sided mostly with the pilots.

Northwest's recent history with employees has been contentious. In 2000, the company sued a flight attendants' union to gain access to computer files related to alleged **sick-outs** used against the company. It fired a dozen employees. In 2005, it also battled an independent union representing 4,750 mechanics, cleaners, and janitors. Northwest hired scabs to replace them, although the final settlement gave displaced workers recall rights and small payments to strikers. In 2007, Northwest gained concessions from flight attendants, but the narrow margin of victory (2,996 to 2,862 votes to approve concessions) makes future disputes likely. Its ongoing financial woes led to a 2008 merger with Delta, but pilots' unions are restive, especially over scheduling disputes.

Current financial uncertainty and a past pattern of troubled labor relations suggest that the airline industry will remain volatile in the foreseeable future. In 2005, United Airlines canceled employee pensions, an action certain to resonate throughout the industry.

Suggested Reading

Aaron Bernstein, *Grounded: Frank Lorenzo and the Destruction of Eastern Airlines*, 1999; James T. Schultz and Marilyn C. Schultz, "Northwest Airlines Strike and Labor Negotiations," http://aabss.org/journal1999/f29Schultz.html; David Walsh, *On Different Planes: An Organizational Analysis of Cooperation and Conflict among Airline Unions*, 1995.

AIR TRAFFIC CONTROLLERS. *See* Professional Air Traffic Controllers Organization Strike.

ALLIANCE FOR LABOR ACTION. *See* American Federation of Labor-Congress of Industrial Organizations; Reuther, Walter; Teamsters; United Auto Workers of America.

AMALGAMATED ASSOCIATION OF IRON, STEEL, AND TIN WORKERS

The Amalgamated Association of Iron, Steel, and Tin Workers (AAISTW) was an early attempt to organize the iron and steel industry, which was among the most union-resistant of all of the heavy industries that emerged from the American **Industrial Revolution**. Iron production was already an important industry at the time of the American Revolution, especially in Massachusetts, Pennsylvania, and New Jersey. By the 19th century, iron ore also was being mined and puddled across the Midwest. Tin mills opened after 1895, when the effects of the McKinley tariff made smelting more profitable. The biggest breakthrough, however, was the introduction of the Bessemer process in 1855; this hot-air extraction system removes impurities from "pig" iron, the brittle product created by mixing coke, limestone, and iron ore. The Bessemer process allowed for the practical production of steel, perhaps the single most important product of the 19th-century Industrial Revolution.

Iron, tin, and steel production was important in industrialization, but these industries were not known for benevolent owners. The first unions evolved from pre-industrial **apprentice** and **journeymen** associations. The AAISTW was formed in 1876 when the Sons of Vulcan; the Associated Brotherhood of Iron and Steel Heaters, Rollers, and Roughers; and the Iron and Steel Roll Hands of the United States merged. Shortly thereafter, the Nailers' union also joined the AAISTW. At the time of the merger, the union had just 3,775 members. It was a conservative **craft union** noted for its cooperation with management and its distaste for **strikes**. In the 1880s, AAISTW president William Weihe did not even resist the 12-hour/7-day work week standard imposed by many employers. When the **Knights of Labor** sought cooperation with the AAISTW, it was usually rebuffed—snubs that led the Knights to form their own prototypical **industrial unions**, which, unlike the AAISTW, did not confine themselves to skilled workers.

The AAISTW's cautious unionism did little to insulate the group from the sting of steel barons such as Andrew Carnegie. The AAISTW was forced into strikes against Carnegie concerns in 1881, 1884, and 1885. In an 1887 action against the Edgar Thompson works in Pittsburgh, Carnegie imported **scabs** to break the strike. In 1887, the AAISTW was a weak organization and joined the newly formed **American Federation of Labor** in hopes of rebuilding its strength. The AAISTW represented about 24,000 workers by the early 1890s, nearly all of whom were

English-speaking, highly skilled workers at a time when waves of immigration and automation were transforming both the composition of the workforce and the production process. This reality set the stage for one of the era's most dramatic clashes, the 1892 **Homestead Steel lockout and strike**. Carnegie's Homestead works, located near Pittsburgh, was managed by Henry Clay Frick. Despite the facility's robust profits, Frick decided to break the union. He instituted large wage cuts, announced that Homestead would operate as a non-union **open shop**, and refused to negotiate with the AAISTW, which represented only 800 of the plant's 3,800 workers. Frick instituted a **lockout** that ultimately resulted in wage cuts as high as 60 percent, the mass firing of many Homestead workers, and a general impoverishment of the region.

The AAISTW was eviscerated by the Homestead strike and was reduced to representing a handful of steel mills, mostly in the West. In 1901, and again in 1910, it attempted to organize workers at U.S. Steel, a corporate conglomerate formed when J. P. Morgan purchased Carnegie assets in 1901. Both attempts failed, and by the 1910s, low pay and six 12-hour days were standard practices at most steel mills. The AAISTW also took part in the nationwide **Steel Strike of 1919** led by **William Z. Foster**, which also failed. In fact, only the **Industrial Workers of the World** (IWW) made any headway in winning concessions from iron and steel companies. In 1907, IWW smelter workers in Tacoma, Washington, won an eight-hour day and pay raises. The IWW also led small strikes in Pennsylvania and Indiana in the first decade of the 20th century, and its 1909 action in McKees Rock, Pennsylvania, is sometimes cited as the first successful **sit-down strike**. The IWW's actions were most isolated, however, and iron and steel remained mostly unorganized.

The AAISTW did not fare well. By the early 1930s, it was a federal labor union within the AFL. In 1935, it had only 8,600 members. That same year, however, **Philip Murray** and the Steel Workers' Organizing Committee (SWOC) made inroads into the steel industry by casting its lot with the **Congress of Industrial Organizations** (CIO). Both SWOC and the CIO revived the Knights of Labor's tactic of organizing steelworkers as a single group rather than subdividing them into craft unions. SWOC's efforts led to the formation of the **United Steelworkers of America**, which joined the CIO and absorbed the AAISTW.

Suggested Reading

David Brody, *Steelworkers in America: The Non-union Era*, 1960; Robert Gordon, *American Iron, 1607–1900*, 2001; Sidney Lens, *The Labor Wars*, 1974; William Serrin, *Homestead*, 1993.

AMALGAMATED CLOTHING WORKERS OF AMERICA

The Amalgamated Clothing Workers of America (ACWA) was one of several garment workers unions formed to combat the exploitation of needletrades workers in the **Progressive Era** and one of the United States' first successful **industrial unions** in that trade. It officially formed on December 26, 1914, to address perceived weaknesses of its predecessor union, the United Garment Workers (UGW), which had been badly weakened during strikes in 1909–1910.

The textile industry was the first large-scale concern of the American **Industrial Revolution** and one of the first to institute an industrial regimen upon workers, especially machine-paced work, time-clock discipline, long hours, and **speedups**. Numerous attempts were made to unionize textile workers, beginning with the **Lowell Female Labor Reform Association** in the 1830s. The annual production of miles of cotton, woolen, and synthetic textiles led to a corresponding explosion in needletrades such as embroidery, garment making, and assorted apparel. Both textile manufacturing and the needletrades, however, were also marked by high turnover, and large numbers of immigrants often made up their workforce. The **Knights of Labor** made inroads in these areas in the late 19th century, as did the **Industrial Workers of the World** in the early 20th century, but the mass-production methods in place in giant industrial concerns—as well as the large numbers of female and immigrant workers—

made needletrades workers a poor fit with the Anglo male- and craft-dominated **American Federation of Labor** (AFL). No union was particularly successful in organizing **outsourced** needletrades work, much of which was done as **homework**. The needletrades also spawned an inordinate number of **sweatshops**, the curtailment of which was a major goal of all garment worker unions.

The ACWA recognized the need to organize immigrant laborers, many of whom worked in sweatshops. Unlike its UGW predecessor, which ignored immigrant tailors toiling in the production of men's suits and coats, the ACWA had numerous Lithuanian, Italian, and Jewish members. **Sidney Hillman**, a Lithuanian Jew, was the first president of the ACWA, and held that post until his death in 1946. Hillman also kept the ACWA outside of the AFL, except for a brief flirtation in 1933. The ACWA embraced both **industrial unionism** and militant tactics. In 1935, it became one of the first unions to affiliate with the **Congress of Industrial Organizations** (CIO). The ACWA also pioneered in delivering union-negotiated benefits for members in such forms as unemployment insurance, free checking

Factory workers like these now enjoy far greater protection under the law due in large part to the work of unions. The Amalgamated Clothing Workers of America, for example, secured better working conditions in garment factories and sweatshops during the early part of the 20th century. (Corel)

accounts, cooperative apartments, employer-paid health and life insurance schemes, and union-operated daycare centers.

The ACWA engaged in numerous acrimonious strikes during its history. A 1919 job action against menswear manufacturer Hart, Schaffner, and Marx established an industry standard of a 44-hour work week. The ACWA also took part in the nationwide **textile strike of 1934**. Although the strike was largely unsuccessful, the ACWA added 50,000 members to its rolls and Sidney Hillman became a key advisor to President Franklin Roosevelt. In 1937, the CIO set up the Textile Workers Organizing Committee, and the ACWA often coordinated its efforts with the newly formed Textile Workers Union of America (TWUA). Despite setbacks while attempting to organize southern workers in **Operation Dixie**, by 1952 the ACWA was able to negotiate the first master agreement in the menswear industry. The ACWA joined the AFL-CIO when the merged federation formed in 1955.

In 1963, the TWUA and ACWA tried to organize J. P. Stevens workers. Although the U.S. Supreme Court upheld a ruling in favor of the unions in 1967, it took a 17-year boycott of Stevens before a contract was finally signed in 1980. (The Hollywood film *Norma Rae* depicts this struggle.) Other bitter battles included a strike and boycott against Oneita Knitting Mills in 1973, and a 22-month campaign against Farrah that ended in 1974; both led to ACWA contracts. The union has also championed investigations into "brown lung" disease, a respiratory ailment associated with long-term inhalation of textile dust.

In 1976, the ACWA and the TWUA merged to form the American Clothing and Textile Workers Union (ACTWU). In the 1990s, ACTWU launched what are now ongoing campaigns for national health insurance, the reform of labor laws, and investigations into capital flight. By then, however, both the needletrades and textiles were in such decline that many analysts consider them to be **sunset industries**. Particularly significant was the ACWA's unsuccessful effort to thwart passage of the **North American Free Trade Agreement**. The clothing industry has been especially hard hit by the closing of U.S. plants, which have relocated in low-wage nations in Latin America, South America, and Asia. In 1995, the various remaining unions, including ACTWU, merged to form the **Union of Needletrades, Industrial, and Textile Employees** (UNITE). In 2004, UNITE merged with the Hotel Employees and Restaurant Employees (HERE) and now calls itself UNITE HERE. The united organization successfully settled a 2005 strike in Atlantic City and negotiated a settlement for 60,000 hotel workers in 2006. As these actions indicate, the union's current focus is on the hospitality industry, as the American needletrades are in severe decline.

Suggested Reading

Sue Davidson and Joan Jensen, eds., *A Needle, a Bobbin, a Strike*, 1984; Foster Dulles and Melvyn Dubofsky, *Labor in America*, 1993; Union of Needletrades, Industrial, and Textile Employees and Hotel Employees and Restaurant Employees, http://www.unitehere.org/about/, accessed April 2010.

AMALGAMATED MEAT CUTTERS AND BUTCHER WORKMEN OF NORTH AMERICA. *See* Butchers.

AMERICAN FEDERATION OF GOVERNMENT EMPLOYEES

The American Federation of Government Employees (AFGE) is the United States' largest union representing federal civil service employees. More than 2.75 million men and women work for the federal government, and approximately 600,000 of them belong to the AFGE. Its 1,100 locals are affiliated with the **American Federation of Labor-Congress of Industrial Organizations** (AFL-CIO).

Although federal employment is often popularly associated with work inside the District of Columbia, just 250,000 federal employees actually work in Washington. The AFGE represents a broad spectrum of workers ranging from food inspectors, janitors, and office workers to park rangers, overseas diplomats, and scientists. The AFGE is a hybrid union representing both **blue-collar** and **white-collar** workers. Its highest levels of representation among the latter include workers in the Department of Veterans Affairs, the Social Security Administration, and the Department of Justice.

Organizing public employees has long been a difficult challenge. Local and state government often took a dim view of union efforts among taxpayer-supported employees, and many federal agencies have their budgets set by the U.S. Congress, a restraint that limits their power of **collective bargaining**. The unique status of public employees also means that the applicability of existing labor laws is not always clear. It was not until the 1912 Lloyd-La Follette Act that federal employees had any official right to organize—and that bill expressively forbade **strikes**. Many government workers are deemed "essential personnel," a designation that limits on-the-job action. In the past, public employee unions often fared poorly during strikes. During the **Boston Police Strike of 1919**, the government of the Commonwealth of Massachusetts fired most of the striking officers. This action had repercussions for federal workers when Congress made it illegal for police and firefighters in the District of Columbia to unionize, a law not repealed until 1939. More recently, more than three-fourths of the nation's air traffic controllers were fired by President **Ronald Reagan** during the 1981 **Professional Air Traffic Controllers Organization Strike**.

Despite these constraints, federal civil service workers have long felt the need to organize. In some ways, federal employees blazed the trail for nonpublic employee union campaigns. In the 19th century, the civil service bureaucracy was small, but federal workers were notoriously overworked and underpaid. Navy yard employees struck for shorter hours in 1835 and 1836. In 1840, President Martin Van Buren signed a 10-hour bill for federal employees, and the **eight-hour movement** found a receptive audience among federal workers. An eight-hour day was granted in 1868, but federal laborers and mechanics struggled for four years to restore the 20 percent wage cuts that came with it. Although government employees often complained that the eight-hour rule was widely violated, they were among the first group of workers to gain a shorter workday and inspired workers seeking to slash hours in the private sphere. Government workers also achieved a victory in 1883, when Congress passed the Pendleton Act, which set up the Civil Service Commission to fill many federal jobs through examinations and qualifications rather than political patronage.

Both the **Knights of Labor** and the **American Federation of Labor** represented small numbers of federal workers, but progress in unionizing such employees remained modest until the establishment of the National Federation of Federal Employees (NFFE), which received an AFL charter in 1917. The Great Depression ravaged the civil service, with layoffs, wage cuts, and supervisor favoritism being the order of the day. The AFGE formed when the NFFE disaffiliated with the AFL in 1931; those workers who wished to remain in the AFL formed the AFGE in 1932. John Shaw was elected the first AFGE president, but the AFGE expanded mostly because of the work of chief organizer Helen McCarthy. Within three years, McCarthy increased AFGE membership to more than 20,000 individuals organized into 13 districts and more than 200 locals. The union's first major campaign was to restore wage cuts, an audacious undertaking during the Great Depression. Wages did slowly rise, although this achievement may have been due to an improving economy rather than AFGE pressure. The AFGE also won the right for workers to determine their own beneficiaries for their retirement funds, and it increased the amount of sick leave an employee could accumulate.

The 1935 **National Labor Relations Act** included protections for government workers, but upheld the 1912 ban on strikes and did little to alter definitions of how essential personnel was defined. During both World War II and the Korean War, the AFGE curtailed some union activities, much of it voluntary but some because perceived national emergencies would have made job actions of dubious legality. Other labor laws have placed federal employees in limbo. The 1939 Hatch Act made partisan campaigning by federal employees illegal and forbade membership in ill-defined "subversive organizations." The Federal Pay Act of 1945 gave government workers a nearly 16 percent pay increase, but placed further restrictions on the union's political voice. The 1947 **Taft-Hartley Act** reiterated the Hatch Act's political restrictions, imposed a **no-strike** clause on federal workers, and reversed some gains under the NLRA by defining government employee groups as "associations" rather than unions. Anticommunist hysteria during the **Cold War** hampered AFGE efforts even further. Senator Joseph McCarthy's (unfounded) accusations of communist infiltration of the U.S. State Department made the AFGE susceptible to **Red Scare** fear tactics. During the 1950s, the AFGE was able to win some concessions on wages, **overtime** pay, and work transfers, but overall it made only modest gains until the 1960 presidential election.

President John F. Kennedy was more sympathetic to federal employees than most of his predecessors, and his Executive Order 10988 established relaxed rules for federal unions by establishing three tiers of representation for federal employees, with those at the highest level enjoying full collective bargaining rights. Workers also gained wage increases, better **pensions**, and improved benefits. AFGE membership jumped from 61,000 in 1942 to more than 108,000 in 1962.

The AFGE enjoyed even greater membership surges after 1964, when President Lyndon Johnson's Great Society programs increased the size of the federal bureaucracy. The **postal strike of 1970** dramatically altered the landscape for public employees. Postal workers committed felonies by the very act of walking out, and stood steadfast despite government threats and the orders of union leadership to raise the strike. Neither NFFE nor AFGE members actually went on strike, and the leadership of each organization appealed to members to stay on the job. AFGE leaders cited the need to remain on the job while the United States was fighting in **Vietnam**—a call that resonated with some employees but alienated others. In the end, all government employees gained a 6 percent pay increase when the postal strike was settled. More importantly, the nation's first successful government employees strike pointed to the potential strength of concerted power.

After 1972, federal employees struggled against changing public opinion and political adversity. Quite often, the AFGE's success has been dependent upon the ideology of the president in power. Taxpayer revolts were exploited by conservatives, who often used civil service employees as rhetorical whipping posts to rail against wasteful government expenditures. President Richard Nixon clashed with the AFGE and, in 1974, the U.S. Supreme Court upheld the ban on political activity by federal employees. Nixon's successor, Gerald Ford, vetoed Congressional reforms of the Hatch Act that would have bypassed part of the Supreme Court's decision. Federal employees cheered the election of Jimmy Carter in 1976, and Carter's 1978 Civil Service Reform Act was a milestone for federal workers. It created a Federal Labor Relations Authority (FLRA) for federal workers, which was modeled after the NLRA's board for private-sector employees. It also established the Merit Systems Relations Board to protect workers not covered by the FLRA.

These gains notwithstanding, the AFGE's bargaining position deteriorated significantly with the election of Ronald Reagan to the presidency in 1980. Reagan's anti-big-government rhetoric was matched by actions found objectionable by the AFGE and the NFFE. Reagan **subcontracted** government work to private-sector employers, threatened to trim the federal bureaucracy, imposed a federal worker pay freeze, fought the union over extending Occupational Safety and Health Administration safety and health rules for federal workers, opposed **comparable worth** legislation, sought to impose mandatory drug testing on federal employees, and supported **decertification** votes by Internal Revenue Service employees. The AFGE responded by supporting the massive 1983 Solidarity Day rally against Reagan policies, and by launching successful organizing drives in the Veterans Administration and Social Security Administration. The union also set up a political action committee (PAC) to raise money for political campaigns. (The creation of a PAC helped members of the union circumvent rules banning direct partisan political activity.)

Relations were equally testy between the AFGE and President George H. W. Bush, who opposed a Government Employee Bill of Rights crafted by the AFGE in 1986. Government/employee relations improved when President Bill Clinton signed a 1993 reform of the hated Hatch Act, which allowed federal employees to engage in political activity outside of the workplace as private citizens. Clinton's Executive Order 12871 created a National Partnership Council (NPC) with presidential cabinet members and representatives of the AFGE, the NFFE, and several smaller federal unions. The NPC is essentially an intermediary body that seeks to resolve problems arising among federal employees before they become serious. In 1994, however, relations soured again when the 1994 Congressional elections returned a Republican majority to Congress. The AFGE and other federal employee unions opposed implementation of House Speaker Newt Gingrich's "Contract with America," which contained anti-union pledges. Employees suffered directly when Republicans shut down the government several times in late 1995 and early 1996, thereby denying paychecks to federal employees. AFGE and its PAC worked hard to reelect Clinton in 1996 and reduce Republican strength. AFGE workers were stunned by the tragic domestic terrorist bombing of a federal office building in Oklahoma City in 1995 that killed 168 employees, and some identified antigovernment rhetoric as a contributing factor in the tragedy.

Shaky relations between the AFGE and Republican Party arose anew when George W. Bush entered the White House in 2001, and Bush's abolition of the NPC served to increase tension. The AFGE opposed Bush's attempt to streamline the Equal Employment Opportunity Commission's complaint-processing guidelines because employees felt the proposed streamlining would eliminate due process protections. The Homeland Security Act passed in the wake of the September 11, 2001, terrorist attacks on New York and Washington, D.C., has also proved contentious. Bush originally wanted to hire private-sector security firms to protect airports and public buildings, largely because he did not want to increase the number of unionized federal workers. Bush also sought the right to hire and fire civil servants in designated security-sensitive positions without going through normal civil service procedures, a move opposed by the AFGE and blocked by the U.S. Senate in 2002. In addition, Bush sought to consolidate numerous agencies and eliminate union jobs in the process. Like most unions, the AFGE found the Bush administration tone deaf to workers' rights to organize. In 2011, the AFGE organized around 44,000 Transportation Security Administration employees, a move Bush resisted when he was in office.

The AFGE has an admirable record on civil rights and gender equity, holds periodic civil rights conventions, and maintains a Women's and Fair Practices Department, whose current head is Andrea Bruce. As of 2012, the president of the AFGE was John Gage. The union enjoys good relations with the NFFE, which is again affiliated with the AFL-CIO as Federal District 1 of the **International Association of Machinists and Aerospace Workers**.

Suggested Reading

American Federation of Government Employees, https://www.afge.org/, accessed April 19, 2010; Kate Bronfenbrenner and Tom Juravich, *Union Organizing in the Public Sector: An Analysis of State and Local Elections*, 1995; Jack Stieber, *Public Employee Unionism*, 1972.

AMERICAN FEDERATION OF LABOR

The American Federation of Labor (AFL) was the one of the forerunners of the **American Federation of Labor-Congress of Industrial Organizations** (AFL-CIO), currently the United States' largest labor federation—that is, an umbrella organization that coordinates policy and actions for various affiliated national and international unions.

The AFL emerged in the late 19th century and is generally considered the nation's second successful labor federation. Forming unions of any sort was difficult in an era in which there was no federal legislation guaranteeing **collective bargaining** rights. For much of the 19th century, labor unions were deemed illegal criminal conspiracies in many parts of the United States. Even where local or state laws were favorable to worker associations, few laws existed to protect workers from reprisals from anti-union employers. Pre-Civil War attempts to form broader alliances between labor groups were mostly abortive. The **National Labor Union** formed in 1866, but its unusual structure and short life span were such that it was more of a prototypical lobby group than a true labor federation. For this reason, many scholars consider the **Knights of Labor** (KOL), formed in 1869, to be the first federation worthy of the label.

At the time the KOL formed, organized labor was particularly vulnerable and many national and local **craft unions** were collapsing. The KOL initially survived by operating in secrecy and by abandoning the craft union model. When craft unions were revived in the late 1870s, discussion of forming a federation of trade unions was rekindled. The AFL is a direct offshoot of a November 15, 1881, meeting of 100 KOL and trade union representatives in Pittsburgh, Pennsylvania, convened by two secret organizations, the Knights of Industry and the Amalgamated Labor. The meeting was chaired by John Jarrett, president of the **Amalgamated Association of Iron, Steel, and Tin Workers**, and delegates announced the formation of the Federation of Organized Trade and Labor Unions (FOTLU). **Samuel Gompers** headed the FOTLU's Committee on Organization.

In its early days, the FOTLU's agenda differed very little from that of the KOL, which initially saw the group as facilitating its own forays into organizing skilled workers. Both organizations called for an end to convict and **child labor**, advocated immigration restriction, and lobbied for the creation of a bureau of labor statistics. The FOTLU did, however, reject as too radical KOL calls for government ownership of railroads and as impractical the KOL's emphasis on forming producer and consumer **cooperatives**. More ominously for the future, the FOTLU restricted membership to skilled workers, unlike the more inclusive KOL. The FOTLU posed little threat to the KOL, however, as it was largely an only-on-paper organization.

The FOTLU evolved into the AFL shortly after the **Haymarket bombing** in May 1886. Trade union leaders convened a December conference in Columbus, Ohio, and announced the formation of the American Federation of Labor. The AFL patterned itself after British trade federations that emphasized member benefits, high dues, centralized control over local unions, and collective bargaining. By 1886, craft unions had reemerged to the point where many skilled workers had come to believe that their interests were best met though separate organizations rather than being subsumed within the KOL's broad reform agenda. Samuel Gompers—who held the AFL's presidency from its founding until his death in 1924, except for a single year—was especially adamant that the KOL did not adequately protect the rights of skilled workers. His own Cigar Makers International Union had feuded with the KOL during the 1880s; hence Gompers launched an aggressive campaign to convince skilled workers to quit the KOL in favor of the AFL. Gompers fervently believed that occupational commonality was the only true basis of labor solidarity, and he found distasteful the KOL's practice of mixing trades in its locals. He also disagreed with the KOL's position that **strikes** should be avoided whenever possible; in his mind, the withholding of labor was organized labor's strongest weapon. Gompers also came to see **capitalism** as a permanent feature of American society. Unlike the KOL, which called for an end to the **wage** system, the Gompers-led AFL was dedicated to a model of **pure and simple unionism** that focused on short-term objectives, relied on point-of-production activism rather than politics to secure worker benefits, limited membership to wage workers, and organized strictly on occupational lines. Gompers saw the AFL as a pragmatic organization as opposed to the KOL, which he saw as unrealistically utopian in nature.

To KOL critics, the AFL was elitist, was insular, and lacked vision. There is no doubt that it was often considerably less enlightened than the KOL and subsequent federations such as the **Industrial Workers of the World** (IWW). The AFL also adopted a policy known as "voluntarism," a component of which gave each constituent union autonomy over its own affairs. As a consequence, each union was free to establish its own racial and gender guidelines. The bulk of AFL unions excluded African Americans and women, made minimal attempts to organize semiskilled or unskilled labor, and were at the fore of calling for immigration restriction. The IWW lampooned the AFL as the "American Separation of Labor." In like fashion, although the KOL was officially a nonpartisan organization, it called upon workers to advance labor's agenda through intelligent voting. The AFL was, at first, aggressively apolitical, as it saw the workplace as labor's arena of struggle, not the ballot box. Moreover, the AFL did not always hold firm to its own principles. Gompers had ridiculed the KOL for allowing employers to join the organization, but the AFL proved even more comfortable working closely with employers. In 1900, Gompers even joined the **National Civic Federation** (NCF) to promote peaceful meditation of labor disputes. To his critics, Gompers's membership in the NCF was viewed as cooperating with organized labor's enemies.

Criticisms of the AFL notwithstanding, by the 1890s it was waxing and the KOL waning. By 1932, 85 percent of all U.S. union workers would be under its aegis. The AFL's brand of pure and simple unionism proved most potent during the first two decades of the 20th century. In cities such as San Francisco, it was so successful in organizing construction workers that the federation began to moderate its position on politics. The AFL remained officially nonpartisan, but whenever possible it informally aligned with pro-labor politicians and their parties. This type of political leverage paid off in the early 20th century. Despite constant attacks by the anti-union **National Association of Manufacturers** (NAM), the AFL's membership exceeded 1.6 million in 1904, which made it the largest federation in U.S. history to that point. Within 10 years, its ranks swelled to 2.6 million despite the fact that the **Progressive Era** was often hostile to organized labor.

By the 20th century, the KOL was moribund. The AFL also benefitted from fears that the IWW was too radical; some employers signed AFL contracts, regarding this organization as a safer alternative. Unlike the IWW, the AFL supported the United States' entry into World War I. AFL membership grew during the war, but so, too, did the number of non-union workers and the membership of independent labor unions. By then, the AFL's racist, sexist, nativist, and conservative policies had come to hinder its expansion. Although the AFL occasionally granted charters to unions with **minority** workers, as in the case of the **Brotherhood of Sleeping Car Porters**, it did so grudgingly. It also often marginalized such unions within the federation. In like fashion, the union's conservative leadership stifled those of a more radical bent, which led activist unions such as the **Amalgamated Clothing Workers** to stay outside the AFL fold. Moreover, Gompers's death in 1924 occasioned the ascendancy of **William Green** to the AFL presidency. Green was less forceful than Gompers at precisely the moment that an anti-union backlash was gathering steam and technological changes were calling craft organizations into question. The 1920s economy was supercharged, but the business community was considerably less reform-minded than the **welfare capitalists** of the pre-World War I era. The NAM spearheaded the **open shop** movement, which sought to operate union-free workplaces. Violence against unionists was commonplace during the postwar **Red Scare**, and the U.S. Supreme Court routinely handed down antilabor decisions during this era. The onset of the Great Depression took a further toll and, by 1933, AFL membership had sunk to pre-World War I levels.

The AFL's fortunes reversed with the advent of the New Deal and President Franklin Roosevelt's support for working-class movements. In 1934, the AFL added nearly 1 million new members. This resurgence took place amid the reality that craft unionism was becoming increasingly archaic in an age of mass industrialization and job deskilling. The AFL's penchant for dispersing **assembly-line** workers among multiple craft unions came under attack by advocates of **industrial unionism**. The AFL had made tentative experiments with industrial unionism in the 1910s and 1920s, but in 1935, an internal cadre—backed by automotive, mine, and rubber workers and led by the **United Mine Workers' John L. Lewis**—created the Committee on Industrial Organizations to pursue industrial unionism on a wider scale. Rather than redouble its efforts, the AFL denounced Committee members as dissidents and, in 1936, suspended unions controlled by them. Those unions promptly bolted from the AFL and, as the **Congress of Industrial Organizations** (CIO), expanded membership in mass industry. Moreover, because the CIO was overtly open to politics, it obtained greater political access than the AFL.

Despite losses in mass-production industries, the AFL made other gains in the 1930s through 1950s, especially in construction, transportation, communication, and service industries. Although the labor history of the 1930s and 1940s often focuses on the CIO, the AFL was actually the more stable of the two organizations. The CIO's organization of mass industry led to clashes with the era's richest and most powerful business interests, some of whom spared no expense in battling unions. Moreover, the CIO's assembly-line workers were more easily replaceable in labor disputes than highly skilled AFL workers. The AFL remained a larger organization throughout the pre-World War II period, and recent scholarship suggests that the CIO's strength may have been exaggerated.

Anticommunism provisions in the **Taft-Hartley Act** proved more of a problem for the CIO than for the AFL and, in 1950, the CIO expelled more than 600,000 members in unions that ran afoul of the Taft-Hartley law. Moreover, the collapse of the CIO's **Operation Dixie** left it bloodied and weakened. The AFL and CIO cooperated with each other in exacting no-strike pledges from members during World War II, and the spirit of cooperation continued after the war. Both federations signed nonraiding pacts, both purged left-wing radicals, both embraced the U.S. government's **Cold War** policies, and both came to embrace **business unionism** precepts. Mutual opposition to the Taft-Hartley Act and the AFL's signaled willingness to compromise on CIO concerns such as advancing racial equality, industrial unionism, and grassroots organizing led to merger talks. In December 1955, the AFL and CIO merged to create the 15.5 million-strong American Federation of Labor-Congress of Industrial Organizations. The AFL's **George Meany** became the first AFL-CIO president.

Suggested Reading

Paul Buhle, *Taking Care of Business*, 1999; Philip Foner, *History of the American Labor Movement*, 10 vols., 1947–1994; Philip Taft, *The A.F. of L. from the Death of Gompers to the Merger*, 1959; Robert Zieger, *American Workers, American Unions*, 1986.

AMERICAN FEDERATION OF LABOR-CONGRESS OF INDUSTRIAL ORGANIZATIONS

The American Federation of Labor-Congress of Industrial Organizations (AFL-CIO) is the United States' largest labor federation. It was formed in December 1955, when the **American Federation of Labor** resolved its differences with its rival, the **Congress of Industrial Organizations**, and the two merged into a single federation. To its critics, the AFL-CIO is a bloated bureaucracy that has neglected grassroots organizing in favor of engaging in political activity with which many of its members disagree. AFL-CIO defenders argue that only a unified organization can be powerful enough to counter the power of organized capital and pressure for the legal and legislative changes needed to protect workers.

After World War II, many of the key differences between the AFL and the CIO had lessened. Both organizations embraced the aggressive anticommunism associated with the **Red Scare**, both accepted much of the logic underlying the **Cold War**, both were bent upon overturning the hated **Taft-Hartley Act**, and both had come to see the Democratic Party as a friend of labor unions. Moreover, both organizations were under new leadership, as both AFL President **William Green** and CIO head **Philip Murray** died in 1952. Their replacements, **George Meany** (AFL) and **Walter Reuther** (CIO), had come to believe that organized labor needed to adopt new tactics to deal with changing social and legal realities. In 1953, the two federations signed a pact to ban **raiding** each other's members, which paved the way for merger discussions. The merger was made possible when the larger AFL agreed to several key CIO demands, including an acknowledgment that **industrial unionism** organizational models made more sense in some industries. An Industrial Union Department (IUD) was established to advance organization in mass industry. The AFL also rhetorically agreed with the CIO's more liberal stand on race and gender. In exchange, the CIO agreed that it would redouble its efforts to remove **communist** influence from its ranks. At the time of the merger, the AFL had 80 affiliated unions and the CIO had 33. It was announced that the combined AFL-CIO had 15.5 million members, although some scholars believe the actual strength was closer to 13 million. Meany assumed the presidency and the AFL's William Schnitzler became secretary-treasurer. Reuther took the third top post, that of executive vice president; he also headed the IUD.

Part of the logic of merger comprised **business unionism**, especially the idea that organized labor's structure had to parallel that of organized **capitalism** so that it could act as a countervailing force within the American economy. Many within the movement hoped that the AFL-CIO could become the de facto left wing of the Democratic Party, thereby steering the passage of labor reform laws, especially the repeal of the Taft-Hartley Act. That outcome did not happen. Agreements on paper notwithstanding, there were great differences between the AFL and the CIO, as well as a deepening ideological divide between Meany and Reuther. Meany interpreted the post-World War II economic boom more optimistically than Reuther, who had been a **socialist** in his youth, with Meany expressing the belief that the working class and middle class were converging, while Reuther emphasized the gaps between the two. More significantly, Meany's strident anticommunism led the AFL-CIO into a reflexive acceptance of U.S. foreign policy objectives. It also led the organization to give short shrift to industrial organizing drives and to improvement of its record on race and gender equity.

The early promise of the AFL-CIO went largely unfulfilled. The AFL-CIO formed the Committee on Political Education (COPE) to help elect politicians sympathetic to labor, but saw many of its endorsed candidates go down to defeat. Even when COPE-endorsed candidates won, as in the case of John Kennedy in 1960, those officials often disappointed the AFL-CIO. Frustration magnified internal differences during the social upheavals of the 1960s. In general, former CIO unions (and Reuther) were quicker to embrace the civil rights movement, criticize the war in Vietnam, and address sexism within organized labor. Meany clashed with black leaders such as **A. Philip Randolph** and numerous constituent unions—mostly former AFL organizations—opposed **affirmative action** policies adopted by Presidents John Kennedy and Lyndon Johnson. Conservative unionists, particularly in the building trades, also clashed with youthful antiwar demonstrators, many of whom were union members. Moreover, AFL-CIO leadership took a dim view of workplace militancy in the 1960s and 1970s, especially groups engaging in **wildcat strikes** and radicals such as the **Dodge Revolutionary Union Movement**.

Meany and Reuther grew to despise each other, so much so that in 1967 Reuther invited the Teamsters—a union Reuther helped expel from the AFL-CIO in 1957—to join his own **United Auto Workers of America** (UAW) union in forming a new federation, the Alliance for Labor Action (ALA). From 1968 to 1972, the nation's two largest trade unions operated outside of the AFL-CIO. The ALA was short-lived and an odd amalgamation of one of the most progressive unions (UAW) and one of the least democratic (Teamsters). It did pay more attention to community organizing than the AFL-CIO did, but it did not long survive Reuther's death in a 1970 plane crash. Even so, animosity remained strong enough that the UAW did not return to the AFL-CIO until 1982 and the Teamsters in 1987.

Interestingly, the AFL-CIO made some of its greatest strides during the period in which its internal and external feuds raged hottest. AFL-CIO support helped secure passage of the 1970 **Occupational Safety and Health Act** and the federation reached its historical apex in the early 1970s, with some of 17 million workers under the AFL-CIO's aegis. It also made tentative strides in casting off outmoded views. "Constituency groups" formed within the federation to address special concerns within the union movement; among them were the **A. Philip Randolph Institute** (1965), the Coalition of Black Trade Unionists (1972), the **Labor Council for Latin American Advancement** (1973), and the **Coalition of Labor Union Women** (1974).

By the 1970s, however, the AFL-CIO was administratively top-heavy and critics continued to complain about its overly conservative leadership, rigid bureaucratic practices, and placement of too much trust in the Democratic Party at the expense of grassroots organizing. Some of these complaints proved prescient when the U.S. economy soured after 1973, when the Organization of Petroleum Exporting Countries (OPEC) withheld petroleum from the world market. Organized labor was badly hurt by the inflation and economic stagnation that ensued. Employers responded to the economic crisis by **downsizing** their workforces and often used the crisis as a way to rid themselves of higher-paid union workers. They also wrested **concessions** from workers and used company resources to promote the passage of anti-union **right-to-work** legislation.

Union workers were especially disappointed by the lack of progress made during the administration of President Jimmy Carter (1977–1981), and some came to question the very wisdom of labor's support for the Democratic Party. The elevation of **Lane Kirkland** to the presidency of the AFL-CIO in 1979 gave hope to reformers inside the federation. Those hopes proved in vain, however, as Kirkland presided over one of the most challenging periods in the history of organized labor. Critics of the AFL-CIO's alliance with the Democratic Party were silenced during the presidencies of Republicans **Ronald Reagan** (1981–1989) and George H. W. Bush (1989–1993). Reagan made no secret of his distaste for labor unions, and his presidency witnessed numerous ruinous strikes that ended in workers losing their jobs; among these were the 1981 **Professional Air Traffic Controllers Organization Strike** and the **Hormel lockout** of 1985. Moreover, Reagan's support for business **deregulation** made it easier for companies to shift jobs out of the United States, which led to a wave of **deindustrialization** that carried off tens of thousands of union jobs. By 1992, AFL-CIO membership was down by nearly

3 million from its 1972 peak and was more than 1 million short of the number of members it claimed at the time of the 1955 merger.

The election of President Bill Clinton in 1992 rekindled complaints that Democrats paid insufficient attention to organized labor. Especially troublesome was Clinton's signing of the 1993 **North American Free Trade Agreement** (NAFTA) and his insistence that **globalism** rendered **protectionism** obsolete. The AFL-CIO did manage to help defeat a "fast track" bill in 1995 that would have made future free trade agreements easier to put into place. Unions within the AFL-CIO also liberalized their practices in the 1990s, including embracing gay rights and protecting the rights of both legal and illegal immigrant workers. By 1995, however, enough AFL-CIO members were discontented to elect **John Sweeney**, an outspoken opponent of both Kirkland and NAFTA, to head the AFL-CIO. Sweeney pledged to devote more resources to organizing and to oppose vigorously the expansion of free trade policies.

Sweeney largely kept those promises, but it did not prove enough to counter the reality of globalism, the virulently antilabor policies of President George W. Bush (2001–2009), or the weakening of the U.S. economy when it went into recession in 2007. In 2003, several unions began to pressure Sweeney to retire and, in 2005, five of them bolted the AFL-CIO to form the **Change to Win Federation**. The renegade unions included Sweeney's own union, the **Service Employees International Union**. Sweeney retired in 2009, and **Richard Trumka** was elected to succeed him. Trumka faces daunting challenges. Many unions have become so weak that they have had to merge with others to survive. As of 2012, the AFL-CIO represented just 56 unions and roughly 11 million workers, which makes it 30% smaller than it was in 1955. Its top agenda items include limiting the salaries of corporate heads, job training, rebuilding the American infrastructure, increasing the **minimum wage**, reindustrializing the U.S. economy, reforming the tax code, and expanding upon President Barack Obama's health care reforms.

The AFL-CIO will face other challenges as well. Critics may well have a point that the AFL-CIO is administratively top-heavy. It has 51 vice presidents and includes 6 departments and 7 constituency groups, plus numerous allied programs, 500 central labor councils, and labor federations in each state. A 2010 U.S. Supreme Court decision removing limits on funding political campaigns will also prove challenging, as the AFL-CIO simply cannot match the resources of corporate interests. This is likely to lead to future internal questioning of the very soundness of business union precepts.

As of 2010, the AFL-CIO's top three offices were held by President Richard Trumka, Secretary-Treasurer Liz Shuler, and Executive Vice President Arlene Holt Baker. Shuler is the first woman to serve in her post, and Baker is the first African American to hold a top federation rank.

Suggested Reading

"AFL-CIO: America's Union Movement," http://www.aflcio.org/, accessed April 21, 2010; Paul Buhle, *Taking Care of Business: Samuel Gompers, George Meany, Lane Kirkland and the Tragedy of American Labor*, 1999; Jo-Ann Mort, *Not Your Father's Labor Movement: Inside the AFL-CIO*, 1998; Edmund Wehrle, *Between a River and a Mountain: The AFL-CIO and the Vietnam War*, 2005.

AMERICAN FEDERATION OF STATE, COUNTY, AND MUNICIPAL EMPLOYEES

The American Federation of State, County, and Municipal Employees (AFSCME) represents approximately 1.6 million correction workers, nurses, early childhood educators, emergency medical care personnel, human services workers, law enforcement officials, public works employees, and numerous others employed in the public sphere. As of 2012 AFSCME was the largest affiliate of the **American Federation of Labor-Congress of Industrial Organizations** (AFL-CIO).

AFSCME, like other unions representing public service workers, is partly a product of the professionalization of civil services that took place in the late 19th and early 20th centuries, an effort that gained steam with the passage of the 1883 Pendleton Civil Service Act. Prior to the Pendleton Act, entry into the bulk of country, state, and federal civil service jobs relied on political patronage rather than competence. This way of filling jobs was riddled with so many abuses that it was dubbed the "spoils system." The assassination of President James Garfield by a frustrated office seeker spurred passage of the Pendleton Act. Although it applied only to the federal civil service, it became the template for state and local civil service jobs.

AFSCME was a direct result of efforts taken by Wisconsin state employees to protect civil service jobs during the Great Depression. In 1932, they formed the Wisconsin State Administrative, Clerical, Fiscal, and Technical Employees Association as a way to protect civil servants from an attempt to reintroduce the spoils system. In 1933, the union—then known as the Wisconsin State Employees Association (WSEA)—gained a charter from the **American Federation of Labor**. WSEA state examiner Arnold Zander expanded organizing efforts to other states and, in 1935, the organization began using the name AFSCME, though it was officially a department within the AFL's **American Federation of Government Employees** (AFGE). In 1936, Zander negotiated separate status and became AFSCME's first president. The group remained small at first, as did AFGE, because most states refused to grant **collective bargaining** rights to civil service employees.

AFSCME grew rapidly after World War II because of the dramatic expansion of public service jobs after 1945. In the 10 years between 1945 and 1955, its membership went from 61,000 members to more than 104,000, despite the fact that no state officially recognized AFSCME's right to bargain until New York did so in 1958. Even after President John Kennedy granted collective bargaining rights to federal employees under Executive Order 10988 in 1962, few states extended this privilege to state or local employees. In 1964, **Jerry Wurf** became AFSCME president. Wurf expressly rejected **business unionism** and embraced militant union tactics that had been common in the 1930s and resonated in the 1960s. By 1977, 20 states had granted bargaining rights to civil servants.

AFSCME has long been one of the more progressive unions inside the AFL-CIO. In 1965, it issued a Bill of Rights for union employees, the first major union to do so. It also organized workers from various minority groups and took an active part in the civil rights movement. In fact, the Reverend Martin Luther King, Jr., had come to Memphis, Tennessee, to assist striking AFSCME sanitation workers when he was assassinated in 1968. AFSCME set up a political action committee in the 1970s, and its membership soared to more than 684,000 by 1975. In many respects, AFSCME's growth during the 1970s presaged the shift from manufacturing to **service industry** jobs that accelerated in the late 1970s because of **deindustrialization**.

Jerry Wurf died in 1981, but his successor and current president, Gerald McEntee, continued the union's militant tradition. In 1981, AFSCME sent the nation's largest union contingent to the Solidarity Day rally that protested the anti-union policies of President **Ronald Reagan**. During the 1980s, AFSCME was one of the few AFL-CIO unions to increase its membership and was able to gain bargaining rights for employees in Alaska, Illinois, Nebraska, and Ohio at a time in which other unions were under attack. AFSCME's militancy also made it an early critic of the AFL-CIO's alliance with the Democratic Party, and it led a fierce, but unsuccessful, battle to sidetrack Democratic President Bill Clinton's campaign to pass the **North American Free Trade Agreement**. It continues to support Democrats overall, however, and McEntee heads the AFL-CIO's political action committee. AFSCME spearheaded the effort to elect **John Sweeney** to the AFL-CIO presidency in 1995 and pushed Sweeney to commit more resources to organizing workers. In the late 1990s, AFSCME expanded its reach into Puerto Rico and Panama, along the way adding 300,000 workers to its membership rolls.

AFSCME now represents state, county, and local employees in general, not just those in posts filled by civil service mechanisms. The union supports most of the AFL-CIO's agenda and is vocal in insisting on racial, ethnic, and gender equity. In 2007, AFSCME scored a major victory by settling a two-year dispute with the University of California that raised pay for the system's lowest-waged workers. AFSCME was also an early supporter of Barack Obama's 2008 presidential campaign.

A major challenge facing many AFSCME unions is the spreading practice of eliminating in-house employment in the public sector in favor of **subcontracting** services to private firms, many of whom which non-union employees. It is also at the forefront of the battle to protect retiree pensions at a time in which state and municipal governments are seeking to trim costs by cutting those pensions.

Suggested Reading

American Federation of State, County, and Municipal Employees, AFL-CIO, http://www.afscme.org/index.cfm, accessed April 21, 2010; Ellen Applebaum and Rosemary Batt, *The New American Workplace*, 1994; Frank Sisya, *The Political Life of a Public Employee Labor Union: Regional Union Democracy*, 2001.

AMERICAN FEDERATION OF TEACHERS

The American Federation of Teachers (AFT) is the second largest union for teachers in the United States, albeit the one that often functions the most like other trade unions. It is affiliated with the **American Federation of Labor-Congress of Industrial Organizations** (AFL-CIO). It claims more than 1 million members, though most observers estimate its 2012 membership at approximately 890,000. The current president of the AFT is Randi Weingarten.

The AFT was founded in 1916, as an outgrowth of unionization efforts commencing in Chicago in 1897. Teaching was predominately a female profession in the 19th and early 20th centuries, with teachers working for low pay and subject to strict moral and personal codes of conduct. Schools, especially in rural areas, were often quite primitive, with rudimentary conditions and heavy demands on teachers. Much as in law, early teachers did not necessarily require any special training to gain a teaching license; in fact, in many areas young women with as little as eight years of formal education could gain a teaching license. "Normal" schools—from the Latin *norma* ("rule")—eventually developed to train teachers. The first state normal school appeared in Massachusetts in 1839, but there were none west of the Appalachian Mountain until 10 years later; indeed, it was not until the early 20th century that all states had formal teacher training program. The AFT's rival, the **National Education Association** (NEA), spearheaded the professionalism of teaching. It formed in 1857, but it first functioned more as a professional guild than as a teacher advocacy group.

Margaret Haley, whose father had been active in the **Knights of Labor**, and Catherine Goggin formed the Chicago Teachers Federation (CFT) in 1897, with Goggin serving as president. In 1902, the CFT affiliated with the citywide Chicago Federation of Labor and soon attracted the attention of several **Progressive Era** reformers, most notably philosopher John Dewey. In 1916, the CFT changed its name to the American Federation of Teachers and secured a charter within the **American Federation of Labor**. Goggin died in a traffic accident, and the new AFT chose Charles Stillman as its first president. The AFT expanded to other cities, even though many states and municipalities, including Chicago, had laws preventing teachers from unionizing. By 1939, the union had 32,000 members. In many cities, women led the charge to organize, with Florence Rood directing efforts in St. Paul, Minnesota, and Mary Barker leading the way in Atlanta.

The AFT remained a small organization until the 1960s. It was the target of **communist** witch hunts during the **Red Scare**, despite very little evidence connecting the union to communism. Some of the animus against the AFT was politically motivated, as the AFT had filed a supporting brief in the case that ultimately became *Brown v. the Board of Education of Topeka, Kansas*—the landmark decision that desegregated public schools. Teachers were especially vulnerable to political retaliation and personal reprisals because they were not protected by the 1935 **National Labor Relations Act**, and most states forbade teacher strikes. The AFT changed the ground rules during the 1960 **New York City teachers strike**, the upshot of which was teachers defying the law to win **collective bargaining** rights. In the next decade and a half, more than 800,000 teachers took part in over 1,000 strikes and the AFT's membership soared to more than 200,000 in 1970. A key leader of the 1960 New York strike was **Albert Shanker**, who assumed the AFT's presidency in 1974. Shanker maintained the AFT's militant stance on teacher rights and, by 1980, more than 70 percent of all public school teachers were covered by collective bargaining agreements and the AFT was strong in every section of the United States except the South.

As part of the AFL-CIO, the AFT has been more political than the NEA, and Shanker advised both Presidents Jimmy Carter and Bill Clinton. Upon his death in

1997, Sandra Feldman was elevated to the presidency, becoming the first woman to hold the post since the 1930s. Feldman endorsed a program called "Kindergarten Plus," a program of compensatory preschool education for disadvantaged children. The AFT has generally taken a different stance from the NEA on controversial educational initiatives such as teacher testing, assessment standards, and the No Child Left Behind Act. Whereas the NEA has often viewed such policies as attacks on teachers, the AFT has taken the position that it would support such programs if they were adequately funded.

The AFT represents K–12 teachers as well as school custodians, guidance counselors, bus drivers, and some university faculty members. It also represents some nurses and state employees. It has approximately 3,000 locals and has been among the few unions to increase its membership in the 21st century.

Suggested Reading

American Federation of Teachers, AFL-CIO, http://www.aft.org/about/, accessed April 21, 2010; Marjorie Murphy, *Blackboard Unions*, 1990; Paula O'Connor, "Grade School Teachers Become Union Leaders," *Labor's Heritage* 7, no. 2 (Fall 1995); Allen Odden and Carolyn Kelley, *Paying Teachers for What They Know and Do*, 2002.

AMERICAN LABOR PARTY (ALP). *See* Labor Parties.

AMERICAN PLAN

The American Plan is the name given to an employer-led **open-shop** movement. It emerged in 1921, when representatives from both houses of Congress, manufacturers associations, and organizations such as the **National Association of Manufacturers** and the League for Industrial Rights gathered in Chicago to coordinate policy on combating the spread of labor unions. Open shops were defended as consistent with ideals of American individualism, a topic much in the public consciousness given the rise of a **communist** government in the wake of the 1917 Russian Revolution. Anti-union employers exploited the post-World War I **Red Scare** to limit organizing by their employees.

Unions were tainted as forms of collective behavior more within the Soviet Union than in the United States. Patriotic appeals, red-baiting, and an economic downturn in 1921 and 1922 combined to weaken organized labor in the 1920s. Manufacturers adhering to the American Plan openly discriminated against union members, maintained a **blacklist** of union activists, and required employees to sign **yellow-dog contracts**. Employers also made extensive use of injunctions to stymie collective action. In the 1920s, union membership fell by one-third.

The American Plan fostered an extensive network of open-shop organizations and greatly crippled unions even in highly unionized cities such as Detroit and San Francisco. The American Plan failed to survive the New Deal era, as its overt anti-union tactics were dubbed **unfair labor practices** under the **National Labor Relations Act**. However, the passage of the 1947 **Taft-Hartley Act** renewed the energy of open-shop advocates, in turn fueling the post-World War II **right-to-work** movement. Anti-union activists have also effectively used the American Plan tactic of tarring collective actions (such as forming unions) as antithetical to American individualism.

Suggested Reading

Irving Bernstein, *The Lean Years*, 1960; Foster R. Dulles and Melvyn Dubofsky, *Labor in America*, 1993; Allen M. Wakstein, "The Origins of the Open-Shop Movement, 1919–1920," *Journal of American History* 51 (1964): 460–475.

AMERICAN RAILWAY UNION

The American Railway Union (ARU) was an attempt to build **industrial unionism** among railway workers. It was founded in Chicago in 1893 as the culmination of numerous attempts to unite separate railway organizations into a single union. Its hope of offering a unified front to counter that of the powerful railroad corporations was crushed by its losses in the **Pullman boycott** of 1894.

Railroads were among the most important of all American industries in the mid- and late 19th century, yet prior to the founding of the ARU, worker organizations were mostly small and weak. Most began life as "brotherhoods," which operated more like fraternities and trade guilds than like modern **craft unions**. Engineers formed a brotherhood in 1863, which one year later became the **Brotherhood of Locomotive Engineers** (BLE). It was followed by organizations of conductors (1868), firemen (1873), and brakemen (1883). Other workers such as cartmen, switchmen, and repair shop workers had their own brotherhoods. Each was craft specific and operated independently of the others. None, except the BLE, was powerful enough to win significant clashes against Gilded Age railroad magnates. Although the BLE occasionally undertook strikes, its membership constituted an **aristocracy of labor** and its highly skilled, well-paid engineers often advocated a **middle-class ideology** and looked down upon the **working class**.

As a result of such fragmentation of employees, it was easy for employers to get members of various brotherhoods to act as **scabs** against one another. The Great Labor Uprising of 1877, which was precipitated by a series of spontaneous railroad strikes, revealed the weaknesses of the brotherhoods. It also had the effect of making the BLE even more conservative and less likely to unite with other rail workers.

The first promising efforts in uniting rail workers took place in the 1880s, when the **Knights of Labor** organized workers in the West and Southwest. Union Pacific workers, in particular, created a prototypical industrial union that became a model for the ARU. The KOL's 1885 victory over Jay Gould's Southwestern Railway conglomerate inspired many rail workers, despite the group's inability to hold on to its hard-fought gains. The KOL also failed to entice either the BLE or the Brotherhood of Locomotive Firemen (BLF) to support the organization. The KOL engaged in numerous **jurisdiction** battles with the BLE. **Eugene V. Debs**, the secretary of BLF, forged a temporary alliance between the BLF and the BLE, but his decision proved unwise. The BLE, led by P. J. Arthur, scabbed on the KOL during its

1887 dispute with the Reading railroad, and some Knights retaliated in kind during the 1888 Chicago, Burlington, and Quincy strike. In the latter strike, the BLE sold out the BLF by obeying a court **injunction** and crossing picket lines.

Angered by the BLE's betrayal and increasingly open to the idea of a broader federation, Debs formed the Supreme Council of the United Order of Railway Employees in 1889. The Council brought together firemen, switchmen, and brakemen and successfully negotiated contracts with several small rail lines. The BLE's refusal to endorse the Council weakened it, however, and the structure disintegrated during an 1892 dispute between brakemen and switchmen. Debs nonetheless remained convinced of the need for united action. To that end, he resigned from the BLF and formed the ARU in June 1893. Unlike the brotherhoods, the ARU opened its ranks to unskilled workers. Unfortunately, ARU leaders rejected the KOL's policy of biracial unionism and maintained racist and exclusionary practices toward **minority labor**. As a result, many former Knights in the West refused to join the ARU.

Despite the severe economic downturn that took place as a result of the Panic of 1893, the ARU grew quickly. Within a year, it represented 150,000 rail workers. In 1894, the ARU helped Union Pacific workers ward off a wage cut and also won a strike against James Hill's Great Northern line. Its success also attracted enmity from the BLE and the **American Federation of Labor** (AFL), which saw the ARU as a threat to craft unionism. Their opposition to the ARU proved critical during the Pullman boycott, which commenced and evolved into a strike during May 1894. Both actions took place against the advice of the ARU. Although Debs personally opposed ARU involvement in the Pullman dispute, he was a diligent advocate for strikers when the Council overruled his advice in June. The ARU stood little chance against the combined opposition of **injunction**-issuing courts, the federal government, the BLE, and the AFL. Despite their moderate counsel, Debs and seven other ARU leaders were jailed when the strike collapsed. As legend holds, Debs converted to the cause of **socialism** as a result of his incarceration. The ARU lingered into 1897, when just two dozen delegates attended its convention and laid the organization to rest.

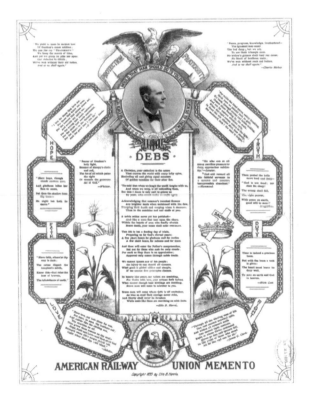

The American Railway Union (ARU) was a labor union formed by Eugene V. Debs in June 1893 that represented members based on their industry association rather than their craft or job skill. (Library of Congress)

Suggested Reading

Stanley Buder, *Pullman*, 1967; Eugene V. Debs, *Writings of Eugene V. Debs*, 2009; Ray Ginger, *The Bending Cross*, 1949; Sidney Lens, *The Labor Wars*, 1974.

ANARCHISM

Anarchism is a general term referring to a broad spectrum of political and social philosophy that views external control of human activity as inherently repressive. Among the many variant (and sometimes competing) forms of anarchism are those that are described as individualist, mutualist, collectivist, **communist**, and **anarcho-syndicalist**. It is sometimes hard to pin down anarchism with precision or to fit it into a conventional political spectrum. Libertarianism, for example, is often viewed as a type of anarchism, yet some libertarians identify with the political left and others with the right. In like fashion, some commentators classify right-wing survivalism as anarchist, though anarchism is conventionally seen as left wing. Adding to the confusion is the fact that accusations of anarchism have been used as a scare tactic with which to slander one's opponents. To the degree that consensus exists, most anarchists argue that it is possible for humans to live cooperatively without external regulation. Most see an essential tension between individual freedom and social organizations and hierarchies, especially governments.

The term derives from an ancient Greek word that means "without leaders" (*archons*), but the ideals of anarchism are as old as human civilization. As commentators as diverse as Plato, Sigmund Freud, Thomas Paine, and Henry David Thoreau have observed, society—especially its customs, laws, and governments—is an artificial concept that constrains human freedom and jeopardizes the liberty of individuals. Suspicion of the potentially coercive nature of government was common among the leaders of the American Revolution, though organized anarchist movements in the United States have largely been European imports that coincided with 19th-century immigration, the **Industrial Revolution**, urban social problems, and capital/labor strife.

Anarchism gained shape during debates between Karl Marx and Mikhail Bakunin in the 1870s about whether the vanguard that Marx argued was necessary to lead a revolution would invariably lead to authoritarianism. There were also debates over whether anarchism could be implemented only through violent, revolutionary actions, or whether society could evolve into it collectively and rationally. Pierre-Joseph Proudhon argued in favor of the latter viewpoint, one that was generally more acceptable among American-born anarchists such as Joseph Labadie and Benjamin Tucker. This position also resonated with the goals of labor unions, which were by nature more collectivist than individualist. In addition, unions emphasized "mutualism," the belief that workers could collectively own the means of production and set up **cooperative** production and distribution networks without the interference of government.

With the heightened social tensions of the Gilded Age and Progressive Era, revolutionary anarchism was much discussed and much feared. During this time, the term evoked fear and was used to justify repression of both true radicals and moderate labor movement leaders. Anarchists were blamed for upheavals such as the **Molly Maguires** troubles of the Pennsylvania coalfields in the 1070s, the Great Labor Uprising of 1877, and the bombing in Chicago's Haymarket Square in 1886. Adding to the fear felt by members of the elite and middle classes were memories of the violence associated with the Paris Commune (1870–1871), in which communists and anarchists declared a radical social agenda and assisted the masses in declaring Paris to be independent of France. As many as 50,000 people died in the suppression of the Paris Commune. The fiery rhetoric found within anarchist journals such as the New York-based *Die Freiheit*, edited by the German-born anarchist Johann Most, did little to quell the broader society's fears.

In the United States, the anarchist threat was more imagined than real, and anarchist involvement in most **working-class** uprisings was more tangential than central. Nonetheless, rumors of anarchist plots proved an effective tool in repressing labor unions. During the Haymarket crisis, for example, eight men were convicted for what most legal scholars consider ideological rather evidential reasons. Of the eight, only Albert Parsons was native born, a situation that fueled nativist fears and further linked radicalism with immigration in the popular mind. The **Haymarket bombing** was also cited to justify repression of the **Knights of Labor** (KOL), even though the KOL had nothing to do with the event, condemned the bombing, and refused to take part in clemency movements that arose after defendants were convicted. For years thereafter, the "Black International"—the anarchist group most closely associated with the Haymarket bombing—was in disarray and anarchism was mostly confined to small numbers of urban Jewish, Italian, and Russian immigrant workers.

The Haymarket crisis also deepened the split among anarchists between those advocating violence ("propaganda of the deed") and those devoted to peaceful measures ("propaganda of the word"). Several events served further to associate anarchism with dangerous extremism. There was, first, the heightened rhetoric of **Emma Goldman**, who immigrated to the United States in 1885 and embraced propaganda of the deed. In 1892, Goldman's lover, the anarchist Alexander Berkman, tried to assassinate industrialist Henry Clay Frick after the **Homestead Steel lockout and strike**. Nine years later, anarchist Leon Czolgosz murdered President William McKinley, a deed that coincided with anarchist assassinations of other world leaders. At least 38 bombings inside the United States were attributed to anarchists in the 1910s, and in several well-publicized cases, letter bombs were mailed to prominent politicians and industrialists. The 1910 bombing of the *Los Angeles Times* building, which resulted in 21 deaths, was blamed on anarchists, though it was not the ideology of the two brothers convicted of the deed. Once again, however, all of organized labor had to defend itself against charges of anarchism, and hostile employers hired private agencies such as the **Pinkertons** and the Burns Detective Agency to infiltrate unions.

The same fate that befell the KOL also became the lot of the **Industrial Workers of the World** (IWW), a group that sometimes embraced anarcho-syndicalism, called for the use of the **general strike**, and spoke of the need for a revolution to destroy **capitalism**. The IWW's grandiose speeches far outstripped reality but they served to justify crackdowns on the group, especially when it opposed U.S. entry into World War I. The 1917 Bolshevik Revolution in Russia made an already tense situation worse. Radicals of all stripes suffered repression during the postwar **Red Scare**, Emma Goldman was deported, and the IWW was eviscerated. In 1921, public sentiment against anarchism contributed to the conviction and eventual execution of two Italian immigrants, Nicola Sacco and Bartolome Vanzetti, for a robbery and murder, though their trial relied upon flimsy evidence. Even moderate organizations such as the **American Federation of Labor** had to fend off charges of anarchism.

After 1921, American and immigrant radicals tended toward involvement in the Communist Party rather than anarchist movements and public fears of radicals tended to shift accordingly. A few anarchists of the word remained, including **Rose Pesotta**, who rose to become vice president of the **International Ladies' Garment Workers' Union**, but she was an exception among labor leaders. By the 1930s, anarchism had largely disappeared from the U.S. labor movement, though a few were among the activists who formed the **Congress of Industrial Organizations**.

Most American anarchists were not violent. Individualist anarchism, including the commune movement, has always existed as an attractive, perhaps utopian vision. Anarchist ideals have also shown up among religious groups, feminists, and black nationalists. In recent years, anarchism has surfaced in association with grunge and punk culture, as well as in radical ecology movements such as EarthFirst! and the Earth Liberation Front. Many recent opponents of **globalization** reference anarchist beliefs when advocating decentralized economics and local control; they are credited with galvanizing protests against the World Trade Organization. Even so, anarchists have generally fared badly in recruiting the masses they champion and valorize. Some critics claim that self-styled modern anarchists are mostly intellectuals and members of the middle class. The history of anarchism in the United States has had moments of great drama, but it has never been a mass movement.

Suggested Reading

Carlotta Anderson, *All-American Anarchist*, 1998; Paul Avrich, ed., *Anarchist Voices: An Oral History of Anarchism in America*, 1996; David DeLeon, *The American as Anarchist: Reflections of Indigenous Anarchism*, 1998.

ANARCHO-SYNDICALISM

Anarcho-syndicalism is a type of **anarchism** whose adherents wish to replace private ownership of production and distribution with departments (syndicates) controlled by workers. Anarcho-syndicalists believe that a network of syndicates could be run cooperatively without government interference, and that such networks would be more rational because they would meet social needs rather than catering to private desires. They would also be more democratic, in that the needs of the masses would be met. Under **capitalism**, supply and demand can be artificially manipulated by advertisers, marketers, monopolists, and speculators. Goods and services are also disproportionately distributed to those with the greatest wealth.

All societies must solve questions related to who will provide goods and services, how much will be produced, how these things will be distributed, and who has access to them. Such decisions become more difficult when society becomes more complex. Many **Native American** cultures sought to be self-sufficient and traded for (or seized through warfare) those goods they could not provide for themselves; the coming of Europeans disrupted those patterns. Mercantilist economic policies placed high value on goods for wider markets, so that soon products such as tobacco, furs, sugar, and forest goods moved across great distances. The search for marketable products undoubtedly fueled the expansion of **slavery**. Even so, most transactions during North America's Colonial and Early Republican periods took place in local or regional markets, often under conditions of barter and reciprocal trade. In an economic system rooted deeply in **agrarianism**, most goods were utilitarian in nature, hard currency was in short supply, and individuals valued self-sufficiency. The coming of the **Industrial Revolution** altered this pattern dramatically. In the mass-production, money-based economy that ensued, goods moved across wide distances, self-sufficiency declined, and unequal access to purchasing goods and services expanded.

Anarcho-syndicalists were among the many ideologues who disagreed with the logic of capital-driven marketplaces. Like other anarchists, they appeared in greatest number after the Civil War as industrialization matured and the social problems associated with it emerged. Many adherents favored revolutionary anarchism and embraced tactics such as **direct action**, **sabotage**, and **general strikes** as avenues for undermining capitalism. As anarchists, they saw formal political, legal, and economic structures as inherently corrupt and irredeemable. As syndicalists, they advocated a post-revolutionary world controlled by workers who would dismantle governments and private enterprises and replace them with democratically run productive and distributive networks. Private profit would be outlawed in such a needs-based society.

In the United States, the organization most associated with the anarcho-syndicalist movement was the **Industrial Workers of the World** (IWW), founded in 1905. The IWW adopted a plan articulated by Thomas Haggerty, a defrocked Catholic priest, who called for seven "departments" (building, manufacturing, public service, distribution, foodstuffs, mining, and transportation). Each department ("syndicate") was subdivided into specific crafts and tasks, and coordination between the departments would be directed by a democratically chosen "general administration." In theory, private profit and private property would disappear as all goods and services would be directed toward the common good. This plan was much discussed among IWW leaders, though its details remained hazy and it seems doubtful that many workers joined the IWW in hopes of implementing it. Although the IWW was often labeled as an anarcho-syndicalist group and such ideals surfaced in speeches delivered during strikes such as those in Lawrence, Massachusetts (1912) and in Paterson, New Jersey (1913), most workers were likely focused on more immediate concerns. Aside from a few forays into **cooperatives**, the IWW's anarcho-syndicalism was mostly theoretical in nature.

Anarcho-syndicalist discussions also took place during the Seattle general strike in 1919, and this ideology remains a tenet of today's IWW. Nevertheless, anarcho-syndicalism failed to catch on the United States as a mass movement. Its major contribution to date has been as an oppositional rhetoric; that is, it calls attention to the problems associated with how goods and services are produced and assigned in society. Most recently anarcho-syndicalist ideas were aired among activists protesting the inequality associated with **globalization**.

Suggested Reading

John Graham Brooks, *American Syndicalism: The I.W.W.*, 1913; "Father Thomas J. Haggerty's Wheel," http://www.iww.org/culture/official/wheel.shtml, accessed May 6, 2010; Rudolf Rucker, *Anarcho-syndicalism*, 1989.

ANTHRACITE COAL STRIKE OF 1902

The Anthracite Coal Strike of 1902 took place in eastern Pennsylvania and was seen as an important victory for the **industrial unionists** of the **United Mine Workers of America** (UMWA). The dispute was the first time in American industrial history in which the federal government did not side with employers in a major industrial dispute.

The roots of this action lay in a 1900 miners' strike in protest of low **wages**, high company store prices, arbitrary work rules, and disputes over how coal was weighed. (Pay scales were partly pegged to tonnage.) The 1900 strike coincided with the presidential election campaign and ended when mine owners accepted a compromise proposed by Republican national party chairman Marcus Hanna, who feared that a long strike would jeopardize William McKinley's reelection chances. Owners agreed to wage increases and minor concessions, but they refused to recognize the UMWA, a still-consolidating union formed in the aftermath of the decline of the **Knights of Labor** and reeling from an 1894 strike among bituminous coal miners that ended ambiguously, from the tragic 1897 **Lattimer massacre**, and from an 1899 strike in the same Pennsylvania coal fields.

The 1900 pact was shaky and collapsed in 1902. UMWA president **John Mitchell** believed that strikes were destructive and was loath to call them. This attitude served him well during the 1902 crisis, as he would ultimately appear more moderate than mine owners. Union delegates met in March 1902 and issued demands that included UMWA recognition, a 20 percent wage increase, an eight-hour work day, standardization of weighing procedures, and clearly defined work rules. Mitchell offered to submit disputes for **arbitration**, as he hoped to save both sides the cost and rancor of a strike. When negotiations mediated by the **National Civic Federation** failed to resolve matters, Mitchell called for a "temporary strike" on May 12. Privately, he told UMWA delegates that a long strike would be disastrous and counseled against extending it, but most **union locals** ignored his advice. Before the strike ended, more than 125,000 miners walked off their jobs.

The strike greatly tested the UMWA, but the union surprised owners by maintaining **solidarity** between ethnic communities they had hoped to pit against one another. Mitchell counseled lawful behavior and, for the most part, strikers obeyed, though some **scabs** were beaten and in some locales police attacked strikers. Mine owners also employed other time-tested strikebreaking methods, such as hiring private security forces and pressuring the Pennsylvania government to deploy the

National Guard in the region. As the strike dragged on into the fall, public opinion was largely on the side of the miners. Mitchell continually called for mediation and appeared a voice of reason in contrast to the steadfast refusal of owners to moderate their position in any way. Theodore Roosevelt—who ascended to the presidency when McKinley was assassinated in 1901—had ordered Labor Commissioner Carroll Wright to investigate the dispute in June. Wright's report mostly sided with the miners, though Roosevelt kept the findings secret for fear of appearing to support unionization efforts. Roosevelt privately tried to convince the UMWA to end the strike, but Mitchell refused to do so without concessions from the mine owners. Pressures to settle rose as anthracite prices rose and the heating season loomed. On October 3, Roosevelt met with mine operators and UMWA representatives, an occasion seen by the UMWA as the president's acceptance of its legitimacy. At that meeting, a respectful Mitchell repeated his offer to submit to binding **arbitration**. By contrast, operators led by George Baer of the Philadelphia and Reading Railroad berated President Roosevelt and demanded that he send troops to the area to force miners to return to work. Roosevelt was outraged by the operators' arrogance, instructed Secretary of War Elihu Root to approach financier J. P. Morgan for help in crafting a compromise, and hinted that he might take action against mine owners.

Morgan, who was also a major stockholder in the Reading Railroad, worked out a face-saving gesture in which employers submitted to arbitration before a presidential commission rather than overtly recognizing the UMWA by negotiating with it directly. Most of owners agreed to this step, fearing that Roosevelt might nationalize the mines. The UMWA called off the strike on October 23, 1902.

The Anthracite Coal Strike Commission met for three months, called more than 500 witnesses, and on March 23, 1903, granted miners gained a 10 percent pay increase and shorter hours. Weighing disputes and UMWA recognition were not settled, but an Anthracite Board of Conciliation was created to handle future disputes. Although the UMWA would become immersed in numerous bitter coal strikes in the following years, the 1902 strike was viewed as a great victory and was used as recruitment tool in organizing campaigns. It also indicated that heavy industries in which **craft** lines were blurred could be organized.

Suggested Reading

Perry Blatz, *Democratic Miners: Work and Labor Relations in the Anthracite Coal Industry*, 1994; Robert Cornell, *The Anthracite Coal Strike of 1902*, 1957; Jonathan Grossman, "The Coal Strike of 1902: Turning Point in U.S. Policy," *Monthly Labor Review* (October 1975); Robert Weibe, "The Anthracite Coal Strike of 1902," *Mississippi Valley Historical Review* 48 (September 1961): 229–251.

A. PHILIP RANDOLPH INSTITUTE

A. Philip Randolph Institute (APRI) is one of five "constituency" groups within the **American Federation of Labor-Congress of Industrial Organizations** (AFL-CIO). Constituency groups are specialized advocacy groups dedicated to the concerns of identity groups inside union movements. There are also advocacy groups for Asian American, African American, Latino, gay, and women trade unionists.

The APRI was formed by Bayard Rustin and A. Philip Randolph in 1965 as a way to merge the interests of the labor movement with the broader social, economic, and political goals of the civil rights movement. One of the motivations for creating the APRI was the AFL-CIO's slowness in embracing civil rights and Randolph's frequent clashes with AFL-CIO President **George Meany**, who failed to comprehend or support many of the progressive social and cultural changes emerging in post-World War II America. By the early 1960s, it was clear to many AFL-CIO leaders—though not to Meany—that organized labor needed to reconsider its response to emerging social activism. The AFL-CIO's relationship to black labor was especially in need of reassessment as many of the federation's constituent unions—especially in construction trades—had racist historical records.

Randolph's lifelong civil rights activism made him a natural to play a key organizing role in the 1963 March on Washington for Jobs and Freedom, best remembered for the eloquent "I have a dream" speech delivered by the Rev. Martin Luther King, Jr. In that same year, the AFL-CIO provided $25,000 in seed money that led to the founding of the APRI in early 1965. In 1965, Randolph and other APRI activists played a key role in securing the passage of the Voting Rights Act, which removed many of the remaining Jim Crow barriers that discouraged African Americans from exercising their suffrage rights. Other past APRI campaigns include supporting the **United Farm Workers of America** boycott of California grapes, supporting striking Memphis sanitation workers in 1968, giving logistical support to striking New York City teachers that same year, and taking part in campaigns to end apartheid in South Africa.

The ARI functions as an internal policy and pressure group inside the AFL-CIO. Although it works closely with the Coalition of Black Trade Unionists (CBTU), a constituency group founded in 1972, the CBTU tends to work exclusively on policy directly germane to AFL-CIO, whereas the APRI has a broader social agenda. It is officially nonpartisan, although it has clashed with several presidential administrations, mostly notably with that of President Richard Nixon, who placed the organization on the White House "enemies list" in the years just preceding the Watergate scandal. The APRI is currently engaged in community organization and policy development in issues such as racial justice, health care reform, tax equity, employer family leave policy, education, job training, and labor law reform. It has 150 chapters active in 36 states. As of 2010, Clayola Brown was president of the APRI.

Suggested Reading

http://www.apri.org, accessed April, 2010; Nina Mjagkij, ed. *Organizing Black America*, 2001; Bayard Rustin, "The History of the A. Philip Randolph Institute," *Debate and Understanding* 1 (Winter 1976): 29–35.

APPRENTICE

Apprentice is the title given to a person who works as a trainee under the supervision of a more skilled person. The use of such training can be traced back to medieval guild societies. Crafts such as blacksmithing, metal work, shoemaking, tailoring, and printing often used apprentices. Work was typically segmented into tasks according to their difficulty, with apprentices performing low-level tasks and the masters applying finishing touches that required great skill. Originally, apprentices were usually children of around 8 years of age who boarded with a **master craftsman**. Apprentices did not receive **wages**, as their remuneration was considered to be their board and the skills they learned from the master. Upon acquiring sufficient skill—generally after 7 to 10 years of training,—apprentices could hire themselves out as **journeymen**, the mid-rung in the work process.

Although most guilds were defunct by the time that Europeans came to North America, guild-like work systems were quite common. Many goods were "bespoken," meaning that they were handcrafted and customized rather than mass produced. The **Industrial Revolution**, the **assembly line**, and mass production deskilled many tasks that were once handicrafts. Today the term "apprenticeship" generally refers to the lowest tier of a training program. It applies mostly in the building and construction trades and is still an important phase of development for carpenters, electricians, plumbers, and technicians. The goal of apprenticeship programs is to ensure proper instruction in skilled work. The duration of training can vary between crafts. A barber serves at this first tier for two years before graduating to journeyman; meat-cutters, three years; electrical workers, three to four years; and printers, five years. Many professions have dispensed with journeymen status altogether, so that workers pass directly from apprenticeship to master status. Of course, **child labor** laws have long outlawed the entry of children into apprenticeship programs and today there is generally no set age at which adults enter apprenticeship programs; in fact, it is increasingly common for older adults who have been forced to change careers to enter apprenticeship programs.

Apprenticeship programs can occasionally be controversial. Labor unions sometimes try to protect the supply of labor in a particular craft by limiting apprenticeships. This has the effect of keeping wages high. There also have been battles over who should control apprenticeship programs—an employer, a union, government, or some combination of interested parties. On a less contentious level, both vocational and technical schools are direct offshoots of the notion of apprenticeship.

Suggested Reading

Robert Glen, *Urban Workers in the Early Industrial Revolution*, 1984; Daniel Jacoby, "Apprenticeship in the United States," *EH-Net Encyclopedia*, http://eh.net/encyclopedia/article/jacoby.apprenticeship.us, accessed May 6, 2010; Bruce Laurie, *Artisans into Workers*, 1989.

ARBITRATION/CONCILIATION/MEDIATION

Arbitration, conciliation, and mediation are terms that refer to ways of resolving capital/labor disputes peacefully. The goal is to avoid an impasse resulting in a **lockout**, **boycott**, **strike**, or court case. "Arbitration" has become the catchall term to describe what might be a multistep process. For the most part, the United States lacks effective national legislation governing how labor disputes are resolved. Peacefully settling conflicts is often left to local or state statutes, or may involve negotiating a separate agreement before the original dispute is tackled.

Mediation is usually (though not always) the first approach tried. It involves bringing in an outside observer who is, in theory, a neutral party. That person (or persons) allows disputants to air their grievances and attempts to find common ground and potential compromises so that the two sides can begin to resolve their difference. Mediation is generally voluntary, though in some cases the dispute may be deemed of such importance to the public interest that state, municipal, or federal governments order mediation. This is particularly the case for crises in the public sector such as those involving municipal services.

Conciliation is the continuing of discussions between parties without a third party present. This step is sometimes skipped. In such cases, either the mediator resolves the dispute or it is advanced to arbitration. Arbitrators generally have more power than mediators. Whereas the latter are mainly facilitators, arbitrators issue "findings" on the dispute and recommend a settlement that can be independent of what either or both sides feel is just. In cases of binding or mandatory arbitration, both sides are legally obligated to accept the findings. In the United States, binding arbitration is relatively rare. It has often occurred that one side—historically management, but more recently labor—refuses to accept the findings and the dispute continues (sometimes with increased rancor on both sides).

Mandatory arbitration laws have been a longtime goal of organized labor. Both the **National Labor Union** and the **Knights of Labor** called for binding arbitration of labor conflicts in the belief that neither employer nor employees recouped their losses incurred during prolonged battles. Social reformers in both the Gilded Age and the Progressive Era also took up the call and argued that arbitration was the answer to many of the inequities of social class that plagued society, disrupted social harmony, and promoted violence. Numerous states set up arbitration boards, but the United States never followed the path of nations such as New Zealand, where government laws made arbiters' decisions binding. The New Zealand model was particularly attractive to American workers, many of whom looked with envy upon the awards given to unions. For the most part, however, U.S. arbitration boards remained weak. During the 1890s, arbiters often ruled in favor of unions but employers refused to comply with their findings and proceeded to crush strikes. In a rare incident, the federal government played an important role in mediating the **anthracite coal strike of 1902** and helping workers obtain a partial victory. Nevertheless, other than those covered by the **Railway Labor Act**, very few American workers enjoyed substantive arbitration rights. The 1925 United States Arbitration Act (USAA) created theoretical dispute resolution systems, but these were seldom invoked for labor disputes.

Some aspects of mandatory arbitration now exist through mechanisms created by the **National Labor Relations Act** (NLRA) in 1935. The NLRA protects both **collective bargaining** and contract arrangements between labor and management. If the National Labor Relations Board deems any action to be an **unfair labor practice** or violation of a contract, it has the backing power of the federal government to enforce its ruling. Another U.S. experiment occurred during World War II, when the government wanted to ensure that vital military production would continue uninterrupted. To that end, President Franklin Roosevelt established the **National**

War Labor Board (NWLB). All disputes within manufacturing concerns related to the war effort were referred to the NWLB, which encouraged mediation, but had the power to impose settlements. Numerous labor unions applauded this effort and nearly all willingly complied.

Arbitration was promoted as a way to ensure industrial peace immediately after World War II. The concept was enshrined in the 1947 **Taft-Hartley Act**, and the Federal Mediation and Conciliation Service (FMCS) was created to encourage mediation, conciliation, and arbitration. The FMCS jurisdiction is mostly confined to cases involving interstate commerce and has been widely perceived as antilabor. Little legislation has been directed at these issues since the FMCS's establishment. In the 1980s and 1990s, even the weak USAA—by then rewritten as the Federal Arbitration Act—was eviscerated by Supreme Court rulings that held that it superseded state and local laws. Most of the latter were far stronger than the USAA.

For most U.S. workers, arbitration remains an elusive goal, with the notable exception of these participating in professional sports. The **Major League Baseball Players Association** has made effective use of arbitration to win lucrative contracts for its members. In the current environment in which labor unions have been shrinking, reformers have renewed the call for stronger arbitration laws as the only effective safeguard against the overwhelming power of global capital. At present, the Arbitration Fairness Act has been discussed by Congress, but there has been little political will to advance such proposals for labor disputes. Arbitration does take place in other aspects of American society, particularly in financial and legal disputes. Numerous private and semi-private mediation and arbitration companies seek to help obtain settlements in capital/labor disputes, but most observers believe that arbitration must be binding to be effective between two parties of unequal power.

Suggested Reading

Walter Baer, *Arbitration for the Practitioner*, 1998; Dennis R. Nolan, *Labor and Employment Arbitration in a Nutshell*, 2006; Katharine V. Stone, *Arbitration*, 2003; Robert Weir, *Knights Down Under: The Knights of Labour in New Zealand*, 2009.

ARISTOCRATS OF LABOR

"Aristocrats of labor" is a controversial term is used to describe an upper tier of wage-earners whose **wages**, skills, working conditions, and aspirations set them apart from other members of the **working class**. They are often considered to be more "respectable" and more politically conservative than other laborers. Although they share the social reality of drawing wages and of being dependent upon an employer class, such workers tend not to identify with the toiling masses. Historically, the label "aristocrats of labor" was applied to highly skilled craft and trades workers whose wage rates placed them well above the average earned by their fellow workers, and to lower-level **white-collar** workers whose salaries were comparable to those of wage-earners even though they did not work with their hands.

Among **Marxist** scholars, the term is typically used in a negative way to reference a person who lacks **class consciousness**, essentially those individuals who fancy themselves to be members of the middle class despite the objective reality that they are not. Extreme critics denounce such individuals as class traitors and enemies of labor **solidarity**. A more charitable view is that it is a mistake to assume that any social class is homogeneous. Aristocrats of labor thus represent groups of workers holding genteel aspirations that could be called "working-class respectability."

Although both views are open to criticism, the existence of individuals whose class identity is ambiguous serves as a warning that social class in the United States is seldom marked by uniformity of values or universal agreement among its members. The difficulties involved in labeling social class have grown more acute in recent years. Polls indicate that a majority of American workers view themselves as members of the middle class, though economic indicators do not support such beliefs.

Suggested Reading

Martin Burke, *The Conundrum of Class*, 1995; Robert Gray, *The Aristocracy of Labour in 19th Century Britain*, 1981.

ARTISAN LABOR

Artisan labor refers to work that is done by a highly skilled worker who has mastered a craft and produces a product from scratch. It is often used as an antonym for machine-made goods. In modern usage, the term "artisan" can be used to designate a worker who has completed training and has passed from **apprentice** to master status. It is also used to label hand-made goods of all sorts, from arts and crafts to bread and beer. The two hallmarks of artisan labor are possession of skill and control over the work process (e.g., pace, hours, conditions, possession of tools). Prior to the emergence of the factory system and the full articulation of **capitalism**, the roles of owner, employer, employee, wholesaler, and retailer were blurred. Most manufactured goods were made for, and consumed in, local and regional markets. This ideal extended to certain services as well, and those who delivered them were called "mechanics" for their mastery of "mechanical arts" such as drafting, engineering, and woodworking.

Today artisanship is considered a highly specialized and individualized pursuit, and an artisan's goods often cost much more than those made in bulk or by machines. Artisanship has long been associated with high-quality production. The term dates to the 16th century in English, but it is essentially an offshoot of the medieval guild system, with "artisan" appearing as another word for **master craftsmen**. Prior to the **Industrial Revolution**, most goods that consumers purchased were artisan crafted, including products that today are made in factories, such as shoes, apparel, tools, paper, leather goods, glass, and textiles. Colonial Americans used the term "bespoken goods" to mean custom-made products. Some artisans—shoemakers and tailors, for instance—were relatively poor, but nonetheless did a substantial amount of bespoken work.

In 1793, Samuel Slater opened a textile mill in Pawtucket, Rhode Island, that is widely regarded as the first factory in the United States. Its founding marked the beginning of a change in how goods were made in the United States, how they were distributed, and how workers were compensated. The spread of factories and the use of machines tended to deskill the workforce. Factory shoemaking, for example, replaced artisan cobblers by segmenting work so that each part of the shoe was made or assembled by a different set of workers—cutters, lasters, stitchers, heel-makers, gluers, polishers, and so on. Although Colonial shoemakers had **outsourced** some tasks, the final product was (at least) overseen by an artisan. Factory work brought all the steps involved in making shoes under one roof, so that shoes could be mass-produced and sold in broader markets. The expansion of markets, in turn, attracted investors who supplied capital needed to purchase new technology, such as sewing machines and MacKay stitching machines. Over time shoe factory owners, managers, production workers, wholesalers, and retailers became separate from one another and had different interests. Those actually making shoes were more likely to be hourly wage-earners rather than artisan cobblers.

What was true in shoemaking was, by the mid 19th century, true in many other trades as well. The transformation of **journeymen**'s associations into labor unions was partly a response to the deskilling of labor; many of these organizations were originally **craft unions** intent upon protecting the integrity of artisanship. For instance, **Samuel Gompers**—the future co-founder of the **American Federation of Labor** (AFL)—was a skilled cigar maker who began his union career trying to protect his craft from threats associated with machine-rolled cigars. Some scholars argue that for many American workers "craft consciousness" was stronger than **class consciousness**. This is a hotly debated topic, but it is certainly true that very few labor organizations fully embraced the idea of **industrial unionism** until the 20th century and that Gilded Age federations such as the **Knights of Labor** (KOL) were badly split over debates between craft and industrial unionists. The AFL survived, whereas the KOL went into severe decline.

By the early 20th century, the craft ideals that the AFL fought so hard to uphold were archaic, and artisanship was well on its way to becoming a niche specialty in most trades. The Arts and Crafts movement (roughly 1910 to 1925) was partly an attempt to rekindle interest in high-quality artisan-made goods, but its products could not compete in price with factory-made items and much of what was made was sold to wealthier individuals, not the masses. Within organized labor, the AFL's failure to appreciate fully the implications of the factory system provoked the rise of the **Congress of Industrial Organizations** (CIO) in the 1930s; the CIO embraced industrial unionism. Automobile manufacturing offers an example of the AFL's dilemma. Although the **assembly line** transformed car manufacturing into unskilled and semiskilled tasks, AFL line workers were subdivided among various "crafts," depending on whether they handled wires, glass, tires, welding equipment, or something else. The CIO's **United Auto Workers of America** affiliate simply classified everyone as an "auto worker." The eventual merger of the AFL and CIO maintained the fiction of craft in some instances, but overall it was very clear that artisan labor was finished in all but a few trades. (Tool making and precision metal work, for instance, remained a very highly skilled profession until the 1980s, when computer-designed and -operated robots began to supplant human workers.)

The current postindustrial economy has sparked new interest in artisan goods. Like items made during the Arts and Crafts movement, though, many of them are pricey. At present, artisan goods are much admired for their quality, but cannot be made in sufficient quantity or cheaply enough to make a dent on the mass market. This reality even extends to goods such as beverages. In 2009, for instance, "craft" beers made by microbreweries (defined as having an annual output of 15,000 or fewer barrels) accounted for just 4.3 percent of all the beer consumed in the United States.

Suggested Reading

Mary Blewett, *Men, Women, and Work: Class, Gender, and Protest in the New England Shoe Industry, 1780–1910*, 1988; Bruce Laurie, *Artisans into Workers: Labor in 19th Century America*, 1997; Roger Penn, *Skilled Workers in Britain and America*, 1990.

ASIAN AMERICAN LABOR

Asian Americans make up slightly less than 5 percent of the U.S. population. Because their median income, household income, and educational attainment levels are higher than the national average and their unemployment and crime statistics are lower than average, Asian Americans are sometimes stereotyped as a "model" **minority** group. Such a label is deceptive in many ways. First, it lumps all persons of Asian descent into a single category and ignores the differing social statistics between ethnic groups. Second, it tends to make invisible the nearly 10 percent of Asian Americans who live in poverty. Third, it draws attention away from a troubled and contentious past in which Asian immigrants were the victims of brutal discrimination. Were it not for this painful history, Asian Americans would undoubtedly make up a higher percentage of the American population.

A disproportionately high percentage of Asian Americans hold professional jobs today, but nearly all Asian Americans were members of the **working class** until after World War II. Small numbers of Asian Americans settled in North America prior to the 19th century, including a community of Filipinos who moved to Louisiana in 1763. The 1790 Naturalization Act restricted citizenship to "free" and "white" males and was the first of numerous immigration bills that discriminated against Asians. Its full impact would be realized during the 19th century when Asian immigration to the United States increased due to population pressures in Asia, economic opportunities in North America, recruitment by American companies, and U.S. foreign policy. Chinese began immigrating to the United States in larger numbers in the 1850s, lured by the West Coast gold rush and pushed out of China by the turmoil caused by European imperialist ventures. They were originally viewed as exotic, but when Chinese laborers began to compete for jobs in the gold fields and with the booming railroad industry, nativism arose. As early as 1854, California passed a law forbidding Chinese individuals from testifying against whites in court. The **National Labor Union** forbade entry to Chinese workers, as did the **Knights of Labor** and most affiliates of the **American Federation of Labor** (AFL). Organized labor as a group clamored to have Congress ban Chinese immigration, and white union members often engaged in both stereotypes and physical attacks on Chinese workers. It did not help the Chinese cause when several employers during the 1870s imported Chinese **scabs** to break **strikes**. Numerous state laws singled out the Chinese, and the 1870 Naturalization Act forbade Chinese immigrants from obtaining U.S. citizenship. Two years later Congress was persuaded to pass the **Chinese Exclusion Act** over the objection of many in the business community who viewed the Chinese as a source of cheap labor. White workers generally refused to work alongside their Chinese counterparts; hence those who remained were employed in jobs viewed as beneath the dignity of whites, or else worked within self-contained ethnic enclaves.

Other Asians suffered similar discriminatory treatment. The 1875 Foran Act banned the importation of contract labor, an act largely seen as targeting Asians (and, to a lesser degree, Italians). Most Asian laborers were ghettoized on the West Coast, including Japanese agricultural, cannery, and fishery workers. Quite a few Japanese operated small farms and strove for self-sufficiency. Numerous laws curtailed Japanese American rights, akin to the discriminatory laws directed at Chinese immigrants. In 1907, Japan and the United States signed the Gentlemen's Agreement, officially a voluntary deal to limit Japanese immigration, but in actuality an exclusion bill. West Coast planters were especially keen to waylay organization of agricultural workers in the wake of the formation of the Japanese-Mexican Labor Alliance in 1903, which directed a strike against Oxnard, California, sugar beet producers. The Gentlemen's Agreement was quickly supplemented by a 1908 executive order that restricted immigration from U.S. territories such as Guam and Hawaii to the mainland, and a 1913 California law forbade "aliens" from buying land in that state.

The latter actions targeted Filipinos as well as the Chinese and Japanese. The 1893 annexation of Hawaii and the 1898 Spanish-American War marked the entry of the United States into foreign imperialist ventures. In particular, the Spanish-American War brought Guam, Puerto Rico, and the Philippines under U.S. control. Numerous Filipinos worked on Hawaiian sugar cane plantations; others migrated to California and worked in agriculture. U.S. foreign adventurism also gave rise to anti-imperialist leagues, many of whose members were motivated more by nativism and racism than by a belief that nonwhite peoples should have self-determination rights.

By the early 20th century, the eugenics movement was going strong, and its adherents argued that miscegenation led to blood "pollution" that threatened the alleged racial supremacy of Anglo-Saxons. Immigration bills passed in 1917, 1924, and 1929 reflected these assumptions. The Immigration Act of 1924 included the National Origins Act, which placed strict quotas on the number of immigrants allowed into the United States by region. For the first time, immigration from the Indian subcontinent was also curtailed. In theory, China, India, Japan, the Pacific islands, Western Samoa, and Thailand were permitted 100 immigrants per year, but a separate Asian Exclusion Act assured that only a handful of professionals were admitted. The 1938 Tyding-McDuffie Act added Filipinos—by then the largest Asian immigrant group—to the growing list of those considered "aliens" and, therefore, ineligible for future entry into the United States. The only positive legislation was a 1918 bill that allowed Asian Americans veterans of World War I to obtain citizenship.

In the wake of such discrimination, it took acts of extraordinary courage for Asian workers to resist discrimination. Nearly 2,000 Filipino sugar cane workers struck against their Hawaiian employers in 1924. In Yakima County, Washington, however, white vigilantes forcibly expelled Filipino agricultural workers in 1928, a pattern repeated elsewhere during the 1930s. In 1924, Japanese American labor leader Karl Yoneda (1906–1999) organized Asian workers in Alaska and California. He went on to become a key organizer in the **International Longshoremen's Union** and would endure numerous beatings for his activities and beliefs. (Yoneda changed his name from Goso to Karl—in honor of Karl Marx—when he joined the **Communist Party** in the 1920s.) The AFL recognized the Cannery Workers' and Farm Laborers' Union in 1933, a largely Filipino union with strength in Washington and Alaska, though it bolted to the **Congress of Industrial Organizations** (CIO) in 1938 and was absorbed by the **United Packinghouse Workers of America**. In 1940, the AFL set up the Filipino Federated Agricultural Laborers Association in recognition of the fact that 15 percent of California's labor force was Filipino.

The December 7, 1941, bombing of Pearl Harbor, Hawaii, occasioned an anti-Japanese backlash that culminated in the issuance of Executive Orders 9066 and 9102 in February and March 1942, which authorized the internment of 120,000 persons of Japanese descent, though nearly two-thirds were American citizens. On the West Coast, internment was accompanied by a property grab in which white farmers bought the land of their Japanese American competitors at rock-bottom prices. When internment ended in 1946, Japanese Americans filed loss claims of more than $148 million, but Congress authorized just $37 million in compensation. Many farmers and small business owners were forced to start over with few resources. (Final restitution was not made until 1999.)

World War II also forced a reevaluation of Asians from nations allied with the United States. The 1943 Magnuson Act repealed the Chinese Exclusion Act, though immigration quotas from China remained extremely low. The 1945 War Brides Act allowed spouses and children of U.S. service personnel to enter the country freely, and emergency consideration was given to Chinese fleeing the communist takeover of mainland China in 1949. Progress toward wider acceptance of Asian Americans remained slow, however. The 1952 Immigration and Naturalization Act theoretically allowed anyone to apply for U.S. citizenship, but kept in place quotas for those of Asian descent. Asian immigration and naturalization did not increase dramatically until after 1965, when the Hart-Celler Immigration and Naturalization Act formally abolished the National Origins Act.

Asian laborers continued to battle for justice. Japanese American labor leader Art Takei led a strike of 10,000 **United Food and Commercial Workers** during 1954. Filipinos were core supporters in efforts that led to the founding of the **United Farm Workers Union** in the 1960s. Since the 1960s, Asian Americans have become more visible both in society and in the labor movement. Asian Americans were active in the civil rights movement and helped secure passage of the 1964 Civil Rights Act. They also took advantage of **affirmative action** laws promulgated and revised in the 1960s. In fact, so many Asian Americans did well educationally that they were the target of lawsuits settled when the 1978 U.S. Supreme Court decision in *Regents of the University of California v. Bakke* affirmed the constitutionality of affirmative action. A wave of post-**Vietnam War** immigrants arrived after 1980 when a United Nations Commissioner for Refugees decision opened the door for immigration of individuals fleeing Vietnam, Cambodia, and Laos.

In 1987, Art Takei formed the Asian Pacific Labor Alliance, a group often cited as the first pan-Asian labor advocacy group. It took up battles against **sweatshops** and forced labor. In 1992, the organization became the Asian Pacific American Labor Alliance (APALA) and entered the AFL-CIO as a constituency group. APALA now claims more than 500,000 members. In the 21st century, APALA has taken up the plight of workers in the electronics, food, garment, health care, and hotel industries. It has also been at the fore of recognizing the need to evolve international organizing plans and has spoken out against labor exploitation in China, India, and elsewhere.

Asian Americans remain vulnerable to both historical prejudices and ongoing political debates over immigration policy. APALA has joined with other civil rights groups in protesting what it sees as overly harsh crackdowns on illegal immigrants. Approximately 12 percent of all Asian American workers belong to labor unions—a share slightly lower than the national average, but one that has remained stable even as most other ethnic groups have witnessed declines in their union membership rates. It is important to reiterate, however, that Asian Americans are not a homogeneous group. Some, for instance, applauded when President George W. Bush made Elaine Chao the first Asian American secretary of labor (2001–2009), whereas many others denounced her as unfriendly to labor unions. There are also historical animosities between groups such as the Vietnamese and Cambodians. Moreover, large gaps persist in relative occupational achievement levels. Laotians, Cambodians, and Vietnamese, for example, are often found in **blue-collar** jobs such as garment production, poultry processing, and service industry work, whereas Indians obtain college degrees at a rate three times higher than the national average and are disproportionately employed in **middle-class** professions such as engineering and the high-tech sector.

Suggested Reading

Seung Hea Han, "Asian Pacific American Immigration and Labor History Timeline," http://www.timerime.com/en/timeline/115774/Asian+Pacific+American+Immigration+and+Labor+History+Timeline/, accessed May 18, 2010; Juanita Tamayo Lott, *Common Destiny: Filipino Generations*, 2006; Kent Wong, Julie Monroe, and Kathleen Yasuda, eds., *Voices for Justice: Asian Pacific Organizers and the New Labor Movement*, 2001.

ASSEMBLY-LINE PRODUCTION

Assembly-line production is a continuous-flow system—often machine driven—in which work comes directly to workers rather than laborers traveling between workstations. It is most famously associated with the pre-1980s auto industry, in which parts were moved along conveyor lines to unskilled or semiskilled laborers who fit together single pieces of the total product. Many types of work—including mail sorting, data processing, **butchering**, and food processing—use assembly-line principles.

Many people mistakenly credit Henry Ford with inventing assembly-line production. In truth, it is a very old principle that has been used for many products that do not depend upon a skilled craft worker to create them from start to finish. Historians generally credit Henry Evans with the first application of assembly lines in America; Evans began using line production in flour mills in 1784. After the Civil War, meatpacking plants also converted to assembly-line work. Assembly-line production is facilitated by the use of interchangeable parts that can be easily installed. In the 19th century, gun manufacturers such as Colt made wide use of such components.

What others pioneered, Henry Ford perfected. In 1914, Ford converted his Dearborn, Michigan, Model-T plant to assembly-line production, and the price of automobiles dropped dramatically. To counter high turnover, Ford offered higher **wages** to his workers than did his competitors. By 1926, a Ford automobile required 7,782 separate operations for completion, but more than three-fourths of all plant jobs required less than a week's training to master. Ford's experiments were hailed by many Progressive Era thinkers as enlightened. The assembly line was in keeping with early Progressive values of efficiency and rationalization, and those seeking social harmony praised Ford's willingness to pay higher wages. Soon most auto manufacturers replicated Ford's assembly line.

For the most part, few workers shared enthusiasm for the assembly line. Work was deskilled, tasks were repetitive, workers lost control over tools, and the pace was set by machines that were subject to **speedups**. Despite Ford's higher wages, turnover on the Ford assembly line was often in excess of 300 percent per year. Adding to worker discontent was the simultaneous articulation of scientific management principles sometimes called **Taylorism**. In an effort to rationalize work even further, time-motion experts studied work efficiency and sought ways to extract greater production from laborers. Workers complained that the pace of work was unnatural and that they were treated as if they themselves were interchangeable machine parts. Many workers sought ways to reestablish control over their work; acts of **sabotage** increased dramatically in factories using assembly-line production. So, too, did informal job actions such as **sick-outs**, deliberate slowdowns, and the implementation of worker-determined **stints**. By the 1950s, many industrial sociologists equated assembly-line production with worker alienation. It proved very hard to sustain assembly-line discipline among younger workers during the social upheavals of the 1960s and 1970s, a factor seen most dramatically among General Motors workers producing the Chevrolet Vega at Lordstown, Ohio. The **Lordstown Strike** and assembly-line problems elsewhere hastened the shift to **automation** in car manufacturing.

Assembly-line production was the norm in American factories from the 1920s into the 1970s, at which time several things occurred to break its monopoly. First, other manufacturers increased the use of robots and other forms of automation, thereby reducing the need for human line workers. Second, the energy crisis of the 1970 touched off the first wave of **deindustrialization**. Third, by the 1980s, some manufacturers began to abandon the assembly line in favor of policies that encouraged a more varied workplace, such as **quality circles**. Finally, as

globalization spread, many manufacturing jobs left the United States. (The assembly line became the manufacturing method of choice in many developing nations to which **runaway shops** have relocated.) Nevertheless, manufacturing remains an important part of the U.S. economy, and assembly lines remain in widespread use despite distaste among workers for how they operate.

The assembly line is also an important concept in intellectual criticism of work. Among radical critics, especially **Marxists**, the assembly line is grouped with Taylorism and is often referred to as "Fordism." It is viewed as a form of labor exploitation that controls work and uses managerial systems designed to maintain a compliant workforce.

Suggested Reading

Harry Braveman, *Labor and Monopoly Capitalism: The Degradation of Work in the 20th Century*, 1974; Mike Davis, *Prisoners of the American Dream*, 1988; David Montgomery, *Workers Control in America*, 1979.

ASSOCIATION OF CATHOLIC TRADE UNIONISTS

The Association of Catholic Trade Unionists (ACTU) was a Roman Catholic lay organization in existence from 1937 to 1950 whose purpose was to give advice to workers joining unions for the first time and to assure that those individuals and organizations acted in accordance with church teachings. An offshoot of the Catholic Worker Movement (CWM) founded by Dorothy Day, it represented a reconciliation between organized labor and the Roman Catholic Church.

Church officials were caught off guard by the rise of labor unions during the 19th century. As the **Industrial Revolution** spread in Western societies, among its effects was a corrosive impact on tradition. **Agrarian** ideals and lifestyles began to give way to urbanism and manufacturing, and many peasants were transformed into industrial workers. Industrialization also led to population shifts and emigration. Catholics had established themselves in North America during the Colonial era, but their overall numbers were so few that in many places churches were officially missionary outposts. The influx of large numbers of Irish immigrants in the wake of famine during the 1830s stimulated growth in the Catholic Church in North America. So, too, did the arrival of southern Germans, Italians, Poles, and others who arrived seeking jobs in the expanding industrial economy. Many Catholic prelates were surprised by how easily new industrial workers gravitated to the labor movement, and they were shocked by the overt **socialist** and **anarchist** views held by many. Traditionalists who insisted upon customary deference to priests and church discipline found that many Catholic workers ignored threats of excommunication and were more willing to take guidance from their unions than the church.

The church had a particularly rancorous relationship with the **Knights of Labor** (KOL), whose members included very large numbers of Irish and other ethnic Catholics. For the first 14 years of its existence (1869–1883), the KOL operated in oath-bound secrecy, which some clerics insisted was in violation of church doctrine. Despite dutiful efforts of KOL leaders to appease clerics, some insisted that Catholics had to quit either the church or the Knights. In the mid-1880s, KOL membership soared and increasing numbers of Catholic workers opted for the KOL over the church. Intense lobbying, much of it led by James Cardinal Gibbons, convinced the Vatican to rethink its views on unions. In 1891, Pope Leo XIII issued the encyclical **Rerum Novarum**, which condemned both socialism and laissez-faire **capitalism**. In doing so, Leo also upheld the right of workers to form unions as long as their actions were consistent with Catholic social and moral teachings.

In the next few decades, the Catholic Church was influenced by the rising **Social Gospel** movement and spoke out against the abuses associated with **social Darwinism**. Despite the church's discomfort with socialism, many Catholics embraced some of its economic and social ideals. Dorothy Day was among those who came from a socialist background. The success of the CWM, the outbreak of the Great Depression, and the issuance of *Quadregisimo Anno* (a 1931 encyclical from Pope Pius XI) inspired a group of Catholics to consider more deeply the church's social teachings. *Quadregisimo Anno* reiterated *Rerum Novarum* by condemning individualism for denying social and public rights, and by debunking most forms of collectivism for disrespecting private property. Pope Pius advocated instead a "corporatist" view of society in which a community of individuals united organically and functionally without strife and antagonism. How to bring this ideal into reality was among the ideas discussed by New York City Catholics such as John Cort, George Donohue, Edward Squitieri, and Martin Wersing. They created ACTU to put church encyclicals into practice, and became convinced that labor unions were the vehicle for doing so.

The ACTU was a lay organization, but it operated with explicit Catholic Church approval. It would eventually form chapters in 20 cities, each with a supervising pastor under the authority of a diocesan bishop. The ACTU sought both to educate Catholic workers about the importance of supporting trade unions and to bring Catholic teachings into those unions. In keeping with the corporatist ideals of *Quadregisimo Anno*, the ACTU insisted that harmony could exist between labor and management and that differences should be settled through reasoned cooperation instead of hostile confrontations. Such a suggestion was, in many ways, rooted more in the guild system of the past than in the realities of modern industrial relations, but the ACTU had the good fortune to form at an opportune moment.

The 1930s were marked by rising labor activism and the formation of new unions, many of which were associated with the emergent **Congress of Industrial Organizations** (CIO). The ACTU assisted in many organizing drives and, on occasion, supported **strikes**. When it held its first convention in 1940, however, the ACTU deemphasized strikes and reemphasized organizing and worker education. It also created several labor schools that taught Catholic trade unionists parliamentary procedure, labor history, Catholic social doctrine, ethics, public speaking, and union leadership for rank-and-file activists seeking top positions in their local unions. It also helped launch newspapers and speakers' forums. At its peak in the mid-1940s, the ACTU had more than 10,000 members.

The early days of the **Cold War** rekindled the Catholic Church's distaste for **communism** and hastened the ACTU's demise. Some ACTU-allied priests, such as Monsignor Charles Owen Rice in Pittsburgh, became increasingly involved in union factional battles between the left and the right. The ACTU supported, encouraged, and created anticommunist factions inside CIO unions such as the **United Electrical, Radio, and Machine Workers of America**, the **United Auto Workers of America** (UAW), and the Newspaper Guild. It had its greatest success in helping assemble an anticommunist coalition that elected **Walter Reuther** as CIO president in 1946. The ACTU also supported the CIO's decision to expel 11 unions in 1949 and 1950 because they were communist dominated. In doing so, however, the ACTU ceased to be an active organizing and coordinating body. Shortly after the expulsions, the ACTU also faded from existence.

The ACTU helped bridge the gulf between the Catholic Church and the **working class**. It also provided organizing energy and logistical support during a crucial moment in U.S. labor history. Some scholars link its demise to the church's return to a more conservative stance toward organized labor, while others argue that it and the CWM laid the foundation for socially active priests and nuns in the civil rights movement and in subsequent reform movements.

Suggested Reading

Aaron I. Abell, *American Catholics and Social Action: A Search for Social Justice*, 1980; John C. Cort, "The Association of Catholic Trade Unionists and the Auto Workers," *U.S. Catholic Historian* 9, no. 4 (Fall 1990): 335–353; Douglas P. Seaton, *Catholics and Radicals: The Association of Catholic Trade Unionists and the American Labor Movement, from Depression to Cold War*, 1981.

AUTO-LITE STRIKE (1934). *See* Depression-Era Strikes.

AUTOMATION

Automation refers to manufacturing processes in which machines perform tasks with little or no human interaction. The term was first coined by Ford Motor Company Vice President Del Harder in 1947 to describe the mechanical work-feeding and material-handling devices on auto **assembly lines**. It came into broader use in the 1950s to describe self-setting and numerically sequenced machines controlled by pre-semiconductor computers. Later it would be applied to the use of robots on the assembly line and to manufacturing processes in which computers regulate machine functions and monitor employee output. Most recently the term has surfaced to reference developments such as computer-activated telephone messages and answering services.

Though the term "automation" is both loosely applied and of relatively recent vintage, it describes a much older principle. Many labor-saving devices incorporate the principles of automation to varying degrees. Automation becomes controversial when it replaces human labor which is the reason why labor unions have had a conflicted relationship with it. On the one hand, automated machines can perform repetitive and dangerous tasks; on the other hand, machines often supplant skilled labor, as has happened in the machine-tool industry. Machine-tool workers were once among the most highly skilled and well paid of all **blue-collar** workers, but by the 1980s computer-programmed machines were able to grind metals, glass, and other materials to the same fine tolerances as skilled workers and a once-thriving trade collapsed.

Historically, workers have initially resisted automation. In England, for example, the introduction of mechanical weaving looms threatened the livelihood of hand weavers. In 1811 and 1812, a loose vigilante movement known as the Luddites smashed machines. The term "Luddite" was first associated with acts of **sabotage** but subsequently took on a secondary meaning to describe anyone who is suspicious of innovation and new gadgets. American workers have also resorted to sabotage, though such acts have generally been related to acrimonious conflicts with employers rather than attempts to get rid of machines themselves. Instead, **craft unionism** has been the vehicle through which mechanization and automation have been resisted.

A central tenet of the **Industrial Revolution** was the use of machines to mass-produce goods. Factory production both creates and destroys jobs. Skilled jobs are often eliminated or downgraded to semiskilled or unskilled labor; hence unions have historically waged struggles to preserve skilled labor. Many of these efforts been rearguard actions, however, and craft unions at best delayed the implementation of machines. By the 1830s, the textile industry had been thoroughly redefined by machine production; by the 1920s, labor-saving machinery was commonplace in the automobile, candy, rubber, and shoe industries. It was, in fact, the erosion of craft work that led to the formation of the **Congress of Industrial Organizations** and the articulation of **industrial unionism**.

Post-World War II developments raised new alarm about automation. Old-style factory production eroded craft-based work but, for the most part, remained labor intensive. By the 1950s, however, automation began to reduce the overall need for human labor. Although doomsday and science fiction scenarios of all-robot factories did not materialize, some industries saw dramatic shrinkage in their human workforces. Rank-and-file workers struggled against automation to little avail: On docks, containerization transformed longshoremen's work; in the pressroom, linotype gave way to cold-type composition; and in machine shops, engineers and machinists battled for control of programming functions on the first generation of automated tools. Automation also greatly strengthened the hand of employers; the need for fewer workers reduced the **collective bargaining** power of unions. Even when unions eked out small victories, their short-term gains often came with negative side effects. Attempts to hold onto jobs opened unions to charges of featherbedding, made them appear inefficient, and helped management portray them as relics from an earlier time. Some unions won the creation of "automation funds" to protect senior workers, but this practice both alienated younger workers and failed to direct the shape and character of automation. Union opposition to automation is cited by some critics as a contributing factor in **deindustrialization**. According to this logic, U.S. factories delayed modernizing and became saddled with aging equipment and inefficient work processes that placed them at a competitive disadvantage when **globalism** became apparent.

By the 1960s, automated factory production was commonplace around the world, and its pace has only accelerated since then. Its impact can be seen most dramatically in auto, electronics, machine tools, and steel production, where robots now perform handling, welding, grinding, and assembly tasks once carried out by humans. As automation expanded, it renewed charges that assembly-line work was dehumanizing. Once machines took over judgment tasks, those workers who remained on assembly lines complained that their labor was mindless and oppressive. This was an issue in the 1972 **Lordstown, Ohio, strike** against Chevrolet, and has been an ongoing dispute for aircraft machinists and postal workers since the 1980s. On a more positive note, automation opened doors for women workers by removing many obstacles previously used to justify job typing by sex. As industrial engineers made "heavy" or "male" jobs obsolete, support for **protective legislation** for women no longer seemed compelling.

A new type of automation, however, has roused women and men alike. Advances in computers and communications now allow employers to monitor employees electronically and to impose demanding production quotas. By the 1990s, for example, telephone operators were expected to average no more than 32 seconds with a customer. Since then, the quotas have increased to the point that operators routinely handle more than 1,000 calls per day, a pace critics liken to the worst abuses of **Taylorism**. Such conditions exist in other professions as well, including **white-collar** jobs. It is now possible for employers to monitor employees' email, track the websites they visit, and measure the number of keystrokes they enter on their computers. Not surprisingly, worker-management conflicts have arisen. Unions have made some headway in disputes over issues such as repetitive strain injury, privacy rights, and ergonomic reconfiguration of the workplace.

Suggested Reading

Barbara Garson, *The Electronic Sweatshop*, 1989; "Hello? Is Anybody There? The Evolution of the Telephone and Telephone Operator," http://legacy.lclark.edu/~soan221/99wlc/telephone.htm#AUTOMATION, accessed May 21, 2010; David Noble, *Forces of Production: A Social History of Industrial Automation*, 1984; Harley Shaiken, *Work Transformed: Automation and Labor in the Computer Age*, 1984.

BACON'S REBELLION

Bacon's Rebellion was an uprising in Virginia in 1676—an encounter between humbler backcountry settlers and Virginia's coastal-based elites that threatened to upset existing class and racial distinctions within Colonial America. It took place 100 years before the Declaration of Independence and is sometimes described as the first "American Revolution" for its seeming disdain for hierarchy and deference. Such claims are exaggerated, but the rights of common people received more attention in the rebellion's aftermath and a rejection of aristocracy was indeed enshrined in both the Declaration of Independence and the U.S. Constitution.

Agrarian practices dominated the economic life of European settlers in North America. At the center of Bacon's Rebellion was the attempt of Virginia's wealthy elites to monopolize both arable coastal lands and social privileges within the colony. Such a system was easier to maintain in the early days of Virginia's settlement, when the death rate was high and most agricultural work was done by **indentured servants**, few of whom lived long enough to redeem their "headrights"—lands given to indentures upon completion of their service. The intention of headrights (usually 50 acres) was to help servants make the transition to the status of freeman, but Virginia's high death rate actually produced a situation in which desirable land became concentrated into fewer hands. Elites who sponsored an indentured individual's cost of travel to the colonies also received a headright and absorbed that of the servant if he did not fulfill his contract.

By the late 1620s, the death rate dropped, most hostile **Native American** tribes along the coast had been pacified, the colony's economy had become dependent upon tobacco for export, and the demand for **slave** labor rose. New indentures and their children found that most of the best lands near Jamestown were concentrated in the hands of elites. Freemen seeking land were pushed deeper into the backcountry, where they encountered less fertile land, the challenge of clearing new lands, and threats from Native Americans. Indian relations on the frontier provided the initial cause for Bacon's Rebellion. White settlers in the backcountry suffered raids by hostile Indian groups living in the same remote regions and demanded militia protection. When such protection proved inadequate, Virginia elites bore the blame.

There was merit to the charge that elites did not share the concerns of backcountry farmers. Declining tobacco prices resulting from England's war with the Dutch led many of the wealthier planters to trade with friendly Indians, and officials were reluctant to risk igniting Indian wars because of incidents on the frontier. Along the James River, a group of freemen of humble means took matters into their own hands and began campaigns that made little distinction between friendly and hostile Indians. They were led by Nathaniel Bacon, Jr., who was actually a wealthy planter who harbored personal grievances against the government and deemed it corrupt. Governor William Berkeley invited Bacon to Jamestown to try to resolve the dispute, but when Bacon demanded a militia commission, Berkeley declared Bacon treasonous and ordered his arrest. For reasons not entirely clear, Bacon was released and allowed to contest a seat in the colonial legislature. When Bacon won, Berkeley tried and failed to prevent Bacon from taking his seat. Governor Berkeley himself was faced with violence, and fled Jamestown. With Berkeley out of the way, Bacon increased his militia and plundered the estates of pro-Berkeley elites. Soon Virginia was awash in race and class warfare. Raids against Native Americans increased and in July 1676, Bacon issued a *Declaration of the People of Virginia*, which called for the removal of all Indians from the region. The upshot of this proclamation was to inflame tribes that had hitherto lived at peace with Jamestown settlers.

The class struggle also intensified, with Berkeley offering freedom to indentured servants who joined his militia, and Bacon promising freedom to slaves and indentured servants who joined his cause. Bacon's militia—probably numbering 500 at the height of its popularity—roamed the backcountry in search of Indians and Berkeley supporters. In September, they burned the city of Jamestown.

Frustrated by the colonial government's reluctance to remove Native Americans from lands desired by settlers, Nathaniel Bacon led Virginians in an attack on Native Americans in 1676. Known as Bacon's Rebellion, this civil revolt was the first serious test of British authority in the New World. (Library of Congress)

Governor Berkeley appealed to the English government for troops to put down the rebellion. The uprising fizzled when Bacon fell ill and died in October, probably from dysentery contracted while campaigning in the backcountry. When British troops arrived, they arrested all but 80 of Bacon's followers.

Berkeley exacted harsh justice when he returned to Jamestown, including the hanging of two dozen wealthy Bacon supporters whose estates he distributed as compensation to pro-Berkeley victims whose own properties had been plundered by Bacon's forces. King Charles II was displeased with Berkeley's response and recalled him to England, where he died in 1677. Subsequent legislation loosened Virginia's social system for whites. Most class-based sumptuary laws—those regulating consumption and decorum—were repealed. For instance, after the rebellion any white Virginian male could wear a sword in public or be addressed as "sir"—privileges once reserved for elites. By the same token, laws regulating relations between whites and black slaves were tightened. Many scholars argue that slavery took a harsher turn in the wake of Bacon's Rebellion, and that Virginia officials used racism to deter a possible future alliance between poor whites, indentured servants, and slaves.

Nathaniel Bacon, Jr., is viewed by some as a champion of liberty and his rebellion as a precursor of the American Revolution. Such readings are often overly romantic. Bacon was also motivated by personal ambition and, though he was willing to consider freeing slaves who joined his cause, was a vicious racist insofar as he viewed Native Americans. Less-charitable scholars view Bacon as a power-hungry criminal whose recklessness was responsible for the slaughter of Indians and, ultimately, the worsening of conditions for slaves. Bacon's complaints about unjust taxation in his *Declaration* assuredly had future impact, as did his assault on systems of deference and class-based privilege. The rebellion also played a role in establishing the image of yeomen farmers as symbols of individualism and independence.

Suggested Reading

Declaration of the People of Virginia, http://historymatters.gmu.edu/d/5800, accessed June 8, 2010; Michael Oberg, ed., *Samuel Wiseman's Book of Record: The Official Account of Bacon's Rebellion in Virginia, 1676–1677*, 2005; Wilcomb E. Washburn, *The Governor and the Rebel*, 1957; Stephen S. Webb, *1676: The End of American Independence*, 1984.

BAGLEY, SARAH

Sarah Bagley (April 19, 1806–1884?) was president of the **Lowell Female Labor Reform Association** (LFLRA), regarded by many scholars as the first important woman-led labor organization in the United States. Bagley was the first female labor leader to exert influence outside her local area, and she advanced the role of women in other areas as well. Unfortunately, her biography contains as many holes as highlights.

Bagley was raised in Candia, New Hampshire, one of five children born to Rhoda (Witham) and Nathan Bagley, who farmed. Very little is known of Bagley's life before she arrived in Lowell in 1835, though the eloquence with which she spoke and wrote suggests that she had some formal education. Historians assume that she went to Lowell for the same reason that many New England farm women went there—to earn **wages** to support her family's farm. New England farming was already in decline by the 1830s, and it is known that Bagley's parents also operated a small mill and sold land to keep the farm afloat. Bagley had two brothers and was unmarried when she came to Lowell. Given the **agrarian** ideals that prevailed and the gender assumptions of the day that posited women were naturally suited for domestic duties, Sarah would have been a prime candidate to work outside the home. It was common for rural girls to spend time in domestic service, teaching, or some other money-making activity until they married. At age 28, Sarah would have been considered a "spinster" as she was already nine years past the average age at which her contemporaries married. Lowell was probably chosen as her destination because other New Hampshire women from Bagley's region were there and recommended her to management. Moreover, in 1835 Lowell was a popular tourist destination as well as a thriving industrial concern. Bagley may also have been attracted to the city because it offered cultural, educational, and social activities unavailable in rural New Hampshire.

Bagley began work in the Hamilton Mills. She took part in Improvement Circles, designed to enrich the educational and cultural lives of mill workers. In 1840, she wrote her first known article for the *Lowell Offering*, a paper sponsored by the Boston Associates, the consortium that owned Lowell's textile mills. Lowell was originally designed as a safe haven for New England farm girls, but tensions began to gather. A short walkout by workers occurred in 1834, the year before Bagley arrived. The Panic of 1837 led to wage cuts, **speedups**, and high turnover rates. Ironically, Bagley's career as a labor leader may have begun after she was first a **scab**. Records are not clear, but Bagley left the Hamilton Mills in 1842 and took a job as a weaver in the Middlesex Mills, perhaps assuming the position of a striking weaver.

Subsequent wage cuts, **stretch-outs**, and speedups radicalized Bagley. She became an advocate of the theories of Charles Fourier (1772–1837), a French utopian advocate of **cooperative** production and communal living. When Lowell management restored the wages of men to pre-1842 levels in 1844, but kept in place cuts to women's wages, Bagley cofounded and served as the first president of the LFLRA. By June 1845, the group had more than 500 members, and Bagley left her mill job to expand the association's reach to other cities. Eventually Female Labor Reform groups met in Waltham and Fall River, Massachusetts; Dover, Nashua, and Manchester, New Hampshire; and across western Pennsylvania.

Central to the LFLRA platform was a call for a 10-hour workday. Bagley immersed herself in the shorter-hours struggle and testified before a Massachusetts legislative committee on behalf of the cause in 1845. She also affiliated the LFLRA with the New England Workingmen's Association and served as the editor of its newspaper, *The Voice of Industry*. Her attacks on the *Lowell Offering* hastened that paper's demise, and her organization known as the Industrial Reform Lyceum brought a steady stream of radical speakers to Lowell. Despite Bagley's tireless efforts, the 10-hour plea was rejected by the Massachusetts legislature, though Lowell mills briefly shortened the workday by a half-hour. A call for a **general strike** on July 4, 1846, fizzled and Bagley was fired from *The Voice of Industry* by editor John Allen, who held a low opinion of women in positions of authority.

Friends of Bagley helped her secure a position as a telegraph operator in Lowell's newly opened office, which made her the first woman in U.S. history to hold such a position. In 1847, Bagley was dispatched to Springfield, Massachusetts, where she ran the telegraph office. Bagley was horrified to learn that her salary was a third less than the salary of the man she replaced. Private letters make it clear that Bagley had evolved views of women's equality and rights that today would be deemed "feminist." She left Springfield in 1848 and returned to the Hamilton Mills in Lowell. She continued to seek public forums for her views of women's rights, prison reform, the 10-hour workday, Fourierism, and women's health. In 1850, she moved to Philadelphia, converted to Quakerism, and worked in a home that sought to redeem prostitutes and poor women. It was there that she met James Durno (1796–1873), a New York homeopathic doctor and patent medicine manufacturer.

On November 13, 1850, Bagley and Durno wed. They moved to Durno's hometown of Albany in early 1851 and set up an herbal and homeopathic medical practice for women and children. The couple relocated to Brooklyn Heights, New York, in 1867 and manufactured a medicinal snuff as well as maintaining a medical practice. After Durno died in 1873, Bagley largely disappeared from the historical record. Her death date and final resting place remain mysteries.

Suggested Reading

Eleanor Flexner, *Century of Struggle: The Woman's Rights Movement in the United States*, 1972; Philip Foner, *Women and the American Labor Movement: From the First Trade Unions to the Present*, 1982; Helene Wright, "Sarah G. Bagley: A Biographical Note," *Labor History* 20, no. 3 (1979): 398–413.

BARRY, LEONORA MARIE

Leonora Barry (August 13, 1849–July 15, 1930) was the general investigator for women's work for the **Knights of Labor** (KOL), a pioneer in organizing women into labor unions, and one of the most powerful female labor leaders of the late 19th century. She was one of the first people to compile accurate statistics and reports on women laborers, to bring women into the union fold, and to insist that women's organizing models should reflect their interests, not those of men. Partly due to Barry's efforts, the KOL had as many as 65,000 female members at a time in which very few unions even tried to organize women and quite a few refused to accept female members.

Lenora Marie Kearney was born on August 13, 1849, in County Cork, Ireland, the daughter of John and Honor (Brown) Kearney. The family left Ireland to escape the ravages of the potato blight and immigrated to upstate New York in 1851. Leonora's mother died in 1864 and her father remarried. She quarreled with her stepmother and left home at age 16. Leonora studied at a girls' school in Colton, New York, and obtained a teaching certificate before she was 17. At the time, public education was still in its infancy. Only New England, New York, and Pennsylvania had appreciable numbers of public schools, and just slightly more than half of American children obtained formal education. Rules for licensing teachers varied widely and standards were generally low. Teaching was often viewed as an extension of "republican motherhood"—a loose set of values that placed the duty of moral and civic education upon female heads of households. Primary school teaching was a poorly paid profession dominated by unmarried women.

Most states required female teachers to quit when they wed, as the prevailing values of the time dictated that women were supposed to confine themselves to domestic tasks. As such, Leonora Kearney taught until 1871, when she married William E. Barry, a Potsdam, New York, house painter. She bore three children between 1873 and 1880: Marion Frances (1873), William Standish (1875), and Charles Joseph (1880). House painting was a skilled profession that combined aspects of interior decorating, but it was a poorly paid and dangerous one. Painters often scaled high ladders, and materials often contained high concentrations of lead and other toxins. The Barry family moved several times before settling in Amsterdam, New York. In 1881, both Leonora's daughter and her husband died of lung disease. Barry was forced to seek employment to support her sons and secured it at an Amsterdam hosiery mill after first failing as a seamstress. In 1884, she joined the KOL's Victory Assembly in Amsterdam. Barry rose quickly in the KOL. In 1885, she became Master Workman (president) of District Assembly 65, a body representing 52 local assemblies and more than 9,000 workers, most of whom were men.

Barry also headed Victory Assembly's 900 women and led them during a successful mill strike in 1886. That same year, she helped the national order resolve a dispute with retail magnate John Wannamaker, and so impressed KOL leadership that the 1886 KOL convention appointed her as the union's first general investigator for women's work. Barry put her sons in boarding school and spent nearly four years traveling, lecturing, organizing, and compiling reports on behalf of the KOL. In 1888 alone, she visited more than 100 cities. Her reports detailed low wages, shocking conditions, and abuses against women workers. Barry's reports were so sensational that employers took steps to deny Barry access to their workplaces.

Barry was not afraid to tackle discrimination within the KOL. She routinely chided male Knights for not living up to the organization's platform plank on gender equality, and women workers for their apathy toward organized labor. She was also one of the first union leaders to insist that organizing women required different methods than unionizing male workers. The latter was controversial among some Knights, as the organization originally based much of its ritual and many of its values upon the practices of male-dominated fraternal orders. In addition, male Knights often shared sexist attitudes about women that were in flux in the late 19th century, but remained dominant.

Barry became embroiled in the KOL's internal politics and earned the antipathy of General Secretary John Hayes, who plotted to remove much of Barry's power. In 1888, the Women's Department was placed under Hayes's personal control, and he harassed Barry. In April 1890, Barry shocked the KOL by announcing she was resigning from the organization because of her recent remarriage to Obadiah Reed Lake, a St. Louis editor and printer. In her resignation, Barry opined that a woman's proper place was in the home, a believable and face-saving statement given the values of the day. It was, however, more likely a loyal act on Barry's part rather than a deeply felt conviction. Barry quickly returned to public life to campaign for women's suffrage and to lecture on behalf of the Women's Christian Temperance Union and the Catholic Total Abstinence Society. She retired to Minooka, Illinois, where she died of mouth cancer on July 15, 1930.

Suggested Reading

Philip Foner, *Women and the American Labor Movement*, 1982; Susan Levine, *Labor's True Woman: Carpet Weavers, Industrialization and Labor Reform in the Gilded Age*, 1984; Robert Weir, *Knights Unhorsed: Internal Conflict in a Gilded Age Social Movement*, 2000.

BATTLE OF BLAIR MOUNTAIN

The Battle of Blair Mountain was an armed encounter between miners and deputy sheriffs, state police, the U.S. Army, and Baldwin-Felts detectives. Miners' strikes were noted for violence, but the events at Blair Mountain were particularly bloody. The confrontation took place in West Virginia during August 1921, and ended when President Warren Harding sent federal troops to the area and even ordered the aerial bombing of entrenched miner positions. Many sources claim that Blair Mountain was the largest armed struggle on American soil since the **Civil War**. The Battle of Blair Mountain came near the end of a protracted strike in West Virginia and Kentucky during the years 1920 to 1923, a struggle that included the infamous **Matewan** massacre.

The troubles at Blair Mountain were a direct response to events in Matewan, West Virginia. Matewan police chief Sid Hatfield was on trial in supposedly neutral McDowell County for the murder of detective Albert Felts when, on August 1, 1921, Baldwin agents gunned him down on the courthouse steps. Miners planned to march from Kanawha County to the Logan County Courthouse to protest Hatfield's murder, as well as the ongoing refusal of coal operators to bargain with the **United Mine Workers of America** (UMWA). Angry miners announced their intention to hang the local sheriff, burn the courthouse, and then proceed to Mingo County to free imprisoned miners. The march commenced on August 24, 1921, and was dubbed "Mother Jones's Will," even though **Mary Harris Jones** counseled against it.

The marchers never made it to the courthouse. Instead, they were met by armed resistance organized by Logan County's virulently anti-union Sheriff Don Chafin. At first there were just small exchanges of gunfire, but as more miners streamed into the area, the two forces took up positions in the mountain ridges and the Battle of Blair Mountain ensued. No one knows for certain how many miners were involved; estimates vary from 7,000 to more than 20,000, as miners from nearby counties flocked to give assistance. Despite facing a foe armed with machine guns and private planes dropping homemade bombs, miners routed a force of deputy sheriffs. Miners briefly controlled much of the area south of the state capital of Charleston, West Virginia, plundering stores, waylaying trains, posting sentries, and causing many politicians to flee.

On August 30, President Harding placed all of West Virginia under martial law. On September 1, 2,500 federal troops arrived with more machine guns, percussion and gas bombs, and 14 airplanes commanded by World War I hero General Billy

Mitchell. Bombs rained on miners' positions, though their accuracy was problematic; in the early days of flight, bombs were literally "dropped" from flimsy aircraft. The insurrection soon collapsed, as many miners refused to take up arms against their government and union leaders such as Bill Blizzard realized that miners could not prevail against such overwhelming firepower. Miners began to sneak off the ridges, often hiding guns and ammunition as they beat a retreat.

Exact casualty figures for the 10-day confrontation are unknown. Estimates place miner deaths at between 50 and 100, and those of the coalition between Baldwin-Felts agents, the sheriff's department, West Virginia State police, and the U.S. Army at 10 to 30. Untold hundreds were wounded, and 985 miners were indicted for crimes ranging from murder to treason against the state of West Virginia. Many were acquitted, as there was little love lost between West Virginia citizens and coal mine operators. The last convicted miners left jail in 1925.

The Battle of Blair Mountain broke the strike, though the UMWA did not officially call it off until 1923. UMWA membership plummeted in the aftermath of Blair Mountain, but the harsh conditions of American mines guaranteed that the union's presence would remain. The events also cast a harsh light on the horrendous conditions in the West Virginia and Kentucky coal patches and the tyranny of coal miner operators, which in turn allowed the UMWA to recruit powerful political allies. By the 1930s, the UMWA had reversed its fortunes and its national president, **John L. Lewis**, became a commanding force in capital/labor relations.

Suggested Reading

David Corbin, *Life, Work, and Rebellion in the Coal Fields: The Southern West Virginia Miners, 1880–1922,* 1981; Howard Lee, *Bloodletting in Appalachia,* 1969; Lon Savage, *Thunder in the Mountain: The West Virginia Mine War,* 1990; Robert Shogan, *The Battle of Blair Mountain: The Story of America's Largest Union Uprising,* 2004.

BELLAMY, EDWARD

Edward Bellamy (March 26, 1850–May 22, 1898) was a journalist and writer whose 1888 work *Looking Backward* captured the imagination of Gilded Age readers to such a degree that reform movements worldwide formed to try to implement aspects of his fictional utopian. The U.S. movement was called "Nationalism," and is often referred to as "Bellamyite Nationalism" to differentiate it from the political term "nationalism." Bellamy's book fired the public's imagination to the point where it was selling 1,000 copies per day. It brought fame to the otherwise unassuming western Massachusetts novelist and reporter for the *Springfield Daily Union,* whose previous science fiction novels and plays attracted scant notice.

The narrative of *Looking Backward* centers on Julian West, a member of the 19th-century bourgeoisie, who is placed in a hypnotic trance and awakes in the year 2000. West finds that the strike-plagued, poverty-ridden Boston of his youth has been supplanted by an egalitarian utopia in which all members of society serve in the Industrial Army from age 21 until their retirement at 45. Competitive **capitalism** has been replaced by a network of state-owned production and distribution centers. Also banished are class conflict, money, accumulated wealth, taxes, nonproductive labor, domestic toil, gender inequality (as Bellamy understood it), and most other social problems. Best of all from the viewpoint of Bellamy's readers, who lived amidst the woes described in the book, the transformation from chaos to social harmony occurred peacefully, with Americans simply agreeing that society was in crisis and incrementally voting in necessary changes.

As a work of literature, *Looking Backward* is cumbersome. It is essentially an extended dialogue between West and Dr. Leete, the physician who revived him and patiently explains how the utopia works. Much to Bellamy's surprise, middle-class readers devoured the book with even more gusto than those from the **working class**, even though the world Bellamy described was based largely upon precepts of evolutionary **socialism**. *Looking Backward* captured the nervous Zeitgeist of the late Gilded Age, a time in which the **strikes**, violence, unemployment, and inequality banished in Bellamy's future utopia were a daily reality. Bellamy's peaceful road to reform appealed to genteel citizens weary of economic depression and social conflict. Many took Bellamy's book as a literal blueprint for the future. In 1889, Bostonians set up the first "Bellamy Club"; within a decade, more than 165 such groups had sprung into existence. The movement became known as Nationalism because of the State- (nation-) directed nature of Bellamy's utopian world.

From his home in the small industrial city of Chicopee Falls, Massachusetts, Bellamy was hailed as a visionary and humanitarian. Both the **American Federation of Labor** and the **Knights of Labor** (KOL) endorsed Bellamy's book. *Looking Backward* was a staple inside KOL local assemblies, and numerous Knights joined Nationalist clubs; in turn, several clubs evolved into labor unions. Bellamy's book also made a stir outside of North America; if anything, Australians and New Zealanders were even more enthused about the novel. Bellamy was at first reticent to join the movements that bore his name, but he eventually took an active role in the Nationalist movement. In 1897, he was persuaded to publish a sequel, *Equality*, that addressed criticisms leveled by opponents of his utopia. The book lacked the conventional Victorian romance of its predecessor and its sales languished; Bellamy died the following year.

As science fiction, *Looking Backward* anticipated several future developments, including the invention of radio, credit cards, and shopping malls. Its social aspects are a blend of progressiveness, quaintness, and naiveté. For example, Bellamy described a world in which women married at will, were active in the workforce, and were relieved of the sole responsibility for childrearing and domestic toil. Yet women were also assumed to be unsuitable for certain types of work, uninterested in politics, demure, and almost singularly focused on shopping. The book's critique of Gilded Age problems remains incisive, however, and Bellamy's influence outlived him. His ideas had profound impact on the **Populist** movement, especially in how **cooperation** was understood. He attracted a host of admirers within the labor movement, including **Eugene V. Debs**, **Daniel DeLeon**, **Elizabeth Gurley Flynn**, and Upton Sinclair. *Looking Backward* was also widely read, quoted, and modified among reformers in both the **Progressive Era** and the New Deal era. Later on, proponents, architects, and thinkers associated with the Garden City and New Urbanism movements drew inspiration from some of the physical dimensions of futuristic Boston described by Bellamy.

Suggested Reading

Edward Bellamy, *Looking Backward*, 1888; Peter Coleman, *Progressivism and the World of Reform*, 1987; Franklin Rosemont, *Apparitions of Things to Come*, 1990.

BIG STRIKE. *See* Harry Bridges.

BITUMINOUS COAL STRIKES OF 1974 AND 1977–1978

The two bituminous coal strikes of the 1970s illustrate the ways in which changing economic realities impacted labor unions in the United States.

The Bituminous Coal Strike of 1974 was a curiously timed 28-day **strike** in November and December called by the **United Mine Workers of America** (UMWA) in the "soft" coal fields of the United States. On the one hand, the time was ripe for a confrontation. The first Organization of Petroleum Exporting Countries (OPEC) oil boycott came in 1973, producing shockwaves through the energy sector of the economy. Production increased in bituminous mines as well as in the "hard" coal anthracite mines that provided cleaner, longer-burning fuel. Miners were also in need of a raise, as they worked long hours in dangerous conditions yet made far less than peer workers such as steelworkers. On the other hand, for the UMWA, the strike's timing carried risks. It was still reeling from internal corruption problems, including the murder of **Joseph A. Yablonski** and ongoing allegations that former UMWA President Tony Boyle was responsible for the crime. The new UMWA head, Arnold Miller, pledged to carry out democratic reforms within the UMWA, but he first had to struggle to control various dissident factions, some of whom had conducted **wildcat strikes**. Moreover, bituminous stockpiles were relatively high when the miners walked out on November 12. The UMWA nonetheless demanded massive **wage** increases, larger contributions to miner **pensions**, and better benefits, including an improved health care plan.

The UMWA was forced to call off the strike when President Gerald Ford threatened to issue an executive branch **injunction** as authorized by the **Taft-Hartley Act**. The UMWA did win its biggest wage increase in history, automatic **cost-of-living adjustments** (COLA), and a rich benefits package for working miners. These gains came at the expense of reducing benefits for some retirees and promising to stop wildcat strikes. The contract passed only narrowly and Miller proved unable to rein in wildcatters, a problem that curtailed the promising recruitment drive for new UMWA members that Miller launched in 1972 when he assumed the organization's presidency.

Shortly after settling the strike, Miller was beset by internal squabbles inside the UMWA, including clashes with supporters loyal to the deceased Yablonski. He narrowly won reelection in 1977, but faced pressures to give more power to **union locals**, including the right to call their own strikes. This right became a major sticking point among mine owners and was the major issue that led to another strike in bituminous coal mines in 1977–1978. Those strikes were marred by violence, and President Jimmy Carter once again invoked the Taft-Hartley Act. This step stopped the strike for most miners and forced the UMWA to the bargaining table in March 1978, though numerous locals simply ignored Carter's injunction and their own leadership. Once again Miller had to convince the rank-and-file that UMWA leaders had worked out the best possible **contract**. The new deal contained wage increases and retained COLAs, but it included **concessions** over health care premiums, reduced benefits, and imposed penalties on wildcat strikers. In the end, most miners acquiesced to the contract mainly because the pension fund was nearly depleted.

The 1977–1978 strike, and a heart attack less than two weeks after the new contract was accepted, effectively reduced Miller to a lame duck leader. He resigned as UMWA president in late 1979.

The two strikes taken together show how the 1970s recession influenced the future of organized labor. The 1973 strike took place after the first energy crisis, but before its overall impact was felt. By 1977, the economy was in its fourth year of stagflation. The second strike is viewed as a concessions strike and presaged the pressures that numerous unions would face in the 1980s.

Suggested Reading

John Ackermann, "The Impact of the Coal Strike of 1977–78," *Industrial and Labor Relations Review* 32, no. 3 (January 1979): 175–188; Paul F. Clark, *The Miners' Fight for Democracy: Arnold Miller and the Reform of the United Mine Workers*, 1981.

BLACKLEG. *See* Scab.

BLACKLIST

In labor terms, a blacklist most commonly refers to a record kept by employers of workers who should not be hired because they are deemed troublemakers, union activists, ideologues, or unreliable. This list is shared with other employers, and workers whose names appear on it experience difficulty in securing work. In some instances, a blacklist refers to a register of antilabor employers circulated by unions and reformers. Potential employees are warned to avoid taking jobs with said firms. A blacklist is a type of **boycott**.

Some sources trace the use of the term to the panel of judges who sentenced English King Charles I to death in 1649, but the *Oxford English Dictionary* identifies a 1619 use by Jacobean dramatist Philip Massinger. The first printed reference to a worker being blacklisted occurred in 1774. By the time the *Atlantic Monthly* recorded the first American use in print, it merely gave name to the common practice of employers blacklisting workers who challenged their authority. Landing on a blacklist often had devastating consequences for a worker. At a time before most social safety nets existed, being blacklisted meant that one could not make a living at a given trade. In remote mining towns and in **company towns**, a blacklisted employee might not be able to find any sort of work at all. Many assumed new identities and left the area. Employers often used blacklists punitively. The aftermath of a broken **strike** often saw employers blacklist large numbers of workers, leaders and rank-and-file workers alike. The American workforce was quite mobile until after World War II. Unions issued traveling cards for members journeying to a new town. These were designed mostly to introduce workers to other union members, but another purpose was to help blacklisted laborers forced to wander in seek of employment.

In theory, the 1935 **National Labor Relations Act** (NLRA) outlawed blacklists as an **unfair labor practice** if used to punish workers for criticizing their employers or being pro-union. In practice, blacklists endured and remain common. One way around the NLRA is to base blacklists on other grounds. From 1947 until well into the 1960s, for instance, Hollywood actors, writers, producers, directors, and other entertainers were blacklisted for alleged **communist** sympathies. The 1947 **Taft-Hartley Act** amended the NLRA in two ways that sustained blacklisting. First, it maintained that employers have a right to oppose unions. Critics charge that this constitutes a backdoor blacklist—an employer can sound out potential employees on their views of labor unions and simply not hire those expressing positive views. Second, the act required loyalty oaths for labor leaders, which made unions subject to the same sort of blacklisting suffered by Hollywood. It became easy to blacklist employees during the height of the **Cold War**—a single allegation of holding radical views was enough to justify dismissal and refusal to hire. The folk singer Pete Seeger was one of many who suffered from the blacklist. Although he was one of the most popular performers of his era, from 1953 to 1967 Seeger was banned from television, was denied access to various venues, and had to scramble to find work—all due to his past labor activism and his association with the Communist Party in the 1930s.

Blacklisting remains a troublesome part of contemporary labor relations. In lieu of producing physical proof, it is exceedingly hard to prove. Employer associations and networks maintain blacklists informally, and the spread of telephones after World War II made it easy for employers to receive hard-to-trace details about workers. Whistleblowers who expose corporate malfeasance are often dismissed for invented reasons; the very act of suing one's employers in such cases makes the worker a public person and dissuades potential employers from hiring the individual. Lawsuits based on blacklisting and wrongful dismissal have, however, been numerous. Employers and personnel office staff have been required to testify under oath about conversations held regarding particular workers and letters thought to be confidential have been subpoenaed. Legal challenges have led to a modern variant of the blacklist. Rather than discuss or commit any views of an employee to paper, employers often simply refuse to comment on a worker's performance. This has become a code that other employers recognize as a veritable do-not-hire suggestion.

Suggested Reading

Paul Buhle and David Wagner, *Hide in Plain Sight: The Hollywood Blacklistees in Film and Television, 1950–2002*, 2003; David K. Dunaway, *How Can I Keep from Singing: The Ballad of Pete Seeger*, 2008; John Earl Haynes, *Red Scare or Red Menace?: American Communism and Anti Communism in the Cold War Era*, 2000.

BLACK LUNG DISEASE AND STRIKE

The Black Lung Strike was a short coal strike in West Virginia in 1969 that resulted in the recognition that miners' pneumoconiosis ("black lung" disease) is an occupationally induced illness for which **workman's compensation** is entitled. Black lung disease is caused by breathing pulverized silica particles within the coal dust that results from blasting and drilling. A form of bronchitis, it is also known as silicosis, anthracosis, and miners' asthma. More colloquially, it is called black spittle, a reference to the dark sputum that results from black lung's most common symptom: a chronic, hacking cough. Difficulty breathing and shortness of breath are other common symptoms. There is no cure for black lung disease, and many people who suffer from it develop accompanying medical problems such as heart disease. The disease is also quite debilitating in its advanced stages; many who suffer from it depend upon external oxygen supplies.

Rank-and-file miners have known about black lung disease for centuries, but until the advent of x-rays there was no way to verify its existence. Mine operators often claimed that black lung was a myth and blamed miners' coughs and black sputum on unhealthy lifestyles such as smoking or careless work habits. The advent of mechanization made the problem more acute. It also had an ironic effect in that **United Mine Workers of America** (UMWA) leaders suspected the reality of black lung disease, but chose not to press the issue. Many miners received bonus pay when they surpassed production **quotas**, and the drills responsible for increased dust helped them achieve it. During the Great Depression, UMWA head **John L. Lewis** opted to not pursue black lung complaints in favor of keeping miners' **wages** at the highest possible levels.

As late as the 1950s, the causes of black lung were still being debated. As scientific evidence mounted, a younger generation of miners began to push the UMWA to take action. In 1968, miners set up the Black Lung Association and engaged in several **wildcat strikes** to publicize the dangers of black lung disease. The campaign to force the coal industry to recognize the ravages wrought by black lung gathered strength during a dispute over other issues between the UMWA and Westmoreland Coal's East Gulf Mine in Rhodell, West Virginia. A strike began on February 18, 1969, and soon spread; within days, more than 40,000 miners were off the job. A key UMWA strike leader was Arnold Miller, a reformer within what was then an autocratic union. The strike lasted 23 days and saw the miners muster a mass demonstration at the state capital in Charleston. Although West Virginia Governor Arch Moore was angered by the 1968 wildcat strikes and the 1969 UMWA protest in Charleston, he signed legislation making black lung eligible for compensation, and the strike ended on March 11, 1969.

Later in 1969, Congress passed the Coal Mine Health and Safety Act and placed enforcement of the bill under the auspices of the Mine Safety and Health Administration. Numerous miners filed for compensation immediately after the bill's passage. Congress funded awards from the Black Lung Disability Trust from a special federal tax on coal. Mine operators agreed to support the bill after provisions were added that required a minimum of 10 years' employment in the mines before compensation would be paid. The UMWA, in turn, received a guarantee that workers exhibiting symptoms of black lung would be transferred to non-dust-producing jobs at no reduction in pay. The successful fight also hastened changes inside the UMWA. Miller headed Miners for Democracy (MFD), a rank-and-file insurgency group that sought to cleanse the UMWA of corruption. In the wake of the dramatic murder of **Joseph A. Yablonski**, of which opponent Tony Boyle was convicted, the MFD gained control of the UMWA. In 1972, Arnold Miller was elected UMWA president.

Black lung is now recognized as an occupational disease associated with coal mining. Awareness of black lung and related diseases—such as "brown lung" and "white lung" among textile workers and stonecutters, respectively—has led to changes in factory ventilation and dust control systems to control the ingestion of airborne particulates. The changes have had mixed success. After an immediate and dramatic drop in black lung rates—up to 90 percent by some estimates—black lung claims rose in the first decade of the 21st century. More than 10,000 deaths have been attributed to black lung since then, and current research suggests that a miner who works 25 years underground has a nearly 10 percent chance of developing the disease.

Suggested Reading

Alan Derickson, *Black Lung: Anatomy of a Public Health Disaster*, 1998; Kim Moody, *An Injury to All: The Decline of American Unionism*, 1989; National Institute for Occupational Safety and Health, "Occupational Respiratory Disease Surveillance," http://www.cdc.gov/niosh/topics/surveillance/ORDS/ecwhsp.html, accessed May 26, 2010.

BLUE-COLLAR LABOR

Blue-collar worker is an older term used to refer to members of the **working class**. The first use of the phrase is unknown, but it was in wide circulation by the 1940s, and was a commonly used category in sociological studies in the 1950s. Blue-collar workers are those who do manual labor. They are generally contrasted with persons in "white-collar" or "pink-collar" jobs, with white referring to office workers and professionals, and pink to clerical workers who, beginning in the 20th century, were often women. Blue-collar work is often associated with factory labor, though other manual laborers, especially construction workers—sometimes also called "hard hats"—also fit the bill. **Service industry** workers are generally not called blue-collar, though their economic status does not conform to the middle-class standards.

The term likely has its origins in several fashion standards of the early 20th century. First, turn-of-the-century shirts often came with detachable and replaceable collars—the inference being that manual workers get dirty in their jobs and would ruin a white collar. Second, coveralls, jeans, and other clothing were often made of denim and other blue-colored materials. These were worn specifically as work uniforms that could be soiled.

It is often claimed that blue-collar workers toil with their hands, while white- and pink-collar workers work with their minds. Blue-collar jobs have historically required less formal education. These generalizations should be viewed with caution, however. **Apprentice** programs, for example, often require levels of training commensurate with that provided in the classroom.

In the 1950s, strong labor unions, booming industrial output, and government-subsidized programs such as the G.I. Bill and federal housing loans made it possible for blue-collar workers to obtain the trappings of American prosperity such as appliances, automobiles, and home ownership. By the 1960s, however, social analysts began speaking of the "blue-collar blues," a growing disillusionment among manual laborers that employers and society undervalued their work, their values, and their well-being. The work itself was often viewed as demeaning, especially on **assembly lines**. Younger workers found factory discipline distasteful; many engaged in rank-and-file rebellions during the 1960s, and took part in **wildcat strikes** and social protests during the period. Other, often older, workers complained that Baby Boomer children claimed privileges denied to hard-working "average" Americans. Some were deeply troubled by social unrest in the 1960s. In 1970, an incident dubbed the "**hard-hat riot**" saw several hundred New York City construction workers attack anti-Vietnam War protestors on Wall Street. Some observers began to speak of "working-class conservatism." Politicians such as George Wallace, Richard Nixon, and Patrick Buchanan fashioned appeals to supposed working-class conservatives. Although their numbers were exaggerated by the media, the Democratic Party largely underestimated worker resentment. Since the New Deal, blue-collar voters had been a core Democratic constituency, but many blue-collar voters cast presidential ballots for former segregationist Wallace in 1968, and for Nixon in 1968 and 1972. A majority of blue-collar voters opted for **Ronald Reagan** in 1980 and 1984, and a sizable portion of the white working class for Republican candidates since then.

By the 1970s, the "blue-collar blues" were compounded by rising unemployment, inflation, and factory closings. **Deindustrialization** ravaged once-vaunted American industries such as steel, rubber, mining, and electronics, making it appear that blue-collar workers were an endangered species. This decline, coupled with lingering ideological clashes from the 1960s, contributed to the blue-collar voter shift toward the Republican Party. The trend continued despite the implementation of Republican-led policies in the 1980s that exacerbated the decline in blue-collar work. By the 1990s, commentators spoke of the "betrayal" of manual workers, though the term "blue collar" had passed out of common usage. Some observers noted the rising anger among manual workers—especially men—who found that the ideals and implied promises of American society were no longer attainable. Hard work alone no longer guaranteed that a worker could support his family and live in material comfort. Although blue-collar families often decried the privileges of the middle class, increasing numbers dissuaded their children from following in their footsteps and encouraged them to obtain college degrees that would allow them to escape blue-collar employment. Between 1973 and 1995, real **wages**—those adjusted for inflation—tumbled in many construction and manufacturing jobs. Real wages have waxed and waned since then, but the fate of semiskilled and unskilled workers is uncertain in the age of **globalization**, **runaway shops**, and movable capital.

Although manufacturing remains an important part of the American economy, it is clearly in decline. In 1960, manufacturing employed about 28 percent of the U.S.

workforce; by 2006, that figure declined to less than 10 percent. An industrial sector that once produced 53 percent of the economy's net worth now creates just 9 percent, and economists now routinely speak of a postindustrial economy in which service-sector and retail jobs proliferate while blue-collar work continues to decline. On average, the new postindustrial jobs pay 25 percent less than most manufacturing jobs and only about half of the wages available in construction. If such trends continue, "blue-collar" will likely become a historical term referencing bygone work patterns. It, as well as the term "working class," has already fallen from popularity. American workers of all income levels prefer to think of themselves as middle class, though materially speaking, many manual or service industry workers make considerably less than the 2007 median income of $45,113.

Suggested Reading

Barbara Ehrenreich, *Fear of Falling*, 1990; Susan Faludi, *Stiffed: The Betrayal of the American Man*, 2000; Robert Morley, "The Death of Manufacturing," *Trumpet Magazine*, February 2006, http://www.thetrumpet.com/index.php?page=article&id=1955, accessed May 28, 2010; Studs Terkel, *Working*, 1974.

BOSTON POLICE STRIKE OF 1919

The Boston Police Strike of 1919 resulted in a loss by striking city law enforcement officers. Although it was confined to the Commonwealth of Massachusetts, the principle that public employees should be forbidden to **strike** was quickly extended across the United States. For many decades thereafter, civil servants and teachers had to defy state and local laws if they chose to redress their grievances by walking off their jobs. Massachusetts Governor Calvin Coolidge won national acclaim for his handling of the Boston Police Strike. The very next year he was the Republican candidate for vice president of the United States; in 1923 he assumed the presidency when Warren G. Harding died in office. In 1924, Coolidge was elected president in his own right.

The years before the United States' entry into World War I saw the enactment of reforms associated with the **Progressive Era**, but most organized labor groups and **socialists** felt that these measures did not go far enough in protecting working people. Some groups, especially the **Industrial Workers of the World**, engendered fear among the **middle class** because of their radical rhetoric and, ultimately, because they opposed U.S. entry into the war in Europe. During the war, the czar of Russia was overthrown and the rise of a **communist** government under V. I. Lenin added to middle-class anxieties. When World War I ended in 1919, the United States was beset by new rounds of labor conflict, of which the Boston Police Strike was one of the most dramatic.

In that year, more than 3,000 work stoppages occurred, idling approximately 4 million workers. Some Americans feared that these uprisings were precursors to a **working-class** revolution similar to the one that had occurred in Russia in 1917. Others worried that the unionization of public employees endangered civic order and the protection of private property.

Officials in Boston and elsewhere were reluctant to allow police unions to affiliate with larger labor federations. Opponents argued that federations constituted

dual unionism that undermined local control and employees' loyalty to the state. The **American Federation of Labor** (AFL) countered that public employees were skilled **artisans** and, therefore, entitled to union protection. Boston police were ripe to test these competing ideals because they suffered from low **wages** and poor working conditions. Police had received only two raises since 1898, and these failed to keep pace with postwar inflation. Police also routinely worked between 70 and 90 hours per week. The immediate cause of the strike was over union recognition. After 1906, the sole vehicle for addressing grievances was a weak organization called the Boston Social Club, which was controlled by a commissioner appointed by the governor. Realistically speaking, police had no effective **collective bargaining** rights. In August 1919, Boston police formed an independent union. The AFL, which had already organized police in 37 other cities, gave Boston police an AFL charter several weeks later. This action angered Police Commissioner Edward Curtis, who ordered police officers to disband their union. When they refused, Curtis issued Order 110 on August 11, which forbade police from joining any outside organizations except for approved veterans' groups. On September 7, Curtis suspended 19 suspected union leaders. The next day, the Boston Police Union voted to strike by a vote of 1,134 to 2, and on September 9, 1,117 of Boston's 1,544 police officers walked out.

The timing of the strike proved poor. The United States was in the midst of a **Red Scare** that began in earnest with the passage of the 1918 Sedition Act. Several **anarchist**-associated bombings in April 1919 provided a pretext for repression of groups deemed radical and/or detrimental to public order. Boston police were furthered compromised when the first night of their strike saw city residents engage in open gambling, rioting, destruction of property, store looting, and assaults on bystanders, public safety volunteers, and nonstriking police. Mayor Andrew Peters called out the Massachusetts National Guard the next day and personally assumed control of the police department. Peters, a Democrat, probably hoped to embarrass Republican political rivals, including Commissioner Curtis and Governor Coolidge. He also appointed a respected reformer to **arbitrate** the strike. By September 11, calm was restored—with most of the property damage and casualties having been inflicted by the Guard rather than residents.

The police strike might have ended peacefully had not hysteria and politics intervened. Public outrage erupted over the strike, fueled in no small part by city newspapers that labeled it as the leading edge of a "Bolshevik" revolution. This opening provided Curtis and Coolidge with rationale for smashing the strike. Coolidge removed Peters as emergency head of the police department and restored control to Curtis, who announced his intention to fire striking police and replace them with new recruits. Coolidge also rejected the original arbitrator's report and an appeal from AFL President **Samuel Gompers** to raise the strike and await a mediator's report. Coolidge tartly replied, "There is no right to strike against public safety by anybody, anywhere, anytime." His hard-line stance frightened the Boston Central Labor Union, which voted against a **sympathy strike** in support of the police.

By September 13, the strike was effectively broken. True to his word, Commissioner Curtis fired 1,100 police officers and replaced most of them with unemployed army veterans. The new hires received virtually all of the wage and hour concessions that would have averted the strike, though recruits worked in civilian clothing for a time because local garment workers denounced them as **scabs** and refused to sew uniforms. The defeat of the strike weakened attempts to form public-sector unions. Public-sector workers would be excluded from protection under the **National Labor Relations Act**, and it was not until the 1960s that the federal government provided some protection for such workers—and only then after several teachers' and civil servants' unions defied existing laws. Many states still lack laws granting collective bargaining rights to public employees. Coolidge's actions during the Boston Police Strike of 1919 are sometimes viewed as a precursor to those of President **Ronald Reagan** during the 1981 **Professional Air Traffic Controllers Strike**.

Suggested Reading

Ann Hagedin, *Savage Peace: Hope and Fear in America, 1919*, 2007; Francis Russell, *A City in Terror: 1919, The Boston Police Strike*, 1975; Joseph Slater, "Public Workers: Labor and the Boston Police Strike of 1919," *Labor History* 38, no. 1 (1997): 7–27.

BOULWARISM

Boulwarism is an out-of-fashion term that refers to a "take it or leave it" bargaining position assumed by management during a labor dispute. Its source is Lemuel Boulware, who was the chief labor negotiator for General Electric (GE) after World War II. In 1946, the leftist **United Electrical, Radio, and Machine Workers of America** (UE) won a strike against GE. In its wake, GE officials sought ways to cripple the UE by keeping it on the defensive. The plan designed by Boulware combined marketing principles with hardball negotiating. Some tactics were practical, such as studying employee concerns, correcting easily fixable problems, and improving communication between management and employees. Such adjustments were not entirely benevolent, however; they were designed to create the impression that workers did not need a union to resolve disputes. In essence, it was a strategy of giving a little to prevent having to give a lot.

Boulwarism took its most controversial form during **collective bargaining** sessions. GE placed a single and "final and best" offer on the table, which it refused to moderate or alter in any way, and challenged the UE to accept it or reject it. Boulware's strategy came at an opportune time. The second **Red Scare** and the pressures for conformity during the **Cold War** took their toll. In 1949, the **Congress of Industrial Organizations** expelled the UE for alleged **communist** influence. The UE was challenged by the rival **International Union of Electrical, Radio, and Machine Workers**, which engaged in **union raiding** of UE members. In that same year, the UE was forced into an unfavorable settlement with GE.

During the 1950s, other companies adopted Boulwarism. In 1964, the National Labor Relations Board (NLRB) ruled that Boulwarism constituted an **unfair labor practice** and outlawed it. The NLRB decision withstood legal challenges and, in theory, made Boulwarism obsolete. In practice, Boulwarism served as a model for future corporate intransigence. What was outlawed was merely the practice of refusing to negotiate. Under existing labor law, it is very hard to prove that a "best and final" management offer was preconceived rather than the end product of prolonged negotiation. In essence, as long as management talks, it can claim it has bargained in good faith.

Boulwarism also continues to be masked as either/or dilemmas. For instance, in 2010 Hershey Chocolate Corporation announced its intention to close its downtown Hershey, Pennsylvania, plant. Union workers were asked to vote on transferring operations to a factory on the town's outskirts and the elimination of 600 jobs, or face the possibility that all Hershey operations might leave the town.

Suggested Reading

Lemuel Boulware, *The Truth about Boulwarism*, 1969; "Final Whistle," *The Patriot-News*, June 2, 2010; James Matles and James Higgins, *Them and Us*, 1975.

BOYCOTT

A boycott occurs when supporters of organized labor or customers refuse to purchase products or services from concerns whose actions are deemed unfair. As a labor action, a boycott is sometimes used instead of a **strike**. The idea behind a boycott is to bring economic pressure to bear upon a more powerful adversary. In some cases, boycotts are used by organized capital. A notorious example of the latter is the 1973 boycott by the Organization of Petroleum Exporting Countries (OPEC). OPEC deliberately withdrew oil supplies from world petroleum markets to create a surge in prices. Political boycotts are also possible, as in the United States' boycott of the 1980 Olympic Games in Moscow to protest the Soviet Union's invasion of Afghanistan, and in the 2010 tourist boycotts of Arizona to register disagreement with the state's harsh crackdown on illegal immigrants.

The term "boycott" itself is borrowed from Irish nationalists. In the mid-1800s, Captain Charles Cunningham Boycott managed lands in Ireland for an absentee English landlord. When tenants requested rent deductions, Captain Boycott refused and tenants launched a protest that included refusing to work and snubbing him in the community. By 1880, Charles Stuart Parnell and the Irish Land League were using boycott as a general term to mean nonpatronage of a hated rival.

Among 19th-century American workers, boycotts were often preferred to strikes, as the latter incurred economic hardship for both workers and employers. Groups such as the **Knights of Labor** (KOL) were officially opposed to strikes, but ordered untold numbers of boycotts. The KOL sought to publicize boycotts, encourage widespread compliance with them, and apply such economic pressure on employers that they would be forced to bargain with unions in exchange for lifting the boycott. Although boycotts never lived up to the exalted expectations of the KOL, they did force some employers to settle labor disputes. In general, KOL boycotts were most successful when applied against smaller business concerns that lacked reserve capital to weather a prolonged avoidance of their products or services.

There are two types of labor boycotts: primary and secondary. Primary boycotts involve direct refusal to patronize a single employer or corporation, whereas a secondary boycott targets distributors and others who do business with the concern in dispute. In a struggle against a newspaper, for example, a secondary boycott would discourage purchasing any product from a store carrying the boycotted newspaper. An example of a secondary boycott occurred in 1894, when the **American Railway Union** refused to make up trains that included Pullman cars during the 1894 **Pullman strike/lockout**. Secondary boycotts often prove more successful than primary boycotts, but they have been more difficult to launch since 1947, when the **Taft-Hartley Act** banned most types of them. One of the most successful uses of the boycott was instigated by the **United Farm Workers of America** (UFWA), which promoted a five-year boycott of table grapes from 1965 to 1970. Because farm workers are exempt from most national labor laws, the UFWA was able to launch a secondary boycott without running afoul of the Taft-Hartley Act. Another partially successful boycott targeted the Coors Brewing Company, which refused to negotiate with strikers in 1977, fired them, and **decertified** the union when production resumed. Its sales were hurt by the 10-year boycott that ensued, though the brewer remained non-union. A form of secondary boycott that passes legal muster is certain aspects of a **corporate campaign**. During 1991–1992 **Ravenswood lockout**, for instance, unions withdrew pension funds invested in banks that also dealt with the steel firm.

Suggested Reading

Philip Foner, *History of the Labor Movement in the United States, Vol. II*, 1955; Lawrence Glickman, *Buying Power: A History of Consumer Activism in America*, 2009; Daniel Jacoby, *Laboring for Freedom*, 1998; Robert E. Weir, *Beyond Labor's Veil*, 1996.

BRACEROS

Bracero is a Spanish slang term that roughly translates as "strong-arm worker." It is also the name of a controversial labor program that existed between 1942 and 1964 in which Mexicans were recruited to work in the United States as temporary, guest workers. The program's roots go far deeper, however, and its impact continues to resonate. More broadly, *braceros* is a shorthand reference to historical and ongoing disputes over the place of Mexican and Mexican American labor in the United States.

Immigration policy is one of the most contentious issues facing contemporary America, especially insofar as it pertains to undocumented workers coming to the United States. These debates have more greatly affected Latinos than other ethnic groups. Stemming the tide of illegal border crossings by Hispanics has become a bellwether issue for conservatives. Indeed, in 2010, the state of Arizona passed laws designed to curtail illegal immigration that critics view as draconian.

Contemporary discussions of Mexican immigration often ignore the fact that trans-border labor has a long history. Borders between the United States and Spanish Latin America were fluid in the 18th and 19th centuries. Mexico obtained its independence from Spain in 1810, but its northern borders and those of the Louisiana Purchase lands obtained by the United States from France in 1803 were sparsely populated and imprecisely surveyed. By the early 19th century, Mexico

Braceros hear their employment contract explained to them in Spanish during the application process for temporary employment in the United States in 1943. (Howard R. Rosenberg, "Snapshots in a Farm Labor Tradition," *Labor Management Decisions*, Winter–Spring 1993)

was beset by a problem of illegal immigration—namely, white, southern slaveholding Americans crossing into the province of Téjas in defiance of Mexico's ban on both American settlement and **slavery**. This problem lay at the core of the move to separate Texas from Mexico, and contributed to border disagreements that led to the Mexican War of 1846–1848. When this conflict was settled by the 1848 Treaty of Guadalupe Hidalgo, Mexico ceded nearly half its territory to the United States. Instantly, more than 100,000 Mexicans found themselves to be "Americans."

The border between the United States and Mexico remained porous throughout the 19th century, though little attention was paid as the United States was under-populated, Mexicans seldom competed with Anglo wage-earners, and the specialized skills of the *vaqueros* were valued by **cowboys** and ranchers. To the degree that borders were recognized at all, the United States routinely violated Mexican sovereignty by pursuing warring Native American tribes into Mexico. The border received more attention during the Mexican Revolution of 1910. Warfare and deprivation led thousands of peasants to cross into the United States in search of safety and opportunity. This wave of immigration occurred at a time of heightened rhetoric about Anglo-Saxon racial superiority and fueled a call for curtailing immigration and tightening border security. Mexicans were not subject to a restrictive 1924 immigration act, but the Border Patrol was established in that year.

Many Americans supported the exclusion of Mexican immigrants when the **Great Depression** started, but this perspective changed dramatically during World War II, when the United States experienced a labor shortage in agriculture.

Under a 1942 bill officially titled "For the Temporary Migration of Mexican Agricultural Workers to the United States," Mexican workers were recruited to cut sugar beets and harvest crops such as cotton, cucumbers, and tomatoes. This program was popularly called the *Braceros* program; before it ended in 1964, as many as 4 million Mexican workers had entered the United States at the bidding of the U.S. government.

Under the treaty signed with Mexico, immigrants older than the age of 14 were entitled to have their transportation and living costs paid and receive at least $0.30 per hour in **wages**. In practice, the $0.30 wage became the de facto floor and ceiling, living quarters were often substandard, and birth certificates were falsified to facilitate **child labor**. The 1942 bill also provided for repatriation of workers once harvests were completed, but it was quite easy for both employers and laborers to avoid this clause. The *Braceros* program was unpopular among the general public, but corporate agribusiness resisted calls to end it as it had come to depend upon cheap Mexican labor.

Officially the program expired in 1964, but in effect all that happened was that the hiring of Mexican labor shifted from official sanction to customary practice. **Latinos** became viewed as a cheap and readily available labor supply; in fact, some employers preferred to hire illegal workers as they were less likely to complain about poor treatment. The general exploitation of immigrant and migrant labor was among the issues that led to the formation of the **United Farm Workers of America** (UFWA) union in 1966.

The porous border between the United States and Mexico has been an increasingly contentious political issue since the official end of the *Braceros* program. It is likely to remain a source of dispute as long as financial incentives remain for Mexicans to cross the border and for U.S.-based employers to hire them. The U.S. government issues approximately 140,000 official "green cards" each year for Mexican citizens to work in the United States legally, but it is estimated that more than 6 million Mexicans reside in the United States illegally. U.S. policymakers also continue to hold contradictory views on the subject. On the one hand, a border barrier between the United States and Mexico has been expanded, Border Patrol budgets have increased, and stricter laws have gone into effect. On the other hand, in 2004 U.S. President George Bush and Mexican President Vincente Fox discussed the possible creation of a new *Braceros* program. The idea did not survive the recession that began shortly thereafter, but it did not prevent critics from decrying the Bush-Fox plan as a scam to ensure a supply of cheap farm labor for agribusiness, underpaid workers for the **service industry**, and a supply of domestic servants for self-indulgent Yuppies.

Many labor unions have changed their views on immigrant labor. Most **American Federation of Labor-Congress of Industrial Organizations** (AFL-CIO) affiliates once saw unrestricted and illegal immigration as a threat to jobs and maintaining high wages. The social activism of the 1960s, the success of the UFWA, and the integration of Latino workers into labor unions has caused many unions to reconsider their views, especially unions that have sizable Latino membership, such as the **Service Employees International Union** and the **United Food** and Commercial Workers Union. The passage of the **North American Free Trade Agreement** led many union activists to raise questions about why goods should be considered to be free trade, but not labor. Organized labor has been at the forefront in protesting Arizona's immigration law and for calling for a general overhaul of U.S. immigration policy.

Suggested Reading

Ernesto Galarza, *Merchants of Labor: The Mexican Bracero Story*, 1978; Erasmo Gamboa, *Mexican Labor and World War II: Braceros in the Pacific Northwest 1942–1947*, 2000; Carlos Marentes, "Los Braceros 1942–1964," http://www.farmworkers.org/benglish.html, accessed June 16, 2010.

BREAD AND ROSES STRIKE. *See* Lawrence Textile Strike.

BREWERY WORKERS

Brewery workers have been important to American society for a long time. The religious fervor of some Colonial Americans notwithstanding, European settlers of all classes and backgrounds drank alcoholic beverages. The numerous local ordinances against public drunkenness that one finds across Puritan New England are testament more to common practice than to personal piety. By the time of the American Revolution, alcohol consumption was an established tradition and brewing was a lucrative venture; even George Washington distilled whiskey, though the first crisis he faced as president was the 1794 Whiskey Rebellion led by western Pennsylvania farmers who opposed his excise tax on spirits.

Consumption of alcohol rose so dramatically in the early 19th century that visitors to the United States commented on the prodigious amounts consumed and some reformers worried that the new nation was becoming a nation of drunkards. One factor in promoting alcohol consumption was the growth of cities. Urbanization outstripped the building infrastructure such as water treatment facilities; thus distilled spirits and brewed beverages were safer to drink than nontreated water. Moreover, some beverages, especially beer, contained far more nutrients than today's counterparts; beer often provided many of the calories that sustained factory workers. In fact, until the 1840s, it was standard practice for workers to consume beer on the job. Many also drank heavily when not at work, so much so on Sundays that "Blue Mondays" were common—high absentee rates for the opening of the new work week.

As a large-scale industry, however, brewing was an immigrant import, with Germans leading the way in its establishment. During the **Industrial Revolution**, some breweries emerged as corporate giants. As such, they also became battlegrounds between capital and labor. Breweries were seldom unionized in Germany, and they proved hard to organize in the United States as well, despite the long hours and poor conditions endured by factory hands. Failed attempts to organize were made in St. Louis in 1850 and in New York City in 1860. Brewery workers figured prominently at an August 1866 rally in Baltimore, where they demand an **eight-hour** workday in an industry in which 13 hours of work per day was the norm. They also joined Eight-Hour Leagues and participated in a building trades **strike** in New York City in May 1872. In that action, brewery workers made demands for a shorter workday and higher wages. The event ended badly; clashes with police contributed to the strike's collapse and many workers were **blacklisted**. Conditions in the breweries worsened during the Panic of 1873, with many workers writing letters to the German-language *New Yorker Volkszeitung* (*NYVZ*) detailing the horrendous conditions under which they worked.

Brewery workers were inspired by the Great Labor Uprising of 1877. Workers in Cincinnati organized the Brauer Gesellen Union (BGU) in December 1879, a prototypical **industrial union**. The BGU allied with the city's Central Trades Assembly and demanded a 10½-hour workday, a minimum wage of $60 per month, the freedom to secure board and lodging of workers' own choosing, and a reduction of working hours on Sunday from 8 to 4 hours. Four breweries granted these demands, but 19 others refused, and a failed 1881 strike led to the BGU's demise. In that same year, St. Louis workers tried and failed to form a union. In New York City, however, workers formed the Brewery Workers Union (BWU) in the wake of a fire at the Peter Doelger Brewery that killed several employees and complaints that a foreman routinely physically assaulted workers.

The BWU showed early promise and was spearheaded by *NYVZ* journalist George Block, a German-speaking immigrant. It soon expanded across Manhattan, Brooklyn, Union Hill, Newark (New Jersey), Staten Island, and other nearby locales. The BWU's growth frightened brewers, and large firms such as J. Ruppert, Ringler, and Schaefer fired those viewed as union members. The *NYVZ*, the Cigar Makers International Union, the Piano Maker's Union, the **Central Labor Union**, the Socialist Labor Party, and the **United Brotherhood of Carpenters and Joiners** collectively launched a **boycott** of beer from union-breaking brewers. The boycott was successful, but the 1881 strike collapsed in five weeks, blacklists ensued, and the BWU withered.

One remnant of New York's BWU joined the **Knights of Labor** (KOL), but widespread organization was deterred until 1884, when New York's Central Labor Union helped create Brewers' Union #1, which eventually became the United Brewery Workmen of America. Brewers' Union #1 also affiliated with the KOL, which launched a successful 1885 boycott of the Peter Doelger Brewery. Workers in Baltimore, Detroit, Newark, Philadelphia, San Francisco, and St. Louis also joined the KOL, which chartered the Brewery Workers International Union in 1884. The KOL also organized brewery workers in Chicago, Cincinnati, and Milwaukee. Brewery workers and the Knights proved a poor match, however, as the KOL was officially in favor of temperance and its president, **Terence V. Powderly**, was a teetotaler activist.

In 1886, Brewers' Union #1 withdrew from the KOL and set up a national organization. By 1889, nearly all brewery unions had quit the KOL, largely over its temperance policies. Several subsequently affiliated with the **American Federation of Labor** (AFL). Also in 1886, brewery workers in Cincinnati, Baltimore, Chicago, Newark, St. Louis, Philadelphia, Detroit, and Buffalo organized unions of their own.

On August 29, 1886, the first national convention of brewery workers was held in Baltimore; the National Union of the Brewers of the United States (NUB) was formed, to be based in New York City. The NUB began with 2,700 members, and its membership grew to more than 4,000 by January 1887. Union membership was overwhelmingly German in origin, and the NUB published a German-language journal called the *Brauer Zeitung*—later the *Brauerei Arbeiter*—that continued until 1917.

By the time the NUB held its second convention in 1887, brewery workers in Albany, San Francisco, Cleveland, Milwaukee, New Haven, Boston, and other cities had also organized. The name of the organization was changed to the National Union of United Brewery Workmen of the United States, delegates condemned Powderly's recent comments in support of prohibition, and debates raged over whether to admit coopers, teamsters, maltsters, and firemen—a decision ultimately left to each local. The new union was so heavily German that it showed little interest in organizing Irish workers working in the ale and porter breweries. In fact, Local #1 in New York City closed its ranks to new immigrants altogether in 1887, a stance that hampered it during strikes that occurred in 1887–1888. Milwaukee workers walked out in 1887 and the call went out for a boycott of the city's beer. Non-German consumers were disinclined to honor the boycott, however. When the strike spread in the summer of 1888, brewers found it easy to tear up union **contracts**, recruit **scabs** among Eastern European and Italian immigrants, and pressure saloonkeepers who had initially supported the unions. With support outside of the German community nearly nil, the strikes failed. In New York, brewery worker unions were not revived until 1902, and in most locales, only those locals affiliated with the AFL retained vitality, albeit at the cost of jettisoning their socialist and German character.

Under the AFL, unions launched organization drives and boycotts in the larger breweries such as Pabst and Anheuser-Busch. The brewery workers union changed names three times between 1899 and 1918 as it combined with several smaller other bodies to form the International Union of United Brewery, Flour, Cereal, and Soft Drink Workers of America, a name that was maintained until 1947. In that year, the union began publication of its first English-language publication, the *Brewery and Soft Drink Workers' Journal* (which also changed names numerous times).

The organization of soft drink workers partially sustained the union during the period between 1919 and 1933, when the Eighteenth Amendment to the U.S. Constitution outlawed the manufacture, sale, and transportation of alcoholic beverages. The passage of the Twenty-First Amendment and the repeal of Prohibition in 1933 rekindled the driving force behind the alcoholic beverage industry, but for the most part unions began from ground zero once production resumed. From 1933 through 1973, the primary union organizing bottlers and distillers was the International Union of United Brewery, Flour, Cereal, Soft Drink, and Distillery Workers of America. (From 1963 to 1973, it was known as the International Union of United Brewery, Flour, Cereal, Malt, Yeast, Soft Drink, and Distillery Workers of America, at which time it merged with the **Teamsters**.) During the 1930s, the United Brewery union was troubled by **jurisdiction** battles with the

Teamsters and, in 1946, disaffiliated from the AFL and joined the **Congress of Industrial Organizations** (CIO). Its battles against the Teamsters were more dramatic than those against brewers, especially in Pittsburgh, where clashes grew so violent that they were dubbed the "Pittsburgh beer war." The union did, however, affiliate with the merged AFL-CIO in 1955.

Changes after World War II made it difficult to sustain a stand-alone international brewery workers union. This was especially true in the beer industry, which was beset by waves of consolidation. By the 1950s, regional breweries began closing as industry giants such as Anheuser-Busch, Coors, and Miller asserted dominance. For example, northern New Jersey was once home to more than two dozen brewing companies; by 1983, however, only a single Anheuser-Busch plant in Newark remained. The Teamsters had long organized brewery workers, and by 1973 it made sense to merge these workers with the more powerful Teamsters, a task accomplished with the formation of the Teamsters' Brewery and Soft Drink Workers Conference. Most national brands of beer in the United States are today produced by union workers, approximately 80 percent of whom are Teamsters. The same union organizes workers in soft drink firms.

Consolidation in the brewing industry has placed brewery workers at a bargaining disadvantage in recent decades. This weakened position was made manifest in the battle against Coors, a notoriously right-wing and anti-union corporation. The company gave money to such right-wing groups as the John Birch Society and the Heritage Foundation, touted its actively anti-gay policies, and even offered its trucks to California grape growers trying to break the **United Farm Workers of America** boycott. A series of strikes in the 1960s and 1970s against Coors mostly ended in defeat. In 1974, workers walked out over wage issues and a company policy of administering lie-detector tests to employees in which, among other things, they were asked about their sexual preferences. A major strike was launched in 1977, and the AFL-CIO promoted a boycott of Coors. The company broke the strike and returning workers **decertified** the union. The retained boycott hurt Coors' sales but it remained non-union. In 1987, Coors struck a deal with the AFL-CIO in which the boycott was lifted with Coors' agreement not to interfere with future union drives. In 1988, however, the Teamsters failed to win a certification vote. Eventually, workers at the Golden, Colorado, plant affiliated with the Operating Engineers Union, and those at its Memphis brewery signed with the Teamsters. Coors has also instituted domestic partnership benefits, thereby reversing its pattern of past discrimination against gays.

The future of independent brewery worker unions is uncertain. Most organized workers currently belong to the Teamsters, with smaller numbers spread across other unions, including the **United Auto Workers of America**. Very little organizing has taken place in the "microbrew" industry, which began to grow in the 1980s. Many of these concerns are no longer small companies, and several have acquired by larger corporations and may be ripe for unionization. Teamster brewery workers quit the AFL-CIO in 2005, when the Teamsters bolted to the **Change to Win Federation**. In 2007, Teamster brewers were decertified at D. G. Yuengling and Sons, which has led to a union boycott of that brand. In 2010, David Laughton became the head of the Teamsters' Brewery and Soft Drink Conference and threw himself into opposition to a proposed tax on soft drinks that supporters see as a weapon in combating obesity, but which the union sees a threat to jobs.

Suggested Reading

Russ Bellent, *The Coors Connection: How Coors Family Philanthropy Undermines Democratic Pluralism*, 1991; W. J. Rorbaugh, *The Alcoholic Republic: An American Tradition*, 1979; Norman Ware, *The Labor Movement in the United States, 1860–1895*, 1929.

BRIDGES, HARRY

Harry Bridges (July 28, 1901–March 30, 1990) was an important leader of the International Longshoremen's and Warehousemen's Union (ILWU) and a person who stood up to the repression associated with both **Red Scares**. He was born Alfred Renton Bridges, as the son of a prosperous real estate dealer, in Melbourne, Australia. He took the name "Harry" in honor of a favored **socialist** uncle, was thrilled by the novels of Jack London, rejected his father's bourgeois lifestyle, and became a merchant seaman at the age of 16.

Bridges emigrated to the United States in 1920. The next year, he joined the **Industrial Workers of the World** (IWW). By then the IWW was in decline, a victim of the first Red Scare and the target of vigilante justice because of its opposition to U.S. entry into World War I. The collapse of a national seaman's strike in 1921 shook Bridges's faith in the IWW, and he drifted away from both the IWW and life at sea. Ultimately, he settled in San Francisco, took up dock work, and began organizing longshoremen and weaning them away from a **company union**. Bridges was frequently **blacklisted** for his union activities and survived by doing odd jobs and securing occasional work on the docks.

The passage of the 1933 **National Industrial Recovery Act** (NIRA) revitalized weak longshoremen's unions and launched Bridges's career. The NIRA—which was superseded by the **National Labor Relations Act**—provided labor organizers with needed legal protections. Bridges immersed himself in a circle of activists known as the Albion Hall Group, whose name was derived from the building in which they met. The Albion Group was a hodgepodge of former IWW members, Communist Party members, socialists, and disgruntled unionists affiliated with the **American Federation of Labor** (AFL), who felt that its International Longshoremen's Association (ILA) was overly cautious. This assemblage planned a strike of West Coast longshoremen that became the largest **general strike** in American history, and Bridges led it. In 1934, Bridges called for a walkout of San Francisco longshoremen. The 1934 action, sometimes called the "Big Strike," was marked by violence in which San Francisco police joined company detectives in shooting down workers, killing two and wounding scores of others. This action served to infuriate dock workers and was the catalyst for the general strike. Longshoremen in Oakland, Portland, Seattle, and smaller ports joined the 83-day walkout.

Bridges served as chief negotiator in ending the strike. Although the immediate result was ambiguous, longshoremen eventually won control of their own hiring halls, which ended notorious hiring abuses on the docks such as favoritism and daily shape-ups in which job-seekers lined up to be picked for work and many paid kickbacks to foremen for choosing them. In 1937, Bridges led longshoremen to abandon the ILA, form the ILWU, and affiliate with the **Congress of Industrial Organizations** (CIO). Bridges was popular among the rank-and-file, many of whom credited him with changing the image of longshoremen from "wharf rats" to "lords of the docks."

Bridges led the ILWU until 1977 and remained a controversial figure. He was an unapologetic radical, denounced the New Deal as hopeless, and openly supported the Soviet Union, including its brief 1939 alliance with Nazi Germany. His outspoken views led to deportment proceedings in 1939 and again in 1941 on the grounds that he was a communist. The U.S. House of Representatives went so far as to pass a bill calling for his deportation in 1940. Bridges defiantly battled each attack. When the Supreme Court ruled the House act unconstitutional in 1945, Bridges became an U.S. citizen. World War II tempered Bridges's views somewhat, and he supported both wartime production emergency **speedups** and the CIO's **no-strike pledge**. Even so, he continued to infuriate conservatives. Bridges supported an aggressive organization drive among Hawaiian pineapple and sugar field hands in 1944–1946, which was not fully resolved until 1954 and served to break the autocratic grip that big planters had on politics, tax policy, and labor relations in Hawaii's pre-statehood days. Bridges also supported the controversial presidential campaign of Henry Wallace in 1948. The latter action led the CIO to remove him as its West Coast director. The CIO expelled the ILWU in 1950 as part of its purge of allegedly communist-dominated unions. (The ILWU did not join the AFL-CIO until 1988.)

Conservatives continued to go after Bridges. In 1950, he was convicted of perjury for testifying at his naturalization hearing that he had never been a member of the Communist Party. One again the Supreme Court came to Bridges's rescue; in 1953, it voided his conviction and five-year prison sentence. In 1955, the Justice Department finally announced it was ending efforts to deport Bridges, though it would be another three years before he was issued a U.S. passport. Bridges never backed away from controversy. In 1958, he married Noriko Sawada, a woman of Japanese descent and in so doing forced the state of Nevada to repeal its anti-miscegenation laws.

In 1961, Bridges convinced the ILWU to sign a controversial mechanization and modernization agreement that provided workers with protection from the loss of jobs that would result from the introduction of containerization and innovation. Bridges sought to minimize the impact of labor-saving technology on the economic well-being of his union's members. In return for a reduced workforce on the docks, employers created a trust fund for workers' pensions and guaranteed a no-layoff agreement for registered workers. The latter action initially angered some younger workers who lacked seniority. The impact of technological change was blunted when the **Vietnam War** made West Coast ports busier; Bridges used this opportunity to promote the hiring of more African American dock workers. In 1971–1972, Bridges directed a strike that tied up the West Coast waterfront for 135 days.

Although he angered those in power, Harry Bridges was respected by waterfront workers, who saw him as a leader who put their concerns first. He outspokenly led the way on issues of workplace safety, holidays and holiday pay, pensions, health care, and racial equality. Bridges retired in 1977 and died in 1990. The city of San Francisco, which once sought to rid itself of Harry Bridges, now has a plaza named in his honor.

Suggested Reading

"Harry Bridges: A Biography," *ILWU History*, http://www.ilwu19.com/history/biography .htm, accessed June 11, 2010; Charles P. Larrowe, *Harry Bridges: The Rise and Fall of Radical Labor in the U.S.*, 1972; Estolv E. Ward, *Harry Bridges on Trial*, 2010.

BRIDGESTONE-FIRESTONE STRIKE, 1994–1995

On November 4, 1996, members of the **United Steelworkers of America** (USWA) ended a bitter 28-month labor dispute involving more than 4,000 rubber workers when they ratified a contract with Bridgestone-Firestone. This agreement ended a dispute that embodied many of the issues that have confronted organized labor in the past several decades: industrial consolidation, **globalism**, and demands for **concessions** from unionized workers. It also involved the use of a **corporate campaign** against Bridgestone-Firestone.

The roots of the conflict lay in the 1988 decision of the Japan-based Bridgestone firm to acquire Firestone Tire and Rubber Company as a way of breaking into the American tire market. Although Firestone was a revered and iconic firm that dated to 1900, by the late 1970s its plants were antiquated, the company was saddled with debt, and it had a reputation for producing poor-quality goods. Firestone was restructured in 1979, closed numerous factories, and trimmed its workforce. Bridgestone nonetheless got into a bidding war and eventually paid $2.6 billion for Firestone, far more than the firm's fair market value. When the time came to negotiate a new contract with the **United Rubber Workers of America** (URWA) in 1994, Bridgestone demanded huge **wage** and benefit concessions, the elimination of American national holidays, and union protections such as **arbitration** of disputes. Among Bridgestone's demands were a 30 percent wage cut for new hires, 12-hour work shifts, and a 7-day work week. The company also steadfastly refused to view URWA contracts with competitors such as Goodrich and Goodyear as **pattern bargaining** models.

On July 12, 4,000 workers walked out of six Bridgestone-Firestone plants. The URWA launched a national **boycott** of the company's tires, though it lacked the funds to promote this measure effectively. As the strike lingered into the fall, the company employed hardball tactics that were later deemed illegal actions. It even rebuffed an October request from Secretary of Labor Charles Reich to meet with company officials. In early 1995, the company hired 2,300 **scabs**, an action that led President Bill Clinton to issue a March 8 executive order terminating federal contracts with employers that permanently replaced legally striking workers. Numerous complaints of **unfair labor practices** were filed against Bridgestone, but the slowness of the National Labor Relations Board (NLRB) in acting on these disputes put the URWA in a bind. In May 1995, the URWA called off the strike in hopes of saving union jobs and because its treasury was depleted. URWA members who returned to work found themselves working alongside scabs and were assigned the worst jobs in the plants. They were also harassed and intimidated, and were constantly monitored by in-plant security cameras. Moreover, Bridgestone refused to rehire 700 union workers.

On July 1, 1995, the URWA merged with the USWA, and the steelworkers brought their clout to bear on the ongoing dispute. The USWA initiated a world-wide campaign similar to the one used in the **Ravenswood lockout** to force Bridgestone to negotiate a new contract. Demonstrations against the company were held in the United States, Japan, and Europe, and a new boycott was launched. Leaflet distribution and demonstrations were conducted at retail outlets and at auto-mobile trade shows and car races. The **American Federation of Labor-Congress of Industrial Organizations** (AFL-CIO) lent support to the USWA, as the battle involved one of the largest uses of scab replacement labor in U.S. history. In its international campaign, the USWA publicized the company's pollution problems, its workplace safety and health violations, its lack of civic responsibility, and the intolerable conditions under which workers had to toil. It also forged an important link with a militant Japanese union, Zenryoko, raising fears that the strike could spread to Bridgestone's homeland operations. A January 31, 1996, initial NLRB report sustained eight unfair labor charges and found merit in back pay demands by former strikers. The USWA kept up its pressure in the first half of 1996, through measures including protest marches, demonstrations at NASCAR events, and pressure on both General Motors-Saturn and Ford to stop purchasing Bridgestone tires. As global protests mounted and with an NLRB hearing looming, pressures increased for Bridgestone to settle. On November 4, 1996, Bridgestone rehired all former strikers, granted a wage increase, and agreed to all of the workers' demands except for stepped-up production. The campaign was the largest world-wide campaign against a single company in American labor history.

Suggested Reading

Jeremy Brecher, *Strike!*, 1997; Tom Juravich and Kate Bronfenbrenner, "Out of the Ashes: The Steelworkers' Global Campaign at Bridgestone/Firestone," http://digital commons.ilr.cornell.edu/cgi/viewcontent.cgi?article=1037&context=articles, accessed June 11, 2010.

BROTHERHOOD OF LOCOMOTIVE ENGINEERS

The Brotherhood of Locomotive Engineers (BLE) is part of the **Teamsters** union and is the oldest railway union in North America. Today it represents the interests of approximately 55,000 engineers and train dispatchers in the United States and Canada and operates much as other trade unions do. For much of its history, how-ever, its mode of operation was one that scholars invoke as an example of conservative unionism. Early BLE members are often seen as "**aristocrats of labor**," who saw themselves as superior to others and lacked **class consciousness**. More progressive unions frequently vilified the BLE, and its own refusal to cooperate with other groups did little to discourage this attitude.

The first major railway strike occurred on the Baltimore and Ohio line in 1854. This action led engineers to form a short-lived organization that was sidetracked by the onset of the **Civil War**. Representatives meeting in Marshall, Michigan, created the BLE on May 3, 1863, and chose William Robinson as "grand chief engineer." The BLE sought to create favorable relations with management and insisted on the mutuality of capital/labor interests. In 1864, however, Robinson was ousted when the BLE lost a strike against the Michigan Southern and Indiana Railroad. His successor, Charles Wilson, shifted the BLE's emphasis to one of "moral uplift." Great authority was placed in the hands of the BLE chief, and rule changes demanded that a majority of affiliates had to approve a strike before any local could take action. Wilson cooperated with the American Railway Association, an employers' consortium. In 1873, he refused to endorse the BLE's strike against the St. Louis, Kansas City, and Northern, an act that led to his replacement by Peter M. Arthur the next year.

Arthur was a dynamic and powerful leader, but also one of the century's most controversial labor-related figures. He sought to convert the BLE from a guild-like society into a modern trade union, though he did not complete that process. In 1875, Arthur negotiated with William Vanderbilt's New York Central System and signed the nation's first union railroad contract, which was also the first to contain provisions for a guaranteed daily wage. The lost Boston and Maine strike of 1876 and the upheaval of the Great Labor Uprising of 1877 shook both Arthur and the BLE. During the latter struggle, the BLE briefly cooperated with attempts by the Trainmen's Union to unite railroad workers, and it struck an alliance with the **socialist** Workingmen's Party of the United States. When the nationwide rail strikes collapsed and backlash set in, the BLE grew more insular. Only white, literate, experienced engineers aged 21 or older could join the BLE. Most strikes were discouraged and, in 1885, a BLE bylaw forbade members from belonging to other labor organizations.

Arthur shepherded steady growth of the union, such that by 1887, the BLE represented more than 25,000 engineers. The BLE negotiated contracts with more than 100 employers in the 1880s, helped define seniority rules, and set up model insurance and employee benefit schemes. The BLE's relationship with other organized labor groups was tense, however, especially in regard to the **Knights of Labor** (KOL) and the Brotherhood of Locomotive Firemen (BLF). Both condemned BLE exclusivity as a guild-like tactic of preventing their members from rising to an engineer's rank. Moreover, the BLE's lack of **solidarity** with other unions, made manifest in its refusals to endorse or honor the strikes of the KOL or other railroad brotherhoods, had severe consequences. When BLE members crossed picket lines during the 1887 Philadelphia and Reading strike, the KOL and BLF responded in kind during the BLE's disastrous 1888 action against the Chicago, Burlington, and Quincy lines. This behavior escalated into tit-for-tat retaliation that weakened organized labor overall. The BLE refused to support the KOL's 1890 strike against the New York Central and sandbagged the efforts of **Eugene V. Debs** and the **American Railway Union** to make labor gains in 1893–1894.

By the early 20th century, the BLE's stock was so low among other labor organizations that **Industrial Workers of the World** songwriter **Joe Hill** even lampooned BLE martyr John Luther "Casey" Jones as a union **scab**. Arthur died in 1903, and

new BLE chief Warren Stone invested BLE resources in real estate and bank holdings that made the brotherhood wealthy, but struck many observers as inappropriate. In 1915, the BLE finally cooperated with other railroad brotherhoods to secure
passage of the 1916 **Adamson Act**, which granted rail workers an eight-hour workday. Railroads were controlled by the U.S. government during World War I, but
thereafter the BLE engaged in a short progressive burst in which it supported
Robert La Follette's quixotic 1924 bid for the presidency and divested many of its
holdings to make union insurance funds solvent.

Later in the 20th century, the advent of automobiles, the consolidation (and overall decline) of railroading, and changing government roles led to upheaval in the rail
industry and changes for the BLE. The 1934 Railway Labor Act set up government
boards to mediate grievances, settle disputes, and facilitate contract negotiations,
but it also thrust the federal government into the collective bargaining process.
When the BLE called a 1946 strike, it had to weather President Harry Truman's
threat to draft strikers before it won wage concessions. By the 1950s, the BLE was
fighting a rearguard action to salvage jobs in the wake of closing rail lines and management assaults on featherbedding. Nor did it dramatically improve its relationship
with the BLF, with which it rejected amalgamation in 1964, and from which it
turned back a court challenge for a BLE **apprenticeship** program that BLF officials
insisted was an attempt to monopolize engineer training. The BLE also battled the
rival United Transportation Union (UTU) in the 1980s, with the BLE being the only
former railroad brotherhood not to join the UTU when it formed in 1969.

In 1971, the bulk of the United States' passenger intercity rail service was reorganized under Amtrak; in 1976, many of the nation's freight carriers were placed
in the ConRail system. These government-run carriers further complicated BLE relations with federal authorities, as did the passage of the 1980 Staggers Rail Act, which
deregulated the rail industry. BLE officials complained that vital safety issues were
being ignored. A 1982 BLE strike ended after only five days when President
Ronald Reagan imposed an agreement forcing employees to abide by a commission
report that took three years to issue. Many BLE members were infuriated by provisions for a two-tier wage system for new hires and for mandatory drug tests they felt
were demeaning. A 1987 train collision that killed 16 people and injured 170 served
to validate BLE safety concerns.

In 1988, U.S. chapters of the BLE became affiliated with the **American
Federation of Labor-Congress of Industrial Organizations** (AFL-CIO). The
AFL-CIO sanctioned a 1991 strike when a government mediation board failed to
resolve wage and safety disputes, but President George H. W. Bush ordered workers
back on the job within 24 hours. In the mid-1990s, the BLE enjoyed some success
with "dual-track bargaining," in which wages, hours, and benefits were negotiated
on a national level while locals bargained over local concerns. By then, however,
the future of the BLE was akin to that of railroads themselves: uncertain. In 2005,
the BLE was absorbed by the Teamsters, which means it also left the AFL-CIO and
became part of the **Change to Win Federation**. The BLE's very existence is likely
more dependent upon how the future national transportation grid is configured
than on BLE tactics.

Suggested Reading

Brotherhood of Locomotive Engineers and Trainmen, http://www.ble-t.org/links/ble.asp, accessed June 11, 2010; Walter Licht, *Working for the Railroad*, 1983; Shelton Stromquist, *A Generation of Boomers*, 1987

BROTHERHOOD OF SLEEPING CAR PORTERS

The Brotherhood of Sleeping Car Porters (BSCP) was the first African American labor organization to affiliate with the **American Federation of Labor** (AFL) and was an important early voice for civil rights.

African American porters began serving on Pullman Palace cars in 1870, and by the turn of the 20th century nearly all porters were black. Within the black community the Pullman uniform conferred great status, though porters worked long hours, were at the beck and call of railroad patrons, relied upon tips to supplement their meager wages, and had to tolerate abuse from racist passengers. By the 1920s, Pullman porters complained of long travel times, low pay, and company practices such as not paying porters for work performed when trains were not in motion. **A. Philip Randolph** created the BSCP in 1925, after two earlier unionization attempts failed. He served as union president until his retirement in 1968.

Randolph functioned as the spokesperson for the BSCP and often relegated administrative details to capable leaders such as Milton Webster, Ashley Totten, and C. L. Dellums. Pullman cars were usually leased rather than purchased, so porters worked for the Pullman Company rather than the rail lines on which they traveled. The company generally took a hard line against labor unions, as witnessed during the bitter 1894 **Pullman lockout** of production workers. Not surprisingly, Pullman refused to recognize the BSCP and insisted that workers were already represented in what was, in fact, a **company union**. It was only the passage of the **Railway Labor Act of 1926** (RLA)—which set up a National Mediation Board (NMB) to **arbitrate** railroad disputes—that gave the union needed breathing room. Randolph bluffed calling a strike in 1928, using the threat of NMB intervention to stave off Pullman's attempts to crush the BSCP. In that year the BSCP petitioned the AFL for a charter. AFL President **William Green** ostensibly rejected the application because of low BSCP membership. A more likely reason is that the BSCP was not a logical fit inside the AFL. Its membership consisted of what are today called **service industry** workers, whereas the AFL represented **craft unions**, many of which were racist and did not allow black members.

Nonetheless, BSCP organizers gained access to Green's inner council, and 1934 amendments to the RLA allowed sleeping car employees to organize legally. The BSCP won **collective bargaining** rights in June 1935 and, one year later gained a long-sought-after charter from the AFL. Randolph, though a **socialist**, kept the BSCP inside the AFL instead of bolting to the newly formed **Congress of Industrial Organizations** (CIO) because most other railroad brotherhoods were affiliated with the AFL and because he did not wish to bring extra controversy down upon the organization. Even so, he was never completely comfortable with the AFL, whose racism he admonished on regular occasions both in his union role and as a civil rights leader.

In 1937, the BSCP exacted a contract from Pullman that improved working conditions and won wage increases. The BSCP's greatest achievements, however, came in the field of civil rights rather than labor organizing. Railroads were already in decline by the time the BSCP gained its AFL charter, and Randolph was a well-known spokesperson for African American equality. His actions were instrumental in securing passage of the 1941 **Fair Employment Practices Act** and in ending racial segregation in the U.S. military. BSCP activists could be found in most of the key civil rights battles of the 1950s and 1960s and several—notably E. D. Nixon—assumed important leadership roles.

The BSCP began to decline after World War II as rail passenger service dwindled and other rail unions removed racial barriers. The union had more than 15,000 members in the early 1940s, but just 3,000 by the late 1960s. Even as the BSCP eroded, however, Randolph's personal prestige was so high that he was among those who negotiated the 1955 AFL-CIO merger and was the founder of the Negro American Labor Council and its president from 1960 to 1966. He also served on the AFL-CIO's executive council and often clashed with **George Meany**, whom he considered tone deaf on matters of racial equality.

The rise of air travel and changing social attitudes about personal service doomed the BSCP as an independent union. In 1978, the BSCP merged with a larger AFL-CIO union, the Brotherhood of Railway and Airline Clerks, now known as the Transportation Communications International Union. which completed its merger with the **International Association of Machinists** in 2012. Some porters continue to work as baggage handlers and receive tips in addition to the wages, but most today perform functions such as clerking and maintaining railroad cars rather than acting as personal valets.

Suggested Reading

William Harris, *Keeping the Faith*, 1977; William Harris and Martin Schipper, *Records of the Sleeping Car Porters*, 1990; David Perata, *Those Pullman Blues: An Oral History of the African American Railroad Attendant*, 1996; Larry Tye, *Rising from the Rails: Pullman Porters and the Making of the Black Middle Class*, 2005.

BROWDER, EARL RUSSELL

Earl Browder (May 20, 1891–June 27, 1973) was a Communist Party and labor leader. He was born in Wichita, Kansas, to William and Martha (Hankins) Browder. As one of eight children, Browder grew up in poverty. He had to leave school and enter the work world at the age of 10 when his father, an elementary school teacher, suffered a nervous breakdown. He eventually completed correspondence courses in law. His father tutored him in politics, often lecturing him on the virtues of the Populist Party. In 1906, Browder joined the Socialist Party. In 1911, he married the former Gladys Grooves.

Browder quit the **socialists** in 1913, when the party abandoned both its commitment to **syndicalism** and the possible use of **sabotage** as a tactic. One year later he became the president of his local Bookkeepers and Stenographers Union, which was affiliated with the **American Federation of Labor** (AFL). By 1916, he was living in

Kansas City, where he worked in a **cooperative** store. Like many radicals, Browder opposed U.S. involvement in World War I and was twice jailed for antiwar activism. While in jail, he studied **Marxist** theory and became enamored with the Russian Revolution. Upon his release in 1920, he deserted his wife and child, moved to New York City, and joined the nascent Communist Party (CP). The next year, Browder became an organizer for the party's Trade Union Educational League (TUEL). The TUEL was a CP front group dedicated to a strategy often called "boring within," the idea being that CP activists would infiltrate and transform AFL unions. Browder also began editing the TUEL's journal, the *Labor Herald*.

Browder made several trips to the Soviet Union. During a 1926 visit, he began a long affair with legal scholar Raissa Luganovskaya, with whom he had two children. His Russian divorce from his first wife and his subsequent marriage to Luganovskaya were of doubtful legality within the United States. In 1930, Browder became general secretary of the U.S. Communist Party (CPUSA). Two years later, he became chairman when **William Z. Foster** suffered a heart attack, and he held that post until 1945. Under Browder's leadership, the CPUSA took an active role in creating Unemployed Councils and leading rent strikes, both of which were needed grassroots responses to the ravages of the Great Depression. Unemployed Councils sought to mobilize out-of-work laborers into unions and political pressure groups, while rent strikes aimed to fight evictions and force owners to lower rates.

Communist policy and cooperation with **capitalists** shifted several times during the depression. In 1929, the CPUSA abandoned the TUEL and set up its own unions under the aegis of the **Trade Union Unity League** (TUUL), when the party decided that the AFL was irredeemable. The TUUL promoted the concept of **industrial unionism** and denounced AFL **craft unionism** as antiquated, autocratic, and exclusionary. At the direction of communist leaders in Moscow, Browder at first denounced the New Deal as a sham that would not help workers. In 1935, however, the CPUSA entered a phase called the **Popular Front**, in which the rise of German fascism and its potential threat to the Soviet Union (USSR) led communists to cooperate with capitalists. The TUUL was abandoned in 1935, and Browder oversaw a period in which the CPUSA enjoyed its greatest growth spurt. CPUSA labor organizers were respected for their energy and dedication, and they provided tremendous logistical support during the formative period of the **Congress of Industrial Organizations** (CIO), though the CIO was not a communist group and would later expel communist members.

The Popular Front era came to an abrupt halt in 1939, when the USSR signed a non-aggression pact with Nazi Germany, and Browder was ordered by officials in Moscow to again denounce capitalism. When the pact fell apart in 1941 and Germany invaded the USSR, the CPUSA just as quickly reversed course. Browder had run for U.S. president in 1936 and was in jail for a passport violation in 1940, but in the wake of the outbreak of World War II and the alliance between the United States and the USSR, Browder threw his full support behind the war effort. Communists were among the most zealous supporters of **no-strike pledges** during the war, and Browder rallied support for the party under the slogan "Communism is

20th-century Americanism." In 1944, Browder oversaw the official dissolution of the CPUSA and the formation of the Communist Political Association, which endorsed President Franklin Roosevelt's reelection.

Although Browder led the CPUSA to its greatest strength, oversaw several difficult ideological shifts, and coordinated the struggle against fascism, he was ultimately a victim of Moscow's inconsistent policy. In 1945, Browder was forced out as party chair and Foster returned to the position. In 1946, Browder was expelled from the CPUSA; in 1949, his policy of strategic cooperation with capitalism was denounced as a perversion of communist ideals and labeled "Browderism." By then the CPUSA was in steep decline, a victim of the second **Red Scare**. Browder remained defiant despite his fall from grace and failed attempts to rehabilitate his image. He accused former communist allies of degenerating into a sect that had little to offer American workers. Browder also steadfastly denied engaging in acts of espionage, though the opening of records after the collapse of the USSR reveal that he did recruit spies for the USSR and that members of his family engaged in espionage in the 1930s. The most serious allegation against Browder—still highly debatable—is that he helped plot the assassination of Leon Trotsky. Before his death in 1973, Browder authored 65 pamphlets. His stewardship of the CPUSA remains the most vital in party history, though he died outside of the CPUSA fold.

Suggested Reading

Mari Jo Buhle, Paul Buhle, and Dan Georgakas, *Encyclopedia of the American Left*, 1990; John Haynes, Harvey Klehr, and Fridrikh Igorevich Firsov, *The Secret World of American Communism*, 1995; Maurice Isserman, *Which Side Were You On?*, 1982; Harvey Klehr, *The Heyday of American Communism*, 1984.

BUCK'S STOVE & RANGE CO. V. AMERICAN FEDERATION OF LABOR ET AL.

Buck's Stove & Range Co. v. American Federation of Labor et al. was an extensive and expensive court battle that drained the energies and resources of the **American Federation of Labor** (AFL) between 1907 and 1914. The **Progressive Era** is often interpreted as a period of liberal reform in the United States, but it was not always very "progressive" insofar as labor policy was concerned. The *Buck's* case illustrates this fact.

The Buck's Stove and Range Company was headquartered in St. Louis and had long been known for its anti-union bias. In the 1880s and 1890s, the **Knights of Labor** (KOL) battled with the company. Company president James Van Cleave was a leading member of the American Anti-Boycott Association and president of the **National Association of Manufacturers**, which called for **open shops**. He was known for his use of labor spies and for seeking any pretext to void union contracts. In 1907, Van Cleave increased the workday from 9 to 10 hours for nickel plating workers in St. Louis. This move led to a showdown between the company and the Founders' Association and the Iron Moulders and Metal Polishers' Union, both of which were AFL affiliates. Van Cleave fired protesting workers, precipitating a **strike**. Van Cleave refused an offer from AFL President **Samuel Gompers** to mediate the dispute. In turn, AFL issued a call to **boycott** Buck's products and listed the firm in the "We Don't Patronize" columns of its official journal, the *American Federationist*.

On August 19, 1907, the Buck's Company asked the Supreme Court of the District of Columbia for an injunction against the boycott, claiming that it constituted an illegal restraint of trade under the provisions of the 1890 **Sherman Antitrust Act**. On December 18, the D.C. court issued a temporary **injunction**, which was later made permanent on March 23, 1908. This decision set off a round of court challenges and attempts to limit labor's boycott power through a broad reading of the Sherman Act. The *Buck's* case coincided with that of **Loewe v. Lawlor** (1908), another boycott case. The two taken together threatened to make illegal virtually any action on the part of labor unions that harmed a company financially. They also raised serious questions about fundamental issues such as the right to free speech.

The D.C. injunction forbade the AFL, its leaders, and its members from in any way restricting Buck's business through writing or speech. The union was not even allowed to criticize the company within its own journal. Gompers declared the decision a violation of fundamental constitutional rights, and the AFL appealed the decision to the federal Court of Appeals of the District of Columbia. On July 20, 1908, before the appeals court could hear the case, the Buck's Company asked the original court to hold the AFL in contempt of the first injunction. On December 23, 1908, AFL leaders Gompers, **John Mitchell**, and Frank Morrison were convicted of the charge and sentenced to jail terms of one year, six months, and three months, respectively. These convictions were also appealed.

On March 11, 1909, the appeals court modified the original injunction slightly, making it illegal to conspire to boycott, but removing individuals from the injunction. This ruling led to appeals to the U.S. Supreme Court by both the Buck's Company and the AFL. On November 2, 1909, the appeals court reversed itself and upheld the convictions of Gompers, Mitchell, and Morrison. This ruling led to another AFL appeal to the Supreme Court. These bitter and expensive court battles threatened to drain the AFL treasury, and the federation had to undertake numerous fundraising efforts to sustain the legal fight. The AFL also did not find many "progressive" allies in Congress, where its solicitation for political relief fell largely upon deaf ears.

The AFL received some solace in 1910, when Van Cleave died and the Buck's Company settled with its striking employees. On February 20, 1911, however, the U.S. Supreme Court dismissed both company and union appeals on the grounds that the recent strike settlement rendered the question moot. This move left open the entire question of whether the injunction had been legitimate in the first place. The conviction of AFL officials was reversed, but on a technicality that again left fundamental questions unresolved. The Supreme Court ruled that only the courts—not companies—could initiate contempt charges. The Supreme Court of the District of Columbia proceeded to do exactly that; on June 16, 1911, new charges were brought against Gompers, Mitchell, and Morrison. They were convicted anew on June 24, 1912, and again appealed. Once again, a district appeals court upheld the convictions, and though it drastically reduced penalties, the AFL again appealed to the federal Supreme Court.

The *Buck's* case came to an inglorious and ill-defined end on May 11, 1914, when the U.S. Supreme Court overturned the labor leaders' convictions, but again dodged essential legal questions by ruling, simply, that the new charges against AFL officials came after the three-year statute of limitations had expired. Repercussions of the *Buck's* case reverberated for quite some time as the Supreme Court's ambiguous resolution of the dispute left the door open for future capital/labor struggles over the boycott. The case and others like it have led labor historians to reinterpret the period of American history known as the Progressive Era (c. 1901–1917). Although the period ushered in many needed reforms, it also saw many attacks on personal liberties and was largely a difficult time for organized labor. Labor historians often view the concerns of Progressive Era reformers as elitist and point to the various ways in which corporate and middle-class interests superseded those of the **working class**.

Suggested Reading

Melvyn Dubofsky, *The State and Labor in Modern America*, 1994; Daniel Ernst, *Lawyers against Labor: From Individual Rights to Corporate Liberalism*, 2002; Benjamin Taylor and Fred Witney, *U.S. Labor Relations Law: Historical Development*, 1992.

BUMPING

Bumping is a procedure in which a laid-off or demoted worker displaces a worker in another job who has less seniority. Bumping clauses are usually outlined in the job security clauses of union and civil service **contracts**. Non-union employers that do not recognize seniority rights may or may not follow the practice.

Under union contracts, seniority usually determines an individual's place on the bumping rights ladder, presuming that the employee has the minimum qualifications to do the job of the worker he or she displaces. Seniority can be calculated in numerous ways—overall company service, time within a department, or time on a specific job. It is also generally defined by contract language. The most common reason for invoking bumping rights is a situation in which workforce reductions take place. In an anticipated temporary layoff, a senior worker might "bump" a less-senior one, who might then be laid off instead. If the layoff is permanent, as in a situation in which an entire division or department is eliminated, bumping might entail less-senior workers losing their jobs altogether.

Bumping is not as automatic as it sounds. Workers subject to workforce reductions are usually given timely written notice of those events. At that point an individual may or may not have an individual decision to make. In some cases, contract language automatically kicks in to determine who will be transferred and who will lose their places. This practice is especially common in the "two-tiered" contracts dating from the 1970s, under which new hires often come into jobs with fewer benefits than workers with longer service. If an individual does have a choice, he or she can elect to exercise seniority to displace a worker in the same, equal, or lower-level classification; take a workforce reduction furlough for a specified period of time, with recall rights when the same or equal job becomes available; accept severance pay; or receive a pension if eligible. Bumping then moves down the chain, with the worker who has been bumped pursuing his or her own seniority options. Although bumping is seldom accomplished without anguish, both employers and labor unions generally prefer to operate according to specified bumping procedures as they are understandable, are roughly as fair as any standard that could be devised, and bring some stability to the workplace by assuring that the most-experienced workers remain on the job when job cuts are made.

Nineteenth-century unions often found bumping to be one of the easier benefits to negotiate in post-**Industrial Revolution** America. Even before it was written into formal contracts, bumping was a customary practice among **artisans** and was in place in many non-union workplaces because it was easy to administer, rewarded seasoned employees, and improved morale by assuring job security. It was also routine practice among 19th-century railroad workers. Customary practices were formalized in contracts during the upsurge of mass-production unionism in the 1930s and 1940s. The **United Auto Workers of America** secured bumping rights in 1934 and the Commercial Telegraphers Union in 1946. Bumping rights are standard operating procedure in many businesses, including non-union establishments. In recent decades bumping clauses have sometimes proved contentious because of **affirmative action** hiring. Some argue that the last-hired, first-fired principle that is central to seniority puts **minority labor** at a permanent disadvantage and undermines the very principle of affirmative action. Both unions and civil servants have been very protective of bumping rights. In 2009 and 2010, for example, New Hampshire state employees sued state and county governments to retain their bumping rights.

Suggested Reading

David Brody, "Workplace Contractualism," in *Industrial Democracy in America*, ed. Nelson Lichtenstein and Howell Harris, 1993; L. Dulude, *Seniority and Employment Equity for Women*, 1995.

BUREAU OF LABOR STATISTICS

The Bureau of Labor Statistics (BLS) is the office within the **Department of Labor (DOL)** that collects economic data on **unemployment**, **wages**, consumer spending, labor productivity, inflation, and the cost of living. These data are categorized in various ways. For example, the national unemployment rate is broken down by geographic region, seasons of the year, work sectors, gender, age, and race. These data are important to labor advocates, the business community, and government planners.

Today the BLS is a seldom-considered part of the federal bureaucracy, but before it came into being, the very idea of creating such an agency inspired hope among **working-class** Americans. Labor unions played an integral role in establishing the BLS. Many 19th-century advocates for the BLS believed that a scientific collection and presentation of employment statistics and data on working-class life would spawn reform. They argued that the data would shock Americans, especially the middle class, into supporting labor unions and reform. Pressure to pass pro-labor legislation would then be applied upon local, state, and federal governments. Such reasoning appears naïve in retrospect, but it was in keeping with the evangelical fervor of northern antebellum reform movements such as abolitionism and temperance, much of which was shaped by perfectionist ideals embedded in the Second Great Awakening. It was also in keeping with arguments in favor of expanding free public education to create an enlightened citizenry. As recently as 1910, fewer than 10 percent of Americans obtained a high school education; hence labor unions and other reform groups placed a high value on disseminating information to the public.

In 1871, Massachusetts became the first state to set up a BLS. Not coincidentally, it was also the first state to mandate free public secondary schools. In 1884, a federal BLS was set up, with Massachusetts BLS head Carroll Wright being recruited to direct it. Its founding became a cause célèbre for the **Knights of Labor** (KOL), which had lobbied for its creation. The KOL shifted emphasis after the agency's establishment, and argued in favor of increasing the BLS budget and expanding its powers. When the **American Federation of Labor** (AFL) formed in 1886, it also saw the BLS as a possible source of pressure for labor reform. For the most part, however, the BLS failed to justify the faith placed in it by the KOL and the AFL. The BLS was placed under the auspices of the Department of Interior, but operated both independently and without a clear mission. Ironically, the BLS slowly became more useful to business leaders than to labor unions or elected officials. Many of its staff statisticians came from the business sector, and business leaders found BLS data useful for economic development plans. Labor statistics were not central to government planning until 1913, when the DOL was created and the BLS was transferred to its control.

The AFL pressed for many of the reforms that led to the creation of the DOL and reform of the BLS. The birth of the DOL also led to the creation of a new Cabinet post, that of secretary of labor. William Wilson, who had been an administrator for the **United Mine Workers of America**, was the first to fill this position. After 1913, labor statistics factored more prominently into government planning. Nonetheless, the BLS became and remains more of an accounting and bureaucratic tool than a vehicle for social change. It has, however, pioneered in developing statistical measurements by which the health of the economy and of laborers can be measured. For example, the BLS created the Cost of Living Index to assess how World War I disrupted what people paid for basic items such as food, housing, and clothing. In 1919, the BLS launched the Consumer Price Index, which charted industrial growth in various sectors. Labor unions used both indices to lobby for wage increases and, after World War II, several negotiated automatic **cost-of-living adjustments** tied to BLS data.

Data are neutral, but the way the BLS collects data and the way those outside the agency interpret labor statistic have often been politicized. During the Great Depression, the BLS was accused of weak collection methods responsible for inaccurate undercounting of unemployment. President Franklin Roosevelt ordered a revamping of BLS methodology, but how the BLS measures unemployment remained contentious. Allegations of undercounting surfaced again in the 1960s, the 1980s, and during the recession that began in 2007. Today many social scientists argue that official unemployment and poverty levels seldom reflect actual rates.

At its best, the BLS provides data deemed key to economic planning. During World War II, for example, the BLS provided important information to the War Labor Board and the Office of Price Administration, agencies charged with steering the volatile war economy. President Richard Nixon drew upon BLS data (and scores of economists) when he imposed wage and price controls in 1971 in an unsuccessful attempt to regulate inflation. In like fashion, presidents from Jimmy Carter onward have consulted BLS statistics when contemplating their budgets or imposing austerity measures. The BLS also sometimes mediates disputes between corporate and union economists, whose cost-of-living and inflation calculations often differ. For better or worse, BLS indices and data impact all Americans. The BLS never became the reform vehicle its early advocates dreamed it would be, but BLS data influence interest rates, wages, cost-of-living allowances, and investment decisions. Although BLS methodology is often challenged, the importance of its mission remains intact. Its annual market-basket report on the cost of key goods and services is central to union **collective bargaining** strategy, just as the business community draws upon BLS inflation calculations to frame employee raises.

Suggested Reading

Ewan Clague, *The Bureau of Labor Statistics*, 1968; Joseph Goldberg and William Move, *The First Hundred Years of the Bureau of Labor Statistics* (U.S. Government Bulletin 2235), 1985; U.S. Bureau of Labor Statistics, http://www.bls.gov/, accessed June 15, 2010; Donald Whitnah, ed., *Government Agencies*, 1983.

BUSINESS AGENT

A business agent is a person employed by a **union local** to negotiate with employers, help settle **grievances**, and see that both parties observe the terms of the **collective bargaining** agreement. The business agent is a paid, full-time officer who is either elected by the members of the local or appointed by a higher union official. Such a person is akin to the manager of the local and takes on such public tasks as answering correspondence, issuing press releases, calling union meetings, and fielding outside queries. The business agent is independent of any workplace covered by the union agreement, but usually has knowledge of the industry through previous employment.

Business agents run **craft union** locals, but unlike the officers in an **industrial union** they frequently deal with multi-employer contracts or multiple contracts with several companies. Because the union's members frequently move from one job site to another, the business agent represents a source of stability between the worker and the job. Some of the business agent's other duties include overseeing the organization of non-union craft workers within their territory, administering employee benefit programs, political lobbying, administering grievance hearings and, in some unions, maintaining the union's hiring hall.

The development of paid, full-time local union officials is, in the United States, largely associated with the rise of the **American Federation of Labor** (AFL) in the late 19th century. Earlier unions felt that most officials should themselves be work-ers and assumed that capital/labor interests were antagonistic. The AFL also assumed that employers would be reluctant to grant concessions to workers, but it accepted the permanence of the **capitalist** system and argued that capital and labor were dependent upon each other. It was, however, necessary for unions to develop bureaucratic structures that mirrored those of organized capital. The business agent is part of an overall strategy called **business unionism**. Business agents became common in AFL affiliates, but radical critics such as the **Industrial Workers of the World** argued that they were emblematic of the AFL's attempt to build an **aris-tocracy of labor**.

The business agent system worked well into the post-World War II period, but with the overall decline in union membership since the 1970s, a new generation of critics has sometimes condemned business agents as symbols of how labor unions have become overly bureaucratic, have deemphasized organizing, and have fallen out of touch with rank-and-file workers. Defenders reply that many of the critics are romantics living in the past and that unions must operate according to the same professional standards as business.

Suggested Reading

Phil Dine, *State of the Unions: How Labor Can Strengthen the Middle Class, Improve Our Economy, and Regain Political Influence*, 2007; Terry L. Leap, *Collective Bargaining and Labor Relations*, 1995; Florence Peterson, *American Labor Unions: What They Are and How They Work*, 1963.

BUSINESS ROUNDTABLE

The Business Roundtable (BR) is a conservative consortium of more than 1,000 cor-porations whose chief executive officers (CEOs) attempt to influence government policy on civil rights, education, labor, tax policies, and numerous other issues. Most of its members are so virulently opposed to labor unions that it is often compared to the **National Association of Manufacturers** (NAM).

The BR formed in 1972 and exercised tremendous influence on presidencies from Richard Nixon through Barack Obama. Jimmy Carter's cordial relations with the BR—as well as those of Bill Clinton—especially infuriated organized labor and caused numerous activists to argue that labor needs to reexamine its long-time links to the Democratic Party.

The genesis of the BR can be found in the business community's desire to derail union-led efforts to pass labor law reform. NAM led such efforts in the early 20th century and also strongly supported the passage of the **Taft-Hartley Act** in 1946. Since then much labor legislation has favored business over unions. This reality was one of the major factors leading to the 1955 merger of the **American Federation of Labor** (AFL) and the **Congress of Industrial Organizations** (CIO). The combined AFL-CIO hoped to pressure Congress into repealing the Taft-Hartley Act. That did not happen, but AFL-CIO political action committees (PACs) began raising money to support pro-labor candidates, most of whom have been Democrats.

Despite the protections afforded to them by the Taft-Hartley Act, corporations continued to complain that labor laws saddled the business community with needless regulations that left it at a competitive disadvantage in the increasingly global marketplace. In 1965, CEOs from AT&T, Bechtel, Exxon, General Dynamics, General Electric, General Motors, Union Carbide, U.S. Steel, and others formed the Labor Law Study Group (LLSG) to promote business interests. The LLSG spawned several spinoff groups, one of which represented building contractors opposed to **prevailing wage** laws protected under the **Davis-Bacon Act**. In 1972, three antilabor groups merged to create the Business Roundtable, whose leaders believed that groups such as the Chamber of Commerce and the NAM were not doing enough to influence public policy.

Publicly, the BR stated its goals were to promote charitable work, to help CEOs coordinate efforts to stimulate the economy, and to provide government and the public with statistics and information germane to keeping American business strong. Privately, the BR's agenda included an assault on organized labor and on labor laws. It especially desired repeal of the Davis-Bacon Act and the **National Labor Relations Act** (NLRA). The BR also launched a massive public relations campaign to sell the idea that labor unions are outmoded and no longer have a place in American society. By the 1980s, it had succeeded so well that the media and many high school textbooks regularly put forth that proposition. In addition, the BR stole a page from labor's playbook and took advantage of laws passed in the early 1970s that made it easier for businesses to form PACs of their own. Corporate PACs were able to amass sums far beyond those which unions could muster, and the BR handed out financial support to both political parties.

This financial generosity began to bear fruit in the late 1970s. The BR met regularly with President Carter, who did little to advance legislation favored by unions. An attempt to increase the **minimum wage** failed in 1977, and a 1978 tax code reform greatly reduced corporate taxes. If Carter was banking on BR support, he badly miscalculated, however. The BR joined many other business groups to support **Ronald Reagan**'s successful bid to unseat Carter in 1980. Reagan proved an even stronger BR ally. Business **deregulation** had long been a centerpiece of the BR agenda, and Reagan proved amenable to it. In addition, Reagan-era tax cuts dwarfed those of the Carter years, and tax code changes made it easier for businesses to write off expenses. These changes paved the way for accelerated **deindustrialization** in various sectors of the U.S. economy, as numerous corporations closed plants, shifted assets, and invested in the stock market rather than replacing aging machinery. The effort to overturn the NLRA directly was turned aside, but the BR helped choose several Reagan appointees who indirectly subverted it. Under Reagan, appointees to the National Labor Relations Board often had anti-union track records. The BR also exerted influence more directly; for example, former Bechtel executive George Shultz became Reagan's secretary of state and most unions opposed all three of the individuals who served as secretary of labor under Reagan. The BR applauded Reagan's handling of the **Professional Air Traffic Controllers Organization strike**, an action that many analysts believe emboldened corporate CEOs to refuse labor demands and precipitated numerous **downsizing,**

decertification, and concessions strikes during the decade. The BR also aided numerous campaigns to repeal prevailing wage laws as well as efforts to increase the number of **right-to-work** states.

The Democratic Party's response to BR influence on Republican Party policy in the 1980s disappointed labor activists. The Democrats actively courted BR CEOs—actions fueled in no small part by the fact that BR PACs continued to dole out money to both parties. Thus, while President Clinton raised the minimum wage and slowed the assault against organized labor, he also supported programs favorable to the BR and opposed by labor, most notably the **North American Free Trade Agreement** and American participation in the World Trade Organization. These actions increased the call within organized labor ranks to sever links with the Democratic Party.

The BR is also opposed by civil rights and women's organizations, as part of its agenda calls for easing workplace rules on **affirmative action**. Consumer groups also decry BR's push to limit consumer liability suits, change **workman's compensation** laws, and place caps on punitive damage awards.

The administration of President George W. Bush was particularly receptive to BR ideals. The BR enthusiastically supported Bush's "No Child Left Behind" legislation and teacher-testing educational objectives, which raised the ire of both the **American Federation of Teachers** and the **National Education Association**. The BR, in turn, advised the Bush administration on energy policy and sought his support for objectives such as market-based health care cost containment and voluntary cuts in greenhouse emissions (in lieu of mandated controls on health costs and pollution limits). It also lobbied to privatize **Social Security**, a proposal strongly opposed by organized labor and one that fell by the wayside when the economy went into a recession in 2007.

Barack Obama won the presidency in 2008 and promised an administration more friendly to organized labor, yet President Obama also proved tractable to large parts of the BR agenda. The BR praised Obama's 2009 bailout of financial institutions, various parts of his economic stimulus package, and his willingness to continue the "No Child Left Behind" program; the last move has proved a huge disappointment to teachers' unions. One of the more surprising recent developments has been the willingness of the **Service Employees International Union** to join the BR, NAM, and other business interests in supporting the "Divided We Fail" initiatives on passing health care reform that relied heavily on the private sector.

The BR is headed by a chairperson who serves up to two one-year terms. The chair reports to a policy committee made up of CEOs, which meets four times per year. The BR also has numerous task forces that develop policies and strategies on specific topics. Its day-to-day activities are supported by a full-time staff of lawyers, specialists, and policy analysts. To its many critics, the BR and like groups are a major threat to American pluralism and the embodiment of a controlling "power elite," whose influence sociologist C. Wright Mills warned against in 1956. Its resources are enormous; BR-allied businesses employ more than 12 million workers and, in 2009, had more than $6 trillion in revenues. By comparison, all of organized labor (unions) contains just roughly 15 million members and the entire AFL-CIO has just $83 million in assets. A 2010 U.S. Supreme Court decision that uncapped the amount of money corporations and advocacy groups can spend on elections means that forces such as the BR will remain powerful in the foreseeable future. Labor unions rightly view it as a powerful foe against which they continue to struggle.

Suggested Reading

Business Roundtable, http://www.businessroundtable.org/, accessed June 15, 2010; G. William Domhoff, *Who Rules America?*, 2005; A. J. Lichtman, *White Protestant Nation: The Rise of the American Conservative Movement*, 2008; Kim Moody, *An Injury to All: The Decline of American Unionism*, 1989.

BUSINESS UNIONISM

Business unionism is the name given to a form of organization in which a **union local** or **labor federation** maintains bureaucratic structures and emphasizes pragmatic goals. It is the type of organization that describes the operation of the **American Federation of Labor-Congress of Industrial Organizations** (AFL-CIO) and most of its affiliates. It is also an increasingly maligned practice. Critics from outside the labor movement dub its emphasis "Big Labor" and present business unionists as ruthless, power-hungry obstructionists who are the union equivalents of robber barons. Internal critics agree with some of those charges and blame business unionism for much of the decline in union membership since the 1970s. They further charge that the labor movement has become mired in bureaucracy at the expense of activism and organizing.

Business unionism evolved from the ideas of Adolph Strasser and **Samuel Gompers**, two cigar makers devoted to **craft unionism** and the chief architects of the American Federation of Labor, which formed in 1886. Gompers believed strongly that **collective bargaining** was the best way to achieve fair wages and working conditions. He rejected the **socialism** of his youth, and clashes between his cigar makers union and the **Knights of Labor** (KOL) soured him on the concept of **social reform unionism**. Strasser and Gompers came to emphasize what was dubbed **pure and simple unionism**, a focus on improving **wages**, reducing work hours, and improving working conditions. Unlike the KOL's leadership, most AFL organizers accepted the permanence of **capitalism** and turned away from radical ideas for transforming American society. At the time, this was a controversial idea in its own right. Although the **Industrial Revolution** had clearly reconfigured the American economy, it did so on a scale that disrupted older models of **paternalism** and individual proprietorship. Numerous 19th-century reformers questioned the morality of an economic system dominated by investment and corporate capital.

Gompers and fellow business unionists believed that workers and management shared mutual interests. They did not think that individual capitalists would always understand that, or would willingly share their bounty with workers. Whereas the KOL saw **strikes** as a desperate last resort to be avoided, business unionists saw the withholding of labor as its strongest weapon in compelling businesses to negotiate with unions. Strikes did, however, need to be carefully managed by a central union organization; in fact, unions themselves needed to operate in a businesslike fashion and hold enough financial reserves to sustain themselves through hard times. High initiation fees and **dues** provided funds to help keep strikes going. They also allowed unions to provide sick and death benefits, thereby encouraging rank-and-file loyalty.

Not all AFL members agreed with business unionism. In 1894, John McBride, the president of the **United Mine Workers** and a **Populist**, briefly unseated Gompers as AFL president by presenting a more militant platform. For the most part, though, Strasser and Gompers proved prescient on the permanence of capitalism, and business unionism served the AFL well from its founding into the Great Depression. It came under attack again during the 1930s when CIO dissidents bolted the AFL, turned toward **industrial unionism**, and emphasized grassroots militancy. By the time World War II commenced, however, the CIO had also adopted many business union principles. The **Red Scare** and anti-union atmosphere after the war, which included passage of the **Taft-Hartley Act**, eventually led the CIO to reunite with the AFL and operate most of its departments and locals according to business union models.

Business unionism proved successful at raising wages and winning benefits for union members in the 1950s and 1960s, but it made little headway on the legislative front. The passage of the **Landrum-Griffin Act** in 1959 served to frustrate further the broader reform desires of some unions. During the 1960s, several unions, including the **American Federation of State, County, and Municipal Employees** and the **Service Employees International Union** (SEIU), adopted methods more in keeping with early CIO militancy than with business union methods. The period was also marked by spontaneous **wildcat strikes**.

Business unionism particularly came under attack when the American economy soured during the waves of stagflation, **deindustrialization**, and **globalism** that ensued in the wake of oil boycotts in the 1970s. As **blue-collar** work declined, unions began to hemorrhage members, and employers seized the opportunity to **decertify** unions and to wring **concessions** from those that remained. All of this unrest served to fuel critics who complained that business unionism is more bureaucratic than democratic, and that it fosters career-path administrators who are insulated from the concerns of the rank-and-file. They called upon the AFL-CIO to curtail spending on bureaucracy and its political action committees, and to devote more resources to organizing. They also demanded that leadership be less conciliatory to management and rekindle the activist spirit of the 1930s and 1960s. Business unionists often retorted that its critics were living in the past and did not understand the complex economic and political forces against which organized labor was arrayed. In 1995, however, SEIU President **John Sweeney** was elected president of the AFL-CIO, and promised to enact many of the demands of business unionist critics.

Sweeney's promises proved easier to make than to keep. Although he devoted more resources to organizing, the results were disappointing. Moreover, his attempts to streamline the AFL-CIO's bureaucracy angered as many as it pleased—eliminating departments often alienated those groups who lost power. Both transportation and carpenters' unions quit the AFL in the early 21st century, and Sweeney himself had to face charges that he had become a business unionist. In

2005, Sweeney was challenged by Andrew Stern, the leader of Sweeney's own SEIU and a man whom he had mentored. Sweeney was reelected as president of the AFL-CIO, but Stern, SEIU, and approximately one-third of the AFL-CIO's membership quit the federation in favor of the newly formed **Change to Win Federation**. It has pledged to maintain high levels of militancy and recruit new members rather than rigidly adhering to business union procedures, drawn-out negotiations, and complex chains of command.

Suggested Reading

Paul Buhl, *Taking Care of Business: Samuel Gompers, George Meany, Lane Kirkland, and the Tragedy of American Labor*, 1999; Philip Dine, *State of the Unions: How Labor Can Strengthen the Middle Class, Improve Our Economy, and Regain Political Influence*, 2007; Kim Moody, *U.S. Labor in Trouble and Transition: The Failure of Reform from Above, the Promise of Revival from Below*, 2007.

BUTCHERS

The term "butcher" conjures up images of neighborhood stores and kindly proprietors slicing individually ordered cuts of meat for their clientele. In truth, since the mid-19th century, the meat industry has been among the largest industrial concerns in the United States, and most "butchers" involved in the organized labor movement could be better be described as "slaughterhouse workers," meat "cutters," meat "packers," "industrial workers," or **service industry** workers.

During the last quarter of the 19th century, meat processing was dramatically transformed by urbanization, the expansion of railroads, and new technology. Growing cities led to increased demand for dressed beef and pork; hence cities at railheads such as Abilene, Kansas City, Chicago, and Omaha developed as centers where **cowboys** and herders drove their animals. Some animals were slaughtered in these cities; others were fed and then placed onto cattle cars and shipped to their final destination for processing. Refrigerated railroad boxcars—nicknamed "reefers"—dramatically reshaped the industry. Prototypes had been in widespread use since the 1850s, but the perfection of them in the 1880s led to further centralization that concentrated butchering in large mass-production settings. Chicago emerged as the largest of these centers, with stockyards once dominating the city's south side. The dramatic expansion of railroad mileage after the Civil War served to encourage consolidation in the meat processing industry. By the end of the 19th century and continuing into the 1970s, the "Big Four"—Armour, Cudahy, Swift, and Wilson—controlled more than three-fourths of the total U.S. meat production.

The **Knights of Labor** (KOL) was the first union to realize that meat production was no longer a **craft** industry for most workers, and it attempted a rudimentary form of **industrial unionism** that proved briefly successful, especially in Chicago. The KOL's efforts collapsed in the wake of a failed 1886 stockyards strike, however. The Amalgamated Meat Cutters and Butcher Workmen of North America (AMCBW) was originally sanctioned by the **American Federation of Labor** (AFL) in 1897. It was an unusual experiment for the AFL, in that it acknowledged the industrial nature of packinghouse work and attempted to organize both skilled

Meat inspectors at the Swift & Company packinghouse in Chicago, circa 1906. Both hygiene and labor conditions within the meatpacking industry came under close scrutiny by muckraking journalists at the turn of the century. Exposés by writers such as Upton Sinclair helped bring about the passage of the 1906 Federal Meat Inspection Act. (Library of Congress)

and unskilled workers, although skilled butchers made up the bulk of the early leadership.

The need for worker organizations in the meat industry was clear. Large-scale production was aided by the use of hoists, conveyors, endless chains, chutes, and moving benches. Workers toiled long hours, wielded sharp knives, and often worked at fast paces on what were veritable *dis*assembly lines. Workers often toiled in cold and bloody conditions, and industrial accidents were very common. The meat industry was labor intensive, and the continual deskilling of production meant that it also evolved into lower-paid labor with high concentrations of immigrants, women, and African Americans. Many of the messier and brutal aspects of meatpacking were assigned according to the national origin, gender, and race of workers. The horrors of the industry were chronicled by Upton Sinclair in *The Jungle*. Although Sinclair's 1906 book was a novel, it was rightly hailed for its realism.

The AMCBW grew slowly until 1898, when Michael Donnelly, a South Omaha sheep butcher, assumed its presidency. By the middle of 1900, the group had 4,000 members. Donnelly expanded the union by organizing workers by department rather than skill—a tactic that often put him at odds with the AFL hierarchy. By 1904, however, the AMCBW was able to call out 28,000 Chicago packinghouse workers to strike for shorter working hours and better conditions. They were joined by thousands of packinghouse workers across the country. Donnelly's efforts notwithstanding, the packinghouses were simply too strong for the AMCBW and the workforce was too divided. Both the 1904 strike and another during 1921–1922 failed; in each case, African Americans were imported from the South to work as **scabs**. Most were later fired when the strikes were settled, but a legacy of fragmentation and racial animosity endured within the industry.

The failed strikes so weakened the AMCBW that it largely retreated from the packinghouses to concentrate on organizing skilled butchers in commercial and retail enterprises, who could be organized like most AFL craft unions. As a consequence, the large meatpacking firms remained without strong unions until the 1930s, when the **United Packinghouse Workers of America** (UPWA) was organized by the **Congress of Industrial Organizations** (CIO). The UPWA openly embraced industrial unionism and was able to forge solidarity among immigrant, African American, and women workers. It was a rival of the AMCBW, though the two groups did cooperate to some extent. For the most part, however, the AMCBW ceded packinghouse organization to the UPWA and concentrated on organizing butchers in small retail shops and chain stores. It also extended its efforts to food processing plants, fur and leather workers, and sheep shearers, and made tentative attempts to organize migratory agricultural workers.

When the AFL and CIO merged in 1955, the AMCBW and the UPWA maintained their separate identities and stood as starkly different from each other. By 1964, the AMCBW had approximately 350,000 members, making it one of the AFL-CIO's larger unions. By then, it was known as a conservative **business union** that sought to avoid strikes or political controversy. For example, the AMCBW officially supported U.S. actions in the Vietnam War through 1973, by which time a majority of the American public opposed government policy. By contrast, the UPWA gained a reputation for being both more militant and more progressive than the AMCBW. It made inroads into organizing black workers and supported the civil rights movement well in advance of most AFL-CIO unions. Mechanization of line production and the increasing reliance on trucking rather than railroad transportation led to a decentralization of meatpacking industry, such that cattle, hog, poultry, and sheep processing took place closer to feedlots. The decline of massive stockyards and employer campaigns to weaken unions led to the eventual demise of the UPWA, which merged with the AMCBW in 1968.

Corruption charges dogged the AMCBW, and in the late 1970s several officials were convicted of **racketeering**, conspiracy, extortion, illegal labor payments, tax evasion, and perjury. These problems, plus continuing decentralization within the meat industry, led the AFL-CIO to reorganize. In 1979, the **United Food and Commercial Workers Union** (UFCW) was formed by a merger of the Retail Clerks International Union, the **Boot and Shoe Workers' Union**, and the AMCBW. Today, most butchers are service workers employed by grocery chain stores. The UFCW continues to organize packinghouse workers, but the numbers of organized packinghouse workers has dropped due to mechanization, increased importation of foodstuffs, and difficulties in organizing immigrant labor. Modern meatpacking plants have been accused of harboring large numbers of illegal and undocumented immigrants. Moreover, many plants are located in the South and in **right-to-work** states. Unions charge that meatpacking remains among the most dangerous and abusive industries in the United States, and employee injury data suggest that these charges have merit.

Suggested Reading

James Barrett, *Work and Community in the Jungle: Chicago's Packinghouse Workers, 1894–1922,* 1987; David Brody, *The Butcher Workmen: A Study of Unionization,* 1964; Rick Halpern, *Down on the Killing Floor: Black and White Workers in Chicago's Packinghouses, 1904–1954,* 1997.

C

CAPITALISM

Capitalism, also known as the "free enterprise system" and the "free market economy," is an economic system rooted in ideals of private property, individualism, and (relatively) unregulated access to markets. It is the dominant economic system in the United States and many other industrial and postindustrial societies. It should not be confused with representative democracy, which is a political system, although the two terms are often incorrectly used interchangeably in contemporary American rhetoric.

Capitalism stands in marked contrast to competing economic systems such as **socialism** or **anarcho-syndicalism**, which emphasize planned economies in which decision making is dictated by collective need. Proponents of capitalism uphold the liberty of individual producers, distributors, and consumers to make economic decisions. In classical theory, **wages** and prices are determined by what the market will bear. Thus the proper role of government in economics should be confined to guaranteeing access to free markets; most other forms of government intervention and regulation are viewed as harmful intrusions that disrupt the natural working of markets. In most capitalist economies, the right to private property—construed broadly to include personal goods and such public forms of wealth as land, natural resources, businesses, stock, and money (capital)—is a sacrosanct ideal. In like fashion, capitalist economies generally place most goods, services, financial systems, and production in private hands. The pursuit of personal profit, another key capitalist concept, is viewed as positive and natural.

The roots of capitalism can be traced to medieval Europe, where urban guild members, merchant traders, and a small band of commercial lenders articulated a money-based economy that rivaled traditional land-based wealth systems. In broad practice, however, capitalism is of more recent vintage. In 1776, Scottish thinker Adam Smith published *Inquiry into the Nature and Causes of the Wealth of Nations*, a book considered path breaking in defining capitalism. Smith's ideas gained acceptance as revolutions engulfed the North American colonies and France. Although many aspects of capitalism were already in place by the 18th century, the American colonies were part of a larger economic system known as mercantilism. In a mercantilist economy, national power, a positive balance of trade, and global competition took precedence over individual pursuits of wealth. Access to raw materials, colonies, and precious metals were linked to national might, and regulations governed numerous economic transactions. Some American historians cite the desire of prototypical capitalist merchants to break free from colonial constraints as among the causes of the American Revolution.

The spread of American capitalism largely coincided with the country's **Industrial Revolution**, but it did not enjoy an unchallenged rise. In capitalism, labor is viewed as a commodity like any other, and it is in the best interest of those who pay workers or answer to profit-seeking stockholders to keep wages low. Moreover, the very idea of lifelong wage-earning conflicted with older American ideals of independence and self-reliance. For most of the 19th century, **agrarian** production outstripped production of industrial goods and services, and even traditional elites were suspicious of unbridled capitalism because its implications included a society in which prestige and power were based in money rather than breeding and deference. In the 19th century, labor unions formed to secure better wage bargains for workers, and every **labor federation** except the **American Federation of Labor** (AFL) paid at least lip service to ending the wage system as a permanent condition for employees. Many labor activists equated wage labor with **slavery** and accused capitalists of desiring a nation in which chattel labor served the interests of a moneyed minority. The rise of amoral robber barons after the **Civil War** advanced capitalist principles, but at the price of sparking fierce opposition and of calling capitalism's very soundness into question. Various **anarchists**, **communists**, and socialists challenged the emerging capitalist class, as did **craft unions** and the **Knights of Labor** (KOL). Labor groups proposed alternatives to capitalism, especially **cooperatives**. By the end of the 19th century, however, capitalists had largely turned aside their challengers, and the 20th century was marked by capitalist dominance.

American capitalism in practice seldom resembled Smith's classical model. Smith inferred that economic forces were natural, as if they were sentient biological organisms capable of imposing imperial control over systems of exchange. In-place economic systems do not operate independently from political, social, and cultural realities, nor do economic models take into account the personalities called upon to enact or react against them. Despite investor calls for a laissez-faire approach, degrees of government regulation are also a feature of American capitalism. Factors such as national trade goals, economic crises, development schemes, wartime emergencies, and demands to correct harmful business practices have taken priority over the desires of individual profit-seekers. In some cases, capitalists themselves have called upon the government to enact regulations. Throughout the 19th century, investors in nascent industries appealed to government to enact tariffs and other forms of **protectionism** to shield their interests from outside competition. Such calls remain commonplace.

Moreover, social ills such as poverty, industrial accidents, long workdays, and poor working conditions have often resulted from the actions of unscrupulous capitalists, which fueled the reform calls of labor activists. During the **Progressive Era** (roughly 1901–1917), numerous restraints were placed on business, and capitalism suffered a near-crippling blow during the Great Depression (1929–1941). New Deal programs during the 1930s and early 1940s further curtailed laissez-faire practices. In some cases, the federal government set up enterprises in direct competition to private concerns. Since the 1940s, unions, reformers, and progressives have pushed agendas that circumscribe the free market in a number of ways, ranging from minimum wage laws and collective bargaining rights for unions to ending discriminatory hiring practices and ensuring consumer safety.

Most Americans now accept capitalism as a permanent feature of the economy, but labor unions have been at the forefront of lobbying efforts to establish regulations such as those related to the eight-hour workday, workplace safety standards, child labor, workman's compensation, unemployment benefits, environmental regulations, vacation pay, and product safety codes. More recently unions have battled international capitalism and have sought to frustrate efforts of groups such as the World Trade Organization to erode global trade barriers that unions fear will undermine needed regulations on capital. Capitalism dominates the American economy, but as in most nations the overall U.S. economy is most accurately labeled as "mixed." Monetary and military policy owe much to a mercantilist worldview, while programs such as public education, Social Security, Medicare, and agricultural subsidies are (mildly) socialist in nature. The United States does, however, allow individual investors, entrepreneurs, and merchants far more economic freedom than is common in European and Asian capitalist economies. Conservative efforts at deregulation since the 1970s have both broadened capitalist opportunities and intensified calls for more control. Since the presidency of Ronald Reagan, emboldened conservatives have promoted economic models that would have been more at home in the late 19th century. At the same time, such calls underscore the fact that economic policy and politics are linked. Far from being synonymous with democracy, some aspects of American capitalism are incompatible with a political system in which a majority could, in theory, vote to regulate business. Many labor activists today fear the rise of oligarchies and power elites more than they fear capitalism per se.

Suggested Reading

Robert Asher, *Concepts in American History*, 1996; Robert Heilbroner, *The Making of Economic Society*, 1985; Nikos Passas and Neva Goodwin, *It's Legal but It Ain't Right: Harmful Social Consequences of Legal Industries*, 2005; Adam Smith, *An Inquiry into the Nature and Causes of the Wealth of Nations*, 1776.

CAREY, JAMES BARRON

James Barron Carey (August 12, 1911–September 1, 1973) was the president of several electrical workers' unions, an anticommunism crusader, and an architect of the merger between the American Federation of Labor (AFL) and the Congress of Industrial Organizations (CIO). His career embodied many of the divisive issues facing organized labor in the mid-20th century, such as the struggle between activists and business unionists, how to respond to the Red Scare, labor's position on civil rights, and the proper political course for labor to hew during the Cold War.

Carey was born in Philadelphia, the son of John and Margaret (Loughery) Carey. He attended public schools in Glassboro, New Jersey, before going to work at Philco Radio, where he became a devotee of industrial unionism. From 1921 to 1931, Carey also attended Drexel Institute, where he studied electrical engineering. He studied finance at the Wharton School of the University of Pennsylvania during

1931 and 1932. Like many Roman Catholics inside the labor movement, Carey was strongly influenced by the papal encyclicals **Rerum Novarum** and *Quadregisimo Anno*. In his case, Carey became a devoted labor union supporter, but also fiercely anticommunist; his anticommunism was reinforced through contact with **socialist** hosiery workers in the Philadelphia area. A lifelong Democrat, Carey admired President Franklin Roosevelt and his New Deal policies.

In 1933, Carey played a key role in the formation of a Philco Radio **union local**. That local became a major building block for the **United Electrical, Radio, and Machine Workers of America** (UE). Carey led a successful strike for union recognition at RCA's Camden, New Jersey, plant in 1936. The arrest of the youthful Carey during the strike vaulted him into prominence in the national labor movement, where older colleagues dubbed him a "boy wonder." The 25-year-old Carey was elected as the first president of the UE.

Carey soon faced charges that the UE was dominated by **communists**—charges that Carey denied. By 1941, however, Carey faced opposition inside the UE general executive board, some of it coming from communists angered by Carey's outspoken criticism of the Hitler-Stalin pact. In that year he lost the UE presidency to Albert Fitzgerald, though UE colleagues supported his successful candidacy to become the CIO's secretary-treasurer in 1942. During World War II, Carey served on several government boards, and was a CIO delegate to the 1945 World Trade Union Conference. In addition, he became an avid supporter and member of President Harry Truman's Committee on Civil Rights. Carey became the CIO's chief spokesperson in support of progressive civil rights legislation.

The 1947 passage of the **Taft-Hartley Act**, the post-World War II Red Scare, and the emergence of the Cold War led the CIO to revisit allegations that many of its affiliates had been infiltrated by communists. CIO President **Philip Murray** shared both Carey's Catholicism and his anticommunism, which made him the logical point man for settling disputes within the UE. In 1947, the UE came under attack for harboring communists, which facilitated **raiding** by rival unions. The CIO tried to resolve this issue at its 1949 convention when it chartered the new **International Union of Electrical, Radio, and Machine Workers of America** (IUE), with Carey as its president. Carey and the IUE attempted to purge all communists from the electrical manufacturing industry and the CIO. Carey made frequent appearances before Congressional committees investigating alleged subversion inside the labor movement. He also supported raids on UE locals, promoted **decertification** elections of UE locals, and filed complaints with the National Labor Relations Board (NLRB) to weaken the UE's influence. Carey's ardent anticommunism earned him enemies as well as friends. The civil war between the UE and the IUE wounded both sides, making it easier for management to frustrate the agendas of each organization.

Carey played a key role in negotiating the 1955 AFL-CIO merger. He served as a vice president and an executive board member of the AFL-CIO, and was an officer in the federation's Industrial Union Department. The latter post made much sense given Carey's devotion to industrial unionism and the department's stated commitment to advancing the industrywide model of organizing. Ironically, Carey found himself under attack as an early example of a careerist business unionist. This hostility became vividly clear in 1964 when Carey's IUE presidency was challenged by Paul Jennings, a former protégé. Carey's apparent slim victory was overturned in 1965 when the NLRB ruled that Carey's supporters had rigged the election. Carey was never prosecuted, but Jennings reversed many of Carey's cautious policies in favor of infusing militancy within the IUE.

After leaving the IUE, Carey served as a labor representative to the United Nations and did work for the Democratic Party but quickly passed out of the public eye. He died in Silver Spring, Maryland, in 1973.

Suggested Reading

R. L. Filippelli and M. D. McColloch, *Cold War in the Working Class: The Rise and Decline of the United Electrical Workers*, 1995; Steven Rosswurm, "The Wondrous Tale of an FBI Bug: What It Tells Us about Communism, Anti-communism, and the CIO Leadership," *American Communist History 2*, no. 1 (2003): 3–20; Ron Schatz, *The Electrical Workers: A History of Labor at General Electric and Westinghouse, 1923–1960*, 1983; Robert Zieger, *The CIO, 1935–1955*, 1995.

CATERPILLAR STRIKE

The Caterpillar Strike was a disastrous struggle between the **United Auto Workers of America** (UAW) and Caterpillar, one of the world's largest manufacturers of earth-moving equipment. The **strike** took place between 1991 and 1995 and ended in a complete victory for the corporation. It dealt a blow to the power and prestige of the UAW, and led to great dissatisfaction among the union's rank-and-file members. The UAW's failure at Caterpillar is a dramatic chapter in a series of **downsizing, decertification, and concession strikes** that have marked capital/labor relations since the 1970s. It is also emblematic of the challenges that **globalism** poses for the American labor movement.

Caterpillar is headquartered in Peoria, Illinois, and has large plants in Decatur, East Peoria, and other Midwestern cities. The UAW and Caterpillar enjoyed relatively good relations into the 1980s, when the company nearly went bankrupt and began to lay off workers. At its 1983 convention, the UAW unveiled its "Blueprint for a Working America: A Proposal for an Industrial Policy," which set up union-management committees to resolve disputes over production quotas, layoff decisions, and work rules. UAW President Owen Bieber hailed the plan as giving organized labor a say in the production process. It also moved the union into a managerial role, which tended to distance it from rank-and-file workers, many of whom wondered why the UAW remained silent as Caterpillar expanded its operations in Indonesia, Mexico, and Scotland while reducing its U.S. workforce by nearly 30 percent. Few UAW workers were aware of the strikes against Caterpillar that took place in Scotland in 1987 or in Canada in 1991. This lack of knowledge made them ill prepared to call upon allies outside the United States when their own troubles began in 1991.

When the Caterpillar/UAW contract expired in 1991, Caterpillar demanded concessions from its U.S. workforce, including the introduction of a two-tier wage system under which new hires would receive lower wages, changes to health care coverage, and a redefinition of **overtime**. When workers balked, Caterpillar instituted a **lockout**. In November 1991, the UAW voted to strike against several Caterpillar plants in Illinois, Pennsylvania, and Tennessee. The strike held for five months, but in April 1992 Caterpillar announced its intention to hire permanent **scabs**. The UAW called off the strike and workers returned to their jobs without a contract. The union banked partly on the hope of a political solution, and it campaigned on behalf of Bill Clinton in the U.S. presidential election.

Workers continued to labor for two and a half years without a contract, with Caterpillar imposing concessions at will despite the fact that its stock price was soaring. The period saw numerous acts of rank-and-file militancy, however, with several **wildcat strikes** taking place that UAW officials worked hard to suppress, thereby further alienating rank-and-file activists. Local militants maintained levels of **solidarity** by wearing provocative shirts, emblems, and badges that lampooned the company and scabs, and sometimes vilified UAW leaders. Conditions at Caterpillar deteriorated so badly that the UAW authorized a new strike in June 1994. Once again, the UAW faltered badly. It refused to authorize mass **picketing**, partly out of fear that militants would commit acts of **sabotage**, and partly from the mistaken belief that Caterpillar would not be able to assemble enough skilled workers to maintain production. In addition, instead of calling out all 13,000 Caterpillar workers, it ordered engine assemblers and parts workers not directly involved in the disputes to remain working. In all, just 4,000 workers actually left their posts.

The strike was doomed when President Clinton failed to support a bill that would ban replacement workers. The company once again hired scabs and quickly increased its production, even though the National Labor Relations Board upheld more than 150 complaints of **unfair labor practices** pending against Caterpillar and barred it from firing strikers. After 17 months of conflict, UAW leaders accepted Caterpillar's offer and, on December 3, 1995, called off the strike.

The union's leadership received a shock when more than 80 percent of the strikers rejected Caterpillar's offer. The UAW was forced to order workers back to the job and told them that no more strike benefits would be paid. The UAW and its new president, Stephen Yokich, tried to save face by officially referring to the strike as in recess, and by claiming that strike solidarity had been compromised by UAW members crossing picket lines, but there was little it could do to sugarcoat the harsh conditions imposed by Caterpillar. After more than three years of struggle, workers faced a settlement that was worse than the deal they could have accepted in 1991. Caterpillar's six-year contract imposed a pay scale for new hires that was 30 percent lower, the right to hire more part-time workers, and changes in grievance, medical insurance, sick leave, and layoff policies. The company also demanded that workers divest themselves of anti-Caterpillar and anti-scab clothing and paraphernalia; it reserved the right to assign more than 8 hours of work without paying overtime until a worker logged more than 40 hours for the week; and it refused to pay overtime for weekend work. In addition, Caterpillar began to **outsource** work more aggressively and to pursue a "southern strategy" in which more work was sent to **right-to-work** and scab-friendly states.

Since 1995, the UAW has managed to modify some of Caterpillar's conditions. Nevertheless, the fact that one of the richest unions in the United States could be so thoroughly routed does not bode well for the future of industrial unionism, nor does Caterpillar's increasing acquisition of overseas ventures. The city of Decatur, the center of the maelstrom, was also engulfed by the **Staley lockout** and the **Bridgestone-Firestone strike** during the Caterpillar struggle, with only the Bridgestone dispute ending on a note of hope.

Ideological radicals tend to blame leaders' betrayal, **business unionism**, and misguided political alliances for organized labor's reversals. Those charges appear to have some merit, though the Caterpillar debacle was due as much to pressures of globalism as UAW errors and misalliances. Caterpillar was able to remain profitable throughout the fight, largely by decentralizing production, outsourcing, and diversifying its assets. Dispassionate observers cite the Caterpillar strike as a lesson about why American organized labor cannot win consistently by using strategies honed in the 1930s. It suggests a need to organize globally and across decentralized production lines, perhaps even to outsourcers and subsidiaries. Tensions between the UAW and Caterpillar remain high and a new strike in 2004 was just narrowly averted.

Suggested Reading

Victor Gary Devinatz, "A Heroic Defeat: The Caterpillar Labor Dispute and the UAW, 1991–1998," *Labor Studies Journal*, 30, no. 2 (Summer 2005), 1–18; Stephen Franklin and William Serrin, *Three Strikes: Labor's Heartland Losses and What They Mean for Working Americans*, 2002; Virginia Postrel, "Unions Forever? A New Vision for America's Workers," *Reason*, May 1998, http://reason.com/archives/1998/05/01/unions-forever, accessed June 22, 2010.

CENTRALIA MASSACRE

Centralia, Washington, was the center of an infamous 1919 shootout between members of the **Industrial Workers of the World** (IWW), the American Legion, vigilantes, and the local sheriff's office. It is often cited as a particularly grim example of the **Red Scare** that accompanied U.S. involvement in World War I.

Exactly who precipitated the violence is a matter of dispute, but tensions between authorities and the IWW were ongoing at the time of the incident. The IWW was strong in the Pacific Northwest, where it had success in organizing timber workers, despite their often peripatetic lifestyles. West Coast members (**Wobblies**) were often more militant and less theory minded than their counterparts in the East. Washington had seen several IWW "free speech" battles in which IWW members defied local and state laws aimed at breaking up the IWW by limiting the size of public assemblies and restricting street solicitation and public speaking permits. Washington's powerful timber barons sought to rid the state of the IWW. In Centralia, an April 1918 IWW parade provoked local vigilantes—some of whom equated Wobblies with the Bolsheviks who took over Russia in 1917—into smashing local IWW offices. Heated talk of driving out the IWW led some Wobblies to arm themselves; the group's attorney, Elmer Smith, assured them it was legal to use arms to ward off attacks on the IWW hall, though he was a pacifist and counseled the IWW not to take up weapons.

The IWW opposed U.S. entry into World War I, for which members suffered persecution. An Armistice Day parade celebrating the war's end curiously (and probably deliberately) involved a route that twice took marchers past the IWW hall, despite pleas from the hotel owner renting space to the IWW that such a course was provocative and dangerous in the wake of ongoing threats against the IWW. The route choice and the decision of American Legion members to march with rubber hoses and pipes suggest that a smash-up of IWW headquarters was planned. Likewise, a former mayor's choice to march carrying a length of rope ending in a hangman's noose suggest premeditation. When the unruly mob finally surged into the hall, armed Wobblies shot and killed three vigilantes. All of the Wobblies inside were beaten and arrested, except for Wesley Everest, who was, ironically, a military veteran. Everest refused to submit to arrest by vigilantes, though he offered to submit to a law enforcement official. When the crowd attempted to take him, Everest killed one of his attackers before he was subdued, beaten, and jailed. That evening an enraged crowd broke into the local jail, seized Everest, and tortured and mutilated him before hanging him from a bridge. Official town records listed Everest's death as a "suicide." By day's end, four Legionnaires, a deputy sheriff, and Everest were dead, and five Legionnaires were wounded.

Ten individuals, including attorney Smith, were tried for second-degree murder in a trial that left more questions than it answered. No convincing testimony emerged as to who had fired the first shots, and even observers from the **American Federation of Labor**, which despised the IWW, felt the trial was unfair and that all 10 men were innocent. In a curious move perhaps aimed at separating the events from the popularity of returning veterans, the IWW's lead defense attorney exonerated the American Legion and blamed the violence on the Citizens' Protective League, the local vigilantes. Smith and one Wobbly were acquitted, one man was found insane, and seven others were sentenced to 25 to 40 years in prison. Smith, who died in 1930, spent the remainder of his life vainly attempting to get each man released.

The Centralia Massacre unleashed wholesale raids on radical groups across the Northwest and contributed to the IWW's demise in the region. By 1925, the IWW's once-powerful Lumber Workers Industrial Union was defunct.

Suggested Reading

Centralia Massacre Collection, http://content.lib.washington.edu/iwwweb/, accessed June 25, 2010; Tom Copeland, *The Centralia Tragedy of 1919: Elmer Smith and the Wobblies*, 1993; Fred Thompson and Patrick Murfin, *The I.W.W: Its First Seventy Years 1905–1975*, 1976.

CENTRAL LABOR COUNCIL. *See* Central Labor Union.

CENTRAL LABOR UNION

A central labor union (CLU) is a coordinating body for various unions within a given geographic area. The idea behind such bodies is to ensure that workers in the same region are not pitted against one another over issues that affect them all. The term CLU was popular in the 19th and early 20th centuries; today it is often called a central labor council (CLC). A CLU or CLC is an intermediary level between a **union local** and the federation with which it is affiliated, although bodies such as statewide labor councils also exist. In many cases, a CLU makes more sense a state labor council; for example, the greater New York City metropolitan area extends into New Jersey and Connecticut, so a CLU covering workers in both states is more appropriate.

The idea behind a CLU is that issues sometimes arise that involve workers generally, irrespective of their individual unions. A CLU brings together leaders from various unions to plan regionwide strategy for issues that do not necessarily involve workers outside the area. This need can be something as noncontroversial as coordinating parade routes for a **Labor Day** parade, or something as controversial as publicizing a **boycott**, organizing a **picket** line, calling a **sympathy strike**, launching a **general strike**, or securing allies for a **corporate campaign**. Building local coalitions assures that unions respect one another's issues and do not work at cross-purposes. A CLU or CLC also seeks to give organized labor a unified voice on political issues such as endorsing candidates, lobbying for health care reform, or attempting to influence impending legislation.

Larger cities generally foster the most powerful CLUs. The New York City CLU planned what is considered to be the first Labor Day in 1882, and Chicago's CLU aided in the **May Day** events of 1886 that culminated in the **Haymarket bombing**. In the 1960s, New York City's CLC played a key role in helping organize hospital and health care workers and exerted an important political role within the city. More recently, councils in Los Angeles, Boston, and elsewhere have given important logistical support to the "Justice for Janitors" movement. CLCs also coordinate union charity work, such as aid for Haitian earthquake victims or helping rebuild U.S. regions ravaged by hurricanes.

The 19th-century CLUs had more autonomy than modern labor councils, which must have their actions approved by the federations of constituent unions. Past CLUs often coordinated workers irrespective of their affiliations; by contrast, New York City's current CLC is an arm of the **American Federation of Labor-Congress of Industrial Organizations**. Such entities remain important sounding boards for discussing issues of mutual importance as well as fostering ties across the labor movement.

Suggested Reading

Stanley Aronowitz, *From the Ashes of the Old*, 1998; R. Emmett Murray, *The Lexicon of Labor*, 1998; "State and Local Union Movements," http://www.aflcio.org/aboutus/unioncities/, accessed June 23, 2010.

CERTIFICATION

Certification is the official recognition by the National Labor Relations Board (NLRB) that a labor union has the right to engage in **collective bargaining** for its members. Under federal law, a union must be certified before it can formally negotiate a contract on behalf of workers. Although it is possible for an employer to recognize a union without resorting to casting secret ballots, in nearly all cases a formal vote is taken. NLRB officials supervise such votes, and close results can be challenged by either side.

The 1935 **National Labor Relations Act** (NLRA) established a procedure for recognizing unions. At the time, it corrected abuses on both sides. Unions generally collected authorization signatures to assess the interest of workers to form a collective bargaining unit. During this process employers used tactics ranging from dismissal to (sometimes violent) intimidation to get rid of union activists and to dissuade workers from signing such cards. Unions also occasionally engaged in shady tactics such as misrepresenting the number of employees who expressed interest in having a union. The NLRA deemed certain methods on both sides to be **unfair labor practices** and set up formal channels for holding union elections. At least 30 percent of employees within a potential bargaining unit must sign cards indicating a desire for a vote before an election can be held. In theory, signing the cards merely indicates desire to call for a vote, not necessarily an endorsement of the union itself. In practice, most of those who do not wish a union refuse to sign cards. Given that the union itself must request a certification election, many err on the cautious side and try to acquire in excess of 30 percent approval.

The NLRA provided for secret ballots or "any other suitable method." The latter clause angered employers who argued that unions were using "card check" methods to try to force employers to bargain. The 1947 **Taft-Hartley Act** amended the NLRA and made the secret ballot the only method of forcing an employer to recognize a union. This, too, led to controversy as numerous employers returned to pre-vote intimidation practices such as those that preceded the NLRA. A 1954 ruling established "blue flash" rules—named for the anti-union Blue Flash Express Company— that forbade employers from making reprisals against employees involved in union certification votes.

Labor union certifications peaked in the late 1960s. By the 1990s, unions were losing more than half of all votes taken; they did not win as many as 51 percent of votes taken until 2002. Employers have seized upon such data to argue that unions are outmoded and unwanted. That position is undermined by a 2007 Gallup poll indicating that 60 percent of Americans approve of unions. Union officials have argued that procedures developed in 1935 and 1947 are outmoded and unfairly empower employers. From their point of view, the current system is so slow and cumbersome that it gives employers time to poison opinions about unions in advance of a vote. There is no set time period in which an election must be held, and recalcitrant employers often delay agreeing on a time and date for as long as they can. Employers may not punish workers for seeking a union vote, but expressing their own opinions about labor unions is also protected free speech. Moreover, employers sometimes express the view that a union would ruin their business, which fearful workers might interpret as a threat to eliminate jobs.

In recent years, organized labor has lobbied for an "Employee Free Choice Act." Under such a bill, a union would be certified if it collected card signatures from more than 50 percent of employees, and no formal vote to join a union would be needed.

Union officials argue that this process would do away with subtle intimidation, eliminate delays, and provide workers with greater anonymity. These so-called card check procedures face long odds at present. Since the passage of the Taft-Hartley Act, U.S. courts have consistently upheld elections as the sole established involuntary procedure under which employers must unionize. Most employers are strongly opposed to card checking and there does not seem to be much political will to force the issue.

Suggested Reading

Charles Caulkins, "The Facts on Union Certification by Card Check," http://library.findlaw.com/2006/May/1/241516.html, accessed June 29, 2010; Gerald Mayer, "Labor Union Recognition Procedures: Use of Secret Ballots and Card Checks," CRS Report for Congress, http://www.policyarchive.org/handle/10207/bitstreams/2453.pdf, accessed June 29, 2010.

CHANGE TO WIN FEDERATION

Change to Win (CTW) is a labor federation rival to the **American Federation of Labor-Congress of Industrial Organizations** (AFL-CIO), which it criticizes as mired in **business unionism** and neglectful of the need to conduct grassroots organizing. CTW formed in 2005. As of 2010, it represented between 4.7 million and 6 million workers, with the discrepancy in membership data indicative of some of the controversy surrounding it.

The federation's largest constituent union is the **Service Employees International Union** (SEIU)—somewhat ironic, in that SEIU was at the forefront of a movement to reform the AFL-CIO. In 1995, SEIU President **John Sweeney** became head of the AFL-CIO. At the time, unions represented 14.9 percent of the American workforce. Sweeney pledged to reverse labor's slide by devoting more AFL-CIO resources to organizing. He did allocate more money for this purpose, but ran into organizational obstacles that caused dissidents within the AFL-CIO to complain that the pace of change was too slow and that AFL-CIO bureaucratic procedures blocked the path to substantive reform. In 2003, amidst continuing declines in union representation, SEIU, **UNITE HERE**, and several other unions formed the New Unity Partnership (NUP) to press for greater emphasis on organizing. The NUP was the genesis of CTW. SEIU President Andy Stern openly broke with his former mentor Sweeney in 2004.

In 2005, the NUP was laid to rest and CTW was founded. It originally contained SEIU, UNITE HERE (the two unions merged in 2004), the **United Brotherhood of Carpenters and Joiners** (UBC), and the Laborers' International Union of North America. Upon its founding, CTW was joined by the **Teamsters** and the **United Food and Commercial Workers Union**. In all, approximately one-third of the AFL-CIO's membership bolted to CTW. CTW began with optimism and its rhetoric was filled with references to the need to organize and maintain a militant, rather than a bureaucratic, demeanor. Some of the same problems that plagued the AFL-CIO arose within CTW, however.

One of the bigger internal squabbles was been over **jurisdiction**. As once-large **international unions** have declined in size, many have streamlined their operations by merging with other unions. HERE and UNITE merged in 2004, even before CTW formed, but that merger was not an easy one. In 2009, approximately one-third of the merged union's membership quit and joined SEIU; the remaining UNITE HERE members rejoined the AFL-CIO. That same year the UBC also quit the coalition and returned to the independent status it had before joining CTW. CTW did, however, add the **United Farm Workers of America** in 2006, and it has kept its promise to focus on organizing by devoting 75 percent of its resources to such activities. It has launched several high-profile campaigns, such efforts to organize employees of CVS, Smithfield Foods, and Wal-Mart. What it has not done is make a dent in organized labor's overall decline. By 2010, just 12 percent of American workers were unionized.

In 2009, talks were held to discuss the possibility of re-merging CTW and the AFL-CIO. The meetings between the two groups were cordial, but vast differences remain over questions such how much federation income should be earmarked for organizing, how to respond to **globalization**, how high member **dues** should be, and how much power CTW would have within a merged federation. Although CTW supported the election of U.S. President Barack Obama, it has also called for reducing ties between labor and the Democratic Party—a major sticking point given that the AFL-CIO regards political ties as key to enacting labor reform. CTW's more militant members also oppose a merger on the grounds that the AFL-CIO is inherently undemocratic.

Suggested Reading

Elizabeth A. Ashack, Bureau of Labor Statistics, "Major Union Mergers, Alliances, and Disaffiliations, 1995–2007," http://www.bls.gov/opub/cwc/cb20080919ar01p1.htm, accessed June 30, 2010; Change to Win, http://www.changetowin.org/about-us.html, accessed June 30, 2010; Tom Leedham, "Reunification without Democracy: What's the Point?" *Labor Notes*, January 21, 2009.

CHÁVEZ, CÉSAR ESTRADA

César Estrada Chávez (March 31, 1927–April 23, 1993) was the cofounder of the **United Farm Workers of America** (UFWA) and one of the most influential Hispanic leaders of the 20th century. He receives credit for bringing to public attention the plight of West Coast agricultural workers, for forcing Americans to reconsider how the food they eat is produced, and for making them confront nativism, racism, and other forms of discrimination against ethnic groups.

Chávez was born near Yuma, Arizona, the son of Librado and Juana Chávez. The couple operated a small store after emigrating from Mexico, but lost it during the Great Depression and were forced to become migrant farm workers. César's mobile lifestyle led him to attend countless elementary schools; he left school before completing the eighth grade to become a full-time agricultural laborer, a move that became necessary when a car crash left his father unable to work. His first encounter with labor unions came when he was just 14 when the **Congress of Industrial Organizations** (CIO) approached his father to discuss organizing farm workers.

Details of Chávez's early life are hazy and differ according to sources. Chávez probably served in the U.S. Navy in 1946–1947—some sources say he joined in 1944, when he would have been just 17. He worked as a field hand when he left the military, and joined the National Agricultural Workers Union, the first labor organization to which he formally belonged. In 1948, he married Helen Fabela, with whom he eventually had eight children. Despite his lack of formal education, Chávez impressed all who encountered him with his knowledge and eloquence. He and his wife often taught migrant farm laborers how to read and helped them register to vote and become U.S. citizens.

Chávez's life took a dramatic turn in 1952, when he joined the Community Service Organization (CSO), a grassroots group associated with activist Saul Alinsky. The CSO schooled Chávez in the tactics of Mahatma Gandhi, in combating racism, and in urban community organizing, Chávez, in turn, transplanted these strategies to the countryside. He was the CSO organizer for California from 1952 to 1962 and its national director from 1960 to 1962, at which time he split with Alinsky over the usefulness of organizing farm workers. Chávez was a devout Roman Catholic, and he often built coalitions

Labor activist César Chávez (1927–1993) walking with farm workers during the 1,000 Mile March in California, summer 1975. Tens of thousands of farm workers marched and attended evening rallies to hear Chávez speak. (Photo by Cathy Murphy/Getty Images)

with the Catholic Church for campaigns to improve the lives of the poor. Those actions centered on nonviolent protest, including marches, hunger strikes, and rallies—tactics Chávez would also use once the UFWA formed.

In 1962, Chávez moved to Delano, California, where he, Gilbert Padilla, and **Dolores Huerta** set up the National Farm Workers Association (NFWA), and led several **strikes** against growers. Chávez joined a 1965 **Agricultural Workings Organizing Committee** (AWOC) strike and **boycott** against Delano grape producers, which united Hispanic and Filipino workers, drew national attention, and thrust Chávez into the public limelight. The Delano actions attracted support from influential labor and political leaders such as **Walter Reuther** and Senator Robert Kennedy. The struggles of farm workers captured the national imagination throughout the 1960s. The UFWA's tactics and objectives resonated with those of other social change movements in the period; many Americans saw the union's actions as a veritable Latino civil rights movement. This view had an ironic side to it, as the UFWA under Chávez often supported immigration restriction and Chávez had been among those calling for an end to the *Braceros* program. Although Spanish-language slogans were commonplace in UFWA campaigns, the union had numerous non-Hispanic members, especially Filipinos, and the UFWA feared that unfettered immigration would undermine pay structures—a position it maintained into the 1990s.

AWOC and the NFWA emerged as the UFWA during the 1965 strike, and Chávez sought to expand its organizing efforts. In that task the UFWA faced stiff competition and **raiding** from the **Teamsters**. Disputes between the rivals went on for years. In 1966, Chávez and the UFWA won contracts from several corporate farms, including Schenley and DiGiorgio. This success led to support from the **American Federation of Labor-Congress of Industrial Organizations** (AFL-CIO). In 1967, Chávez called for a lettuce boycott to protest low **wages** and poor conditions in the fields, including the heavy use of health-damaging pesticides. By 1967, the UFWA had secured wage increases, union hiring halls, improved field conditions, and pesticide-use agreements throughout California. Its successes spawned the birth of similar unions in other parts of the country. In 1968, the AFL-CIO formally chartered the UFWA, although the union struggled with Teamsters' raiding until 1977.

By 1970, most West Coast grape growers had signed agreements with the UFWA, though Chávez led a campaign against vegetable growers who signed contracts with the Teamsters. When grape producers tried to wring **concessions** from the UFWA in 1973, Chávez, Huerta, and the UFWA renewed their call for a nationwide boycott of U.S.-grown grapes. In 1975, growers conceded the right of farm workers' rights to **collective bargaining** under California's **Agricultural Labor Relations Act**. Although it is the only law formally recognizing the right of farm workers to unionize, the California law has become a template for other states. Throughout the 1970s, the UFWA held union recognition votes and negotiated health, pension, and wage benefits for its members.

At its height in the mid-1970s, the UFWA had more than 50,000 members. Declining activism and the economic downslide of the 1970s led to a drop-off in union membership. In the 1980s, Chávez switched his attention to campaigns to end pesticide poisoning. In 1986, he fasted for 36 days to call attention to health risks involved in pesticide use and in support of a new boycott against grapes. By the early 1990s, however, UFWA membership had fallen to approximately 15,000.

Chávez critics argued that the UFWA often operated more as a César Chávez cult than as a true labor union. Still others complained of autocratic rule and self-aggrandizement, though Chávez's salary never exceeded $5,000 per year and he often did not even head the UFWA. His unexpected death both shocked the UFWA and gave credence to arguments that the UFWA had become too closely associated with Chávez. More than 40,000 people attended his funeral, and in 1994 Chávez was posthumously awarded the Presidential Medal of Freedom, only the second Mexican American to be so honored. In 1998, he was elected to the Labor Hall of Fame. The UFWA, however, struggled to regain traction. Although it has rebounded to more than 27,000 members, it is no longer in the public eye as it was under Chávez. Moreover, the union evokes Chávez's legacy at every turn. The long-term wisdom of this strategy is uncertain given the relative youth of many farm workers.

Suggested Reading

Roger Bruns, *César Chávez: A Biography*, 2005; Juan Gonzalez, *Harvest of Empire*, 2000; David Goodwin, *Great Lives: César Chávez*, 1991; Ilan Stavans, ed. *César Chávez: An Organizer's Tale: Speeches*, 2008.

CHECKOFF

Checkoff is the practice wherein an employer automatically deducts union **dues** from an employee's paycheck. Securing checkoff rights was a major breakthrough for funding unions, which hitherto had to collect all dues individually and maintain complex accounting records.

Checkoffs were rare until the 20th century. Insofar as historians can determine, in 1889 Ohio coal miners were the first to negotiate checkoffs, and the **United Mine Workers of America** was the first national union to do so in 1898. Checkoff rights were negotiated on a case-by-case basis throughout the early 20th century, and the practice gained momentum when adopted by the **National War Labor Board** during World War I. Although checkoffs are not specifically guaranteed under the **National Labor Relations Act**, since this legislation's passage most employers have viewed checkoffs as an easy concession to grant during **collective bargaining** sessions. Federal labor laws allowing checkoffs have withstood legal challenges and by the 1980s, most unionized workplaces had checkoff systems in place. Most of the workplaces without checkoff systems are located in **right-to-work** states.

The 1947 **Taft-Hartley Act** allows checkoffs only for those employees who individually authorize the employer to make such withholdings. The 1959 **Landrum-Griffin Act** enables employees with ideological or religious objections to opt out of checkoffs. If there is no automatic checkoff, then the shop steward or another union official must collect dues from each member. Union officials dislike this method of funding because it casts officials as bill collectors. Most employers that sign union contracts also see the checkoff method as less disruptive than having union officials collect dues on company property during work hours. Moreover, they are called upon to collect **agency fees** from recalcitrant employees, or perhaps even dismiss them—a possibility that places employers in the midst of disputes not of their making.

The checkoff procedure is generally quite straightforward. When workers are hired, they sign authorization forms allowing the employer to deduct a specified amount from their paycheck. These fees are transferred into the union's account. If a worker chooses not to use checkoff, the union contract determines how dues will be collected.

Some unions, especially the **Industrial Workers of the World**, have argued that dues checkoffs isolate union officials from the rank-and-file workers, associate the practice with **business unionism**, and oppose it. For the most part, the push to eliminate dues checkoff comes from right-wing ideological opponents of labor unions rather than employers who have used the practice. Occasionally attacks on the checkoff system are part of hardball negotiating tactics or attempts to break unions. In 2010, Detroit Mayor Dave Bing announced his intention to terminate the contracts of city workers and end the checkoff system in an attempt to wring **concessions** from public employees.

Suggested Reading

"Checkoff," *West's Encyclopedia of American Law*, http://www.answers.com/topic/checkoff, accessed June 23, 2010; Terry L. Leap, *Collective Bargaining and Labor Relations*, 1995; U.S. Department of Labor, Bureau of Labor Statistics, *Major Collective Bargaining Agreements: Union Security and Dues Checkoff Provisions*, 1982, 1425–1431.

CHILD LABOR

Child labor refers to the employment of individuals younger than the age of 18 years. Although teen employment is considered an American rite of passage, child labor becomes a social problem when those younger than age 18 are forced to labor, work longer than federal laws allow, or toil under dangerous conditions. Many Americans mistakenly think that child labor abuses are a thing of the past, and official policy often encourages such views. It is even difficult to find out how many children younger than the age of 18 are working in the United States, though most estimates run in excess of 5.5 million. According to the International Labor Organization, in 2009 more than 400,000 children worked in agriculture, many of them younger than the age of 12. The National Consumer League notes that in 2007 alone, on average, an American teenage worker died every five days.

Four young boys pose outside of the coal mine where they worked in Pittston, Pennsylvania, in 1911. (Photograph by Lewis Hine. Library of Congress)

Child labor has been a standard feature in North America since the first Europeans settled there. In the Colonial period, children worked in numerous capacities. Boys were generally part of the **agrarian** economy, girls were trained in household tasks, and quite a few girls were hired out as domestic servants. Puritan ideology equated idle time with mischief and bedevilment, so children were immersed in trade and work from an early age. The advent of the **Industrial Revolution** saw the influx of children into factories; in fact, they were often among the earliest industrial workers, as their labor was the least valuable in an agrarian economy and sending children into **wage** labor helped supplement family farm incomes. Immigration and urbanization also contributed to rising levels of child labor. By the latter part of the 19th century, children could be found in all manner of jobs—from tending machines and picking the slate from coal chutes to hawking goods on urban streets. Many of their tasks involved long hours and were menial or dangerous in nature. Children also received the lowest wages of any category of worker; hence labor unions championed child labor restrictions as a way of protecting wage rates. Public school and child welfare advocates also argued that children's health was being abused and their educational opportunities ignored when child labor was allowed. Groups such as the **Knights of Labor** issued shocking reports on child labor, filled with data that were largely substantiated by the **Bureau of Labor Statistics** and exposés such as *How the Other Half Lives* (1890) by Jacob Riis.

Employers resisted child labor laws, as it was in their economic self-interest to do so. High levels of poverty and **unemployment** made it easy to recruit children as low-paid workers, especially among immigrants. In 1900, at least 1.7 million children worked in American factories. By then, however, the tide was turning. Ending child labor was a major issue for **Progressive Era** reformers. The National Child Labor Committee (NCLC) was founded in 1904 to document child labor and advocate for national legislation to control it, and photographers such as Lewis Hine and writers associated with the muckraking era kept the issue alive in the public consciousness. The NCLC and other reformers encountered fierce opposition from business leaders, especially in southern states where national legislation was couched as an infringement of states' rights, and from business-friendly courts. In 1916, Congress passed the Keating-Owen Act to regulate child labor, only to have it struck down by the U.S. Supreme Court, which declared the law unconstitutional in 1918. A revised law passed in 1919 was also struck down in 1922, and a proposed child labor amendment to the Constitution failed to achieve ratification.

Although various states enacted their own laws, there was no federal statue regulating child labor until 1938, when the **Fair Labor Standards Act** (FSLA) established minimum age and hour limits for under-18 laborers. The FSLA set 14 as the minimum age for employment and placed an 18-hour per week limit on the number of hours that a child can work when school is in session. (Children can work as many as 40 hours per week in the summer.) The FSLA created separate standards for farm employment, however, which has been a source of ongoing contention. The **United Farm Workers of America** complained that children as young as age 5 may work up to 10 hours per day—abuses that are hard to track down because many of these children are the offspring of undocumented migrants.

Abuses have not been limited to field workers. Each year states collect millions of dollars in fines from employers that violate hour laws. The NCLC estimates that as many as 150,000 children per week are working when they should be in school. In addition, approximately 50,000 children remain involved in street peddling, convenience stores and fast-food restaurants routinely work children off the clock, corporations such as Wal-Mart have been fined for placing children in dangerous work conditions such as driving forklifts, and agricultural states such as Iowa see thousands of child labor violations filed each year. The **Department of Labor** estimates that children suffer an average of 158,000 work-related injuries each year. Lax enforcement under President George W. Bush led to climbing numbers of both child workers and on-the-job injuries. Secretary of Labor Hilda Solis pledged in 2009 that the administration of President Barack Obama would enforce child labor laws more aggressively. The **American Federation of Labor-Congress of Industrial Organizations** insists that child labor is a serious contemporary problem that must be curtailed.

Suggested Reading

Sandy Hobbs, Jim McKechnie, and Michael Lavalette, *Child Labor: A World History Companion*, 1999; National Child Labor Committee, http://www.nationalchildlabor.org/index.html, accessed June 25, 2010; Laurence Steinberg, Sanford Dornbusch, and B. Bradford Brown, *Beyond the Classroom*, 1997; Walter I. Trattner, *Crusade for the Children: A History of the National Child Labor Committee and Child Labor Reform in America*, 1970.

CHINESE EXCLUSION ACT

The Chinese Exclusion Act was an 1882 Congressional action signed into law by President Chester Arthur that curtailed Chinese immigration into the United States. It stands as a grim testament to popular racist sentiments in the United States during the Gilded Age—views that penetrated even the most progressive elements of society. It culminated more than a decade's worth of intense lobbying on the part of organized labor, which saw imported Chinese labor as a threat and was not above trading in vicious ethnic stereotyping in support of such a bill.

The first Chinese immigrants who came to North America were viewed as exotic, and few laborers saw them as competition. That perception changed quickly when gold seekers poured into California in 1849. Large numbers of Chinese came to California to pan for gold and to provide services such as cooking, laundering, and retail activity. During the 1870s, Chinese workers also toiled in railroad construction. Although Chinese immigration never posed the threat alarmists claimed, the overall population of Chinese west of the Rocky Mountains increased dramatically, with the heaviest concentrations found in California and the Pacific Northwest. By 1870, roughly 50,000 Chinese lived in California, often clustered into enclaves dubbed "Chinatowns." Caucasian labor organizations accused Chinese workers of undermining local **wage** structures and of diverting jobs from white workers. Local and state restrictions often confined Chinese workers to menial positions, subjected them to special taxes, and limited their opportunities.

For example, the Chinese largely panned for gold because in many places they were not allowed to open mine shafts; alternatively, they might be allowed to pan for gold only downstream from claims worked by Caucasians. Despite early discrimination, Caucasians grudgingly tolerated the Chinese population until the economic downturn that occurred in the West after the **Civil War**.

During the Panic of 1873, whites complained that Chinese "coolie" labor contributed to white **unemployment**. Most whites using the term misunderstood that coolie labor was a form of domestic servitude imposed by British imperialists inside China. Technically, very few Chinese laborers came to North America under the coolie system, but the tendency of employers, especially railroad builders, to hire work gangs through third-party contractors fueled hysteria over coolie labor. In California, organized labor took up the cause of Chinese exclusion. Fear of Chinese labor was further exacerbated by incidents in which employers recruited Chinese **scabs** during labor conflicts, as happened during a shoemakers' **strike** in North Adams, Massachusetts, in 1870. Such cases were relatively rare, but they were well publicized. In 1875, Congress passed the Page Act to disqualify undesirables such as prostitutes from entering the United States. This law had the net effect of excluding nearly all Chinese women. Because of a gross gender imbalance among Chinese immigrants, prostitution was high in some Chinatowns, but for the most part, the Page Age added a sexist twist to prevailing nativist beliefs about the Chinese.

By 1877, the Workingmen's Party had gained traction in California. Operating as a **labor party**, it promoted general labor reform, but banning Chinese immigration was its touchstone cause. Ironically, the most prominent national figure in the Workingmen's Party, Denis Kearney, was himself an immigrant from Ireland. Kearney embarked on a national tour on behalf of Chinese exclusion in 1878. His reception was mixed in the East and numerous newspapers denounced him as a buffoon, but Kearney nonetheless helped turn anti-Chinese agitation into a national issue. Even the central leadership of the **Knights of Labor** (KOL), which organized African Americans and unskilled immigrants on an equal basis with white, native-born, skilled workers, supported Chinese exclusion, though several **union locals** ignored the call and organized Chinese workers into KOL assemblies.

As organized labor lobbied for curtailment of Chinese labor, it initially found itself on the opposite side of prevailing politics. In 1864, President Abraham Lincoln signed into law "An Act to Encourage Immigration," which required enforcement of labor contracts drawn abroad. The **National Labor Union** opposed this legislation and all forms of contract gang labor. The bill gave ammunition to those spreading rumors that Chinese workers were coolies and was unpopular among many laborers. So, too, was the 1868 Burlingame Treaty, which gave China most-favored nation status in trade relations with the United States and encouraged immigration. Labor groups denounced the Burlingame pact as a plot by robber barons to undermine wages—a charge not completely without merit, as employers generally supported Chinese immigration and some benefited greatly from patterns in which Chinese workers often *did* work for lower wages than Caucasians. By the 1870s, however, some national politicians joined with organized labor in support of anti-Chinese laws. This behavior was particularly noted among those candidates seeking working-class support in close electoral races, although by then anti-Chinese hysteria was rampant in most Western industrial nations. New political alliances secured passage of both the Page Act and the 1879 Fifteen Passenger Bill, which limited the number of Chinese passengers entering the United States on any ship. President Rutherford B. Hayes's veto of the latter served mainly to whip hysteria to higher levels and to drive eastern laborers uncomfortable with Kearney into the anti-Chinese cause.

In the 1880 election, both Republicans and Democrats called for restricting Chinese immigration, which made some form of restriction a foregone conclusion. The 1882 bill passed by Congress and signed by President Arthur banned any new Chinese immigration for 10 years and required Chinese living in the United States to secure a residency permit. It did little to appease those activists who, under the slogan "The Chinese Must Go," called for deportation of all existing Chinese inside the United Sates. There had been acts of violence against Chinese immigrants in the 1870s, but some of the worst incidents occurred after the 1882 law went into effect. One of the uglier confrontations happened in Rock Springs, Wyoming Territory, in 1885, when gangs of white workers, including KOL members, rioted and killed as many as 40 Chinese. There were also vicious anti-Chinese riots in cities such as Seattle, Tacoma, and San Francisco. Congress tried to suppress the anger through the passage of the Foran Act in 1885, which essentially repealed the 1864 bill signed by Lincoln. By the 1880s, however, the Chinese were viewed in popular culture as virtually subhuman and incapable of being assimilated.

Congress extended the Chinese Exclusion Act thought the Geary Act in 1892 and, in 1902, continued the ban indefinitely. The 1907 Gentlemen's Agreement with Japan imposed similar restrictions upon would-be Japanese immigrants. Japan, however, would be the pathway through which the Chinese Exclusion Act would be reversed. Following the bombing of Pearl Harbor on December 7, 1941, anger was directed against persons of Japanese ancestry. China was a U.S. ally against Japan in World War II, which led to a 1943 repeal of the Chinese Exclusion Act.

There is dubious merit in debating the relative oppression of groups suffering discrimination. Nonetheless, a good case can be made that few groups endured the overall oppression suffered by Chinese living in the United States between 1878 and 1943.

Suggested Reading

Andrew Gyory, *Closing the Gate: Race, Politics, and the Chinese Exclusion Act*, 1998; Alexander Saxton, *The Indispensable Enemy: Labor and the Anti-Chinese Movement in California*, 1971; Robert Weir, "Blind in One Eye Only: Western and Eastern Knights of Labor View the Chinese Question," *Labor History* 41, no. 4 (November 2000), 421–436.

CIVIL RIGHTS MOVEMENT AND LABOR

The problem of race is a vexing one that has proved a challenge for organized labor as well as society as a whole. Paradoxically, labor unions have been among both the more progressive and the most regressive forces in American society in the overall struggle for racial equality.

For most of American history, white privilege was a given in the nation's social makeup. Much of the need for antebellum labor was filled through **slavery**, with only people of color serving as chattel. Racial prejudice was the norm, even among northern abolitionists. The **Civil War** ended slavery, but racism remained entrenched both ideologically and institutionally. In the South, formal "Jim Crow" labor systems relegated African Americans to some of the lowest-paying and most dangerous jobs in America; in the North, informal social arrangements accomplished the same effects. It took **William Sylvis** several years to convince white colleagues in the **National Labor Union** to offer fraternal affiliation to the **Colored National Labor Union**, though that alliance quickly dissolved. Among 19th-century **labor federations**, only the **Knights of Labor** (KOL) sought to organize African Americans on an equal basis with whites, and even it battled fierce opposition from some members, especially in the South. Such generally progressive groups as the **American Railway Union** and **Populists** excluded African Americans, as did most of the **American Federation of Labor** (AFL). Although the AFL often paid lip service to the need for cross-racial labor **solidarity**, the principle of **voluntarism** allowed affiliates to set their own membership criteria. In turn, many unions explicitly forbade black members, and quite a few extended exclusion clauses to **Asians** and **Latinos** as well. Only a handful of unions—most notably the **United Mine Workers of America** (UMWA) and **butchers**—made much effort to recruit black members. Unions' neglect of African American employees was a target of complaints by black leaders such as Booker T. Washington and Richard Davis. Well into the 1950s, fewer than 20 percent of AFL affiliates had antidiscrimination clauses in their charters.

In the early 20th century, the **Industrial Workers of the World** called for the organization of black workers, though it took only tentative steps to do so. African Americans were largely left to form their own unions, as laundresses, sharecroppers, shipyard workers, and others tried to do. Unfortunately, such groups were vulnerable to racist backlash and seldom exercised more than local influence. A rare exception to nationwide organizing in the pre-World War II era was the **Brotherhood of Sleeping Car Porters** (BSCP), whose president, **A. Philip Randolph**, emerged as the most important black labor leader of the first three-fourths of the 20th century. The AFL's reluctance to approach people of color meant that radical left labor groups associated with **communists** and **socialists** did the bulk of black organizing. The BSCP gained a rare AFL charter and did not join the **Congress of Industrial Unions** (CIO) in the 1930s, although the CIO's blend of **social unionism** and its willingness to call upon radical left organizers made it far more open to recruiting black members. It is not certain how many African Americans the CIO organized, but the **United Auto Workers of America** had about 100,000 black members by 1940, and the **United Steelworkers of America** (USW) had approximately 70,000 black members, giving them the largest presence inside the CIO. Other CIO unions with significant black membership included the UMWA and the **United Packinghouse Workers** (UPHW). The CIO, like the KOL before it, had to endure outbreaks of rank-and-file racial tension. During the 1940s, the CIO held several congresses to address union racism, efforts that met with mixed success.

Randolph used both clout and bluff to force President Franklin Roosevelt into signing a 1941 executive order that ended racial discrimination in defense industries, an action often viewed as prelude to President Harry Truman's 1951 order to desegregate the military, and the 1954 *Brown v. Board of Education* decision, which desegregated public schools. World War II revitalized the civil rights movement, which posed new dilemmas for labor. Although the CIO's record was much stronger on civil rights, even it faced charges that its unions treated African Americans as second-class citizens. Moreover, after the passage of the **Taft-Hartley Act** and the outbreak of the **Red Scare**, the CIO faced pressure to rid itself of the very radical left members who had been most successful in cross-racial organizing.

In the 1955 merger between the AFL and the CIO, the latter extracted a promise that the federation would be more attendant to civil rights. That initially proved a hollow promise. Individual unions—mostly old CIO bodies—assisted the civil rights movement, but the AFL-CIO executive council remained aloof. The BSCP played a key role during the Montgomery bus boycott, the packinghouse workers assisted the family of Emmett Till, two black members were added to the AFL-CIO board, and a federation Civil Rights Committee was created in 1956. In 1958, however, National Association for the Advancement of Colored People (NAACP) labor secretary Herbert Hill bitterly complained that even old CIO unions practiced systematic racial discrimination, and he questioned the usefulness of the NAACP alliance with organized labor. Hill's salvo shocked the UAW, the USW, the UPHW, and other former CIO unions. They provided seed money, logistical support, and volunteers to civil rights groups such as the Student Nonviolent Coordinating Committee, the Congressional of Racial Equality, and the Southern Christian Leadership Committee. The UAW's **Walter Reuther** took the podium during the 1963 March on Washington in which the Reverend Martin Luther King, Jr., delivered his famed "I have a dream" speech.

Individual unions supported the civil rights movement, but AFL-CIO leaders were slow to change their policy. Job discrimination against black workers remained appallingly high in the building trades. When Randolph—also the titular head of the Negro American Labor Council (NALC)—criticized a whitewashed, self-congratulatory 1961 AFL-CIO report on civil rights, federation President **George Meany** publicly humiliated him; the two maintained frosty relations to the end of their respective lives. Meany's commitment to **Cold War** unionism made him fearful of activism overall, as he often misinterpreted 1960s radicalism as akin to the 1930s left-wing movement.

Meany was not alone in this view. Nearly all AFL-CIO unions eliminated racial barriers by the mid-1960s in the wake of the 1964 Civil Rights Act, but not all Great Society programs meshed well with old union models. **Affirmative action** programs, for instance, met with opposition from unions with **apprentice** programs when those inside programs were passed over for promotion in favor of lesser-trained minority candidates. Affirmative action also proved contentious during layoffs, as union seniority and **bumping** rights largely meant that **minority labor** was the first to go. The changing composition of **blue-collar** labor from the 1960s forced organized labor to come to terms with black laborers, but the urban riots of the mid- and late 1960s and the rise of black power movements made the transition difficult. In 1968, the Reverend King was assassinated in Memphis, Tennessee, where he had gone to offer support for a sanitation workers' **strike**. Black militancy—already on the rise—increased dramatically after King's death. Even the UAW struggled with **wildcat strikes** led by so-called black revolutionary union movements, though it had pulled out of the AFL-CIO in 1968 partly in solidarity with those complaining of the federation's inattention to civil rights.

Rank-and-file rebellion cooled during the stagflation of the mid- and late 1970s. The 1973 creation of the Coalition of Black Trade Unionists also helped build new bonds between black workers and unions, and the impact of affirmative action in bringing thousands of black workers into fields such as public service, construction, health and human services, and education helped erode old racial barriers. So, too, did structural changes inside the AFL-CIO that brought more people of color into direct decision-making roles. By the time of its founder's death in 1979, the **A. Philip Randolph Institute**, created in 1965, had become an effective conduit between civil rights and organized labor. Today's AFL-CIO actively trains minority leaders and openly supports movements that have high minority membership, such as **Janitors for Justice**. The irony is that the greatest racial progress has come during decades in which organized labor's overall vitality has waned in the face of **deindustrialization** and attacks on labor unions.

Suggested Reading

Horace Clayton and George Mitchell, *Black Workers and New Unions*, 2009; Philip Foner and Ronald Lewis, *Black Workers: A Documentary History from Colonial Times to the Present*, 1989; August Meier, Elliott Rudwick, and Joseph Trotter, *Black Detroit and the Rise of the UAW*, 2007; Kim Moody, *An Injury to All: The Decline of American Unionism*, 1988.

CIVIL WAR AND LABOR

Working people determined the outcome of the American Civil War (1861–1865). Commoners made up the bulk of the armies of both the Union and the Confederacy. They also indirectly shaped the war through the ideals they held and through their respective industrial and agricultural productivity.

Colonial labor was rooted in **agrarianism** and the idea that a "natural aristocracy" based on character and breeding should determine social relations. These beliefs persisted in the American South far longer than in the trans-Appalachian West, where individualism was stronger, or in the North, where the **Industrial Revolution** first appeared and where both the **middle class** and the **working class** first took shape. Southern agriculture was also geared more toward the market production of crops such as cotton, indigo, and tobacco rather than foodstuffs, a contributing factor to the region's heavy use of **slave** labor.

In the decade following the War of 1812, many states liberalized their constitutions to place a greater emphasis on commoners. As a consequence, politicians were forced to make appeals to farmers and workers. In the North, the concept of "free labor" took hold in which freedom of contract, freedom of mobility, and ownership of one's labor slowly eroded the Colonial ideal that working for **wages** was a dangerous form of dependency and should be only a temporary phase in one's life. By the 1850s, many northern workers had come to embrace what some observers call "free labor ideology," an acceptance of the value of free labor bolstered by a belief in its superiority to slave labor.

From the 1820s through the 1850s, many Americans, especially among the northern middle class, embraced reform and utopian movements, including temperance and abolitionism. Although the evangelical fervor of the Second Great Awakening (c. 1790–1840) touched all regions of the nation, in the North it first impacted the middle class, which then attempted to redeem workers. Their evangelical efforts coincided with a wave of canal and road building, the expansion of manufacturing, the growth of cities, and an influx of immigrants from Ireland, Germany, and Britain. Although northern workers were not the most enthusiastic supporters of religion, temperance, or abolitionism, their associated ideals contributed to free labor ideology. Moreover, rising levels of immigration brought millions of newcomers who saw slave labor as competition for the unskilled and semiskilled jobs they sought. New York City's population, for example, jumped from 313,000 to 814,000 in just 20 years (1840 to 1860).

During this era, the vast majority of Americans from all regions and classes were profoundly racist. This number included abolitionists, the largest group of which called for an end to slavery and deportation of people of color. Northerners converted to abolitionism generally upheld the superiority of free labor, not racial equality, and they feared the political might of "Slave Power"—the Southern planter elites—rather than the sin of slavery itself. Events that suggested an expansion of Slave Power—including the 1846 Mexican War, the Fugitive Slave Act, and the Kansas-Nebraska Act—met with popular resistance in the North. Some northern workers had joined the antislavery Liberty Party in 1848; many more hastened to the newly formed Republican Party after 1854.

Northern workers embraced free labor ideology, but they were not mere conduits for a middle-class agenda. Numerous **strikes** occurred in the North from the late 1820s onward, and two large ones took place on the eve of the Civil War—a Philadelphia iron molders walkout in 1857 and a strike involving 20,000 Lynn **shoemakers** in 1860. Once the military hostilities broke out, however, workers on both sides were drawn into the conflict. **William Sylvis** personally organized a militia of northern iron molders, and New York's 69th Brigade was assembled mostly from immigrant Irish. Most commoners were motivated by a desire to preserve the Union, not the cause of liberating slaves. Lincoln's Emancipation Proclamation met with scorn among many northerners, and an 1863 military draft associated with ending slavery led to riots and loss of life.

Commoners also flocked to the Confederate cause, but more from a sense of regional pride than from a desire to perpetuate slavery. The notion of a "plantation South" is a myth. Fewer than 1 percent of Southern whites owned more than 50 slaves, at least 80 percent of the white population owned none at all, and a majority of southerners shared the North's contempt for slave-owning elites. The cry of "a rich man's war and a poor man's fight" was heard throughout the South during the war, and there were also food riots in the region.

Northern workers indirectly contributed to the Union victory in a profound way: They gave the North an insurmountable material advantage. The North produced 70 percent of the nation's commodities. It also held two-thirds of all its railroad mileage, two-thirds of the food supply, and 85 percent of all its factories. There were 1.3 million industrial workers in the North, but just 110,000 in the entire South, many of whom were slaves. Throughout the war the Confederacy struggled to manufacture munitions, build ships, replace destroyed rail lines, and feed its population. By contrast, northern production hummed with such vitality that a labor shortage occurred, and more than 700,000 immigrants to fill the gaps were recruited in 1864 and 1865.

As in most wars, commoners did the bulk of fighting, suffered the worst deprivations, and incurred the highest number of casualties. Both Union and Confederate women contributed to the war effort—as nurses, as businesswomen, as farm and home managers, and in other capacities. Small numbers also worked as spies, disguised themselves as men and fought, or serviced soldiers as prostitutes. African Americans took an active role in the North's war effort. Nearly 200,000 fought in official units, and many more took unilateral action. They also replaced northern workers at war; in the Confederacy many slaves were forced to work, but many also sabotaged the war effort and/or escaped to northern lines.

Despite the valiant efforts of African Americans during the war, most white Americans returned to prewar racist views when the hostilities ended. Roughly 90 percent of all African Americans remained in the South after the Civil War, where Jim Crow labor supplanted slavery and equality remained elusive.

Suggested Reading

Eric Foner, *Free Soil, Free Labor, Free Men*, 1970; Benjamin Quarles, *The Negro in the Civil War*, 1953; David Williams, *A People's History of the Civil War*, 2005.

CLASS CONSCIOUSNESS

Class consciousness refers to the awareness by members of a particular social group that their economic, vocational, and cultural status is different from that of other social groups, as are their values and aspirations. It is a key concept in both **Marxist** and contemporary sociological thought. For Marx, the development of a self-aware class consciousness among the **working class** was an essential prerequisite for it to reach its revolutionary potential. For most modern non-Marxist scholars, class consciousness is among the factors used when categorizing individuals within a socioeconomic framework. It helps explain, for instance, the disconnection between the amount that individuals earn and the class to which they think they belong.

Marxists argue that social class is objectively defined by a person's relationship to the means of production, whether "production" is a physical object, a service, or an intellectual product. In most cases, those who control the means of production have greater power than those who merely use those means. That power is often unjust in the sense that those who produce wealth receive a lesser share of it than those whose labor is not directly involved in production. For instance, investment **capitalists** stand to get a higher percentage of profits from building automobiles than workers who actually make the cars receive in **wages**. The only way to correct such inequity is for workers to seize the means of production for the good of themselves and society as a whole rather than allowing benefits to accrue to an elite minority. This cannot happen, however, until members of the working class gain an awareness of themselves as a class apart whose interests are not identical to those of the ruling classes. Class consciousness, then, is the full awareness of the need and ability to further the interests of one's own social group. Many contemporary Marxists note with irony that capitalist elites generally have greater class consciousness than those who serve them.

The social reality of different classes is as old as recorded history. In simplest terms, society is akin to a pyramid with elites at its top. Various subordinate classes form the pyramid's base and are necessary to sustain elites, who are parasitical in the sense that their activities do not directly produce the material goods and services necessary for survival. Class consciousness is the awareness of where one is located on the socioeconomic pyramid. This means, however, that class consciousness is twofold: The first facet entails identification with others in the same stratum; the second aspect is a desire to change one's social position through political action.

The latter is the key consideration. Class conflict occurs only if a group feels its interests clash with those above them. **Middle-class ideology** often rejects such notions. A high-income member of the middle class might, for example, feel that his interests are identical to those of the upper class and might aspire to become part of the elite. Many scholars have noted that the American working class has generally been more quiescent than its counterparts in other Western industrial (and postindustrial) powers. Most agree that it has had a less developed sense of class consciousness, though scholars have been and remain deeply divided over why this has been the case. One explanation suggests that the overall wealth of the nation and dreams of upward social mobility have caused American workers to identify their interests with those of elites. **Samuel Gompers**, for example, argued that capitalists were reluctant to share their wealth, but that their interests were symbiotic. Under his leadership, the **American Federation of Labor** (AFL) sought greater benefits for unionized workers, but did not question the underlying logic of capitalism. By the end of World War II, AFL President **George Meany** remarked, without irony, that the working class and the middle class were becoming indistinguishable.

Other observers have sought different explanations for weak class consciousness among the working class. Some have followed the lead of Antonio Gramsci (1891–1937) and have identified ways in which workers have been seduced into embracing values not in their self-interest. This line of thought is dominant among modern-day Marxist thinkers. Many labor historians have looked at the role that social diversity has played in weakening class consciousness. The United States is and has been a heterogeneous society. Karl Marx saw labor unions as the building blocks of a post-revolutionary society, but in the Unites States unions have never organized more than 35 percent of eligible workers. The existence of so much **minority labor** has made it easier for employers to use divide-and-conquer methods to retard working-class **solidarity**. American workers have been riven by factors such as race, ethnicity, gender, religion, and skill. In addition, the ongoing influx of immigrants periodically changes the composition of the working class.

Competing identities make it harder for individuals to see class as the primary social fact of their existence. Some observers argue that class consciousness is, at its core, a romantic notion and that individuals generally identify more strongly with groups such as family, friends, peers, neighborhoods, and ethnic groups than with abstractions such as class theory. Social scientists generally take a middle position and assert that we must view social class through myriad objective and subjective factors. Class consciousness is a subjective factor and a perplexing one. At present most Americans, to the degree that they have any class consciousness at all, perceive themselves as members of an ill-defined middle class.

Suggested Reading

Karl Marx, *The Communist Manifesto*, 1848; Robert E. Weir, *Class in America*, 3 vols., 2007; Erik O. Wright, *The Comparative Project on Class Structure and Class Consciousness: An Overview*, 1989.

CLAYTON ANTITRUST ACT

The Clayton Antitrust Act was, in theory, a landmark bill protecting labor's **collective bargaining** rights, though in practice it was widely ignored. The act was signed into law by President Woodrow Wilson in 1914.

The Clayton Act revised the 1890 **Sherman Antitrust Act**, which was designed to outlaw monopolies and curtail the power of trusts. Presaging the Clayton Act, the Sherman Act looked very different on paper than in practice. It proved far too weak to hinder trusts, though its provisos defining illegal restraints against trade provided organized capital with an effective tool for repressing labor unions. Businesses often invoked the Sherman Act to argue that unions were illegal combinations that interrupted the free flow of goods. Compliant courts freely handed out **injunctions** against **strikes** and **boycotts**.

Such a reading of the Sherman Act was clearly beyond Congressional intent, and the Clayton Antitrust Act closed some of the loopholes used against labor. The Clayton bill strengthened anti-monopoly provisions in the Sherman Act, established the Federal Trade Commission to protect consumers, and reformed numerous business practices. From the standpoint of organized labor, its most important provisions were those stating that human labor was "not a commodity or article of commerce." As a consequence, antitrust laws did not apply to labor unions, mutual-aid societies, or other groups engaged in lawful strikes, boycotts, **picketing**, or protests. It also meant that unions were not "illegal combinations or conspiracies in restraint of trade."

The Clayton Act was also the first clear statement of the right of labor unions to exist as lawful organizations. In a fit of what proved to be misplaced optimism, **Samuel Gompers**, president of the **American Federation of Labor**, hailed the Clayton Act as "Labor's Magna Carta." It was not. The **Progressive Era** (c. 1901–1917) brought needed reforms to American society, but most of them were adjustments to the status quo rather than serious challenges to it. Progressive reformers tended to put their faith in experts rather than in grassroots reformers, and the over-all sentiment toward organized labor was hostile. Groups such as the **Industrial Workers of the World** suffered even worse repression than that endured by the **Knights of Labor** during the Gilded Age, and Progressive Era courts continued to favor big business in ruling such as *Buck's Stove & Range Co. v. American Federation of Labor et al.* and *Loewe v. Lawlor*. Many in the business community pushed for **open shops**, and most decried Clayton Act sections protecting unions, condemned Congress for drafting them, and pressured courts to ignore them. The 1921 Supreme Court decision in *Duplex Printing v. Deering* outlawed secondary boycotts and reintroduced the use of certain types of injunctions. Moreover, nothing in the Clayton Act defined **unfair labor practices** on the part of employers—an omission that left open the door for all manner of anti-union activity.

The Clayton Act was mostly a symbolic victory for labor. Labor's right to organize would not be protected completely until the passage of the **National Labor Relations Act**.

Suggested Reading

"The Clayton Act," http://www.antitrustupdate.com/Statutes/ClaytonAct/ST-Clayton17-18.html, accessed June 28, 2010; Daniel Ernst, *Lawyers against Labor: From Individual Rights to Corporate Liberalism*, 2002; Herbert Hovenkamp, *The Antitrust Enterprise: Principle and Execution*, 2008.

COALITION OF LABOR UNION WOMEN

The Coalition of Labor Union Women (CLUW) is a nonprofit organization made up of American and international trade union women dedicated to promoting the interests of working women within unions and advancing social justice for women within society. It bills itself as the only national organization for union women, and is one of seven special constituency groups with the **American Federation of Labor-Congress of Industrial Organizations** (AFL-CIO).

The CLUW was founded in 1974 when Olga Madar of the **United Auto Workers of America** and Addie Wyatt of the **United Food and Commercial Workers Union** convened a conference in Chicago that, among other things, addressed issues of sexism within the organized labor movement. When delegate Myra Wolfgang told AFL-CIO President **George Meany**, "We did not come here to swap recipes," the phrase quickly became an identifiable CLUW slogan.

Part union reform movement and part political pressure group, the CLUW has fought for a variety of issues, including an increase in the **minimum wage**, **comparable-worth** legislation, preservation of existing **Social Security** laws, daycare programs for working women, enforcement of **affirmative action** laws, elimination of workplace sexual harassment, women's reproductive rights, women's health issues, workplace safety, organizing women to vote, and overall gender equality. The CLUW was very active in the unsuccessful attempt to add an Equal Rights Amendment to the U.S. Constitution.

At the CLUW's annual conferences, women discuss workplace and union issues that affect all working women. The group took up the issue of gender **equity pay** in 1976; two years later, it established a national Center for Education and Research to train women for leadership roles within their unions. Its ongoing summer institutes have been especially effective leadership training forums. In 1980, CLUW President Joyce Miller became the first woman to be elected to the AFL-CIO executive council, and she helped convene its first conference to discuss strategies for recruiting unorganized workers.

The CLUW filed a brief to the U.S. Supreme Court on sexual harassment that figured prominently in the landmark 1986 *Meritor Savings Bank v. Vinson* case, which helped legally define sexual harassment. It also filed a brief in the 1989 *UAW v. Johnson Controls* case dealing with hazardous chemicals and reproductive health. In 1993, Miller resigned as CLUW president and was replaced by Gloria Johnson, who headed the coalition until 2009, when Karen See became president. Under Johnson, the CLUW took up issues such as the **North American Free Trade Agreement**, international trade, **sweatshop** production, **child labor**, human rights, and women's health. See has advanced issues such as organizing Wal-Mart and anti-sweatshop campaigns.

The CLUW has three staff members at its Washington, D.C., office, a national executive board of 19 members, 3 permanent task forces, and 15 standing committees on issues as diverse as affirmative action, violence against women, and issues germane to older workers.

Suggested Reading

CLUW News, http://www.cluw.org/newsletters.html, accessed June 30, 2010; Coalition of Labor Union Women, http://www.cluw.org/index.html, accessed June 30, 2010; Melvyn Dubofsky and Foster Rhea Dulles, *Labor in America*, 1993.

COAL MINERS STRIKE OF 1943

The Coal Miners Strike of 1943 comprised a series of **strikes** that idled more than a half million miners and were called by the **United Mine Workers of America** (UMWA). The strikes were mainly confined to bituminous fields, though approximately 50,000 anthracite miners also walked off their jobs. The UMWA was one of only a very few unions to strike during World War II—most had taken **no-strike pledges** for the duration of the conflict. To its defenders, the UMWA's actions were bold and strategically brilliant; to its many critics, they were reckless, and perhaps treasonous.

UMWA President **John L. Lewis** had split with both U.S. President Franklin Roosevelt and the **Congress of Industrial Organizations** (CIO) by 1942. Lewis opposed Roosevelt's reelection in 1940 and clashed with the president (and outmaneuvered him) over the question of captive mines in 1941. Lewis was also angered by a perceived lack of support from the CIO and, in May 1942, withdrew the UMWA from the federation.

Lewis was also a critic of boards that emerged to safeguard production during World War II. In January 1942, the **National War Labor Board** (NWLB) was created to resolve industrial conflicts. It consisted of representatives from labor, business, and government who were charged with setting **wage** ceilings for industrial workers and settling workplace **grievances**. Coal miners resented the imposition of the **Little Steel Formula**, a wage settlement for steelworkers that became the guideline used by the NWLB to settle other disputes. It stipulated that wage increases could not exceed the inflation rate between January 1941 and March 1942. For most workers, this formula capped raises at 15 percent. The UMWA and Lewis countered that the NWLB benefited employers and pushed for a $2 per day raise for miners, an increase that exceeded the Little Steel standards.

The walk-offs from coal mine jobs actually began in December 1942 and originated from disgruntlement over union **dues**, which had increased by 50 percent. Lewis helped quash the rank-and-file rebellion, but instead of denouncing strikers he demanded wage increases for UMWA workers and sanctioned official strikes. Throughout much of 1943, Lewis sponsored a series of strikes that were akin to an elaborate cat-and-mouse game between him and President Roosevelt. These strikes threatened to disrupt coal supplies for American battleships, Lewis was denounced as unpatriotic, and some conservatives called for miners to be drafted and for the government to seize the mines. In June, a frustrated Congress passed the Smith-Connally Act after the UMWA launched its third strike in seven weeks. This legislation authorized the government to assume control over strike-threatened industries and to order wartime strikers to return to their jobs. For a brief period in November 1943, the government did, in fact, nationalize the country's mines, though a high percentage of UMWA employees defied the call to return to work. Later in November, the NWLB capitulated to the UMWA and granted miners an increase in pay of $1.50 per day.

Labor analysts have subsequently debated whether this outcome was a victory or a tactical error for organized labor. Among miners, Lewis emerged as a defiant and beloved champion. Many scholars agree with Lewis's assessment that the NWLB favored employers and that the Little Steel Formula was inappropriately applied as a "one size fits all" solution to wage disputes. Recent work also suggests that the nation's coal supply was not seriously jeopardized by on again, off again UMWA strikes, and that the labor action's impact was exaggerated by the business community.

At the same time, the 1943 strikes were a public relations nightmare for organized labor. The strikes were unpopular among the general public, the UMWA was excoriated in much of the press, and Lewis infuriated powerful elements in government. In 1947, Congress passed the **Taft-Hartley Act**, which placed greater restrictions on labor unions. The bill was vetoed by President Harry Truman, but Congress overrode the president. Achieving the necessary votes required a number of Democrats to split with Truman, which suggests that UMWA actions may have cooled the Democratic Party's support for organized labor.

Suggested Reading

James Atleson, *Labor and the Wartime State: Labor Relations and Law during World War II*, 1998; Nelson Lichtenstein, *Labor's War at Home: The CIO in World War II*, 1982; Alan Singer, " 'Something of a Man': John L. Lewis, the UMWA, and the CIO, 1919–1943," in John H. M. Laslett, ed., *The United Mineworkers of America: A Model of Industrial Solidarity?*, 1996.

COEUR D'ALENE

Coeur d'Alene is a lead- and silver-mining town in Idaho that was the site of two infamous labor disputes in the late 19th century. The first occurred in 1892, when silver-mining companies cut workers' **wages** to try to recoup profits lost when railroad companies raised freight rates. At the time, several small unions represented workers and several **union locals** had been infiltrated by **Pinkerton** spies. **Scabs** were imported in an effort to break the **strike**, and more Pinkertons and Thiel Detective Agency personnel arrived to act as private armies to keep the mines open and intimidate workers. Pinkerton spy Charlie Siringo provided up-to-the-moment details of union plans and offered sensational reports that tarred strikers as dangerous **anarchists**. When Siringo's treachery was revealed, the strike turned violent. Shootouts at the Frisco mine led to the deaths of two company men and a dynamite explosion there. Similar patterns of violence followed elsewhere. One company miner and three strikers were killed in incidents around the Gem mine, which led the union to issue a ceasefire.

Martial law was declared and the National Guard was deployed. Approximately 600 union men were arrested and held in impromptu bullpens, and union leader George Pettibone was convicted of criminal conspiracy and contempt of court—verdicts later overturned by the U.S. Supreme Court. Martial law remained in effect for four months, however, and the strike was lost. It did, however, inspire the formation of the militant Western Federation of Miners (WFM), which would soon be embroiled in the **Colorado labor wars**.

Violence returned to Coeur d'Alene in 1899. The Bunker Hill Mining Company continued the practice of using Pinkerton spies, and it dismissed 17 workers said to be union agitators. Approximately 250 men walked off their jobs in protest, and violence flared in which several people died and a mine was dynamited. Governor Frank Steunenberg petitioned President William McKinley to send the U.S. Army to the region. McKinley complied, more than 1,000 miners were taken prisoner, and 3 died from the appalling conditions under which they were held. In the end, the strike was broken.

The second Coeur d'Alene strike is noteworthy for what happened next. Allegations swirled that Governor Steunenberg had received a $35,000 inducement from mine owners to declare martial law, a charge that had considerable merit. In 1905, a spectacular dynamite explosion killed Steunenberg. Harry Orchard, a pseudonym for Albert Horsley, was arrested for the crime and confessed to famed Pinkerton agent James McParland, who had blown open the **Molly Maguires** trials in Pennsylvania. Orchard also implicated WFM officials Pettibone, Charles Moyer, and **Bill Haywood** as co-conspirators. Their trials became the focus of media attention and evoked considerable anger in organized labor's ranks. Pettibone and Haywood were acquitted and charges against Moyer were dropped after testimony revealed that Orchard was probably a Pinkerton agent, that he had greatly embellished his tales, and that he was possibly insane. Orchard spent the rest of his life in prison, and his allegations served only to turn the accused labor leaders into heroes.

Suggested Reading

Albert E. Horsley, *The Confessions and Autobiography of Harry Orchard*, 1907; J. Anthony Lukas, *Big Trouble: A Murder in a Small Western Town Sets off a Struggle for the Soul of America*, 1997; Mark Wyman, *Hard Rock Epic: Western Miners and the Industrial Revolution, 1860–1910*, 1979.

COLD WAR AND LABOR

The euphoria of the West's victory during World War II quickly gave way to the challenges of the Cold War after the military clashes ended. The wartime alliance between the United States and the Soviet Union was mostly one of convenience; once fascism was defeated, the two nations slipped back into their prewar positions of mutual distrust, albeit in a scenario that was complicated further by the Soviet occupation of much of Eastern Europe, a **communist** revolution in China, the specter of the atomic bomb, the space race, and spy rings. The period between 1947 and 1991, when the Soviet Union collapsed, was marked by geopolitical tension broken by short bouts of détente between Western democracies and the communist bloc. Citizens in each sphere lived with the fear that small conflicts could lead to wider war, and possibly World War III. In the United States, this fear inspired outbreaks of domestic paranoia, especially in the years between 1947 and 1966.

The Cold War posed distinct challenges for organized labor. Radicals, including communists and others associated with the **Popular Front**, had played a vital role in organizing workplaces during the 1930s, especially in many of the unions affiliated with the **Congress of Industrial Organizations** (CIO). Labor was now faced with questions of how to respond to the **Red Scare** that ensued during the Cold War, how to protect gains made during the 1930s and 1940s, what its role should be in rebuilding war-torn nations, and how much it should accede to U.S. foreign policy objectives.

The CIO, in particular, faced a dilemma. Although many of its Popular Front allies played a key role in developing international organizations such as the United Nations (UN) and the World Federation of Trade Unions (WFTU), those individuals and their ideologies lost favor during the Cold War and the CIO feared its own fallout, including diminished political clout, from its association with leftists. The 1947 **Taft-Hartley Act** required union leaders to sign loyalty oaths and anticommunist affidavits, which posed a particular problem for leaders such as **Harry Bridges** and for unions with large numbers of radical members. Recent studies indicate that the CIO was in decline by the late 1940s, with one key factor being that the relentlessly anticommunist **American Federation of Labor** (AFL) was better positioned to parlay patriotism into organizing gains.

In 1945, the AFL began working with the newly formed WFTU in ways that made the AFL a veritable arm of the U.S. State Department. AFL officials trained noncommunist labor leaders, cooperated with U.S. security services in Western Europe, and even helped fracture national labor movements in France and Italy where communist labor activism remained strong and the WFTU could not secure popular support. In 1949, the AFL spearheaded the formation of a new body, the

International Confederation of Free Trade Unions, when the WFTU was deemed too sympathetic to communism. The AFL also fully embraced the Marshall Plan for rebuilding Europe, including its anticommunist dimensions.

CIO leaders took steps to reduce their federation's isolation. CIO President **Philip Murray** shared a fear of communists, an influence deepened by his involvement in the **Association of Catholic Trade Unionists**. In 1948, the CIO alienated many of its leftist activists by opposing the presidential bid of Progressive Party candidate Henry Wallace. The CIO similarly embraced the Marshall Plan and, like the AFL, withdrew from the WFTU in 1949. When it became clear that the CIO's **Operation Dixie**, an attempt to organize the South, was not going well, and that red-baiting was often used against the federation, the CIO complied with Taft-Hartley Act bans on communists holding union office. Over the howl of rank-and-file protest, in 1949 and 1950 the CIO removed Bridges and several other leaders, and expelled five unions it considered communist led. In all, the CIO jettisoned approximately one-third of its membership.

This move paved the way for the 1955 AFL-CIO merger, but it also tied the former CIO more directly to Cold War politics. Numerous critics of **business unionism** date its triumph to the CIO's acceding to Cold War fears. During the 1950s, American organized labor's international activism was largely funded by U.S. government agencies. In retrospect, acceptance of this relationship may not have been a wise course. The AFL-CIO budget for global ventures was greater than what it spent on domestic organizing. The linkage with the government also harmed the AFL-CIO's credibility in the long term. For example, during the 1960s the AFL-CIO's American Institute for Free Labor Development ostensibly provided training and logistical support for Latin American union movements but was, in fact, a veritable conduit for the Central Intelligence Agency, which caused havoc in the region. Similarly, the affiliated Agency for International Development served the interests of American-owned multinational corporations rather than those of organized labor. Like institutes in Africa and Asia were also tied to U.S. Cold War objectives, especially those in Kenya, Nigeria, Vietnam, and Indonesia. In most cases, strong union movements failed to materialize, the major exception being in Poland, where the AFL-CIO helped the labor group Solidarity during the 1980s, which in turn led the way to toppling communist governments in Eastern Europe.

Rank-and-file union members had very little input into decisions made at the upper levels of the AFL-CIO. Some critics also have argued that another effect of the organization's outward focus in the Cold War was to discourage grassroots activism and to embolden conservative elements in the union movement. There was very little union opposition to the Korean War, U.S. interventions in the Caribbean, or early U.S. involvement in Vietnam. In 1970, for instance, union construction workers attacked antiwar protestors during so-called **hard hat riots**. These types of clashes were emblematic of the fractures opening within labor's ranks. As union leaders sought respectability through cooperation with foreign policy goals, some became tone deaf to domestic developments such as civil rights and antiwar activism. They also quashed **wildcat strikes**. The AFL-CIO's tepid response to civil rights and support for Cold War foreign objectives led the **United Auto Workers of America** to disaffiliate from the federation in 1967.

Unions enrolled approximately 22 million members by the mid-1960s, but their overall representation within the workforce dipped below 25 percent. This trend led to several years of stagnation of membership, followed by a decline in union rolls that began in the 1970s and accelerated in the 1980s. The **Vietnam War**, the civil rights movement, and the rise of feminism were, in retrospect, watershed events that focused criticism of AFL-CIO leaders. Vietnam, in particular, called into question the Cold War assumptions that undergirded official union policy since the late 1940s. Frustration mounted, but it was not until 1984 that open debate on foreign policy took place at an AFL-CIO annual convention.

By then, organized labor faced a domestic conundrum that was linked to foreign policy. Organized labor's support for Cold War objectives meant that government tolerated labor unions and that labor leaders sometimes enjoyed political access. These arrangements yielded some benefits, albeit at a cost. Labor's alliance with the Democratic Party led to gains such as the **Occupational Health and Safety Act**, Medicare, **minimum wage** increases, and worker training programs. They did little to achieve the overturn of the repressive Taft-Hartley Act, ward off the unpopular **Landrum-Griffin Act**, scuttle **right-to-work** legislation, or mollify the effects of **automation**, containerized cargo systems, the rise of non-union service industries, or **deindustrialization**.

Deindustrialization, globalization, and the stagflation of the 1970s contributed to the erosion of manufacturing jobs in the United States and an overall decline in union membership, as did the blatantly anti-union policies of Presidents **Ronald Reagan** and George H. W. Bush in the 1980s. Reagan's presidency came on the heels of failed promises from President Jimmy Carter. To critics, Carter, Reagan, and Bush were proof of the unsoundness of Cold War unionism. Their critique was seemingly conformed when President Bill Clinton signed into law the **North American Free Trade Agreement** and manufacturing jobs disappeared just as labor had predicted they would.

The collapse of European communism between 1988 and 1991 rendered moot many of the principles of Cold War unionism. Politicians and union activists alike spoke of an emerging "new world order," but organized labor was not well positioned to shape it. The long-term legacy of tying its agenda to that of the U.S. State Department was mostly negative. By the time the impact of **globalization** became apparent in the 1980s and international organizing efforts were needed to blunt the impact of runaway capital, American union movements were the objects of suspicion from potential allies abroad. Some unions have waged successful **corporate campaigns** that have involved transnational alliances, but these have relatively rare. Grassroots labor activists have sought to open new transnational avenues and have been active in North America and abroad in protests against the World Trade Organization and economic summits aimed at reducing existing trade barriers. Union activists taking part in the protests are far removed from their Cold War counterparts, in that they no longer see their role as one in support of official U.S. policies.

This evolution has opened a larger political debate within organized labor's ranks. During the Cold War, Republicans and Democrats largely agreed on foreign policy but differed markedly on domestic issues. The Cold War's end has thus far seen a rough economic consensus emerge between the parties, with both devoted to free trade and dependence upon the private business sector. This agreement has magnified many of the "culture war" issues that divide Republicans and Democrats—such as abortion rights, school prayer, welfare policy, and **affirmative action**—which in turn have galvanized trade union conservatives. In some cases, the union rank-and-file is now less liberal than its leadership. Many union heads, for example, have been highly critical of both Persian Gulf wars, though union members have generally been more supportive of U.S. government actions.

The consensus among scholars is that Cold War unionism was ultimately unwise and its payback disappointing. They remain divided over questions of whether labor leaders could have made other choices during the Red Scare, and to what degree Cold War unionism has contributed to labor's decline since the 1970s. Those who are skeptical of the link argue that the impact of globalization would have negated any ideological positions taken by organized labor.

Suggested Reading

Stephen Burwood, *American Labor, France, and the Politics of Intervention, 1945–1952*, 1999; Mike Davis, *Prisoners of the American Dream*, 1989; Shelton Stromquist, ed., *Labor's Cold War: Local Politics in a Global Context*, 2008.

COLLECTIVE BARGAINING

Collective bargaining is the very reason that labor unions exist. It involves an organized and unified method of negotiating the **wages**, working conditions, and benefits that an employer grants to employees. It is accomplished when employees designate representatives to negotiate a contract on their behalf. Although this can be done without a formal labor union, unions are covered by provisions of the **National Labor Relations Act** (NLRA) that are more easily skirted by employers if a noncertified body negotiates a contract. The core ideal behind collective bargaining is that workers as a body can achieve greater gains than individuals acting on their own accord. In most cases, successful collective bargaining also depends on the existence of labor laws that enforce the provisions of a contract.

British **socialists** Sidney and Beatrice Webb are often credited with coining the term "collective bargaining" in the 1890s, though they simply gave a name to long-standing practice. In the United States, the first known use of collective bargaining occurred in 1799, when a group of Philadelphia **journeymen** (cordwainers) secured an agreement with **master craftsmen** (shoemakers). For much of the 19th century, collective bargaining was stifled by laws that declared labor unions to be illegal combinations and conspiracies that restrained trade. This meant that union strength—and hence collective bargaining—varied according to individual state laws. For the most part, unions gathered strength after the **Civil War**, but collective bargaining remained a fragile and contested right. The 1890 **Sherman Antitrust Act** had the unintended effect of undoing some of the collective bargaining rights won by unions in the previous 20 years as some courts ruled that unions were also illegal trusts.

Collective bargaining received a boost when the 1914 **Clayton Act** exempted unions from antitrust laws, but it did little to ensure that employers negotiate in good faith or comply with agreements. Labor's absolute right to bargain collectively was not established until the passage of the NLRA in 1935. The NLRA defines the legal parameters for collective bargaining. Bargaining is not the same as an agreement—rather, it is merely the first step in securing an agreement. In case of an impasse, both employers and unions may resort to various tactics to achieve their objectives. Unions may engage in practices such as work slowdowns, **boycotts**, **strikes**, **picketing**, and political lobbying. Management might resort to seeking a court **injunction** against a union, enforcing a **lockout**, hiring **scabs**, or threatening to close the business. The NLRA was designed, in part, to defuse such actions by creating a mechanism through which mutually acceptable agreements can be hammered out. Most of the actions noted previously are illegal when a contract is in place. Moreover, the NLRA and subsequently passed labor laws outline various **unfair labor practices** that are not allowed because they undermine collective bargaining. For instance, in most cases unions are not allowed to call secondary boycotts that punish those doing business with the employer with which they are negotiating, nor are employers allowed to refuse to recognize a legally constituted union.

As noted earlier, collective bargaining rights do not ensure that a contract will be successfully negotiated. Collective bargaining laws made capital/labor relations relatively more stable since the NLRA went into effect, but they have not eliminated impasses. In recent years, organized labor has complained that labor laws since the NLRA have unfairly favored management and have eroded labor's collective bargaining strength. There are more restraints on union activity than on management, they argue, and employers use their wealth to draw out negotiations, defy labor laws, and engage in union busting.

Suggested Reading

Michael Carrell and Christina Heavrin, *Labor Relations and Collective Bargaining*, 2009; Thomas Colosi and Arthur Berkeley, *Collective Bargaining: How It Works and Why*, 2006; Walter Licht, *Industrializing America*, 1995.

COLONIAL LABOR

The patterns of work and authority in Colonial America are both familiar and alien to contemporary observers. They are familiar in the sense that labor took place within hierarchical settings in which a small group of elites controlled disproportionate amounts of wealth, power, and prestige. Those same elites very often determined how the masses would toil, which goods and services would be produced, what remuneration workers would receive, and how much say non-elites would have in political, social, cultural, and economic decision making. In some cases, the **masses** were even subject to the will of faraway corporations, though these bore only rudimentary resemblance to today's multinational bodies.

There were, however, significant differences between Colonial-era practices and today's labor market. Colonial society was, at best, proto-capitalist. The dominant economic philosophy was mercantilism, which allowed for individual enterprise but subsumed those activities within a larger system in which the overall wealth of the nation had the highest priority. Colonies, such as those in North America, were part of the mercantilist system in that they were expected to provide both markets and raw materials that enriched the motherland. Joint-stock companies often underwrote colonial settlements, but even these differed from modern corporations in that they often operated within the overall structure of the national economy rather than merely being regulated by it. Policymakers were often themselves key stockholders. Each colonial power sought to sponsor colonies that enriched the nation; hence Spanish explorers were expected to locate valuable minerals, French and Dutch settlers were engaged heavily in fur trading, the French colonists focused on sugar production, and English colonists sent market goods (e.g., tobacco, woodland products, and foodstuffs) back to England.

Hierarchy was also defined differently in colonial society. Authority and deference were based as much on custom, birth, and royal warrant as on merit. The very idea of democracy lay in the future, and social class as currently understood was in its infancy. For the most part, an individual was either a member of the elite or a member of the masses. Toward the end of the Colonial era within English colonies, a group often called the "middling sorts" developed, but there was no true middle class, nor was there a permanent **working class**. Working for **wages** was, for most, a temporary status. **Agrarianism** was the dominant economic ideal within North America into the 20th century; hence the goal of most males was to obtain the status of an independent yeoman, except in towns where **artisan labor** was more common. For the most part, there were no factories or mass-produced goods; with just a few exceptions—especially in goods worn by slaves—most personal items were "bespoken," or custom-made. **Apprentices** and **journeymen** worked for wages for a time, as did unmarried females working as domestics, but this activity was expected to cease when males either obtained a farm or **master** craftsman status. Girls generally ended paid employment upon marriage. Not until the 18th century did prototypical labor unions arise, at a time when economic crises made it harder for journeymen to rise out of wage status—journeymen's associations became the template for trade unions.

In the countryside especially, labor broke down largely into the categories of free and unfree. From the outset elites complained of a labor shortage within the colonies. Those who came from aristocratic or gentry backgrounds were conditioned to see manual labor as beneath them. They attempted to fill the labor void in numerous ways. As early as the 1520s, Spanish landholders enjoyed *encomienda* rights—that is, the land and the labor of those upon it. This often meant the cajoled or forced labor of **Native Americans**, a factor that led to numerous uprisings in Spanish colonies that ultimately weakened them. Dutch, Swedish, French, and English colonies seldom adopted policies as formal as the *encomienda*, but each sought to exploit the potential of Native American labor as well. This practice contributed to tensions between Europeans and Natives, but it also inexorably drove the latter into new forms of economic activity that altered traditional patterns of life and brought groups that had hitherto coexisted into conflict with one another. This was especially the case of tribes engaged in supplying furs to European merchants.

Natives proved an unstable workforce. They knew the land better than the European settlers, knowledge that facilitated rebellion. A much larger problem was that Native Americans proved susceptible to European diseases and died in numbers that made reliance upon their labor unsustainable. Most Europeans sought to entice the lower orders of European society to emigrate to the Americas, either by forcing them to leave their homelands or, as the English perfected the appeal, by enticing them to come as **indentured servants**. In such arrangements, a patron sponsored immigrants by paying their passage and assuming responsibility for their sustenance in exchange for their labor during a set contract period. At the end of their contracts, immigrants received the wherewithal to assume independence, usually in the form of a land grant.

The indenture system was also subject to many abuses, not the least of which was that patrons had little incentive to see indentured servants actually live out their contracts. Moreover, many indentured workers in the Chesapeake region were drawn into the production of non-utilitarian crops such as tobacco and suffered from hunger and malnutrition. The death rate among indentured servants was appallingly high for the first three decades of English settlement in the Chesapeake area. Even when it dropped, the exploitation of indentured servants and poor yeomen was such that there were periodic rebellions in the backcountry, the most famous of which was **Bacon's Rebellion** in Virginia in 1676.

Spain addressed the New World labor shortage problem by introducing **slavery** in 1510. By 1600, more than 250,000 Africans had come to North America. Slaves were also introduced to English colonies in the early 17th century. Although slavery eventually factored more prominently into English colonies in what later became the southern United States, there was no English colony south of Canada that did not have some slaves at the time of the American Revolution. Slaves in the northern colonies were generally household servants or worked alongside yeomen farmers and master craftsmen rather than in large field gangs as in the South.

Within the English colonies that became the United States, several broad work patterns existed by the early 18th century. Southern colonies had very few indentured servants and relied heavily upon slave labor wherever crops such as tobacco, cotton, sugar, rice, or indigo were produced in volume. Backcountry yeomen were generally too poor to have more than a few slaves, and most had none at all. These individuals were independent, but eked out marginal subsistence. Some white manual labor took place in coastal cities, but even this work was increasingly carried out by slaves.

Northern colonies generally had a higher percentage of yeomen farmers, though good lands had long been claimed and settlement moved farther away from the coast, where making a living was more difficult. As less land became available, the indenture system declined. There were more towns in the North; hence more individuals worked in urban trades such as shipbuilding, rope making, bricklaying, fishing, printing, and artisan trades. Again, the ultimate goal for most workers was to escape wage labor. A small, but growing contingent of shopkeepers, tavern owners, and business owners made up the middling classes.

The Mid-Atlantic region also had urban activity and yeomanry, though the legacy of Dutch and Swedish settlement there led to the persistence of a tenant system in which large landowners rented out their land. This system was especially prominent in New York and New Jersey.

The most consistent pattern of labor in Colonial America was a gendered division of labor. Women's domestic production was valued within the context of a family economy, but overall men's labor was deemed superior. Women were largely expected to perform tasks related to childrearing and household maintenance. Even women's right to property was largely determined by their relationship to males. They were also important to the local exchange and barter systems that dominated in rural areas. In addition, women acted as herbalists and midwives. In larger towns, women might be found in occupations such as keeping boarding houses, working in millinery shops, and running taverns. Some poor women engaged in prostitution. Girls from families of modest means often worked as hired hands and servants before marriage.

Scholars now recognize that discontent among free commoners was a major factor leading to and ensuring the success of the American Revolution. According to the best estimates, just 10 percent of English colonists held elite status. Perhaps as many as 30 percent could have been considered middling sorts, and 60 percent were poor. Revolutionary leaders came mostly from the bottom ranks of elites and the middling groups, but they needed to mobilize the poor masses to overthrow British rule. The rural land crisis, rising land taxes, and social upheaval during the 18th-century Great Awakening made the countryside restive. In urban areas, falling wage and prices had impoverished workers in trades such as carpentry and shoemaking. Historians now caution that the a narrative of the American Revolution that concentrates on iconic leaders but fails to take into account the fervor of individuals of few to moderate means is an incomplete one. The revolution succeeded only because those who led it were able to convince those whose labor had long been exploited that they shared mutual interests.

Suggested Reading

Stephen Innes, *Work and Labor in Early America*, 1988; Christopher Tomlins, *Freedom Bound: Law, Labor, and Civic Identity in Colonizing English America, 1580–1865*, 2010; Lawrence Towner and Rachel Raffles, *A Good Master Well Serve: Masters and Servants in Colonial Massachusetts, 1620–1750*, 1998; Alfred Young, *Liberty Tree: Ordinary People and the American Revolution*, 2006.

COLORADO LABOR WARS

During the late 19th and early 20th centuries, Colorado was the scene of violent capital/labor struggles. In its final phase, the battle pitted organized labor against the interests of the richest man in U.S. history, John D. Rockefeller, Jr.

Portrait of men, women, and children at the UMW camp for coal miners on strike against CF&I in Ludlow, Las Animas County, Colorado, 1913–1914. (Denver Public Library, Western History Collection, Bartosch, X-60475)

As in many mining regions, capital/labor relations were tense in Colorado. In 1894, hard-rock miners affiliated with the Western Federation of Miners (WFM) struck Cripple Creek owners who unilaterally imposed a 10-hour day on gold and silver workers accustomed to an 8-hour workday, and did not increase their pay. The **strike** lasted five months and ended in a WFM victory, though participants had to defy **injunctions**, battle the importation of **scabs**, and engage in gun battles with law enforcement and private militias. Colorado Governor Davis Waite, a former **Knight of Labor** and a **Populist Party** supporter, was forced to declare martial law when mine owners defied his authority and their private militias degenerated into uncontrollable vigilante groups that plunged the region into chaos.

The WFM became a dominant union and political force within the region. When the **American Federation of Labor** (AFL) failed to provide support for an 1896 strike in Leadville, the WFM disaffiliated. WFM leaders such as Ed Boyce and **William Haywood** were popular leaders throughout the region, and the WFM's efforts extended to Idaho, where dramatic losses in labor actions at Coeur d'Alene both staggered the union and strengthened its militant resolve. Haywood became more active in **socialist** politics and, in 1904, was a cofounder of the **Industrial Workers of the World** (IWW). The WFM affiliated with the IWW, as the federation was in accord with WFM militancy and its adherence to **industrial unionism** forms of organizing.

The introduction of **Pinkerton** detectives into Colorado mining regions—ostensibly to stop theft—raised tensions. In truth, these private security forces came there in the wake of the WFM's attempt to secure an eight-hour day for miners in the Idaho Springs area. This 1902 strike was defeated by a powerful alliance of Chicago-based employers, which influenced courts and organized a Colorado-based "Citizens Alliance" to oppose the WFM. Several dozen WFM leaders were driven from the area after a strike that, like previous ones in the region, saw shoot-outs and dynamiting. The Pinkertons played a direct role in defeating the WFM's strike by ore mill and smelter workers in Colorado City in 1903. Pinkerton spies fingered WFM activists, who were fired, and manufactured tales of union violence that justified securing scab workers and calling out National Guard troops. Newly elected Governor James Peabody turned against the WFM, after courting union votes the previous November. The governor went so far as to work with employer associations to build private armies, the likes of which former Governor Waite had dismantled. The WFM did, however, convince owners of several Colorado City mills to sign agreements, which Governor Peabody then worked to sabotage. When the agreements fell apart, the WFM called a strike and enlisted workers supplying ore to support it. This action brought the Cripple Creek region into the conflict during August.

Cripple Creek saw the same patterns of dynamite use, expulsion of union members, infiltration of unions by Pinkertons and other labor spies, formation of employer-created anti-union citizen groups, accusations of union **sabotage** (acts that were probably carried out by **agent provocateurs**), trumped-up charges against Haywood and other union officials, and the use of the National Guard. A horrible incident in which the Independence Mine was held responsible for the death of 15 non-union miners did little to help the WFM; when the Independence, Colorado, train station blew up with a loss of 15 lives, Governor Peabody seized upon the incident to clear the region of WFM influence, a task largely accomplished by late spring 1904.

The Cripple Creek region was also the center of coal strikes during 1903–1904. Colorado mines, especially those in Las Animas and Huerfano Counties on the eastern side of the Rocky Mountains, supplied a high-grade of bituminous coal that was converted to coke for the steel industry. By 1892, three-fourths of Colorado's coal came from mines controlled by the Colorado Fuel and Iron Company (CF&I), which was later purchased by John Rockefeller and the heirs of robber baron Jay Gould in 1903. Miners lived in dire **company towns** located in canyons, bought their goods at company stores, and were often paid in scrip redeemable only at the company store. The companies controlled every aspect of life in the mining towns, and the mines were notoriously dangerous. From 1884 through 1912, Colorado miners died at over twice the national average for the industry, though coroner's juries nearly always ruled that the miners caused the accidents that killed them.

Coal miners struck for higher pay, better conditions, union recognition, and an end to company control over their lives. The relationship between the coal strikers and the WFM is unclear. Most unionized coal miners belonged to the AFL's **United Mine Workers of America** (UMWA), not the WFM, and many were recent immigrants who had not been party to the state's long-standing labor conflicts. Moreover, UMWA President **John Mitchell** was a cautious man, the likes of which Haywood and the WFM deplored. Nevertheless, more than 10,000 coal miners walked off their jobs in November 1903. **Mary "Mother" Jones** came to Cripple Creek in October, and her reports helped convince UMWA officials that a strike was justified.

The coal miners and Jones met with the same rough justice that Governor Peabody meted out to the WFM. National Guard commander John Chase imposed martial law in the region and did not hesitate to send charging horses into demonstrations led by miners' wives, hold miners in bullpens, torture and beat prisoners, and jail strikers en masse. Because habeas corpus was suspended, between February and July 1904, Jones was seized several times and forcibly expelled from Colorado. The strike ended in a mixed decision in which miners in the northern coal fields settled, but not those in the south.

The UMWA kept up its efforts in the southern field and had secretly organized workers by September 1913. It then issued demands including the right to trade at noncompany stores, a union check-weight man to end company underpayments on ore loads, and payment for "dead work" such as shoring, timbering, and laying track for which miners were not paid. The CF&I refused to accede to these demands, which led to a 14-month strike that lasted into 1914 and was one of the most violent in American history.

Strikers expected little quarter and were given none. Those in Ludlow and several other towns were expelled from company housing, an action that necessitated constructing makeshift tent colonies at the entries to the canyons in which families lived during the dead of the winter of 1913–1914. The Baldwin-Felts Detective Agency, which specialized in brutal strikebreaking and later gained infamy during the **Matewan** Massacre, guarded scabs and terrorized the region. Among the Baldwin-Felts weapons was the "Death Special," a makeshift armored car with a mounted search light and machine gun that sprayed miners' tents with machine gun fire. Deaths and injuries associated with this type of attack led to the construction of underground pits by the striking miners. Mother Jones, then age 83, visited the area and implored Colorado Governor Elias Ammons to intercede. Ammons sent the National Guard into the region.

Alas, the National Guard was led by the same John Chase who had brutalized miners 10 years earlier. He protected scabs and destroyed tent cities with as much zeal as Baldwin agents had done. The situation deteriorated even further when Colorado ran out of money to pay National Guardsmen. Governor Ammons authorized the CF&I to organize a militia to protect mine property. This unit was responsible for the April 20, 1914, **Ludlow Massacre**, in which 19 people—mostly women and children—died when their tent colony was strafed and set afire. Many perished in the very pits built for self-protection. The massacre so outraged organized labor that it touched off open warfare between miners and the state of Colorado, with UMWA officials openly giving out ammunition. Governor Ammons was forced to seek federal intervention. The UMWA called off the strike in December, when it ran out of strike funds.

In a further outrage, 408 miners were arrested and 332 were charged with murder. Their trials dragged on until 1920, but there were no convictions. Ten officers and 12 enlisted men were court-martialed for the Ludlow Massacre, but all were acquitted. It was cold comfort to miners that John D. Rockefeller, Jr., became a figure of national scorn. Rockefeller turned to Ivy L. Lee and former Canadian Labor Minister William L. McKenzie-King for help in rehabilitating his family's image. The resultant Colorado Plan of Industrial Representation was mostly a **company union**, but it did introduce benefits and improvements that brought industrial peace to Rockefeller-owned enterprises.

During the 1903–1904 troubles, the WFM printed posters that asked, "Is Colorado in America?" The state's two decades of labor brutality between 1894 and 1914 took an untold number of lives and was a shameful period in American history. It is often evoked as an example of robber barony at its most egregious and arrogant. The fact that these bloody events did not lead to immediate rounds of reform and regulation ensured that several more decades of labor wars would take place before legislative actions associated with the New Deal curbed some of the grossest misuses of corporate might.

Suggested Reading

Howard M. Gitelman, *Legacy of the Ludlow Massacre: A Chapter in American Industrial Relations*, 1988; Leonard Guttridge and George S. McGovern, *The Great Coalfield War*, 1972; Elizabeth Jameson, *All That Glitters: Class, Conflict, and Community in Cripple Creek*, 1998; George Suggs, *Colorado's War on Militant Unionism: James H. Peabody and the Western Federation of Miners*, 1972.

COLORED NATIONAL LABOR UNION

The Colored National Labor Union (CNLU) was an attempt to create a body to coordinate the efforts of African American unions. Although it was active only between 1869 and 1871, it paved the way for more extensive organization under the auspices of the **Knights of Labor** (KOL). The CNLU was the brainchild of Issac Myers, a black ship caulker. Myers tried to foster a working relationship between the CNLU and the **National Labor Union** (NLU), an early **labor federation**. Alas, neither the NLU nor the CNLU survived.

Black laborers were especially vulnerable in the immediate aftermath of the **Civil War**. Although **slavery** itself was abolished, the majority of whites, in both the North and the South, held racist views. This was true also of labor unions, many of which excluded black workers. A series of labor congresses was held in the 1860s that took up various issues, including formation of a labor federation and the way in which white workers should view black laborers. When the NLU formed in 1866, delegates at the founding convention split over whether to admit African Americans. The issue proved so divisive that it was tabled. The NLU's guiding spirit, **William Sylvis**, supported admitting African Americans, however, and the 1867 convention appointed a Committee on Colored Labor to explore the possibilities. That group was headed by A. W. Phelps, a carpenter whose union excluded blacks. Not surprisingly the committee's 1868 report recommended against admitting African Americans to the NLU.

Nonetheless, Sylvis continued to push for African Americans' admission to the union, and nine black delegates attended the 1869 NLU convention, including Myers of the Colored Caulkers Trade Union Society. At that meeting, the NLU reversed course and voted to allow black members. Its action was partly due to the fact that African Americans had already begun organizing without the NLU's official sanction, having held their own labor congresses in 1868. In addition, many black workers were organized into trade unions, though they often maintained secrecy to protect their members against retaliation.

In December 1869, Myers convened 214 Negro Labor Congress members in Washington, D.C. Those assembled formed the CNLU. Most of the delegates represented trade unions, though there were also smatterings of ministers, reformers, and Prince Hall Freemasons. The new organization's structure and most of its agenda mirrored that of the NLU, with which it voted to affiliate. The CNLU echoed the NLU's call for an **eight-hour** workday, the establishment of **cooperatives**, free public education, elimination of **child labor**, and women's suffrage. It even followed the NLU's lead in holding yearly labor congresses, in calling for a **Chinese Exclusion Act**, and in renouncing **strikes** in favor of mandatory **arbitration**. Myers was appointed to organize workers in the South, while Sella Martin was sent to Paris to represent the CNLU at the Marxist First International convention.

Only in politics did the CLNU's agenda substantively differ from that of the NLU. Given that the Republican Party had supported abolition and secured ratification of the Thirteenth, Fourteenth, and Fifteenth Amendments ending slavery and extending civil rights to African Americans, CNLU members remained loyal to the GOP and eschewed the third-party call of the NLU.

Racism and politics unraveled the CNLU/NLU alliance before much came of it. African Americans complained bitterly that NLU unions retained racial barriers. In retaliation, an 1870 delegate, J. M. Langston, introduced a resolution to ban whites from the CNLU, an act that led to his exclusion from the NLU's convention in the fall. When that same NLU convention decided to form a third party, Myers led the CNLU's move to disaffiliate with the NLU. That same year, however, Frederick Douglass replaced Myers as CNLU president and temporarily soothed relations with the NLU. In the end, Douglass proved equally incapable of getting the NLU to reverse its racist policies. Indeed, his own son was denied membership in an NLU-affiliated typographers' union.

In an ironic twist, the CNLU's refusal to support third-party efforts came at a time in which some of members had begun to criticize the Republican Party's tepid commitment to African American equality. As **Reconstruction** efforts dwindled, the Democratic Party regained strength in the South, opportunities for black farm laborers declined, and groups like the Ku Klux Klan began terrorizing African Americans. To black critics, the Republican Party seemed little inclined to do anything about the swift erosion of African American rights and the emergence of early forms of "Jim Crow" discrimination. Douglass's support for the GOP came under great criticism at the 1871 CNLU convention, but by then the organization was a spent force.

So, too, was the NLU. The CNLU's skepticism over third parties proved correct. The NLU collapsed quickly after an ill-fated 1872 presidential campaign in which the federation attempted to transform itself into a political party. Several labor congresses were held between 1873 and 1875, but none were held under NLU auspices and no African American delegates attended. Economic crises associated with the Panic of 1873 doomed hopes of reviving either the NLU or the CNLU.

The CNLU's track record as an independent organization was not particularly noteworthy, in part because neither it nor the NLU was a true labor federation. Both were largely extensions of labor congresses—veritable discussion and brainstorm groups. These groups proved more adroit at issuing position papers and editorials than actually organizing workers. In some cases, workers whose unions belonged to the CNLU or the NLU were unaware of their membership in a larger federation. The CNLU's greatest achievement was as a rhetorical force in support of African American rights. Both its yearly congresses and its official newspaper, *New National Era*, exposed the hypocrisy of white workers espousing views of **solidarity** and universal brotherhood while continuing to discriminate against black workers.

That message resonated deeply with key leaders in the Knights of Labor, the first successful labor federation. In the 1880s and 1890s, the KOL organized approximately 90,000 African American workers. The KOL also struggled with racism among its affiliates, but its leadership remained committed to bridging racial barriers.

Suggested Reading

Philip Foner and Ronald Lewis, eds., *Black Workers: A Documentary History from Colonial Times to the Present*, 1989; Peter Rachleff, *Black Labor in Richmond, 1865–1890*, 1989; Robert E. Weir, "Colored National Labor Union," in *Organizing Black America*, ed. Nina Mjagkij, 2001.

COLUMBINE MINE MASSACRE

The Columbine Mine Massacre was a 1927 assault on unarmed strikers in Serene, Colorado, that left six coal miners dead and added to Colorado's reputation as the bloodiest labor state in the union. It also indirectly involved the Colorado Fuel and Iron Company (CF&I), the same firm involved in the 1914 **Ludlow Massacre**, which had been a major player during the **Colorado labor wars**. Serene was a **company town** owned by the Rocky Mountain Fuel Company (RMFC).

The northern mining region where the Columbine mine stood was largely unorganized, though the **Industrial Workers of the World** (IWW) had made minor inroads. Tension in the area began with a series of **sympathy strikes** to protest the August 23, 1927, execution of **anarchists** Sacco and Vanzetti. Most of the region's 12,000 miners—about half of whom worked for CF&I—left their jobs for three days. In the ensuing weeks, the IWW organized some workers and issued a strike call for higher pay and improved safety conditions. The strike did not begin until October 18, as state officials refused to recognize the IWW officials as representatives for the workers. Most of the mines were closed completely, but the Columbine mine was one of a handful kept open by **scabs**. Workers rallied and set up **pickets** in support of the strike, usually gathering in the town of Serene before doing so. The RMFC was actually in the hands of Josephine Roche, who had taken over after her father's recent death and was a supporter of labor unions. She had ordered that coffee and donuts be offered to strikers as they gathered each morning.

The strike was roughly five weeks old in Serene when, on November 21, workers, their wives, and children marching behind a phalanx of American flags found the town gate closed and barred by ex-state policemen associated with the Colorado Rangers, a notoriously anti-union paramilitary force under the control of the governor. The CF&I was in the region to protect scabs and probably had no direct tie to the RMFC. Taunting and scuffles broke out at the gate. When the guards tore flags and clubbed workers, the miners rushed the gate and forced their way inside. There they were fired upon by police with at least two and possibly three machine guns. By the time firing stopped, six miners lay mortally wounded and dozens more had serious injuries. The Colorado Rangers denied using machine guns, but testimony is clear that they were used and that strikers were armed with nothing more lethal than rocks and pocket knives.

RMFC owner Josephine Roche quickly settled with workers at Columbine, though she invited the **United Mine Workers of America** (UMWA) to negotiate a **contract**, not the IWW. The IWW continued to suffer harassment in the region, and a January 12, 1928, raid on its hall in Walsenburg, Colorado, left two IWW members dead. Roche's direct involvement with the unions paid off—UMWA productivity rates were the highest in the state.

Although the facts of the Columbine Mine Massacre were obvious, lawsuits against Colorado's governor, the Rangers, and CF&I were dismissed in 1932. When CF&I records were opened after the company went bankrupt in 1990, they revealed the firm's culpability in many of the region's worst labor conflicts. The Columbine Mine Massacre stands as an egregious example of corporate might and abuse.

Suggested Reading

Lowell May and Richard Myers, *Slaughter in Serene: The Columbine Coal Strike Reader*, 2005; "1927: Colorado Miners Strike and Columbine Mine Massacre," libcom.org, http://libcom.org/history/1927-colorado-miners-strike-and-columbine-mine-massacre, accessed July 20, 2010; Fred Thompson and Patrick Murfin, *The I.W.W.: Its First Seventy Years (1905–1975)*, 1976.

COMMONWEALTH V. HUNT

Commonwealth v. Hunt was an 1842 case heard by the Massachusetts Supreme Court, in which the ruling provided the first legal recognition that labor unions were not illegal conspiracies that restrained trade. Prior to the *Hunt* decision, labor unions were frequently deemed illegal conspiracies pursuant to an 1809 ruling in *Commonwealth v. Pullis*. That Pennsylvania decision drew upon English common law in finding against Philadelphia cordwainers.

The 1842 ruling by Chief Justice Lemuel Shaw of the Massachusetts Supreme Court specifically struck down the part of the *Pullis* decision that defined labor unions as conspiracies. The *Hunt* case was so named because John Hunt's name was the first listed in an indictment against seven members of the Boston Journeymen's Bootmakers' Society. They were charged with conspiracy for leading a **strike** against an employer who refused to honor a closed shop and sought to hire non-union employees. The seven men were convicted of conspiracy in 1839, but appealed the result. The union attorney, Robert Rantoul, argued that English common law was not applicable—a risky strategy give that there was very little case law specifically relating to labor unions. In the void, courts generally upheld the *Pullis* decision and accepted employer logic that unions, strikes, and coerced concessions restrained competition and damaged the economy.

Shaw ruled that unions were legal and that their actions could not be deemed conspiratorial as long as they did not engage in or advocate illegal activity. Moreover, the act of calling a strike was not illegal because it had been voted upon and no worker was compelled to strike. As long as the methods employed by unions were within the law, Shaw argued, unions were free to seek recognition and concessions from their employers.

The *Hunt* decision was the first explicit recognition that labor unions were legal and was often cited by 19th-century labor groups seeking **collective bargaining** rights. The decision was also in advance of its time. It did not define **unfair labor practices**, establish procedures for union **certification**, or compel employers to bargain with or recognize unions, nor did it specify which actions *did* constitute conspiracy or restraint of trade. Nineteenth-century courts generally held that strikes for higher **wages** or shorter hours were legal, but they also routinely issued **injunctions** against strikes and entertained conspiracy charges for other union activities. The overall legal climate was one of hostility toward unions. The full implications of the *Hunt* decision were not made manifest until the 1935 **National Labor Relations Act**.

Suggested Reading

Commonwealth v. Hunt, http://plaza.ufl.edu/edale/Commonwealth percent20vs percent20 Hunt.htm, accessed July 11, 2010; Leonard W. Levy, *The Law of the Commonwealth and Chief Justice Shaw*, 1957; Christopher L. Tomlins, *Law, Labor, and Ideology in the Early American Republic*, 1993.

COMMUNISM AND UNIONS

Communism, as a political ideal, is a form of **socialism** in which private property, the state, and nonproductive social classes are abolished. It mainly derives from **Marxism**—that is, from the works of 19th-century theorist Karl Marx, who saw communism as the final social evolutionary stage in the historical struggle of the **working class** to cast off its oppressors. In 1848, Marx and Friedrich Engels published *The Communist Manifesto*, a work that distilled centuries of proto-communist thought and presented it in an inspirational tract that continues to be read widely. Marx refined these ideas in subsequent, more heavily theoretical writings. A communist society, he argued, would be a collectivist one in which workers would produce according to their abilities and take according to their needs.

It would be democratic, egalitarian, and self-governing; hence there would no need for a central government or any sort of hierarchy.

Pure communism is a utopian ideal that has been practiced only on a small scale and for limited periods of time. Although many people from the time of the publication of *The Communist Manifesto* to the present have lumped all forms of socialist thought together, it is important to note that many varieties of socialism exist, and that for much of American history socialists and communists have been bitter political rivals. Most of the nations dubbed "communist," including the Soviet Union, post-1949 China, and Cuba under Fidel Castro, have been centralized authoritarian states, not utopian communist societies. Critics—including most noncommunist socialists—argue that communism is an unrealistic dream. Most socialists do agree that trade unions are the building block upon which a more just society can be rebuilt.

Communism as an ideal has inspired many within the American union movement, especially in the period between World War I and World War II. The 1917 Russian Revolution, which established the Union of Soviet Socialist Republics (USSR), offered great hope to workers, especially during the Great Depression (1929–1941) when **capitalism** was in chaos. It also resonated with workers familiar with the long history of repression embedded within American labor history. Communism should properly be viewed as one of the alternatives proposed by the radical left to the profound social inequality, abuses, and social ills that were an unintended by-product of the **Industrial Revolution**.

The Communist Party of the United States of America (CPUSA) was created in 1919, as an offshoot of the Third International gathering in Moscow that discussed making communism a worldwide movement. Early American communists included those who found socialist movements overly cautious, members of the declining **Industrial Workers of the World** (IWW), radical trade unionists, and idealistic reformers disappointed by the **Progressive Era**'s antilabor biases. American communism quickly bifurcated into theorists and pragmatists, the latter of whom often proved to be superb labor organizers. The CPUSA had roughly 60,000 members shortly after its founding, which may have been its peak mark.

During its first decade, the CPUSA pursued a policy sometimes called "boring within," meaning that it sought to be the left wing of the **American Federation of Labor** (AFL) and its affiliated **craft unions**. Communists formed the Trade Union Educational League (TUEL), an association designed to advance communist ideals and convince workers that **industrial unionism** was superior to **craft unionism**. AFL President **Samuel Gompers** opposed communists, however, and he clashed with TUEL leader **William Z. Foster**. The AFL attempted to isolate or eliminate communist influence among its affiliates. Resistance, a postwar **Red Scare**, and the pro-business, anti-union climate of the 1920s all came together to blunt communist success.

Because the CPUSA was part of the Communist International (Comintern), it took policy directions from Moscow. In 1929, the CPUSA was ordered to disband the TUEL in favor of the Trade Union Unity League (TUUL). Communists formed parallel unions rather than work within the AFL—a risky strategy given that **dual**

unionism had long been controversial among American workers. Communists formed dozens of new unions, but their antagonistic stance toward noncommunist union leaders probably fractured labor **solidarity** more than fostering it. The TUUL's major accomplishment before it was abandoned in 1935 was to train a competent cadre of leaders. Communists were very active in the early days of the Great Depression, especially in urban areas, where they set up soup kitchens, led rent strikes, created Unemployed Councils to demand relief, and organized groups ignored by the AFL, including black workers, women, and the unskilled. The CPUSA also formed networks with thousands of militant workers deeply committed to industrial unionism.

Several factors led to another shift in CPUSA policy. First, communist leaders in Moscow viewed the rise of European fascism with growing alarm and saw an alliance with Western bourgeois societies as potentially necessary to protect the USSR. Second, TUUL efforts were not very successful. Third, the pro-labor administration of President Franklin Roosevelt touched off a wave of legislation and organizing associated with New Deal unionism that provided opportunity for communist gains in the United States. In 1935, the CPUSA announced its willingness to participate in a **Popular Front** to oppose fascism abroad and build the labor movement at home. Some scholars think that CPUSA membership may have surged to more than 100,000 individuals around 1936, but this may be an inflated figure because the Popular Front included numerous noncommunist militants.

What is clear is that the early **Congress of Industrial Organizations** (CIO) proved more welcoming to communists than did the AFL. Although CIO head **John L. Lewis** was no fan of communism, he had witnessed communists' organizational skills within his own **United Mine Workers of America** and admired their commitment to industrial unionism. CPUSA organizers played a key role in organizing workers in heavy industries such as steel, rubber, and electric. Several assumed communists were found in key CIO positions: Len De Caux served as CIO press secretary, Lee Pressman as CIO counsel, Wyndham Mortimer as **United Auto Workers of America** (UAW) vice president, and Ben Gold as president of the furriers union. **Harry Bridges**, president of the International Longshoremen's and Warehousemen's Union (ILWU), was reputed to be a communist, though this was never authenticated. Indeed, only Gold publicly touted his CPUSA affiliation. It is difficult to determine just how many communist organizers were present in the CIO, but their logistical support is thought to have played an important role in organizing efforts among steelworkers, the UAW, sharecroppers, transport workers, the **United Electrical Workers**, maritime workers, office unions, packinghouse workers, the ILWU, and the **Screen Directors Guild**.

After World War II, it was charged that approximately 25 percent of all CIO members were in communist-controlled unions. At the time, this figure generated great alarm, but it is a deceptive statistic on many levels. First, the CPUSA was a legal party and those joining it broke no U.S. laws in doing so. Second, although communists were generally idealistic, many of the finest organizers were pragmatists rather than theorists or ideologues. Third, it is doubtful that more than a few thousand workers were party members, even when communists led their unions. Finally, during the Popular Front period (1935–1939), the CPUSA worked within American society rather than seeking to overthrow it. The CPUSA gave lukewarm support to Roosevelt and the New Deal, and enthusiastic endorsement to antifascist movements. There was little evidence of Moscow's control over American communists beyond their active involvement in international causes such as the battle against Mussolini's forces in Ethiopia and enlistment in the Spanish Republic's war against Franco.

For the most part, CPUSA organizers were good trade-unionists. The CPUSA consistently fought for racial equality in unions, workplaces, and government policy. Its support for immigrants won it a large following among immigrants. The CPUSA generally supported rank-and-file democracy within unions to a far greater degree than did many AFL affiliates. By 1939, most separate communist units within unions had been dissolved, which both removed communist politics from the shop floor and made it difficult to know who was a communist and who was not. Moreover, communist ideals were not considered especially radical in the 1930s. The USSR still commanded admiration among many noncommunist workers, and the notion of a planned economy and a public welfare state seemed realistic considerations within a depression-mired economy.

Moscow's direction, in fact, sabotaged much of the goodwill generated by CPUSA labor organizers. On August 23, 1939, USSR leader Josef Stalin signed a nonaggression pact with Germany's Adolf Hitler. American communists were ordered to renounce the Popular Front, the alliance with Western governments, and cooperation with bourgeois institutions. Many American communists protested these mandates, and some quit the CPUSA in disgust. When Hitler broke the agreement and invaded the USSR on June 22, 1941, CPUSA leaders were ordered to renew their Popular Front-like cooperation. They did so and cooperated fully with war efforts, including stringent enforcement of **no-strike pledges**, but it proved impossible to rebuild trust among much of the working class. CPUSA head **Earl Browder** tried his best, even going so far as to dissolve the party in 1944, endorse Roosevelt's reelection, and insist that communism and **capitalism** were compatible.

The end of the war led to a second Red Scare, and anticommunism emerged as a key component of **Cold War unionism**. Moscow's directives hindered more than they helped in this regard. Browder was dismissed, and the newly formed Communist Political Association (CPA) essentially reconstituted the CPUSA along TUUL lines. Its support for Henry Wallace's quixotic 1948 presidential campaign served mainly to alienate the Democratic Party and trade-union liberals backing Harry Truman.

Anticommunist sentiment was high in government circles even before the Red Scare. In 1938, the House Special Committee on Un-American Activities (HUAC) opened investigations into the CIO and New Deal agencies for alleged communist infiltration. The 1939 Hatch Act barred suspected communists from federal jobs, and the 1940 Smith Act made it a criminal offense to belong to an organization advocating the overthrow of the U.S. government. After the war, unions came under even greater scrutiny. The 1947 **Taft Hartley Act** required union officials sign loyalty oaths that asserted they were not communists.

Unions initially resisted the Red Scare, but in 1950 the CIO expelled 11 communist-led unions, and key leaders such as CIO President **Philip Murray** and UAW head **Walter Reuther** worked to purge Communists from their organizations. Pressures for conformity and a political climate that equated patriotism with Cold War objectives helped convert rank-and-file unionists to the anticommunist cause. So, too, did fear. From 1945 to 1952, congressional committees conducted 84 hearings on alleged subversive activities—investigations that touched 13.5 million Americans in some form or another. One in five workers was forced to take a loyalty oath, some 15,000 federal and private employees were fired, and countless thousands were blacklisted.

The effects of the Red Scare among unions went beyond the individual level. Red-baiting was (and is) used by employers to combat unions. It played a major role in the collapse of the CIO's **Operation Dixie** efforts to organize the South. Although the AFL and CIO merged in 1955 in hopes of reversing antilabor laws such as the Taft Hartley Act, acceding to anticommunism demands had the overall effect of blunting the very militancy that had made organized labor successful a generation earlier. This factor may have contributed to organized labor's overall slowness in responding to social movements such as civil rights, the peace movement, feminism, and student radicalism during the mid-1950s through the mid-1970s. Many contemporary labor analysts argue that organized labor needs to rekindle the sort of grassroots activism at which communist organizers excelled.

Although several American labor leaders traveled to the Soviet Union before 1950, no serious espionage charges have ever been sustained against an American labor leader. After 1950, the CPA ceased to be a major factor within the U.S. labor movement in more than a rhetorical sense. Black nationalists involved in the **Dodge Revolutionary Union Movement** and some radicals associated with both unions and the New Left during the 1960s and early 1970s claimed to be communists, but they were likely to admire Mao Zedong, Leon Trotsky, or other non-Soviet figures. After the USSR's repudiation of Stalin's leadership in 1956, Moscow's credibility among American communists eroded even further. In 1984, CPA head Gus Hall formalized American communism's separate path. Communism is legal in the United States, but the current movement is very small and is largely a rhetorical body that has very little presence inside organized labor.

Suggested Reading

Bert Cochran, *Labor and Communism: The Conflict That Shaped American Unions*, 1977; Roger Keeran, *The Communist Party and the Auto Workers Unions*, 1980; Tricia Cayo Sexton, *The War on Labor and the Left*, 1991.

COMPANY TOWN

A company town is a village, town, or section of a municipality where a significant number—if not all—of essential housing units, utilities, and services are owned by the region's dominant business. In popular parlance, the term is also used to reference towns in which a single corporation exerts undue political influence due to its economic dominance within the region, though this is an imprecise use of the term.

Company towns evolved from 19th-century **paternalism** and are rare in contemporary America. Critics of company towns complained that company towns were forms of industrial **slavery** in which workers fattened company coffers by returning much of their pay in the form of rent, utility costs, and the purchase of goods and services in company-owned stores. In extreme cases, most commonly in remote coal-mining villages, workers did not even receive **wages**, but were paid in scrip redeemable only within the town. Company towns also frequently made moral demands upon workers, such as sobriety or mandatory church attendance, on the theory that a moral workforce would be more pliable and stable.

In practice, few company towns lived up to the expectations of their founders or investors. Samuel Slater was one of the first entrepreneurs to build company towns. Flush with success at Pawtucket, Rhode Island, where workers lived in company-owned dormitories adjacent to his textile mill, Slater and his partners expanded northward along the Blackstone River valley toward Worcester, Massachusetts. Several factory villages emerged in what are now the towns of Dudley, Oxford, and Webster, Massachusetts. When disputes arose with workers over issues such as water rights or wages, Slater simply opened a new village. The Slater family continued to operate factory villages into the 1870s, but over time these small-scale operations grew antiquated, and absolute control dwindled. As in the case of most future company towns, Slater realized profits from textiles, but seldom on the towns themselves. The infrastructure of even small villages was expensive to build and maintain and employers often ended up subsidizing their towns as they paid their workers wages too meager to pay what the services actually cost.

More famed—and for a time, more successful—experiments in textile-based company towns were those undertaken by a group of investors known as Boston Associates. In 1821, they began construction in Lowell, Massachusetts, and in less than a decade operated a company town of more than 20,000 employees. Lowell opened in a burst of utopian optimism in that it was designed to be the antithesis of nightmarish English factory towns. Lowell featured sturdy boarding houses, tree-lined streets, public gardens, and other amenities amidst its landscaped red-brick factories. Virtually every institution, from schools and churches to the lyceum and the town's literary journal, was controlled by the company. Because Lowell's workforce was largely composed of single farm women, Boston Associates sought to build a moral environment consistent with prevailing gender ideals and assumptions. By the 1830s, Lowell was considered such a wonder that it was a tourist destination for self-congratulatory members of the **middle class**. Lowell workers soon disabused them of that notion. As was the case in most factory towns, **working-class** aspirations were often ignored, and corporate profit took precedence over employee livelihoods. Many workers chafed under excessive company control, long working hours, and wage cuts imposed during economic downturns. Those wage cuts were seldom accompanied by reductions in rent or services. A series of **strikes** rocked Lowell in the 1830s and 1840s, and the **Lowell Female Labor Reform Association**, led by **Sarah Bagley**, is regarded by many scholars as the first women's trade union in the United States.

Conflict plus an influx of Irish immigration led to the steady decline of Lowell as a utopian experiment. Nonetheless, Boston Associates transplanted the Lowell model to Chicopee, Holyoke, and Lawrence in Massachusetts; Dover, Manchester, Nashua, and Somersworth in New Hampshire; and Biddeford and Saco in Maine.

Lowell was merely the most famous antebellum company town. Iron workers in Troy, New York, and textile workers in nearby Cohoes lived in company towns, though their proximity to Albany made total control more difficult than in the Boston Associates communities, which arose in the midst of agricultural regions. Rockdale, Pennsylvania, was also a company-owned textile town.

Many company towns developed at a time in which urban areas were gaining in population, but the modern American city had not yet developed. It was not until the last part of the 19th century that many cities developed such rudimentary amenities of city life as police forces, public sewers, purified water, garbage collection, urban transit systems, zoning regulations, and efficient city government. Company towns often provided services that far exceeded those available elsewhere. This was especially true in company mining towns. Mining operations were often mere villages—called "patches" in some regions—many miles from urban areas of any consequence. Isolation gave mine operators a level of control over workers that only the operators of lumber camps rivaled. Housing was controlled by the company, and the local company store was often the only retail establishment within miles and peddled goods at inflated prices. Payment in scrip was particularly common in mining towns. Moreover, few of them would have been mistaken for utopian experiments. Most patch towns were grimy villages in which upkeep was spotty and access to social services rare. Northeast Pennsylvania sported numerous such villages, and it is hardly surprising that labor agitation was intense there, including the **Molly Maguires** troubles of the 1870s. Coal towns were the site of some of America's bloodiest capital/labor conflicts, including the **Colorado labor wars**, the **Lattimer Massacre** of 1897, the 1914 **Ludlow Massacre**, and conflict among Kentucky and West Virginia coal miners that included the infamous shoot-out at **Matewan**, West Virginia, in 1920.

Violent clashes notwithstanding, many company-town efforts were born out of 19th-century utopian impulses. Before Lowell was built, British reformer **Robert Owen** opened a textile community in New Lanarck, Scotland, that both made a profit and provided a humane quality of life that stood in marked contrast to working-class life in the rest of Britain. His son, **Robert Dale Owen**, came to the United States in 1825 to operate his father's cooperative community in New Harmony, Indiana. It failed within four years, but inspired imitators. The problem with most overtly utopian industrial towns—including the Brook Farm experiments of the 1840s that built upon the **cooperative** ideals of French intellectual Charles Fourier—was that they were undercapitalized. Those with adequate funds succeeded, as did the Hutterite Amana community in Iowa and the Oneida community in New York State. Oneida was founded in 1836 as a religious experiment and turned to industrial production to support its community members' exceedingly unorthodox religious views. In 1881, the religious community was dissolved and Oneida became a joint-stock company producing high-quality tableware.

These utopian communities had an advantage that few industry-sponsored company towns enjoyed: Communalism was their central ideal, rather than corporate profit. The maturation of **capitalism** after the **Civil War** rendered much of the logic of company towns archaic. By the 1880s, most capitalists found greater opportunity for profit in industrial production, stock investment, and selling goods and services than in operating entire towns. Moreover, the spread of **social Darwinism**—which applied the evolutionary principle of survival of the fittest to society and the economy—made American entrepreneurs more comfortable with the cold-blooded logic of their English counterparts. Fewer investors cared about how workers lived or how their moral development proceeded as long as profits were healthy. Thus fewer were interested in the paternalistic motives that fueled the development of Lowell, and even fewer in cooperative or communal principles.

That skepticism was no doubt reinforced by the spectacular failure of Pullman, Illinois. The **Homestead Steel lockout and strike** of 1892 had already dampened enthusiasm; the 1894 **Pullman strike/lockout** seemed to confirm that company towns were neither profitable nor stable. George Pullman constructed an industrial city near Chicago to produce his railroad sleeping cars. Pullman was, in many ways, even more impressive than Lowell. In addition to factories and worker housing, Pullman featured a splendid community center, a luxury hotel, an ornate library, and an artificial lake. The town was also meticulously landscaped. In 1881, the first residents moved in and almost immediately resented Pullman's paternalistic control. Rents in Pullman were higher than those in working-class neighborhoods of Chicago, as were utilities, retail prices, and fares on the only rail line that serviced the town. Workers joked that they lived in Pullman's houses, worshiped in his church, were buried in his cemetery, and would undoubtedly spend eternity in Pullman hell. When the Panic of 1893 caused Pullman to slash wages, but not rent or utilities, a bitter labor conflict ensued that ended Pullman's experiment. By 1899, the factory town was decrepit; in 1904, the land and houses were sold to the city of Chicago.

By the 20th century, the majority of company towns were owned by mining firms. A rare company town start-up was Hershey, Pennsylvania, where chocolate magnate Milton Hershey opened his namesake town in 1903. Hershey was a throwback to 19th-century paternalists and the town operated reasonably well until the 1950s, when town and business operations became increasingly separate from each other. Instead of ownership of most or all city assets, many 20th-century corporations chose instead to flex their economic and political muscle. Numerous towns and cities dominated by a single employer became de facto company towns, even when owning little or no real estate beyond that upon which their factories stood. For all practical purposes, Gary, Indiana, was a U.S. Steel company town, and Flint, Michigan, was the preserve of General Motors. In such places, much of the area's economy relied directly or indirectly upon the health of its corporate giants. The same patterns were found in textile towns in the Southern Piedmont, one-industry New England mill towns, Arizona mining towns dominated by Phelps Dodge, and many other places across America. The Great Depression challenged but did not destroy this new type of company town. A more serious challenge was posed by the waves of **deindustrialization**, **globalization**, and **deregulation** that transformed the American economy from the 1970s onward. It simply makes little sense for most towns and cities to rely on a single industry for their livelihood. A few places persist where older corporations remain dominant and a subtle company-town mentality permeates the community, but few can claim the sort of control of 19th-century paternalist towns or mid-20th-century one-industry towns.

The closest analog to old-style company towns are those dominated by universities ("college towns") and those in which military bases or Defense Department contracts command disproportionate numbers of local employment opportunities. Parris Island, South Carolina—home to the Marine Corps' training base—is akin to a company town. Economists are nearly unanimous in their assertion that company towns past and present are less economically stable than municipalities with diversified economies.

Suggested Reading

Stanley Buder, *Pullman: An Experiment in Industrial Order and Community Planning*, 1967; David Corbin, *Life, Work, and Rebellion in the Coal Fields*, 1981; Stephen Hahn and Jonathan Prude, eds., *The Countryside in the Age of Capitalist Transformation*, 1985; Daniel Walkowitz, *Worker City, Company Town: Iron and Cotton Worker Protest in Troy and Cohoes, New York, 1855–84*, 1978.

COMPANY UNION

A company union is a bargaining unit set up by employers on behalf of their own employees. Also known as employee representation plans, company unions thrived in the 1920s but were outlawed as **unfair labor practices** under the 1935 **National Labor Relations Act** (NLRA). Employers experimented with employee shop committees and worker councils in the 19th century, but most scholars see a 1915 structure put in place by the Colorado Fuel and Iron Company as the prototypical company union. It followed the **Colorado labor wars** and the **Ludlow Massacre** and allowed employees to negotiate **wages**, layoffs, work hours, and a **welfare capitalism** benefit package with the company. That said, the company union was also clearly an attempt to divide workers into those loyal to the company and those who wished to be recognized by the **United Mine Workers of America**.

By 1933, as many as 2.5 million workers were represented by company unions. Like the Colorado Fuel and Iron body, company unions everywhere were problematic. Because the company was, in effect, bargaining with itself, company unions could not hope to compete as equals, nor could their negotiators operate free from potential reprisals. A bigger problem still was that welfare capitalist gains were little more than free-will offerings from the company that could be withdrawn at any time. Whenever stockholders demanded higher dividends or an economic downturn weakened earnings, companies cut benefits. That situation grew particularly acute with the onset of the Great Depression (1929–1941). Company unions were expressly eliminated by Section 8(a)(2) of the NLRA.

Although in a small number of cases company unions delivered superior benefits to those won by labor unions, most observers agree that company unions were typically employer dodges intended to stifle legitimate unionization efforts. Company unions have proved easier to ban in theory than in reality. Many firms operate staff councils, advisory groups, and ad hoc committees that operate much like 1920s-style company unions, except that they are expressly forbidden from negotiating a **contract**. Under the guise of giving staff the right to make "suggestions" and offer "input," these bodies are often touted as examples of how management "cares" about its employees. The lack of rules regulating such bodies allows management to choose who serves in them, if it so chooses, and to receive regular reports on activist and disgruntled employees. In the 1990s, Republican members of Congress proposed amending the NLRA to allow new company unions under the guise of what they dubbed the TEAM (Teamwork for Employees and Managers) Act. This move has been bitterly opposed by the **American Federation of Labor-Congress of Industrial Organizations** (AFL-CIO), and President Bill Clinton vetoed such a measure in 1996. An attempt to pass an amended version faltered in 1997 and such legislation has not made its way before Congress since 1996, though it remains a favored idea among conservatives.

Suggested Reading

Irving Bernstein, *The Lean Years*, 1960; Stuart Brandes, *American Welfare Capitalism, 1880–1940*, 1995; Bruce Kaufman, "The Case for the Company Union," *Labor History* 41, no. 3 (August 2000): 321–350.

COMPARABLE WORTH

Comparable worth is the idea that workers should receive equal levels of pay for jobs that are similar in nature, and that require analogous skills and training. Obtaining comparable worth protection is an important goal among unions, civil rights organizations, and women's rights groups. Comparable worth is similar to **equity pay**, and some people use the terms interchangeably.

Comparable worth has long been a *cause célèbre* among working women. The **Knights of Labor** supported the passage of racial and equity pay laws in the late 19th century, as did the **Industrial Workers of the World** and the **Congress of Industrial Organizations** in the early and mid-20th century. The federal Women's Bureau (WB) has called for comparable worth reform since 1945, and feminists within unions such as the **United Auto Workers of America** began challenging male privilege as early as the 1950s. The WB, the National Council of Women's Organization (NCWO), and the **Coalition of Labor Union Women** have all advocated corrective measures such as periodic data collection to document the effects of job segregation and comparative appraisals of job content, qualifications, and working conditions across occupations.

The **Equal Pay Act of 1963**, which amended the **Fair Labor Standards Act** (1938), outlawed differential **wage** scales for workers doing the *same* job, but since then some employers have perpetuated pay inequity by giving similar jobs different titles and slightly different responsibilities. Although an employer cannot pay women less than men for doing the same job, the 1963 law's literal wording left room for creative job classifications.

Title VII of the 1964 Civil Rights Act extended the comparable worth principle to race, ethnicity, and religion, but allowed exceptions that lawmakers at the time thought were reasonable and natural differences between individuals. Theorists call such assumptions "essentialism"—that is, the idea that men and women (and to a lesser extent, people of different races) have "essential" differences that make them more capable of doing some tasks and less capable of doing others. Only women, for example, can give birth.

By the 1970s, it was obvious that existing laws had too many loopholes. An employer might, for example, require employees to be able to lift objects assumed too heavy for women's "naturally" smaller bodies. Courts, however, ruled that such standards must be reasonable within the job. If, for example, machines are used the move heavy objects, then a woman would need only the strength necessary to operate that machine. Appeals court cases such as *Schultz v. Wheaton Glass Co.* (1970) closed a few loopholes, as did the U.S. Supreme Court's 1974 decision in *Corning Glass Works v. Brennan*. In 1974, Governor Daniel Evans of Washington State ordered the nation's first pay equity wage study in response to pressure from the **American Federation of State, County, and Municipal Employees**. The ensuing report on 121 job classifications revealed that women in state service earned 20 percent less than male public employees in comparable jobs.

Even so, gender and racial bias has persisted, such that work performed by women and people of color earns those employees substantially less than male workers. In 2002, women earned 77 cents for every dollar earned by a man. In April 2004, the Institute for Women's Policy Research (IWPR) reported the earnings of white men and women of different races, concluding that the highest-paid women earned 25 percent less than men. African Americans generally fare even worse on comparable pay scales, earning just two-thirds of what white males earn on the average. In 2007, average family income for African American families was more than $20,000 per year less than that of white families.

Comparable worth battles are ongoing, and the direction of the courts has been ambiguous in all but the most egregious violations of equity pay principles. In 1985, for example, Washington State was ordered to pay $101 million in pay increases for unionized female employees—an award that was promptly overturned upon appeal. That case remains in limbo, as does the largest sex discrimination case ever brought against a private employer, *Dukes, et al. v. Wal-Mart Stores, Inc.* The latter case was first filed in 2004 and has been heard, settled, reversed, and reheard several times.

Many analysts believe that Congressional action is the best way to solve comparable worth disputes, as court rulings have been contradictory and slow in coming. A Fair Pay Act has appeared before Congress several times since 2000, but it has been vigorously opposed by both the business community and the Republican Party. Businesses ostensibly see it as needless regulation, but they stand to lose hundreds of millions of dollars if such a bill ever passes. Republicans call it an anti-business bill. Thus far there has been insufficient political will to break the logjam, but President Barack Obama did sign the Lilly Ledbetter Equal Pay Act of 2009, which clarified the statue of limitations for filing equal-pay lawsuits. Overall action on comparable worth remains slow, though 20 states have undertaken data collection and claim support for pay equity on comparable worth grounds.

Suggested Reading

Linda M. Blum, *Between Labor and Feminism: The Significance of the Comparable Worth Movement*, 1991; Liza Featherstone, *Selling Women Short: The Landmark Battle for Workers' Rights at Wal-Mart*, 2004; Margaret Hallock, "Pay Equity: Did it Work?" in *Squaring Up: Policy Strategies to Raise Women's Incomes in the United States*, ed. Mary C. King, 2001; Alice Kessler-Harris, *A Woman's Wage: Historical Meanings and Social Consequences*, 1990.

COMPUTER REVOLUTION AND ORGANIZED LABOR

Labor unions have made little headway in organizing the high-tech sector of the American economy that boomed in the 1980s and 1990s, and have retrenched their positions since the "tech bubble" burst. One estimate suggests that just 1 in 20 high-tech workers is in a union—a ratio that is considerably lower than the union representation rate in the private sector. Although some commentators have glibly attributed this discrepancy to a lack of interest among independent-minded programmers, **outsourcing**, **globalization**, and **contingent labor** are more likely culprits.

Most high-tech workers are not programmers, a position for which demand is flat and expected to shrink in the second decade of the 21st century. Programmers are well paid, but the majority of high-tech workers are employed in fields such as data processing, hardware assembly, network setup, computer security, information technology services, repair, and product testing. Much of this work is easy to **subcontract**, which means that many—up to one-third by some estimates—jobs are done by nonbenefited freelancers on a for-hire basis. A larger problem, though, has been subcontracting offshore.

Many computer manufacturing jobs have left the United States for low-wage countries, and most of the computers that do not arrive in stores readymade are merely assembled in the United States from parts made elsewhere. High-tech jobs are easily outsourced—and this is precisely what has happened. According to Forrester Research, 27,000 high-tech jobs had left the United States by 1990, and that number is projected to grow to 472,000 by 2015. Some studies dispute such figures, however, and estimate the loss will be in the 2 to 3 percent range; others say the total job loss figures could exceed 3 million.

Unions such as the Communication Workers of America have worked with industry officials to try to retain U.S. high-tech jobs, but the forecast is not good. Information technology and troubleshooting calls, for instance, are now routinely rerouted to India, and even medical x-rays are electronically sent abroad to be read. Not surprisingly, information technology workers are among those white-collar workers most interested in joining unions, and a consumer backlash against outsourcing has slowed its pace. Whether these actions can reverse the impact of globalization within the industry is uncertain at best.

Suggested Reading

Alorie Gilbert, "Labor Activists Picket Outsourcing Event," *CNET News*, September 18, 2003, http://news.cnet.com/Labor-activists-picket-outsourcing-event/2100-1022_3-5077627.html, accessed July 21, 2010; Carrie Kirby, "Techies See Jobs Go Overseas: Opposition to Offshore Outsourcing Beginning to Grow," *San Francisco Chronicle*, June 2, 2003; Steve Lohr, "Study Plays Down Export of Computer Jobs," *New York Times*, February 23, 2006.

CONCESSIONS

In labor history terms, concessions refer to a regressive contract whose terms are less advantageous than those in the contract it replaces. Sometimes called "givebacks," concessions are exacted from employees bargaining from a position of weakness. In essence, unions bargain away power, conceding to management the right to invest, determine production, organize work, and make financial decisions as it sees fit. During negotiations, concessions are often offered as an ultimatum and can involve significant cuts in **wages** and benefits.

Concessions have long been a staple of the **collective bargaining** process. The ideal in a **capitalist** economic system is for both capital and labor to benefit from economic expansion. Nonetheless, capitalism privatizes most forms of wealth, which means that one side seeks to maximize its gain at the other side's expense. Employees seek to build upon gains made in previous contracts, and employers attempt to roll back those gains. Concessions come into play in ways beyond normal give-and-take tactics during economic downturns and in highly competitive industries. In extreme cases, management threatens to lay off workers or cease operations altogether if unions fail to grant economic concessions.

Until the 1970s, concessions were usually negotiated with individual firms or within a particularly vulnerable industry. More common was **pattern bargaining**, in which unions targeted an industry leader and used its contract as the template for others within that industry. Some employers welcomed this as it stabilized wage rates and discouraged employee turnover.

By the late 1970s, however, employers argued that stagflation and the pressures of **globalization** placed U.S. firms at a competitive disadvantage in world markets. They demanded employee givebacks to reduce operating costs and make them more profitable. Typical of this sort of reverse pattern bargaining was what happened in the auto industry. In 1979, Chrysler Corporation declared bankruptcy. To prevent the loss of tens of thousands of jobs, the federal government devised a bailout plan to rescue the ailing firm. As part of its restructuring plan, Chrysler reopened a contract with the **United Auto Workers of America** (UAW) and forced the union to accept $673 million in wage and benefit concessions. Ford and General Motors quickly demanded similar cuts, which the beleaguered UAW was forced to grant.

Unlike earlier versions of concessions, those unleashed in the 1970s were neither isolated nor confined to a single industry; rather, they were part of a concerted business strategy to reduce the power of unions. Many firms, in fact, rejected union concession offers and relocated outside of the United States. The decline and near-disappearance of American basic industries in steel, rubber, glass, and electronics made **blue-collar** workers vulnerable and sent the message that employers were not prepared to negotiate over concessions.

These trends accelerated in the 1980s. The administrations of **Ronald Reagan** and George H. W. Bush were largely hostile to organized labor, which in turn emboldened employers. In addition, the U.S. Supreme Court ruled that employers need not negotiate with unions to close plants, relocate, or transfer work from one site to another. Reagan-Bush tax policies also accelerated the trend of capital flight. In 1981, new union contracts averaged a nearly 10 percent wage increase for members; by 1986, this growth was down to 1.2 percent, a figure that failed to keep up with inflation. Wage concessions were often coupled with deep cuts in fringe benefits, with employees being forced to reduce their number of paid holidays, pay higher premiums for health care coverage, agree to mandatory **overtime**, give up **cost-of-living adjustments**, and allow firms more discretion in investing employee pension funds. Most unions were ill prepared for concessions battles and fought rearguard campaigns in which success was measured by how little they were forced to concede rather than by how much they won. By the late 1980s, some union leaders spoke of "concession bargaining" and argued that the only choice was between givebacks and unemployment. Many unions sought to protect older members by accepting two-tier contracts, wherein new employees began work at lower pay rates and with less attractive benefit packages than those employees already working. Such a strategy might have been necessary, but it did little to endear unions to young workers. The UAW accepted such a contract in 1996.

By the mid-1990s, unions had begun to hold a firmer line on concessions. Studies revealed that employers often squandered employee pension funds in reckless stock market speculation and that there was very little link between granting concessions and saving jobs. Manufacturing jobs continued to evaporate as firms moved outside U.S. borders or invested concessions in the stock market rather than rebuilding aging plants. Unions were also angered by the passage of the **North American Free Trade Agreement**, which facilitated capital flight to Mexico and signaled to some union advocates that organized labor could no longer rely upon the Democratic Party for support. Many became convinced that aggressive resistance to concessions was better than passively hoping for the best. **Corporate campaigns** were launched to expose corporate investment patterns, pressure subsidiaries, and involve workers outside the immediate conflict area.

The overall contraction of manufacturing also meant that unions were left strongest in those businesses least susceptible to capital flight such as the professional, government-work, education, and service industries. Rank-and-file rebellion against concessions-minded **business unionists** also played a part in altering the balance of power. **John Sweeney** made resistance concession-bargaining a centerpiece of his successful 1995 bid for the presidency of the **American Federation of Labor-Congress of Industrial Organizations** (AFL-CIO). The AFL-CIO's mixed record of success on this front was among the issues that gave rise to the rival **Change to Win Federation** in 2005.

Union efforts to roll back concessions remain an unfinished task. The task is complicated by the increase in the number of part-time workers, professional adjuncts, and temporary workers. Soaring health care costs are the source of numerous contemporary employer demands for concessions. The recession of 2007–2010 spurred a new wave of employer-initiated concessions. In 2010, for example, Hershey chocolate workers grudgingly agreed to a plan to fire 600 workers when the company announced it would close all local operations if they refused. It should be noted that in some cases teachers, firefighters, and other municipal workers have also reopened contracts to save the jobs of their colleagues and preserve services.

Suggested Reading

Stanley Aronowitz, *From the Ashes of the Old: American Labor and America's Future*, 1998, Martin Jay Leavitt, *Confessions of a Union Buster*, 1993; Kim Moody, *An Injury to All*, 1988.

CONCILIATION. *See* Arbitration/Conciliation/Mediation.

CONGRESS OF INDUSTRIAL ORGANIZATIONS

The Congress of Industrial Organizations (CIO) reshaped capital/labor relations in the 20th century. During its 20-year existence from 1935 to 1955, the CIO brought **industrial unionism** to the fore and organized industries that had long been resistant to unions. The CIO won **collective bargaining** rights for millions of working people and played a key role in shaping New Deal legislation that benefited workers. At its height around 1940, commentators joked, only half-ironically, that CIO head **John L. Lewis** was the second most-powerful man in the United States, inferior only to President Roosevelt.

The CIO began life in 1935 as the Committee for Industrial Organization, a faction within the **American Federation of Labor** (AFL) that sought to organize mass-production industries such as those producing steel, automobiles, rubber, and electrical appliances. Although these enterprises dominated the American economy, AFL leaders were suspicious of industrial unionism. The AFL was devoted to **craft unionism**, and many of its leaders argued that only skilled workers could build the **solidarity** necessary to unify labor. Several, in fact, were contemptuous of assembly-line workers and viewed them as little more than mindless drones. When the AFL went into mass-production industries at all, it classified workers into skill groups, many of which were arbitrary and nonsensical. An autoworker installing spark plugs on an **assembly line** might find himself classified as an "electrician," for instance. Industrial union advocates argued that such designations merely segmented the workforce and reduced everyone's bargaining power. They proposed that such industries be organized according to the end product they created, not by whatever part a specific worker played in assembling it.

Frustrated by the AFL's inaction and buoyed by a confrontation in which Lewis punched out William Hutcheson of the carpenters' union during the AFL's October 1935 convention, eight union presidents broke with the AFL and announced their intention to begin organizing industrial workers. The Committee for Industrial Organization chose Lewis, the combative president of the **United Mine Workers of America** (UMWA), as its head. Most historians date the CIO's founding to October 1935, though technically it remained a dissident faction within the AFL until the eight original unions and two others that joined were expelled from the AFL in November 1936. The formal name change to "Congress of Industrial Organizations" occurred in 1938.

The CIO began cautiously, quietly sending organizers into the factory towns of the East and Midwest to spread the industrial unionism message. They quickly found receptive audiences, and the CIO found itself coordinating a massive **strike** wave in the American industrial heartland in 1936 and 1937. The usual pattern was to set up an "organizing committee," which converted to a CIO union if a **certification** drive proved successful. The CIO concentrated on shop-floor and grassroots organizing, and made use of local talent, even if organizers were **socialists**, **communists**, or radicals of whatever ilk. It also fostered a rich union-based culture associated with **social unionism**.

In February and March 1936, workers at the Goodyear Tire plant in Akron, Ohio, struck to demand that the company recognize their union, the **United Rubber Workers of America**. A year later, workers at the General Motors (GM) plants in Flint, Michigan, engaged in dramatic **sit-down strikes** to seize control of their factories and secure recognition of the **United Auto Workers of America** (UAW). The strike wave quickly spread to Detroit, where workers at Chrysler and other auto manufacturers insisted on UAW representation. In the spring of 1937, workers in the steel industry struck to win recognition of the Steel Workers Organizing Committee. A few months later, workers at Radio Corporation of America (RCA) struck to gain recognition of their union, the **United Electrical, Radio, and Machine Workers of America** (UE), officially the first union after the CIO's formal founding, though the 1938 ceremony merely confirmed a three-year reality.

A few corporations—most notably in steel, in southern textile plants, and at Ford Motors—held out for a time, but many union officials were stunned by their workers' sudden militancy. Their actions were all the more surprising given that they came in the depths of the Great Depression, during a time of record high levels of **unemployment**. By the close of 1937, the CIO had 3 million members organized into 6,000 **union locals**. In just two years, the CIO had organized workers in the auto, clothing, electric, rubber, and textile industries. Its membership included 600,000 electrical workers alone. "Sit-down fever" swept the nation, with everyone from laundry workers to Woolworth's clerks engaging in **wildcat strikes** inspired by the UAW.

The worker militancy took even CIO leaders by surprise, and the organization eventually opted to place more emphasis on political leverage. In 1936, Lewis forged a relationship with the Democratic Party. This liaison served the CIO well; during the Flint sit-down strike, for instance, Michigan's Democratic Governor Frank Murphy refused GM demands to use the militia to dislodge sit-down strikers. Lewis's CIO colleague **Sidney Hillman** of the clothing workers' union became a key advisor to President Franklin Roosevelt, and CIO leaders had access to the White

House when such landmark labor bills as the **National Labor Relations Act**, the **Social Security Act**, and the **Fair Labor Standards Act** were drafted and enacted. Lewis's successors as CIO president, **Philip Murray** and **Walter Reuther**, also nurtured the CIO's relationship with Democrats, though Lewis eventually broke with Roosevelt.

By the late 1930s and early 1940s, the CIO turned to the slower, less spectacular work of building a stable organization. It continued to organize workers, sometimes through strikes, and sometimes by mounting legal challenges against employers. By the time of U.S. entry into World War II in December 1941, the CIO had even organized Ford Motor Company and Bethlehem Steel, two notoriously anti-union firms. The CIO's penetration into mass-production industries positioned it well during the war—many of the industries in which the CIO organized workers were vital to wartime production and hired new employees during this era. Most CIO affiliates took **no-strike pledges** during the war and, by 1945, the CIO had more than 4 million members despite the departure of Lewis and the UMWA, who left the CIO in 1941 in disputes over support for Roosevelt and the CIO's reluctance to sanction mine strikes.

CIO unions made significant gains and forced corporations to concede benefits now viewed as standard, such as health care, pension plans, and paid vacations. It also brought a measure of justice to the factory floor by setting up formal **grievance** procedures, establishing seniority systems, and helping employers write clearly defined job descriptions. Its brand of social unionism also led it to support a greatly expanded welfare state, vigorous government management of the economy, civil rights for African Americans and other minority groups, and other progressive causes—changes it was in a position to demand because the CIO had become the de facto liberal wing of the Democratic Party. The UAW even secured contract provisions such as **cost-of-living adjustments** that pegged rising inflation to automatic raises, and guarantees that auto companies would pay workers a portion of their wages even when they were laid off.

The CIO's decline was almost as dramatic as its rise. Its aggressive social unionism and past association with political radicals made it a lightning rod for conservatives. As early as 1938, right-wing politicians attacked the CIO as a threat to the American way of life. The post-World War II **Red Scare** and **Cold War** emboldened conservatives, and the 1947 **Taft-Hartley Act** gave them a mallet with which to hammer away at the CIO. The CIO's efforts to organize the South during **Operation Dixie** failed badly and drained CIO coffers. The federation also faced charges that its affiliates were riddled with communists and was forced to jettison nearly a million members between 1948 and 1950 over that issue. In addition, it proved unable to rekindle the militant spirit of the 1930s; unions such as the UAW had largely ceded management's right to operate as it saw fit in exchange for lucrative contracts and a promise of curtailing shop-floor agitation.

Some historians think that the CIO was a declining—perhaps dying—federation by the early 1950s and sincerely doubt that it contained the 6 million members claimed at the time it merged with the larger AFL in 1955. At the time, the CIO was rent by internal dissension—especially a dispute between Reuther and the steelmakers—and weakened by external attack. After prolonged negotiations, a new **American Federation of Labor-Congress of Industrial Organizations** appeared in December 1955. It gave former CIO unions needed security, but lacked the vigor, imagination, courage, and social unionism flair that that had once made the CIO so extraordinary.

Suggested Reading

Irving Bernstein, *Turbulent Years: A History of the American Worker, 1933–41*, 1971; Nelson Lichtenstein, *Labor's War at Home: The CIO in World War II*, 1982; Robert Zieger, *The CIO, 1935–55*, 1997.

CONTINGENCY LABOR

Contingency labor has come to be a synonym for all **part-time labor**, though economists and labor studies experts generally confine its use to labor undertaken for a limited period of time with no promise or expectation that it will be permanent. Contingency labor is an increasingly commonplace and controversial practice that might involve as many as 20 percent of all American workers. Critics refer to it as "disposable labor," reflecting the fact that most contingent workers receive few, if any, **fringe benefits** and often receive lower **wages** than those on full-time staff. Critics also charge that contingent workers are exploited by unscrupulous employers seeking to maximize profits. Union activists deplore the use of contingency labor because it undermines both staffing levels and pay rates for unionized workers. Put simply, if employers can hire contingency labor for less money, they have little incentive to hire full-time workers. Unions assert that contingent workers ultimately harm business as these laborers are less qualified, are less loyal, and have little incentive to care whether the firm does well or poorly.

The 1997 United Parcel Service strike brought to light many of the issues concerning contingent and part-time work in the United States. In settling the strike, the **Teamsters** secured promises to convert part-time jobs into full-time employment. Contingent work tends to be concentrated in the retail and service sector, but it is also found within large firms that could afford to hire more full-time workers. For example, software giant Microsoft employs an estimated 6,000 contingency workers at any given time, a practice so engrained in its corporate culture that it has been the focus of several lawsuits, including the 1999 ruling in *Vizcaino v. Microsoft* that ordered the firm to provide benefits in some cases. Similar rulings involved the DuPont Corporation. The contingent labor practices of Wal-Mart—the world's richest company—have also been scrutinized, especially its habit of working employees just an hour or two shy of the point at which they would become eligible for benefits. An especially egregious employer of contingency labor is higher education; more than half of all classes in many colleges and universities are taught by graduate students and adjunct professors, the bulk of the latter seeking full-time work. When these individuals assume heavier teaching loads, universities save money, but students are denied access to those professors with the greatest expertise in a given subject and promising instructors are driven to seek employment outside of education.

According to the **Bureau of Labor Statistics** (BLS), those persons who work fewer than 35 hours per week are considered part time workers. How many of these workers are coerced to do so or contingent is a matter of some debate. Defenders of current hiring programs claim that only the 20 percent of current part-time employees who are seeking full-time work should be considered contingency labor. They accuse unions and social activists of being alarmist, claiming that the total percentage of part-time workers has remained constant at 18 percent since the 1970s. Moreover, only one in five contingent workers is a head of household, many have health insurance through other family members, and most part-time workers are students, retirees, or women seeking flexible hours. They also point out that of those individuals who are involuntarily working part-time, only one out of five remains a part-time worker after a year. From this point of view, the number of true contingency workers appears quite small, about 5 percent of the total workforce.

The BLS, however, places the percentage of true contingent labor at 10 percent, double what apologists claim, and some labor economists argue that the actual number is closer to 20 percent. Even if one accepts the lowest estimates, between 500,000 and 750,000 workers appear to be seeking full-time employment, but cannot secure it. The issue also has gender and racial dimensions, as a disproportionate percentage of contingency workers are female and people of color. A further problem is that the demand for contingent labor is highest during economic expansion, but its fallout is greatest during downturns. The severe recession of 2007–2010 forced many full-time workers into contingent status, and many former contingent workers were pushed out of work with few safety nets to break their fall; many even lacked **unemployment** benefits. Organized labor has made the plight of contingency and part-time workers a high priority. In some cases, employers have found the problems associated with contingent labor to be more trouble than it is worth. Some have turned to a practice of **outsourcing** tasks instead of hiring in-house contingent labor, while still others have sought to increase staffing levels. The potential cost savings involved in contingency labor means, however, that the practice is likely to remain a hot-button topic in the coming decades.

Suggested Reading

Kathleen Barker and Kathleen Christensen, eds., *Contingent Work: American Employment Relations in Transition*, 1998; "FutureWork," Bureau of Labor Statistics, http://www .bls.gov/opub/ooq/2000/Summer/art04.pdf, accessed July 17, 2010; "Hiring Contingency Workers Becomes a Riskier Business," *IC Law OnLine*, http://www .contingentlaw.com/Hiringpercent20Temps percent20Riskierpercent20Business.htm, accessed July 17, 2010.

CONTRACT

A labor contract is an agreement between two or more parties in which each party is bound to fulfill specified obligations. Labor contracts are usually signed between a union and one or more employers, and their conditions are legally binding. In most cases a union's rank-and-file members must ratify a contract before it goes into effect.

Contracts have governed North American laborers even before there were unions. During the **Colonial** period, contracts were drawn between sponsors and **indentured servants** that specified the length of time an indenture would labor in exchange for his or her patron, usually five to seven years. In exchange, the indentured servant received passage across the Atlantic Ocean from Europe. At the end of the agreed-upon term, workers were free to seek independent situations. Often they received land, money, or goods at the end of their contracts. Later, contracts were set up between **master craftsmen** and their **journeymen** and **apprentices**.

Some early labor contracts were verbal agreements, though most were written. With the rise of labor unions, contracts were almost always written, and they grew more complex over time. It was not unusual, however, for late-19th-century contracts to be rather breezy and straightforward. One reason for this informality was that there was relatively little law governing relations between employers and employees. As labor laws expanded, the number of issues requiring negotiation grew accordingly.

A modern contract between a union and an employer contains many parts. Standard items such as **wages**, hours of employment, and **fringe benefits** are spelled out, but so, too, are highly detailed items such as job classifications, the conditions under which work can be reassigned, and **grievance** procedures. Today's contracts can run hundreds of pages long, take months to negotiate, and need to be reviewed by lawyers. Although unions and management often bitterly contest contract provisions, both like the predictability of contracts once they are in effect. In accordance with provisions of the **National Labor Relations Act**, deviation from the contract by either side constitutes an **unfair labor practice**.

Suggested Reading

Labor Contracts Database, http://www.irle.berkeley.edu/library/index.php?page=3, accessed July 18, 2010; Terry L. Leap, *Collective Bargaining and Labor Relations*, 1995.

CONTRACT LABOR

In labor terms, contract labor is a form of immigrant gang labor. It was vigorously opposed by 19th-century labor groups. The first Contact Labor Law was passed by the U.S. Congress in 1864 in direct response to the labor shortage in the northern states caused by **Civil War** conscription. It was essentially an updated **indentured servant** bill whereby immigrants were advanced passage money in return for a lien upon their **wages**. Encouraged by the act, influential Americans—including Secretary of the Navy Gideon Welles, Senator Charles Sumner of Massachusetts, and the Reverend Henry Ward Beecher—capitalized the American Emigrant Company to the tune of $1 million. The company's announced intention was to import laborers, especially skilled workers, from England, Belgium, France, and other northern European countries, to take posts as miners, puddlers, mechanics, and machinists. The workers were required by law to repay the cost of their passage and other expenses "advanced" on their behalf.

The act proved unpopular among the northern U.S. **working class** from the start. First, during the repayment period, contract workers received no wages, which undercut local wage rates. Second, money advanced for living expenses often trapped contract workers in a debt peonage cycle out of accord with free labor ideals in the North. Finally, contract workers were often recruited as **scabs** during labor conflicts. In very little time, contract labor was also conflated with fears of "coolie" gang labor. Unions generally saw contract labor as a cynical attempt to create a **surplus labor supply** to depress wages artificially and discourage union movements. Both craft unions and the **National Labor Union** made repeal of the Contract Labor Act a key agenda item. The first bill was actually repealed in 1868; however, repeal merely ended government sponsorship for contracted immigrants, and private citizens were free to pursue the practice.

By the 1870s, discussion of eliminating contract labor was inexorably linked to the call for a **Chinese Exclusion Act**. The 1885 Alien Contract Labor Act, popularly known as the Foran Act, prohibited most forms of imported contract labor. It was strengthened by amendments in 1887.

Suggested Reading

Edward Hutchinson, *Legislative History of American Immigration*, 1981; Joseph G. Rayback, *A History of American Labor*, 1966; Paul R. Taylor, *The ABC-CLIO Companion to the American Labor Movement*, 1993.

COOPERATIVES

A cooperative is an enterprise owned and operated for the benefit of those who consume its products or use its services. It also refers to an industrial concern that is owned by the workers who toil in it. Cooperation, as its name implies, is an economic practice that places group needs and interests above the system of private profit that marks **capitalism**. Cooperatives are a very small part of the current economic system, but for much of the 19th century they were touted as an alternative to capitalism and cooperation was widely perceived to be a more just system.

Such enterprises usually operate according to democratic principles and make membership open and voluntary. Although cooperation is an ancient ideal, its practice over the past several centuries has been associated with utopian movements, labor reformers, and laborers seeking to eliminate middle men.

An early inspiration came from philanthropist **Robert Owen** (1771–1858), who established a cooperative store and model **company town** in New Lanark, Scotland. Owen held five conferences on cooperative principles between 1831 and 1833, in which the virtues of his experiments were discussed. Many of the town's 2,000 people were recruited from Edinburgh and Glasgow slums, the town's 500 children attended school, stores sold items at cost, laborers worked an **eight-hour** day, and workers enjoyed profit-sharing plans. Owen's ideals endured even after New Lanark converted to more conventional business methods. Owen purchased land in the United States in 1825, and announced the creation of New Harmony, Indiana. His son, **Robert Dale Owen**, was involved in New Harmony, as was Frances Wright and other members of the **Workingmen's movement**.

American cooperation experiments also drew inspiration from the French social theorist Charles Fourier, whose ideas were introduced into the United States by

Albert Brisbane. Their views on self-sufficient agricultural communities led to the establishment of several short-lived Brook Farm communities in Massachusetts (1841–1846) and a community in Red Bank, New Jersey. English and Scottish cooperationists associated with the Rochdale Society of Equitable Pioneers provided a widely emulated model and statement of principles that seemed both more pragmatic and democratic to 19th-century experimenters. The first Rochdale cooperative in North America opened in Lawrence, Kansas, in 1863. It operated much the way some food cooperatives do today, in that it pooled member capital to buy and sell goods and return profits to members as dividends. Unlike simple profit-sharing programs, however, Rochdale cooperationists hoped to one day abolish the wage system.

Cooperatives generally take one (or more) of three forms: consumption cooperatives, production cooperatives, and credit or financial cooperatives. A consumption cooperative caters to members as consumers by eliminating the merchant's profits and selling goods at or near wholesale cost. Production cooperatives are those in which workers themselves own the means of production and, therefore, control manufacturing processes. All profit accrues to producers instead of being siphoned off by intermediary employers and investors. Credit or financial cooperatives are groups that derive benefit by combining their capital and their credit. The first two types of cooperatives are **socialist** in nature, whereas the third is more akin to an alternative banking system.

The first consumer-cooperative movement in the United States was the New England Workingmen's Association, organized in Boston in 1844. A store was started in 1845, and by 1847, 12 groups of people had banded together to form the Workingmen's Protective Union (later named the New England Protective Union). The **Knights of Labor** (KOL) was devoted to cooperative ideals and started at least 185 production cooperatives, and its local assemblies operated untold numbers of cooperative stores that provided discounts to Knights. When KOL cooperatives generated a profit, some of the excess went into the KOL's Defense (strike) Fund and some into establishing mutual-aid societies and new cooperative ventures. Alas, most KOL cooperatives were undercapitalized and short-lived, but the organization officially called upon the creation of cooperatives to supplant capitalism.

The cooperative movement reached its apex in the 1890s, when various groups linked to Farmers' Alliances and the Populist Party formed cooperatives. Farmers were especially vulnerable to middle men such as grain elevator operators, wholesalers, and railroads, each of which cut into their already thin operating capital. Farmers responded by setting up their own elevators, milling centers, distribution networks, and retail outlets. In some cases they even commanded enough collective volume to secure better railroad freight rates. Farmer co-ops persist as the most enduring example of production cooperatives and have enjoyed a small resurgence among producers of specialty items such as cheese, ice cream, organic food, and fibers. The flip side of this gain is that most conventional farming is now securely in the hands of corporate conglomerates.

Cooperation waned in the first half of the 20th century and the movement faced charges that members advocated socialism or **communism**, ideals that were not as controversial in the 19th century as they became after World War II. Cooperative ideals resonated anew during the 1960s, especially among those seeking alternative lifestyles. Scores of small co-ops opened in college towns, in urban areas activists sought to revitalize, and adjacent to communes. Many such ventures began with great idealism, but simply lacked the resources to compete with large-scale capital concerns. Few co-ops have enough reserve capital to weather economic downturns, nor can they compete with larger stores seeking to supply the same niche markets. A local food co-op, for example, would find to very hard to compete against chain store giant Whole Foods, which holds nearly $4 billion in assets.

Cooperation remains a visible presence in the American economy, mostly in small-scale enterprises such as employee-owned retail stores, cafes, print shops, and small building firms. Food co-ops remain the most visible type of consumption cooperatives, and many are staffed by volunteer members to keep costs low. The most financially successful remnants of the cooperative movement are credit unions, quasi-cooperative financial institutions that deliver some banking services to members at more favorable rates than commercial banks. Numerous labor unions operate their own credit unions. Cooperative housing—or co-housing—has grown in popularity recently. Co-housing complexes are intentional communities that are hybrids of private and community property. In 1995, the International Co-operative Alliance drafted a statement of identity to facilitate the spread of cooperation; its principles hark back to the Rochdale movement.

Suggested Reading

Edward Bemis, *Cooperation*, 1888; John Curl, *History of Work Cooperation in the United States*, 1980, Robert Jackall and Henry Levin, eds., *Worker Cooperatives in America*, 1984; Robert E. Weir, *Knights Unhorsed: Internal Conflict in a Gilded Age Labor Movement*, 2000.

COPPAGE V. KANSAS. See Adair v. the United States.

COPPER MINERS AND STRIKES

Although copper mining does not evoke a history of capital/labor strife parallel to that of coal mining, it, too, has been the backdrop for numerous and violent clashes between corporations and unions. The reasons for conflict are similar: low pay, long hours, dangerous working conditions, the existence of authoritarian **company towns**, and corporations unwillingly to compromise with unions. In addition, many of the copper pits were located in the Rocky Mountain West and Southwest— regions that remained raw and underdeveloped for much of the 19th century. In some areas copper companies were veritable fiefdoms that exercised undue control over political and legal machinery.

Copper mining was mostly done in open pits rather than underground, but the work was still arduous and dangerous, with landslides, accidents with explosives, inhalation of dust, and other such factors contributing to many early deaths. The earliest pits were opened by individual entrepreneurs. Within several decades after the Civil War, however, four major corporations controlled most of the copper mining done in the United States: The Calumet and Hecla Mining Company controlled most pits in Michigan, the Anaconda Copper Company was centered in Montana, the Kennecott Corporation ruled over Utah mines, and Phelps Dodge owned many of the mines in Arizona and New Mexico. Each company experienced numerous clashes with its laborers.

Many Cornish immigrants settled in company towns in and around Calumet, Michigan, though they complained bitterly of low wages and of company paternalism. Calumet and Hecla (C & H) offered more **fringe benefits** than most copper firms and even operated a hospital for employees, but the company broached no challenges to its authority and intruded into workers' lives off the job. In July 1913, the Western Federation of Miners (WFM) tried to organize Michigan copper miners. At issue were demands for union recognition, an **eight-hour** workday, a $3 per day minimum wage, and an end to one-armed jackhammers associated with rising industrial accident rates. C & H agreed to an eight-hour day but refused all other demands. When workers walked off the job, **scabs** were brought in and the National Guard was deployed to keep the mines open. The WFM was nearly broke by the time the strike broke out, and was able to exercise little control over rank-and-file workers. Petty violence and hooliganism were commonplace in the region, with strikers, **agent provocateurs**, and scabs all guilty of provocation. On December 24, 1913, a WFM Christmas party for strikers and their families in Calumet's Italian Hall ended in tragedy when someone cried, "Fire!"; 74 people were crushed to death while attempting to flee the building. The WFM blamed the incident on a local vigilante group, but no culpability was ever proved. The tragedy revitalized the strike, but the WFM ran out of money in April 1914 and called off the strike. Michigan copper mine conditions did get somewhat better in the years to come, but the region's miners did not win **collective bargaining** rights until 1939. Strikes also rocked the area in 1943 and again in 1969, at which time most of the mines closed. The last copper mine in Michigan closed in 1995.

Anaconda Copper—then known as the Amalgamated Copper Mining Company— was successively owned by two of the richest families in American history, the Rothschilds and the Rockefellers. John D. Rockefeller, Jr., proved no more merciful with copper miners than he had during the **Colorado labor wars** when his interests battled against coal miners. Copper and timber interests controlled Montana's economy in the early 20th century, with copper interests centered around Butte, one of the nation's wealthiest cities courtesy of its copper output. Butte was not, however, a company town. Indeed, prior to World War I, it had a **socialist** government and a union hiring hall. It was also a union town, but one riven by conflict between labor organizations. The WFM was the dominant union in the area and had been known for its past militancy. Although the WFM had helped found the **Industrial Workers of the World** (IWW) in 1905, it quit the organization in 1907 in a factional dispute and became affiliated with the **American Federation of Labor** (AFL) in 1911. By 1914, however, the WFM was losing money and membership due to a downturn in industry. A name change to the International Union of Mine, Mill, and Smelter Workers—popularly known as "Mine Mill"—did little to revive fortunes.

In Montana, Anaconda was determined to break miners' control over local affairs. It steadfastly resisted efforts of the IWW to organize copper miners and often enjoyed the assistance of Mine Mill in doing so. Anaconda also exploited the United States' April 1917 entry into World War I by labeling the antiwar IWW as unpatriotic. Nonetheless, the IWW made headway in the region. In June 1917, miners walked off their jobs in the Butte area after a disastrous fire in the Speculator Mine. In that event, an insulated cable frayed and a supervisor's helmet flame ignited the paper covering the cable, sending flames into the pit and asphyxiating 168 miners in the worst single mining accident in U.S. history. The IWW sent veteran organizer Frank Little to area to assist the strikers. On August 1, vigilantes broke into his hotel room, and abducted, tortured, and murdered Little. His murder was never solved.

The IWW was also on the losing end of a 1920 strike against Anaconda. A strike against Butte mines began on April 19 and soon closed all the pits. On April 21, mine guards deputized by a local sheriff opened fire on **pickets** outside the Neversweat Mine, killing one miner and wounding 16 others. No culpability was ever established for what was dubbed the "Anaconda Road Massacre." The IWW called off the strike three weeks later, by which time the postwar **Red Scare** was in full force and the IWW was in no position to rebuild its strength.

It was not until the passage of the **National Labor Relations Act** (NLRA) that Butte miners rebuilt their unions, and it took a 1934 Mine Mill strike by more than 5,000 miners to do so. Mine Mill had, by then, quit the AFL and was again a radical union, with close ties to the Communist Party. The NLRA proved successful in curtailing much of the blatant violence used against workers seeking to organize, but Anaconda hardly became a model of peaceful industrial relations. It diversified its holdings to Chile and endured labor strife there. (It was also implicated in the 1973 overthrow of Chilean President Salvador Allende.) Anaconda endured numerous strikes after 1934, including ones in 1954, 1959, and 1971. By the 1970s, however, most of the company's North American mines were played out. Anaconda has been sold several times and is now part of BP. It is also liable for cleanup of numerous polluted sites.

A famed folk song blames Utah "copper bosses" for framing IWW songwriter **Joe Hill** for a murder that led to his 1915 execution. There is little evidence to support this contention, but plenty to connect Utah copper interests to a systematic effort to purge the IWW from hard-rock regions. Kennecott Copper, a Guggenheim family interest, dominated Utah's copper mines. In 1912, the WFM tried to organize miners, but failed to do so in the wake of lost strikes that were broken in part by the importation of Mexican scab labor. It would officially organize the region as Mine Mill in 1938. Utah proved resistant to unionization for several reasons. First, Kennecott and other firms constructed company towns that were more pleasant than most and considerably more posh than surrounding towns. Second, the firms promoted a form of benevolent paternalism that included active promotion of Latino culture. Third, and most important of all, the companies made an unwavering decision to offer no quarter to the IWW. Strikes were frequent in Utah, but victories were not. By the 1920s, the IWW was driven from the area. Kennecott recognized unions after passage of the NLRA, but many **contracts** came only after bitter strikes. Few of these labor actions, other than a large 1971 strike, garnered much national attention and most were relatively less violent than copper strikes elsewhere, though violence did occur at Kennecott's mines in Chile and Peru.

Kennecott did not escape national notoriety in 1954, when the controversial film *Salt of the Earth* was released. It is said to be the only film officially **blacklisted** and was widely denounced by detractors as a work of **communist** propaganda. The film was made by industry artists already on the Hollywood blacklist, and many of its actors were Mine Mill members and families who had taken part in the actual 1951 strike on which the fictional film was based. Copper (and ancillary zinc) mines in Arizona and New Mexico were less concentrated than those elsewhere; hence single-company dominance was less common in these regions. As a consequence, the 1951 conflict involved both Kennecott and Phelps Dodge. It also came at a time in which a nationwide copper strike was in force.

Salt of the Earth made mockery of company town benevolence, especially in terms of the policy toward Latinos. As in the film, strikers in the Bayard-Hanover, New Mexico, area returned to work when President Harry Truman issued a Taft-Hartley **injunction**. Kennecott workers won a $0.14 per hour raise. The **Taft- Hartley Act** was also invoked in 1953 against Mine Mill strike organizer Clifford Jencks, who gave writers the ideas that became *Salt of the Earth*. Jencks was charged with concealing Communist Party membership when he signed a 1950 Taft-Hartley loyalty oath. Jencks was convicted twice, the second time after his chief accuser admitted he had lied. The conviction was overturned in a famed 1957 Supreme Court decision, *Jencks v. the United States*, in which the Court also ruled that prosecutors had to provide verbatim testimony against a defendant, and could do so only *after* testimony under oath. The *Jencks* case also confirmed what copper unions had long claimed to be the case—that labor spies such as **Pinkerton** detectives had long infiltrated unions and provided secret evidence that was withheld during investigations.

The Phelps Dodge Company has been among the more aggressive anti-union firms in the copper industry. It, too, launched anti-IWW campaigns. In 1917, IWW miners won a short strike in Prescott, Arizona, which led Mine Mill workers in nearby Jerome to issue demands of their own. The IWW agreed to help in this effort, and it proved more effective than cautious Mine Mill. Phelps Dodge responded with a virtual declaration of war on the IWW. Company President Walter Douglas ordered all IWW members to be removed from Jerome. With the help of vigilantes, approximately 100 men were kidnapped, placed on trains, and shipped to Needles, California. This event set the stage for a larger-scale deportation in Bisbee, Arizona, where 2,200 vigilantes rounded up around 2,000 strikers and marched them several miles to a holding area, where they were given a choice of renouncing the IWW or being deported. A total of 1,286 individuals were loaded into 23 railroad box cars—some filled with manure and none with food or water—and shipped to the desert town of Hermanas, New Mexico, where they were thrown out after a 15-hour train ride in 90-degree heat. In the interim, Phelps Dodge took over telegraph offices to prevent news of its actions from leaking and staffed the town with vigilantes. Those who ventured back to Bisbee were turned aside and threatened with death if they returned.

The Bisbee outrage actually met with positive public approval at the height of IWW hysteria, including acclaim from ex-President Theodore Roosevelt. President Wilson, however, was less amused; in 1918, 21 indictments were issued against Phelps Dodge officials. In 1920, the charges were dismissed when the Supreme Court ruled that the Bisbee action was a state matter over which the federal government had no jurisdiction. Arizona did not press the matter, though a few private lawsuits were settled. Most historians now see Bisbee as the template for the Red Scare that broke out in earnest in 1919.

The **Phelps Dodge strike** of 1983 is also infamous in labor history, and the company is generally viewed in negative terms by unions. A recent study also identified it as among the top two dozen polluters in the United States. It ceased operations in 2007, when it was purchased by Phoenix-based Freeport-McMoRan.

Suggested Reading

Melvyn Dubofsky, *We Shall Be All: A History of the IWW*, 1969; Larry Lankton, *Cradle to Grave: Life, Work, and Death at the Lake Superior Copper Mines*, 1993; Laurie Mercier, *Anaconda: Labor, Community, and Culture in Montana's Smelter City*, 2004; Philip F. Notarianni, "Copper Mining," *Utah History Encyclopedia*, http://www.media.utah.edu/ UHE/c/COPPERMINE.html, accessed July 21, 2010.

CORPORATE CAMPAIGN

A corporate campaign is an attempt to force employers to bargain with their workers by applying pressure across the corporate structure rather than concentrating solely on an individual workplace. In traditional disputes and **strikes**, most union activity takes place at the site of the alleged **grievance**, and the bulk of negotiations take place between local management and union officials. Corporate campaigns extend the battle lines and may include such actions as protesting at stockholder meetings, waging public-relations campaigns against companies, calling attention to the holdings and activities of corporate officials, applying pressure to a corporation's subsidiary holdings, filing multiple lawsuits, threatening to withdraw union funds from banks that lend money to a corporation, and blowing the whistle on unpopular or illegal corporate behaviors that are generally hidden from view. The goal is to isolate a company by bringing pressure to bear from many sources that is so expensive and/or damaging to the corporate image that management is forced to the bargaining table.

Corporate campaigns are largely the brainchild of Ray Rogers, who heads Corporate Campaign, Inc. (CCI), in New York City, although many of its tactics evoke those pioneered by the **United Farm Workers of America**. Rogers believed that traditional union strategies no longer worked in the latter half of the 20th century because local shops were seldom owned locally. Mergers, **globalization**, **deregulation**, and **runaway** shops rendered old tactics antiquated. Unions no longer faced local firms with limited resources, but rather multinational companies with stuffed coffers. Rogers first applied a corporate campaign against J. P. Stevens, a southern textile manufacturer that had resisted unionization efforts by the Textile Workers Union of America since 1963, and was infamous for its practices of **blacklisting**, harassing organizers, and threatening employees. Stevens continued its aggressive anti-union campaign even after 1976, when it was cited for more than 1,200 violations of the **National Labor Relations Act**. Rogers and CCI began to bypass Stevens management. Instead, additional lawsuits were filed against the firm, a national consumer **boycott** of Farah—a Stevens line of menswear—was launched, protesters picketed stockholders, and various unions threatened to remove their considerable funds from a bank that provided Stevens's major credit line. The CCI also proved adroit at building alliances against Stevens, arraying local churches against the firm and organizing a consumer boycott of Avon products, as its chair was a Stevens board member. Stevens finally settled with the union in 1983.

The overall record of corporate campaigns has been mixed. In the 1980s, corporate campaigns helped American Airlines flight attendants, Boston hotel workers, and Watsonville (California) cannery workers. There have been equally dramatic failures, however—most notably those involving Phelps Dodge workers in 1983, and Hormel workers in Austin, Minnesota, whose 1985–1887 corporate campaign was undermined by the parent **United Food and Commercial Workers** (UFCW) union. A 1987 corporate campaign against International Paper also failed. Perhaps the most spectacular recent victory occurred during the 1992 **Ravenswood lockout**, when a corporate campaign succeeded in building multinational alliances and linking financier Marc Rich, an international fugitive from justice living in Switzerland, to the dispute in faraway West Virginia. A 1993 corporate campaign against Food Lion ended in a mixed decision that delivered back pay to workers, but left the UFCW unable to organize the non-union chain.

The future of corporate campaigns is uncertain. They seem to some observers to be an innovative alternative to increasingly outmoded tactics from the past and to more realistically address the complex structure of global business. The overall win rate is much higher for unions using corporate campaigns versus traditional strikes. Such measures are, however, expensive and time-consuming. Some ongoing corporate campaigns are more than two decades old, which raises questions about whether the costs of such a strategy can ever be recouped. Some critics argue that corporate campaigns are little more than wars of attrition that pit the financial resources of richer unions against those of deep-pocketed corporations, and are of little use for unions without deep treasuries. Moreover, conservative union leaders have been reluctant to embrace CCI methods, while some progressives believe that some corporate campaigns alone are too inflexible and do not pay enough attention to local concerns and issues. Most strategists favor using corporate campaigns in combination with community organizing, traditional bargaining methods, and **solidarity** building, as was done at Ravenswood. Corporate campaign defenders concede the latter charge and counter that local organizing is a key element of a successful corporate campaign. As of 2010, there were numerous ongoing corporate campaigns. A 1996 attempt by conservatives to outlaw corporate campaigns failed, but this item remains on the agenda of anti-union politicians.

Suggested Reading

Corporate Campaign, Inc., http://www.corporatecampaign.org/, accessed July 20, 2010; Tom Juravich and Kate Bronfenbrenner, *Ravenswood*, 1999; Jarol Manheim, *The Death of a Thousand Cuts: Corporate Campaigns and the Attack on the Corporation*, 2000; Kim Moody, *An Injury to All*, 1989.

COST-OF-LIVING ADJUSTMENT

A cost-of-living adjustment (COLA)—sometimes (inaccurately) called a cost of living allowance—is a negotiated contract clause that automatically adjusts one's **wages** or pension to compensate for inflation. It is generally linked to the cost of living—that is, the amount of money needed to purchase the goods and services necessary to maintain a certain standard of living.

It has long been known that raw economic figures by themselves can be deceptive. For example, a $0.10 loaf of bread sold in 1900 would need to sell for $2.54 in 2009 just to compensate for inflation. In 1919, the **Bureau of Labor Statistics**, by then a division of the **Department of Labor**, began collecting statistics to show the effect of inflation on maintaining an individual's standard of living. One measure, the consumer price index (CPI), is based on monthly prices for a "basket" of various goods and services, including food, shelter, transportation, fuel, utilities, household furnishings, medical care, entertainment, and personal care. The CPI is a controversial instrument that has been criticized for both overestimating and underestimating inflation, but it remains the most commonly used method of determining its effects.

Cost-of-living adjustments were originally created by negotiators of labor **contracts** as a way of fostering industrial peace. It was hoped that automatic adjustments to wages and salaries during the life of a contract would reduce tensions involved in negotiating new deals. This approach was popularized by the post-World War II contracts between the **United Auto Workers of America** (UAW) and General Motors. UAW negotiations during the 1930s had been contentious and difficult, but UAW officials wanted to ensure that the gains it negotiated in longer contracts after World War II were not eviscerated by inflation. Many UAW contracts contained escalator clauses that automatically raised wages and salaries without opening up the contract for further negotiations.

COLAs were commonplace in union contracts from the late 1940s into the early 1970s. During this period many unions also secured COLAs for pensioners. With the decline of **blue-collar** unions in the past four decades, however, COLAs have become less common and many companies have sought to revisit their pension commitments. In some cases, companies have canceled pensions altogether. In recent years, federal employees and members of the civil service are those most likely to have COLA provisions in their contracts. COLAs are also a standard feature in the **Social Security** system, though these adjustments are calculated in a different way and have not kept pace with inflation.

The cost-of-living-adjustments in place in the U.S. military and present as standard negotiated items in many professions are a different type of COLA. These regional standard-of-living measures account for the relative differences in what a person needs to maintain a certain lifestyle. A person living in New York City, for instance, would require a much higher salary than an individual living in the suburban Midwest to sustain the same standard of living. This type of COLA, except in the case of the military, is usually negotiated individually.

Not all labor activists believe that COLAs were a wise choice for unions. Critics claim that a narrow focus on money was a retreat from the **social unionism** that led to union growth in the 1930s.

Suggested Reading

Tammy Flanagan, "COLA Wars," http://www.govexec.com/dailyfed/0906/090806rp.htm, accessed July 20, 2010; Steve Greenhut, *Plunder! How Public Employee Unions Are Raiding Treasuries, Controlling Our Lives, and Bankrupting the Nation*, 2009; Thomas Stapleford, *The Cost of Living in America*, 2009.

COUNTERCULTURE AND LABOR

The relationship between labor unions and the rising counterculture of the 1960s and 1970s is analogous to the relationship between unions and the **civil rights movement** in that it often vacillated between fruitful and antagonistic. In the long run, brushes with the counterculture diversified organized labor in much needed ways.

Labor groups with a progressive past were mostly among the first to seek accommodation. Students for a Democratic Society (SDS), for instance, emerged in part from an old **socialist** organization, the League for Industrial Democracy, and it got seed money from the **United Auto Workers of America** (UAW) union, which also gave it use of the union's retreat where the Port Huron Statement was drafted. Unions—including the UAW, the **United Packinghouse Workers**, and the **American Federation of State, County, and Municipal Employees** (AFSCME)— often contributed to SDS Economic and Research Action Projects (ERAP) set up in inner cities to organize urban dwellers to battle racism and poverty. Student radicals, in turn, were important in assisting unions such as the **United Farm Workers of America** in their battles for recognition. Students were also found on the **picket lines** of numerous union **strikes**, and many counterculture figures adopted **blue-collar** garb as a symbol of **solidarity** with labor unions.

There were, however, built-in tensions between student and labor groups. Organized labor represented the Old Left at a time in which student thinkers were fashioning a New Left that jettisoned what it saw as needless baggage from the past. Part of that baggage was fear of **communism**, which the New Left rejected and which was a bad fit with the **Cold War unionism** that had dominated the **American Federation of Labor-Congress of Industrial Organizations** (AFL-CIO) since its 1955 merger. Although the subject was politely avoided, the bureaucratic **business unionism** practices of the AFL-CIO were also despised by New Left radicals, many of whom privately complained of the endless deliberations that ensued whenever unions were approached for support.

The counterculture and organized labor frequently clashed over two major issues: black nationalism and the Vietnam War. In each case AFL-CIO President **George Meany** championed those within the labor movement who thought the New Left too radical, disapproved of countercultural lifestyles, and saw opposition to the Vietnam War as disloyal. Although many unions were more in accord with the New Left than with Meany and conservative AFL-CIO affiliates, opposition from on high fueled those within the New Left who argued that liberalism was the enemy of progressive change—a charge that stung the UAW's **Walter Reuther**. Overall, much of organized labor continued to support the Vietnam War long after public opinion had shifted on the issue and New Left energy was thrown into the antiwar movement. Meany—furious over antiwar protests at the AFL-CIO's 1965 convention—was contemptuous of unions allied with the antiwar group SANE and associated the Labor Leadership Assembly for Peace (LLAP) with labor's left fringe.

LLAP was far more than a fringe group, however; its November 1967 founding meeting attracted 523 labor leaders. What it really represented was how countercultural causes further bifurcated the labor movement. Young people moving into the workforce also hastened this division. Union membership peaked at 39 percent of the private workforce in 1958, but its share was still 32 percent 10 years later. Unions did not, however, represent the same workers. Younger workers rejected the factory discipline of the **assembly line** and spoke of the deep alienation they felt in their work lives. Conditioned directly or indirectly by countercultural values, they also proved prone to rank-and-file rebellion against their own unions, tendencies made manifest in rising levels of **wildcat strikes**. Moreover, they vexed unions with their tendency to take matters into their own hands through acts of **sabotage**, a problem among **Lordstown** autoworkers, or they joined radical groups such as the **Dodge Revolutionary Union Movement**. Women infused with the spirit of new feminist movements also challenged entrenched patterns of discrimination.

The split between old and new came to a head in several incidents, including the **hard hat riots** in which union construction workers attacked antiwar protesters. It also factored into the decision of the UAW to quit the AFL-CIO, which cited the organization's poor civil rights record and its continuing support for the Vietnam War as among its reasons for leaving. By 1970–1971, commentators routinely spoke of blue-collar conservatism and a gathering backlash against countercultural values.

In retrospect, much of that analysis was flawed. Observers often saw emergent trends in what were, in fact, long-time splits within organized labor. They also ignored the way in which the counterculture transformed aspects of the labor movement. Unions such as the **American Federation of Teachers**, AFSCME, the **International Union of Electrical, Radio, and Machine Workers of America**, the International Longshoremen, and the Mine and Mill workers were infused with new bursts of energy courtesy of the New Left. When union labor began its precipitous decline in the late 1970s, the trend occurred not because former countercultural figures had abandoned the labor movement, but rather because changes in political and economic realities had taken place that old-style unions were slow to grasp.

The legacy of the counterculture can be seen in the fact that organized labor is today among the most diverse sectors of American society and generally supports agendas that are to the left of prevailing political winds. Union movements actively recruit, train, and promote women and people of color and have been at the fore of causes such as gay rights, **comparable worth**, gender equity, and anti-globalization. Several New Left figures, including Andrew Stern of the **Service**

Employees International Union, are now labor leaders. The AFL-CIO's "New Voices" movement that transformed how it has done business since 1994 is easily traceable to countercultural influences.

Suggested Reading

Jeffrey Coker, *Confronting American Labor: The New Left Dilemma*, 2002; Peter Levy, *The New Left and Labor in the 1960s*, 1994; Jo-Ann Mort, *Not Your Father's Union Movement: Inside the AFL-CIO*, 1998.

COWBOYS

Cowboys are herders and livestock specialists who assist ranchers and herd owners. The term derives from *vaca*, the Spanish word for "cow," and from the fact that the profession has traditionally been dominated by males. As understood in North America, cowboys of all sorts took inspiration from Mexican *vaqueros*, who drove range animals from horseback.

The image of American cowboys as models of rugged individualism and self-reliance is steeped in romance and generally bears little resemblance to reality. Although cowboys were originally independent herd owners, by the mid-19th century most cowboys were wage-earners and casual and seasonal laborers. Quite a few did not even negotiate their own **wages**; they were recruited by foremen who divvied out shares from contracts they signed with herd owners. A substantial number of 19th-century cowboys—more than one-third by most reckonings—were African Americans, Mexicans, or Native Americans. As individuals who made up the secondary labor force, these groups were able to obtain employment as cowboys because it was a notoriously unpleasant occupation that involved long hours, very low pay, and danger in the form of everything from stampedes, bad weather, snakebites, horse accidents, and attacks from hostile Native tribes. Moreover, the long cattle drives that later became a staple of imaginative films and television programs over-emphasize what was a very short period of American economic history, roughly a 20-year period from 1866 to the mid-1880s.

The heyday of cowboys was occasioned by the development of the American West after the **Civil War**. Although the United States expanded its territory dramatically in the early-19th century, courtesy of the Louisiana Purchase and lands ceded after the Mexican War, much of the American West was sparsely developed and Native American populations were small. The discovery of gold in California in 1848 led to rapid population growth on the West Coast, but much of the trans-Mississippi region east of the Sierra Nevada Mountains remained frontier insofar as Euro-Americans were concerned. Denver's population, for example, did not reach 5,000 citizens until 1870, a year in which Dallas and Phoenix would have been sparsely inhabited backwaters.

The 1862 Homestead Act opened vast swaths of Kansas and Nebraska to settlement, but it was the **Industrial Revolution** and the expansion of railroads that created the brief cowboy heyday. Industrial expansion was accompanied by urbanization and by large numbers of immigrants coming to the United States seeking work. A demand for food, especially beef, accompanied the growth of cities.

Open grasslands in the trans-Mississippi West were used to graze and fatten cattle. In some areas, especially in Texas, herds of unclaimed wild cattle could be rounded up and sold. Cattle drives developed for the simple reason that most American railroads terminated near the Mississippi River. The first transcontinental railroad was not completed until 1869. Five others would follow in the next forty years, but even before then a spider-web pattern of branch lines connected to major trunk lines. The cowboy era mostly occupied the interim period between the end of the Civil War and the full articulation of the rail system. During this period it was necessary to fatten cattle on grazing lands, round them up, and then drive them to the nearest railhead for shipment to major stockyard centers such as Chicago, Kansas City, and Omaha.

Profits were high for cattle owners feeding hungry eastern and midwestern city dwellers. By 1870, meatpackers often paid as much as $40 per head for animals that sold for one-tenth of that amount in Texas. Regular trails developed—so chosen because they could provide needed water and pasturage—in which cowboys would move cattle to railroad stock pens for shipment to the slaughterhouses. Railhead towns such as Wichita, Dodge City, and Abilene, Kansas, and San Antonio, Fort Worth, and El Paso, Texas, became veritable boom towns because of the cattle drives. El Paso, for example, grew from a remote outpost to a town of more than 10,000 in the decade between 1880 and 1890, and the populations of Dallas and Fort Worth tripled.

Ultimately, the cowboy system proved untenable. First, cattle drives were long—often 1,000 miles or more, with herds that averaged around 3,000 head seldom traveling more than 25 miles per day. During the roughly 6-week journey, cattle lost weight, which reduced profits for owners. As railroads expanded, it simply made more sense to run branch lines closer to where livestock grazed. Railroads themselves soon became large landowners by either purchasing acreage along their lines or receiving it in the form of grants. By the late 1870s, railroads wielded corporate power in rural America, where they operated branch lines, built grain elevators, or rented stock pens that determined the value of produce and livestock far more than grazing conditions or the skills of farmers, ranchers, and cowboys. The invention of barbed wire—patented by Joseph Glidden in 1874—also spelled doom for cattle drives. For a time there was tension between free-range herders and settled ranchers in the trans-Mississippi West, but the ideology of private property ultimately prevailed. In 1890, the Census Bureau declared that there was no more unclaimed land in the continental United States and that the frontier was "closed." Established ranches and farms soon dominated the region. Ranchers still needed the assistance of cowboys and herdsmen, but the employee/employer relationship in rural America was analogous to those of urban/industrial relations—that is, "cowboys" were really just agrarian wage-earners. By the time Buffalo Bill's Wild West Show began touring in 1873, cowboy life was already waning in many areas.

The romantic image of American cowboys was partly the product of tales collected by 20th-century folklorists—the cowboy songs published by John Lomax in 1910 were very influential—as well as popular-culture products such as the novels of Zane Grey (1872–1939), the musical recordings of Gene Autry (1907–1964), and the movies of John Ford (1894–1973). The first known American rodeo took place in 1872, but the articulation of an established circuit in the early 20th century also served to romanticize cowboys. During the **Cold War**, cowboy imagery enjoyed resurgence in popular film and on television, its ideological associations with American individualism and democracy standing as a counterpoint to collectivist Soviet authoritarianism.

Suggested Reading

Terry L. Anderson and Peter Hill, *The Not So Wild, Wild West: Property Rights on the Frontier*, 2003; William Cronon, Miles Jay, and George Jay, eds., *Under an Open Sky: Rethinking America's Western Past*, 1994; David Dary, *Cowboy Culture: A Saga of Five Centuries*, 1989; Jon Nicholson, *Cowboys: A Vanishing World*, 2001.

COXEY'S ARMY

Coxey's Army was a comic-dramatic 1894 march of unemployed citizens on Washington, D.C. According to some sources, it was the first major orchestrated demonstration inside the District of Columbia and the template for future protests in the nation's capitol.

Jacob Coxey vividly dramatized the plight of the unemployed in the United States by leading a march on Washington, known as Coxey's Army, to demand relief during the depression of the 1890s. (Library of Congress)

The event is named for Jacob Sechler Coxey, Sr. (1854–1951), an offbeat **socialist** politician from Massillon, Ohio. Coxey was also involved in the Populist Party and was such a devotee of monetary reform that he named one of his sons Legal Tender. Coxey's plan was to amass vast industrial armies in various parts of the country and generate publicity that would force Congress and President Grover Cleveland to fund public-works relief projects to assist the country's unemployed. Coxey also took up the Populist demand for **greenbacks** and free silver by calling upon the government to print more money to stimulate the economy. The idea of marching the industrial armies across the land and converging at the capitol came from Carl Browne, an eccentric California politician who agreed with many of Coxey's economic ideas. Coxey and Browne hoped to rendezvous an army of more than 400,000 on **May Day**, 1894.

What in retrospect seems a harebrained scheme was born out of desperation. In U.S. economic history, the Panic of 1893 ranks second in severity only to the Great Depression of 1929–1941. By 1894, the unemployment rate in the United States stood at nearly 20 percent. The flamboyant Browne proved good at public relations, and groups from as far away as Los Angeles and Seattle began trekking toward Washington, D.C. In all, eight armies massed, each headed by a "general." Coxey left Massillon at the head of approximately 100 men and dubbed his group the "Commonweal of Christ." The entire affair was ill conceived from the start. There was no central coordination of efforts, and each army was left to its own devices on how to get to Washington. Some tramped their way along the rail lines or rafted down dangerous rivers, others commandeered wagons and horses, and one group actually stole a locomotive. Neither Coxey nor Browne fit the profile of the men whom they led. Coxey's zeal was unquestionable, but he was a man of substantial means. Browne, who dressed as Buffalo Bill for the march, was a first-rate eccentric who had failed at numerous business ventures and was thought by many to be unstable. Neither he nor Coxey bivouacked with their armies; rather, the pair stayed in rooming houses and hotels en route.

The march generated great publicity and inspired acts of charity, such as a donation of five tons of food by Pennsylvanians, but it sparked more curiosity than commitment. Only Coxey's Army reached Washington intact, and the actual massing was closer to 500 rather than 400,000. On May 1, 1894, Coxey and Browne entered the city, but Coxey was dragged away before he could speak, and mounted police clubbed demonstrators. Coxey was arrested for trespassing on the Capitol lawn, and by May 2, police had chased most of his army out of the District of Columbia.

As a reform movement, Coxey's Army was an utter failure. The heavy-handed manner in which was dispatched did, however, focus attention on the economic ills plaguing American society. In the same year the **Pullman boycott and strike** met with similar iron-fisted reactions that soured industrial workers on the Democratic Party, stimulated interest in farmer-labor alliances, and focused public attention on the plight of the unemployed. The fact that the depression lingered into 1897 and that the government approached industrialist J. P. Morgan for stimulus money also raised questions about corporate power in America. Many historians place Coxey's Army among the crises of the 1890s that inspired **Progressive Era** reforms from 1901 to 1914. A few also link Coxey's monetary ideas to the passage of the **Social Security Act**. The thrice-married Coxey remained a political maverick, running for political office 17 times between 1894 and 1942, but managing to win just a single term as Massillon's mayor.

Suggested Reading

Lyman T. Sargent, *Extremism in America*, 1995; Udo Sautter, *Three Cheers for the Unemployed: Government and Unemployment before the New Deal*, 1991; Carlos Schwantes, *Coxey's Army: An American Odyssey*, 1985.

CRAFT UNIONISM

Craft unionism is the organizational principle holding that **solidarity** is best maintained in an organization of one's peers within a given trade. The practice was born in an age of **artisan** labor—a form of labor that is, by nature, exclusive to members of a particular craft. Its supporters argue that only peers can make intelligent decisions about proper **wage** rates and conditions within an occupation, whereas past and present critics argue that craft unions encourage parochial thinking that retards the development of **class consciousness** and is inattentive to how work tasks are actually assigned. Historically, craft unions as a whole have tended to be more moderate and suspicious of radical theories, though some trades have also been hotbeds of radicalism.

The trade union movement in the United States emerged from the breakup of work patterns established during the **Colonial** era that made sharp distinctions between **master craftsmen**, **journeymen**, and **apprentices**. Because most goods were bespoken, craft labor was the norm and all nonfarm laborers generally maintained relations akin to those in medieval guilds. The emergence of the factory system and the advent of the 19th-century **Industrial Revolution** severed the connection between masters and journeymen, with the latter evolving their associations into trade unions, though craft ideals remained dominant. Craft-based trade unions emerged in the industrial cities of the East, though even those strong enough to form national organizations, such as the iron makers union (Sons of Vulcan), were so fragile that their fortunes waxed and waned according to nationwide economic conditions. Prior to the **Civil War**, must unions and factories remained small concerns. Only shoes and textiles presaged the enormous industrial expansion of the post-Civil War era.

Modern craft unions and their alternatives both took shape after the Civil War. By the 1870s, many crafts had national and international unions. Craft workers generally owned their own tools and possessed specialized knowledge and skills that were essential to expanding industry, but those monopolies did not last long. This history of the American factory system is one in which technological change deskilled the workforce and broke down production into various subtasks. Many of the early post-Civil War craft unions, such as the Knights of St. Crispin (shoemakers) and the Cigar Makers International Union, fought rearguard actions that sought to preserve traditional craft privileges from technological obsolescence. Most were unsuccessful. The **Knights of Labor** (KOL) was formed in 1869 from the remains of a failed tailor's union and explicitly rejected craft unionism as an outmoded model. The KOL's own inchoate brand of unionism was a hodgepodge of proto-**industrial unionism**, **social unionism**, mystical idealism, political activism, and selective craft unionism, but its critique of craft unionism struck many as sensible, especially leftist groups such as **socialists**, **communists**, and **anarchists**, who placed class identity above craft identity.

Even so, craft union ideals prevailed among many American workers. In 1881, the Federation of Organized Trade and Labor Unions (FOTLU) attempted to organize craft unions into a **labor federation**. The FOTLU foundered, but it provided the inspiration for the 1886 creation of the **American Federation of Labor** (AFL). Unlike the KOL, which espoused a broad reform agenda, idealism, and political involvement, the AFL confined itself to "pure and simple" issues of wages, hours, and working conditions. It was also the first labor federation to accept the permanence of **capitalism**, though it insisted that labor's share of capitalist wealth had to be vigorously defended by **strikes**—which the KOL abhorred—when necessary. Many on the political left decried the AFL's exclusivity and accused it of betraying class solidarity, but when the AFL largely supplanted the KOL by the 1890s, its defenders hailed AFL policy and craft unionism as "prudential" unionism.

Craft unionism has been inaccurately dismissed as "conservative" based on the proclivities of a few unions such as the **Brotherhood of Locomotive Engineers** and the **United Brotherhood of Carpenters and Joiners** (UBC). Numerous craft unions have a long history of activism, including the **United Mine Workers of America** (UMWA), and the UBC's founder, Peter J. McGuire, was a socialist. It was true, however, that craft unions overall tended to exclude vast sections of the American workforce—not just the unskilled, but also most women, recent immigrants, and **minority labor**. It is also generally the case that craft unions were less interested in reforms not directly tied to **pure and simple union** objectives. The **Industrial Workers of the World** (IWW) often ridiculed the AFL as the "American Separation of Labor" and an enemy to class solidarity. The spread of mass-production techniques proved craft unionism's biggest challenge, however. The **assembly line** rendered many "craft" designations absurd. In the automobile industry, for example, those workers installing wiring were placed in an electricians' union and those who simply snapped windshields into place became "glassmakers." To a large degree, the AFL simply ignored noncraft workers.

In the 1930s, the **Congress of Industrial Organizations** (CIO) rekindled the IWW's call for industrial unionism, a drive reinforced both by industrial reality and the fact that several important unions, including the UMWA, were already operating according to those principles. When the CIO captured the bulk of workers in heavy industries such as automotives, meatpacking, mining, rubber, steel, and textiles, the AFL was forced to reconsider the outmoded way in which it defined craft.

The AFL and CIO merged in 1955, with the latter often complaining that the former still did not grasp fully the importance of industrial unionism, but ensuing technological and economic changes took their toll and further eroded the vitality of craft unionism. Outside of a handful of trades such as engineering and printing, craft designations in most **blue-collar** fields typically evoke heritage or mark rites of passage for union-run apprenticeship programs. Those with the greatest levels of craft identity today are found in white-collar professions such as teaching, law, medicine, and journalism, and many of those workers are not organized. The most successful craft unions today are those found in the entertainment industry and in professional sports, such as the **Screen Actors Guild** and the **Major League Baseball Players Association**.

Suggested Reading

Julie Green, *Pure and Simple Politics: The American Federation of Labor and Political Activism, 1881–1917*, 2006; Philip S. Foner, *History of the American Labor Movement in the United States*, 10 volumes, 1947–1994; Bruce Laurie, *Artisans into Workers*, 1997.

CRIPPLE CREEK STRIKE OF 1894. *See* Colorado Labor Wars.

D

DAVIS-BACON ACT

The Davis-Bacon Act is a federal law passed that requires contractors working on any federally funded construction projects of more than $2,000 to pay local **prevailing wages** to their workers. It is named for the two Republicans who sponsored the bill, Senator James Davis (Pennsylvania) and Representative Robert Bacon (New York). The Davis-Bacon Act has been a frequent target for conservatives in the past several decades, but thus far efforts to repeal it have been rebuffed. To both its original sponsors and current supporters of the law, the Davis-Bacon Act prevents the importation of out-of-state workers or third-party contractors who would undermine **wages** within an area. It is not, as critics sometimes charge, a bill that requires the hiring of union labor. It also applies only to projects that receive federal funding, though many states have their own prevailing wage laws.

Although numerous states had prevailing wage laws before the Davis-Bacon Act took effect, the current law took shape in 1927. The construction industry had declined in advance of the onset of the Great Depression and wages had been cut in many states. In 1927, an Alabama contractor won a bid to build a Veterans Bureau hospital on Long Island, New York. Congressman Bacon filed "A Bill to Require Contractors and Subcontractors Engaged on Public Works of the United States to Comply with State Laws Relating to Hours of Labor and Wages of Employees on State Public Works" to prevent Alabama workers—some of whom were African Americans—from migrating north with the contractor unless the contractor paid them wages comparable to those commanded by workers in the metropolitan New York City area. Bacon's original bill failed, but he filed 13 similar bills in the next four years, all modeled after his 1927 draft. A federal bill cosponsored with Senator James J. Davis was signed into law by President Herbert Hoover in 1931.

The Davis-Bacon Act proved very important during the early days of the Great Depression, when half of all money spent on construction in the United States went toward federal projects. Union labor, especially in larger cities, benefited from the bill because it prevented their wages from being undercut, but there is no requirement within the bill that unions receive any sort of preferential treatment. In fact, some unions complained that Davis-Bacon rates, which are generally determined by complex **Department of Labor** formulae, set minimal rates below what union workers received. African American contractors also complained that they were effectively shut out of bidding on many federal jobs because they lacked sufficient capital to guarantee Davis-Bacon rates. Over time, however, the bill has proved very popular among most construction workers. The National Association for Advancement of Colored People has come to be one of the most ardent supporters of the bill.

The Davis-Bacon Act has been amended three times. In 1935, protections were added to make certain that contractors did not win low bids by slashing wages. A 1964 revision allowed **fringe benefits** to be added to wage calculations, and a 1994 revision required that Head Start projects had to comply with the act. The Davis-Bacon Act has spawned numerous imitators, with many states and cities passing their own versions of the legislation to cover construction funded by state and local tax money.

The business community has sought to refine or repeal the law, often resorting to histrionic claims of how the Davis-Bacon Act stymies investment, causes taxes to rise, and rewards corrupt union labor. They have also sought to dodge the law by sponsoring state ballot initiatives that would repeal state prevailing wage laws. Most efforts have failed and, if ever passed, would certainly be tested in federal courts if a project involved federal money.

Certain provisions in the act allow for temporary suspension of its mandates. These have used, but only for short periods of time. President Franklin Roosevelt suspended the act for 3 weeks in 1934, President Richard Nixon suspended it for 28 days in 1971, and President George H. W. Bush tried to suspend it indefinitely in 1992, but President Bill Clinton immediately restored it upon taking office in 1993. A public outcry forced President George W. Bush to restore the Davis-Bacon Act after 6 weeks when he suspended it in the wake of Hurricane Katrina. Efforts of conservative Congressional members to repeal the bill failed in 1993, 1995, and 2004.

Suggested Reading

John Gould and George Bittlingmayer, *The Economics of the Davis-Bacon Act: An Analysis of Prevailing Wage Laws*, 1980; Armand Thieblot, Jr., *Prevailing Wage Legislation: The Davis-Bacon Act, "Little Davis-Bacon" Acts, the Walsh Healey Act, and the Service Contract Act*, 1986; "Wage Determinations Online.gov," http://www.wdol.gov/, accessed July 28, 2010.

DEADHEADING

In labor terms, deadheading refers to long-distance haulers who are not carrying freight or passengers on the return trip to their original destination. Deadheading is anathema to shippers, as they incur fuel costs in returning to base but derive no economic benefit from the trip.

The term's origin derives from a 19th-century practice of passengers traveling without a ticket, particularly preachers and politicians returning to their constituencies. It also referred to people occupying theater seats for which they were given free tickets as a way to make the "house" seem more impressive. It came into wider use in the railroad industry, where it came to mean locomotives pulling empty cars (or none at all). By the 1930s, it also passed into use to refer to taxicabs and trucks without passengers or cargo. By the late 20th century, deadheading was applied most often to the trucking industry, and it continues to be an important labor issue for truckers. Deadheading was common in the trucking industry prior to **deregulation** of the industry in the early 1980s. Union drivers, especially **Teamsters**, negotiated strict controls on the number of loads for which drivers were responsible, which meant they often hauled empty trucks back to the terminal—a practice deemed unproductive by shippers. Deregulation removed controls on freight delivery, which in turn led to consolidation of the trucking industry. Freight rates dropped, but so too did **wages**, union representation, and the overall number of employed drivers. Many trucking companies, particularly unionized companies with higher wages and **fringe benefit** structures, went out of business.

At a glance, an end to deadheading seems a logical and positive reform, but reality is a bit more complex. Consolidation in the trucking industry also led to an increase in tandem trailers, which have higher rates of serious accidents and whose overall weight strains infrastructure. Independent owner-operators have also become more vulnerable in an age of consolidation. A loaded truck consumes more fuel than an empty one, so many independent truckers are forced to accept return cargoes at rates that barely enable them to meet fuel costs, just to remain competitive. In the 21st century, the desire to avoid deadheading and acquire backhauls has forced many truckers to depend on cell phones, laptops, and the Internet to search for work. There are even websites devoted to finding backhauls.

Suggested Reading

Michael Agar, *Independents Declared: The Dilemmas of Independent Trucking*, 1986; "FreightFinder," http://www.freightfinder.com/, accessed July 28, 2010.

DEAD TIME

Dead time refers to lost time for which an employee is not responsible and for which he or she must be paid. For example, a delivery person might arrive at a location to find that an office is closed for lunch, or bricklayers might be idled as they await a delivery of more bricks. Dead time can be controversial when employers and employees disagree over why it exists, or if an employer refuses to pay workers for dead time. It may also involve disputes over the very nature of work.

One of the first industries to struggle over dead time was mining. For workers in underground pits, it sometimes took a long time to move miners from the mine's entrance to the seam being worked. The **United Mine Workers of America** (UMWA) argued that workers should be compensated for time spent in transit. In 1938, the Supreme Court agreed that not paying workers for dead time was a violation of the 1938 Wages and Hours Act. The ruling was controversial because it also forced companies to pay **overtime** premiums if the added transit time made the workday in excess of eight hours. Nonetheless, the UMWA's "portal-to-portal" victory became the standard, and other industries reluctantly adopted it when it was further enshrined in the **Fair Labor Standards Act** (FLSA).

The construction industry has seen battles over dead time. On most projects built by union labor, strict **jurisdiction** rules exist about who is allowed to do what. A mason, for example, is not permitted to do carpentry work. This restriction enrages some employers, who see it as a form of featherbedding and argue that dead time simply drives up costs. These employers argue that a work crew should be able to perform multiple jobs. In some states, this battle has led to attempts to deny **wages** for dead time as well as lobbying efforts to change regulations regarding the awarding of construction **contracts**. Thus far most of these challenges have been turned aside.

Unions counter that these employers are merely seeking to keep workers at their beck-and-call without paying for that service, and that they seek to assign complex tasks to those lacking the expertise to do them properly. Dead time is especially a problem in the trucking industry. In the past, the **Teamsters** were successful in winning dead-time pay for drivers forced to sit at terminals waiting to load or unload. The union now charges that independent truckers and non-union drivers are often subject to dead time abuses.

Dead time rules also apply to occupations such as firefighting and law enforcement. A professional firefighter is "on duty" even if asleep in the station and must be compensated for that time; the same is true for a police officer "on call." Moreover, employers are not allowed to count "breaks" of less than 20 minutes as nonwork time. The FSLA does not require employers to offer breaks or time off for meals, but most state laws do. In most cases, employers can require employees to clock out for breaks of more than 30 minutes as long as there is no expectation that employees will perform any duties whatsoever during this time. Several companies, including Wal-Mart, have been sued for working employees off the clock.

Portal-to-portal and dead time pay requirements as covered by the FSLA have been amended several times. In 1947, laws were clarified that excluded commuting time. In addition, FSLA provisions protect companies from financial ruin involved in altering customary practices and numerous other refinements. Current law is governed by Title 29, Chapter 9 of the United States Code.

Suggested Reading

" 'Downtime' Pay: When to Pay for Travel, Rest, On-call Time," *Business Management Daily*, http://www.businessmanagementdaily.com/articles/3182/1/, accessed July 30, 2010; "Title 29," Cornell University Law School, http://www.law.cornell.edu/uscode/29/usc _sup_01_29.html, accessed July 30, 2010; "Wages and Salaries: Portal-to-Portal for All," *Time*, December 16, 1946.

DEBS, EUGENE VICTOR

Eugene V. Debs (November 5, 1855–October 20, 1926) was a **socialist**, labor leader, and five-time presidential candidate. To many students of labor history, Debs is a heroic figure.

Debs was born in Terre Haute, Indiana, the son of Jean Daniel and Marguerite Marie Debs, French immigrants who operated a grocery store. At age 15, he left school to work as a locomotive paint scraper but within two years became a locomotive fireman. At age 20, he helped organize a Terre Haute local of the Brotherhood of Locomotive Firemen (BLF) and served as its secretary. In 1878, Debs became an associate editor of *Locomotive Firemen's Journal*; he became its editor-in-chief two years later. He also became active in local **Democratic Party** politics and was elected city clerk in 1879, followed by his election to the Indiana legislature in 1884.

Debs continued his rise within the BLF, becoming national secretary, and then vice president. He became increasingly dissatisfied with the BLF, however, as it continued to operate more as a fraternal organization than as a labor union. Debs was an ardent supporter of emergent **industrial unionism** and wished to merge the numerous and separate railroad brotherhoods into a single union. He resigned his BLF offices in 1892 to assume the presidency of the newly created **American Railway Union** (ARU), an industrial union that formed when the **Knights of Labor** (KOL) began its precipitous decline. The ARU absorbed several KOL bodies.

The ARU's successful 1893 **strike** against James Hill's Great Northern line catapulted Debs and the ARU into the limelight. As had happened to the KOL in 1886, however, the ARU's rapid growth brought in new members whose expectations were higher than the union's realistic ability to deliver them. As such, Debs opposed the 1894 **Pullman strike** because he felt the ARU was not ready to tackle such a formidable foe as the Pullman Palace Car Corporation. Although his counsel was rejected, Debs dutifully assumed leadership of the ensuing **boycott** of Pullman cars. He was arrested for violating a federal **injunction** prohibiting interference with delivery of the U.S. mail and was sentenced to six months in the federal penitentiary in Woodstock, Illinois. Legend holds that Debs converted to socialism while in prison, though in truth his political thought was evolving along those lines before he was jailed.

In 1898, Debs founded the Social Democratic Party (SDP), a socialist organization. Two years later, he garnered 96,000 votes in his first bid to become president of the United States. In 1901, Debs merged the SDP with another party to create the Socialist Party of America (SP), a body dedicated to electing socialists to political office by mobilizing the votes of the majority **working class**. Debs quickly became the nation's most prominent socialist spokesperson, crisscrossing the country to make speeches and authoring numerous pamphlets. He was present at the 1905 founding convention of the **Industrial Workers of the World** (IWW) and helped draft its preamble, though he resigned from the IWW in 1908, when the organization rejected ballot-box politics.

Debs ran for president in 1904, 1908, and 1912, increasing his vote total in each election. As the United States moved toward involvement in World War I, however, Debs denounced the hostilities as a **capitalist** war and urged workers to avoid it. He was convicted of violating the wartime Espionage Act. His sentencing speech is considered a classic and has inspired reformers ever since, including the Reverend Martin Luther King, Jr. In 1918, Debs entered a federal prison in Atlanta to begin a 10-year sentence; he was still in prison in 1920, when he ran for president and gathered more than 915,000 votes. He remained in jail until Christmas Day, 1921, when President Warren G. Harding pardoned him. By then he was in frail health and spent much of the rest of his life working on his prison memoir, *Walls and Bars*, which was published posthumously in 1927.

Debs is credited with removing much of the stigma that socialism was a foreign import. To the degree that socialist ideals took any root in American soil, Debs played an influential part. He is also an exemplar of a principled individual who placed the good of the working class above his own self-interest.

Suggested Reading

Eugene Debs, "Statement to the Court," http://www.wfu.edu/~zulick/341/Debs1918.html, accessed July 30, 2010; Ray Ginger, *The Bending Cross*, 1949; Ronald Radosh, ed., *Debs*, 1971; Nick Salvatore, *Eugene V. Debs*, 1982.

DECERTIFICATION

Decertification is the process by which an employee-approved union can be stripped of its right to represent workers. In recent decades decertification votes have increased as employers seek to rid themselves of unions. They often argue that unions are an outmoded relic from another era, whereas unions counter that many of the decertification votes would be considered as **unfair labor practices** if labor laws and courts were not so unfairly stacked against unions.

Procedures for decertifying a union are outlined in the 1935 **National Labor Relations Act** (NLRA). Under the NLRA, a decertification vote is held if 30 percent of those workers legally defined as a bargaining unit petition the National Labor Relations Board to hold such a vote. Just as in the certification process, however, a majority must agree before a union is decertified. The 1947 **Taft-Hartley Act** also facilitates decertification. In particular, it guarantees an employer's right to free speech, including the right to voice anti-union opinions. It had also made **right-to-work** laws easier to pass, which had smoothed the way for decertification in some states. In addition, the union members' "bill of rights" in the 1959 **Landrum-Griffin Act** has made it easier for workers to vote out unpopular unions.

Workers may decide to decertify their unions for a number of reasons. After World War II, for example, some workers left unions that members felt were too radical. In the late 1940s, some locals of the **United Electrical, Radio, and Machine Workers of America** (UE) disbanded in light of charges that the UE was dominated by **communists**. Many UE members joined the more conservative **International Union of Electrical, Radio and Machine Workers of America**. In rare cases, workers may decertify their union or strategically threaten to do so because they feel leadership is too conservative. The latter was the case in 2000, when Union Pacific rail workers sought to leave the United Transportation Union and join the **Brotherhood of Locomotive Engineers**.

Union **raiding** has also led to decertification votes. For example, the Hollywood-based International Alliance of Theatrical Stage Employees and Moving Picture Machine Operators (IATSE) routinely used decertification votes to lure away members of the Conference of Studio Unions (CSU) during the 1940s. IATSE often resorted to red-baiting to convince former CSU members to change allegiance. In the 1960s, the **Teamsters** tried to use decertification votes to raid members of the **United Farm Workers of America**. Some unions have been decertified because of union corruption, as in the case of some dockworkers' locals in the 1950s.

In recent years, most decertification drives have been employer instigated and (often) employer financed. Decertification votes have been part of an overall strategy to put unions on the defensive and give management the right to conduct business affairs, such as mergers, without union interference. This trend has been noticeable in the newspaper industry, where mergers and declining readership have threatened the existence of the Newspaper Guild. Newspaper unions in the South were largely broken in the 1950s, a harbinger of things to come. In the 1980s and 1990s, media conglomerates such as Gannett and the Hearst Corporation sought to destroy the Newspaper Guild in cities such as Cincinnati, Detroit, Tacoma, San Antonio, and Santa Barbara. At the *New York Daily News*, management precipitated a **strike** in 1990, hired **scabs**, and then encouraged its new employees to decertify the Newspaper Guild. That effort did not succeed entirely, but it has worked elsewhere, including in San Diego in 1998.

Many law firms have partners who specialize in assisting firms bring forth decertification votes. These efforts are often undertaken in right-to-work states. Employers may resort to a variety of tactics to produce decertification, ranging from **paternalistic** promises to threats of job elimination. Another common tactic has been to wring **concessions** from the union as a prelude to attacking unions as outmoded, ineffective, or corrupt. By the 1980s, for every three new members whom unions gained, one member was lost in a decertification drive. This trend slowed slightly in the 1990s, though unions continue to lose more votes than they win. In 1998, 475 decertification votes were held, with unions losing 71.1 percent of the time and suffering a net loss of 12,879 members. In 1999, there were 373 decertification votes, with unions winning only 35.7 percent of the time and hemorrhaging an additional 9,400 members. In recent years, unions have taken a more proactive approach to avoiding decertification votes, but the practice remains a potent challenge to organized labor's future. In 2004, for example, unions still lost two of every three decertification votes. Although this rate improved by 2009, unions still lost 56 percent of all decertification votes. The Teamsters have the dubious distinction of having been decertified at the highest rate in 2008–2009, having lost 67 percent of said votes.

These grim statistics do not bode well for the immediate future of unions, but current polls indicate that it is simplistic to interpret the decertification trend as reflective of worker disinterest in labor unions. Some decertification votes result from overall frustration on the part of workers lashing out against unions forced to give back **wages** and **fringe benefits**, but the vast majority of decertification votes are orchestrated by very powerful and well-funded anti-union business interests and conservative ideologues. These groups often form what appear to be independent advocacy groups but are, in fact, front organizations. According to a 2007 Economic Policy Institute report, a majority of non-union workers would organize if they felt that they could do so without repercussions. There is also an indication that overtly anti-union policies may be backfiring and that worker distrust of management is rising.

Suggested Reading

Richard Freeman, "Do Workers Still Want Unions? More than Ever," *Economic Policy Institute Report*, February 22, 2007; Lawrence Richards, *Union-Free America: Workers and Antiunion Culture*, 2008; Patricia Sexton, *The War on Labor and the Left*, 1991; Steve Simurda, "Sticking with the Union?," *Columbia Journalism Review* (March/April 1993).

DEINDUSTRIALIZATION

Deindustrialization refers to the processes through which investment in and production of durable goods has declined, resulting in plant closings, mass layoffs, and the loss of U.S. manufacturing dominance in the global market. Some analysts locate its genesis in the 1973 Organization of Petroleum Exporting Countries (OPEC) oil boycott, the hyperinflation of the late 1970s, and the economic policies of **Ronald Reagan** in the 1980s. These factors played a significant part, but so, too, did the post-World War II recovery of European and Asian economies as they became manifest in the 1960s and numerous other factors. It is now customary to refer to the U.S. economy as "postindustrial" in nature, though such a designation exaggerates the magnitude of economic transformation and ignores the fact that manufacturing remains an important component of the national economy.

From the early 20th century through the 1960s, the United States dominated the global economy in terms of the production of industrial goods such as automobiles, steel, electronics, rubber, and textiles. This situation changed dramatically beginning in the 1970s. In 1946, American firms provided 60 percent of the world's steel; by the late 1970s, this share fell to 16 percent, and by 2006 to just 8 percent. In 1963, the United States imported approximately 2 percent of the clothing sold by its domestic retailers; by 1980, U.S. imports of clothing had risen to 50 percent, and today it is increasingly rare to find American-made garments. Even the venerable automobile industry has suffered from deindustrialization, with imports capturing more than 30 percent of the U.S. market by 1987. By 2009, the United States was only the third-largest producer of automobiles. The loss of market shares in such industries led to a decline in **blue-collar** jobs and has pushed venerable firms such as General Motors—once the world's largest and most profitable corporation—to the brink of bankruptcy.

The decline in manufacturing has had an impact on the traditional **working class**. Real **wages** fell for American workers from 1975 until 1992. Inflation in the 1970s badly crippled the ability of U.S. manufacturers to compete in the global market. American factories were older than those in emerging economies such as those of Germany and Japan. Faced with soaring labor costs and the high costs of retooling, many U.S. manufacturers decreased their investments, thereby conceding much of the domestic market to cheaper imported goods. As companies folded, reconfigured, or relocated their operations, vast swaths of the former industrial heartland of the upper Midwest and Northeast were devastated and cities such as Detroit, St. Louis, and Cleveland faced declines in population and standards of living. New York City had more than 1 million industrial jobs in the metropolitan area in 1950; it now has approximately one-fifth of that number. Overall, employment within the manufacturing sector fell from 25.1 percent of the workforce in 1959 to 18.5 percent in 1984, and again to 9.25 percent in 2005. Deindustrialization is the single biggest reason for declining membership in labor unions, as historically these groups' members have been concentrated in manufacturing. In the period between 1984 and 1997, union members accounted for 80 percent of the jobs lost in manufacturing and gained just 5 percent of the jobs in new enterprises. A majority of union workers now work in government jobs, not the manufacturing sector.

Labor critics also blame the financial policies of presidents Ronald Reagan and George H. W. Bush for exacerbating the problem. They particularly blame **deregulation** policies that encouraged **downsizing**, mergers, investment abroad, **runaway shops**, and stock speculation rather than direct investment in manufacturing. President Bill Clinton signed the **North American Free Trade Agreement** (NAFTA) in 1994, an act to which the loss of hundreds of thousands of jobs can be directly linked. There is considerable truth to the complaints of those who blame government action and inaction for deindustrialization, though factors such as technological change, increased demand in the economy's service sector, an overpriced U.S. dollar that discouraged foreign investment, and advances made by developing nations also played a part in hastening this trend. By 2010, American manufacturers were globally dominant only in military hardware and pharmaceutical production.

Deindustrialization has changed many aspects of American life. **Globalism** is now an established fact, for good or ill. Employers increasingly demand high skills, exacting work, and longer hours from employees under the rubric of maintaining global competitiveness. Organized labor often fears that lower global standards of worker safety, environmental protection, wages, and working conditions will lead to erosion of hard-won rights within the United States. Many union workers participated in protests outside of the World Trade Organization meetings in Seattle in 1999 and Geneva in 2009. They have also become a visible presence at global economic summits. Many unions fear that globalization will produce a "race to the bottom" in terms of wages, working conditions, and environmental standards.

Although its manufacturing base has declined, the United States is far from being a manufacturing-free nation. In steel, for example, U.S. dominance of global markets has declined, yet America remains the world's third-largest producer (after China and Japan) and overall production has increased in recent years. Likewise, although much has been written about the decline of the U.S. auto industry, American manufacturers produced 5.7 million vehicles in 2009. As of June 2010, more than 11.6 million workers were employed in manufacturing in the United States. There has also been a backlash against imported goods, especially from China, and a minor resurgence in some industries. Unions have long sponsored campaigns to buy American-made goods, though it remains to be seen whether consumers will continue to be motivated more by price than by national pride.

Suggested Reading

Donald Bartlett and James Steele, *America: What Went Wrong?*, 1993; Barry Bluestone and Bennett Harrison, *The Deindustrializing of the United States*, 1982; Michael Dertouzos et al., *Made in America*, 1989; "Industries at a Glance," Bureau of Labor Statistics, http://www.bls.gov/iag/tgs/iag31-33.htm#about, accessed August 2, 2010

DELEON, DANIEL

Daniel DeLeon (December 14, 1852–May 11, 1914) was a radical Marxist labor leader and theorist. Although DeLeon was a deep thinker, he was often rigid and disputatious. He is sometimes invoked as an example of a doctrinaire leader whose refusal to compromise made him more fiery than effective.

DeLeon was a distant relative of Juan Ponce de León, the 16th-century Spanish explorer who dreamed of finding the Fountain of Youth. Daniel DeLeon was born on the Caribbean island of Curaçao, off the northern coast of Venezuela. He was the son of Salomon de Leon and Sarah Jesurun DeLeon, Dutch Jews. DeLeon left Curaçao to go to Germany, where he studied medicine and languages before immigrating to the United States in early 1874. He taught Latin, Greek, and math at a school in Westchester County, New York, and also studied law at Columbia University, from which he obtained a law degree in 1878. He worked as an attorney for six years, first in Brownsville, Texas (1878–1882) and then in New York City (1882–1884).

In 1882, DeLeon he briefly returned to Curaçao to marry Sara Lobo, the 16-year-old daughter of a wealthy Jewish family. They moved to the Lower East Side of New York City. Sara bore two sons, the second of whom died in infancy; Sara herself died while giving birth to stillborn twins in 1887. DeLeon also suffered a career disappointment in 1889, when he failed to secure a permanent professorship at Columbia University, where he had taught off and on since 1883. In 1892, DeLeon married Bertha Canary, a Kansas school teacher with whom he had five children.

DeLeon's chaotic personal life coincided with a time in which his political consciousness was in flux, and he later came to believe he had been dismissed from Columbia because of his radical beliefs. Bitterness and conflict seemed to follow DeLeon. He became involved with the **Knights of Labor** (KOL) sometime in the mid-1880s and, though he had named one of his children for Democratic President Grover Cleveland, by 1886 he was immersed in **socialist** politics. He was an ardent supporter of **Henry George** and, later, of **Edward Bellamy** and the Nationalist movement.

In 1890, DeLeon joined the Socialist Labor Party (SLP), embraced doctrinaire Marxism, and quickly rose through its ranks. As editor of the SLP's English-language journal *People*, DeLeon again had a lectern, and he filled the publication's pages with articles urging workers to support independent labor parties. He ran for governor of New York on the SLP ticket in 1891, 1902, and 1904. He also translated Karl Marx and the works of other European radicals into English.

DeLeon transformed the SLP into a doctrinaire Marxist organization and sought to do the same to the KOL. By 1890, the KOL was in steep decline and had lost more than three-fourths of the members it contained when it peaked in 1886. In New York City, the KOL was embroiled in a doctrinal debate in which the **Lassallean** socialists who had controlled affairs were being pressured by orthodox Marxists. DeLeon and like-minded individuals such as Lucien Sanial sought to make the KOL overtly Marxist. Indeed, between 1892 and 1894, DeLeon was probably the most influential KOL leader in the New York City area.

Both the KOL and the SLP disappointed DeLeon by embracing what were seen as pragmatic agendas rather than the purist line pushed by DeLeon. In response, DeLeon tore both groups asunder in 1895. From the breakaway Knights and renegade SLP members, DeLeon formed the Socialist Trades and Labor Alliance (STLA), which he hoped could become an alternative to the **American**

Federation of Labor (AFL), which was by then the dominant labor federation in the country, but one that DeLeon despised for its exclusionary craft unionism and its lack of class consciousness. He is sometimes credited with first calling the AFL the "American Separation of Labor," an oft-repeated smear among radical labor leaders. The STLA failed to make major inroads among American workers, however, and its tenure was marked by intense internal doctrinal conflicts.

DeLeon made many enemies. Critics accused him of being an unyielding ideologue whose dogmatism weakened the labor movement. Among his detractors was Eugene V. Debs of the Socialist Party of America (SP), who admired DeLeon's energy and commitment but felt his purist attitudes harmed the socialist cause. By 1904, both the SLP and the STLA were on the verge of collapse, and DeLeon briefly reevaluated the wisdom of combining political action and labor reform in a single organization. In 1905, both DeLeon and Debs attended the founding convention of the Industrial Workers of the World (IWW). DeLeon embraced its vision of overthrowing capitalism, though he had come to doubt that unions were sufficiently revolutionary bodies and lobbied for a separate IWW political strategy. He did, however, embrace the IWW's industrial unionism policy.

Once again DeLeon proved fractious, and many felt he was using the IWW merely to recruit SLP members. As had happened in the KOL, DeLeon immersed himself in a larger political dispute within the IWW, one that can be roughly understood as a debate between centralizers and decentralizers. Eastern-based IWW members favored coordinated policy, were more willing to engage in ballot-box politics, and formed union locals that looked similar to other unions, albeit more radical. Western IWW members favored increased use of direct action to destabilize capitalism, were more loosely organized, and doubted the value of politics. In 1908, the latter faction—based in Chicago—was powerful enough to expel DeLeon. Debs, who also believed in political action, left the IWW of his own accord and concentrated on the SP. DeLeon once again formed a splinter organization, which became known as the Detroit IWW, after insulting the Chicago-based IWW by calling it "bummery" and "slum proletarians." DeLeon led the splinter group, which was renamed the Workers' International Industrial Union in 1915 (a year after DeLeon's death from heart disease). The group folded a decade later. The only socialist group to which DeLeon belonged that survives is the SLP, and it remains a very ideological (and very small) third party.

DeLeon deserves some credit for making socialism more palatable to English speakers at a time when it was seen as a foreign import, though Debs certainly accomplished far more on this score by adopting a less strident tone. DeLeon was clearly an intellectual, as can be seen in his three books and numerous pamphlets. His writings gained more currency in Europe than in the United States. Overall, DeLeon was a difficult man who split every organization to which he belonged.

Suggested Reading

Stephen Coleman, *Daniel DeLeon*, 1990; L. Gene Seretan, *Daniel DeLeon: The Odyssey of an American Marxist*, 1979; Socialist Labor Party of America, http://www.slp.org/, accessed August 3, 2010.

DEMOCRATIC PARTY AND LABOR

Of the two major political parties in the United States, the Democrats have long been considered friendlier to organized labor, which has reciprocated by offering more support for Democratic than Republican candidates. This relationship was forged during the New Deal and for a time it looked as if unions might become the veritable "labor party" wing of the Democratic Party. That did not happen, however, and over the years the relationship has grown strained. Numerous labor activists have argued that organized labor needs to return to its militant roots and abandon the belief that the Democratic Party is an ally of labor unions. Still others argue that the United States needs to form a progressive third party along the lines of early 20th-century European Labor parties. Defenders counter that the alliance with Democrats gives labor opportunities to influence policy it would not otherwise have.

Historically the **working class** has been the largest segment of the American electorate, making it necessary for both parties to court support among **blue-collar** voters. Neither party held a significant edge after the Civil War. Although northern Irish-heritage working-class voters were loyal to the Democrats, the Republican Party was generally perceived to be more progressive and it made inroads among workers through promises to keep commodity prices low. This effectively balanced the support Democrats drew from southern and midwestern farmers. A significant amount of third-party experimentation also occurred in the late 19th century, which further fragmented the labor vote.

The Democrats made their first significant inroads into the working-class vote in the late 19th century by co-opting labor **populism**. Democrats embraced moderate aspects of the populist agenda, such as electoral reform and implementation of a graduated income tax, and rejected **socialist** ideas such as nationalizing communications and transportation or manipulating commodity prices. Many northern workers cast ballots for Democrats for the first time in 1896 and 1900, albeit not in great enough numbers to derail the presidential bids of Republican William McKinley.

During the **Progressive Era**, working-class voters again split their votes. Progressivism was a decidedly elitist approach to reform, and neither party seemed particularly inclined to court organized labor, though the Democrat Woodrow Wilson signed the **Clayton Act**, which was hailed by unions. For the most part, the Progressive Era was a challenging time for unions. **Samuel Gompers**, president of the **American Federation of Labor** (AFE), sat on boards such as the **National Civic Federation** and there was cooperation between organized labor and government during World War I, but this rapprochement failed to translate into a significant political role for labor.

The postwar **Red Scare** led to assaults on radicalism that rippled across the labor movement; in turn, union strength declined. The Republican Party openly courted support from Big Business during the 1920s, embraced **open-shop** policies, and largely pegged party policy to the booming business prosperity of the decade. The 1929 stock market crash was destined to change the political landscape. President Herbert Hoover's ineffective response to the crisis, the outbreak of **Depression-era** strikes, and the resurgence of the political left combined to create a perception of the Republican Party as callous and heartless. Franklin Roosevelt rode the ensuing mass discontent to a convincing victory in 1932. He would be reelected three times, in each case drawing the bulk of the working-class vote.

Roosevelt fashioned what political scientists dubbed the "New Deal coalition," a Democratic Party juggernaut that drew support from blue-collar workers, second- and third-generation immigrants, southern and midwestern farmers, women, and African Americans. Although Democrats did not always hold power in Congress or the White House, this coalition made Democrats the dominant political party for the next 50-plus years. As president, Roosevelt both signed into law bills favorable to labor unions and expressed the view that unions were good for American workers. During the 1930s, labor union membership soared and the new **Congress of Industrial Organizations** (CIO) brought organization to heavy industries that had been resolutely hostile to unions for many decades. Moreover, prominent labor leaders such as **John L. Lewis** enjoyed access to the president and **Sidney Hillman** became one of Roosevelt's advisors.

By the mid-1930s some observers opined that the United States did not need a separate Labor Party because the Democrats filled that role. In retrospect, such an assertion was overly optimistic. Much of labor's success in the 1930s was the product of grassroots militancy that involved alliances with the radical left. Even pro-labor bills such as the **National Labor Relations Act** had to be enshrined through industry-by-industry **strikes**. Embattled workers averaged more than 2,000 strikes per year in the 1930s. In many ways the Democratic Party reluctantly followed organized labor's lead. Moreover, the alliance between labor and the Democrats was mostly informal; the role of men such as Hillman notwithstanding, labor had no formal role in the party and had no representatives who helped shape party policy aside from advisory roles during World War II, when labor gave input to the **War Labor Relations Board** (WLRB).

Unions gave **no-strike pledges** during the war, and some union leaders hoped that the WLRB would become the template for a managed economy in the postwar period in which industrial councils would assist in planning. The 1942 Congressional elections, in which Democrats nearly lost the House of Representatives, signaled that conservative forces intended to battle both the New Deal and labor unions. The CIO set up its political action committee (PAC) in 1944 in response to the 1943 Smith-Connally Act, which banned direct union contributions to candidates and allowed the president to take over strike-torn industries—the latter provision being a direct response to the **United Mine Workers of America's** refusal to agree to no-strike pledges.

The war's end put labor further on the defensive, despite a massive strike wave that idled 5 million workers between August 1945 and January 1946. Attacks on the left that had begun before the war accelerated during the second Red Scare and, in 1947, a conservative Congress enacted the hated **Taft-Hartley Act** over President Harry Truman's veto. It placed so many restrictions on unions that its repeal became the top legislative goal for both the CIO and the AFL, which set up its own PAC in advance of the 1948 election.

Both **labor federations** contributed heavily to the Truman campaign in 1948, though their support was often overlooked by those commenting on Truman's surprise victory over Thomas Dewey. Many CIO leaders saw Truman as the only hope to save the New Deal, and several argued that the United States was rapidly moving toward a political realignment in which there would be a liberal party that contested power with a conservative party. The cost of supporting Truman in 1948 was abandoning his more progressive opponent, Henry Wallace. This decision marked the beginning of the CIO's move to isolate radicals.

Organized labor made a series of decisions in the early postwar years that have subsequently provided fodder for critics. Truman's "Fair Deal" policies proved milder versions of the New Deal, and the president did not seem inclined to equate his upset victory with the need to repay labor allies. The 1949 Housing Act rewarded private contractors—many of whom were non-union enterprises—over labor's objection, and Truman's use of presidential **injunctions** and periodic threats to draft strikers shocked unions. He also gave what labor saw as undue attention to the party's conservative southern wing, the segregationist and anti-union "Dixiecrats." The collapse of the CIO's **Operation Dixie** attempt to organize the South ensued, as did significant amounts of red-baiting.

Rather than seeking to rekindle 1930s-style grassroots militancy, organized labor largely sought to become team players in hopes of strengthening its alliance with the Democratic Party. The AFL became an early and enthusiastic support of **Cold War unionism** that tied labor to foreign policy objectives. For its part, the CIO purged much of its membership in an effort to remove unions too closely associated with **communist** leadership, a veritable acquiescence to the very Taft-Hartley Act it hoped to overturn. In 1950 the **United Auto Workers of America** (UAW) signed five-year no-strike contracts with automakers that ceded the right to manage in exchange for exceedingly lucrative **wage** and **fringe benefits** packages. Some analysts date the end of CIO militancy to this pact.

Labor benefited financially in the 1950s but had very little else to show from its decisions. Access to the Democratic Party decision- and policy-making apparatus remained elusive, and Adlai Stevenson's loss to Republican Dwight Eisenhower in 1952 further isolated labor politically. The Taft-Hartley Act remained more entrenched than ever, despite the 1955 merger of the AFL and the CIO motivated in part by a determination to rid unions of the act's restrictions. Most AFL-CIO affiliates opted for **business unionism** methods of conducting their affairs, which brought economic gain in many cases, but little political power.

Many union leaders cheered the elections of John Kennedy and Lyndon Johnson in 1960 and 1964, respectively. Johnson's "Great Society" and "War on Poverty" programs contained numerous provisions favorable to labor unions. Union leaders were quick to attribute progressive legislation to unions' ability to influence the Democratic Party, though historians generally see these gains more as spillovers from the **civil rights** movement and agitations from the New Left than as evidence of organized labor's political clout. The Republican Richard Nixon, no friend of unions, was elected in 1968, and the AFL-CIO's refusal to endorse his Democratic opponent George McGovern in 1972 strained already thin relations between unions and Democrats. The economic crisis of the 1970s highlighted the myriad ways in which the Democratic Party was not a surrogate labor party. Although Democrats as a whole were more likely to speak favorably of labor and meet with union leaders, President Jimmy Carter gave more credence to the advice of **Business Roundtable** leaders than to organized labor. Unions were unable even to secure passage of a bill that would curtail *illegal* behavior on the part of employers, let alone secure positive labor reform. The early effects of **concessions**, **downsizing**, and **deindustrialization** were felt during the Carter years.

The Republican presidencies of **Ronald Reagan**, George H. W. Bush, and George W. Bush were very challenging for organized labor, as none of the three made much effort to hide their disdain for labor unions. What was more troubling for organized labor was the reluctance of erstwhile Democratic allies to champion labor's cause. "Neo-liberal" Democrats, as they have been dubbed, sought to promote business growth, embrace **deregulation** and free trade policies, and empower the private sector at the expense of the public realm. When President Bill Clinton signed the **North American Free Trade Agreement**, some labor activists called for an end to labor's support for Democrats.

The historical fact is that labor did not become the progressive wing of the Democratic Party. Organized labor now faces a dilemma largely of its own making. At present there is no viable alternative to the Democratic Party from labor's perspective. Much of the Republican Party is openly hostile to unions, and some labor leaders blame labor's flirtation with the Green Party for Al Gore's narrow loss to George W. Bush in the 2000 presidential election. The complaints of labor radicals notwithstanding, supporters of the Democratic Party are correct in arguing that organized labor has a political forum within the party that it would not have on its own. They further argue that labor has subtly influenced numerous bills to make them more responsive to working people. Moreover, there is currently no sizable militant labor wing and unions are hemorrhaging members. It is also clear that the Democratic Party often counts on labor's financial and electoral support, though the latter has become less reliable since the 1980s. Organized labor will, however, need a significant revitalization of strength if it hopes to pressure Democratic Party policy in the future.

Suggested Reading

Kevin Boyle, *The UAW and the Heyday of American Liberalism, 1945–1968*, 1998; Taylor Dark, *The Unions and the Democrats: An Enduring Alliance*, 2001; Mike Davis, *Prisoners of the American Dream*, 1988.

DEPARTMENT OF LABOR

The Department of Labor (DOL) is part of the executive branch of the federal government and was created to promote and develop policies to benefit working Americans. It also seeks to improve working conditions and mediate between the interests of capital and labor.

Thoughts of creating a labor department first emerged in the 1860s, with **William Sylvis** often given credit for the idea, although the modern DOL dates only to 1913. Groups such as the **National Labor Union** and the **Knights of Labor** supported the formation of a national **Bureau of Labor Statistics** (BLS), patterned on a body founded in Massachusetts in 1871, that would gather information on **wages** and working conditions. Many activists felt that educating the public would be the first step to labor reform. A national BLS was founded in 1874 and is today a division of the DOL.

In 1884, Congress created the Bureau of Labor as part of the Department of the Interior. It operated independently of the Department of the Interior from 1888 until 1903, when it was placed under the jurisdiction of the Department of Commerce and Labor. Immigration policy consumed much of the DOL's work in its early days. President William Taft signed legislation in 1913 that created the modern DOL, elevating its secretary to a Cabinet-level position. William B. Wilson, who served as the first secretary of labor, began the process by which agencies such as the BLS, the Bureau of Immigration, and the Children's Bureau were consolidated by the DOL. Wilson also appealed to labor unions to allow the DOL to mediate disputes, but **arbitration** was not made mandatory, and it was not until 1916 that Congress allocated money to assist DOL mediation efforts. Wilson also used DOL resources to set up employment bureaus, and during World War I, to maintain wartime production codes that included the **eight-hour** day for some workers.

Between 1921 and 1933, the DOL mostly concerned itself with curtailing **child labor**. A special Women's Bureau was set up to address child care and maternity leave and to expand work opportunities for women, though the latter effort stalled at the onset of the Great Depression. The DOL expanded its role during the period from 1933 to 1945, when **Frances Perkins** held the position of secretary of labor. The department was directly involved in establishing New Deal programs such as the Works Progress Administration, **Social Security**, and **minimum-wage** legislation. During Perkins's tenure, the eight-hour day became standard for many American workers. The DOL also directed wartime production efforts during World War II.

Politics have sometimes hampered DOL efforts since World War II. The **Taft-Hartley Act** curtailed labor rights and a Republican-controlled Congress rejected all modifications to the act, causing President Dwight Eisenhower's Labor Secretary, Martin Durkin, to resign. Aside from directing production during the Korean War, the DOL remained relatively quiescent until 1961, when it was called upon to administer parts of the Area Redevelopment Act. In 1962, the DOL began overseeing the Manpower Development and Training Act, a retraining program for long-term unemployed workers. This effort dovetailed with the Economic Opportunities Act of 1964, in which the DOL oversaw a program designed to train disadvantaged youth. The DOL also played a central role in President Lyndon Johnson's "War on Poverty."

Administering the 1970 **Occupational Safety and Health Act** (OSHA) is perhaps the DOL's most important post-World War II initiative. Each year, the DOL is called upon to set safety and health standards in American workplaces and to use the power of the executive branch to enforce these standards and seek penalties against violators. Another important program was the 1983 Job and Training

Partnership Act, which sought to build alliances among government, workers, and the private sector to promote job training. Critics, however, charged that the DOL was weakened by an antilabor political climate in the 1980s and early 1990s. Alexis Herman, secretary of labor under President Bill Clinton, is credited with restoring the morale of beleaguered DOL employees, though unions maintain that they were kept in low profile. The DOL became the center of controversy again during the administration of George W. Bush, who placed the Center for Faith-Based and Community Initiatives under its aegis—an act that rankled civil libertarians and others who asserted that Bush's action violated the principle of separation of church and state.

Today the DOL administers 17 separate operating units, ranging in responsibility from law enforcement to international labor standards. Among the issues addressed and overseen by the DOL are campaigns to curtail child labor globally, protect funds that workers have invested in **pensions**, make certain that terminated workers receive proper continuation of benefits rights, and enforce labor law standards related to points such as **overtime** pay, the **minimum wage**, and workers' entitlement to benefits such as breaks, vacation pay, and sick leave. In all, the DOL is responsible for executing approximately 180 federal laws. In 2008, President Barack Obama appointed Hilda Solis as secretary of labor; Solis is the first Latina to hold a Cabinet-level post.

Suggested Reading

United States Department of Labor, http://www.dol.gov/, accessed August 3, 2010; Donald Whitnah, ed., *Government Agencies*, 1983.

DEPRESSION-ERA STRIKES

The stock market collapse of October 1929 occasioned the greatest economic collapse in American history. The U.S. economy sank into a depression from which it did not emerge fully until 1941. Paradoxically, what scholars call the "Great Depression" provided an opportunity for labor unions to recover many of the gains they had lost in the anti-union and **open-shop** climate of the 1920s. In similar fashion, though unemployment rates routinely climbed above 20 percent, the 1930s were also marked by an increase in labor activism and **strikes**.

When the depression first began, President Herbert Hoover's response was timid, as he and his advisors believed the downturn would be short-lived. In fact, Hoover's initial actions were aimed at stimulating the business sector rather than at aiding the unemployed. By 1932, however, approximately 15 million people were unemployed and Hoover found himself increasingly unpopular. The number of hobos and homeless people increased, midwestern farmers destroyed products and animals to protest low commodity prices, and Harlan County coal miners struck rather than accept starvation-level **wages**. Millions of workers lucky enough to keep their jobs suffered repeated wage cuts and periodic layoffs, and legions more endured underemployment in that they were forced to take jobs far beneath their levels of experience and training. In the spring of 1932, in scenes reminiscent of **Coxey's Army**, "bonus armies" of World War I veterans descended upon Washington, D.C., to lobby Congress for early payment of bonuses due in 1945. They were routed violently by the standing U.S. Army, with several veterans being killed and hundreds of others wounded. Anger and desperation levels rose and large cities saw an increase in unemployment demonstrations and rent strikes, often led by **communists** and/or **socialists**. Some alarmists worried that **capitalism** was on the verge of collapse, a fear reinforced by the fact that the depression was global in span.

Working people overwhelmingly voted for Democratic presidential candidate Franklin Roosevelt in November 1932. Roosevelt was aware that the **working class** was one of the constituencies responsible for his election and immediately launched programs aimed at getting relief to the needy and providing jobs for the unemployed. He also took steps to protect the right of workers to join labor unions. In June 1933, Roosevelt signed the **National Industrial Recovery Act** (NIRA), which gave workers the right to form, join, or assist unions of their choosing and closed many of the loopholes in the **Clayton Act** that allowed employers to engage in anti-union activities.

Although Roosevelt's New Deal provided far more protections for workers than the programs of his predecessors, not all of these policies were granted as top-down forms of benevolence. Roosevelt was also pushed by increasing levels of labor activism. Both the **American Federation of Labor** (AFL) and independent unions such as the Mechanics Educational Society of America and the Automotive Industrial Workers Association increased their membership. In 1933—the first year of the New Deal—more than 1.2 million workers went on strike, a 600 percent increase from 1930. In August 1933, nearly 95 percent of San Francisco's longshoremen joined the International Longshoremen's Association (ILA), the first successful organizing drive since the **Industrial Workers of the World** (IWW) enrolled dock workers in the 1910s; the ILA immediately launched campaigns to increase wages and end management prerogatives such as the **shape-up**. When faced with resistance, the ILA struck back. On May 9, 1934, more than 12,000 dock workers from British Columbia to San Diego walked off the job. Under the leadership of **Harry Bridges**, another 10,000 workers were on strike within weeks. In July, the city of San Francisco was virtually shut down by a four-day **general strike** that idled more than 125,000 workers from a variety of occupations. Although the strike fizzled out, management was pushed by government officials to set up boards to **arbitrate** disputes. Dockworkers remained restive, however, and more than 350 additional strikes broke out by mid-1938.

The ILA actions were examples of the willingness of workers to take matters into their own hands when private or government action proved too slow during the Great Depression. A violent strike at the Auto-Lite Plant in Toledo, Ohio, in April 1934 shocked authorities when unemployed workers came to the aid of strikers. The National Guard had to battle enraged workers to break the strike; troops killed 2 workers and wounded 15. But even then Auto-Lite workers were not truly subdued: The company's owners found they could not operate the plant under their own terms and agreed to worker demands, including rehiring most of the former strikers.

A similarly violent clash occurred in Minneapolis, where coal haulers associated with **Teamsters** Local 574, fed up with low wages, long hours, and being cheated at the scales, struck coal yards. Within days, nearly all the city's coal yards were shut down. After three days, the owners recognized the Teamsters and the strike was called off, but when owners reneged on promises during contract negotiations, a second strike quickly ensued. Elites were surprised to find local citizens joining the strikers; one rally saw more 25,000 people turn out in support of the union. During the month-long second strike, police killed 2 workers and wounded 67. In the end, though, management conceded to most of the union's demands.

· Textile workers conducted a nationwide strike in 1934. Poor working conditions, **speedups**, **stretch-outs**, and layoffs were commonplace among textile workers. By September, a three-month walkout of Alabama mill hands had escalated into a **general strike** involving more than 400,000 textile workers in 20 states. The strike ended ambiguously when President Roosevelt appointed a board to mediate the dispute, but the 1934 strikes paved the way for the **Congress of Industrial Organizations** (CIO) to organize textile workers in 1936 and 1937. In all, some 1,856 separate strikes involving nearly 1.5 million workers occurred in 1934.

Worker militancy pushed Roosevelt to act. When the NIRA was struck down as unconstitutional in 1935, the president quickly readied the **National Labor Relations Act** (NLRA), which supplanted it and is arguably the single most important pro-labor bill in American history. Where NIRA had guaranteed a union's right to exist as part of industry agreed-upon "codes of fair competition," the NLRA made the right of workers to organize unions a matter of law. Thousands of workers took advantage of the NLRA and joined unions, especially in manufacturing, where **industrial unionism** ideals were on the rise. The CIO formed to advance those ideals. Its willingness to draw upon the expertise and organizing savvy of leftwing radicals alarmed many, but the Roosevelt administration took the view that repressing labor unions was far more dangerous for the long-term health of American society.

The NLRA was, however, a legal guarantee that had to be won in the workplace. From 1936 onward, workers engaged in numerous battles aimed at forcing recalcitrant employers to recognize their right to belong to unions. One method used was the **sit-down strike**. In the six months between September 1936 and June 1937, more than half a million workers engaged in sit-downs. The most dramatic of these actions occurred in early 1937, when members of the **United Auto Workers of America** (UAW) won a strike in Flint, Michigan, by barricading themselves inside a General Motors plant for 44 days. The actions at Flint did much to secure the existence of the UAW and give credibility to the still-fledgling CIO. Flint became the template for other disgruntled employees, including production workers in rubber, textile, and glass as well as waitresses, newspaper delivery boys, truck drivers, sewer workers, and teachers.

Strikes remained part of the social landscape throughout the Great Depression. Industries once immune to labor organizing, such as steel, found themselves unionized during this era. The **United Steelworkers of America** (USW) organized U.S. Steel in early 1937. Once again, though, unions learned that militancy was often needed to secure their legal rights. The USW discovered this fact during a campaign to organize smaller steel mills. It lost the Little Steel strike in 1937, when management used extreme violence against workers. The Memorial Day Massacre saw Chicago police murder 10 picnicking steelworkers and wound more than 100 others. The USW kept up pressure, however, and Little Steel was organized in 1941. In similar fashion, the UAW successfully organized General Motors and Chrysler, but had to battle **goons**, labor spies, and aggressive anti-union tactics until it won recognition from Ford in 1941.

Between 1933 and 1938, workers engaged in an average of 2,541 strikes each year. In 1937, an astounding 4,740 work stoppages took place. These strikes forced organized capital to consider organized labor as a countervailing force in American society, politics, and economics. Worker militancy is especially important to keep in mind when discussing the New Deal. Many New Deal programs, such as the NIRA, the NLRA, the **Social Security Act**, and the **Fair Employment Practices Act** were inspired as much by grassroots pressure as by political debate.

Suggested Reading

Irving Bernstein, *Turbulent Years: A History of the American Worker, 1933–1941*, 1969; Jeremy Brecher, *Strike*, 1997; Lizabeth Cohen, *Making a New Deal: Industrial Workers in Chicago, 1919–1939*, 1990; Sidney Lens, *The Labor Wars*, 1973; David Selvin, *A Terrible Anger*, 1996.

DEREGULATION

Deregulation is the reduction of state and federal laws that place restrictions on how a company can conduct its business. A host of regulations generally apply to businesses, including those related to **minimum wage** rates, **child labor** restrictions, environmental standards, safety, and competition, market shares, investment policies, **outsourcing**, and pricing. Indeed, wages, hours, employment standards, and safety are generally covered by numerous laws. Although many business leaders would like laws pertaining to these matters to be softened, deregulation generally refers to business practices related to how companies manage their capital.

American industries were loosely regulated until after the **Civil War**, but regulatory practices gradually emerged from the efforts of laborers and unions to curtail abusive employer practices. They also resulted from the business community's own contradictory demands. On the one hand, business leaders insisted that the economy functioned best under laissez-faire conditions in which the government ceded economic decisions to the private sector. On the other hand, numerous businesses pressured elected officials to adopt **protectionist** policies such as high tariffs to ward off foreign competition. The latter desire violated classic **capitalist** theory, which asserted that uncontrolled supply and demand within a free market system provides natural regulations. The widespread abuses of 19th-century robber barons led to intense capital/labor conflict, and eventually even members of the growing **middle class** embraced the idea that some business regulations were in order. During the **Progressive Era**, regulations were enacted to break up trusts, guard against consumer fraud, govern interstate commerce, protect public health, monitor the money supply, and tax wealth.

Regulations expanded during the New Deal. In addition to closing loopholes that had led to reckless speculation, President Franklin Roosevelt signed into law a host of bills protecting labor's right to **collective bargaining**, curtailing the hours of employment, ending child labor, creating a minimum wage, and establishing an unemployment compensation system. The banking industry came under special scrutiny and numerous regulations were enacted to stabilize it, though bankers (both then and since) complained of overly restrictive rules.

Despite business's complaints, a regulated economy served the nation's economic health well until the 1960s, when American businesses began to feel the pressures of **globalization**. Business leaders sought allies among conservative politicians and asserted that regulations made American business less competitive on a global scale. Those arguments gained traction during the crippling stagflation that ensued after the first Organization of Petroleum Exporting Countries (OPEC) boycott in 1973, which made energy prices soar. Deregulation became a centerpiece of reform emerging in think tanks such as the Brookings Institute and from associations such as the **Business Roundtable**. Government-directed deregulation from the 1970s onward eliminated numerous regulations, many of which hit unionized industries quite hard. The trucking industry was deregulated in 1976, which led to consolidation, relaxation of **deadheading** rules, and expanded rules on how much freight a trucker can handle. Not coincidentally, it also led to a decline in the **Teamsters** union.

Other transportation groups were deregulated around the same time. The deregulation of the airline industry in 1976 and of railroads in 1980 took away many price controls, which opened the door for intense competition. Consumers benefited briefly from reduced fares, but mergers eventually dramatically reduced the overall number of carriers. Once famed carriers such as Eastern, Pan Am, and TWA eventually went out of business. Most communications industries were deregulated in 1981. Soon workers within these industries—especially airline and communications employees—complained that deregulated firms were operating like 19th-century oligarchies. Many deregulated firms were non-union, which enabled them to undercut **prevailing wage** structures. This trend forced numerous unionized companies to shut down or sell inefficient production units, thereby reducing the number of organized workers.

The 1980s saw a wave of deregulation, and President **Ronald Reagan** made it a centerpiece of his economic policy. Some deregulation efforts backfired disastrously—few more so than the deregulation of savings and loan (S&L) institutions under Reagan's 1986 Tax Reform Act. Stripped of much of this law's oversight, S&Ls engaged in unwise speculation that eventually led a crisis that required a $160 billion taxpayer bailout in 1989, and reregulation of numerous S&L practices. Nonetheless, the 1999 Graham-Leach-Biley Act actually deregulated various aspects of commercial banking, despite the hue-and-cry that this bill was unwise. The economic crisis of the early 21st century seemingly validated critics, and mild banking and financial market reforms were passed in 2010, albeit over the howl of business community protests.

Reagan-era policies also made it much easier for companies to shift assets between their internal divisions, draw upon employee **pension** accounts, and reduce **fringe benefits** for employees. Critics, especially in the labor movement, charged that few of the new rules were used to make businesses more competitive globally; instead, employers exploited them to move jobs from high-wage to low-wage states or out of the country altogether. They also argued that firms used tax savings for speculative and merger purposes, not to retool their operations.

Nonetheless, the workplace has been dramatically reconfigured from the 1980s onward. Companies demanded and got relaxed work rules that altered restrictions on job assignments, maintenance schedules, promotions, job security, handling of **grievances**, wage scales for new hires, and transfers. Deregulation often went hand in hand with demands for **concessions** from union employees. Critics blame the federal government for the poor labor/management relations that ensued after deregulation, with some charging that conditions have reverted to a state paralleling those in the Gilded Age. Organized labor has struggled to cope with the loss of members, benefits, and safety regulations undermined by deregulation. In 2010, deregulation was discussed in the wake of an explosion of an oil rig off the coast of Louisiana that sent millions of gallons of crude oil into the Gulf of Mexico. It was telling that President Barack Obama's attempt to regulate future drilling in the region met with failure. Although most organized labor groups support regulation of business, neither political party is presently inclined to reverse deregulatory practices in a proactive manner.

Suggested Reading

John Barnum, "What Prompted Airline Deregulation 20 Years Ago?," http://library.findlaw.com/1988/Sep/1/129304.html, accessed August 9, 2010; Dedria Bryfonski, *Deregulation: Opposing Viewpoints*, 2010; Paul Joskow, *Deregulation: Where Do We Go from Here?*, 2009.

DETROIT NEWSPAPER STRIKE

The Detroit Newspaper Strike was an unsuccessful 1995 work stoppage called by six unions against the *Detroit News*, owned by the Gannett Corporation, and the *Detroit Free Press*, part of the Knight-Ridder chain. The **strike** began on July 13, 1995, and involved more than 2,500 reporters, printers, circulation workers, and support staff; it ended in defeat five and half years later. It has been studied as an example of a **downsizing, concessions, and decertification strike** by analysts who think that management precipitated the dispute solely to increase profits and force non-union **open shops** upon employees. It has also been studied by those concerned about media consolidation in contemporary America and, more recently, by those who see what happened in Detroit as a harbinger of cataclysmic changes in the newspaper business that became more widespread in the 21st century. The strike certainly illustrates that **solidarity** alone cannot sustain a strike under current labor law.

The Detroit strike had its genesis in media mergers and changes in communications laws that emerged in the 1970s, accelerated during the **deregulation** wave of the 1980s, and have gained momentum since then. Well into the 1960s, most metropolitan areas had competing newspapers, and laws regulated the number of outlets that any one corporation could control. The economic crisis of the 1970s began a trend in which many city newspapers either went out of business or were absorbed by corporate chains such as Gannett, Hearst, or Knight-Ridder. The situation was especially acute in cities that shed population in the aftermath of **deindustrialization**.

By 1988, Detroit was one of the few metropolitan areas that still had viable competing papers. In that year, however, the *News* and the *Free Press* set up the joint operating agreement (JOA) to fuse the advertising and circulation departments of the two papers, even though the plan was opposed by the mayor's office and the Justice Department's antitrust division, which denied the JOA petition. Both corporations vigorously lobbied Attorney General Edward Meese III, who headed President **Ronald Reagan's** Justice Department. In the deregulatory climate of the 1980s, Meese moved swiftly to overturn the Justice Department's decision, and the newly christened Detroit Newspaper Association (DNA) began publishing both papers. The ruling came at a particularly opportune time for Gannett, which had launched the national paper *USA Today* in 1982 and was keen to divert resources from its metropolitan papers to prop up the money-losing and critically panned national venture.

As critics had warned, once the papers were no longer in direct competition, advertising rates soared, staff was trimmed, and harsh **concessions** were demanded from remaining workers, including **wage** cuts and higher medical insurance copayments. These demands were made despite the fact that both chains posted record profits. Reporters and newsroom personnel belonging to the Newspaper Guild voted to strike after the implementation of a **merit raise** system, which came after six years of pay freezes. Circulation department employees joined the strike after further layoffs of what management deemed featherbedding jobs, a transparent claim in light of the fact that nearly all of those let go were union workers. Workers represented by the Communication Workers of America and the International Brotherhood of Teamsters (IBT) also took part in the strike and **boycott**. In retrospect, the unions walked into a management trap. Once workers struck, both companies hired **scabs** and announced their intentions to operate as union-free papers. It was later revealed that the DNA had contacted Alternative Work Force (AWF) months before the strike, so preparations to replace workers were in place well in advance of the walkout.

The strike was marked by acrimony and violence from the start, nearly all of it precipitated by management. Private security guards contracted from Huffmaster Security clashed with picketers and beat them. In a 1996 incident, two Gannett delivery trucks rammed **picketers**. Huffmaster was later replaced by Vance International, a firm that specializes in security during labor disputes and that has been charged by labor unions with inciting violence through the use of **agent provocateurs**. Very little news of the strike made its way into the mainstream media, leading media critics to charge that corporate control of newspapers leads to a de facto censoring of information; in essence, it is unrealistic for one paper under corporate control to report positively on a dispute involving another within the same chain.

On the local level, striker resolve remained high during the strike's early days. Union networks worked to spread information not covered in the mainstream news and boycotts dramatically reduced revenues for both papers. Several unions aided strikers in underwriting the *Sunday Detroit Journal*, an alternative to the *News* and *Free Press*. Deprived of a broader public platform, however, the strike began to fizzle and about half of the Newspaper Guild's strikers drifted back to work. On February 14, 1997, more than a year and a half after the initial walkout, the strike was called off and unions unconditionally offered to return to work. The DNA responded by placing a small number of workers on a preferential hiring list for future openings, but declared that the vast majority had forfeited their jobs. Merit pay, wage cuts, open-shop policies, and other concessions remained in effect.

Although the strike was officially over, the boycott remained in effect. In June 1997, Detroit hosted a huge solidarity march in which unions such as the **United Farm Workers of America**, the **United Auto Workers of America**, and the **Industrial Workers of the World** pledged support, as did international officers of the **American Federation of Labor-Congress of Industrial Organizations** (AFL-CIO). Weeks earlier, the National Labor Relations Board (NLRB) ruled that Gannett and Knight-Ridder were guilty of **unfair labor practices**; both appealed the ruling and then ignored it. In September 1998, the NLRB again found unfair labor practices and ordered that former strikers be rehired. That decision was also appealed.

Numerous labor activists were critical of the strike tactics used by the Detroit workers. Strikers did not stop production of a single issue, causing some activists to question the wisdom of relying too much on boycotts and not enough on militancy. Others charged that AFL-CIO president **John Sweeney** placed too much faith in political pressure. He met several times with President Bill Clinton, but little came of those meetings. Sweeney also drew criticism for being too slow to organize rallies in support of the original job action. Strikers also were criticized. A significant number of AWF scabs were African Americans, and picketers occasionally hurled racist epithets at them—an act of political and social suicide in a city whose population is predominately black. The interjection of race served only to harm the union cause. Remaining hope dissipated in July 2000, when the U.S. Court of Appeals reversed NLRB findings against the DNA. Judge Laurence Silberman ruled that because the strike was called over economic issues, the DNA had not engaged in unfair labor practices by hiring replacement workers. In December 2000, the last remaining strikers settled when IBT drivers and mailers ratified an agreement. Teamsters president James P. Hoffa ruffled feathers when he asserted it was time for labor to cut its losses. With the IBT settling its dispute, the last remaining boycott call was removed.

The Detroit newspaper strike was a disaster for organized labor. The IBT alone spent more than $30 million in the unsuccessful fight against Gannett and Knight-Ridder. There is no question that both companies suffered losses as well; most estimates place revenue losses at more than $100 million, in addition to the $650 million spent to combat the strike and boycott. Paper circulation dropped dramatically. In 2002, the combined circulation of the daily papers was approximately 604,000, down from 900,000 before the 1995 strike. Sunday sales plummeted from 1.1 million to 750,000 copies. In 2005, Gannett sold the *Detroit News* to

MediaNews Group, though it bought the *Free Press* from Knight-Ridder. Both papers continue to be published jointly, and both continue to lose readers. By April 2010, Sunday readership of the *Free Press* dropped to 511,742, a decline of 12.1 percent in just six months. A Sunday paper that was once the nation's sixth largest is now its ninth largest. Daily circulation dropped to 252,017, a 13 percent decline, and the paper now makes home deliveries only on Thursdays and Fridays. Although newspapers nationwide have suffered lost readership, the Detroit decreases are substantially steeper than the national readership declines of 6.5 percent for Sunday papers and 8.7 percent for daily paper. The smaller *Detroit News* circulates just 149,872 issues on Monday through Saturday. Labor activists point to a recent decision on the part of the *News* to launch an all-conservative website as further proof that the paper's labor woes are, at heart, ideological in nature.

The Detroit battles are a late example of the downsizing and concession strikes of the 1980s and a poignant reminder that corporations generally have far deeper pockets than labor. It is hard to defeat employers determined to implement long-term programs to crush unions via traditional tactics. The failed efforts in Detroit have fueled the call for increased militancy among organized labor. Activists point once again to the inability (or unwillingness) of the **Democratic Party** to intervene on behalf of unions; some radicals have called for the repeal of *all* existing labor laws, charging that alleged legal protections are chimeras that lead to false hopes and provide management with delaying tactics. In their view, workers would be better served by fighting management at the point of production or by waging **corporate campaigns**. More cautious observers counsel that assessment of the Detroit losses must be balanced by recent victories like those of **Ravenswood** steelworkers and United Parcel Service employees. At the very least, the Detroit strike and boycott raise questions of the efficacy of traditional tactics.

Suggested Reading

"Business as Usual Lost the Newspaper Strike," *Labor Notes* (February 2001); Shannon Jones, "Unions Settle with *Detroit News* and *Free Press*: Lessons of Another AFL-CIO Debacle," http://www.wsws.org/articles/2001/jan2001/news-j04.shtml, accessed August 10, 2010; "One Love, Too Little Too Late for Detroit Newspaper Strikers," *Love and Rage*, 8, no. 4 (August/September 1997); Robert G. Picard, Stephen Lacy, and Robert H. Giles, "Lessons from the Detroit Newspaper Strike," *Newspaper Research Journal*, 18, 1997.

DIRECT ACTION

Direct action is a loosely defined but basic **anarcho-syndicalist** concept associated with the **Industrial Workers of the World** (IWW). Among the founding ideals of the IWW was a belief that traditional labor unions were slow and deliberative in their responses to injustice. Direct action is a demonstration of ongoing worker power in the workplace and can be applied without the formality of going through union bureaucratic channels. Its basic premise is to address unfairness in a militant way that punishes employers. It could take the form of a **strike**, but also involves strategies such as a deliberate slowing of production, shaming, or **sabotage**. The last was often defined as a strategic withdrawal of efficiency and might involve feigned incompetence or using deliberately labor-intensive work methods, but it also occasionally meant damaging machines. Direct action also entailed aggressive responses against **scab** labor or abusive bosses. Although violence committed by IWW members was greatly exaggerated and more was done *to* them than *by* them, intimidation of scabs and bosses was certainly part of the IWW repertoire. One IWW tactic involved meting out justice to railroad "bulls" (police) known for brutalizing tramps. Such individuals were sometimes lured into situations in which a gang would administer a demonstrative beating.

In general, direct action is associated with militant and immediate actions taken to assert labor's rights. The IWW claimed that direct action would be a mechanism in the ultimate destabilization and destruction of **capitalism**, but working people in general have viewed direct action as justified tit-for-tat responses to intolerable conditions. Most cases of direct action involve decisions in which workers on the job determine which responses should be taken, not absentee union officials. The IWW found it easier to embrace direct action because it rejected many of the standard operating principles of less-militant unions. Power was concentrated as much as possible in individual members and **union locals** rather than in national organizations, and those locals did not need to seek permission to launch job actions. The IWW also rejected automatic dues **checkoffs**, high dues, and paycheck deductions for things such as health and life insurance, which it viewed as **welfare capitalist** tricks designed to blunt militancy. Many IWW locals even refused to sign written **contracts** with employers, lest workers be hemmed in by stipulations that would prevent direct action to redress **grievances**.

The IWW lost much of its influence after 1919, but direct action continued to be a powerful concept, even if it did not always go by that name. Perhaps the most notable example was the **sit-down strike**, an IWW tactic revived by the **United Auto Workers of America** at Flint, Michigan, in 1936. **Wildcat strikes** are often framed in direct action terms. Other forms of direct action involve spontaneous **picketing**, holding impromptu rallies, occupying private property, defacing property with graffiti, rioting, and blocking roads. In recent years some labor activists have argued that current conditions are so unfairly stacked against working people that they need to revisit the use of direct action and act in defiance of, rather than in accordance with, existing labor laws. They cite recent examples from the civil rights and radical environmental movements as examples of strategic use of direct action. Recent disruptions of World Trade Organization meetings have involved labor militants.

Suggested Reading

Melvyn Dubofsky, *We Shall Be All: A History of the Industrial Workers of the World*, 1969; Joyce L. Kornbluh, *Rebel Voice: An IWW Anthology*, 1972; William Mellor, *Direct Action*, 1920.

DIVISION OF LABOR

Division of labor is a self-defining term that refers to how work is divided among those to whom it is assigned. Other than in some cases of **artisan labor**, most work tasks are broken into smaller subtasks, either for efficiency's sake, in the case of

assembly-line production, or because certain individual workers are more skilled at carrying out a specialized job.

A division of labor is as old as civilization; indeed, many scholars see its development as a hallmark of the Neolithic Revolution that gave rise to permanent settlements. Ancient writers such as Plato wrote of a division of labor as a prerequisite for the smooth functioning of society, though such discussions generally extended to society as a whole rather than to individual jobs. The first division of labor was probably that between rulers, soldiers, and workers (broadly defined as those who produced the food, implements, and services necessary to sustain the other two groups).

Although little about the concept is inherently controversial, the social applications of division of labor are often contentious, and they became even more so after the advent of the **Industrial Revolution**. In **agrarian** America, work usually involved a division of labor, with men often assuming responsibility for the bulk of outdoor tasks and women taking on the burden of domestic toil, including the raising of children. The lines between the tasks were often blurred, however, and independent yeomanry was understood to require a cooperative approach for success. Because most goods were produced for consumption or local barter (a system often known as closed household economy), task assignment was customary but not rigidly observed. Women, for example, took to the fields during plowing and harvest season and worked alongside men.

Division of labor becomes more controversial when certain types of labor are valued more highly than others, or if it is reserved only for certain groups. When factory production matured in the United States during the early 19th century, work was often segregated along the lines of gender, racial, ethnic, skill, and age. For the most part, white men of Western European backgrounds who possessed skills not yet replaceable by machine labor stood at the top of the labor hierarchy. By mid-century, most male work was valued and remunerated above work associated with women. It became intertwined with prevailing views of biology now dubbed essentialism that held that men and women were, by nature, suited to certain tasks. Historians speak of domestic ideology, a division that prevailed until well into the 20th century and held that women were naturally suited for unpaid work revolving around child care and taking care of the home, while it was a man's natural sphere to work outside the home for **wages**.

Gender views dovetailed with those on race. Antebellum **slavery** and post-Civil War "Jim Crow" systems guaranteed that African Americans would be assigned work thought to be unworthy of whites. The same thinking extended to immigrants, with most new immigrants being assigned poorly paid work that was dirtier, harder, and more dangerous, and with groups such as the **Chinese** thought to be unfit to work around whites in any capacity. Similarly denigrated were white workers who did manual, semi-skilled, or unskilled labor; those at the top of their crafts and pay scale—sometimes called the **aristocracy of labor**—looked down upon such workers. Ironically, the division of labor that was least controversial among workers themselves was **child labor**, a widespread practice that would not be curtailed until the 20th century. Children were often viewed as most suitable for menial tasks, many of which involved long hours and deplorable working conditions.

The values associated with division of labor have generated great debate since industrialization. They have been vigorously defended by apologists for **capitalism** such as Adam Smith and hotly contested by **socialists**, labor unions, and social reformers. In recent years the **globalization** of the economy has extended the debate beyond North American borders. Intense debates continue to roil over child labor and **sweatshop** practices in the developing world. Within the United States, controversy persists over remaining wage disparities in the relative pay of white males compared to women and **minority labor**. Many ongoing battles over pay equity are rooted in division of labor ideals that critics declare are outdated. In like fashion, feminist activists and scholars have called attention to the many ways in which working women continue to shoulder an undue share of household work.

Suggested Reading

Gary Becker, *A Treatise on the Family*, 1991; Harvey Braverman, *Labor and Monopoly Capitalism: The Degradation of Work in the 20th Century*, 1974; Andrew Sayer, *The New Social Economy: Reworking the Division of Labor*, 1992; Marcus Taylor, *Global Economy Contested: Power and Conflict across the International Division of Labor*, 2008.

DODGE REVOLUTIONARY UNION MOVEMENT

The Dodge Revolutionary Union Movement (DRUM) was the most famous of a series of Marxist labor action groups formed in the late 1960s and active into the 1970s. DRUM inspired a series of Revolutionary Union Movements (RUMs) that galvanized African American, Asian American, Latino, and Native American workers. At the time many RUM members called themselves **communists**, though in retrospect most seem to have been reacting to urban chaos and racism rather than to the seductions of Marxist ideology. The most significant RUMs were inside the auto industry, and the pressures they exerted led to changes with organized labor's structure. They also contributed to white flight to the suburbs, especially in Detroit.

DRUM came to public light on May 2, 1968, when 4,000 workers at Chrysler Corporation's Dodge Main plant in Hamtramck, Michigan, held a five-day **wildcat strike** that caught both the company and the **United Auto Workers of America** (UAW) by surprise. Although the immediate cause of the strike was worker complaints about assembly-line **speedups** and racist foremen, its roots lay in the rising tide of black militancy that peaked in the 1960s. During that decade, civil rights groups, students, and antiwar activists transformed American political and social dialogue. By the middle of the decade, some African American leaders came to question the pacifist strategies that had hitherto governed civil rights protests. Black organizations such as the Student Nonviolent Coordinating Committee (SNCC) and the Black Panther Party touted militant Black Power as the antidote to what they saw as the implicit accommodationism of passive-resistance tactics. Urban areas became a powder keg of racial tension. Beginning with Harlem (New York) in 1964 and Watts (Los Angeles) in 1965, a series of racially charged riots engulfed

American cities. One of the very worst disruptions occurred in Detroit in July 1967. Large sections of the "Motor City" burned, snipers fired from vacant buildings and highway overpasses, and near-anarchy reigned for more than a week before some 4,700 U.S. Army paratroopers and 8,000 National Guardsmen imposed heavy-handed order. At least 43 people died in the riots, hundreds were injured, and nearly 4,000 were arrested.

The Detroit riots reflected the city's changing face. The city had long been the preserve of native-born whites and European immigrants. It was they who led the labor battles of the 1930s and made Detroit a UAW stronghold. By the 1960s, however, Detroit was an increasingly black city with an entrenched, conservative white power structure. The city's police force, in particular, was viewed as brutal and racist to the core. White privilege extended to Detroit's auto industry and unions. In the suburb of Hamtramck, 85 percent of all Dodge workers were black, but only 2 percent of its foremen were people of color. Unions were no better; black autoworkers complained that UAW stood for "U Ain't White."

The Hamtramck wildcat strike of May 1968 was as much a critique of the UAW and liberalism as of Chrysler. Detroit elected Jerome Cavanaugh as mayor in 1961; Cavanaugh was an advocate of liberal policies during the administrations of John Kennedy and Lyndon Johnson. Local black leaders complained of the slow pace of reform, and Cavanaugh was mayor when both the 1967 riot and the 1968 wildcat strikes took place. The latter shocked the UAW, which had long fancied itself to be one of the more progressive labor unions in the United States. UAW President **Walter Reuther** supported black rights, and the UAW frequently gave money to assist civil rights groups. In 1967, the UAW ceased paying dues to the **American Federation of Labor-Congress of Industrial Organizations** (AFL-CIO), in part because Reuther felt it was too slow to embrace civil rights and the antiwar movement. To DRUM activists such as General Gordon Baker, Luke Tripp, and John Watson, however, Reuther and local UAW officials were paternalistic, condescending, and out of touch with changing urban realities. Some also argued that racism was inextricably linked to unsound economic assumptions. DRUM leaders schooled themselves in the theories of Karl Marx, V. I. Lenin, and other radical theorists. Instead of the UAW's program of higher **wages** and behind-the-scenes political lobbying, DRUM called for a revolution to cast off both white oppression and **capitalism**.

Revolutionary fervor was probably more deeply ingrained among leaders than amidst the DRUM rank-and-file, but their impassioned rhetoric tapped into simmering anger and rubbed salt into festering racial wounds. DRUM inspired copycat organizations. African American Cadillac assemblers formed the Cadillac Revolutionary Union Movement (CADRUM), Chrysler workers formed CHRYRUM, and Detroit's Elron Avenue axle-makers formed ELRUM. Ford workers in Detroit and Mahwah, New Jersey, created the Ford Revolutionary Union Movement (FORUM), and RUMs appeared at United Parcel Service, at the *Detroit News*, and among autoworkers in California and Maryland. Black steelworkers at Sparrow's Point, Maryland; Birmingham, Alabama; and elsewhere formed RUM-like groups of their own. Some of these groups cultivated ties with other black militant groups such as SNCC and the Black Panthers. In 1971, Detroit-area RUMs created the League of Revolutionary Black Workers (LRBW), a loose federation that attempted to coordinate efforts among militant groups. Its membership was closed to whites, though Asians, Latinos, and Native Americans were represented. The LRBW issued fiery statements, but its achievements were modest as the RUM movement was already losing steam by then.

The bulk of DRUM activities took place in Detroit. John Watson took over editorship of Wayne State University's paper, *South End*, and converted it into a **socialist** daily with links to the Black Panthers, much to the chagrin of university officials. Copies were distributed to autoworkers. The LRBW's most dramatic action was to underwrite the defense of James Johnson, who murdered two foremen and a coworker in 1971. Johnson's defense team successfully argued that on-the-job pressures at Chrysler and a lifetime of exposure to racism had driven him criminally insane. Until the judgment was overturned on appeal, Chrysler even had to pay **worker's compensation** to help defray Johnson's mental health care costs.

DRUM and other RUMs fizzled shortly after the Johnson verdict and, by the mid-1970s, quietly faded from existence. In Detroit, the mayoralty in 1969 went to a conservative, Roman Gribbs, who campaigned on a law-and-order platform and unleashed Detroit police to crack down on black militants. Although local RUMs succeeded in forcing changes upon the police force, their venture into mainstream politics in 1973 was out of synch with Marxist rhetoric. RUM candidates fared poorly, but galvanized enough voters to secure the election of Coleman Young, Detroit's first black mayor. In like fashion, the UAW began electing more black officials and placing them in high positions of authority.

As DRUM and its imitators declined, some radicals blamed the slide on factors such as complacency, oppression, and the abandonment of a revolutionary workers base. From a historical viewpoint, though, the case can be made for viewing RUMs as expressions of a particular historical moment—one infused with anger, rising racial consciousness, and heightened social tensions that created opportunities for leaders and organizations to express and channel fury. The RUMs parallel the experience of the **Industrial Workers of the World** in that they often enjoyed their greatest success when responding to local and immediate incidents, but had trouble in keeping alive the passions they inflamed. Structural changes also explain the passing of DRUM and the LRBW. These groups tapped into anger over the slowness of reform, but by the early 1970s initiatives such as the Civil Rights Act and the Equal Employment Opportunity Act finally began to have the impact that those who created them had hoped. Detroit's power structure changed dramatically, with African Americans winning control of the mayor's office and city council. In general, the mid-1970s saw a cooling of the activist fervor of the previous 10 years.

Scholars are divided over whether the net effect of RUM activity was positive or negative. There is no question that DRUM gave voice and power to groups long denied these privileges. Nor is there argument over the impact RUMs had on changing the composition of union leadership; even the stodgy AFL-CIO placed more people of color in top leadership posts. These gains came at the cost of stifling rank-and-file activism, however. Wildcat strikes had the effect of leading the UAW deeper into a business unionism mode of operation, the inclusion of black leaders notwithstanding.

It is also true is that the white flight to the suburbs accelerated dramatically in the 1960s and 1970s. By the time African Americans took over Detroit's political structure in the 1970s, its economic base was in a deep downward spiral and the city's population was shrinking. In 1950, Detroit had 1.8 million residents; today it is barely half that number. In like fashion, in 1973, one of six jobs in Detroit was linked to the auto industry. In that year, however, the auto industry was devastated by the first Organization of Petroleum Exporting Countries (OPEC) oil boycott and began to hemorrhage jobs. Soaring gasoline prices, inflation, and imported vehicles also challenged Detroit's near-monopoly on auto sales. Lagging sales led to layoffs and plant closures; by the 1980s, **deindustrialization** ravaged Detroit. Since 1989, the city has lost 70 percent of its auto-industry jobs, with this retrenchment coming on the heels of huge losses prior to that. The city now has one of the highest **unemployment** rates in the nation. For thousands of Detroit residents, immediate needs for economic survival take precedence over a revolutionary future.

Suggested Reading

Dan Georgakas and Marvin Surkin, *Detroit: I Do Mind Dying*, 1998; Philip Levine and Andrew Moore, *Detroit Disassembled*, 2010; Heather Thompson, *Whose Detroit? Politics, Labor, and Race in a Modern American City*, 2001.

DOMESTIC IDEOLOGY. *See* Division of Labor.

DOWNSIZING

Downsizing refers to a deliberate company strategy to reduce a firm's workforce so as to cut costs and/or increase profits. A wave of downsizing occurred in the 1970s and 1980s that involved plant shutdowns, mergers, **outsourcing**, and technological updating of manufacturing facilities. The recession of the early 21st century led to a new wave of downsizing that has lingered into the century's second decade. Unlike layoffs in which workers are thrown out of work temporarily during periods of weak demand, downsizing involves the permanent elimination of positions. Workers involved in downsizing are forced to exist on unemployment benefits until they can secure new jobs. Downsizing often goes hand in hand with **deindustrialization**. The resulting economic dislocation means that workers who stay in the area where downsizing occurs often have difficulty securing new jobs that pay as well as the ones they lost. Thus downsizing has also been linked to a lifestyle diminishment for millions of Americans.

In the 1990s, many labor unions responded to downsizing by negotiating explicit employment security clauses as part of their **collective bargaining** agreements. Seniority clauses have long been important, but they have received renewed attention given that layoffs usually start with the least senior workers. Downsizing also led to joint management/labor partnerships as unions, fearing the increased loss of members, worked with employers to reduce inefficiencies and retain as many workers as possible.

Unions have largely conceded that certain efficiencies are needed to keep American business competitive, but downsizing is extremely controversial when it takes place within profitable firms that seek to increase value to shareholders at the expense of workers. Much of the downsizing has also come at a time of skyrocketing executive salaries. In more egregious cases, executives have won bonuses for reducing payroll, even though their companies' production and profits failed to increase. Unions charge, with considerable merit, that such downsizing is little more than disguised union-busting. Many union activists call for stricter controls on the conditions under which a profitable firm can downsize its workforce.

Recent studies indicate that downsizing often fails to secure the benefits companies intended. In many cases, the outcomes of poor employee morale, lower-quality products, the loss of valuable expertise, and the inefficiency of overworked surviving employees more than negate payroll savings.

Suggested Reading

W. J. Baumol, A. S. Blinder, and E. N. Wolff, *Downsizing in America: Reality, Causes and Consequences*, 2003; James P. Guthrie and Deepak K. Datta, "Dumb and Dumber: The Impact of Downsizing on Firm Performance as Moderated by Industry Conditions," *Organization Science*, 19, no. 1 (January–February 2008), 108–123; David Hornestay, "Downsizing Dilemma," http://www.govexec.com/reinvent/downsize/0896s3.htm, accessed August 10, 2010.

DOWNSIZING, DECERTIFICATION, AND CONCESSIONS STRIKES

"Downsizing, decertification, and concessions strikes" is a catchall phrase that refers to a series of actions that peaked in the 1980s and 1990s, in which businesses launched an assault against organized labor. Most of the associated **strikes** and **lockouts** were initiated by the business community to increase corporate profits and/or weaken labor unions. To a large extent, this corporate strategy was successful; by the mid-1990s, union workers represented just 15.5 percent of the American workforce, and today that figure now stands at less than 13 percent.

The U.S. economy sputtered after 1973, falling into a condition economists labeled stagflation, one marked by flat growth, yet high inflation. Some companies—particularly in the **blue-collar** manufacturing sector—were saddled with outmoded equipment and high-waged workers that made it difficult to compete with cheaper foreign imports. Between 1969 and 1976 alone, some 22 million jobs were lost due to plant closures. Most of the new jobs created during the period paid lower **wages**. Employers that stayed in business demanded **concessions** from workers in the form of wage freezes (or cuts), reduced benefits, and/or increased production rates. Unemployment rose to its highest levels since the Great Depression. In 1979, the Chrysler Corporation declared bankruptcy, and only a huge taxpayer-funded bailout saved the company from disappearing altogether. The **United Auto Workers of America** agreed to a concessions package to help keep the company afloat. The net effect, however, was for other employers to jump on the concessions bandwagon and make similar demands of their employees.

By the 1980s, buzzwords such as "competitiveness," "becoming lean," and "downsizing" (or the more euphemistic "rightsizing") became corporate policy. Workforces were trimmed, concessions imposed, and productivity quotas increased as employers sought to cut costs and compete in the global economy.

Economists continue to debate how much cost cutting was legitimate and how much simply padded the bottom line of already profitable companies. Nevertheless, trends begun in the 1970s accelerated in the 1980s, and few sectors of the economy were spared. Even states and municipalities were forced to cut budgets in the wake of taxpayer revolts like Proposition 13 in California and Proposition 2½ in Massachusetts. That situation was worsened by Reagan-era cutbacks on social spending.

In 1980, **Ronald Reagan** was elected president, and the country's mainstream politics moved sharply rightward. A sizable part of the American business community has always opposed labor unions, and it found an ally for this position in the White House. When Reagan fired striking **Professional Air Traffic Controllers Organization** (PATCO) workers in 1981, he emboldened anti-union forces across the nation. The decade was marked by bitter **strikes** and **lockouts**, almost all of which were initiated by management. Southwestern copper miners—many of whom were Hispanic—were routed by **Phelps Dodge** during 1983 and 1984, as were Midwestern meatpackers during a 1985–1986 confrontation with **Hormel**. The Hormel strike was marked by ugly internecine struggles between local unions and the parent **United Food and Commercial Workers Union** (UFCW), with Austin, Minnesota, workers attempting to decertify the UFCW. Workers also suffered stinging defeats in battles against Eastern Airlines, Greyhound, International Paper, **Pittston Coal**, and USX (the former United States Steel Corporation), to name just a few.

In all, the 1980s saw the largest assault against labor unions since the **open-shop** drives of the 1920s, though the situation in the 1980s was, in many ways, more dire. The **American Federation of Labor-Congress of Industrial Organizations** (AFL-CIO) failed in its attempts to get labor law reforms passed during the presidency of Jimmy Carter (1977–1981), opening the door for the aggressive anti-union tactics of the Reagan and George H. W. Bush administrations (1981–1993). Openings on the National Labor Relations Board (NLRB) often went to individuals more sympathetic to management than to labor and, in a few cases, to those with track records of aggressively opposing unions. Law firms sprouted that specialized in helping employers launch **decertification** drives against unions, while numerous consultant agencies counseled corporations on how to keep their workplaces free of unions. The Chamber of Commerce set up a National Right-to-Work Committee, which churned out negative publicity about unions, and the **National Association of Manufacturers** unveiled its Committee on a Union Free Environment. More damaging still was the use of replacement workers—that is, **scabs** hired on a permanent basis to take the jobs of strikers. These types of hirings came to the fore during the PATCO walkout, and courts have upheld the right of corporations to hire replacement workers during economic strikes in which there are no findings of **unfair labor practices**. With the rightward shift of the NLRB, fewer such findings were made, but even when they were, a favored corporate tactic was simply to tie up cases in lengthy appeals that few workers could weather and even well-heeled unions found expensive.

Corporations received a further boost from Reagan tax reforms in 1981 and 1986 that dramatically slashed taxes for corporations and high-income individuals. In 1977, 8.1 percent of corporate profits were taxed; by 1985, that figure was nearly halved (4.2 percent). Generous tax write-offs allowed companies to shield profits, and they also benefited from **deregulation**. The cornerstone of Reagan-Bush economics was adherence to the supply-side economic ideas of Arthur Laffer and George Gilder. In theory, tax cuts and laissez-faire policies encourage corporations and wealthy individuals to invest in the economy. This, in turn, creates opportunity for all Americans. That outcome, however, was not the reality. Many companies used tax loopholes to close factories, sell the assets, and invest in the stock market. By the mid-1980s, economists spoke of the **deindustrialization** of America; the U.S. share of the world's industrial output slipped from 50 percent in 1960 to less than 25 percent by 1985. Fully three-fourths of *Fortune* magazine's top 100 new companies of the 1980s were, in fact, the product of mergers; U.S. Steel, for example, reemerged as USX Corporation and derived more income from shopping malls, real estate, golf courses, and insurance than from steel. Some 57 percent of the jobs that were created in the 1980s paid wages that sank a family of four below the poverty line. A substantial number were **part-time** jobs. Adjusted for inflation, real wages fell by 9 percent from 1980 to 1989.

Globalization posed the biggest challenge of all. A 1976 tax revision encouraged American companies to set up subsidiaries in U.S. possessions. By the 1980s, many went a step further and simply moved their operations overseas to take advantage of lower wage structures, lax environmental laws, and union-free workplaces. Between 1980 and 1995, more than 2,200 factories employing in excess of 800,000 workers were built in Mexico, the vast majority of them by American-based firms. President Bill Clinton earned the enmity of many union workers for signing the 1993 **North American Free Trade Agreement** with Canada and Mexico, a bill that hastened relocation of manufacturing plants to Mexico.

Organized labor fared only slightly better during the **Democratic** administration of the Clinton years (1993–2001) than under Republicans Reagan and Bush. The 1990s saw bitter battles like the **Staley lockout**, and strikes against Bridgestone/Firestone, Caterpillar, General Motors, and newspapers in Detroit and Seattle. Organized labor managed to win several key battles. Favorable settlements for workers at Bridgestone/Firestone, Fieldcrest, United Parcel Service, NYNEX, and Ravenswood during the 1990s slowed the decline of unions and gave rise to new hopes. AFL-CIO President **John Sweeney** pledged to renew union militancy and reverse patterns of downsizing, decertification votes, and concessionary givebacks. To date, the results of this effort have been mixed. The administration of George H. W. Bush saw a return to open hostility between labor and the government. Union membership continued to slide and Sweeney has himself become the target of union activists who claim he is too cautious.

To many observers, the troubles of the 1980s and beyond signal a need to rethink how organized labor conducts itself. Prevailing labor law is slanted toward employers, and the threats of globalization and movable capital render old union tactics obsolete. The most successful work stoppages of recent years have come from service and public-sector workers who are not threatened by capital flight. Deindustrialization, outsourcing, and the rise of a service economy have led to structural changes in the U.S. economy to which old-style unions have not yet adapted. Unions remain optimistic that global organizing, new tactics, and political pressure will revitalize the labor movement. Less sanguine observers suggest that unions should abandon organizing **sunset industries** and concentrate on the service sector, white-collar workers, and professionals.

Suggested Reading

Stanley Aronowitz, *From the Ashes of the Old: American Labor's Future*, 1998; Donald Bartlett and James Steele, *America: What Went Wrong?*, 1993; Thomas Geoghegan, *Which Side Are You On?*, 1992.

DUAL UNIONISM

Dual unionism refers to a situation in which an individual worker (or group) belongs to more than one labor federation or **international union** at the same time. In most cases, unions frown on dual unionism, and many have specific constitutional bylaws forbidding it. It is seen as dividing workers' loyalty and, in some cases, forcing them to choose among competing ideals or to take sides in **jurisdiction** disputes. Some dual union activities are forbidden under the **National Labor Relations Act**. For instance, only one union can be recognized as the **collective bargaining** agent for employees of a particular workplace.

Numerous dual unionism disputes have marked American labor history. During the late 19th century, many workers were simultaneously members of the **Knights of Labor** (KOL) and of specific **craft unions**. This proved problematic in situations in which a local or international union authorized a **strike**, **boycott**, or decision with which the KOL disapproved, and it led to several bitter clashes that forced members to choose sides. For example, the KOL sided with a renegade faction of the Cigar Makers International Union (CMIU) in New York City in 1884, which led the CMIU to disaffiliate from the KOL two years later. This experience had a profound influence on CMIU officials **Samuel Gompers** and **Adolph Strasser**. When they founded the **American Federation of Labor** (AFL) in 1886, many of AFL constituent unions expressly forbade dual membership in the KOL. Later in the century, **Daniel DeLeon** set up the Socialist Trade and Labor Alliance, seen by both the KOL and the AFL as a dual union. In the 20th century, the AFL urged members to avoid the **Industrial Workers of the World** (IWW), which sometimes had overlapping memberships. Although the IWW was contemptuous of the AFL, it did not impose restrictions against dual unions on its members.

Workers who join more than one union generally do so for a combination of pragmatic and ideological reasons. For example, many workers trusted their craft unions to represent their immediate occupational interests, but admired the KOL for its broad reform agenda and its long-term plan for remaking society. Sometimes dual unionism is a deliberate tactic used by movements seeking to alter existing organizations, protect themselves, or both. This was the strategy of the Communist Party of the United States of America (CPUSA) on several occasions. The **Red Scare** after World War I made it difficult for **communists** to espouse their views openly. The CPUSA set up the Trade Union Educational League to bore within existing AFL unions. The hope was that CPUSA members would eventually convert fellow workers to the communist cause. That did not happen on a large scale, but skilled leaders such as **William Z. Foster** demonstrated some success in leading AFL workers to a more militant stance. In 1929, the CPUSA abandoned boring within, set up its own **Trade Union Unity League** (TUUL), and moved away from dual unionism. Nonetheless, the experience left the AFL so shaken that many of its more conservative leaders viewed advocates of **industrial unionism** as supporters of dual unions. The inability to resolve that clash led to the establishment of the **Congress of Industrial Organizations** (CIO). Ironically, the CPUSA later dismantled the TUUL and returned to working within existing unions. Until a renewed Red Scare after World War II led the CIO to purge communists, some of its best organizers had ties to the CPUSA.

Most analysts assumed that serious dual unionism disputes would disappear after the 1955 AFL-CIO merger. That was not the case. Occasionally, **wildcat strikes** were denounced by international unions as a form of dual unionism, as were reform groups such as the Teamsters for a Democratic Union, which sought to democratize the International Brotherhood of Teamsters. More recently, dual unionism charges have been leveled against rank-and-file militants who battle against what they see as entrenched **business unionist** bureaucrats. The decline of labor unions since the 1970s has led some to head **decertification** drives against their own unions to establish independent militant organizations, or to join another union they deem better able to represent them. For example, in 2002, the Transport Workers Union leveled charges of dual unionism against American Airline mechanics contemplating affiliation with the **International Association of Machinists and Aerospace Workers**. In an age of union mergers, overlapping jurisdictions, and broader worker representation, jurisdictional and dual unionism debates are likely to continue.

Suggested Reading

AFL-CIO, http://www.aflcio.org; Bert Cochran, *Labor and Communism: The Conflict That Shaped American Labor*, 1977; Harvey Klehr, *The Heyday of American Communism*, 1984.

DUES

Dues are the money paid by union members to a labor organization. These funds provide income for the union and defray the costs of operating it. Most union dues are automatically deducted from workers' paychecks through a system known as **checkoff** and are tax deductible. The checkoff replaced a system in which **shop** stewards collected dues individually. Although not everyone likes the checkoff system, unions operating in the pre checkoff days often found themselves chronically short of cash. A few unions, most notably the **Industrial Workers of the World**, oppose automatic payment of dues on principle.

Although most **labor federations** also rely upon investments, donations, and other revenue streams, dues provide much of the needed operating capital for unions. This is especially the case for **union locals**, which rely upon dues to pay staff salaries and fund initiatives such as scholarships and educational programming. Locals are also responsible for collecting assessments that go any international unions or labor federations with which they may be affiliated. When the **American Federation of Labor** (AFL) was established in 1886, high dues became a centerpiece of the federation, as founder **Samuel Gompers** believed that the AFL could operate effectively only if it was well endowed.

In the current **American Federation of Labor-Congress of Industrial Organizations** (AFL-CIO), approximately 40 percent of the money collected by local unions goes to the parent organization. In addition to salaries and programs, part of a member's dues is dispersed to intermediate bodies such as citywide labor councils and state federations. A portion of the dues may be deposited in special **strike** funds in advance of an anticipated tough contract negotiation. All union funds are subject to rapid depletion, so unions need to make careful decisions on which portion of its funds should remain liquid and which should be invested.

Most local union stewards are known in their community and the portion of member dues used locally generally engenders far less controversy than the amount that goes to labor federations. The AFL-CIO, for example, spends a lot of money each year on political activity such as lobbying and donations. Some members resent money being spent on causes or candidates they find objectionable, and still others believe that more money should be spent on organizing and education. Some workers also charge that AFL-CIO **business unionists** spend too much money to sustain a bloated bureaucracy.

Suggested Reading

Harry Katz and Thomas Kochan, *An Introduction to Collective Bargaining and Industrial Relations*, 2000; Terry Leap, *Collective Bargaining and Labor Relations*, 1991.

EFFICIENCY. *See* Taylorism.

EIGHT-HOUR MOVEMENT

The eight-hour movement began in the 19th century and was a concerted effort to reduce the hours of employment. The creation of a permanent **working class** was among the many changes brought by the **Industrial Revolution**. Farmers and independent proprietors often worked long hours, but they had great control over the pace of their work and the length of time for which they labored. This was not true for most wage-earners, nor were there many laws governing how long an employee could be required to toil. As early as the 1810s, factory workers, miners, quarry workers, and others complained that most of their waking hours were devoted to labor. By the 1830s, 12- to 14-hour workdays were commonplace. Many workers received only Sundays and half of Saturday off, and quite a few did not enjoy even this small luxury. In 1791, **Philadelphia carpenters** struck for a 10-hour workday; New York City shipbuilders and caulkers battled for a 10-hour day in 1806. An 1824 strike by female weavers at Slater's Mill in Pawtucket, Rhode Island—birthplace of the American Industrial Revolution—was partially in support of reduced hours, and the call for shorter hours by was taken up by the **Workingmen's movement** in the 1820s and 1830s. Numerous strikers included a 10-hour workday among their demands, and the **Lowell Female Labor Reform Association** pressured the Massachusetts legislature to take up the question in 1845. The Massachusetts legislature declined to pass a 10-hour bill, though Pennsylvania enacted such a bill in 1849.

Eight hours was, however, the ultimate ideal. Many sources place the birth of the eight-hour movement in the 1860s, but the idea had been floating around decades earlier. British philanthropist **Robert Owen** began championing an eight-hour workday in 1817, and many New Zealand laborers obtained it by 1840. U.S. labor journals began calling for eight hours as early as 1836, and Boston shipyard workers obtained it in 1842. For the most part, though, the number of hours fluctuated by industry and region, and the eight-hour movement did not become well organized until after the **Civil War**. The **National Labor Union** took up the eight-hour cause in 1865, but the movement's greatest champion was Boston machinist **Ira Steward**, who is sometimes cited as "the father of the eight-hour movement." Boston's Eight-Hour League became the template for others and, by 1869, a Grand Eight-Hour League was in place as a nationwide lobbying body. Numerous **anarchist** and **socialist** groups also took up the cause and many

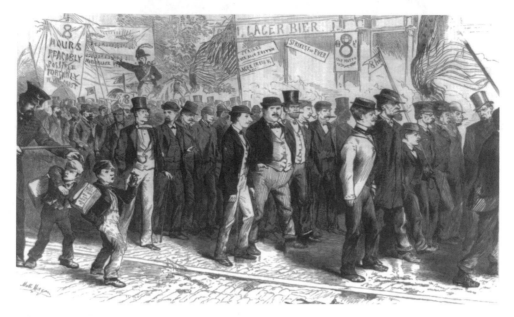

Laborers march in New York City on June 10, 1874, in support of an eight-hour workday. The eight-hour workday was a major issue taken up by the National Labor Union. (Library of Congress)

of the Gilded Age's most prominent labor agitators were involved with the eight-hour cause.

In 1869, Congress passed an eight-hour bill for federal employees only, but the legislation added a layer of contention to the debate. Workers could opt for a workday of eight hours, but at a reduced **wage**, or they could "choose" to continue working 10 hours at the original rate. For the rest of the century, the eight-hour cause was linked to questions of pay, and reducing work hours was contested on a case-by-case basis for most workers. It was a struggle whose progress was marked by progress and retreat. Many **strikes** resulted in workers gaining reduced hours that were lost in subsequent strikes, or were withdrawn by employers pleading economic hardship. In some industries—notably shipbuilding—the eight-hour workday was common; in others, such as textiles, a 13-hour day was standard. Complicating the issue even further was the widespread existence of **protective labor legislation** that mandated shorter hours for women and children, but insisted upon "freedom of contract" principles for men.

In the 1870s and 1880s, the **Knights of Labor** (KOL) led the crusade for eight hours as the length of the workday. A popular poem turned into a song and slogan summed up labor's position: "Eight hours for work; eight hours for rest; eight hours for what we will!" Numerous KOL affiliates battled for eight hours, but the KOL as an organization sought a political solution and argued that the existing ad hoc situation bred chaos that could be remedied only by the adoption of federal legislation that applied to all businesses. This was also the position of many non-KOL trade unions, as it would be that of the **American Federation of Labor** (AFL) when it formed at the end of 1886, but trade unions were more willing than the KOL to endorse strikes in support of the eight-hour ideal.

The KOL did not officially endorse a nationwide call for an eight-hour workday on May 1, 1886, partly because of its reluctance to approve of strikes and partly because of the presence of anarchists among the event's planners. At least 200,000 workers walked off the job on May 1, and approximately one-fifth of them won reduced work hours. Although the KOL would be excoriated for withholding its support, its warning about the chaos of the status quo on eight hours came to tragic light in Chicago, where the presence of eight-hour agitators and an ongoing strike against a major employer led to violence. When workers gathered on May 4 to protest a police killing of a striker several days earlier, a bomb went off, injuring and killing protestors and police alike in Haymarket Square. Chicago had been an epicenter of eight-hour movement and the bloodshed from the **Haymarket bombing** tainted the movement as anarchist and retarded its progress.

After Haymarket, the battle for eight hours returned to the local level, though the AFL held rallies on the question at its annual conventions and formalized its support for a national law in 1890. It also opted for an industry-by-industry campaign for shorter hours. The struggle for shorter working hours waxed and waned, though overall the ideal served as a unifying symbol for labor **solidarity**. The **United Mine Workers of America** secured an eight-hour workday in 1898, San Francisco construction workers in 1900, and printers in 1905. Oddly enough, the eight-hour day received one of its greatest boosts from **capitalist** Henry Ford, who granted his autoworkers reduced hours (at higher pay) in 1914 in an effort to curtail turnover on Ford **assembly lines**. Another important moment was the 1916 **Adamson Act**, which gave railroad workers an eight-hour work schedule.

These milestones notwithstanding, there was no universal standard on how long workers should toil until the onset of the Great **Depression**. In the face of high unemployment, some advocates offered the eight-hour day as a way to increase the workforce; for example, three 8-hour shifts at a factory instead of two 12-hour shifts had the potential to increase the workforce by a third. There was even discussion of reducing the workday to six hours, a notion first advanced by the **Industrial Workers of the World** (IWW)during the first decade of the 20th century. Worker militancy during the 1930s probably applied more pressure on New Deal planners than the reasoned logic of eight-hour lobbyists, but the 1935 **Fair Labor Standards Act** (FLSA) finally defined an official workday as eight hours and mandated **overtime** pay for all work beyond 8 hours per day or 40 hours per week.

For a while, some unions continued to discuss the merits of the IWW's call for a 30-hour work week, but World War II production helped enshrine the 40-hour week. During the postwar period, organized labor largely opted for higher wages and greater **fringe benefits**, not reduced work time, shorter days, or longer vacations. Gradually, the lure of a consumer society trumped that of working-class leisure time.

The eight-hour battle did not end with passage of the FLSA, however. The pressures of **globalization**, the **deregulation** climate of the 1980s, and the push for **concessions** by employers led to longer hours for many American workers. At first many of these hours were absorbed by unionized workers who received overtime and premium pay, but declining union membership has left many workers with few ways to resist forced overtime or to assure that they were not working off the clock. Moreover, some members of the business community have allied with conservative politicians who have voiced a willingness to amend the FLSA.

Another area of concern is in the rising **white-collar** sector of the economy. Salaried workers are not subject to the FLSA and a work week in excess of 40 hours with no additional compensation is expected in many occupations. Indeed, professionals such as lawyers, professors, public relations experts, and computer programmers routinely put in workdays analogous to those of the early 19th century. The battle for reduced hours is returning as a union and social concern.

Suggested Reading

David R. Roediger and Philip S. Foner, *Our Own Time: A History of American Labor and the Working Day*, 1989; Peter Scheckner and M. C. Boyes, eds., *The Way We Work: Contemporary Writings from the American Workplace*, 2008; Juliet B. Schor, *The Overworked American: The Unexpected Decline of Leisure*, 1991.

ENVIRONMENT AND LABOR

In recent years, organized labor has become very interested in finding synergy between itself and the environmental movement. Its past record on the environment is spotty, however.

In fairness to organized labor, environmental concern is a relatively recent phenomenon in the United States. American society has long had wilderness champions and conservationists, but prior to the 1960s only a handful of environmental action groups existed and groups such as the Audubon Society, the Izaak Walton League, and the Sierra Club had reputations as genteel organizations rather than militant pressure groups. Most government policy related to environmental stewardship was collected under the aegis of the Department of the Interior. The unleashing of atomic weapons during World War II, the development of nuclear weaponry during the **Cold War**, concern about global population explosion, new scientific data on toxins, and a spate of alarmist but popular books led to growing public awareness of the dangers involved in mismanaging natural resources. Social activists in the 1960s formed organized ecology movements, many of which were more confrontational than established groups. The first Earth Day was held in 1970, the same year that the Environmental Protection Agency (EPA) was established and the Clean Air Act was passed. In short order, other landmark bills were passed, including the Water Pollution Control Act (1972), the Endangered Species Act (1973), the Safe Drinking Water Act (1974), and the Clean Water Act (1976).

The American **Industrial Revolution** transformed the nation into a global power, but it was neither clean nor eco-friendly. Steel cities such as Pittsburgh and Gary, Indiana, were infamous for foul air. In 1948, the town of Donora, Pennsylvania, suffered a temperature inversion that trapped zinc and coal fumes in the air; two dozen people died and more than 7,000 people were sickened by the air pollution. It was not an isolated incident. Factory smokestacks lacked "scrubbers" that filtered out heavy metals and particulates, dyes and chemicals were routinely flushed into rivers and streams, and chemical fertilizers were sprayed onto fields. By the mid-20th century, one of the biggest polluters was the automobile.

In the 1960s and 1970s, environmental activists became more aggressive at calling attention to eco-nightmares. They were aided by such media-reported events as a 1969 incident in which chemicals dumped into Cleveland's Cuyahoga River caused the waterway to catch on fire, and reports on the unhealthy layers of smog—mostly from auto exhaust—that enveloped cities such as Los Angeles, Phoenix, Houston, and New York.

Environmental insight did not necessarily mesh well with traditional **blue-collar** unions. Many equated environmental safeguards with a loss of jobs, a doomsday scenario often encouraged by business owners reluctant to invest in pollution-control measures. The **United Auto Workers of America** (UAW)—one of the nation's more progressive unions on many social issues—lagged behind in environmental awareness from the 1970s through to the 21st century. The UAW was reluctant to endorse any fuel-efficiency requirements that might close down existing production lines or involve long periods of downtime for retooling. Only recently has UAW President Ron Gettelfinger endorsed higher fuel efficiency for automobiles, and that decision has not been popular among many rank-and-file members.

Other unions and groups of workers have similarly opposed environmental regulations. The Endangered Species Act led to controversy when a dam project in Tennessee was delayed for six years because of a diminutive endangered fish called the snail darter, and loggers in the Pacific Northwest have clashed with the EPA and environmental groups over spotted owl habitats. That region, in fact, has seen fierce clashes between loggers and radical environmental groups such as Earth First! over clear-cutting of trees and logging in old-growth forests. The fishing industry has also been at odds with environmentalists. Studies indicating dangerous depletions of fish resources have led to numerous restrictions on catches; numerous boat owners have been unable to adjust to those changes and gone out of business. In many cases, unions have opted for jobs over the environment. Oil and chemical workers, for instance, have little vested interest in ending America's dependence on fossil fuels, and uranium miners do not share the concerns of antinuclear activists. The **Teamsters** union generated enormous controversy in 2001 when it embraced President George W. Bush's call to drill for oil in the Arctic National Wildlife Refuge on the grounds that it would create jobs.

In contrast, some other unions embraced environmentalism early in their history. The **United Farm Workers of America** (UFWA) alerted Americans of the dangers of chemicals in advance of science that proved the UFWA correct, and it currently champions controls on pesticide use. The **United Steelworkers of America** (USW) were among the groups that lobbied for the Clean Air Act, and several unions defied the leadership of the **American Federation of Labor-Congress of Industrial Unions** (AFL-CIO), ignored warnings of job loss, and embraced the passage of the 1970 **Occupational Safety and Health Act**. Unions also discovered that exposing employer pollution practices during **corporate campaigns** often garnered support they would not have otherwise had. Workers employed on "Superfund" cleanup projects resulting from the 1980 passage of the Comprehensive Environmental Response, Compensation, and Liability Act also followed the UFWA's lead and embraced the dangers of working on toxic worksites.

The 21st century has seen renewed emphasis on becoming "green," and organized labor now often leads on environmental issues on which it once dragged its feet. Thirty unions signed on board to the Apollo Alliance, a 2001 project aimed at making the United States energy independent through the development of clean and efficient energy sources. USW President Leo Gerard was among the founding board members. The USW also forged a partnership with the Sierra Club in 2006 that became the Blue Green Alliance; this federation currently includes nine unions—including the **Service Employees International Union** and the Communications Workers of America—and is endorsed by the AFL-CIO. The Alliance calls for reforms that will develop clean energy policies geared toward reducing global warming, protect labor's **collective bargaining rights**, control the use of toxic chemicals, and adopt trade policies that adhere to standards of environmental, labor, and human rights.

The **American Federation of State, County, and Municipal Employees** (AFSCME) took part in a United Nations-sponsored conference in 2006 and endorsed its recommendations on reducing global warming. It is also part of ongoing discussions on resource management. The 2006 conference revealed some alarming statistics: Since 1900, commercial logging has reduced the reserves of the globe's forested areas by at least 20 percent and perhaps as much as half; likewise, fish stocks have dropped by 70 percent, and 60 percent of the earth's rivers have been severely compromised by ecosystem-altering dams.

Before his death in 2002, Tony Mazzochi of the Oil, Chemical, and Atomic Workers Union warned union members that they should abandon their fears over lost jobs and embrace the green future. As he saw it, clinging to **sunset industries** and environmentally damaging jobs simply meant that union workers would lose out on future jobs. Many have taken his warning to heart. Organized labor now routinely sends representatives to climate change conferences and meetings of the World Trade Organization. In 2009, the AFL-CIO created its Center for Green Jobs.

Fear of job loss continues to be a concern for many workers, and both the environmental and labor movements are often targets for right-wing ideologues. The administration of **Ronald Reagan** in the 1980s attacked both unions and environmentalists as "special interests" that unduly hindered the private sector in exploiting natural resources. Such attacks remain potent. During the 2010 BP oil spill in the Gulf of Mexico, conservatives railed against the Barack Obama administration's application of the 1920 Jones Act, which confines merchant marine activity in American waters to American crews aboard American ships. When the president declined offers from other nations to help clean up the spill, he was attacked for caving into unions. Those attacks fell upon deaf ears, but the same forces—aided by some **union locals**—turned aside a proposed moratorium on deep-water drilling on the grounds that it would result in job losses.

Suggested Reading

"Labour and the Environment. A Natural Synergy," http://www.unep.org/labour_environment/PDFs/UNEP-labour-env-synergy.pdf; Brian Orbach, *Labor and the Environmental Movement: The Quest for Common Ground*, 2004; Craig Slaiton, *Environmental Unions: Labor and the Superfund*, 2009; Adam Werbach, "Bridging the Labor-Environment Gap," *In These Times*, January 20, 2004.

EQUAL PAY ACT OF 1963

The Equal Pay Act of 1963 amended the **Fair Labor Standards Act** and prohibits employers from discriminating against workers on the basis of sex when tasks require equal skill, effort, and responsibility under similar working conditions. It also mandates equal pay for equal work. In lieu of an equal rights amendment to the U.S. Constitution, the Equal Pay Act stands as one of the most important legal guarantees for the rights of female employees.

The bill was a centerpiece of President John F. Kennedy's "New Frontier" programs. It was also an acknowledgment on the part of Congress that social changes were in the process of rendering obsolete older views of male-supported households. The pressures of consumer society, rising divorce rates, and the increasing presence of women in the workforce required a new look at household income. Those headed by women were at a particular disadvantage, as women in 1963 earned just 60 cents on average for every dollar paid to male workers. Moreover, champions of the bill argued that the traditional use of women as a secondary labor force suppressed **wages** for all workers and created tensions that interrupted commerce. The Equal Pay Act was intended as part of an overall plan to elevate the position of women in American society. Title VII of the 1964 Civil Rights Act expanded the Equal Pay Act by forbidding job discrimination based on race or sex, and by extending the act to include **white-collar labor**.

The Equal Pay Act led to both hope and frustration. Women's pay vis-à-vis that of men rose, but only slightly; by 1970, it was just 62 cents for every dollar paid to men, and is still roughly a fifth lower than that of men. The Equal Pay Act is just 150 words long and both its supporters and detractors agree that its language is imprecise. The lack of detail in the bill also opened many doors for those seeking to circumvent it. One could, for instance, get around "equal pay for equal work" provisions by making minor changes in job titles and job descriptions. This has given rise to a move to enact **comparable worth** legislation.

Feminists also charged that the bill's rhetorical force was offset by lax enforcement. They noted, with considerable merit, that the Equal Pay Act did little to break up entrenched gender segregation in the labor market. Certain professions—elementary school teaching, nursing, clerical work—remained veritable "pink-collar ghettoes" dominated by women and in which women were paid far less than workers in comparable male-dominated fields. Senator Hillary Rodham Clinton introduced a Paycheck Fairness Act in 2007 that was designed to close the pay gap between men and women; it has not yet passed. In 2009, however, President Barack Obama signed the Lilly Ledbetter Fair Pay Act, which revised a crippling 180-day statute of limitations for filing violations of either the Equal Pay Act or Title VII. The law now allows a complaint to be filed within 180 days of each discriminatory paycheck.

Suggested Reading

"Equal Pay Act of 1963, as Amended," U.S. Department of Labor, http://www.dol.gov/
oasam/regs/statutes/equal_pay_act.htm, accessed August 11, 2010; Walter Fogel, *The
Equal Pay Act*, 1984; Catherine Selden, *Equal Pay for Work of Comparable Worth: An
Annotated Bibliography*, 1984.

EQUITY PAY. *See* Comparable Worth; Equal Pay Act of 1963.

ERDMAN ACT

The Erdman Act was passed in 1898 in response to the **Pullman strike and boycott**
of 1894 and the findings of the United States Strike Commission. It prohibited
interstate railroads from imposing **yellow-dog contracts** on their employees. The
act also allowed for voluntary **arbitration** of labor disputes. At the time of its passage, the Erdman Act was a stunning victory for working people, as it imposed regulations on one of the Gilded Age's most powerful industries, and one whose labor
relations had been marked by some of the period's most bitter **strikes**.

The 1908 Supreme Court decision in *Adair v. The United States* declared the
Erdman Act unconstitutional and allowed the reinstatement of yellow-dog contracts.
In the regulatory climate of the **Progressive Era**, however, pressure quickly mounted
to replace the Erdman Act with a bill that could withstand legal challenges. With a
nationwide rail strike in the offing, Congress passed the **Adamson Act** in 1916,
which improved conditions for railroad workers and gave those involved in interstate
commerce an **eight-hour** workday. This legislation was followed 10 years later by the
Railway Labor Act, which gave railroad workers even greater protections.

The Erdman Act is an example of how labor law evolves in the United States. The
same pattern of legal challenge followed by revised bills has often been followed in
the United States, a prime example being the **National Labor Relations Act**, which
came to pass when the **National Industrial Recovery Act** was struck down.

Suggested Reading

Jay Finley Christ, "The Federal Courts and Organized Labor. II. From the Sherman Act to
the Clayton Act (Continued)," *Journal of Business of the University of Chicago* (1930):
341–375; Paul R. Taylor, *The ABC-CLIO Companion to the American Labor Movement*,
1993.

ESCALATOR CLAUSE. *See* Cost-of-Living Adjustment.

ESSENTIALISM. *See* Comparable Worth.

EVERETT MASSACRE

The Everett Massacre was a shootout between local vigilantes and members
(**Wobblies**) of the **Industrial Workers of the World** (IWW) that took place in
the state of Washington on November 5, 1916.

At the time, the IWW was split into factions that argued over tactics. Western militants, such as those in Everett, favored **direct action** confrontations, while Wobblies in the East were more open to ballot-box politics and conventional union tactics such as coordinated **strikes**. Because western Wobblies were often more unpredictable, and because they had made inroads among occupations that had hitherto been hard to organize (e.g., hard-rock miners, transient harvest workers, and loggers), local authorities throughout the West were equally aggressive in trying to break up the IWW.

A favored tactic was a broad application of criminal **syndicalism** laws that denied speaking permits for IWW agitators, limited the size of crowds that could gather in public, restricted the distribution of IWW literature, and, in some cases, banned certain individuals from entering towns and states. The Wobblies saw such restrictions as violations of the First Amendment, but instead of launching legal challenges, they engaged in what they dubbed "free speech" battles. A favored tactic was to send out a call for Wobblies to descend upon a restrictive town and hold mass rallies in defiance of the laws. Another part of the strategy was to have so many members arrested that the towns would run out of jail space and exhaust municipal coffers in feeding and guarding imprisoned Wobblies. IWW members often suffered violence at the hands of their captors, but despite horrendous hardships—including the mass deportation of **copper mine strikers** in Bisbee, Arizona—the IWW conducted at least 30 free speech fights between 1907 and 1916. They were also largely successful, as the laws Wobblies resisted were, in fact, violations of the First Amendment that would also have put other public organizations out of business, most notably the Salvation Army. The IWW free speech battles (and persecution of Americans opposed to World War I) inspired the lawyer Roger Baldwin (1884–1981) to found the American Civil Liberties Union.

The free speech battles and the reputation of the IWW formed the backdrop for the Everett Massacre. The IWW did not have a union hall in Everett, though it was very active in Seattle and Spokane. When Everett shingle workers went on strike after a **wage** cut, the IWW signaled a willingness to assist them. On October 30, 41 Wobblies came to Everett and began high-profile public organizing effort that angered city officials. When word came that more Wobblies were on the way, the county sheriff's office—headed by Donald MacRae—deputized local vigilantes in an effort to keep them out of the city. The city also enacted revised ordinances designed to curtail IWW organizing. Ferries named the *Verona* and the *Calista* left Seattle with several hundred Wobblies aboard determined to enter Everett, assist the shingle workers, and hold a free speech battle. As the ferry approached Everett, MacRae allegedly yelled, "Who is your leader?" When the reply came, "We all are!", shots rang out that killed five Wobblies and two deputies. Approximately 50 people were wounded.

It was never determined who fired the first shots, though it seems highly probable that the deputies did so. The two deputies who died appeared to have been shot in the back by their own comrades during the fusillade on the docks. Seventy-four Wobblies were arrested when they returned to Seattle, and Thomas H. Tracy was charged with murder. All the Wobblies were ultimately released, as there was no direct evidence to tie them to the shootout. In like fashion, Tracy was acquitted after a two-month trial.

The Everett Massacre is a vivid example of the ferociousness with which organized **capitalism** was determined to resist the IWW. It is also an example of the limits of **Progressive Era** reforms, efforts that were uncomfortable with grassroots movements or radical challenges to authority. Scholars also generally agree that the IWW free speech battles exemplify the way in which Progressive Era courts often reflected views more in accordance with Gilded Age **social Darwinism** than with the changing social climate of the 20th century.

Suggested Reading

Stewart Bird, Dan Georgakas, and Deborah Shaffer, eds., *Solidarity Forever—The IWW: An Oral History of the Wobblies*, 1985; John McClelland Jr., *Wobbly War: The Centralia Story*, 1987; Walker Smith, *The Everett Massacre: A History of Class Struggle in the Lumber Industry*, 1916/1965.

EXCEPTIONALISM

Exceptionalism is a controversial theory that seeks to explain the relative lack of **socialism** and **class consciousness** in the United States vis-à-vis other Western industrial democracies. According to those who uphold the doctrine of exceptionalism, the United States developed uniquely because it lacked an aristocracy of birth, possessed an abundance of available land for settlers, and evolved a political system that granted basic liberties and individual freedoms much earlier than peer nations. As such, American prosperity begat political quiescence.

The term originated with Alexis de Tocqueville and appeared in his four-volume work, *Democracy in America* (1835–1840). Tocqueville juxtaposed American liberty, equality of birth, individualism, popular democracy, and laissez-faire business practices against the feudal background of Europe. Americans, he argued, felt loyalty to their families and to a vaguely constructed notion of their nation, but were not burdened by obligations to social class and hierarchy. His ideas echoed the rhetoric of those European settlers to North America who deliberately fashioned new colonies based on ideals that ran contrary to Old World values.

The exceptionalism thesis has waxed and waned among scholars. During the 19th century, exceptionalism was often invoked by elites seeking to justify the United States' Manifest Destiny. It was also an important component of the **middle-class ideology** used by members of that rising class to celebrate its own achievements or, more ominously, to defend **social Darwinism**. Some Gilded Age apologists for ruthless business practices appealed to exceptionalism by associating the alleged merits of individualism with the collectivist ideals of labor unions. More benignly, exceptionalism also showed up in Frederick Jackson Turner's 1893 "frontier thesis," in which he argued that the availability of free land in the United States functioned as a "safety valve" that blunted radicalism.

In labor terms, exceptionalism was thrust to the fore of academic debate by German scholar Werner Sombart. His 1906 book *Why Is There No Socialism in the United States?* argued that American workers were less likely to embrace socialist principles or form an independent **labor party** because they were prosperous vis-à-vis their counterparts in other industrial nations. Sombart's prosperity thesis was hotly debated, but in the 1920s scholars working at the University of Wisconsin, such as John R. Commons and Selig Perlman, echoed Sombart's argument to a degree and asserted both that American workers were more wage-conscious than Europeans, and that American democracy provided them with more political power.

A belief in American exceptionalism dovetailed with America's emergence as a dominant global power in the 20th century. Exceptionalist themes such as the glory, genius, and power of the United States were commonplace in American history texts. Many of America's most eminent 20th-century historians—including Charles Beard, Daniel Bell, Daniel Boorstin, Henry Steele Commager, Richard Hofstadter, Horace Kallen, Seymour Lipset, Vernon Parrington, Henry Nash Smith, and Arthur Schlesinger—have, to varying degrees, evoked exceptionalism.

In the 1960s, however, scholars associated with the "New Social History" began to call into question the underlying assumptions of American exceptionalism. First, they argued that exceptionalism is at its core a flawed concept. Most nations evolve laws, social customs, and histories that are outwardly different from those of others, but these are often merely surface variations regarding how similar problems and issues are addressed. For example, workers worldwide have struggled for more power and higher wages for the same reason—the **working class** is not the ruling class, so it must wrest political and economic power from elites. It is a mistake, critics argue, to apply an ex post facto exceptionalist reading to the relative success (or failure) of social movements to achieve reform. For example, New Zealand workers faced most of the same problems facing American workers in the late 19th century, but the former achieved political success that would escape American wage-earners until the 1930s. Examples such as these have led scholars questioning exceptionalism to caution that one should not assume consensus on social values without paying attention to the role of class power. One cannot say, for instance, that American workers rejected radicalism without paying attention to the concerted efforts of organized **capitalism**, court systems, and politicians to crush radical movements. The **Industrial Workers of the World** is a case in point. This group's history is littered with acts of violence directed at the organization and wholesale violation of what were supposed to be the Constitutional guarantees of all Americans. In fact, one of the few ways in which American labor history does exhibit unique characteristics is that it has been far bloodier than that of other Western industrial democracies.

Historians have also thoroughly demolished the assumption of working-class prosperity. The data simply do not support such a claim for the past or the present. In contemporary America, for example, more than 7 million full-time workers in the United States earn wages that are below the poverty level for families, and nearly one-third of all laborers earn just above that level. The most severe critics of exceptionalism charge its defenders with historical amnesia, reductionism, or deliberate ideological distortion.

Despite attacks on exceptionalism from the 1960s on, the theory remains vital. Some scholars argue that the United States was not born exceptional, but rather became so after the defeat of radical movements that might have brought American history more in line with that of Europe. As such, they represent a middle ground between those advocates who defend exceptionalism and those critics who would deny it altogether.

Exceptionalism also remains an attractive to political conservatives, especially in the post-**Cold War** period. From their viewpoint, America's "victory" in the Cold War is testament to the superiority of its political, social, and cultural institutions. Exceptionalism also meshes well with social views that celebrate the opportunities conservatives believe are inherent within American capitalism.

Most current scholars hold that American exceptionalism has been overstated and its resiliency is due mostly to a dearth of comparative studies. Many scholars do agree, however, that a belief in exceptionalism is useful in explaining the tendency of some Americans toward xenophobia and the nation's awkwardness in international relations. This theory also retains the loyalty of a devoted core of intellectuals who feel the concept holds merit.

Suggested Reading

Rick Fantasia and Kim Voss, *Hard Work: Remaking American Labor*, 2004; Martin Seymour Lipset and John Laslet, eds., *Failure of a Dream? Essays in the History of American Socialism*, 1974; Kim Voss, *The Making of American Exceptionalism: The Knights of Labor and Class Formation in the 19th Century*, 1993.

EXECUTIVE ORDERS

Executive orders (E.O.) are a controversial maneuver in American politics whereby the president of the United States issues a directive to an agency controlled by the executive branch of government; the order requires that body to enact a new policy or to interpret old ones in new ways. Such mandates are controversial in that they have the force of law and skirt the Constitutional borders between the executive and legislative branches. To critics, executive orders dangerously expand the power of the president and can be used in an authoritarian manner, though they are reviewable by the Supreme Court.

Until recent years, executive orders were used rather sparingly—government agencies thrive on consistency and clear directives—and most presidents have chosen not to politicize them. The efficient running of government can be interrupted if policies are blatantly political; an incoming president might reverse directives from a previous administrations. Executive orders can also be contradictory in nature. For example, President Franklin Roosevelt issued two executive orders related to Japanese Americans during World War II: E.O. 9066 allowed for the internment of Japanese Americans, and E.O. 9102 allowed for their forced relocation. Both of these directives had profound racial implications, yet Roosevelt also issued an executive order forbidding discrimination against people of color in the defense industry and President Harry Truman's 1948 E.O. 9981 desegregated the U.S. military.

Some executive orders have been of the utmost importance to working people. The first such directive to affect workers directly came in 1935, when President Roosevelt issued E.O. 7034 to create the Works Progress Administration, a federal project aimed at putting unemployed Americans to work during the Great Depression. Roosevelt also signed into law E.O. 8802 in 1941; this landmark action ended discriminatory hiring and treatment of African Americans in the defense industry. Roosevelt created the **Fair Employment Practices Committee** to oversee enforcement of the order. He did so as much to avert a planned civil rights demonstration threatened **by A. Philip Randolph** as out of concern for racial equity, but this action is now generally hailed as anticipating the rebirth of the modern civil rights movement during the 1950s.

Executive orders can also be used against working people. In 1945, President Truman enacted E.O. 9835, which required government workers to sign anti-communist loyalty oaths; some workers lost their jobs as a result. Truman's E.O. 10340 (1952) demanded that the secretary of commerce seize steel mills to avert a planned strike, an action struck down as unconstitutional by the U.S. Supreme Court in *Youngstown Steel & Tube Company v. Sawyer*.

In 1961, President John F. Kennedy issued E.O. 10925, which set up the Equal Employment Opportunities Commission, the forerunner of the similarly named Equal Employment Opportunity Commission (EEOC) created by Title VII of the Civil Rights Act of 1964. The EEOC and its predecessor established federal protections against discrimination in the workplace because of sex, race, national origin, and creed. The 1964 bill has been altered by other executive orders that have extended its protections to categories such as age and disabilities. President Lyndon Johnson's E.O. 11246 (1965) extended these principles to hiring decisions, President Richard Nixon's E.O. 11478 ordered that mandates applied to civilian federal employees also be binding on military contracts, and President Bill Clinton's E.O. 13087 (1998) added sexual orientation to the protected categories list. More famously, Clinton's order established the controversial "Don't ask, don't tell, don't pursue" policy for U.S. military personnel, which allowed homosexuals to serve in the military as long as their orientation remained private.

President Kennedy's E.O. 10988 (1962) was an extremely important mandate for workers, as it established **collective bargaining** procedures for unions representing employees of the federal government who had been denied bargaining rights under the 1935 **National Labor Relations Act**, including postal workers and some employees of the Tennessee Valley Authority. This had long been an objective of the **American Federation of Labor-Congress of Industrial Unions** (AFL-CIO), as there were numerous quasi-public government agencies and "associations" whose bargaining rights were ambiguous prior to the Kennedy decision. E.O. 10988 allowed unions, after winning a representation election, to bargain with a federal agency. It prohibited **union shops**, continued the ban on **strikes** by federal employees, and prohibited recognition of unions that supported the right to strike, but allowed negotiations over issues such as job descriptions, working conditions, **subcontracting**, and **grievance** policies. Although the directive was limited in scope, it led to explosive growth in unionization of federal employees—from 19,000 in 1963 to more than

670,000 almost overnight. Public employee unionization became the major growth sector for organized labor in the 1960s. The original order was superseded by President Nixon's E.O. 11491 (1969), which ended informal consultation with employee associations, altered the ways bargaining units would be determined, expanded the range of negotiable issues, and provided for **arbitration** of disputes.

In the past several decades, executive orders have been very controversial. A 1997 order by President Clinton that would have banned awarding federal contracts to employers who hired **scab** labor was struck down by federal courts. President George W. Bush issued more executive orders than any other previous chief executive, and many of them have caused political disputes. Several orders (especially E.O. 13198 and E.O. 13217, both in 2001, and E.O. 13397 in 2004) allowed for the creation of faith-based agencies that were exempt from discriminatory practices that applied to secular groups; human rights and labor activists decried these measures. Critics charged that other Bush orders signaled the president's personal distaste for labor unions and were bad policy. An airline mechanics union objected to Bush's interference in its dispute with Northwest Airlines by attempting to impose mediation through E.O. 13205 (2001). Bush's E.O. 13202 (2001) mandated that the government take a neutral position when considering contract bids from contractors embroiled in labor disputes.

Unions also strongly objected to E.O. 13201 (2001), which directed the National Labor Relations Board to establish procedures that would allow union members to object to political spending by their unions and withhold **dues** that go toward that purpose. The AFL-CIO strongly objected to this mandate, as similar restrictions are not placed on how much a corporation can spend on objectionable political activity. President Barack Obama revoked this order in 2009 via E.O. 13496. Bush's E.O. 13228 (2001), which laid the groundwork for establishment of the Homeland Security Office, was also contentious, as Bush originally wanted new security positions to be union-free. The AFL-CIO aggressively objected to this provision, Bush modified his stance, and Obama further eased restrictions on unions.

President Obama has reversed several Bush executive orders, but this has created the very confusion within federal agencies that critics of the executive order practice feared. Nonetheless, executive orders are likely to play an important role in the federal government's future approach to workers, workplace issues, and labor unions because Congress is so deeply divided that it will be hard to muster support for legislative action on labor law reform.

Suggested Reading

Irving Bernstein, *Promises Kept: John F. Kennedy's New Frontier*, 1991; "Executive Orders Disposition Tables Index," http://www.archives.gov/federal-register/executive-orders/disposition.html, accessed August 15, 2010; Michael Moskow, J. Joseph Loewenberg, and Edward Koziara, *Collective Bargaining in Public Employment*, 1970.

•

F

FAIR EMPLOYMENT PRACTICES COMMISSION

The Fair Employment Practices Commission (FEPC) was created by an **executive order** (E.O.) in June 1941. Its mandate was to curtail race-based discrimination in the federal government and in the defense industry. Although the FEPC found it hard to enforce its decisions, its very existence marked a return of the federal government's willingness to intervene in civil rights issues, a willingness that had waned since the collapse of **Reconstruction** in the 1870s. It also inspired more permanent change.

The FEPC had not been among President Franklin Roosevelt's New Deal priorities; in fact, Roosevelt moved very slowly on racial justice issues for fear of alienating the Democratic Party's southern wing. It was largely forced upon the president by **A. Philip Randolph** and the National Association for the Advancement of Colored People (NAACP). They demanded that black Americans be given a fair proportion of new jobs emerging in the defense industry and threatened a march of more than 100,000 African Americans on Washington, D.C., if the president did not comply. Although the United States was not yet at war, Roosevelt foresaw the coming of conflict and American manufacturers began to churn out defense materiel at a rate that at long last ended the Great Depression, which had begun in 1929. Randolph's threat posed a serious challenge to Roosevelt, both politically and in terms of its potential to interrupt factory production. Randolph was almost certainly bluffing; few historians now believe that he could have attracted 100,000 marchers, or that he had even taken all the necessary steps necessary to launch such a protest. Nonetheless, Roosevelt was embarrassed in both the white and black press, and the administration was accused of hypocrisy for denouncing fascism abroad while coddling racism at home.

Roosevelt met with NAACP President Walter White and agreed to meet certain demands if the planned march was canceled. Roosevelt's E.O. 8802 created the FEPC, which had the authority to investigate complaints, hold hearings, and issue directives to correct discriminatory practices in defense industries and federal agencies. The FEPC was more important symbolically than in reality. The military itself remained segregated until 1948, and E.O. 8802 did not preclude government contracts with discriminatory employers, or grant the FEPC power to force compliance with its directives. Roosevelt also appointed white Louisville publisher Mark Etheridge as its first chair. Etheridge was a man of moderate temperament whose decisions placated a critical mass of white southerners, but disappointed most African American leaders. Criticism led Etheridge to resign only a few months into his tenure, and he was replaced by Malcolm MacLean, who held publicized hearings into employment discrimination in Birmingham, Alabama. The hope that the FEPC would become more aggressive diminished once wartime hostilities commenced in December 1941. In July 1942, the FEPC was placed under the aegis of the War Manpower Commission headed by Paul McNutt. McNutt was antagonistic toward black civil rights and placed restrictions on field personnel that so muted the FEPC's effectiveness that MacLean resigned as FEPC head in protest. President Roosevelt was forced to reorganize the FEPC and give enforcement authority to the agency. This was done through E.O. 9346 on May 27, 1943. After initially sputtering as badly as its predecessor, the revamped FEPC finally began to fulfill its promise when Malcolm Ross took over as chair in October 1943. Ross pressed cases that included complaints against Washington and Philadelphia transit companies, southern railroads, and midwestern defense plants. In all, the FEPC processed more than 12,000 cases and settled nearly 5,000.

The invigorated FEPC raised the ire of conservatives and southern politicians such as Mississippi Congressman John Rankin, who accused the agency of trying to force whites to accept African Americans as social equals. Virginia Representative Howard W. Smith, a staunch segregationist, demanded that the FEPC be investigated for harboring **communist** subversives. Although the **Congress of Industrial Organizations** (CIO) supported the FEPC, it was opposed by **American Federation of Labor** (AFL), as many of its affiliates practiced discrimination against African Americans. The AFL helped lobby for deep cuts in the FEPC's budget.

The FEPC passed from the scene after June 1946 when Congress eliminated all of its funding. Any chance it had of being revived vanished when the Republican Party took control of the House of Representatives in the November elections. Republicans were not inclined to enact legislation necessary to make the agency permanent, and Democrats were even more deeply dependent upon shoring up party support in the South. President Harry Truman made a public appeal for a permanent FEPC in 1948 and Congress took up the issue two years later, but a filibuster led by southern Democrats killed the bill.

The FEPC was ultimately more important for what it inspired than for its modest achievements. It engendered great opposition, but the racial equality principles it upheld were the centerpiece of a revived civil rights movement that came of age in the 1950s. The FEPC was also the role model for several provisions in the 1948 Fair Employment Practices Act and for the 1964 creation of the Equal Employment Opportunity Commission, the federal agency that today oversees issues related to hiring and workplace discrimination (broadly defined).

Suggested Reading

Keith M. Finley, *Delaying the Dream: Southern Senators and the Fight against Civil Rights, 1938–1965*, 2008; Herbert Garfinkel, *When Negroes March*, 1959; Andrew Kersten, *Race, Jobs, and the War*, 2000; Merl Reed, *Seedtime for the Modern Civil Rights Movement*, 1991.

FAIR LABOR STANDARDS ACT

The 1938 Fair Labor Standards Act (FLSA) was the last major piece of New Deal labor legislation. It remains one of the most important labor laws ever passed, as it established precedents that remain benchmarks, such as the **eight-hour** workday, the 40-hour workweek, a **minimum wage**, a **child labor** law that withstood Constitutional challenges, and requirements that employers pay time-and-a-half **overtime** rates. The provisions of the FLSA are enforced by the Wage and Hour division of the **Department of Labor**.

Not all workers were covered by the FLSA in its original form; among those excluded were farm workers, domestic servants, salaried employees, babysitters, some government employees, and journalists. It has also been amended numerous times since it was passed, and numerous legislative acts that many Americans think of as stand-alone bills are actually amendments to the FLSA. A 1947 amendment called the Portal-to-Portal Act addressed the question of **dead time**, and there have been numerous changes that raised the minimum wage and clarified the eight hours clause. The **Equal Pay Act of 1963** protected wage rates for women. The FLSA has also been expanded to cover groups that were not included in the 1938 bill. A 1967 amendment outlawed age discrimination, some farm workers came under FLSA protection in 1966, all government wage-earners fell under the FLSA in 1974, and migrant labor was included in 1983. The 1993 **Family and Medical Leave Act** was also an amendment to the FLSA.

The FLSA is an important protection for American workers, but it has not been a perfect bill, nor has it been immune from political maneuvering. President **Ronald Reagan** pushed through a 1986 amendment that removed overtime pay protections for workers on federal contracts, and changes made in 1996 under President Bill Clinton allowed small businesses to change the way tips were counted in calculating the minimum wage for many service industry employees. Far more controversially, in 2004 President George W. Bush granted numerous exemptions to overtime pay requirements for small businesses. These moves were opposed by the **American Federation of Labor-Congress of Industrial Organizations** (AFL-CIO), but it was unable to overturn Bush's actions. They were more deeply enshrined in the 2007 Fair Minimum Wage Act, changes Bush insisted upon before permitting an increase in the minimum wage. According to the AFL-CIO, these changes have forced millions of workers to toil extra hours for inadequate compensation, and the definition of small business has been abused.

Suggested Reading

"Fair Labor Standards Act Advisor," Department of Labor, http://www.dol.gov/elaws/flsa.htm, accessed August 17, 2010; Barbara Repa, *Your Rights in the Workplace*, 2000.

FAIR SHOP FEE. *See* Agency Fee.

FAMILY AND MEDICAL LEAVE ACT

The Family and Medical Leave Act (FMLA), a bill supported by most labor unions, was passed by Congress and signed by President Bill Clinton in 1993.

It amended the **Fair Labor Standards Act** to allow some employees to take as much as 12 weeks of unpaid leave per year to address family needs. Employees in firms with 50 or more employees are legally entitled to leave to attend to their own "serious health conditions," or those of a spouse, parent, or child. Leave is also granted for the birth, adoption, or establishment of foster care for a child. Employers must allow employees to return to their old jobs when their leave expires. The FMLA sets a minimum base for family leave practices, and does not override existing employer parental or personal leave policies that go beyond its scope.

The FMLA was bitterly opposed by the business community, which complained that it would lead to serious declines in productivity, and that it constitutes needless government regulation of the private sector's affairs. Their fears have proved alarmist. If anything, labor and social activists who complained that the FMLA was too weak have proved more accurate. The FMLA is very limited when compared with family legislation in other industrialized nations. Some New Zealand employees, for example, are entitled to a full year's leave at partial pay to attend to newborns, and nearly every European democracy grants more liberal leave. Moreover, the FMLA has numerous restrictions. Data compiled since 1993 indicate that less than 20 percent of eligible employees take family leave in a given year. The data further indicate that the FMLA has had no discernible impact on productivity.

To be eligible for this benefit, an employee must have worked at least 1,250 hours during the course of 12 months with the employer from which leave is requested. While on leave, employees might be required to pick up their own health care premiums and are not entitled to seniority rights. Under some conditions, employers can actually terminate a position while an employee is on leave. The law also allows employers to require periodic reports on their employees' leave status. Some employees have complained that they have been pressured into not taking leave or that they were pressured to return early. Most critics contend, however, that the biggest shortfall of the FMLA is that leave is unpaid. They suggest that most employees cannot sustain three months of **wage** losses and, therefore, are forced to substitute vacation leave, sick days, and personal days for the FMLA benefit. In addition, the FMLA applies only to larger firms with more than 50 employees, thereby leaving millions of Americans beyond the law's reach. Because of the FMLA's limitations, six states and the District of Columbia have enacted more generous versions of the act. The District of Columbia and nine states have also enacted legislation that adds eligibility categories not present in the federal bill. In 2002, California became the first state to institute paid family leave. In 2009, President Barack Obama called for expansion of the FMLA, but aside from minor clarifications over defining parental authority over nonbiological children, this has not yet occurred.

Despite the law's limitations, most labor unions have hailed the FMLA as an important first step in making American work policies more pro-family. The FMLA is administered by the Wage and Hour Division of the U.S. **Department of Labor**.

Suggested Reading

"Family and Medical Leave Act," U.S. Department of Labor, http://www.dol.gov/whd/fmla/, accessed August 17, 2010; Paid Family Leave California, http://www.paidfamilyleave.org/, accessed August 17, 2010.

FAMILY WAGE

Family wage is the outmoded idea that a male breadwinner should earn **wages** sufficient to support himself, his spouse, and their offspring. Although multiple wage-earning families are now the norm in the United States, the family wage remains a potent and sometimes troubling social ideal.

The concept of the family wage coincided with the **Industrial Revolution**, though its roots run even deeper. Many of the first industrial workers were women and children whose wages supplemented family farm incomes. During the early 19th century, **agrarianism** declined in the Northeast and industrialization expanded. As more men moved into paid labor, the family wage ideal developed. Farm labor divided numerous tasks along gender lines, but these did not carry the broader social implications associated with life in industrial towns and cities. Even though economic reality often forced women and children to work, there was great social pressure for **working-class** families to conform to social patterns in which women assumed all domestic roles and took care of their households. As early as the 1830s, labor organizations championed the family wage. Unions argued that male workers needed wages high enough to support their families.

In the post-**Civil War** period, male workers felt even greater pressure to obtain a family wage. The middle class expanded dramatically during the latter part of the 19th century, and a key component of **middle-class ideology** was the belief that a woman's proper "sphere" was to be the moral guardian of her home. Although the working class vastly outnumbered the middle class, this ideal—variously called domestic ideology, the doctrine of separate spheres, and Victorianism—became the dominant social norm. The uneven development of the **Gilded Age** economy, the **social Darwinist** practices of employers, and low wages meant that the reality for many working-class families was that they could not survive on a single income. This often induced shame among men whose family members had to work.

The **Knights of Labor** (KOL) was among the first **labor federations** to support equal pay for women workers, but even most KOL members saw the very presence of women in the workplace as a symptom of **capitalist** abuse. In similar fashion, the KOL championed the abolition of **child labor**. By the end of the 19th century, the **American Federation of Labor** (AFL) had become adamant in its support for the family wage, albeit for a different reason than earlier advocates. The AFL was a federation of **craft unions** and it (correctly) viewed women and children as a secondary labor force whose lower wages were used by employers to drive down the wages of male workers. This had the paradoxical effect of making a family wage harder to obtain.

The family wage ideal notwithstanding, working families were the norm for millions of Americans. In an unexpected twist, the Great Depression gave the family wage a temporary boost when the federal government reacted to high unemployment rates by enacting legislation that limited the employment of married women. World War II abruptly ended that practice and legions of women entered the workforce. The postwar years saw an immediate dip in women's employment and the reemergence of the family wage ideal. Both were temporary responses to an economy in transition. Although the family wage remained a powerful rhetorical force, the postwar economic boom, the emergence of a consumer society, family financial pressures associated with the "Baby Boom," and increasing discontent with domestic confinement led millions of women to enter the workplace. The image of the 1950s as a decade of stay-at-home women is deceptive; by 1950, more than half of all married women worked for wages outside of their homes and women made up more than a third of the total workforce. These figures have steadily grown; in 2010, women surpassed men as a percentage of the total workforce and now constitute the majority of American workers.

Social pressure and data such as these rendered the family wage unrealistic. Nevertheless, there has been a backlash associated with women entering the workforce and against dual-income families in general. The family wage has never been realistic for many American families, but its very existence has led many men to feel as if they have failed because they cannot support their families solely on their wages. Some commentators see male anger and aggressive masculinity as partial responses to the unrealistic pressures induced by a belief in the family wage. In addition, some conservatives link working parents to rising divorce levels, delinquency rates, perceived declines in morality, and alleged neglect for children. Some advocate a return to domestic ideology, though relatively few have rekindled a call for a family wage. It is improbable that the family wage will become a realistic option in the near future. Most labor unions abandoned the family wage by the early 1960s and are more likely to call for a gender-neutral **living wage** instead.

Suggested Reading

Susan Faludi, *Stiffed: The Betrayal of the American Man*, 1999; Martha May, "Bread before Roses: American Workingmen, Labor Unions, and the Family Wage," in *Women, Work and Protest: A Century of U.S. Women's Labor History*, ed. Ruth Milkman, 1987; Robert Pollin and Stephanie Luce, *The Living Wage: Building a Fair Economy*, 1998.

FARMER-LABOR ALLIANCES

Farmer-labor alliances comprise efforts to fuse the interests of wage-earners with those who till the soil. In theory, a bridge between the two largest constituencies of the **working class** would create a powerful political and social force. In practice, these alliances—though numerous—have proved fragile and relatively short-lived. Political parties created through such liaisons have been difficult to sustain because of the winner-takes-all nature of the American electoral system, which makes it hard for third-party movements to gain traction and easier for the major parties to siphon strength from farmer-labor parties. The latter task is also facilitated by the fact that the economic interests of the two groups often differ. Farmers, as producers, often favor inflationary economic policies that drive up commodity prices; wage-earners, as consumers, tend to favor low commodity prices. Nonetheless, there have been numerous moments in American history in which farmer associations and labor unions have united to battle against power elites viewed as oppressing the masses.

The **Workingmen's movement** of the 1830s was decentralized in nature, but in many locales farmer-labor alliances emerged. In Massachusetts, for instance, several groups contested elections under the name of the Association of Farmers, Mechanics, and Other Workingmen. Like future farmer-labor groups, their platform consisted of a hodge-podge of issues designed to attract working-class and farm votes. Candidates called for such changes as free public education, the abolition of debtor prisons, an end to land speculation, currency reform, banking regulation, and restrictions on monopolies. Overall, however, the Workingmen enjoyed its greatest success in urban areas, but did not succeed in unifying the working class or in surviving the Panic of 1837.

After the **Civil War**, farmers began to organize in the face of heavy debt, sinking commodity prices, and rising railroad freight and grain elevator storage rates. For their part, wage-earners were challenged by new breed of industrial and investment **capitalists** who offered little quarter to trade unions. In 1866, trade unionists and **socialists** created the **National Labor Union** (NLU), which issued an appeal to farmers. Several rural groups—especially those interested in monetary reform—sent representatives to NLU congresses. In 1872, the NLU reorganized as the National Labor Reform Party (NLRP), sometimes cited as the first nationwide farmer-labor organization, but the NLRP fared poorly in the fall elections and soon both it and the NLU collapsed. In the wake of the NLRP's demise, farmer organizations such as the Patrons of Husbandry (Grange) continued to agitate for regulating monopolies, especially railroads. This call resonated with urban workers with greater clarity after the nationwide rail strikes associated with the Great Labor Uprising of 1877. In the late 1870s and early 1880s, farm and labor interests unified over the issue of currency reform, with both groups advocating the printing of government **greenbacks** to alleviate the credit crunch occasioned by hard-money policies that favored lenders. Unions were convinced that greater access to credit would stimulate business growth and result in higher **wages**, while farmers again saw the potential for higher commodity prices. The Greenback-Labor Party (GLP) emerged and did very well in local and state elections into the mid-1880s, though it faltered on the national level. Future **Knights of Labor** (KOL) President **Terence Powderly** was elected mayor of Scranton, Pennsylvania, on the GLP ticket, a post he held through 1884. Fifteen GLP candidates won seats in Congress.

The GLP faded when the economy revived in the 1880s, but many greenbackers later took part in the "free silver" movement. Farmers and urban workers alike also gravitated to the KOL, which actively recruited in the countryside and whose platform contained cherished objectives such as opening public lands for settlement and money reform. Many Knights upheld **agrarianism** as morally superior to **capitalism** and viewed the countryside as a possible refuge for the urban poor. Although the KOL waned in urban areas after 1888, it retained vitality in rural America into the early 20th century.

In the countryside, the KOL was often indistinguishable from the 19th century's most important farmer-labor alliance, the **Populists**. Rural America suffered economic woes in advance of the Panic of 1893, a worsening of conditions that precipitated unrest in the South, the West, and rural pockets of the Northeast. Local and state People's parties contested elections beginning in the mid-1880s and high tariffs, tumbling grain prices, and crop lien systems in the South led groups such as the Grangers, state Farmers Alliances, the KOL, and labor activists to launch a national People's Party (Populists) at a gathering in Omaha, Nebraska, in 1892. The Populists took a page from the KOL's platform and fashioned a call to action that addressed rural concerns yet appealed to urban workers. Among the Populist agenda items were a call for government ownership of railroads and the adoption of an **eight-hour** workday. The declining KOL endorsed the Populists, but the **American Federation of Labor** (AFL) declined to do so, ostensibly because of its principles of nonpartisan politics and **voluntarism**. Populist presidential candidate James Weaver attracted more than 1 million votes and won 22 electoral votes in 1892 but, distressingly, most of his support came from farm-state voters. Urban workers were briefly more favorably disposed to the Populists in the immediate aftermath of the **Pullman boycott**, in which President Grover Cleveland's use of federal troops against railroad workers rekindled both their hatred of railroad monopolies and their distrust of the **Democratic Party**. In 1896, however, Democrats nominated William Jennings Bryan for president. Bryan co-opted enough of the Populist platform to win its endorsement, but Populists lost many urban voters in the process. Bryan lost the presidential election to William McKinley in both 1896 and 1900, and the Populist movement dissipated. In both elections, many urban workers voted for McKinley, who successfully argued that free-silver monetary policies would result in soaring food prices.

Farmer-labor alliances formed anew during World War I, especially in northern Plains states, where the Citizens' Nonpartisan League promoted farmer interests and attracted urban voters through mildly socialist rhetoric that championed commoners and lambasted entrenched power. This message played especially well in North Dakota, where the League captured the governorship and enough seats in the legislature to secure laws making farm foreclosure difficult.

The post-World War I period was a difficult time for organized labor. In 1920, some union members cast their lot with the newly formed Farmer-Labor Party, which included progressive labor platform planks. It drew most of its strength from farm states, especially those in the West and upper Midwest. These efforts peaked in 1924, when representatives from railroad unions, the Nonpartisan League, socialists, progressive reformers, and the Minnesota Farmer-Labor Party created the Progressive Party. There was so much enthusiasm for the party's 1924 presidential candidate Robert La Follette that even the AFL endorsed him, but the Progressives ultimately fell prey to the vagaries of the electoral system. Although La Follette polled more than 5 million votes, he won only his home state of Wisconsin. The party also made the tactical error of not contesting state or local races, so it lacked a sufficient grassroots presence to recover from La Follette's quixotic run for the presidency. The Progressives disappeared in most parts of the country, though

Farmer-Labor parties in the Midwest survived. Easily the most successful of these entities was the Minnesota Farmer-Labor Party (MFL), which controlled the governorship of its home state throughout the 1930s. The New Deal lured many farm-labor advocates to the Democratic Party and, in 1944, the MFL merged with them.

The Great Depression was especially harsh in rural America and dealt a blow to independent yeomanry from which it has never recovered. Corporate farming has continued to supplant individual farmers, thereby rendering the notion of a farmer-labor alliance problematic. The 1948 presidential campaign of former secretary of agriculture and vice president Henry Wallace was the last serious attempt to unite farmers and laborers. He headed a new Progressive Party and attracted great attention from political left, which ultimately was a mixed blessing. Wallace received a million votes, but he was viewed by many as a dangerous radical and his campaign was marred by red-baiting that, in retrospect, was an early salvo in the post-World War II **Red Scare**.

The term "populist" remains a commonly used term in American politics, but it no longer carries rural associations and is largely a synonym for a candidate who is trying to pass as an "average" American or as a champion of a supposedly neglected group. Farming is now agribusiness and the opponents of unions such as the **United Farm Workers of America** (UFWA). Groups like the UFWA are more likely to seek alliances with the Democratic Party than to form a third-party movement. If farmer-labor alliances have a future, such groups will probably emerge as the result of international and transborder organizing rather than domestic efforts.

Suggested Reading

Nathan Fine, *Labor and Farmer Parties in the United States*, 1961; Matthew Hild, *Greenbackers, Knights of Labor, and Populists: Farmer-Labor Insurgency in the Late-19th-Century South*, 2007; Elizabeth Sanders, *Roots and Reform: Farmers, Workers, and the American State, 1877–1917*, 1999.

FASANELLA, RALPH

Ralph Fasanella (September 2, 1914–December 16, 1997) was an American folk artist who produced iconic images of American labor struggles and urban life. He was born in New York City on **Labor Day**, September 2, 1914, to Italian immigrant parents from the Apulia region. His father, Joseph Fasanella, was an ice delivery-man, and his mother, Ginevra (Spanoeletti), was a buttonhole maker and a **socialist**. Both were devoted to labor unions and opposed the rising fascist tide in their native Italy.

Ralph grew up in immigrant neighborhoods in Greenwich Village and the Bronx, but led a troubled childhood. He was frequently truant and was sent to several Catholic reformatories. He later claimed to have been sexually assaulted by priests, and he became a militant anticleric and suspicious of authority in general. Fasanella dropped out of school at an early age when his father abandoned his family to return to Italy. Much of his political consciousness was shaped by his mother, who, in addition to her socialism, marched in demonstrations and worked on a small, Italian-language antifascist newspaper. During the **Depression era** Fasanella worked in the garment and textile industries, as a truck driver, and as a machinist. In the last position, he joined the **United Electrical, Radio and Machine Workers of America** (UE) union. Before the 1930s closed, he joined the Young Communist League and went to Spain to support the Loyalist cause in the Spanish Civil War. He drove a truck for the Abraham Lincoln Brigade during the conflict.

When Fasanella returned to the United States in 1940, he joined the UE staff as an organizer. His experiences during several New York City electrical workers and machinist **strikes** led him to begin sketching, a short-lived experience that ended when he developed arthritic pain in his hands. Fasanella began painting in 1944, when an artist friend suggested it as a form of physical therapy. Within a year he was teaching painting. In 1945, Fasanella quit his job as a union organizer to take up painting full-time. He later commented that he was disillusioned with organized labor's turn toward **business unionism**, though his compulsive interest in art may have been the real reason. Fasanella's art is often grouped with the primitive school of American folk art, but he disliked that label and his style also borrowed from surrealism and the mural art of the 1930s.

A short marriage in 1943 ended in divorce a year later, but in 1950 Fasanella married Eva Lazorek, a teacher with whom he had two children. His radically themed art of strikes, injustice, and **working-class** life did not mesh well with the **Red Scare** of the 1950s, and he was banned from many galleries. Fasanella eked out a living as a painter and by occasionally pumping gas at his brothers' service stations until 1972, when a cover article in *New York* magazine hailed him as the "best primitive painter since Grandma Moses." Fasanella was suddenly the latest sensation, and his cityscapes of street festivals, stickball games, Yankee Stadium, Coney Island, union meetings, strikes, and political rallies were in high demand. Critics hailed his use of detail and the exuberant manner and bright colors with which he depicted working-class culture. Fasanella remained faithful to his ethnic, working-class roots and insisted he did not want his work to "hang in some rich guy's living room." This attitude led him to display his work in public spaces and in museums where workers and their families would see them, such as the Ellis Island Immigration Museum, the Baseball Hall of Fame, the 53rd Street subway station in New York, and the Heritage Park Visitor's Center in Lawrence, Massachusetts. His painting titled *Lawrence 1912: The Bread and Roses Strike* is one of America's most reproduced images pertaining to labor history, and works such as *May Day, Iceman Crucified*, and *Meeting at the Common* also remain popular. Fasanella died December 16, 1997, at his home in Ardsley, New York.

Suggested Reading

Peter Carroll, "Ralph Fasanella Limns the Story of the Workingman," *Smithsonian* 24, no. 5 (August 1993); Paul D'Ambrosio, *Ralph Fasanella's America*, 2001: 58–69; Jerry Saltz, "Working-Class Hero: 'Ralph Fasanella's America' at The New York Historical Society," *Village Voice*, June 10, 2002; Patrick Watson, *Fasanella's City*, 1973.

FAST-TRACK LEGISLATION

Fast-track legislation is a controversial practice that applies to international trade agreements. Under the U.S. Constitution, the president of the United States can negotiate treaties with foreign powers, but the U.S. Congress must approve them. In most circumstances Congress has the ability to make amendments and individual members can assert the right to filibuster against a treaty. In fast-track agreements, the president negotiates the treaty and it goes to Congress for acceptance or rejection, with no provision for making changes. This practice was first established by the Free Trade Act of 1974 and must be renewed periodically. Fast-track authority expired in 1994, was renewed in 2002, and expired again in 2007.

Fast-track options are generally favored by those who believe that unfettered free trade is sound economic policy, and opposed by those who advocate **protectionism**, but there is plenty of debate terrain lying between these two poles. Congress has approved free trade agreements via fast-track methods in the past, but this practice's use to secure the 1993 **North American Free Trade Agreement** (NAFTA) met with great controversy and was bitterly opposed by the **American Federation of Labor-Congress of Industrial Organizations** (AFL-CIO), which complained that NAFTA would result in jobs lost to Mexico. When this prediction turned out to be true, the AFL-CIO aggressively lobbied against other fast-track free trade agreements. The AFL-CIO has ultimately been unsuccessful in warding off such agreements. When authority to fast track was restored in 2002, President George W. Bush fast-tracked free trade agreements between the United States and eight other nations. Numerous other agreements are pending and await either Congressional action or renewal of fast-track authority. For its part the AFL-CIO seeks the repeal of several fast-track agreements, especially NAFTA.

Organized labor generally opposes fast-track agreements, as do many non-organized American workers, for several reasons. First, they argue that removal of trade barriers allows employers to shift work to low-**wage** nations, which leads to lost jobs in the United States. Second, they argue that fast-track legislation, as well as agreements signed by international bodies such as the World Trade Organization, violates national sovereignty by creating standards that are beyond the say of American voters. American companies are allowed to engage in labor and environmental practices outside U.S. borders that would be illegal inside them. Moreover, foreign importers can flood U.S. markets with goods manufactured under conditions long ago made illegal in the United States. The fast-track process, then, becomes little more than global **capitalism** seeking to drive down labor costs, dodge questions of human rights, and circumvent environmental concerns. In essence, opponents of this practice see expedited agreements as a race to the bottom that endangers workers worldwide.

Defenders of fast-track bills see such actions as good for American consumers, as fostering international cooperation, and as inevitable nods to the reality of **globalism** and world markets.

Suggested Reading

I. M. Destler, *The New Politics of American Trade: Trade, Labor and the Environment*, 2000; Todd Tucker and Lori Wallach, *The Rise and Fall of Fast Track Trade Authority*, 2009.

FEDERAL EMERGENCY RELIEF ADMINISTRATION

The Federal Emergency Relief Administration (FERA) came into being in 1933 and was perhaps the first federal agency to administer poor relief programs aimed at assisting Americans in times of economic hardship. It began a controversial practice in which the federal government gives direct aid to distressed individuals.

The very idea of the federal government administering poor relief is of relatively recent vintage. It was not until the **Progressive Era** that a well-articulated notion of "social" problems first became widespread. Prior to this time, poverty and misfortune were often linked to character and moral flaws. Relief was viewed as a matter of charity and was a matter left to state and local governments and to private religious and philanthropic institutions. Most people took their cue from the Puritan belief that poverty should be shameful; hence relief programs were often unpleasant and demeaning. Debtors' prisons and workhouses were widespread, and social disapproval was high for those who needed external support. One of the few nods given to extenuating circumstances was the distinction made between the "deserving" and "undeserving" poor, the latter group made up of those unable to work for their sustenance—the elderly, the blind, the insane, and mothers with young children. Caring for such individuals was regarded as an act of generosity, not as a civic duty.

The **Industrial Revolution** exposed the inadequacy of private charity. Throughout the 19th century cities expanded, **agrarianism** declined, and the number of Americans dependent upon **wages** grew. Although the U.S. economy expanded dramatically after the **Civil War**, the pace of growth was uneven and was blemished by periodic downturns and recessions. In a nation that provided no unemployment compensation or entitled relief of any sort, families that experienced wage cuts or loss of employment frequently slid into crippling poverty. As sociologists later came to realize, poverty is often linked to other forms of social strain. The late 19th century was marred by **strikes**, urban unrest, high infant mortality rates, soaring alcoholism levels, and other social ills. The need for social reform sparked change during the Progressive Era, but few of the new laws directly targeted distressed individuals.

The onset of the Great Depression altered the federal government's role in delivering services to individuals. Its severity was such that the old distinction between the deserving and undeserving poor was rendered moot. When the economic decline first began in 1929, President Herbert Hoover insisted that the federal government should not provide poor relief as it would entail tax increases, and that direct handouts bred dependency. He also held the naïve belief that private charities would bridge the gap between the downturn and the return to prosperity he thought would soon emerge. By early 1933, however, the official unemployment level reached 25 percent and in some areas was much higher.

The deepening depression led to the presidential election of Franklin Roosevelt in 1932. A centerpiece of Roosevelt's New Deal program involved direct relief to poor and unemployed Americans. Roosevelt had previously served as governor of New York, and he used the New York State Temporary Emergency Relief Association (TERA) as the template for creating a national agency to administer emergency relief. In like fashion, he appointed former TERA head Harry Hopkins to direct the newly formed Federal Emergency Relief Administration, whose establishment was approved by Congress on May 12, 1933. The FERA began with a budget of $500 million, half of which was distributed to the states as matching grants at a rate of $1 to every $3 each state provided. The other half of the fund was reserved for discretionary spending. Critics charged that some of those funds were distributed for political reasons.

FERA funds were supposed to be directed at work relief, but the federal bureaucracy was small at the time and lacked the ability to oversee state and local projects. In some states and locales work relief gave way to direct handouts to individuals, a practice decried both by workers and by opponents of the FERA. A much bigger problem, however, was that the lack of federal oversight meant that local authorities often made it difficult for potential recipients to obtain FERA aid, and many complained that they were subjected to humiliating and invasive means testing. Immigrant and **minority labor** groups experienced even greater difficulty in accessing FERA funds. Overall the FERA enjoyed its greatest successes among those workers forced by economic conditions to become transient and migrant workers. An estimated 20 million individuals obtained work on FERA projects.

The FERA was beset by great criticism, though it was popular among the **working class** and most labor unions, both of which appreciated the effort to link relief to work. Most workers had long internalized the social shame associated with taking handouts and decried misuse of FERA funds directed away from work projects. The FERA was dismantled in 1935 and replaced with programs more explicitly linked to employment, including the Works Progress Administration (WPA). Hopkins had already been transferred to the Civil Works Administration (CWA) at that point, and he later headed the WPA. Both the CWA and the WPA proved better at providing jobs for the unemployed, though they were best by controversies of their own.

The FERA was a stopgap measure that provided relief that states and private charities could not during the depression. Roosevelt's quick response to the economic crisis won admiration among those most affected by the economic crisis. In retrospect, the FERA had lasting effects on American society. By changing the relationship between the government and society, it opened the door to future social programs and, therefore, was a component of the emergence of the welfare state. The FERA also began the process by which the very notion of taking aid from the government became more acceptable. Although some forms of federal aid are controversial, others— including **Social Security**—are now institutionalized. Moreover, the FERA played a role in making millions of Americans feel that public welfare is ultimately a civic responsibility. The term "welfare" continues to carry a negative connotation for many Americans, but the idea that the federal government should intervene during an economic crisis is no longer unthinkable. In many ways President Barack Obama's 2009 American Recovery and Reinvestment Act traces its origins to the FERA.

Suggested Reading

Lorena A. Hickok, *One-Third of a Nation: Lorena Hickok Reports on the Great Depression*, 1981; Harry L. Hopkins, *Spending to Save: The Complete Story of Relief*, 1936; Jeff

Singelton, *The American Dole: Unemployment Relief and the Welfare State in the Great Depression*, 2000; Fiona Venn, *The New Deal*, 1998.

FEDERAL SOCIETY OF JOURNEYMEN CORDWAINERS

The Federal Society of Journeymen Cordwainers (FSJC) is often considered to be the first true labor union in the United States. Although earlier workers formed short-term alliances, in 1794, Philadelphia **journeymen** bootmakers and shoe-makers were perhaps the first to contemplate an ongoing organization to protect **wages** and pressure **master craftsmen** for better working conditions.

At the time, American industry was in its infancy, and its work structure mirrored the guild system. Most production was done in small shops owned by masters, who hired journeymen for wages and maintained unpaid **apprentices**. Journeymen cordwainers were among the poorest craftsmen in pre-Revolutionary America and among the most ardent supporters of independence from Britain. Many hoped that independence would result in better conditions. On the contrary, the American Revolution disrupted trade, and its conclusion threw the economy into a temporary tailspin. Work was irregular, wages declined, and markets contracted. The economy recovered somewhat in the early 1790s, but opportunities were rare for journey-men. The ideal of the guild-like structure of early industry was that journeymen could expect to obtain master status in roughly seven years, at which time they would cease working for wages and take on their own apprentices and journeymen. By 1794, an increasingly closed economic system meant that fewer than one-tenth of all journeymen cordwainers were able to rise to master status. Some journeymen complained that the power of master shoemakers was as arbitrary as that of the British government.

Threatened with lifelong status as wage-earners—a degraded and dependent sta-tus by the ideological standards of the day—cordwainers formed the FSJC. The FSJC struck several Philadelphia masters in 1799 and is credited with launching one of the first successful **boycotts** in post-Revolutionary America. Although the FSJC blazed the trail for other workers to combine forces, it also proved to be the first victim of problems that beset future worker organizations. It passed out of exis-tence in 1806, when the organization ran afoul of the legal system and was judged an illegal restraint of trade. The resulting court case, *Commonwealth v. Pullis*, proved a challenge for the upcoming decades, as labor unions seeking to follow in the FSJC's footsteps were deemed criminal conspiracies. In some states, legislation soft-ened the blow of the *Pullis* decision, but the right to form unions was not guaranteed in total until the passage of the **Clayton Antitrust Act** in 1914, and even it had numerous loopholes that were not addressed until the 1935 **National Labor Relations Act**.

The FSJC folded at a time in which the shoemaking industry was on the cusp of great change. Shoemaking and textile manufacturing (and, to a lesser extent, iron production) were the first American industries to move toward large-scale factory production, with masters becoming owners and journeymen becoming factory hands. Mechanization further transformed the profession by deskilling it and by segmenting work tasks. By the 1840s, few shoemakers produced their wares from start to finish; instead, workers performed specialized tasks such as leather cutting, hole punching, lasting, stitching, and so forth.

The spirit of the FSJC lived on within the trade. By 1815, most cities had similar cordwainer associations, though they, too, suffered legal setbacks that destroyed them. However, later shoemaker organizations such as the Knights of St. Crispin and the Boot and Shoe Workers' Union were the ideological offspring of the FSJC. In the 1830s, journeymen papers like *The Awl* drew upon FSJC experiences, and **strikes** like that undertaken by Lynn shoe workers in 1860 can be viewed in the context of a pattern of strained employer/employee relations within the industry.

The FSJC was also important because it was part of a broader pattern of discontent among journeymen in the early American republic. New York printers set up a lasting typographical society later in 1794, while others created organizations that led to the 10-hour movement. While the FSJC and like-minded early groups were destroyed by a combination of legal obstacles, employer intransigence, and severe economic downturns during the 1820s, their pioneering efforts were the very foundations upon which the American union movement was built.

Suggested Reading

Foster Dulles and Melvyn Dubofsky, *Labor in America*, 1984; Victoria Hattam, *Labor Visions and State Power*, 1993; Billy Smith, "The Vicissitudes of Fortune: The Careers of Laboring Men in Philadelphia, 1750–1800," in *Work and Labor in Early America*, ed. Stephen Innes, 1988.

FEDERATION OF ORGANIZED TRADES AND LABOR UNIONS. *See* American Federation of Labor.

FIELDCREST SETTLEMENT

The Fieldcrest settlement took place in June 1999. A long and bitter union recognition struggle between the textile company and the **Union of Needletrades, Industrial, and Textile Employees** (UNITE) ended when 5,200 Pillowtex workers at the Fieldcrest Cannon plant in Kannapolis, North Carolina, secured union protection for the first time. On February 10, 2000, more than 90 percent of UNITE's membership voted to approve a contract that called for a 9 percent raise in hourly and **piecework** rates, increased retirement benefits, and included the company's first-ever sick-pay policy. At the time it was seen as an important victory that would revitalize organized labor. The UNITE contract culminated more than a decade of union struggle and activists hoped that it would become a model for future organization of the South, a notoriously union-resistant region. Those hopes proved overly optimistic.

Fieldcrest was a remnant of the once-powerful Cannon Mills, a family-owned enterprise that incorporated in 1887. Like many southern textile concerns, Cannon controlled workers through **paternalism** and political influence. Kannapolis was largely a **company town** and its blend of family paternalism endured well into the 20th century. By the 1930s, Cannon Mills was the nation's largest textile manufacturer, with more than 18,000 employees. This made it a lynchpin of the post-World War II attempt by the **Congress of Industrial Organizations** (CIO) to organize the South in its **Operation Dixie** campaign. That effort stalled due to a combination of Red-baiting, racism, and strong-arm tactics. Although the Cannon family maintained a façade of paternalist concern for its workers, conditions at Kannapolis were notoriously poor, and **wages** were low even by debased Piedmont standards.

Conditions continued to decline in Kannapolis as Cannon struggled to maintain its market share for its major product: towels. In 1962, the company was briefly delisted from the New York Stock Exchange. It soon returned to profitability, but remained vulnerable and, in 1982, was taken over in a leveraged buyout by California financier David Murdock, who made improvements to the plant, but also eliminated jobs and implemented a **stretch-out**. The **Amalgamated Clothing and Textile Workers Union** (ACTWU) attempted to organize Cannon workers, but a 1985 recognition vote lost by nearly a 2:1 margin of the 9,512 factory hands.

That same year, Cannon was sold again, this time to the larger Fieldcrest Corporation. At the time, orders had increased and employment surged, but Fieldcrest Cannon faced stiff competition from overseas manufacturers. Conditions deteriorated further, and more jobs were lost. In August 1991, the ACTWU again forced a union recognition vote. Fieldcrest Cannon used a variety of scare tactics to dissuade pro-union votes, including threats to hire **scabs** or to close Kannapolis operations. The latter threat was made more palpable by the fact that Fieldcrest Cannon had recently closed two other operations organized by the ACTWU. Even with such threats looming, the union failed to win certification by the scant margin of 3,233 to 3,094. The ACTWU charged that its loss was the result of illegal votes from clerical workers and it petitioned the National Labor Relations Board for a revote. That request came to naught, but conditions remained tense and Fieldcrest's 1994 purchase of Amoskeag Mills raised questions about how corporate funds were being used.

In 1995, the ACTWU and the **International Ladies' Garment Workers' Union** merged to form UNITE and launched a new campaign against Fieldcrest Cannon. This dispute was inherited by the Pillowtex Corporation, which purchased Fieldcrest Cannon in 1997. The unionization campaign finally succeeded in 1999 when employees accepted UNITE by a wide margin, though just 5,200 votes were cast, an indication of the continuing hemorrhaging of textile jobs in the Piedmont region. The union victory ended a 93-year anti-union epoch in the southern textile industry and heartened UNITE activists who hoped to use the Fieldcrest settlement as the basis for expansion.

Industry analysts were less optimistic, as most viewed domestic textile production as a **sunset industry**. This perception proved to be correct. Paternalism and hardball anti-union tactics were no longer the biggest obstacles for unionization, but rather **deindustrialization** and **globalism**. After it purchased Cannon, Pillowtex was pressured by Wal-Mart, its largest customer, to close U.S. operations and move jobs to low-wage overseas. Pillowtex refused and dropped its Wal-Mart account. Competition crippled the company, however, and it declared bankruptcy in 2000. It reorganized in 2002, but in 2003 it failed. This resulted in the largest mass layoff in North Carolina history, with more than 7,600 workers losing their jobs, of which 4,340 were located in Kannapolis. Demolition of the former Cannon Mills property commenced in 2005 and a biotechnology plant now stands on part of the property. A Hong Kong firm now owns the Fieldcrest brand.

What was once viewed as hope for organized labor's future is now fodder for those who argue that unions should not waste resources in dying industries and should concentrate its organizational efforts in stable and emerging occupations.

Suggested Reading

Clete Daniel, *Culture of Misfortune*, 2001; "Fieldcrest-Cannon Workers Vote to Ratify Historic Union Contract," *Business Wire*, February 10, 2000, accessed September 12, 2010; Gwen Laird Perney, "Former Fieldcrest Cannon Plant Yields to North Carolina Research Campus," *Waste Handling Equipment News*, February 2007.

FILM AND LABOR

One of world's earliest films, the Lumiere brothers' *Workers Leaving the Factory* (1895), put the **working class** on the silver screen. But this was a chance debut— the Lumieres filmed employees because they were handy, not for any political purpose. Throughout the first century of American film, viewers had to look hard for depictions of unionization or working-class life. Feature films addressing these themes have been scarce, leaving documentarians, unions, and radical organizations to fund and produce most labor images on the screen. When workers are on film, they are typically caricatured as wild-eyed, uncontrollably violent mobs stirred up by outside agitators and foreign radicals. Organized labor is generally seen as comprising mindless factory drones and corrupt officials eager to sell out the rank-and-file. Rarely does one see the underlying causes of labor/capital conflict or the legitimacy of workers' concerns.

The early years of American film were the heyday of labor cinema. Costs were low, so films could be made by anyone with a story to tell. Some 600 films were created by labor unions, workers, and radicals before 1917. Unfortunately, few have survived and most are known only from written accounts. Nevertheless, they represent a parallel cinema stream to the mass-market pictures created by the emerging film industry.

Worker-owned film companies made social class central and featured **strikes**, union organizing, and even radical challenges to dominant American values and institutions. In D. W. Griffith's 1908 *The Song of the Shirt*, audiences were asked to contrast heartless business owners with exploited workers. Other films included the pro-socialist *From Dusk to Dawn* (1913); the meatpacking industry exposé *The Jungle* (1914); *Why?* (1913), which questioned the humanity of **child labor**; and *The Blacklist* (1916), which featured violent strikebreaking thugs.

Until the 1920s, film audiences were overwhelmingly working class. Many were immigrants who learned both English and American values from those flickering images. Censors and government figures rallied to keep viewers away from "radical" ideas. While leftist organizations tried to inspire **class consciousness** by showing films about labor/capital conflict, mainstream features that used working-class characters largely ignored class issues or promoted sanitized images of harmony between the classes.

By the 1920s, mainstream studios had a selfish reason to avoid depicting capital/labor tensions: The emerging Hollywood film industry coalesced around studios that had relocated to California in part to avoid unionized workforces back East. Studios controlled what was produced and how it was distributed. In addition, middle-class censors feared that showing labor unrest on the screen would encourage such actions off-screen. The Hollywood system largely blocked worker-made films from reaching mass audiences. Grandiose film palaces built in the 1920s convinced middle-class audiences that films were respectable, and a change in content followed. Filmmakers less often featured working-class characters, assuming that middle-class patrons wished to see people like themselves on the screen.

By the 1930s, films had sound and occasionally addressed social concerns and working-class life. During the Great Depression, ignoring labor altogether would have been problematic, and a wave of "social-problem" films took a liberal or radical perspective. Independent filmmakers and union-sponsored productions had been pushed to the fringes, but they were able to find audiences for projects that tried to educate and inspire workers to organize. Their genres of choice were often documentaries and docudramas such as *Native Land* (1942) and *The Wave* (1937), in which Mexican fishermen strike for a living **wage**. Conservatives controlled the studio system, however, and they often succeeded in blunting radicalism. For example, the original pro-labor screenplay of 1935's *Black Fury* criticized mine owners; it was gutted in favor of a script that depicted union workers as bigoted and violent. A few films made it to the screen with a pro-labor slant. Among them are Charlie Chaplin's blistering anti-**Fordism** classic *Modern Times* (1936) and King Vidor's vision of a **co-operative** workers' experiment *Our Daily Bread* (1934), though the latter was attacked vigorously by conservatives.

The 1940s brought more labor-themed features. Pro-labor sensibilities were obvious in *The Grapes of Wrath* (1940), which showed the gritty determination of displaced farm workers, and in *How Green Was My Valley* (1941), which chronicled the family devastation caused by conditions in Welsh coal mining towns. Even in the commercial *The Devil and Miss Jones* (1941), a boss works undercover in his own department store and learns a lesson about workers' lives. Labor-oriented films became scarcer as the decade progressed, especially as World War II brought a wave of feature films supporting the war effort.

The post-World War II **Red Scare** further decimated the number of pro-labor productions. In 1947, the House Un-American Activities Committee (HUAC) began investigating alleged **communist** subversion in the film industry. Its efforts were aided by internal battles between the conservative International Alliance of Theatrical Stage Employees and Moving Picture Machine Operators (IATSE) and the Conference of Studio Unions (CSU), whose ranks included communists. IATSE exploited anticommunist fears to win **contracts** for its members at the CSU's expense. In so doing, it also brought the entire industry under closer scrutiny.

In 1947, the "Hollywood Ten," a mix of writers and directors, were hauled before HUAC, convicted of contempt of Congress, and served jail terms. The HUAC hearings caused a ripple effect through the industry. Studios **blacklisted** actors, writers, technicians, directors, and anyone else whose political views rendered them controversial. Numerous individuals, including Screen Actors Guild President **Ronald Reagan**, cooperated with government attempts to ferret out left-wingers in Hollywood.

Widespread prosperity in the 1950s led Hollywood to disingenuously portray a nation where harmony reigned. It also avoided controversial content. When workers appeared onscreen, individual heroism, rather than collective action, was championed. *On the Waterfront*, a 1954 classic about New York City dockworkers and their corrupt union, bears witness to this theme. Although set in a unionized world, problems are solved by Karl Malden's tough-kind clergyman and Marlon Brando's loner longshoreman. An outstanding exception to this generally conservative period in film is one of the most progressive, pro-labor films ever made, *Salt of the Earth* (1954), which shows how a strike changed individuals and their community. It also interwove class and gender more effectively than most films of any age. Director Herbert Biberman faced stiff opposition at every stage of production and distribution, and despite the film's cinematic merits, it largely went unseen by the public.

Labor was seldom seen on American screens for the next decade and a half. Among the very few films of the late 1960s and early 1970s to feature working-class people were *The Pawnbroker* (1965), with its elements of working-class despair; *Joe* (1970), about a hard-drinking, working-class bigot who exacted vigilante justice on counterculture figures; and *The Molly Maguires* (1970), which depicted the 19th-century rebellion of Pennsylvania coal miners. In the late 1970s and 1980s, workers made a comeback. Even apolitical films such as *Saturday Night Fever* (1977), *Blue Collar* (1978), *An Officer and a Gentleman* (1982), and *Flashdance* (1983) had working-class settings, characters, or subplots. Though studio features often exploited or trivialized their labor themes—unions are in cahoots with organized crime in *Blue Collar*, for example—their very presence stands in contrast to most films of the preceding decades.

Several features actually made working-class life central. *Breaking Away* (1979) follows a bicycle-racing enthusiast whose working-class roots set him apart in a university town. *Twice in a Lifetime* (1985) gives a full and realistic portrait of a steelworker's life. *Bound for Glory* (1976) is a biopic of folk singer and labor organizer Woody Guthrie; *Silkwood* (1983) shows a working-class heroine battling corporate lies; and Woody Allen's *The Front* (1976) dramatizes the blacklisting of Hollywood leftists during McCarthyism. *Reds* (1981) went even further, following the triumph of Soviet **socialism** and sympathetically portraying American communists *Norma Rae* (1979) was a rare commercial feature that sympathetically showcased union organizing. More radical than the features was a string of superb documentaries focusing on labor unions and workers' lives: *Union Maids* (1976), *Harlan County, USA* (1977), *With Babies and Banners* (1978), *The Wobblies* (1979), *The Life and Times of Rosie the Riveter* (1980), *You Got to Move* (1985), *American Dream* (1989), and *Roger and Me* (1989). Equal in power and scope to *Norma Rae*, and appearing a decade later, is John Sayles's 1987 *Matewan*, which follows a bitter strike in the West Virginia coalfields. Sayles's stark portrayal of unionists, miners, and socialists battling against the evil corporate bosses nonetheless used classic Hollywood entertainment structure. Sayles is one of the few contemporary filmmakers openly favorable to workers, as seen also in his film *Eight Men Out* (1988).

Labor-themed films largely faded from view during the 1990s. A rare example of a major studio film about labor is the 1992 Jack Nicholson vehicle *Hoffa*. This biopic of the **Teamsters** boss is union centered, but focuses on the drama of Hoffa's life rather than on the workers he leads or the causes of the strikes they undergo. At the turn of the millennium, labor-themed films were still rarely seen, other than in documentaries such as Michael Moore's anticorporate *The Big One* (1997), *Sicko* (2007), and *Capitalism: A Love Story* (2009); these films carried the same working-class-friendly ethos of Moore's 1989 debut, *Roger and Me*, which took an often humorous look at **deindustrialization** in his hometown of Flint, Michigan.

In the new century's opening decade, which coincided with the worst economic downturn in the United States since the Great Depression, working-class characters started to reappear in feature films, though by no means often. Representative movies that did not tackle labor issues directly but whose main characters happened to be blue-collar workers included *The Perfect Storm* (2000), about commercial fishermen fighting the sea's power; *Billy Elliot* (2000), set during a strike in a northern English mining town; *The Good Girl* (2002), in which Jennifer Aniston played a discount-store clerk; *Mystic River* (2003), a tense drama taking place in blue-collar Boston; *The Machinist* (2004), in which a lathe operator fears sleeplessness is sapping his sanity; and *Sunshine Cleaning* (2008), in which a cash-strapped mother starts a crime-scene-cleaning business to put her son through school.

A handful of films made labor issues their plot anchors, but few enjoyed commercial success at the box office. For example, *New in Town* (2009) starred Renee Zellweger as a hard-charging corporate minion assigned to restructure a manufacturing plant in Minnesota. It is a romantic comedy, but one whose climactic moment comes when the protagonist is ordered to close the plant and fire everyone, including her new love, the union representative. Given that the film had a mere $16 million gross box office, few people found out which side she was on.

A much more serious—and successful with critics if not at the box office (it made $18 million)—was 2005's *North Country*. Its topic was America's first major sexual harassment case by a female worker. A-list stars Charlize Theron and Frances McDormand, both Oscar nominated for their roles, reveal the effects of uninvited sexual advances and general disrespect showed to the first female miners at Eveleth Mines in Minnesota by their male coworkers, and the tough legal battle they fought to secure a workplace free of harassment.

Labor-themed films are generally cast in *North Country*'s mold—serious, well-crafted, but small-budget pictures created as labors of love. The one major exception so far this century has been *Up in the Air* (2009), which earned $83 million, critical acclaim, six Oscar nominations (including best picture), and 45 other awards. Here, corporate callousness is front and center. The "hero," played by George Clooney, is a "career transition counselor"—in business-speak, that means he fires people. Director Jason Reitman deliberately and boldly included montages of real life laid off workers speaking to the camera about what effect job-loss had on them and what they wish they had told the person who fired them. Although these moments occupy only a sliver of screen time, the emotional weight amplifies the entire film's impact. Moreover, although themes of romance, competition, business ethics, and aging all vie for attention in the plotlines, the emotional and practical effects of turning good workers into ex-workers is the film's emotional heart.

In general, however, working-class heroes—unless they are police or firefighters—get little screen time in nondocumentary American movies.

Suggested Reading

Geoffrey Nowell-Smith, ed., *The Oxford History of World Cinema*, 1996; Steven Ross, *Working-Class Hollywood: Silent Film and the Shaping of Class in America*, 1998; Peter Stead, *Film and the Working Class*, 1991; "Worker/Union-Themed Movies," http://www.cgeu.org/wiki/index.php/Worker/Union-themed_Movies, accessed October 8, 2010.

FLINT SIT-DOWN STRIKE. *See* General Motors Sit-down Strike.

FLYNN, ELIZABETH GURLEY

Elizabeth Gurley Flynn (August 7, 1890–September 5, 1964) was an important leader of the **Industrial Workers of the World** (IWW) in the early 20th century, and later became an activist in the Communist Party. Her radical left politics notwithstanding, Flynn is an example of an independent woman who broke with social convention and followed her ideals rather than caving in to cultural expectations.

Elizabeth was born in Concord, New Hampshire, and was one of three daughters raised by Irish Americans Tom and Annie Flynn. When she was in her teens the family moved to New York's South Bronx, where the Flynns introduced their daughters to **socialist** ideals. Her father, a civil engineer, suffered from periodic bouts of unemployment, and the family frequently depended upon Annie's wages for sustenance. Mrs. Flynn worked as a tailoress, an occupation that spawned numerous female labor leaders during the late 19th century, including **Leonora Barry**. Annie Flynn was also well read, instructed her daughters in feminist and socialist literature, and encouraged them to break free from traditional gender roles. Elizabeth made her first public speech at a labor rally when she was just 15, and both parents urged her to cultivate her talent as a speaker.

One year later, in 1907, Elizabeth dropped out of high school to become an organizer for the IWW, a union rhetorically in favor of a revolutionary overthrow of **capitalism** through the applied use of **general strikes**. Flynn quickly became acculturated into the IWW's polyglot world. Unlike the more conservative **craft unions** affiliated with the **American Federation of Labor** (AFL), the IWW was devoted to **industrial unionism** and organized workers whom the AFL often ignored: unskilled and semiskilled laborers, women, African Americans, and recent immigrants, including those who spoke little or no English. Flynn traveled extensively for the IWW and took part in the organization's 1909 free speech battle in Spokane, Washington. Back East the writer Theodore Dreiser was so captivated by Flynn's electrifying rhetorical gifts that he dubbed her "an East Side (of New York) Joan of Arc." Flynn had minimal foreign language skills, but her striking good looks and passion made her a favorite among workers of all tongues, and the IWW generally paired English-speaking organizers with those who could address workers in their native languages. Flynn also took her mother's lessons to heart and upheld the rights and power of women.

Flynn and the IWW proved the AFL wrong in its assumptions that women and immigrants could not be organized. She played a key role in two of the IWW's most dramatic East Coast strikes. During the 1912 Lawrence, Massachusetts, "bread and roses" strike, Flynn helped organize mothers to send their children out of the city during the conflict. This generated so much negative publicity for the textile firms and the city that they attempted to halt the practice. When that effort turned violent, the resulting public revulsion was instrumental in helping workers win the **Lawrence textile strike**. Flynn was also active in a 1913 strike in Paterson, New Jersey, and helped organize a pageant that generated great publicity. Although the Paterson strike did not succeed, Flynn's efforts were praised by supporters and foes alike. Her charisma also served on the legal front; between 1907 and 1916 she was arrested at least 10 times, but was never convicted of an offense.

Flynn's lively speaking style, her straightforward language, and her charm attracted many workers to the IWW. She was also a strong advocate for birth control and economic independence for women, and realized that female workers had needs different from those of males. True to her IWW beliefs, Flynn saw social class as more important than gender, but in retrospect she was an early adopter of woman-centered organizing models. She also expressed sympathy for the suffrage movement and even cooperated with middle-class women's rights leaders on occasion.

Flynn was expelled from the IWW in 1916 after a quarrel with **Bill Haywood** over her handling of a Minnesota miner strike. She was accused of bungling a plea bargain that sent three immigrant miners to prison for 20 years instead of being set free. It is unclear whether Flynn made her way back into the IWW, but the organization was badly crippled by the post-World War I **Red Scare** and the ensuing persecutions led Flynn to become a cofounder of the American Civil Liberties Union (ACLU) in 1920. She was also a cofounder of the Workers Defense Union, which provided legal and financial aid to victims of the Red Scare. During the 1920s Flynn was very active in ACLU campaigns to free Sacco and Vanzetti, and she was drawn deeper into the birth control cause.

Flynn's whirlwind activism took its toll and, in 1926, she moved to Portland, Oregon. Although she was in poor health for much of her 10-year stay in Portland, she took part in the city's 1934 longshoremen's strike. Like many leftists during the Great Depression, she came to believe that this era signaled the imminent demise of capitalism. Flynn had been enthralled by the 1917 Bolshevik Revolution in Russia and she was convinced that **communism** would soon supplant capitalism. In 1936, she joined the Communist Party of the United States of America (CPUSA) and began writing a regular column for its official journal, the *Daily Worker*. As a well-known rabble rouser, Flynn soon attracted the attention of conservatives. She eventually became too controversial for even her allies. In 1940, she was dismissed from the ACLU's governing board. Flynn advocated for women's causes during World War II and, in 1942, ran an unsuccessful congressional campaign. The war's end touched off a second Red Scare and the aging Flynn would be among its victims.

In 1948, Flynn took part in a legal effort to dismiss the charges against 12 CPUSA colleagues convicted under the 1940 Smith Act, which made it illegal to advocate the violent overthrow of the U.S. government. The convictions and the Smith Act were upheld by a 1951 Supreme Court decision that opened the door for Flynn's own arrest. Flynn spent 28 months in the Federal Reformatory at Alderson, West Virginia. There, she wrote her autobiography, *The Rebel Girl*, and assisted poor and uneducated inmates. Her time in prison did little to chasten Flynn, and she resumed her work with the CPUSA upon her release. From 1961 to 1964, she chaired the CPUSA and made several trips to the Soviet Union, where she died in 1964. According to her wishes, her ashes were sent to Chicago and interned at a site containing the remains of anarchists convicted for the 1886 **Haymarket bombing**. Although Flynn died a communist, she was an activist rather than an ideologue. Her life was that of a woman who cared more about social justice than social norms.

Suggested Reading

Rosalyn F. Baxandall, *Words on Fire: The Life and Writing of Elizabeth Gurley Flynn*, 1987; Helen C. Camp, *Iron in Her Soul: Elizabeth Gurley Flynn and the American Left*, 1995; Elizabeth Gurley Flynn, *The Rebel Girl, An Autobiography: My First Life (1906– 26)*, 1955.

FORDISM

Fordism refers to specific **assembly-line** production methods and management techniques associated with the Ford Motor Company. Marxist and radical critics also use the term as a synonym for industrial exploitation. Central to assembly-line production is a machine-driven, continuous flow of parts and material to individual workstations where unskilled or semiskilled laborers fashion or install single pieces of the total product. It also refers to management methods in which work is simplified, supervisors hold all decision-making power, and workers are expected to be compliant and efficient.

Henry Ford did not invent assembly-line production. Instead, flour mills were the first American businesses to use the assembly line, adapting methods pioneered by Oliver Evans around 1784. In the 19th century, meatpackers and gun manufacturers also adopted the assembly line. Ford did, however, apply assembly-line production on a hitherto unprecedented scale. In 1914, he converted his Dearborn, Michigan, Model-T plant to assembly-line production, and the price of automobiles dropped dramatically. The implementation of this approach was accomplished, in part, by a radical deskilling of the workforce. By 1926, a Ford automobile required 7,782 separate operations for completion, but more than three-fourths of all jobs required less than a week's training to master.

Assembly-line workers complained that the new production methods distanced them from the final product, were mind-numbing, robbed them of control over tools, and were dehumanizing to the point that laborers were as interchangeable as the parts that flowed to their workstations. To get workers to accept the machine-driven pace and monotony of the line, Ford offered higher **wages** than other manufacturers. Nonetheless, Ford often experienced yearly turnover in excess of 300 percent.

Fordism was also marked by devotion to efficiency, though it was often Ford's competitors that first subjected the assembly line to the scientific management principles and time-and-motion studies associated with **Taylorism**. Efficient mass production was the primary goal of Fordism, and plants operating under its principles were (and are) often fast-paced. Monetary incentives were used to reduce turnover, especially such things as piece-rate pay and bonuses.

By the 1950s, many industrial sociologists equated assembly-line production with worker alienation, and in the 1960s and 1970s, younger autoworkers resorted to **stints** and sabotage to resist the tedium of the line. General Motors was particularly hard hit by resistance from Chevrolet Vega workers at its Lordstown, Ohio, facility. Despite resistance, by the 1930s assembly-line production was the norm in many American factories until the full effect of **automation** began to transform manufacturing in the 1970s. By the 1980s, some manufacturers had begun to abandon the assembly line in favor of a more varied workplace, such as the **quality circles** model. However, the line remains in widespread use in the United States and is the method of choice in many developing nations to which **runaway shops** have relocated. Among radical critics, Fordism is a catchall label that refers to any excessively exploitative labor system that encompasses mass production and managerial systems designed to maintain a compliant workforce.

Suggested Reading

Harry Braveman, *Labor and Monopoly Capitalism: The Degradation of Work in the 20th Century*, 1974; Robert Burrows, Nigel Gilbert and Anna Pollert, eds., *Fordism and Flexibility: Divisions and Change*, 1992; Mike Davis, *Prisoners of the American Dream*, 1988.

FOSTER, FRANK KEYES

Frank Keyes Foster (December 18, 1855–June 27, 1909) was a leading trade-union journalist of the late 19th and 20th centuries and cofounder of the **American Federation of Labor** (AFL).

Foster was born in Palmer, Massachusetts, the son of Charles Dwight and Jane Elizabeth (Burgess) Foster. He was educated at Monson Academy, and learned the printing trade in Hartford, Connecticut, while working for the publication *Churchman*. Although Foster joined the Hartford Typographical Union and was elected secretary of that organization, labor unions were weak in the aftermath of the Panic of 1873. Numerous trade unions collapsed after the nationwide rail strikes during 1877. Foster moved to Cambridge, Massachusetts, in 1878, and was elected president of the Cambridge Typographical Union, one of the few trade unions that maintained its vitality during this era. He also served as a delegate to its international union. Foster married Lucretia Ella Ladd on May 22, 1879, and within a year the couple moved to Boston, where Foster became active with the Boston Central Trades and Labor Union, serving as secretary for the organization. In 1883, he joined the **Knights of Labor** (KOL) and served on executive boards on the local, district, state, and national levels. By the mid-1880s, Massachusetts's District 30 was the largest district assembly in the KOL, and Foster was one of its leading lights. He was a frequent contributor of poetry, short stories, news, and editorials to KOL publications. In 1884, Foster assumed the editorship of the *Haverhill* (Massachusetts) *Daily and Weekly Laborer*, which served as the KOL's official journal in Massachusetts. In 1886, he became the editor and the publisher of the *Liberator*, a short-lived eastern Massachusetts labor journal.

Foster was an ardent trade unionist, a commitment that led to his estrangement from the Knights, who viewed them as exclusionary. Trade unions were revived during the 1880s, and by mid-decade often battled the KOL over such issues as **jurisdiction** and **dual unionism**. Foster tended to side with trade unions in those disputes; he also disagreed with KOL leaders over the organization's opposition to **strikes** and over the **socialist** principles held by numerous individuals. Foster had been a socialist in his youth, but became an ardent Democrat, even making an unsuccessful bid to become Massachusetts lieutenant governor in 1886. He was especially distrustful of a **Lassallean** clique said to control the KOL. Foster slowly drifted away from the KOL and became more deeply immersed in trade union causes. After helping found the AFL in December 1886, Foster's career was more closely aligned with that federation.

In 1887, Foster began working with **George E. McNeill** on the official paper of the Massachusetts Federation of Labor, the *Labor Leader*. McNeill went on to edit a book, *The Labor Movement: The Problem of Today* (1887), to which Foster contributed a chapter on shoemakers. McNeill retired as *Labor Leader* editor within a year of Foster's arrival, and Foster took over that role. He would edit the paper until 1897, and also contributed articles on Boston-area labor. His steady hand made it one of the few labor newspapers to enjoy a long life.

As an AFL stalwart, Foster became increasingly opposed to Marxist ideals, especially Marx's emphasis on revolution. Foster argued for evolutionary change instead, and was enamored with the philosophy of Herbert Spencer, particularly his Law of Equal Freedom, a mildly libertarian view that emphasized complete individual freedom for those persons who did not infringe on the self-expression of others. He also espoused pragmatic, **pure and simple** trade unionism, often echoing the ideology of **Samuel Gompers** and the AFL. Foster eventually split acrimoniously with the KOL, when he deemed that organization to be hostile to trade unions. Numerous *Labor Leader* editorials condemned the KOL. In fact, Foster and Gompers became so critical of the Knights that their critiques often colored how future historians of late 19th-century labor movements judged the KOL.

Foster dubbed his belief in both individualism and working-class associations "collective-individualism." Much of his justification for that hybrid view was outlined in a semi-autobiographical novel, *The Evolution of a Trade Unionist* (1901). Foster also penned a volume of poetry, *The Karma of Labor* (1903). His reputation as a dynamic speaker on labor issues put him in demand as a **Labor Day** orator, and he ultimately spoke in 23 states. Foster was also a civic-minded individual who was a member of numerous Boston boards, committees, and fraternal organizations.

Suggested Reading

Joseph DePlasco, "The University of Labor vs. the University of Letters in 1904: Frank K. Foster Confronts Harvard University President Charles W. Eliot," *Labor's Heritage* 1, no. 2 (April 1989): 52–65; Arthur Mann, *Yankee Reformers in the Urban Age: Social Reform in Boston, 1880–1900*, 1966; Robert E. Weir, *Knights Unhorsed: Internal Conflict in a Gilded Age Social Movement*, 2000.

FOSTER, WILLIAM ZEBULON

William Zebulon Foster (February 25, 1881–December 1, 1961) was a fiery and controversial labor leader active in the first half of the 20th century. An unrepentant radical, he passed through the Socialist Party (SP) and the **Industrial Workers of the World** (IWW) before becoming a mainstay of the Communist Party of the United States (CPUSA).

Foster was born in Taunton, Massachusetts, the son of James, an Irish immigrant rail yard worker and Elizabeth (McLaughlin) Foster. His poverty-stricken youth was spent in a Philadelphia Irish slum known as "Skittereen," and Foster was forced to leave school at the age of 10. He was apprenticed to an artist in 1891 and learned rudimentary stonecutting, but over the next decade worked jobs as diverse as railroading, fertilizer production, dock work, mining, farming, and operating a streetcar.

Foster joined the SP in 1901, by which time he was living in Washington State. Although he had little formal education, Foster possessed great raw intelligence and curiosity. He immersed himself in Marxist literature, an exercise that made him critical of the SP, which he saw as too cautious. His barbed criticisms led to his expulsion from the SP in 1909, the same year he joined the IWW. Foster took part in the IWW's "free speech" battle in Spokane during 1909 and became a convert to the group's emphasis on **anarcho-syndicalism**. He traveled to Budapest in 1910 to attend a labor conference, but delegates refused to seat representatives from the radical IWW. Foster left Budapest, but spent much of 1910 and 1911 traveling across Europe to observe and study syndicalism. In an ironic twist, this experience estranged him from the IWW. Foster grew convinced that the IWW was not fully committed to syndicalism and that its independence from the larger labor movement was a tactical mistake. He quit the IWW in 1912, convinced that a policy of radicals "boring within" existing trade unions was the surest path to syndicalism. Foster authored the pamphlet *Syndicalism* that outlined the goals of the newly formed Syndicalist League of North America (SLNA), a propaganda organization aimed at converting the rank-and-file of the **American Federation of Labor** (AFL) to syndicalist principles. Although the SLNA was never a large organization, numerous important individuals passed through the group, including future CPUSA head **Earl Browder**, future **Trotskyite** James Cannon, and Tom Mooney, who became a labor *cause célèbre* when he was convicted of a 1916 Preparedness Day bombing in San Francisco, in what many observers felt was an unjust verdict.

The SLNA folded in 1914 and Foster took work as a business agent for a Chicago railroad union. He also worked as an AFL organizer, a task at which he so excelled that AFL officials chose to ignore his radical politics and his burgeoning commitment to the principles of **industrial unionism**. Foster also managed to stay out of the limelight by being one of the few leftist radicals to *not* speak out against America's involvement in World War I. He was able to leverage the war to his advantage, however. In 1917 Foster took charge of a **strike** of approximately 50,000 meat packinghouse workers, and his leadership in this action is often studied as a portrait in the potential of interracial organizing. Foster was able to get numerous (and often competing) packinghouse unions to form a single organization and to get white workers to cooperate with **minority labor**. President Woodrow Wilson was anxious to settle the dispute so that food delivery would not be interrupted as war clouds gathered and forced industry leaders to settle questions of union recognition, **wages**, and hours through **arbitration**. Foster became the secretary of the newly formed Stockyards Labor Council (SLC). In 1918, he married Ester Abramovitch.

At about the time it seemed as if Foster was on the verge of professional success, his life took another radical turn. Foster's industrial unionism was not a good match with AFL **craft unionism** and the SLC was subject to **raiding** from other AFL affiliates. A 1919 Chicago race riot quickly reestablished the back/white animosities and Jim Crow practices that Foster had labored so hard to break down, and soon employers refused to bargain with the SLC; in turn, it became defunct.

That same year Foster led the **Steel Strike of 1919**. Once again, he maintained rare levels of racial solidarity between white and African American workers. At the time, very little of the steel industry was unionized in any capacity, and Foster believed that a nationwide organizing campaign was necessary. Despite very weak support from the AFL, he formed the National Committee for Organizing Iron and Steel Workers (NCOISW) and led 250,000 steelworkers in a strike that lasted from September 22, 1919, to January 1920, when it was crushed by business-hired vigilantes, private armies, and active resistance from state governments. At least 14 strikers were murdered during the strike.

The steel strike deepened Foster's radicalism and, in 1920, he founded the **Trade Union Educational League** (TUEL), a group partly patterned on the SLNA. He was also enamored of the 1917 Russian Revolution, visited the Soviet Union in 1921, and joined the CPUSA. From this point on, Foster was a devoted **communist**. He advocated the formation of a separate labor party, but most of his positions were in line with those formulated by in Moscow and he became embroiled in many of the CPUSA's numerous internecine struggles. Foster was arrested for criminal syndicalism in 1922, but was acquitted. He also sought to undermine the control

John L. Lewis held over the **United Mine Workers**, a role that Lewis never forgot. Foster was the CPUSA presidential candidate in 1924, 1928, and 1932. His greatest success came in 1932, the year in which he became national chairman of the CPUSA. Foster received more than 103,000 votes in his symbolic campaign for the presidency. He also suffered a heart attack and an emotional and physical breakdown during the campaign from which he did not recover until 1935.

The TUEL received money and policy directives from Moscow. In turn, Foster reflexively embraced Stalinism in the 1930s, and his convalescence further contributed to his uncritical view of the Soviet Union. Foster's ill health also saw control of the CPUSA shift to Earl Browder, with whom Foster frequently clashed ideologically and tactically. He was especially critical of the CPUSA's no-strike pledge and of the party's 1944 endorsement of Franklin Roosevelt's reelection. When Browder was discredited in 1945, Foster regained control of the CPUSA and served as its chair until 1957. During this tenure, he headed the party at a time in which it would soon find itself on the defensive on numerous fronts—the postwar **Red Scare**, suspicions of disloyalty associated with the CPUSA's opposition to anti-Soviet **Cold War** politics, and an overall climate of anticommunist hysteria. Foster threw his energy into newspaper writing, pamphleteering, and speechmaking, but the CPUSA declined precipitously. Foster was also badly stung by Soviet Union Premier Nikita Khrushchev's 1956 denunciation of the crimes of Joseph Stalin, whom Foster had dutifully defended to the end. He stepped down as CPUSA chair in 1957 and was replaced by Gus Hall. Foster died during a 1961 visit to the USSR.

Foster's long association with the CPUSA and Stalinism have obscured his overall contributions to the labor movement. His racial organizing models during 1917 and 1919 remain admirable efforts, and his commitment to working people was sincere. Moreover, his leadership of the 1919 steel strike became the model through which the steel industry was finally organized and the **United Steelworkers of America** union was formed.

Suggested Reading

James Barrett, *William Z. Foster and the Tragedy of American Radicalism*, 1999; William Z. Foster, *Pages from a Worker's Life*, 1939; Edward Johanningsmeier, *Forging American Communism*, 1998; Arthur Zipser, *Workingclass Giant: The Life of William Z. Foster*, 1981.

FRASER, DOUGLAS ANDREW

Douglas Andrew Fraser (December 16, 1916–February 23, 2008) headed the **United Auto Workers of America** (UAW) union between 1977 and 1983. Although Fraser was had been among the "pioneer generation" whose members had founded the UAW, he served as president during a turbulent time that saw the union hemorrhage members and decline in strength. As such, his reign was controversial. To his supporters, Fraser boldly held the fort at a time in which organized labor came under attack and was able to stave off even deeper declines. To his many critics, he was a dinosaur whose outmoded thinking and tactics facilitated the decline.

Douglas Fraser was born in Glasgow, Scotland, but his family moved to Detroit in 1922, before he was six. The ravages of the Great Depression forced him to leave high school in 1934 and secure work in a Dearborn machine shop. Fraser, however, was caught up in the rising labor militancy of the age and was soon fired for union organizing. In 1936, he was hired as a metal finisher at Chrysler's Dodge Main assembly plant in Hamtramck, Michigan. A year later, Fraser moved to the De Soto assembly plant, where his UAW activism came into full bloom. He took part in a 1937 **sit-down strike** against Chrysler that was inspired by the UAW's 1935–1936 strike against General Motors (GM). Like the GM workers, those at Chrysler secured **collective bargaining** rights that led to higher pay, improved **fringe benefits**, and better working conditions. Fraser rose in the ranks of UAW Local 227 in Detroit, became its president in 1943, and continued in that role through 1946, even though he served in the Army during World War II. In 1950, Fraser joined the UAW's international staff. His experience proved invaluable during the UAW's 104-day strike against Chrysler in 1950, and his negotiation skills caught the attention of UAW President **Walter Reuther**, who made Fraser his administrative assistant in 1951. Thereafter Fraser's career trajectory was that of the classic union insider. In 1959, Fraser won election to become UAW Region 1A co-director; in 1962, he was selected to the UAW executive board. He was best known for helping negotiate agreements that enabled UAW members in Canada to secure wages comparable to those paid to their counterparts in the United States.

Fraser became a UAW vice president in 1970, the same year that Walter Reuther perished in a plane crash. Fraser was favored to succeed Reuther, but lost the presidency to Leonard Woodcock (1911–2001) by a single vote. In 1973, Fraser led the first strike against Chrysler since 1950 and settled it in five days. Upon Woodcock's retirement in 1977, Fraser finally succeeded to the presidency of the UAW. It was a difficult time to come to power. Several boycotts by the Organization of Petroleum Exporting Countries (OPEC) hastened the development of the deep recession that struck the United States after 1973 and lasted into the 1980s. American automakers were already facing stiff competition from Japanese and German imports, most of which were more fuel efficient than the gas-guzzling models produced in Detroit. As gas prices skyrocketed, imported cars captured a growing slice of the U.S. market, which in turn led to layoffs in North American plants. Fraser faced criticism for not doing enough to form new union **locals** or to encourage member militancy, though he was generally seen as a hard-working executive who cultivated rank-and-file support. Fraser often paid visits to factory workers and was a familiar face on picket lines, in civil rights marches, and at meetings with politicians. He also advised several presidents, though he did not hesitate to lambaste politicians whom he perceived to be antilabor. In 1978, Fraser resigned from the Labor-Management Group when Congress failed to enact labor-law reform and delivered a blistering denunciation of business leaders he viewed as waging class warfare against workers. He also charged that there was little difference between the labor policies of Republicans and Democrats.

Fraser's tenure as UAW president is best remembered for the role he and the union played in the 1979 government bailout of Chrysler Corporation. As the smallest of the "Big Three" automakers—which also include Ford and General Motors (GM)—and as a maker of an inefficient and outmoded fleet, Chrysler was deeply hurt by the 1970s recession and was mired in unsustainable debt. It was clear to Fraser that Chrysler needed to retool, restyle, and reorganize. He cooperated with the lobbying efforts of Chrysler President Lee Iacocca and called upon UAW allies such as Detroit Mayor Coleman Young to help Chrysler negotiate a $1.2 billion federal bailout. Fraser's role was controversial on several levels. Notably, the bailout involved **concessions** on the part of Chrysler workers. Some militants decried these givebacks, but Fraser defended his actions and argued that without them Chrysler simply would not have survived.

A second controversy ensued in 1980, when Fraser joined the Chrysler board and became the first American labor leader to sit on the board of directors of an American corporation. Under Iacocca's leadership, redesigned Chrysler products returned the firm to profitability. In retrospect, though, Chrysler enjoyed a reprieve, rather than a return to economic health. It began to lose money again in the 1980s, and in 1998 it and its subsidiaries were purchased by Germany's Daimler-Benz. Chrysler's new owners also struggled. In 2001, the company discontinued its once-robust Plymouth line. Six years later, Daimler dumped 80 percent of its Chrysler stock. It offloaded the remainder in 2009, and Chrysler declared bankruptcy. A new corporate entity was formed in 2009, relations were severed with more than 750 dealers, and Chrysler entered into an agreement with Italian automaker Fiat. Each realignment of the firm has come with new rounds of layoffs and concessions from UAW and non-union members. The long-term viability of the firm remains uncertain.

Fraser's negotiated concessions proved quite controversial. The pattern established at Chrysler became an unintended norm. A 172-day strike against International Harvester ended inconclusively and involved UAW concessions. The concessions trend accelerated during the 1980s during the presidency of **Ronald Reagan**, a foe of organized labor. Although the UAW resisted concessions at General Motors and Ford, it as soon forced to give in; in 1982, the UAW negotiated a contract involving substantial givebacks. The year before, Fraser had presided over negotiations that led the UAW to reaffiliate with the **American Federation of Labor-Congress of Industrial Organization**s. Fraser hoped that this alliance would bolster UAW efforts to resist Reagan-era concessions, but it has borne mixed results at best.

In 1983, Fraser retired from the UAW. He continued to speak on behalf of both organized labor and civil rights. He and his wife, Winnie, taught labor studies courses at Detroit's Wayne State University; the university's Center for Workplace Issues now bears Fraser's name. Labor reformers and academics continue to debate whether Fraser's decisions as UAW president were the best that could have been made under the circumstances, or if a very different path should have been taken. He is certainly vulnerable to the charge that the UAW often resisted—in the name of minimizing layoffs—technological changes that would have made American automakers more competitive globally. The UAW, once one of the most powerful unions in the country, has struggled since Fraser's retirement and its long-term health is also uncertain.

Suggested Reading

Kevin Boyle, *The UAW and the Heyday of American Liberalism, 1945–68*, 1995; Douglas A. Fraser Center for Workplace Issues, http://www.clas.wayne.edu/fraser/, accessed October 4, 2010; Lee Iacocca, *Talking Straight*, 1988; Nelson Lichtenstein, *The Most Dangerous Man in Detroit: Walter Reuther and the Fate of American Labor*, 1997.

FREE LABOR

Free labor is a term that implies the ability of American workers to bargain for **wages** and conditions within an open and competitive labor market. It first gained currency in the early 19th century and was tied to the ability of **journeymen** to make wage deals with **master craftsmen**. As the century progressed, however, the idea of free labor emerged as an attack on **slavery**. According to the promoters of the free labor ideology, the ability of northern laborers to negotiate their own **contracts** and move about society freely created an economic system that was incentive driven and, therefore, more efficient and profitable than that found in the South. In theory, free labor also afforded workers the possibility of upward mobility and independence.

Apologists for slavery countered that free labor was a myth that masked an overall degradation of northern labor that was worse than that of chattel slaves, who never suffered from homelessness or unemployment, and were cared for when sick, infirm, or elderly. The northern **working class** as a whole was generally unsympathetic to the plight of slaves until the passage of the Fugitive Slave Act in 1850. It is uncertain how many northern workers embraced free labor ideology in the decade before the outbreak of the **Civil War** and the majority of white northern workers remained racist, but most scholars now argue that a critical mass of laborers embraced free labor ideals. Many did so out of fear that an expansion of slavery would endanger the wage structure by placing wage-earners in competition with unpaid chattel. Free labor ideology proved an important component in contributing to the sectional tensions between North and South that led to war in 1861.

After the Civil War, free labor mutated into a defense of individual wage bargaining. Many employers used free labor logic to attack **collective bargaining** and oppose the recognition of labor unions. From the 20th century onward, free labor has been used by management to defend **open shops**, **right-to-work** laws, the hiring of **scabs** during labor disputes, and the calling of **decertification** votes. Free-labor ideology meshes well with cherished notions of individualism and has proved especially attractive to the middle class, a factor that has retarded the growth of **white-collar** unionism.

Suggested Reading

Mike Davis, *Prisoners of the American Dream*, 1986; Eric Foner, *Free Soil, Free Labor, Free Men: The Ideology of the Republican Party before the Civil War*, 1995; James Schmidt, *Free to Work: Labor Law, Emancipation, and Reconstruction, 1815–1880*, 1998.

FREE RIDERS: refers to individuals who benefit from labor unions without paying dues. *See* Agency Fee.

FREE SPEECH BATTLES. *See* Everett Massacre.

FREE TRADE. *See* Fast-Track Legislation; Protectionism.

FRINGE BENEFITS

Fringe benefits are forms of compensation given to employees in addition to their regular **salary** or **wage**. They are typically important negotiated items in a union **contract**. Examples include health insurance, profit-sharing plans, paid holidays and vacations, sick leave, **pensions**, and unemployment insurance.

The very existence of fringe benefits reflects social changes that have taken place in American society. Many things that are now part of union and non-union contracts were once absent in the American workplace. In the 19th century, worker associations, **working-class** clubs, and labor unions often also acted as mutual aid societies. Typically, members paid into a fund whose monies were dispersed in the form of sickness or death benefits. Charities were mostly in private hands, there were no accident insurance plans until after 1850, and medical benefit plans were unknown until 1890. When they could, labor unions negotiated fringe benefits, but they were mostly confined to items such as profit sharing, disability payments, and modest death benefits for families of workers killed in industrial accidents. For the most part, workers were expected to be frugal and save for things such as retirement.

Unions began to concentrate more on fringe benefits in the 20th century. Ironically, unions were given a boost by employers in negotiating benefits. During the **Progressive Era** a growing number of entrepreneurs espousing **welfare capitalism** principles granted benefits to workers out of benevolence and as a strategic way of getting employees to perceive capital/labor interests as mutual. In addition, some advocates of **Taylorism** put into place benefits such as profit sharing in the hope of increasing worker output. Even so, it was not until the 1940s that fringe benefits became standard in union contracts. During World War II, the **National War Labor Board** encouraged bargaining over fringe benefits to hold down wage increases that would otherwise jeopardize pay scales put into place as safeguards against inflation. Thereafter, unions sought to make fringe benefits part of each contract, and to broaden their scope. They were bolstered by a 1948 National Labor Relations Board decision ruling that pensions and retirement funds were, indeed, items that fell under the purview of **collective bargaining** rights. In the 1950s, supplemental unemployment benefits, paid vacations, and holiday pay became standard provisions in almost all union contracts. In subsequent years, benefit packages expanded to include dental and eye care, life insurance, sick leave, childcare assistance, moving costs, and personal days. Many unions negotiated extensions of benefits to the families of workers. Later, legal insurance and finance-based extras such 401(k) savings options were added to many contracts.

Fringe benefits were among the first casualties in capital/labor battles over **concessions**. When the U.S. economy soured after 1973, numerous employers sought to roll back generous benefits packages. This trend accelerated in the 1980s when Republican presidential administrations hostile to organized labor largely sided with business leaders, arguing that American firms needed to trim costs to compete in the global market. Soaring health care costs added to the contentious atmosphere. In 1960, health care spending consumed 5.2 percent of America's Gross Domestic Product. By 2007, that share had more than tripled to 16 percent. Rising health insurance premiums led many employers to insist that employees pay for part of their coverage; in quite a few instances, employers simply dropped health care coverage altogether.

Battles over pensions have been equally acrimonious. Inflation, longer life spans, aggressive stockholder demands, and (in some instances) corporate greed have led some companies to seek changes in what workers view as earned entitlements. A few firms "raided" pension funds that were earmarked for retirees and shifted those resources to other uses. In some cases—including California and Connecticut—state governments have raided pensions of teachers and state employees in an effort to close budget deficits.

The decline in labor union strength in the past several decades has made it easier for both private- and public-sector employers to reduce fringe benefits, but in so doing a new host of social problems have emerged. Skyrocketing medical costs have made it potentially financially ruinous not to have medical insurance, yet in 2010 some 46 million Americans were uninsured, mostly because they could not afford the premiums. In like fashion, the elimination or reduction of private pension funds threatens to strain social services, as **Social Security** is designed to be a source of supplemental income and is wholly inadequate as the sole support for the elderly and disabled.

Some analysts see the battle over fringe benefits as an area that organizers can exploit as they seek to rebuild the labor movement. To that end, most American unions call for pension protection legislation, affordable health care, Social Security reform, and an expansion of the government's role in caring for its citizenry. Given that such calls are anathema to conservatives, future political battles over benefits are quite likely.

Suggested Reading

Donald Barlett and James Steele, *America: What Went Wrong?*, 1992; Barbare Ehrenreich, *Nickel and Dimed: On (Not) Getting by in America*, 2007; Harry Katz and Thomas Kochan, *An Introduction to Collective Bargaining and Industrial Relations*, 2000; Jerry Rosenbloom, *The Handbook of Employee Benefits*, 2005.

GASTONIA STRIKE

The Gastonia Strike was a violent episode in the unsuccessful effort to organize textile workers in the Deep South during the spring of 1929. It involved workers at the Loray Mill in the **company town** of Gastonia, North Carolina, and featured efforts by **communist** activists to organize the community.

By the 1920s, a process was well under way in which northern textile manufacturers had begun to relocate their mills to the South, where far fewer workers were unionized and where the overall **wage** structure was lower. New England textile workers averaged $21.49 for a 48-hour workweek, whereas those in the South earned just $15.81 for a 55-hour schedule. **Child labor** was also widespread throughout the region. Organizing the South became a priority for numerous labor unions, especially the United Textile Union (UTW), an affiliate of the **American Federation of Labor** (AFL). The UTW, however, made little headway in the region and its overall campaign to organize workers in North and South Carolina had foundered by September 1928, when the National Textile Workers Union (NTWU) formed in Gastonia and sought to supplant the UTW. The NTWU was associated with the Communist Party of the United States of America (CPUSA) at a time in which the CPUSA had abandoned its policy of "boring within" existing AFL unions and had set up a separate **Trade Union Unity League** (TUUL) to compete with the AFL. Goals of the NTWU included not only organizing the South, but also establishing support for the Soviet Union.

In early 1929, Fred Beal, a young communist who had organized textile workers in Massachusetts, came to Gastonia. On April 1, some 1,800 Loray Mill workers walked out, demanding higher pay, a reduction in the work week, an end to the notorious **stretch-out** system, and recognition of the NTWU. They met with stiff resistance. Mill owners obtained an **injunction** to end the **strike**, and North Carolina Governor Max Gardner ordered the National Guard to enforce a ban on **picketing**. These standard tactics were supplemented by intensive red-baiting. With memories of the post-World War I **Red Scare** still fresh, the local press incited the general public to violence by whipping up fears of a communist conspiracy. About two weeks into the strike, the NTWU union hall in Gastonia was destroyed by a mob, and strikers—mostly women and children—were beaten and jailed.

Violence took its toll and by the third week of April, the strike was in collapse. It may well have ended more quickly had local and company officials acted with greater wisdom and compassion. In May, the families of holdout strikers were evicted from company housing. They set up a hastily built tent colony, which, on June 7, was attacked by local officers. When tent dwellers fought back, the chief of police was killed in the gunfire. Beal and several other organizers would be convicted of murder and sentenced to lengthy prison terms. Through the efforts of the American Civil Liberties Union, the strike leaders posted bail and fled to the Soviet Union.

The strike's most infamous event occurred on September 14, when armed thugs ambushed a truck full of strikers headed for a union rally and murdered Ella Mae Wiggins. Wiggins was a well-known local figure who was dubbed the "Bard of Gastonia" for her self-composed ballads addressing the plight of the workers. In contrast to the outcome in the shooting of the local police chief, Wiggins's killers were never convicted despite the testimony of dozens of eyewitnesses.

Defeated Loray Mill employees returned to a slightly reduced work week and the elimination of night work for women and children. The strike failed to bring about unionization of Loray Mill, however, and the collapse of the Gastonia strike mirrored the defeats union organizers experienced throughout the Piedmont region. The NTWU largely disappeared, though some workers surreptitiously retained NTWU membership for a while. The UTW also went into decline.

The strike's most enduring legacy came after its defeat. Ella Mae Wiggins became a labor martyr, and both her songs and new ones composed about her became staples in country, folk, and labor music repertoires. Her memory was also invoked during the post-World War II musical phenomenon known as the Folk Revival. The Gastonia Strike also provided fodder for fictionalized works by Mary Heaton Vorse, Sherwood Anderson, Grace Lumpkin, Dorothy Myra Page, William Rollins, and Olive Tilford Dargan. Scholars often draw upon the strike to study the significant role that women played in labor organizing. Students of gender and labor militancy remain intrigued by the community-organizing efforts of Gastonia women. The strike also stands as an example of the symbolic power of anticommunism as a tool for derailing social movements.

Suggested Reading

Fred Beal, *Proletarian Journey: New England, Gastonia, Moscow*, 1947; Bert Cochran, *Labor and Communism: The Conflict That Shaped American Unions*, 1977; Cletus E. Daniel, *Culture of Misfortune: An Interpretive History of Textile Unionism in the United States*, 2001; Liston Pope, *Millhands and Preachers: A Study of Gastonia*, 1942; Vera Buch Weisbord, "Gastonia, 1929: Strike at the Loray Mill," *Southern Exposure*, 1, nos. 3 & 4 (Winter 1974).

GENERAL AGREEMENT ON TARIFFS AND TRADE

The General Agreement on Tariffs and Trade (GATT) was a trade agreement that lowered trade barriers between member nations. It was the forerunner of the work done by the World Trade Organization (WTO), which was created in 1995. The GATT, WTO, and numerous global banking and trade conferences became the target of labor unions and social activists ranging from conservative nationalists to **anarchists** to advocates of **protectionism** as a bulwark against the dangers of **globalism**.

The GATT was a product of post-World War II attempts to integrate and stabilize global trade. It was initiated in 1947, when 23 nations agreed to an ambitious agenda of raising global standards of living, implementing full-employment policies, regulating demand, developing global resources, and expanding international trade. Signatories believed that lower tariffs and adherence to free trade principles were essential to achieving these goals. They made, at best, modest progress in achieving most of their goals, but reduced tariffs stimulated trade and paved the way for the development of today's global marketplace in which goods move easily from one part of the world to another. The same has not been true of labor, however, as most nations more strictly regulate the movement of peoples. Labor unions often opposed both the GATT and the WTO. Another article of faith among defenders of the GATT and the WTO has been the elimination of quotas on imported goods. Those who support tariffs, quotas, or both argue that unregulated trade serves mainly to enrich investors to the detriment of workers by encouraging capital flight to low-**wage** nations. Far from advancing rising standards of living, they claim, the GATT and the WTO perpetuate poverty and threaten to add to it by diminishing those standards for workers in high-wage countries.

When the GATT was introduced, critics expressed concerns about its principle of nondiscrimination between signatory nations. Those countries joining the GATT were obliged to open their markets to all other signatory nations equally. This mandate extended even to tariff reductions directly negotiated between two nations, even if one was not a GATT member. "Most-favored nation status"—as it is officially known in diplomatic language—was automatically granted to every other GATT member. This served to make protectionism even more difficult, though escape clauses could be invoked if policymakers determined that trade terms caused serious damage to a national economy. Unions and critics argued, however, that automatic provisions undermined the democratic processes of some nations. In the United States, for example, the U.S. Constitution asserts that the Senate must approve foreign treaties. Critics also feared that various "side agreements" violated national sovereignty by setting up global standards for items such as labor rights or environmental quality that superseded much stronger laws within member nations. This has proved to be a burning issue among activists opposed to the WTO.

The GATT was born out of the economic and political chaos of World War II and advanced **capitalism** around the globe. It was expanded several times at various meetings that were generally dubbed "rounds," of which there were seven before the GATT was scrapped in 1994. Although the primary focus of the GATT was trade issues, various multilateral agreements expanded its purview.

The 1986–1994 Uruguay Round had a sweeping impact in advancing economic globalization. Negotiators aggressively pursued worldwide expansion of free trade and even addressed the implications for the service sector of the global economy. The GATT was dissolved in 1994 in favor of setting up a stronger organization, the WTO, which came into being the next year.

In 1995, 125 nations transferred their membership from the GATT to the WTO. A key difference between the two entities is that the GATT was a set of rules applied on a provisional basis, whereas the WTO is an enduring institution to which member nations commit permanently. In addition, the GATT applied to trade in material goods, whereas the WTO also covers trade in services such as information technology, data processing, and intellectual property.

Since the WTO's creation, an increasingly mobile and vocal opposition movement has challenged its authority to dictate national behavior, with labor and environmental standards ranking high among their concerns. The anti-WTO opposition has evolved into a broad coalition of environmentalists, labor unionists, human rights groups, economic justice groups, and anarchists on the left, but has also drawn support from groups on the political right who fear the loss of national power, oppose what they see as encroaching "one-world" ideals, or are xenophobic. American labor unions are outspoken in what they see as an erosion of hard-fought campaigns to raise wages, establish work safety standards, and create humane working environments. As they see it, the lack of global environmental accords threatens to undermine American wages by flooding the market with goods produced in nations unencumbered by pollution controls. They also argue that jobs will be lost to nations that lack even basic protections for workers such as **minimum wage** laws. Most unions have demanded international labor and environmental bills of rights as a minimal precondition for supporting the WTO. Thus far, unions have proved correct in their predictions that American jobs would flee to low-wage nations, that **sweatshop** goods would appear in American markets, that global manufacturing would degrade the environment, and that American workers would be asked to swallow deep **concessions** in the name of global competitiveness.

Much to the shock and chagrin of globalism supporters, the WTO has met with fierce opposition worldwide. The template for global opposition was set when the WTO met in Seattle, Washington, in late 1999. Between 50,000 and 100,000 protestors representing 1,434 separate organizations descended upon the city, among them dozens of labor unions. Labor unions repudiated the violent clashes between police and political radicals, but those skirmishes and the property damage that ensued served notice that globalization faced formidable challenges. Since 1999, all WTO meetings and those of other groups associated with global capitalism—such as the International Monetary Fund, the World Bank, and G8 summits of industrial nations—have had to contend with protest and opposition. Like capital itself, these protests have become global. A 2001 G8 meeting in Genoa attracted 250,000 protestors to the Italian city, and one person was killed by police gunfire. Protestors also disrupted a WTO meeting in Hong Kong in 2005, and a 2009 WTO meeting in Geneva saw mobs set cars ablaze, loot shops, and battle police.

American labor unions have distanced themselves from these violent protests, but they largely share the view that the WTO, which as of 2009 contained 153 member nations, is a threat to national sovereignty, is inherently undemocratic, and has done little to improve the economic well-being of the masses.

Suggested Reading

Susan Aaronson, *Trade and The American Dream: A Social History of Postwar Trade Policy*, 1996; Peggy Ann David and Ronald Reis, *World Trade Organization*, 2009; Carolyn Rhodes, *Reciprocity, U.S. Trade Policy, and the GATT Regime*, 1993; Thomas Zeiler, *Free Trade Free World: The Advent of GATT*, 1999.

GENERAL MOTORS SIT-DOWN STRIKE

The General Motors Sit-down Strike of 1936–1937 is probably the most famous labor conflict in American history. Also known as the "Great Flint Sit-down Strike," it saw autoworkers resurrect a tactic that was perhaps first used by the **Industrial Workers of the World** (IWW). When negotiations stalled between their union and General Motors (GM), workers inside several Flint factories barricaded themselves inside the buildings. They held out from December 30, 1936, to February 11, 1937, when GM finally capitulated. This **strike** is often credited as establishing the legitimacy of both the **United Auto Workers of America** (UAW) union and the **Congress of Industrial Organizations** (CIO). The UAW's victory at Flint buoyed the spirits of workers across the United States, spawned numerous imitators that observers at the time dubbed "**sit-down** fever," and led to a resurgence of union-organizing activity.

The American auto industry boomed during the 1920s, a time in which Americans came to see cars as a necessity and the nation's infrastructure adjusted to accommodate them. Nonetheless, the industry was badly hurt by the Great Depression, which began in 1929. Economic collapse occasioned numerous layoffs and **wage** cuts that brought hardship to autoworkers, but the traditional **craft unionism** of the **American Federation of Labor** (AFL) proved inadequate. By the mid-1930s, most autoworkers drew about one-third less pay than they had before 1929, and overall employment in the industry plummeted from more than 435,000 workers in 1929 to just 244,000 in 1935. Manufacturers also took aggressive steps to deter unionization. Plants were riddled with stool pigeons, **agent provocateurs**, and labor spies. According to a 1937 **La Follette Committee** report on labor strife, GM spent nearly $1 million on labor spies between 1934 and 1936. Efforts to combat GM were also hampered by AFL organizing principles. Workers on auto **assembly lines** were dispersed among countless craft unions, even though most workers performed repetitive tasks that made a mockery of the designation "skilled labor." By the mid-1930s, craft unionism had become an obstacle in creating **solidarity** among workers. Some groups, such as the Mechanics Educational Society of America (MESA) advocated **industrial unionism** as a better alternative for autoworkers, a sentiment shared by **communist** organizers and **socialists** associated with the labor movement. This was precisely the position taken by CIO rebels inside the AFL, who eventually bolted and formed a new labor federation.

The UAW-CIO was relatively weak when the Flint strike began. Key leaders such as Wyndham Mortimer, **Walter Reuther**, and Homer Martin discussed the possibility of shutting down GM's Fisher Body plants in Cleveland and Flint, as these facilities produced the body and chassis needed for every GM car. For the most part, though, UAW leaders clashed over strategy, and there was personal conflict between the cautious Martin, who was the UAW president, and the vice president Mortimer, who had ties to the Communist Party and advocated a more aggressive response against GM. Flint workers were also deeply divided. Most belonged to a **company union** hostile to the UAW, and an organization known as the Black Legion recruited white Protestant workers with a message of antipathy toward African Americans,

Catholics, and Jews. In the 1930s, the UAW began to make inroads, often because of the dogged efforts of left-wing organizers. Bud Simons, for example, was sympathetic to the communists, and Bob Travis was a veteran of the 1934 Auto-Lite Strike in Akron, Ohio, that was led by MESA. Travis, like the Reuther brothers—Walter, Victor, and Roy—was a socialist, and Flint also had a smattering of **Trotskyites**.

The radicals were heartened by an incident in Flint in November 1936. When Fisher Body Number One reduced its three-man crews to two members, one team refused to work. When they were fired, 700 workers sat down at their machines, and GM was forced to rehire the men. Travis began both to enroll workers in the UAW and to rethink the effectiveness of the sit-down strike, which the IWW had used against General Electric in Schenectady, New York, in 1919. There had also been numerous sit-down strikes during 1935 and 1936 that predated actions in Flint, including several in which the Reuthers had participated. While UAW officials debated their next move, Fisher Body workers in Cleveland spontaneously sat down on the job on December 28, 1936, to protest a delayed meeting with GM management. Two days later, Flint workers also took matters into their own hands. In all, Flint workers at Fisher Number One and Two would spend 44 days inside the plant.

Although the UAW did not plan the actions at Flint, it proved adroit at organizing the spontaneous strike. At any one time, there were between 500 and 1,000 men inside Fisher One. Simons and other UAW leaders molded the strikers into a disciplined industrial army. Women were sent home to avoid any hint of impropriety, alcohol was banned, and destruction of property was prohibited, lest it be used as a pretext for forcibly evicting strikers. The UAW also organized the workers into 15-member "families," each headed by a "captain." Work groups, recreation committees, labor-history classes, and food details were established, and a sentry rotation schedule was put in place. When GM sent alcohol and prostitutes to the plant on New Year's Eve for the pleasure of GM foremen and police still inside the plant, the UAW expelled all GM management personnel. Absolutely vital to the UAW's success was the creation of the Women's Emergency Brigade (WEB), spearheaded by Genora Johnson (Dollinger). Most of the approximately 350 WEB members—identified by their red berets—had family members inside the plant, and they took charge of getting food to workers, often through smuggling and subterfuge. They also coordinated protests, launched public relations campaigns, and relayed vital information between UAW leaders and the sit-down strikers.

The UAW also benefited from a change in gubernatorial administrations when, on January 1, 1937, Frank Murphy took office as governor of Michigan. Murphy was a New Deal Democrat who owed his election to the state's **working classes** and was loath to side with GM. Attempts to serve an **injunction** to key leaders failed when they were tipped off, and revelations that the issuing judge was a major GM stockholder quelled Murphy's incentive to assist GM in enforcing an injunction. Appeals to President Franklin Roosevelt and CIO President **John L. Lewis** also fell upon deaf ears, and the UAW steadfastly refused to cave in to GM's negative publicity campaign or take the bait of its offer to negotiate once the plant was evacuated.

A key moment of the strike occurred on January 11, 1937, when GM foolishly stormed Fisher Number Two, which was not essential to production. Heat and power to the plant were cut off, and GM guards stopped food deliveries. A squad of **goons** went into the plant and fought with workers; tear gas was fired into the building, and armed sheriff's deputies stood ready to charge the factory. Outside, Victor Reuther manned a sound truck. As tear gas was launched, Genora Johnson went to the microphone and exhorted the women of Flint to protect their husbands, brothers, and fathers. Women surged toward the plant, smashed windows to ventilate the factory, and tossed tear-gas canisters back at the deputies. Inside the plant, workers rained down a fusillade of car-door hinges using makeshift slingshots and turned high-pressure water hoses against their attackers. The goons and deputies retreated, and the "Battle of the Running Bulls" ended in victory for the strikers and the WEB. ("Bull" was a slang term for policeman.)

As a result of the incident, Murphy stationed 1,500 National Guard troops around the plant, but refused GM's calls to have them evict strikers. GM was beginning to feel the pinch, as weekly production fell from more than 6,100 cars to just 3,800. Yet it continued to play hardball. GM tried to take a tougher approach; UAW workers were beaten in Anderson, Indiana, and several other locales, and Travis, the Reuthers, and several others were charged with inciting a riot. The harder GM pushed, however, the higher UAW signups soared. A tentative agreement reached on January 16 fell apart when GM reneged on its promise to recognize the UAW. Flint workers once again forced GM to act. The UAW decided to occupy Chevrolet Number 4 on February 1, a plant crucial to production. Knowing their ranks were filled with stool pigeons, Walter Reuther, Travis, and other leaders discussed taking Chevrolet Number 9 instead. As expected, GM guards converged at Number 9, where workers inside feigned a takeover and gave the UAW the time needed to occupy Number 4. Governor Murphy was furious about the deception, and authorized another 1,200 National Guard members to deal with the strikers. Officials briefly cut off power and food supplies to the facility, but services were restored when Walter Reuther threatened to light bonfires inside the plant to ward off the winter's chill. In the end, Governor Murphy did not execute a new court order requiring the UAW to vacate all buildings by February 3. With its production down to just 1,500 cars per week and dividends slashed by 50 percent, GM relented. On February 11, GM and the UAW struck a final agreement, and workers left the plants behind a marching band, singing lusty choruses of "Solidarity Forever," and enjoyed a citywide celebration.

The UAW was still in a precarious situation. Its agreement with GM was only for six months, and the union was not recognized as the sole bargaining agent for GM workers. Moreover, the agreement covered just 17 of GM's 69 plants. The UAW gambled that Flint would be a symbolic victory that would increase its strength, and that assumption proved to be the case. Even so, it took several years of hard negotiations and new strikes before all GM workers could opt for representation by the UAW, and the union also had to negotiate with Chrysler and Ford, the latter of which was not organized until 1941.

The immediate aftermath of the Flint strike was an electric atmosphere that benefited labor organizers. Workers across the nation were inspired by the UAW's victory. Between late 1936 and the end of 1937, nearly half a million workers sat down; their occupations ranged from rubber workers to Woolworth's clerks. The Steel Workers Organizing Committee was especially energized by the events at Flint, and union-resistant steel soon found itself organized. The strike also made the CIO into a legitimate alternative to the AFL and catapulted John L. Lewis into the national limelight.

Historians and union activists have debated the long-term significance of the Flint strike, especially since the 1980s, when labor unions began to lose strength. To some, the contemporary labor movement needs to rekindle the militancy of the sit-down strikers, and they call upon today's workers to replicate the latter's willingness to defy court orders, public opinion, and corporate might. Historians are generally less sanguine. Courts ruled the sit-down strike illegal in 1939, and the success at Flint was achieved within a specific political context in which national New Deal leaders and elected Michigan officials refrained from using state power against workers. Such conditions would be difficult to duplicate today. Regardless of the conclusions one draws, the General Motors Sit-down Strike was a pivotal moment in American history and a testament to the bravery and persistence of the men and women who took part in it.

Suggested Reading

Carlton Jackson, *Child of the Sit-downs: The Revolutionary Life of Genora Dollinger*; 2008; Nelson Lichtenstein, *Walter Reuther: The Most Dangerous Man in Detroit*, 1995; Victor Reuther, *The Brothers Reuther and the Story of the UAW: A Memoir*, 1976.

GENERAL MOTORS STRIKE OF 2007

The General Motors Strike of 2007 was a mass protest staged by the **United Auto Workers of America** (UAW) that ultimately yielded little benefit to General Motors (GM) workers. Some observers cite it as an example of organized labor's diminished influence, and still others see it as emblematic of the challenges of **blue-collar** organizing in the declining manufacturing sector.

The strike took place on September 24–26, 2007, and focused primarily on discontent over the progress of a new national contract between GM and the UAW. It came on the heels of cost-cutting measures on the part of GM during a recession that saw what had long been the world's largest automaker slip to second place behind Toyota and hemorrhage cash. In 2005, the company lost an astronomical $10.6 billion; in 2006, it reported another loss of $2 billion. In the wake of dismal financial reports, GM took measures aimed at returning the company to profitability. By enacting cost-cutting measures in 2007, it was able to post an impressive $891 million in earnings during its second quarter.

With its contract with the UAW expiring, GM saw a chance to further reduce costs by scaling back on the generous **pension**, **fringe benefits**, and health care packages UAW workers had enjoyed for decades. Central to GM's savings plan was the Voluntary Employee Beneficiary Association (VEBA).

In 2007, GM unleashed the VEBA, in essence a capped trust fund that would be financed by company payments but ultimately controlled by the UAW and a board of trustees. It was planned to dispense employee health care benefits in a manner determined by the board. Because those payments would be capped under the VEBA, GM would be able to forgo health care payments and costs altogether. The UAW vigorously opposed such a plan. Under the direction of President Ron Gettelfinger, the UAW called a walkout. On September 24, UAW workers flowed onto the streets to protest and form **picket** lines.

News of the strike electrified the media, as it was the first mass strike at GM since 1970. Unlike the 1970 job action, which lasted 67 days and idled nearly 400,000 workers, the 2007 strike lasted a mere 51 hours. Gettelfinger and the UAW declared victory, but the strike did little to prevent GM from getting what it wanted. GM was a radically different company in 2007 than it had been in 1970, when the UAW wrested provisions to strengthen **cost-of-living adjustments** (COLAs) to **wages** and secure lucrative pensions. GM had only half as many employees in 2007, and the contract signed with the UAW belied Gettelfinger's upbeat public declarations. It contained numerous **concessions** foisted upon UAW workers for the first time, including implementation of a two-tier wage system that instituted a lower rate for new hires, a four-year wage freeze, the diversion of COLA funds to pay for employee health care, and implementation of the controversial VEBA. Other than GM's promise to make 3,000 temporary workers into permanent employees and a small increase in retirement benefits, the UAW obtained very little from the strike. Critics charged that the UAW had become subservient to the demands of corporate boards and that it backed down when its members needed the union to stand up and protect rights and benefits.

It is noteworthy that the contract has not had a short-term benefit for GM either. In 2008, the company discontinued pension payments for more than 100,000 **white-collar** workers. In 2009, the company filed for bankruptcy protection, reorganized, trimmed its workforce, and eliminated model lines such as Pontiac, Saturn, and Hummer. Many industry analysts see it as inevitable that issues arising from the 2007 strike will resurface when the current UAW contract expires. GM has been the subject of much speculation and is widely seen as participating in a **sunset industry** with a questionable future.

Suggested Reading

Dianne Feeley and Tiffany Ten Eyck, "UAW General Motors Proposed Contract at a Glance," *Labor Notes*, http://labornotes.org/node/1347, accessed October 9, 2010; Paul Ingrassia, *Crash Course: The American Automobile Industry's Road from Glory to Disaster*, 2010; Michelle Maynard, "73,000 U.A.W. Members Go on Strike against G.M." *New York Times*, September 25, 2009.

GENERAL STRIKE

A general strike is the organized withdrawal of labor by workers in many industries and services at the same time. Several 19th-century American work stoppages qualify as general strikes, including the railroad strikes of 1877 and the 1886

Confrontation between a police officer wielding a night-stick and a striker during the San Francisco General Strike in 1934. A general strike seeks to unite workers from various occupations and thus cause greater political and economic disruption that pressures employers to settle with unions. (National Archives)

nationwide strike for the eight-hour workday that, in Chicago, culminated in the **Haymarket bombing** tragedy. The term is most closely associated with radical movements seeking to disrupt or overthrow **capitalism**. Among many **anarcho-syndicalists**, the general strike is viewed as the very weapon that will usher in a new society. Some leaders of the **Industrial Workers of the World** (IWW) were so enamored with the potential of general strikes that they refused to sign **contracts** after a successful labor dispute, lest that action be viewed as acknowledging the legitimacy of capitalism. The IWW hoped that members of the **working class** would ultimately embrace the concept of one big union and launch a truly national general strike that would collapse existing economic and political systems and abolish the **wage system**.

In practice, most general strikes have been more localized and modest than ideologues envisioned. The 1886 general strike, for example, was not as widespread as **May Day** organizers had hoped it would be, and it was not endorsed by the **Knights of Labor**, which repudiated the violent rhetoric of its planners. This is not to say that such strikes were not disruptive, or that they were not legitimate expressions of working-class grievances. Several general strikes have involved massive resistance on the part of working people. The 1919 Seattle general strike saw at least 65,000 workers walk off their jobs, and an action in Winnipeg, Manitoba, that same year precipitated political realignment. A 1934 dock workers strike tied up shipping traffic on much of the U.S. and Canadian West Coast. Both sets of strikes entailed social and political issues that went beyond the workplace and wages. Major strike waves also occurred following both World War I and World War II that some scholars interpret as general strikes. There is, however, no clear definition of what constitutes a general strike if the groups leading it do not frame it as such, or if they do not articulate goals suggestive of transforming society as a whole. Many strikes that began in a single industry have led to **sympathy strikes** in other professions, but there is no clear answer as to how many occupations must coordinate for a strike to be considered "general." Some observers, for example, would classify the 1934 Toledo Auto-Lite and the Minneapolis **Teamsters** work stoppages as general strikes, but others would not.

The same debate rages over how to classify protests against the **World Trade Organization** that coincide with labor walkouts.

What is clear is that general strikes can paralyze sizable segments of the economy and society, which is one reason why they often meet with fierce resistance. They disrupt society to a far greater degree than conventional actions involving a single union. Concerns that such actions are led by revolutionary anarchist, **communist**, and **socialist** groups is another reason why general strikes are feared. Violence has been common in general strikes, and it is often precipitated by business and government officials, **agent provocateurs**, and self-appointed citizens' groups rather than by workers.

The general strike is now infrequent in the United States, but it remains a weapon among labor movements in some regions, especially Western Europe and South America.

Suggested Reading

Jeremy Brecher, *Strike!*, 1997; Ann Hagedon, *Savage Peace: Hope and Fear in America, 1919*, 2007; David Selvin, *A Terrible Anger: The 1934 Waterfront and General Strikes in San Francisco*, 1996.

GEORGE, HENRY

Henry George (September 2, 1839–October 29, 1897) was a journalist, social philosopher, economist, Irish nationalist, and labor advocate. Among 19th-century reformers, few had the influence of George.

Henry George was born in Philadelphia, the second of 10 children to Richard S. H. and Catherine (Vallance) George. He was raised in a devout Protestant household, left school at age 14, and worked as a clerk for two years before signing on as a cabin boy for an around-the-world voyage on the *Hindoo*. George kept a detailed account of his travels and later won acclaim for his writings. He returned to Philadelphia in 1857, and briefly worked as a typesetter before setting sail again in 1858. Later that year he disembarked in San Francisco, where he worked for several newspapers and the local Democratic Party. An independent publishing venture failed, and George and his wife, the former Annie Fox—an 18-year-old Australian Catholic whom he married in 1861—were deeply in debt. Henry's political appointment as a gas meter inspector rescued the Georges from poverty.

The job also afforded George the opportunity to complete his seminal work, *Progress and Poverty* (1879), a book that catapulted him to fame and set the framework for an economic debate that continues to resonate. His ideas almost died in their infancy, however. George could not find a publisher to take his manuscript and was forced to scrape together enough money to self-publish 500 copies. Once unleashed on the public, however, it quickly sold 3 million copies. Millions worldwide embraced *Progress and Poverty* as the solution to economic inequity. Writing at a time in which the United States did not yet tax personal income, George made the bold suggestion that all of society's taxes could be abolished and replaced by just one tax on the unearned increments generated by land. His "single tax," as George called it, addressed the rising trend of land speculation and resonated with a swelling social movement to reserve unclaimed land for actual settlers. His unique proposal called for a 100 percent tax on land value increases that resulted from social advances rather than improvements made by those who owned land. **Agrarianism** and a belief in a **labor theory of value** remained powerful ideals, so many Americans applauded George's assertion that no one was entitled to reap profit from land merely by holding onto it. If social improvements caused land values to rise, then society as a whole was entitled to all of the value beyond whatever improvements the land's owner had made to the property. George believed that such a tax would generate sufficient revenue to fund government and needed social reforms and would obviate the need for any other taxes. He argued that ultimately all land should belong to the state and should be leased from the government. He also called for the nationalization of all transportation and communications systems. George's views found favor with **socialists** and he considered himself one of their number, though he took pains to insist he was not a **Marxist**.

George's work also attacked landlords, which also struck a responsive chord on the heels of the Panic of 1873, an economic depression that stretched into 1878. Not coincidentally, his anti-rent sentiments made him a hero in Ireland.

Progress and Poverty went through numerous printings and soon George became an international celebrity. He moved to New York in 1880, where he joined the **Knights of Labor** (KOL) and immersed himself in politics. His travels to Ireland and England in 1881 and 1882 led to a series of blistering articles in American newspapers attacking English landowners, which further enhanced his reputation in the swelling Irish American community. In 1884, George published *Social Problems*; it was followed in 1886 by *Free Trade*. The latter work cooled the ardor of some **protectionism**-minded reformers, but the labor community wholeheartedly endorsed his 1886 third-party bid for New York City's mayoralty. Irish American KOL members worked the polls on George's behalf, and he received more than one-third of the total vote. Although he lost to Democrat Abram Hewitt, George outpolled the Republican candidate, Theodore Roosevelt. Many of George's supporters claimed that only fraud prevented him from winning New York City's mayoral race. Historians have found little evidence to support that claim, but most agree that George's 1886 bid for office was a key moment in the **Great Upheaval**. Although George lost, his United Labor Party (ULP) briefly challenged two-party hegemony in many communities; in quite a few, ULP candidates won their election battles.

In 1888 and 1889, George again traveled to Great Britain. In 1890, he visited Australia and New Zealand, where his single-tax proposal spawned social experiments and government policies that surpassed those in the United States. George returned home in 1891 and suffered a stroke. He nonetheless continued to write and lecture. He published a synopsis of his theories in *The Science of Political Economy* in 1897. In that year, the ailing George made another quixotic bid to become mayor of New York, but died of another stroke a week before the election. His son, Henry Jr., took his place but attracted just 22,000 votes. Nonetheless, more than 100,000 people were said to have attended the funeral of Henry George, Sr.

Although George's single-tax plan never came to fruition in its entirety, it did become the basis for land tax reforms across the globe. Many land taxes based on the valuation of the property owe their inspiration to George, and numerous architects of said taxes envisioned them as the first step toward implementation of a single-tax system. George's ideas also inspired reformers during both the **Progressive Era** and the New Deal, and at least one utopian experiment, that of Fairhope, Alabama, sought to put George's ideals into practice. For the most part, though, Henry had more direct influence abroad than in the United States, which did not develop **labor parties** akin to those of other industrial democracies. Even so, George continues to inspire some Americans, and various societies dedicated to his ideals remain in existence.

Suggested Reading

Charles Barker, *Henry George*, 1955; Steven Cord, *Henry George: Dreamer or Realist?*, 1965; Henry George, *Progress and Poverty*, 1879; Henry George Foundation of America, http://www.ourcommonwealth.org/, accessed October 31, 2010; "Special Issue Commemorating the 100th Anniversary of the Death of Henry George," *American Journal of Economics and Sociology* 56, no. 4 (October 1997) 385–683.

GLASS CEILING

The term "glass ceiling" refers to barriers that prevent women and **minority labor** from advancing in the workplace. It is dubbed a "glass" ceiling because those who encounter it are aware of the customs and discriminatory practices that impede their upward mobility, though those policies may not be written down. In essence, they can "see" what's above them, but find it difficult to shatter the barrier. Those trapped beneath the ceiling often complain that they are better qualified than those above them. In some cases, they have actually trained their future supervisors. The earliest known coinage of the phrase was by Henry Bradford Smith in 1932, in a review article about geometry and inductive reasoning. It appears to have been given its current meaning by a 1984 *Adweek* magazine article and passed into the common vernacular shortly thereafter.

White males historically have dominated skilled positions and management, but social changes after World War II challenged that hegemony. Both the civil rights and women's movements stimulated important legal changes that opened society to those once marginalized. The **Equal Pay Act of 1963** stipulated that those who do the same job must receive identical pay. In like fashion, the Civil Rights Act of 1964 tore down most of the remaining racist "Jim Crow" barriers that excluded people of color, and Title VII of that bill extended civil rights protections to women. **Affirmative action** programs forced employers to consider women and minorities when hiring and promoting staff. By the 1960s, women and minority groups could be found in many occupations once considered reserved for white males. Nevertheless, it soon became apparent that the penetration of said groups into the workplace was shallow—often mere tokenism that circumvented substantive social change. This was especially noticeable at the upper levels of work. A 1986 survey of *Fortune* 1,000 industrial firms and *Fortune* 500 service corporations revealed that

95 percent of all senior managers were male and that 97 percent of them were white. Of the remaining 5 percent of senior managers who were female, 95 percent of them were also white. These percentages have changed only slightly since then, despite the fact that by 2010, 49 percent of the workforce was female and a mere one-third was male and white.

The 1991 Civil Rights Act established the Federal Glass Ceiling Commission to study ways to redress this imbalance, but has achieved only modest success. A 1996 report indicated that female managers and chief executives worked as many hours as their male counterparts, but received on average only two-thirds as much compensation. By 1999, this ratio had improved to just 74 cents for every dollar earned by males; a decade later, it had risen to just 77 cents per dollar. Studies also indicate that women and minorities usually advance in large firms only when they adopt the management styles of entrenched white males. In 2006, Catalyst, a non-profit research group tracking women in management, reported that a mere 15.7 percent of *Fortune* 500 firms were controlled by women, though those few companies far outpaced male-headed firms in stock performance. The record is better with smaller firms, as women controlled around 35 percent of small businesses by the year 2009, but nowhere are the numbers encouraging for people of color. For example, in 2010, a mere 3 percent of *Fortune* 1,000 companies had as many as a single African American on their boards of directors.

Most labor unions oppose the glass ceiling, and in the past several decades have taken proactive steps to counter past practices in which union hierarchies mirrored business in being dominated by white males. These changes often came as a result of upheaval inspired by the **counterculture** during the 1960s and 1970s. The **United Auto Workers of America** (UAW), for example, was rocked by challenges from rank-and-file women and minorities. The UAW responded to these challenges, albeit during a time in which overall UAW membership has been on the wane. Groups such as the **Coalition of Labor Union Women** and the **A. Philip Randolph Institute** have struggled to increase the number of women and people of color in union leadership ranks. Unions have fought hard in recent years to eliminate wage discrimination, but they have largely refrained from taking a position on representation at the management level as this is beyond their purview. In 2010, women—one of whom is African American—held two of the top three positions in the **American Federation of Labor-Congress of Industrial Organizations** (AFL-CIO). The AFL-CIO also maintains various internal constituency groups and has ties to allied groups that advance the positions of women, African Americans, Asian Americans, Latinos, and Jewish laborers. There is room for improvement within the labor movement, but overall unions have generally done more to shatter glass-ceiling barriers than either the private sector or the government.

Suggested Reading

AFL-CIO, http://www.aflcio.org/aboutus/allies/, accessed November 3, 2010; Christine Cross, *The Glass Ceiling: A View from the Middle*, 2009; Nancy Gabin, *Feminism in the Labor Movement: Women and the United Auto Workers, 1935–1975*, 1990; Glass Ceiling Research Center, http://www.glass-ceiling.com/, accessed November 3, 2010.

GLOBALISM. *See* Globalization.

GLOBALIZATION

Globalization—also called globalism—is a catchall term that refers to aspects of modern society in which economic decisions, trade, culture, and politics are considered in a worldwide context. It is an outgrowth of the post-World War II expansion of multinational corporations and represents the ascendancy of free trade policies over those of **protectionism**. Champions of globalization see the world as a vast open market for capital investment opportunities, the procurement of labor and resources, efficient manufacturing, and sales. Critics of globalization—such as the protestors who have disrupted **General Agreement on Tariffs and Trade (GATT) and World Trade Organization (WTO)** meetings—see globalization as a threat to national sovereignty, a blow to American workers, and a license for amoral investors to pursue higher profits without regard to human costs. Labor analysts generally agree that it is a major obstacle in organizing workers into unions.

The current parameters of globalization were largely forged after 1945, but globalization has long been an aspect of economic life. Before **capitalism** was fully articulated in the 19th century, mercantilist nations exploited colonies for raw materials and cheap labor. In like fashion, forced labor systems such as **indentured servitude**, **slavery**, and imported work gangs could be viewed as perverse forms of globalization, and serve as reminders that goods and laborers have long been part of global networks. Long before the United States existed, imported Africans mined Spanish silver in South America, planted French sugar cane in the Caribbean, and harvested English tobacco in North America, with these raw materials becoming items of global trade. They often toiled alongside indentured servants or enslaved **Native Americans**. In Colonial America, one manifestation of globalization was the infamous triangle trade in which slave-produced sugar in the Caribbean was made into molasses, shipped to New England and made into rum, which was then traded in West Africa for more slaves to be sold in the Caribbean. After the American Revolution, slavery continued to support global trade, though the popularity of indentured labor slowly faded. Slave-tended cotton left the South for New England textile mills; much of the cloth produced at these mills was then sold abroad and enriched American investors.

The **Industrial Revolution** brought the United States into a broader global market of raw materials and markets. Nineteenth-century economists such as Jean-Baptiste Say and David Ricardo argued that the global economy would be self-correcting and that nations would naturally develop relations to their mutual advantage. In practice, global competition was often cutthroat and ruinous, and many within the American labor movement argued for protectionist policies to ensure the survival of American businesses and stabilize jobs for workers. Nonetheless, the world appetite for stable gold specie exchange encouraged expanding globalization. So, too, did American industry. During the 19th and early 20th centuries, a mobile global workforce filled the demand for industrial labor. Millions of immigrants were forced from their homelands and into expanding factories.

Competing imperialist claims, World War I, the Great Depression, and the decline of gold as an international standard of exchange slowed the growth of globalization in the early 20th century. In the United States during the 1920s, rising isolationist sentiment and the passage of draconian immigration laws also retarded globalization. The worldwide depression in the 1930s led other nations to look inward and rekindled protectionist sentiment. Globalization was further disrupted by the military conquests of Germany, Italy, and Japan in the 1930s and the economic sanctions taken against expansionist powers. The United States, for example, restricted the trade of commodities such as scrap iron and oil to Japan, a decision that may have factored into Japan's decision to bomb Pearl Harbor.

Globalization gained new life after World War II. In 1947, the General Agreement on Tariffs and Trade reduced trade barriers among twenty-three nations. The number of GATT-compliant nations expanded many times before the GATT was disbanded in 1994 and replaced by the WTO. Both the GATT and the WTO removed many tariffs and other barriers to free trade. The development of the International Monetary Fund in 1947, the emergence of the European Economic Union in 1951, and the passage of the **North American Free Trade Agreement** (NAFTA) and various **fast-track** bills have also facilitated the spread of globalization. The United Nations and the World Court promote globalization in social and political matters.

Globalization was not widely discussed in the United States when it reemerged after World War II, partly because new global arrangements benefited the United States and its **working class**. As the world's dominant economic power, the United States saw its goods, services, and technology flood the global market. American factories operated at near capacity, unemployment was low, and retail shelves were stocked with American-made consumer goods. By the 1960s, however, Europe and Asia had recovered from the ravages of war, their economies often rebuilt courtesy of American capital infused into the regions to stabilize them and create reliable **Cold War** allies. This process had the unintended effect of underwriting state-of-the-art manufacturing facilities that began aggressively competing with the United States in the global market. U.S. dominance slipped at precisely the time energy prices soared in the 1970s, and the domestic economy soured. By the mid-1970s, American factories producing steel, rubber, textiles, electronics, and consumer appliances began to fail, unemployment soared, and inflation ran rampant. Inflation, in particular, made U.S. goods less competitive and encouraged foreign importers. Treaties such as the GATT precluded protective tariffs; hence many **blue-collar** jobs simply disappeared, and with them many union jobs.

A resurgent conservative movement, buoyed by the election of **Ronald Reagan** in 1980, also advanced free trade and globalization. Tax credits allowed U.S. firms to set up operations abroad, which supporters claimed made U.S. firms more competitive, but which cost untold thousands of jobs on the domestic front. "Capital flight" became the watchword of the 1980s, with corporations taking full advantage of Reagan-era tax cuts to relocate operations outside the country, usually within low-**wage** countries. Tax code changes also made it easier for foreign firms to open U.S. subsidiaries. Since the 1980s, the guiding principle governing the

U.S. economy has been a perceived need to be competitive in the global market. This principle was, in turn, used to tar labor unions as impediments to economic growth and as relics from a bygone era. The 1980s and early 1990s saw employers wring **concessions** from employees, launch **decertification** drives against unions, and expand the number of **right-to-work** states, all of which made union-led campaigns harder to sustain.

Competitiveness is more attractive to entrepreneurs than to workers. There has been a marked increase in fortunes among the upper class, albeit at the expense of others. NAFTA, for example, resulted in a loss of more than 200,000 American jobs in its first decade of existence. Globalization has been a disaster for the labor movement, which has seen its strength among industrial workers evaporate in the wake of **deindustrialization**. Promised shifts in the economy to replace lost high-wage jobs have not materialized; instead, economic growth has occurred in **service industries**. It also appears that the middle class is shrinking. In addition, the United States faces a massive balance of trade deficit, as it is now so reliant upon imported goods; in 2006, the deficit soared to more than $817.3 billion. Although it has fallen since then, many economists worry that the trade deficit remains far too high. By 2007, the value of U.S. exports marginally outstripped the value of imports, the United States' reliance upon foreign energy sources and manufactured goods quickly erased that advantage. In February 2012, for example, the United States ran a balance of trade deficit of $46 billion, a figure driven by increased demand for energy and foreign-made consumer goods. More troubling to anti-globalization experts has been what has been labeled the "race to the bottom," in which goods once made by relatively well-paid American workers are now manufactured in lands with deplorable labor and environmental standards. Despite well-publicized campaigns against **sweatshop** goods, global **child labor**, and revelations that, in some places, slave labor has been reimposed, price has proved to have a greater allure than morality. As unions have long argued, American workers simply cannot compete in a world without labor standards. Moreover, organized labor warns that the long-term effects of globalization will be that the United States evolves into a society of have and have-nots. Such predictions may be alarmist, but since the 1980s the gap between rich and poor has widened significantly and **unemployment** levels that would have been viewed as unacceptable in the 1950s and 1960s are now the new norm.

American activists assert that globalization is simply a rush to exploit labor in the developing world, evade environmental standards, avoid taxes, and subvert U.S. laws. These concerns have also gone global. The race to the bottom has affected other industrial democracies such as those in Western Europe, South Korea, and Japan. Growing anxiety has fueled worldwide protests at WTO meetings and has accelerated discussions of reconfiguring unionization as a global movement. The challenge, however, is that U.S. unions have hemorrhaged so many members since the late 1960s that they are struggling to maintain a national presence, let alone launch worldwide campaigns. Both the **American Federation of Labor-Congress of Industrial Organizations** and the **Change to Win Federation** are rhetorically committed to global organizing, but whether they have the clout to launch such action programs is an open question. Most labor scholars argue that they have little choice other than at least making the effort.

Protests notwithstanding, globalization shows little sign of abating, there is little political support for American protectionism, and the American public demonstrates little inclination to wean itself from the material by-products of globalization. Nonetheless, anti-globalization protests are quite likely to continue into the foreseeable future as promises made by globalization boosters of rising global economic conditions, greater stability, international justice standards, and the promotion of international understanding have not materialized. Suspicion remains that globalization is little more than the exploitation of the poor on a worldwide basis.

Suggested Reading

Thomas Friedman, *The World Is Flat: A Brief History of the 21st Century*, 2005; Manfred Steger, *Globalization: A Very Short Introduction*, 2009; Joseph E. Stiglitz, *Globalization and Its Discontents*, 2003; Martin Wolf, *Why Globalization Works*, 2005.

GOLDMAN, EMMA

Emma Goldman (June 27, 1869–May 14, 1940) was an **anarchist** and one of the most feared radicals of the early 20th century. Although Goldman was devoted to the liberation of the **working class** and had many admirers, her career has sparked fierce debate over whether her actions advanced or retarded the efforts of the labor movement.

Emma Goldman was born into a Jewish family in Kovno, Russia (Kaunas in modern Lithuania), the daughter of Abraham and Tuave Goldman. Abraham Goldman was Tuave's second husband, and their union was ill fated, as it was an arranged marriage and Abraham was abusive to his wife and children. Emma was often the target of her father's attempts to break her indomitable will through physical intimidation. Goldman's family moved to St. Petersburg in 1881, and Goldman left school to work in a factory, where she was sexually assaulted, perhaps raped. This experience, her abusive father, and an attempt to force Goldman into an arranged marriage colored Goldman's views of relationships for the rest of her life. She soon became a free-love advocate in the belief that patriarchal patterns of treating women as chattel should be replaced by free-will relationships that paid little heed to prevailing social conventions. While in St. Petersburg Goldman also immersed herself in radical politics, and joined small circles of anarchists and nihilists.

When she was just 15, Goldman joined a sister who had already settled in Rochester, New York. Goldman quickly realized that America was not the promised land of myth, especially for Jews, for whom the U.S. experience was often one of toil, **sweatshops**, and slums. Her anarchism deepened in the wake of the **Haymarket bombing** of 1886, though Goldman later fancifully claimed that she became an anarchist the day those convicted of the bombing were hanged. In 1887, Goldman married Jacob Kershner, a laborer who helped Goldman supplement her interrupted education, but with whom she was physically and emotionally incompatible. At age 20, the recently divorced Goldman moved to New York City, and became the protégé of Johann Most, editor of a German-language anarchist newspaper. Most helped Goldman develop as both an intellectual and a public speaker. She soon became such a fiery advocate for the overthrow of **capitalism** that she turned her back on such cherished working-class goals such as the fight for an **eight-hour** workday. As her political views gained greater depth, she even repudiated Most's teaching in favor of the views of the Russian anarchist Peter Kropotkin. Kropotkin's **anarcho-syndicalist** writings resonated with Goldman's own beliefs in the individual, self-expression, and the repressive nature of state power. She embraced free speech, free love, personal freedom, birth control, and women's equality. Goldman took numerous lovers, and her personal life shocked conservatives almost as much as her ideology. The record is unclear as to whether Goldman engaged in same-sex relationships, but she was outspoken in her defense of homosexuality.

In 1892, she and fellow anarchist Alexander Berkman—also her lover—planned the assassination of Henry Clay Frick, who had suppressed the **Homestead Steel lockout and strike**. Following the lead of Kropotkin, Goldman and Berkman argued that violence was necessary in achieving widespread social change, and they hoped that Frick's death would raise comrades-in-arms. The assassination attempt failed, and Berkman was sentenced to a lengthy prison term. Goldman's role escaped detection, but she was sentenced to one year in prison in 1893 for allegedly inciting a riot among impoverished workers protesting conditions resulting from the depression that began that year. It was the first of many arrests for Goldman, whose jail terms included those for distributing illegal birth-control literature, for advocating that hungry workers take bread by force, and for setting up "No Conscription" leagues during World War I. She was not convicted of involvement in the 1901 assassination of William McKinley, though she met with assassin Leon Czolgosz, refused to condemn his action, and was widely rumored to have been part of a conspiracy to murder the president.

By the opening of the 20th century, Goldman was a professional agitator and lecturer for the anarchist cause. She met with various anarchists and often published their writings in *Mother Earth*, an anarchist journal she established in 1906. When Alexander Berkman was released from prison after 14 years, he and Goldman resumed their affair, though Goldman was also having a relationship with Chicago slum physician Ben Reitman. According to some biographers, Goldman was so infatuated with Reitman that their relationship challenged her free love ideals. Reitman, however, had no desire to be monogamous and he and Goldman parted ways in 1908. Around this period Goldman also immersed herself in free speech battles. Roger Baldwin, founder of the American Civil Liberties Union, acknowledged Emma Goldman as a civil liberties tutor. Goldman often coordinated her own free speech campaigns with those led by the **Industrial Workers of the World** (IWW). Goldman was briefly an IWW member, but she soon drifted away from the IWW and deemed it insufficiently ideological. Like the IWW, however, Goldman suffered for her views on World War I. She opposed the military draft, U.S. involvement in the war, and the very idea of workers battling other workers on the fields of combat. In 1917, she and Berkman were arrested for obstruction of the draft. In 1919, during the postwar **Red Scare**, Goldman was stripped of her citizenship and deported to Russia. At her trial future Federal Bureau of Investigation (FBI) director J. Edgar Hoover called Goldman "one of the most dangerous women in America."

Goldman put on a bold face and declared it an honor to be deported to Russia, where the 1917 Bolshevik revolution brought **communists** to power. Once in Russia, though, Goldman quickly grew disenchanted, considered the Bolsheviks to be a counterrevolutionary, and penned her dismay in two books: *My Disillusionment in Russia* (1923) and *My Further Disillusionment in Russia* (1924). She left Russia in 1921, moved briefly to Berlin, lectured in Great Britain, and wrote her autobiography, *Living My Life* (1931). In 1925, Goldman entered into a marriage of convenience with James Colton, a Scottish anarchist miner, so that she would not be deported. She used her British passport to travel to Canada and across Europe to agitate on behalf of anarchism. She made numerous efforts to be readmitted to the United States, but was allowed just one brief visit in 1934, and only then under the stipulation that she could not lecture on politics.

In 1936, her beloved comrade Alexander Berkman committed suicide when it was clear he was dying of prostate problems. At the age of 67, Goldman ventured to Spain to support the Republican cause during the Spanish Civil War. She soon returned to Canada, where she made repeated attempts to gain permanent entry into the United States, but she got no closer than Toronto, where she was aiding Spanish refugees. She died in 1940 and was granted posthumous reentry to the United States to be buried in Chicago near where the Haymarket anarchists were laid to rest.

Goldman represents the revolutionary pole of the labor political spectrum. She was convinced that no worker could ever be free under capitalism, and devoted her life to denouncing that system and calling for its overthrow. In her lifetime she was a controversial figure even within the radical movement, and many within the organized labor movement went out of their way to repudiate her lest the union movement be tarred with guilt by association. In death Emma Goldman has often been romanticized, and it is difficult to determine which deeds and plots were hers and which were events in which she probably had no hand. Goldman's most enduring legacy perhaps lies in the realm of sexual politics, with her views on sexuality, free choice, and birth control anticipating those associated with second-wave feminism by many decades. Goldman's contributions to class struggle, the topic that most interested her, are far more ambiguous.

Suggested Reading

Candace Falk, *Love, Anarchy, and Emma Goldman*, 1990; Candace Falk et al., eds. *Emma Goldman: A Documentary History of the American Years*, 2 volumes, 2003, 2004; Emma Goldman, *Living My Life*, 1931; Alice Wexler, *Emma Goldman in America*, 1988.

GOMPERS, SAMUEL

Samuel Gompers (January 27, 1850–December 13, 1924) was a co-founder of the **American Federation of Labor** (AFL) and served as its president from 1886 until his death in 1924, with the exception of 1896. He is considered one of the iconic figures of the American labor movement.

Gompers was born to a **working-class**, Dutch Jewish immigrant family in London, England. His father, Solomon, was a cigar maker—the trade that Samuel would also make his own. The Gompers family floundered in London, and Solomon's union provided assistance that allowed the family to immigrate to the United States in 1863. They settled in New York City, where Samuel initially worked alongside his father, rolling cigars in their Lower East Side tenement. Cigar rolling was then an **artisan** trade, though one threatened by the introduction of machinery. Gompers joined the Cigar Makers International Union (CMIU) in 1864, after securing work in a cigar factory. As in the case of many 19th-century artisan workplaces, it was customary for cigar factories to have a "reader" who read aloud while the others worked. Gompers would eventually become a self-taught scholar in his own right, but factory readers first made the teenaged Gompers aware of political and social issues, and acquainted him with the works of labor champions such as Karl Marx and **Ira Steward**.

Gompers was soon part of a group dubbed "the 10 philosophers," who met after work to continue discussions over matters such as **craft unionism, socialism**, politics, and encroaching mechanization of the cigar trade. Gompers witnessed the latter effects firsthand, as employers were keen to introduce machines that could displace highly paid artisan cigar makers. Gompers and a fellow cigar maker and local union leader, Adolph Strasser, came to see mechanized production as inevitable, and they began to discuss ways of maintaining CMIU strength in the face of technological challenge. In 1873, Gompers secured employment with David Hirsch and Company, where he encountered German-speaking **Marxists** whose militant spirit he admired. He became president of CMIU Local 144 in 1875. Although Gompers would later downplay (and occasionally deny) it, he also joined the **Knights of Labor** (KOL) during the 1870s, when his Local 144 union briefly affiliated with the KOL. The CMIU was in decline by 1878, and it nearly collapsed altogether in the wake of the prolonged Panic of 1873 and the assault on trade unions following the **Railroad Strike of 1877**. It was a testament to Adolph Strasser, who assumed the presidency of the national CMIU in 1877, that the organization survived.

Although Gompers did not become a national CMIU official until 1880, when he became CMIU second vice president, he and Strasser were close allies who began brainstorming ways to strengthen the CMIU by introducing union benefit packages such as unemployment compensation, sick relief, travel assistance for those searching for work, and **strike** funds administered by the CMIU and funded by high **dues**. These policies allowed the national union to exert power over the **locals** and contain rash actions on the part of rank-and-file workers. The chaos of the 1870s and the weakness of the CMIU convinced Gompers that only through strong national unions, and not through independent but weak locals, could organized labor combat hostile employers, courts, and politicians. He abandoned his youthful flirtations with socialism following the **Tompkins Square Riot**, and declared socialism romantic and unrealistic.

These ideals placed him on a collision course with the KOL, which by 1880 was a surging force in the greater New York City area. Many Knights in New York were **Lassallean** socialists, and most of them had come to believe that craft unionism divided the working class and promoted parochial trade interests rather than class **solidarity**. This group included a substantial number of cigar makers as well. In 1880, a renegade faction of New York City cigar rollers was expelled from the CMIU. In 1881, that faction declared itself the Progressive Cigar Makers Union (PCMU) and announced that it intended to operate in accordance with KOL principles rather than the narrow precepts of craft unionism. Both the CMIU and the PCMU appealed to the KOL's executive board to resolve the dispute. Before the KOL ruled on the matter, Gompers and other trade unionists gathered in Pittsburgh in November 1881 and announced the formation of the Federation of Organized Trades and Labor Unions (FOTLU). Gompers, as president, sought to exclude all but skilled workers and to minimize the influence of the KOL. Although many Knights took part in the FOTLU convention, Gompers's actions angered KOL leaders and earned him the enmity of KOL head **Terence V. Powderly**. Gompers and Powderly would clash repeatedly over the next several decades, and their personal rancor seldom served their organizations well. In the short term, the KOL sided with the PCMU against the CMIU—an action that led Gompers to declare war against the KOL. Gompers's anger toward the KOL was so intense that many future students of American labor often uncritically accepted his critique of the KOL.

The FOTLU failed to thrive even though trade unions were revived in the 1880s. It did, however, give birth to the American Federation of Labor in December 1886. Gompers was elected AFL president and served as head of the organization until his death in 1924, with the exception of 1895–1896, when socialist John McBride of the **United Mine Workers of America** ousted him from that position. Gompers's early tenure with the AFL was marked by internecine wars in organized labor's ranks between the AFL and the KOL. Unlike the KOL, the AFL sought to attract only skilled craft workers, and it promoted the idea that craft workers were ill served by the Knights. Both sides engaged in **raiding** and, in some places, disputes were so rancorous that members of one federation did not hesitate to serve as **scabs** during strikes led by its rival. During the **Great Upheaval** of the mid- and late 1880s, Gompers was able to position the AFL to better weather the coming backlash against organized labor. The 1886 **Haymarket bombing** assisted business leaders in tarring labor unions as repositories for radicals, **anarchists**, and assassins. The KOL, which also repudiated violence, had a larger presence in mass industry than the AFL. Rising unionization rates and the success of **labor parties** during the elections of 1886 and 1887 precipitated a capitalist counter-assault that weighed most heavily upon the KOL. Its broad-based membership included radicals, its extensive reform platform included a call for the abolition of the **wage** system, and its local assemblies were often found in shops controlled by the most powerful captains of industry— the group sometimes dubbed "robber barons."

The AFL survived the backlash because it was, in many ways, less ambitious than the KOL. It affirmed the principle of **voluntarism**, by which it meant both the autonomy of individual national unions and their right to join (or to leave) the federation, and the need for workers acting through their unions to win improved conditions in the workplace. Unlike the KOL, Gompers rejected the role of government interference in industrial relations. Workers themselves, he believed, must solve their own problems. In the AFL, the national unions had **jurisdiction** within their own crafts and were regarded as independent from both other national unions and the AFL itself as long as their affairs were self-contained. As a consequence, AFL disputes were confined to single industries and were unlikely to become **general strikes** or lead to secondary **boycotts**. The AFL also rejected as utopian most of the KOL's reform agenda. Its brand of militancy was dubbed **pure and simple unionism** as it was mostly confined to raising workers' wages, reducing the hours of employment, and improving the conditions under which they toiled. The AFL accepted the permanence of **capitalism** and spoke little of remaking society as a whole. To some employers, the AFL and Gompers appeared as more respectable and reasonable than the KOL. Moreover, although mechanization had transformed factory labor, those skilled workers who remained were integral to production and hard to replace, which often gave AFL workers more bargaining power than the unskilled and semiskilled workers in the KOL.

Where Gompers was resolutely militant, however, was over the issue of strikes. Whereas the KOL called for mandatory **arbitration** of labor disputes and generally refrained from endorsing strikes, Gompers and the AFL saw them as labor's primary weapon in compelling employers to improve the lot of their workers. AFL unions won strikes during the Great Upheaval, though few of them took place in mass industry and Gompers sought to keep the AFL out of what he saw as hopeless frays. Events in the early 1890s led some critics to question the AFL's faith in strikes. Both the **Homestead Steel lockout and strike** and the **Pullman strike/lockout** ended in spectacular losses, though neither was an AFL-led action. The Pullman action was, however, directly responsible for Gompers's loss of the AFL presidency for a year. Gompers refused to assist the **American Railway Union** as he saw it as a **dual union**, and he repudiated the strike leadership of **Eugene V. Debs**, though he had once courted Debs on behalf of the AFL cause. The Pullman strike, though lost, became a cause célèbre among radicals and, at the 1895 AFL convention, John McBride supplanted Gompers as AFL president.

Gompers regained his presidency the next year. Although the United States was still suffering the effects of the crippling Panic of 1893, AFL membership was on the rise. By 1904, the AFL contained 1.7 million members, making it nearly twice as large as the KOL had been at its height. Gompers's desire to gain acceptance of the labor movement nationally led him into controversy. In 1904, he joined the **National Civic Federation** (NCF), a **Progressive Era** group that labeled itself as a business reform organization. On paper the NCF certainly looked progressive. Its members pledged to implement such social welfare plans as employee stock option plans, company **pensions**, and other **fringe benefit** plans. In exchange for generous **welfare capitalism** packages, however, labor conceded the principle of management's right to set conditions of employment. Gompers justified his co-operation with the NCF by arguing that it gave labor influence among the captains of industry, thereby promoting mediation during industrial disputes; it was, in essence, a voluntarist form of the KOL's call for mandatory arbitration. Gompers's hopes soon proved naïve and the Progressive Era as a whole was a challenging time for the AFL. Although some business leaders signed contracts with the AFL in hopes of derailing organization by the radical **Industrial Workers of the World** (IWW), the AFL could not boast of having led any labor action as militant as the 1909 **Uprising of the 20,000** led by the **International Ladies' Garment Workers' Union**, or as successful as the IWW's 1912 **Lawrence textile strike**. Nor did Gompers's alliance with the NCF help stave off **open-shop** drives by the rival **National Association of Manufacturers**, or help the AFL when the Danbury hat makers were socked with damages associated with a boycott they had called. The 1908 Supreme Court case *Loewe v. Lawlor* that punished the hat makers would also threaten Gompers. In 1911, Gompers found himself facing a year in prison for adding his name to a boycott call against the Buck's Stove and Range Company of St. Louis, with which AFL affiliates were feuding. Gompers's conviction would eventually be overturned, but the overall antilabor climate of the Progressive Era convinced radicals involved in movements such as the Western Federation of Labor and the IWW that the AFL was naïve in its belief it could win concessions from management through cooperation with capitalists. The IWW accused the Gompers-led AFL of betraying the working class and often mockingly referred to the organization as the "American Separation of Labor."

Gompers's pragmatic views eventually captured the bulk of the labor movement, though scholars remain divided over whether the AFL's philosophy were prudent in the long term. Gompers was, however, able to parlay politics and the coming of World War I into an advantage for the AFL. His involvement in civic affairs led him to abandon his earlier avoidance of partisan political commitment. Gompers sought support from both Republican and Democratic leaders, but, by 1912, he had allied himself with the Democratic Party. The 1914 **Clayton Antitrust Act** revised the 1890 **Sherman Antitrust Act** in ways that made it harder to prosecute labor unions as illegal conspiracies in restraint of trade. Gompers hailed the legislation as "Labor's Magna Carta." In practice the Clayton Act was considerably more modest in its effects, but it did provide the base from which Gompers's 1911 conviction was overturned. The Woodrow Wilson administration also signed into law several other bills favorable to labor, including the **La Follette Seamen's Act** (1915) and the **Adamson Act** (1916). By 1917, the AFL contained 2.4 million workers, and its support for **no-strike pledges** during World War I further cemented the alliance between labor and the Wilson administrations. Not coincidentally, this positioning also served to further distance the AFL from the IWW, which opposed American entry into the war, and it allowed Gompers to promote the AFL as a respectable, patriotic, and reasoned alternative to left-wing radicalism. Gompers strongly supported the war effort and refused to tolerate antiwar sentiment within AFL affiliates. He welcomed the creation of the **National War Labor Board** (NWLB) as a vehicle for enforcing labor/capital accord and for assuring uninterrupted wartime production. The board guaranteed labor's right to organize, and unions used the wartime détente imposed by the NWLB to increase union membership to 4 million by war's end. Moreover, Gompers used the board to increase his personal influence and the clout of organized labor, both of which reached their high-water mark by the end of the war. Gompers was a delegate to the Paris peace delegation, but he soon lost most of his political clout and came to doubt that organized labor should depend upon government.

The end of the war saw employers attempt to reassert their prewar autonomy and reverse the gains made by labor during the war. Gompers opposed continuation of sedition laws applied during the war and was fearful of the implications of the **Red Scare**, even though it often targeted groups with which he disagreed, such as IWW members and **anarchists**. Gompers was, however, nervous about the militancy of labor's response to employer rollbacks, especially the strike wave of 1919. He offered only tepid support for the **steel strike of 1919**, and some strikers blamed him for its collapse. Gompers largely retreated to the voluntarism principles upon which the AFL was founded, even to the point of opposing calls for programs such as government-funded old-age **pensions**, unemployment compensation, national health care, **child labor laws**, and compulsory **arbitration**, as he argued that labor needed to secure these rights on its own.

The 1920 election of Republican Warren G. Harding to the presidency served to sever most of Gompers's remaining civic ties and ushered in an era that was even more challenging to organized labor than the Progressive Era had been. Gompers spent his remaining years writing and attempting to halt a precipitous decline in union membership in the face of increased employer hostility. His one success with the Harding administration was the use of his remaining influence to secure a presidential pardon for his one-time friend, then nemesis, Eugene V. Debs, who had been imprisoned for his antiwar activities. Samuel Gompers died on December 13, 1924, as he made his way home from the inauguration of Mexican President Plutarco Calles. His successor, **William Green**, often struggled with Gompers's legacy, as Gompers was truly the founding and guiding spirit of the AFL for the first 36 years of its existence.

Scholars are often divided over the Gompers legacy, in part because Gompers was an enigmatic figure who exhibited a difficult-to-pigeonhole mix of militancy and caution. He lacked the visionary spirit of contemporaries such as Powderly, Debs, or **William Haywood**, yet he was more than willing to battle capitalism through strikes. Gompers rejected socialism as impractical, and under his tutelage many AFL members improved their lives, yet the AFL's principles and actions sacrificed class consciousness in favor of craft consciousness. Scholars continue to debate whether Gompers and the AFL pursued a realistic and prudential path, or whether both sacrificed ideals and tactics that delayed securing greater rights for working people.

Suggested Reading

Paul Buhle, *Taking Care of Business: Samuel Gompers, George Meany, Lane Kirkland, and the Tragedy of American Labor*, 1999; Julie Greene, *Pure and Simple Politics: The American Federation of Labor and Political Activism, 1881–1917*, 1998; Harold Livesay, *Samuel Gompers and Organized Labor in America*, 1987; Samuel Gompers Papers Web Project, http://www.history.umd.edu/Gompers/index.htm, accessed November 18, 2010; Gerald Emanuel Stearn, ed., *Gompers*, 1971; Philip Taft, *The AFL in the Time of Gompers*, 1957.

GOON

A goon is a thug hired by management to intimidate and, if necessary, commit acts of violence against workers. Goons are mercenaries in the service of their employers, and many have unsavory reputations that may include associations with organized crime.

In popular culture, a goon is a stupid person. "Goon" is likely a shortened form of "gooney," which traces its origins to a cartoon character created by E. E. Segar in 1921. Its first known application in labor terms occurred in the timber fields of the Pacific Northwest during 1938. Lumber camps were often located in remote areas and some timber companies were known for harsh treatments of their work-forces, which included the maintenance of veritable private armies to enforce employers' wills. The term "goon" emerged to stereotype such enemies of organized labor. It implies that hired enforcers are more brawny than brainy, so much so that they are subhuman and should not be expected to act with compassion or be shown any.

Although the term comes from the 20th century, goons as ruthless private merce-naries have long been a staple of American capital/labor relations. In many cases, the introduction of hired thugs, such as **Pinkerton**, Burns, and Baldwin-Felts detec-tives, caused the very violence they were hired to curtail. Hired thugs precipitated bloody episodes in American labor history such as the **Homestead Steel lockout and strike**, violence at **Matewan** and **Ludlow**, and the 1937 **Memorial Day Massacre**. The term "goon" came into wider parlance after the 1937 La Follette Subcommittee on Violation of Civil Liberties revealed the widespread practice of hiring temporary strong-armed mercenaries to smash picket lines, guard **scabs**, and intimidate workers on the eve of a union recognition vote. In theory the use of goons is an **unfair labor practice** outlawed by the **National Labor Relations Act**, but the distinction between a goon and a guard is often subjective. Ford Motors made widespread use of goons prior to being unionized in 1941.

The term "goon" is no longer in widespread use, partly because modern-day efforts to harass organizers, break strikes, and intimidate workers are seldom as overtly violent as they were in the past. Companies are now more likely to hire anti-labor lawyers and contract with **white-collar** firms that specialize in breaking unions. Moreover, goons often generally thrived in isolated regions far from media attention. With improved communications and transportation, it has become much harder to use violence in a cavalier or unprovoked manner.

Suggested Reading

James David Horan and Howard Swiggett, *The Pinkerton Story*, 1951; Stephen Norwood, *Strikebreaking and Intimidation: Mercenaries and Masculinity in 20th-Century America*, 2002.

GRANITE WORKERS

Granite workers include those who quarry, cut, shape, polish, install, and carve the stone. Granite workers are generally not as well studied by historians as coal miners, but they, too, have fought important battles in improving the lives of working

Americans. Granite and marble workers have been at the forefront of campaigns against silicosis, a deadly lung disease whose very existence was once denied. The struggles of granite workers parallel those of others who have attracted less scholarly attention, including marble workers, glassblowers, construction blast crews, and others who breathe air laden with particulates.

Granite workers have generally been better organized than marble workers, though work routines are similar within the industries. Granite was a key building material for public structures from the early 19th through the mid-20th centuries, and it remains a much-in-demand commodity. Numerous unions emerged within the granite industry. One of the earliest to appear was the Granite Cutters' National Union, which was formed in 1877 and was based in Quincy, Massachusetts. In 1905, it changed its name to the Granite Cutters' International Association (GCIA). The GCIA represented carvers, cutters, and polishers. It was an early leader in protesting prison labor and took that battle to Texas in 1885, when it learned that the new state capitol was being built in part by prisoners. The GCIA received a charter from the **American Federation of Labor** (AFL) in 1888, but quit the organization two years later when the AFL tried to impose an assessment to support the carpenters' union's battle for an **eight-hour** day. At the time, the GCIA complained that the carpenters were stealing jobs from GCIA members. The GCIA rejoined the AFL in 1895, and in 1900 the AFL supported the granite cutters in their own battle for an eight-hour day. Quarry workers who blasted the stone from the pits also formed unions. Many of them joined forces in 1903 to create the Quarry Workers International Union of North America (QW), with headquarters in Barre, Vermont. The QW also joined the AFL. Marble workers were less successful in their efforts to form unions, though the **Knights of Labor** briefly organized the sheds and pits around Rutland, Vermont, in the late 1880s.

From the outset, stoneworkers faced daunting obstacles. Quarries were often owned by self-made entrepreneurs who were loath to deal with unions. Many enterprises were small, and competition was fierce. These factors made owners reluctant to invest in either expensive equipment to improve safety for quarrymen or dust ventilation systems for workers in the polishing and carving sheds. The granite cutters was probably the first union in the United States to win sick-leave benefits for its members, but that was cold comfort in an industry where, in the early 20th century, the average age at death for carvers and cutters in Barre, Vermont, was 42.

Both the GCIA and the QW organized workers as far away as Indiana, Kansas, Missouri, and Texas, though their strength was usually greatest in the Northeast, especially Vermont, Maine, New Hampshire, and New York. Stoneworkers belied the AFL's assumption that immigrant workers were difficult to organize. By 1900, only the textile industry could rival stoneworkers for ethnic diversity. Much of the industry in the Northeast was established by Scots in the 1870s, but within two decades there were also Italians, Spaniards, Germans, Norwegians, Swedes, Finns, French Canadians, Poles, and others working in this arena. Politics helped establish a cross-ethnic class identity, with many immigrants holding **socialist** or **anarchist** beliefs. By 1900, more than 90 percent of all Barre stoneworkers were unionized.

Many stoneworker families in Quincy and Barre took in children from Lawrence, Massachusetts, during the famed 1912 "Bread and Roses" strike.

Worker solidarity was tested sorely after World War I when the **open-shop** movement spread to the stone industry. Workers who had gained a 44-hour work week only in 1914 found themselves facing longer hours and renewed anti-union sentiment on the part of larger employers within a consolidating industry. Unsuccessful strikes in 1922 and 1933 further curtailed GCIA and QW demands for higher **wages** and improved health standards. Although silicosis was recognized as an occupational disease in 1917, and states passed bills to reduce the amount of dust inhaled by workers, ventilation systems within the stone industry proved inadequate to ward off this threat to workers' health.

Quarry workers expressed their frustration with conservative AFL leaders. Many within the QW felt they received little support in their attempts to organize marble workers. In 1938, the QW left the AFL for the new **Congress of Industrial Organizations** (CIO). In 1940, it changed its name to the United Stone and Allied Products Workers of North America (USAPW). The USAPW continued to press for improved safety conditions and engaged in periodic strikes, usually localized and of brief duration. In 1971, the USAPW was absorbed into the **United Steelworkers of America**, and today it is an affiliate of the **American Federation of Labor-Congress of Industrial Organizations (AFL-CIO)**.

The GCIA continued as an AFL union. Some **locals**, including those throughout Vermont, unsuccessfully struck for a seven-hour day in 1952. The Northeast granite industry was also struck in 1970 and 1980. Technological changes led to a contraction of employment throughout the stone industry and, in the early 1980s, the GCIA and most of its locals merged with other groups to form the Tile, Marble, Terrazzo, and Granite Cutters Union. It, in turn, was absorbed into the Brotherhood of Carpenters and Joiners in the 1990s. Two 1996 Supreme Court decisions (*Acme Tile and Terrazzo Company v. NLRB* and *Roman Tile and Terrazzo Company v. NLRB*) dealt a serious blow to organizing efforts by ruling against closed-shop provisions in several union **contracts**.

Despite recent challenges in the industry, stone workers achieved great success in calling attention to the dangers of silicosis and played a key role in pressing for national legislation to control dust. Their efforts culminated in important legislation such as the 1969 Mine Safety and Health Act and the 1970 **Occupational Safety and Health Act**. Today, the bulk of stonework is found in memorials, building trim, and curbs. There are fewer workers within the industry now than in the early 20th century. Some former GCIA locals, including those in Barre, Vermont, resented the high **dues** associated with the AFL-CIO and disaffiliated in 1986. Numerous small unions among granite workers remain independent of the AFL-CIO. Several local unions are affiliated with the Laborers International Union of North America, but the bulk of unionized granite workers do belong to the AFL-CIO and can be found in construction industry unions that once catered to specific trades such as bricklayers, masons, and carpenters. The **United Mine Workers** also organizes granite and marble workers.

Suggested Reading

Mike Austin, *Stories from Vermont's Marble Valley*, 2010; Public Occurrence, *Vermont's Untold History*, 1976, David Rosner and Gerald Markovitz, *Deadly Dust: Silicosis and the Politics of Occupational Disease in the 20th Century*, 2006, Philip Taft, *The A.F. of L. in the Time of Gompers*, 1957.

GRAPE BOYCOTTS

Grape boycotts were the most publicized of a series of actions taken by California farm workers to publicize the plight of field hands. The first **boycott** of 1965 to 1970 was the seminal event that led to the formation of the **United Farm Workers of America** (UFWA) and catapulted UFWA leader **César Chávez** to international fame. Although grape boycotts have gotten the most publicity, the UFWA has also led boycotts of other commodities, most notably lettuce.

The grape boycott grew out of disputes between California grape growers in the Delano/Bakersfield area and Filipino pickers, who complained of low wages, horrendous sanitary conditions, a lack of potable water in the fields, and brutal treatment. Most of the workers were American citizens, but their wages were lower than those of guest ***braceros*** still working in the fields, despite the official termination of that program a year earlier. On September 8, 1965, Filipino workers organized the Agricultural Workers Organizing Committee (AWOC) and struck nine California farms. An attempt to import Chicano **scabs** backfired when Chávez convinced his National Farm Workers Association (NFWA) to support the **strike**. By September 20, pickers on more than 30 farms had walked out.

The strike was marked by violence on the part of growers, but the AWOC and the NFWA used tactics of passive resistance that were en vogue in the African American civil rights movement and studiously practiced by the deeply religious Chávez. Chávez was able to convince numerous Roman Catholic clerics and Protestant ministers to join the cause. Violence against strikers and the arrests of peaceful pickets galvanized support for the workers. Chávez and **Dolores Huerta** convinced the NFWA/AWOC coalition to call for a boycott of California grapes. Chávez proved a skilled grassroots organizer, and soon boycott support chapters crisscrossed the United States. Chávez also engaged in a fast and led a 340-mile march from Delano to Sacramento to call attention to the farm workers' cause. Because most agricultural workers are not covered by the **National Labor Relations Act** and its various amendments, questions concerning the legality of secondary boycotts were ambiguous. Chávez, Huerta, and Larry Itliong applied great moral pressure and convinced churches, citizens' groups, student organizations, and social activists to pressure local supermarkets to stop carrying grapes until the growers settled. The first to do so were corporate giants Schenley and DiGiorgio, which settled in the spring of 1966. In August, the NFWA and the AWOC officially merged and the United Farm Workers of America was born. It took nearly five years to bring most growers into compliance, at which time the grape boycott was called off. The UFWA then stood at its peak membership of approximately 80,000 members. The events of 1965 to 1970 stand as one of the most successful uses of the boycott tactic in American labor history.

The UFWA called two more grape boycotts whose achievements were more modest. In 1972 and 1973, the group renewed its grape boycott to call attention to growers who were still not in compliance with UFWA demands, as well as to protest the **raiding** practices of the **Teamsters**. That boycott, which included lettuce, most famously targeted E. J. Gallo & Company, one of California's largest bottlers and distributors of wine. It took until 1978 to settle, but the UFWA's victory over Gallo had the secondary effect of forestalling attempts by the Teamsters to usurp the UFWA's jurisdiction. Violence committed against farm workers during the boycott were among the factors that led California to enact its **Agricultural Labor Relations Act**, the nation's most comprehensive bill regulating the treatment of farm workers. A third boycott lasted from 1984 to 2000 and was called to attract attention to pesticide dangers that cause cancers and miscarriages among farm workers. The third boycott began with a flourish, but passed from public awareness as it lingered.

Chávez's death in 1993 also diverted attention from the boycott. By the time it was called off in 2000, some UFWA activists questioned whether the boycott remained an effective tactic. Nonetheless, in 2002, the UFWA announced a boycott of Pictsweet mushrooms. In 2005, the union launched a new boycott against Gallo on behalf of part-time workers. That dispute was resolved within three months, but in 2010 new problems with Gallo led to renewed calls to boycott the company's many holdings and products. The UFWA has also been boycotting Giumarra Vineyard since 2005.

Suggested Reading

Farmworker Movement Documentation Project, http://www.farmworkermovement.org/, accessed November 16, 2010; Susan Ferriss, Ricardo Sandoval, and Diana Hembree, *The Fight in the Fields: Cesar Chávez and the Farmworkers' Movement*, 1998; Douglas Hurt, *American Agriculture: A Brief History*, 2002; Patrick H. Mooney and Theo J. Majka, *Farmers' and Farmworkers' Movements: Social Protest in American Agriculture*, 1995.

GREAT LABOR UPRISING. *See* Railroad Strike of 1877.

GREAT MIGRATION

The Great Migration refers to internal population shifts in the United States between 1910 and 1940. Although the term is usually associated with African Americans leaving southern states and relocating in northern, midwestern, and western industrial cities, there was also movement of whites out of Appalachia, movement of Latinos into urban areas, and movement among other established immigrant groups leaving rural regions to seek jobs. In each case, the lure of industrial employment was among the incentives for relocation. The Great Migration's effects on the nation were magnified by the fact that there was considerably less overseas immigration during a period marked by two world wars, economic depression, and the enactment of immigration restriction laws. It should be noted that some scholars speak of a "Second Great Migration" after World War II to discuss the flight from the

"Rustbelt" to the "Sunbelt." For many African American families, this change in residence represents a reverse migration.

When the **Civil War** ended, and as late as 1900, more than 90 percent of all African Americans resided in the South. The collapse of **Reconstruction**, an increase in lynching incidents, the emergence of hate groups such as the Ku Klux Klan, and the rise of "Jim Crow" discrimination provided powerful incentives for African Americans to consider migrating, but most lacked the wherewithal to do so. Nonetheless, flight to the North remained an ideal. Black Pullman porters working on interstate trains often returned to the South with tales of the nonsegregated North and of visits to black enclaves in Chicago and New York. The maturation of the **Industrial Revolution** provided more economic opportunity for domestic migrants. Midwestern steel mills and meatpacking plants often lured immigrant Slavs, Poles, and other Eastern Europeans from farming regions to urban factories and some companies, including Ford and Youngstown Sheet and Tube, operated Americanization programs to assimilate foreign-born workers into American society. Many other industries simply sought manpower.

When World War I depleted the pool of white workers and postwar immigration revisions cut off the source of new immigration, manufacturers turned to African American, Latino, and transplanted Appalachian whites to fill the void. As many as 500,000 southern whites came north between 1910 and 1920, as did an equally large number of African Americans. The black populations of cities such as Chicago, New York, Gary, Indiana, and Pittsburgh grew by as much as 40 percent in just two decades (1910–1930), and Detroit's by 20-fold. Ford Motor Company actively recruited black workers, many of whom repaid Henry Ford by rebuffing unionization efforts at Ford into the 1940s. The same pattern held among black stockyard workers in Chicago and among Mexican American shipyard workers in Los Angeles. The openly racist policies of numerous **American Federation of Labor** (AFL) affiliates did little to encourage new migrants to join unions and some black leaders—most notably W. E. B. Du Bois and Booker T. Washington—went so far as to assert that in some cases it was acceptable for African Americans to serve as **scabs** during **strikes** called by white racists. Although the **Industrial Workers of the World** federation and individual AFL unions such as the **United Mine Workers of America** and the **United Packinghouse Workers of America** sought to reduce racial tensions and recruit black workers, they were not able to do so in great enough numbers to reverse racist practices within the larger labor movement.

African Americans did not find utopia when they ventured north. Although most cities north of the Mason-Dixon Line may not have been segregated by law, most were divided by social custom and most white Northerners shared the views of Anglo-Saxon racial supremacy held by whites in the South. Many white workers resented the very presence of blacks in their factories and some conducted **wildcat strikes** in protest. Cities also witnessed race riots when African Americans sought to move into white neighborhoods, with the worst occurring in East St. Louis, Illinois, in 1917; Chicago in 1919; Tulsa, Oklahoma, in 1921; and Detroit during 1943. The Detroit event resulted in 34 deaths.

African American men and boys stand outside of the glass factory where they worked in Alexandria, Virginia, circa 1911. Poor wages and working conditions caused many African Americans to flee the South in pursuit of better opportunities provided by jobs in the North. (Library of Congress)

Mexicans and Mexican Americans experienced similar prejudice. As many as 200,000 Mexicans had crossed the border in the United States by 1910, many of them illegally, as they sought to flee to ravages of civil war. Many first settled in the Southwest, often in remote smelter towns, or toiled as agricultural workers in California, Texas, and Colorado. Roundups and deportations of illegal immigrants were commonplace. Over time, however, ethnic enclaves emerged in the border regions that served to attract new cross-border influxes. Like African Americans, many Latinos also ventured farther north to work in auto factories, the rubber industry, and steel mills. Still others worked on West Coast docks and in the ship-building industry. During 1943, Latino youths were attacked by white sailors stationed in Los Angeles. These "Zoot Suit riots"—named for the distinctive baggy garb favored by Latino teens—spread to other cities.

The labor of African Americans and Latinos was essential during World War II. Smaller percentages of African Americans joined the U.S. military, which was segregated until 1948, but they were a strong presence in the defense industry and helped prepare war materiel. Similar patterns prevailed among Latinos. White Appalachia transplants—attracted by high-paying factory jobs—also faced challenges, many of which were cultural and religious in nature. The newly formed **Congress of Industrial Organizations** (CIO) had a much better record on organizing people of color, women, and transplanted southern whites than most AFL unions, and in 1941 the **United Auto Workers of America** won the loyalty of black workers during a union recognition strike against Ford. Nevertheless, it would take the efforts of the post-World War II **civil rights** movement to improve conditions for ethnic minorities, and this movement would entail even more struggle than occurred during the Great Migration.

The Great Migration irrevocably changed American society, culture, and labor patterns. By 1940, more than 3 million Latinos resided in the United States and as many as 2 million African Americans had left the South. Both cities and workplaces that had hitherto been the bastion of northern-born Anglo-Saxons and assimilated European immigrants were forced to confront the realities of multiculturalism. Labor unions would also be forced to grapple with the choice of either organizing workers across racial and cultural divides or facing competition from the groups they ignored.

Suggested Reading

James Grossman, *Land of Hope: Chicago, Black Southerners, and the Great Migration*, 1991; Nelson Lichtenstein, Susan Strasser, and Roy Rosenzweig, eds., *Who Built America? Vol. 2, Since 1877*, 2000; Isabel Wilkerson, *The Warmth of Other Suns: The Epic Story of America's Great Migration*, 2010.

GREAT UPHEAVAL

The Great Upheaval is a somewhat vague term used by historians to designate the period between roughly 1885 and 1888 (or 1890). A portion of the Gilded Age, this era had a social climate marked by labor organizing, **strikes**, third-party electoral success, and widespread unrest. The term describing it passed into wider use among scholars influenced by what was called the "new social history" that emerged in the 1960s and calls attention to the manner in which the very essence of history changes when it is refracted through different lenses. On the level of national politics, for example, the late 1880s can appear staid and conservative, whereas the same period was a chaotic and creative period in local and state politics. It also looks very different if viewed from the perspective of **working-class** activism rather than the Victorianism of middle- and upper-class elites. Historians now routinely connect the **railroad strike of 1877** to labor turmoil in the 1880s, and see the late 19th century as a period marked by great social and economic challenges. Few, for example, would now see the century's last decade as the "Gay '90s," as older studies had designated it.

The Great Upheaval was a pivotal period in American history that, in the end, solidified the permanence of industrial **capitalism**. Its signal event occurred in September 1885, when the **Knights of Labor** (KOL) won an unexpected strike victory against Jay Gould and his Southwestern Railway conglomerate. Gould was one of the most hated robber barons of the Gilded Age, and his capitulation led tens of thousands of workers to join the KOL. KOL membership mushroomed from fewer than 112,000 before the strike to between 729,000 and 1 million by mid-1886. Although the KOL lost many of its 1885 gains in a new strike against Gould during early 1886, the initial victory unleashed pent-up frustrations across the country. The Great Upheaval reached its zenith in 1886. During that year, more than 1,400 strikes took place, idling more than 400,000 workers. This level of activity posed a dilemma for the KOL, which officially opposed strikes, though its discomfort did little to deter an aroused working class. The **eight-hour movement** designated May 1, 1886, as the occasion of a nationwide **general strike** for shorter hours. The world's first **May Day** protest did not command as much interest as organizers hoped, but it did lead to one of the most traumatic episodes in American history: the **Haymarket bombing** in Chicago, which resulted in the deaths of eight policemen and an untold number of workers. The wrongful arrests of eight anarchists and the execution of four of them precipitated massive protests and grassroots organization. In the fall, workers cast ballots and working-class candidates running on third-party and **labor party** tickets swept to victory in numerous municipalities. A dozen members of Congress claimed sympathy with the KOL. **Henry George** narrowly lost his bid to become New York City mayor as a United Labor Party (ULP) candidate, but his run inspired a flurry of organizing work on behalf of the ULP. **Socialist** parties also experienced a surge in membership, while more cautious skilled craftsmen found expression in the newly formed **American Federation of Labor** (AFL).

Strike pressure mounted in 1887, and some employers granted an eight-hour day rather than face labor's fury. The KOL, however, found itself the victim of a fierce capitalist backlash, as its strength was more concentrated in mass-production industries than the AFL. Cash-rich industrialists often incited KOL strikes as a pretext for quashing the organization. Labor candidates also lost ground in the 1887 elections. Industrial capitalists and their political allies succeeded in generating fear among the middle class. In the minds of many, the labor movement was associated with bomb-throwing **anarchists**, immigrant radicals, violence, and misrule. By 1888, the tide was turning, though the publication of **Edward Bellamy**'s utopian novel *Looking Backward* inspired myriad Bellamyite Nationalist clubs to seek a peaceful means to dismantle capitalism. The Nationalists notwithstanding, the KOL was reeling from strike losses, bitter **jurisdiction** battles with the AFL, internal dissension, a shrinking membership base, financial woes, and negative publicity. Across the nation Republicans and Democrats frequently cooperated to defeat third-party candidates, while mainstream politicians and judges used their powers to stymie workers. By 1890, most third-party officials had lost reelection bids. In that same year, the KOL lost a strike against the New York Central Railroad, which set off a cascade effect that eviscerated the organization in most eastern and midwestern cities.

The Great Upheaval ended in a rout, with the forces of organized capital prevailing over those of organized labor. Had the tables been turned, subsequent American history would have unfolded quite differently. Despite the collapse of the Great Upheaval, not all was lost. The 1890s were also an unstable decade, with hundreds of strikes occurring each year from 1890 to 1896. The political challenge shifted to rural America, where populists battled the entrenched two-party system. The decade was also marked by a prolonged financial crisis that lasted from 1893 into 1897. The Great Upheaval, coupled with the crises of the 1890s, did much to convince the urban middle class of the need for social reform. The ensuing **Progressive Era** was hardly what Great Upheaval activists had envisioned, but it did institute needed business regulations, social reforms, and political changes.

Suggested Reading

Leon Fink, *Workingmen's Democracy*, 1983; Bruce Laurie, *Artisans into Workers*, 1989; Michael McGeer, *A Fierce Discontent: The Rise and Fall of the Progressive Movement in America, 1870–1920*, 2010; Alan Trachtenberg, *The Incorporation of America: Culture and Society in the Gilded Age*, 2007; Robert E. Weir, *Beyond Labor's Veil*, 1996.

GREEN, WILLIAM

William Green (May 3, 1870–November 21, 1952) is best known for serving as the second president of the **American Federation of Labor** (AFL), a position he held from the death of **Samuel Gompers** in 1924 until his own demise in 1952. Prior to heading the AFL, Green served in numerous union offices for the **United Mine Workers of America** (UMWA). He is often evoked as an example of a pragmatic and cautious labor leader. To his critics he was overly cautious; to his defenders he was the kind of careful and respectable leader needed to direct organized labor during periods of chaotic upheaval.

Green was born in Coshocton, Ohio, the eldest of the five children of Welsh immigrants Hugh and Jane Oram Green. Hugh Green was a miner who provided his offspring with poor but secure childhoods. William developed an early interest in religion and had aspirations of becoming a Baptist minister. This was not to be; he completed just eight years of formal schooling and entered the mines when he was 16 years old. At the age of 19, he married the former Jennie Mobley, with whom he would have six children. Green supported his growing family by spending 22 years as a miner. This work led him into union activities. He joined the National Progressive Miners Union in 1886, and remained an active member when it merged with the former National Trade Assembly 135 of the **Knights of Labor** (KOL) to form the UMWA in 1891. Green would eventually serve as his local's secretary-treasurer, **business agent**, vice president, and president. He would also serve as a subdistrict president of Ohio in 1900 and as president of the entire Ohio district in 1906. In each role he mixed his desire to improve the lot of miners with his deep commitment to Christian idealism and the Social Gospel movement. As such, Green eschewed radicalism and spoke of the need for capital/labor cooperation. He attracted attention among the UMWA rank-and-file, though he lost bids for the UMWA presidency in 1909 and for secretary-treasurer in 1910.

Green fared better in mainstream politics. Running as a Democrat, he was elected to the Ohio State Senate in 1910, and was reelected to that seat in 1912. He served as senate president pro tempore in both terms. Green successfully guided legislation that provided worker's compensation and better safety measures for Ohio miners. He also presented legislation aimed at developing better labor/management relations. Green returned to UMWA activities in 1913, and was elected national secretary-treasurer of that organization. That same year, UMWA President John White turned down a position as a vice president on the AFL executive council and offered it to Green instead. In 1916, Green was elected as the AFL's secretary-treasurer. In 1919, he was one of the five labor representatives to go to the Versailles peace conference that negotiated the treaty officially ending World War I. Green rose in AFL ranks just as his star was waning in the UMWA. In 1920, **John L. Lewis** became president of the UMWA, and he and Green had a problematic working relationship that deteriorated steadily.

Long-time AFL President Samuel Gompers died in 1924, touching off a bitter succession battle. The leading candidates to fill his seat were Lewis and Matthew Woll of the Photo Engravers' union, but the convention deadlocked and Green emerged as the successful compromise candidate. Green's tenure at the top of the AFL was both long and controversial. In keeping with the AFL's principle of **voluntarism**, Green saw himself primarily as a facilitator and servant of the executive committee. He also remained unwavering in his devotion to Christian idealism and labor/management cooperation. As such, Green often functioned as a public relations leader for organized labor and as a missionary to the non-union world. As an ardent adherent of the free-enterprise system, a rabid anticommunist, and an outspoken patriot, Green spoke before various business groups, churches, and fraternal organizations. Although he may have helped labor's public image, his civic boosterism did little to advance organized union strength during the 1920s, a decade that saw a counter-assault on labor that rolled back many of the gains made during World War I.

The ensuing Great Depression also proved challenging to the AFL. Green shared the distrust of radical activism held by the leadership of many AFL affiliates. He also deferred to conservative **craft unionists** within the AFL and moved to isolate rising sentiment favoring **industrial unionism**, although he actually agreed that it made sense in mass-production factories. The AFL had several industrial unions, but they were organized into federal unions that were designed to be temporary. By the early 1930s, industrial unionists had grown restive and resentful of their second-class membership status. Green's overarching belief in the mutuality of capital/labor interests served to further isolate him from rank-and-file workers in mass production. New Deal legislation proved to be a catalyst for union organizing drives and Green both supported and lobbied for such important bills as the 1932 **Norris-La Guardia Act**, the 1935 **National Labor Relations Act**, and the 1938 **Fair Labor Standards Act**. At the same time, he naively believed that industrialists would allow unions to organize workers. As a result, Green strongly opposed militant organizing campaigns and acceded to the AFL's expulsion of unions supporting the AFL's rebellious Committee for Industrial Organizations faction. The rebels, in turn, ignored AFL sanctions and reorganized as the separate **Congress of Industrial Organizations** (CIO). In a defiant and symbolic move, new CIO President John L. Lewis retaliated by expelling Green from the UMWA. During the late 1930s and into the late 1940s, the AFL and CIO would engage in fratricidal union **raiding** and **jurisdiction** battles.

Some historians argue that by 1940 Green was no longer the most important figure within the AFL and that power had shifted to the AFL's secretary-treasurer,
George Meany, though Green remained president until his death in 1952. Green
continued to believe that corporations would work with organized labor and was
devastated when conservative business leaders spearheaded efforts to pass the
Smith-Connally Act and **Taft-Hartley Act**, which placed greater restrictions on
unions. It would be Meany, not Green, who would most directly shape the parameters of **Cold War** unionism following World War II. Shortly before his death, however, Green did serve on President Harry Truman's advisory board for mobilization
for the Korean War.

William Green may well have overstayed his effectiveness as AFL head.
Nonetheless, his long service to organized labor led to his 1996 induction into the
Labor Hall of Fame.

Suggested Reading

Irving Bernstein, *The Lean Years: A History of the American Workers, 1920–33*, 1970; Irving
  Bernstein, *The Turbulent Years: A History of the American Worker, 1933–41*, 1969;
  William Green, *Labor and Democracy*, 1939; Craig Phelan, *William Green: Biography of a
  Labor Leader*, 1989.

GREENBACKISM

In labor terms, greenbackism refers to various philosophies and organized movements from the 1860s to the turn of the 20th century in support of changing
American monetary policy. For most of the 19th century, the United States adhered
to a gold standard as part of its monetary system. Such a "hard money" policy—as it
was called at the time—greatly curtailed the amount of money in circulation. It kept
inflation in check and greatly favored lenders, which could charge high interest
rates. This practice often hurt those who produced goods and services, especially
farmers dependent upon annual loans to provide needed supplies, equipment, and
seeds. Even a minor dip in crop prices could spell the difference between successfully paying back loans or slipping into debt peonage. Farmers and some (but not
all) **wage**-earners favored "soft money" policies, usually the printing of paper money
("greenbacks"), which (in theory) would increase the overall supply of money, cause
prices to rise, and interest rates to fall.

Greenbackism had its ideological roots in the **Jacksonian Era**, especially among
shopkeepers, small businesses, and farmers. Numerous advocates of the
Workingmen's movement supported systematic banking and currency reform.
More directly, Greenbacks—the name generally used for supporters—drew upon
the precedent set by the **Civil War**. Both the United States and the Confederate
States of America faced the need to stimulate domestic commerce and overseas
trade, and to finance the war. Both governments floated paper money during the
war, with the currency used in the North being dubbed "greenbacks." Confederate
currency was declared worthless after the war, but the more than $430 million of
greenbacks in circulation proved popular among the laboring classes of the North,
where the push for banking reform fused with social class concerns over the rising

power of industrial and investment **capitalism**. The call for permanent monetary reform grew even more passionate in rural America, where farmers had grown increasingly dependent upon monopolistic railroads to move their goods to market. Rising railroad rates and the fees charged by grain elevators served to strengthen calls for inflationary currency policies.

The 1870s witnessed intense political debates over the fate of greenbacks. Fiscal conservatives—dubbed "Goldbugs"—called for reestablishing the gold standard, regulating financial markets, reducing the volume of paper money in circulation, and allowing the National Banking System (NBS) to manage currency and credit. Opponents saw the Goldbugs as monopolists who wished to return to return to a prewar status quo that enriched a small elite by exploiting the laboring masses. The 1873 Coinage Act engaged Greenback activists by putting into place mechanisms through which paper money and silver coins would give way to gold. It was dubbed the "Crime of '73" by farmers, bank reformers, and Western silver miners who felt their livelihoods would be endangered by lower demand for silver ore.

The first Greenback Party (GP) was organized by farmers in 1874. GP activists quickly broadened the party's appeal by adding labor reforms such as the **eight-hour** workday to its platform. In 1876, the GP nominated the elderly and eccentric New Yorker Peter Cooper, a veteran of Jacksonian monetary reform, as its presidential candidate. Cooper fared poorly, but the party attracted the attention of labor activists such as **Ira Steward**, John Siney, George Trevellick, and Uriah Stephens, the founder of the **Knights of Labor** (KOL). The **National Labor Union** was especially enamored of the greenback cause, with **William Sylvis** openly embracing theories developed by Edward Kellogg in the 1840s. Kellogg had argued in favor of putting interest-bearing notes into circulation that would break the power of banking monopolies. Farmers, he asserted, would benefit immediately from issuing bank notes, but the rate of inflation could be controlled through the amount of interest those notes accrued.

The GP—often known as the Greenback Labor Party (GLP) in many parts of the country—was an important third-party movement on the state and local levels. In 1874, the GLP was especially successful and 14 of its members were elected to Congress. In 1878, **Terence Powderly**, the head of the KOL, was elected mayor of Scranton, Pennsylvania, on the GLP ticket. In many ways the GLP served as a transitional party at a time in which the Republicans and Democrats were redefining themselves. Among the emerging differences was that Republicans eventually committed to the gold standard, while Democrats became more sympathetic to parts of the greenback agenda. The Resumption Act of 1875 forced the issue as it irrevocably returned the United States to the gold standard by calling for the conversion of all greenbacks to specie as of 1879.

The coming withdrawal of greenbacks led to the slow demise of the GLP, but it did little to bury the issues gave rise to demands for monetary reform. Myriad local movements emerged, and several—including the GLP, the Labor Reform Party, the Anti-Monopoly Party, and the Union Labor Party—tried to build national organizations. The GLP managed to field presidential candidates until 1884, at which time it faded from view, but its 1880 ticket leader, James B. Weaver, of Iowa, would resurface as a Populist Party standard bearer. Because it embraced many issues, greenbackism attracted urban labor, small businessmen, farmers, craftsmen, and especially southerners and westerners resentful of the growing power and influence of the northeastern establishment. In fact, by the mid-1880s greenbackism had evolved into a catchall movement that gathered the discontented from groups as diverse as **socialists** and old-style conservatives who distrusted nouveau riche monopolists. Greenbacks were most prevalent among farmer groups, KOL members involved in **cooperative** experiments, and assorted labor reformers, though specific plans for banking reform were often hazy in detail or subsumed under a welter of other agenda items. Nonetheless, greenback principles were found amidst the rhetoric of most third-party campaigns during the **Great Upheaval**.

By then, many Greenbacks no longer entirely associated currency reform with the issuance of paper currency; many had embraced the "free silver" movement. Technically, hardcore Greenbacks wanted little or no restrictions on the amount of currency in circulation, while many free-silver advocates advocated a bimetallic system in which silver coins would also circulate and their value would be guaranteed by government fiat. During most of the late 19th century, the relative value of an ounce of silver versus an ounce of gold was 16:1, which meant that "free coinage" of silver would dramatically increase the amount of money in circulation and, in theory, control rates of inflation. Given that many free-silver advocates also felt that paper money could be used in combination with silver, the two movements tended to merge. By the late 1880s, various **populist** parties formed. Many of them—especially in New York and in the South—attracted support from organized labor, again because many also endorsed labor reforms such as the eight-hour day, the establishment of cooperatives, mechanics' lien laws, and other reforms important to urban workers. These parties enjoyed local success and, in 1891, the formation of a national party was announced. The following year delegates gathered in Omaha, Nebraska, where they were joined by numerous KOL members and social reformers and issued the official platform for the People's Party, better known as the Populists. Free silver was the lynchpin of the Populist platform.

The Populists formed their organization in a flurry of promise and optimism. Farmers hoped to obtain higher commodity prices that would allow them to pay off crippling mortgages, and many workers hoped comprehensive banking reform would facilitate the establishment of cooperatives. Many also believed that the Populists' overall effect would be to break the power of banks and railroads. According to their logic, political success would create a force powerful enough to break the stranglehold of banks and large corporations. This idea had an especially attractive allure for the KOL members, whose own organization was in severe decline. The KOL virtually fused with the Populists in many parts of rural America. Between 1893 and 1900, the Populists would elect 10 governors, 6 U.S. senators, and 45 Congressmen. In 1892, the Populist presidential candidate James Weaver received more than a million votes and won electoral votes from six states.

The election of 1896, however, exposed a basic contradiction in the farmer/labor alliance, which Republican candidate William McKinley parlayed into victory over William Jennings Bryan, a Democrat who endorsed enough of the Populist platform to capture its endorsement. McKinley's campaign realized that both greenbackism and the free silver movement often rested upon fast-fading agrarian ideals. Farmers—whose percentage of the workforce dwindled each year—were producers whose income was derived entirely from commodity production. As such, they desired high prices. Industrial workers, in contrast, were largely consumers for whom high farm prices translated into lower earning power. Fear tactics succeeded in eroding populism's urban support. McKinley's victory sent the Populists into steep decline, and his reelection in 1900—also over Bryan—sealed the party's fate. In 1900, McKinley signed the Gold Standard Act, which required all paper money and silver to be backed by gold. This move was made more palatable by the opening of new gold fields that promised to increase the money supply, but it proved only a temporary balm.

Labor and farm groups continued to lobby for monetary reform in the 20th century. The gold standard was relaxed somewhat by the Federal Reserve Act (FSA) of 1913, which made the money supply more flexible and decentralized banking by creating 12 federal district banks that could lend money to commercial banks and raise or lower interest rates to control the amount of money in circulation and regulate inflation. The full power of the FSA did not become apparent until 1933, however, when President Franklin Roosevelt took the United States off the gold standard. Since 1933, labor groups have continued to press for banking reforms, though they now tend to center on investment policies rather than currency issues. The Federal Reserve Board is often the main battleground, with unions and labor leaders often calling on the board to loosen credit by lowering interest rates.

Suggested Reading

Norman Pollock, *The Populist Response to Industrial America*, 1962; Gretchen Ritter, *Goldbugs and Greenbacks: The Antimonopoly Tradition and the Politics of Finance in America*, 1997; Allen Weinstein, *Prelude to Populism: Origins of the Silver Issue, 1867–78*, 1970.

GRIEVANCE

A grievance is a complaint arising in the workplace. The ability to resolve grievances through formal procedures outlined in a **collective bargaining** agreement is one of the fundamental rights guaranteed by a union contract and one of the most important privileges that union employees enjoy over those who are not in bargaining units. Although U.S. labor law protects all employees from some abuses by management, most workers who fall into the category of "employee at will" have no formal method of resolving disputes. Although complaints about management are often exaggerated, a 2007 survey conducted by Career-Builder.com indicated that only a bit more than half of American workers were satisfied with management and nearly one-fourth held extremely negative views of their bosses. The use of arbitrary power ranks high among employee complaints.

Most union contracts specify the ways in which grievances are to be handled. In general, if informal attempts to resolve a complaint fail, the employee files a formal grievance. If management's behavior violates terms of the contract, that behavior can be deemed an **unfair labor practice** under the **National Labor Relations Act** (NLRA), which also specifies the steps that can be taken. In practice, the bulk of grievances are resolved well in advance of such drastic measures. Often a union **business agent** meets with management to find a solution to the complaint. Formal grievances frequently end with no more formal actions than a warning from the union and a promise by management to correct the practices than resulted in filing. In many cases, however, union employees have won back-pay and damages if they were dismissed without cause. Such a scenario is rare for employees who are not in unions. Employees-at-will must file claims in civil courts—often a long and expensive process that results in a settlement that does not include job reinstatement. They also lack the collective dispute resolution power of union members and the union's resources to battle management.

Grievance language is now standard in union contracts, though it was not widespread until the 20th century and did not become ubiquitous until after World War II. It is important to note that under the NLRA and its **Taft-Hartley Act** revisions, either unions or management can file grievances. There have also been occasions in which unions and management have been on the same side in disputes. This has especially been the case in spontaneous **wildcat strikes**, which violate terms of a contract. Most unions prefer to invoke dispute resolution and **arbitration** to resolve complaints. The final step in most grievance procedures is binding arbitration.

Suggested Reading

Henry Campbell Black, *Black's Law Dictionary*, 1999; Harry C. Katz and Thomas A. Kochan, *An Introduction to Collective Bargaining and Industrial Relations*, 2003.

GUARANTEED ANNUAL WAGE

A guaranteed annual wage—also called guaranteed minimum income, supplemental unemployment benefit, or basic income guarantee—is an increasingly rare negotiated provision within a union contract that specifies a minimum sum or minimum number of hours per year that a worker will receive. Under such terms, the employee will draw pay for that minimum even if a reduction in output or other work slowdown means that he or she does not actually work for those **wages**. Unions prefer such provisions because they provide members with more financial security. The incentive for employers to grant a guaranteed annual wage is that it stabilizes the workforce and decreases the likelihood that skilled and highly qualified workers will seek alternative employment during slack economic conditions.

Most guaranteed annual wage provisions have been negotiated in industries that are subject to seasonal downturns and those that sometimes need to shut down to retool for a new product line. As a response to the frequent layoffs in the post-World War II workplace, unions began to seek more security for their members, and employers in the automobile and household appliances industries were among the first to use the guaranteed annual wage as a way to secure their workforces. In 1955, the **United Auto Workers of America** negotiated the world's first

Supplemental Unemployment Benefit Plan, a private, employer-financed plan providing payments to laid-off workers in addition to unemployment insurance benefits.

The guaranteed annual wage began to fade from union contracts with the coming of **deindustrialization**, and it was among the first **fringe benefits** to be cut during the rounds of **concessions** and **downsizing** battles that occurred between unions and management during the 1970s and 1980s. By 1995, just 16 percent of all union contracts provided work or pay guarantees—a percentage that has steadily fallen since then. In recent years the battle for a guaranteed annual income has shifted to policy experts, economists, and social critics, who argue that it will be a necessary feature of future society as automation, **outsourcing** of production, and **globalism** will make work unpredictable. They argue that only a guaranteed annual income can provide a stable financial foundation for the future; without it, social chaos may ensue in the United States as there would simply be too many people without resources.

Suggested Reading

Harry Katz and Thomas Kochan, *An Introduction to Collective Bargaining and Industrial Relations*, 2000; "Labor Fight for the Annual Wage," *Time*, February 7, 1955; R. Emmet Murray, *The Lexicon of Labor*, 1999, Jeremy Rifkin, *The End of Work*, 1995.

H

HARD HAT RIOTS

The "hard hat riots" refers to several incidents that took place during the 1970s in which **blue-collar** construction workers clashed violently with student antiwar protestors. The term "hard hat" refers to the protective headgear worn on building sites. The worst of these incidents took place in New York City on May 8, 1970, when an estimated 200 construction workers attacked a group of approximately 1,000 individuals—mostly high school and college students—protesting continued U.S. involvement in the **Vietnam War**. Workers severely beat several individuals and then went on a rampage down Wall Street and onto the grounds of Pace University, where they broke windows, attacked students, and hurled threats and obscenities. In all, some 70 people suffered injuries that needed treatment, a toll that included four police officers trying to contain the violence. Six people were arrested. There were also smaller, less serious copycat incidents in other cities, but New York City became the symbol for those postulating that organized labor and blue-collar labor in general had grown conservative. The reality was more complex, but the hard hat riots did magnify schism and unresolved tension within the labor movement.

The deep roots of the hard hat riots lay in the 1930s. During the New Deal, many labor unions embraced the Democratic Party and came to view the government as a guarantor of the rights of working people. This perception came at a cost. Organized labor took steps to tame (or expel) militants within the rank-and-file, accelerate the transition to **business unionism**, and emphasize political lobbying rather than grassroots activism. Cooperation with government also meant acceding to **Cold War** foreign policy objectives and many of the domestic crackdowns on radicals associated with the second **Red Scare**. Much of organized labor likewise supported the remilitarization of the United States, the deployment of U.S. troops abroad, and U.S. involvement in the Korean War. Acceptance of anticommunism was among the preconditions for the 1955 merger between the **American Federation of Labor** (AFL) and the **Congress of Industrial Organizations** (CIO).

Problems emerged in the 1960s with the rise of New Left critics of U.S. policy. The AFL-CIO merger looked much stronger on paper than it was in reality, and lingering ideological splits within the alliance would be magnified by the social protest and unrest of the 1960s. It is important to remember that the AFL-CIO is a federation of unions, each of which retains a great degree of autonomy over its internal policies. As a consequence, each affiliated union had to wrestle with its response to the social challenges of the New Left. For the most part, former CIO unions proved more comfortable with the New Left than those associated with the former

AFL. This was especially the case with **civil rights**, with ex-CIO bodies such as the **United Auto Workers of America** (UAW) and the **United Packinghouse Workers of America** offering financial and logistical support to civil rights activists. The UAW also gave seed money and other aid to the founders of Students for a Democratic Society (SDS). AFL-CIO President **George Meany** was far less comfortable with social movements, however, and soon he and more liberal members of the federation such as **A. Philip Randolph** and **Walter Reuther** found themselves at loggerheads, with Meany emerging as the self-proclaimed spokesperson for conservative politics. Meany seethed when Reuther, Randolph, Herbert Hill, Joseph Rauh, and others simply ignored his counsel for caution and plunged headlong into support for the civil rights movement.

The infusion of American ground troops into Vietnam after 1965 brought the divisions within organized labor to the forefront. Meany supported the war and never wavered in his belief. When Reuther added his name to the newly formed Labor Leadership Assembly for Peace (LLAP) in 1967, Meany denounced him as a "kook," seemingly oblivious to the fact that 522 other labor leaders also endorsed the LLAP. As younger workers entered the workforce—the leading edge of the Baby Boom generation—Meany also struggled to understand them; in fact, his rhetoric against antiwar demonstrators and members of the **counterculture** was often as harsh as that of conservatives such as Spiro Agnew, Barry Goldwater, George Wallace, and Richard Nixon. By 1967, Reuther had grown so disgusted with Meany and the conservative clique of old-line **craft unionists** who supported him that he withdrew the UAW from the AFL-CIO and denounced both as devoid of new ideas and wedded to an outdated past. Shortly thereafter Reuther formed the **Alliance for Labor Action**, a new federation that challenged the AFL-CIO.

Meany may have been correct to see Reuther as being on the fringe of public opinion over the Vietnam War in 1967, but the 1968 Tet Offensive changed perceptions among the U.S. public. The ease with which North Vietnamese forces invaded the South in early 1968 made many Americans question whether the war was winnable and whether the costs were worth it. Despite swelling protests against the war, Meany remained steadfast in his support for it, and his stance remained the AFL-CIO's official position. The year also saw President Lyndon Johnson's decision not to seek reelection, the assassinations of Martin Luther King, Jr., and Robert Kennedy, the chaos of the Democratic national convention in Chicago, increased numbers of urban riots, and rising levels of campus protest. The November presidential election, which brought Richard Nixon to power, served only to exacerbate tensions within the working class. Numerous conservative white workers, fearful of civil rights militants and disapproving of the counterculture, cast their votes for either Nixon or the segregation-based third-party campaign of George Wallace.

Nixon, and his running mate Agnew, openly encouraged the bifurcation within labor's ranks and saw it as a way to court blue-collar voters. By 1969 analysts routinely spoke of blue-collar conservatives and of general alienation among white male wage-earners who felt cheated by **affirmative action**, threatened by feminism, and disgusted by the privilege and antipatriotism of the New Left and counterculture.

That year the **film** *Joe* depicted a blue-collar worker driven to rampage and murder by his declining status and his anger over hippies.

The hard hat riots did not go to that extreme, but they did pit one of the AFL-CIO's most conservative groups, construction workers, against student antiwar demonstrators. The riots came just four days after four students were killed during antiwar protests on the campus of Kent State University in Ohio. The New York City event had been called to protest the deaths at Kent State and to demand an immediate end to the war in Vietnam. As protestors gathered in front of Federal Hall, flag-waving construction workers shouting slogans and making racial and homosexual slurs broke through a police line and attacked them. Many singled out males with long hair and beat them. Some protestors fled down Wall Street, and accounts differ about whether financial district workers sought to harbor them or pointed out their positions to pursuers. The rioters also entered City Hall, ripped a Red Cross flag from Trinity Church, and entered the grounds of Pace University to beat students and smash windows.

In the weeks to come, Peter J. Brennan, president of the Building and Construction Trades Council of Greater New York, emerged as a hero for those applauding the attacks. On May 20, Brennan convened a pro-war rally attended by at least 60,000 people—including construction workers and longshoremen—that also turned into a vitriolic protest against the policies of New York City's liberal mayor, John Lindsay. Two days later Brennan and 22 other union leaders were invited to the White House, where President Nixon greeted them warmly. Brennan was a major supporter of Nixon's reelection campaign in 1972 and among the centerpieces of Nixon's plan to win blue-collar votes. In 1973, Nixon appointed Brennan to be his secretary of labor. His tenure proved to be an unpopular one that angered even George Meany, especially when Brennan compromised over **minimum wage** increases and delayed affirmative action implementation in the building trades.

The hard hat riots arose from deep-seated and unresolved divisions among blue-collar workers. In retrospect, they appear to be a generalized response to simmering alienation and presaged the frustration that would attend the overall decline of blue-collar work looming on the horizon. Nixon's embrace of the rioters was clearly part of an orchestrated plan to wean wage-earners away from the Democratic Party and into the Republican fold. It is difficult to know how many workers shared conservative values and how many simply felt threatened by the myriad social changes of the period, but the hard hat riots do reflect a splintering of the New Deal Democratic/organized labor alliance. Although many analysts overestimate the number of formerly working-class votes that shifted allegiance during this period, there can be little doubt that increasing numbers of blue-collar voters were willing to cast ballots for Wallace, Nixon, **Ronald Reagan**, and other conservative candidates. The riots also served to magnify organized labor's inability to come to grips with demographic change and probably played a role in distancing younger workers from unions.

There is another sad and ironic footnote to New York City's hard hat riots. Many of the workers present in that section of New York on May 8, 1970, were working on the construction of the World Trade Center, which would be destroyed by terrorists on September 11, 2001.

Suggested Reading

Joshua B. Freeman, "Hardhats: Construction Workers, Manliness, and the 1970 Pro-War Demonstrations." *Journal of Social History*, June 1993, 725–739; Peter B. Levy, *The New Left and Labor in the 1960s*, 1994; Jonathan Schell, *The Time of Illusion*, 1975.

HAYMARKET BOMBING

The Haymarket bombing occurred on May 4, 1886, in Chicago's Haymarket Square, when a dynamite bomb was thrown at the end of a protest rally. The explosion and subsequent gunfire from police left eight police officers and four workers dead, and scores more were wounded. Although the identity of the bomber was never established, eight anarchists were convicted after a trial that most legal scholars agree was a miscarriage of justice. In the short run, the Haymarket bombing galvanized workers already caught up in the **Great Upheaval** and helped labor parties at the polls. In the long run, it was a public relations and political disaster seized upon by opponents of organized labor as pretext for crushing working-class movements. The **Knights of Labor** (KOL) was particularly hurt by the Haymarket event.

The Haymarket Square protest took place against the backdrop of struggles related to the **eight-hour** movement. Although some federal employees and a few workers in the private sector had won the eight-hour day by 1886, most workers toiled 10 or more hours. Various groups discussed a nationwide general strike to pressure employers to grant shorter workdays. Those groups included the KOL; the Federation of Organized Trades and Labor Unions (FOTLU), the forerunner of the **American Federation of Labor** (AFL); and the International Working People's Association (IWPA), a radical group that blended **socialism** and **anarcho-syndicalist** precepts. The IWPA was instrumental in pushing for a general strike, and the May 1 date set for this action is now widely recognized as labor's first **May Day** show of strength. At the time, however, the very presence of the IWPA led KOL leaders to back away from the protest; indeed, its executive board refused to endorse it and cautioned Knights to avoid all association with May 1 events. That advice would appear prescient in the wake of what ensued, though at the time it was motivated mostly by the KOL's internal challenges and by its distrust of the IWPA.

The KOL's unexpected strike victory over hated robber baron Jay Gould had led to explosive growth in the federation that overwhelmed the KOL's central administration. Many new members of the KOL had scant understanding of the organization or its principles. In particular, the KOL repudiated the use of violence, which many IWPA leaders seemed to embrace. Several key KOL local and district assemblies were influenced by **Lassallean** socialists, who saw the ballot box as the key to labor's emancipation and, therefore, were distrustful of both FOTLU craft unionism and the perceived recklessness of the IWPA. This was particularly true in New York, where many local leaders were Lassalleans, and where the organization maintained friendly ties with the Socialist Labor Party, which advocated a peaceful road to social change. Moreover, as the KOL expanded, its national leader, Terence Powderly, grew more cautious, hoping to foster a positive public view of the KOL. Much of the KOL's platform rested upon the hope of government-led reform, and Powderly sought to distance the KOL from association with anarchism. This would prove a challenge, as anarchists of various persuasions were certainly found among the KOL rank-and-file. Powderly nonetheless ordered Knights to stay away from the May 1 demonstrations.

The KOL was far and away the largest labor federation of the day, and the withdrawal of its endorsement meant that the May 1 **general strike** was a bust. Organizers had hoped for 1 million demonstrators, but fewer than one-third of that number participated. May 1 would have likely passed without notice had it not been for conditions in Chicago, where anarchist ideals were much stronger and this position's advocates less prone to ideological debates that caused schisms elsewhere. Many Chicago Knights defied Powderly and joined the city's eight-hour protest. In fact, at least 80,000 workers turned out, a figure that represented nearly 20 percent of the nationwide total. Moreover, Chicago was also home to a key IWPA leader who also held KOL membership: **Albert Parsons**, a Texas-born white radical married to **Lucy Parsons**, an African American woman who was his equal in radical passion. The two were perhaps the nation's most-famous left-wing couple.

Albert Parsons led Chicago's May 1 parade, and the day passed without incident. Two days later, flush with feelings of solidarity, some veterans of the May 1 demonstration joined protestors on **strike** against McCormick Harvester Machine Company, a manufacturer of mechanical reapers and one of the city's largest employers. At the behest of police captain John Bonfield, Chicago police beat strikers, fatally shot two (some accounts say six), and wounded several others. In the wake of the unprovoked attack on unarmed workers, the IWPA called for a protest to be held the next day in Haymarket Square. Fiery IWPA leaflets were peppered with provocative language such as "revenge" and a call "to arms." Haymarket Square could accommodate up to 20,000 people, but the actual turnout on May 4 was disappointing, with estimates varying from 1,800 to 3,000 protestors. Numerous speeches were given, most filled with anger and anguish, but the gathering was peaceful. Chicago's mayor, Carter Harrison, attended and left satisfied that no trouble was brewing. As the last speaker, Samuel Fielden, was finishing his remarks, Captain Bonfield marched 180 policemen into Haymarket Square. Fielden's remark, "We are peaceful," was interrupted by a bomb blast that killed policeman Mathias Degan. Police opened fire, and several of the seven other officers who subsequently died may have been crossfire victims. At least four protestors were killed, and approximately 50 were wounded.

The death of police officers led the mainstream press and political conservatives to demand a crackdown on anarchism. Within three weeks, 31 people were indicted for Degan's murder, his death being the only one directly attributable to the bombing. Only eight men actually stood trial in June: August Spies, Adolph Fischer, George Engel, Michael Schwab, Oscar Neebe, Louis Lingg, Samuel Fielden, and Albert Parsons. (Parsons had not been apprehended when the trial opened; he dramatically turned himself in as jury selection was taking place.) The presiding judge was Joseph Gary. None of the defendants was charged with actually throwing the bomb; rather, they stood accused of conspiracy to commit murder. Judge Gary allowed prosecution such wide latitude in defining conspiracy that, in essence, it was anarchism itself that was on trial. The eight men stood accused of creating the very atmosphere of violence that led to the bombing. Despite world-wide protests—only Parsons was native born—and the general perception that the trial was a farce, on August 19, 1886, all eight men were convicted. All but Neebe—who got a 15-year sentence—were sentenced to hang. Amnesty groups formed across the world in the hope that political pressure could save the convicted men, but to no avail. By November 2, all appeals were exhausted and the first round of executions was scheduled.

The last appeals coincided with the fall elections. The trial, the failed appeals, and the repression of radical groups initially galvanized American workers. Most labor organizations, except the KOL, protested the arrests, trial, and sentences. Powderly still hoped to distance the KOL from anarchism, but he succeeded mainly in angering workers, including many Knights who were furious that he refused to support either Parsons or Spies, both of whom held KOL membership. Powderly's intransigence notwithstanding, the aftermath of the Haymarket bombing actually stimulated more strikes for the eight-hour day, and trade unions picked up strength. (In December, the surging FOTLU reorganized as the AFL.) In elections held days after the final appeals, working-class voters turned out in droves and many rejected Republicans and Democrats with equal fervor. In New York, **Henry George** came close to being elected mayor of New York. Numerous **labor party** candidates else-where bettered George's effort and won elected office. In several locales, KOL candi-dates gained control of city government. As the first executions grew nearer, clemency movements arose to pressure officials to spare the condemned men, and many cities witnessed renewed strikes, with clemency among the demands. Lucy Parsons embarrassed Illinois governor Richard Oglesby by "confessing" her own guilt and demanding that she, too, be hanged.

Labor flexed its muscles in the short run, but its hopes were soon dashed. Powderly shocked many labor supporters by refusing even to endorse clemency and in joining the conservative call for the annihilation of anarchism; thousands of workers quit the KOL in disgust, and many KOL elected officials were repudiated in subsequent elections. (KOL strength in Chicago fell from around 400,000 to around 17,000 despite the fact that the city's KOL paper published autobiographies of each of the eight convicted Haymarket men, and despite bitter denunciation of Powderly by local KOL leaders.) The clemency movement did help convince Governor Oglesby to commute the sentences of Fielden and Schwab, but on November 11, 1887, Parsons, Spies, Fischer, and Engel went to the gallows. Louis Lingg would have joined them, but he committed suicide in his cell by biting a dynamite cap the day before his scheduled execution.

Radical groups embraced their departed comrades as martyrs, but the general crackdown on left-wing groups continued unabated. In fact, the success of labor parties during the fall elections helped precipitate a capitalist backlash against organized labor in general. This left the KOL particularly vulnerable, as it had more members in mass industry than did the aspirant AFL. Many of its skilled members bolted to the AFL, leaving the KOL's semiskilled and unskilled workers even more vulnerable.

By the early 1890s, much of the challenge to the status quo related to the Great Upheaval had been turned aside. Anarchists found themselves targeted, a campaign that had the unintended effect of encouraging those groups that espoused violence while weakening those organizations of more moderate disposition. In 1893, Illinois Governor John P. Altgeld pardoned Fielden, Schwab, and Neebe and denounced the trial itself, implying that none of the men were guilty. Altgeld's courageous actions cost him his political career; he was another casualty of what many historians now call the "crisis of the 1890s," an expansion of the capitalist backlash that began in the wake of the Haymarket bombing. Progressives and radicals alike have subsequently used Haymarket as a symbol of capitalist repression, justice miscarried, and idealism trampled. Historians tend to view it as a key moment in capital/labor struggles in which capital gained the upper hand. Many also see capital's response as a heavy-handed one that ignored the root causes of the unrest, a blindness that paved the way for **Progressive Era** reforms.

Suggested Reading

Paul Avrich, *The Haymarket Tragedy*, 1984; Philip Foner, ed., *The Autobiographies of the Haymarket Martyrs*, 2001; Bruce Nelson, *Beyond the Martyrs: A Social History of Chicago Anarchism, 1870–1900*, 1988.

HAYWOOD, WILLIAM DUDLEY

William Haywood (February 4, 1869–March 18, 1928) was a colorful and dynamic organizer and activist in the Western Federation of Miners (WFM), Socialist Party, and the **Industrial Workers of the World** (IWW). To his friends and supporters, Haywood was the very embodiment of a **class-conscious** militant labor leader. To many in the middle class and within more moderate wings of the labor movement, Haywood was unrealistic and recklessly incited workers to violence and to lost cause battles with organized capital.

Haywood was born in Salt Lake City. His father, a Pony Express rider, died when Haywood was three, and his mother remarried a miner. At the age of nine, Haywood lost his right eye in a home accident, a misfortune that brought him the nicknames "Squint Eye" and "Dick Dead-Eye." His formal education ended at age 15, when he left home and took a series of cowboy and mining jobs in Nevada and Idaho. Despite leaving school, Haywood fit the classic **Marxist** profile of an organic intellectual—quick-minded, well read, articulate, and analytical. Although he was less than six feet tall, his fellow miners bestowed upon the burly-framed Haywood a nickname he much preferred: "Big Bill." In 1889, he married Jane Minor, a rancher's daughter, with whom he fathered two daughters. Haywood was largely an absentee parent due to his activism and a penchant for heavy drinking and womanizing. His wife, dubbed "Nevada Jane," fit the profile of a pioneer woman. She remained devoted to her wayward husband, even though he largely ignored her and separated from her in the 1890s.

In 1894, Haywood moved his family to Silver City, Idaho, where he joined the WFM, an early **industrial union**. He rose quickly within the WFM hierarchy, joining the executive board in 1900, becoming secretary-treasurer the next year, and developing a reputation as a spellbinding speaker and rabble-rouser. Haywood helped convert the WFM into an organization that espoused revolutionary unionism. He took part in numerous WFM strikes, including one in Idaho in 1899 that was broken when Governor Frank Steunenberg declared martial law. In 1901, Haywood moved to Denver and took part in several bitter Colorado coalfield strikes. Haywood was also present at the 1905 founding of the Industrial Workers of the World. Like many who passed through the IWW, Haywood held utter contempt for the **American Federation of Labor** (AFL), which he saw as complicit in promoting **capitalism**. In return, AFL President **Samuel Gompers** saw Haywood as unprincipled and dangerous, and viewed the IWW as injurious to the cause of labor. The AFL occasionally enjoyed success by presenting itself as a safe, patriotic, and respectable alternative to the IWW.

In 1906, Haywood, WFM President Charles Moyer, and two others were jailed on a charge of murdering ex-Idaho Governor Steunenberg in 1905. Haywood and his compatriots were acquitted when their defense team, led by the famed lawyer Clarence Darrow, demolished the testimony of **Pinkerton** agent James McParland, who had once claimed he infiltrated the **Molly Maguires**. The court victory valorized Haywood among labor radicals. He was briefly a victim of internal fighting within the IWW, causing him to leave that group, and from 1908 through 1912 was an organizer for the Socialist Party. Haywood rejoined the IWW just in time for its victory in the 1912 **Lawrence textile strike** and became general secretary of the IWW (its highest office). He led the IWW to the height of its influence and presided over the group's drive to organize agricultural workers in the Midwest. Haywood's fiery rhetoric led to his expulsion from the Socialist Party in 1913, when that group renounced violence and put its faith in electoral politics. Like many IWW members, Haywood had little faith in the ballot box as a means of social change, and thought the American electoral system was a sham in which elites exploited the **working class** by creating an illusion of democracy. Haywood advocated the abolition of the **wage** system and a future society based on **anarcho-syndicalist** ideals.

Haywood's militancy led to his arrest in 1917. He and other IWW members vehemently opposed militarism and U.S. involvement in World War I. Haywood interpreted the war as a conflict among elites in which working people were being used as pawns, so he encouraged workers to avoid it. In a U.S. court, his comments were found to be in violation of the 1917 Espionage Act. On August 17, 1918, he was sentenced to 20 years in prison. Haywood appealed his conviction, but the outbreak of the **Red Scare** convinced Haywood that that the courts would not vindicate him or uphold the sanctity of free speech. Haywood skipped bail, and fled to the Soviet Union in 1921. His flight was much criticized, as several supporters forfeited cash and property that had underwritten his bail. Haywood also left behind his legal wife and bigamously married a Russian woman who spoke little English. He managed a mine in the Soviet Union, set up an international fund for imprisoned radicals, and wrote his autobiography. When he died in 1928, he was buried in the Kremlin wall.

Suggested Reading

Peter Carlson, *Roughneck: The Life and Times of Big Bill Haywood*, 1983; Joseph Conlin, *Big Bill Haywood and the Radical Union Movement*, 1969; William Haywood, *The Autobiography of Big Bill Haywood*, 1929.

HERRIN MASSACRE

The Herrin Massacre was an organized bloodbath in Herrin, Illinois, in Williamson County, that took place on June 22, 1922. Twenty-one deaths occurred in a labor dispute that is less noteworthy for its bloodiness than for the fact that it marked a rare time in which more strikebreakers than strikers died.

The tragedy was an outgrowth of a nationwide coal **strike** that had started just two months earlier. Initiated in April, the strike had begun to take its toll by June. Losing money steadily, owners searched for ways to keep their operations running without conceding to the demands of the **United Mine Workers of America** (UMW) union. The Southern Illinois Coal Company, owned by William J. Lester, initially tried to stay aloof from the battles by forging an agreement in which miners would produce coal from his strip mine, but he agreed not to ship it until the strike was settled. Rising coal prices proved too tempting, however, and on June 13, Lester imported 50 **scabs** to move the coal and private mine guards to facilitate their work and protect them from reprisal. News of Lester's actions sparked deep anger among Williamson County workers. Lester's actions were all the more shocking given that he was counseled against importing scabs or guards by the Illinois Attorney General's office. As was feared, Lester's private forces—overseen by mine superintendent C. K. McDowell—proved a rogue operation that quickly gained an unsavory reputation for rash behavior and harassment of local citizens. McDowell hoped that a heavy-handed approach would cause the miners to back down, but it merely strengthened their resolve and heightened the defiance of UMW President **John L. Lewis**, who had been on the job for less than two years and was anxious to show the world that the UMW was a force with which to be reckoned.

As matters began to spiral out of control in Williamson County, Colonel Samuel Hunter of the Illinois National Guard journeyed to the region to plead with Lester and the local sheriff, Melvin Thaxton, to defuse tensions and to warn that the mine could not be easily defended. Unfortunately, his pleas fell upon deaf ears. The UMW had a strong presence in the area, its members were accustomed to hardship, and the union's resolve was great. Armed with weapons looted from local hardware stores, an angry mob surrounded the mine on June 21, 1922, and began to shoot at the guards. The attack came on the heels on an early-morning ambush of a car carrying scabs that left the driver dead and resulted in several scabs being beaten.

The mob continued to grow in size throughout the day of June 21, but Colonel Hunter was able to fashion a compromise that led to a temporary ceasefire. The matter might have been resolved without further violence, except that severed phone lines led to confusion and delayed the arrival of the National Guard. What ensued might also have been avoided if Thaxton had taken his deputies to the mine and evacuated the strikebreakers immediately, as he was urged to do. Instead, he insisted on waiting until the morning to retrieve the men.

Anger and sniper fire simmered throughout the night and tempers were high when the surrounded private guards and strikebreakers surrendered. As they were marched toward Herrin, the scabs were beaten, insulted, and harassed. Witnesses later testified that an unknown person yelled out that the scabs should be killed. One of the first to be killed was McDowell, and as the procession approached a wooded area and a barbed-wire fence, strikebreakers were told to run for their lives. A melee ensued in which fleeing scabs were fired upon. Those who escaped were pursued, and gunfire and execution-style killings continued into the morning of June 22. In all, 19 strikebreakers and two UMW members were killed. No law enforcement officials ever appeared, and Sheriff Thaxton reportedly slept through the entire massacre. By the time he appeared at his office at 8 A.M., two hours late for a meeting with Hunter, 21 men were dead.

National sentiment was overwhelmingly against the UMW, though several observers felt that all of Herrin was culpable. President Warren G. Harding expressed his outrage, but the overall chaos of the situation was such that responsibility was nearly impossible to determine. A board of inquest determined that all victims died by the hands of unknown assailants. Eventually 214 indictments were issued, but no one was convicted of any sort of crime. The Herrin massacre is a stain on organized labor's record, albeit an exceedingly rare blemish. Although workers often **sabotaged** property during labor disputes and gunfire exchanges during mine strikes were not unusual, labor was usually on the defensive in such violent outbursts. The Herrin massacre did little to advance the UMW's cause, but rather was cited as justifying organized capital's assault on unions during the 1920s. Oddly enough, the Herrin massacre was quickly forgotten. The UMW naturally wished to distance itself from association with the violence, but organized capital had equally little desire to advertise the fact that scab labor had met such a bloody end.

Suggested Reading

Paul M. Angle, *Bloody Williamson: A Chapter in American Lawlessness*, 1992; David Goldberg, *Discontented America: The United States in the 1920s*, 1999; Chatland Parker, *The Herrin Massacre: A Fair and Impartial Statement of All the Facts; The Trial, Evidence, Verdict*, 1922.

HIGHLANDER FOLK CENTER. *See* Labor Colleges.

HILL, JOE

Joe Hill (October 7, 1879?–November 19, 1915), born Joel Haggland and also known as Joseph Hillstrom, was a songwriter for the **Industrial Workers of the**

World (IWW or **Wobblies**) and a member of that organization. In the history of **music and labor**, Hill is probably the most famous songwriter of all time. His compositions include "Union Maid," "The Preacher and the Slave," "There Is Power in a Union," "Casey Jones, the Union Scab," "Mr. Block," and "The Rebel Girl," the last composition being Hill's tribute to **Elizabeth Gurley Flynn**.

Details of Hill's personal life are sketchy and, in many ways, the legend of Joe Hill has been more valuable to labor organizers than the reality of his life. He was born Joel Emmanuel Haggland in Gavle, Sweden, one of nine children to Olof and Margaerta Haggland. His father was a railroad worker who died when Joel was eight. Joel's formal education ended early, as he was forced to work to help keep his family afloat. He worked in a rope factory, shoveled coal for a construction firm, and was rumored to have been a seaman. Three of his siblings died before he was age 10, and Joel almost perished when he contracted tuberculosis at age 12. He survived the disease, but several operations left him with distinguishable nose and neck scars. He supposedly learned English at the YMCA in Gavle and perfected his language skills on ships plying the North Sea between Sweden and England. He may have started going by the name of "Joe" at this time. When his mother died in 1901, Joel and his brother Paul decided to immigrate to the United States, landing in New York in October 1902.

Very little is known about Hill until he surfaced at a 1910 IWW-led dock strike in San Pedro, California. Fragmentary evidence suggests that he drifted first to Cleveland, then to the West Coast, where he worked aboard merchant ships and as a longshoreman. At some point he went by the name of Joseph Hillstrom. Exactly why he changed his name is unknown, though it was common at the time for immigrants to adopt more "Americanized" names, either by choice or because others imposed them. From there it was an easy transition to "Joe Hill," which was probably first a pen name. One unconfirmed story holds that Joel Haggland was a vagrant and thief who changed his name to escape from the notoriety of several minor arrests. Equally speculative is how Hill came to be associated with the Wobblies. The IWW had been founded in 1905, and it placed early emphasis on recruiting roustabouts, migrant workers, and other semiskilled and unskilled workers deemed unworthy of notice by the **American Federation of Labor** (AFL). Hill may have been among that teeming labor underclass targeted by the IWW's Overalls Brigade to lead free-speech fights across the West. Numerous towns fearful of radical groups adopted ordinances designed to limit public speech and the size of gatherings. From 1907 through 1916, the IWW conducted at least 30 separate free-speech campaigns to protect basic constitutional rights. Hill's song "The Preacher and the Slave" indirectly and humorously addresses the attempts made in some towns to exempt religious groups like the Salvation Army from newly passed ordinances. Such hypocrisy was challenged and lampooned by the IWW.

For reasons unknown, the IWW's revolutionary fervor found a receptive audience in Hill. The few contemporary accounts of Hill describe him as distant and cynical. How many IWW actions Hill actually took part in is as speculative as most of his biography, though it appears he participated in the San Pedro strike in 1910, an ill-fated 1911 attempt to overthrow the Mexican government and make Lower

California a workers' commune, and the 1912 San Diego free-speech battle. His first piece for the IWW was a 1910 letter to the IWW journal *Industrial Worker*, in which he claimed to be a member of a Portland, Oregon, local. He was said to have spent 30 days in a San Pedro jail for vagrancy, though the police claimed he was a robbery suspect whom they were forced to release for lack of evidence. Hill also claimed he was beaten by police during the 1911 Fresno free-speech campaign.

Hill was a self-taught musician who dabbled with violin, piano, and guitar. He claimed that his songs were based on "scribbles," his notes on his travels and of labor struggles. In 1910, Hill's "Workers of the World, Awaken" was published in an IWW newspaper; it may have been his first published song contribution to the Wobblies. Like many labor songwriters, Hill's favorite tactic was to take an existing tune and set new lyrics to it. Since much labor singing was done on **picket** lines, known tunes made it easier for strikers to learn new songs. For example, Hill's "There Is Power in a Union" used the music of the well-known gospel song "There Is Power in the Blood," and "The Preacher and the Slave" was a lyrical adaptation of "Sweet Bye and Bye." Labor songwriters frequently used church music, though only a handful did so with the irreverence and skill of Wobbly bards such as Hill. By 1913, Hill enjoyed minor fame for his songs, several of which appeared in print to support ongoing IWW struggles.

In that year, Hill went to Utah, perhaps to work in the Park City silver mines. He was living in a Salt Lake City boarding house on January 10, 1914, when two masked men entered a local grocery store. The ensuing gun battle left owner John Morrison and his son, Arling, dead. (Some sources give the son's name as Alving.) A second son, Merlin, saw two men fleeing the store when he rushed to assist his father and brother. Police investigators concluded—though the only material evidence to support the hypothesis were a few bloodspots in an outside alley—that Arling had wounded one of the assailants. They also speculated that a vendetta was involved, as John Morrison's wounds were made at close range and no money was taken from the cash register.

The night, Joe Hill was treated for a gunshot wound, which he told Dr. Frank McHugh had resulted from a jealous fight over a woman. Hill was carrying a gun at the time, though he allegedly tossed it into a field during the carriage ride back to his boarding house. When Dr. McHugh heard that police were seeking a wounded suspect in the Morrison murders, he dutifully notified them of his treatment of Hill's wounds. Officers rushed to the boarding house, awoke Hill from his sleep, and shot him in the hand as he reached for his trousers. Rather than treat Hill's wound, police charged him with the Morrison murders and imprisoned him. Hill remained in jail for five months, awaiting trial. Once Hill's identity and IWW affiliation became known, public sentiment ran high to convict Hill. The Wobblies were especially feared in Utah, a state where anti-union feelings were strong and where the Mormon Church controlled much of the state's political and social life. Hill acted as his own counsel during his arraignment hearing, but was given two court-appointed attorneys for the trial that opened on June 10, 1914. Hill fired both of his lawyers midway through the trial, after an outburst in which he claimed they were in cahoots with the prosecutor. Toward the end of the trial,

O. N. Hilton, a lawyer with experience in defending miners, was appointed as Hill's counsel, though Hill apparently seldom followed Hilton's advice.

Hill sealed his own fate, either by deciding to represent himself or by taking bad advice from Hilton. (The latter seems implausible given Hilton's hitherto stellar record.) The prosecution's case was weak, relying entirely on the timing of Hill's gunshot wounds and two shaky eyewitness accounts claiming that Hill's tuberculosis-ravaged face matched that of a man seen fleeing Morrison's store. Missing from the account was the fact that Morrison was involved in a shootout months before and had told police that his attackers were trying to settle an old grudge from Morrison's days on the police force. No murder weapon was produced, nor did Dr. McHugh retrieve a bullet when he treated Hill's wounds. But Hill did not acquit himself well, either. He never took the stand in his own defense, his alibi was shaky, and his refusal to name his assailant or the woman in question made his story appear even more dubious. His gallant claim that he was defending a woman's honor was out of keeping with known aspects of his character, and his steadfast refusal to provide more details of his alleged domestic quarrel as the firing squad loomed suggests that either Hill was guilty as charged or he longed for a martyr's death. After a 10-day trial, a jury convicted Hill of both murders, and he was sentenced to death. Hill was allowed to choose between hanging or the firing squad, and chose the latter.

With his execution nearing, Hill's case received much more attention than it had previously attracted. The Wobblies defended Hill and accused "copper bosses" and the Mormon church of framing Hill. The IWW spent so much on Hill's appeals that it had very little money left to assist Wobblies elsewhere with their own legal woes. The case received worldwide publicity, with more than 10,000 letters and telegrams flooding state capital offices when the Utah Supreme Court refused to hear Hill's appeal. Death threats were levied against Utah governor William Spry. But Hill again did nothing to assist his own cause. He refused to give any more details of his shooting to the Board of Pardons when it met on September 18 and sat idly as protests erupted around the country. In his final days, luminaries such as the Swedish ambassador to the United States, the AFL's **Samuel Gompers**, and Virginia Snow Stephen, the daughter of the president of the Mormon Church, appealed for clemency, but President Woodrow Wilson refused to grant it. Before he faced the firing squad on November 19, 1915, Hill penned a note to the IWW's **William Haywood** urging him, "Don't waste any time mourning. Organize!"

That advice quickly became an IWW slogan, and it factored prominently in the song "Joe Hill," penned by poet Alfred Hayes and composer Earl Robinson in 1925, which entered the folk-music canon and remains a staple of that genre. At his request, Hill's body was removed from Utah. He was cremated, and small packets of his ashes were distributed to be cast across the world and the United States (except Utah). In death, Hill became a martyr and a legend. In IWW lore, Hill, Frank Little, and Wesley Everett stand as testaments of organized capital's resolve to smash the IWW. (Little was lynched by vigilantes in Butte, Montana, in 1917, and Everett died in a shootout with American Legion thugs in the **Centralia massacre** in Washington in 1919.) Given that "reasonable doubt" is the standard of

American jurisprudence, Hill's conviction is troubling, though his case is hardly on par with egregious miscarriages of justice like the executions of alleged **Molly Maguires**, the **Haymarket** anarchists, or Sacco and Vanzetti. The best available evidence suggests that Hill was a flawed individual, perhaps the petty thief and murderer his prosecutors claimed. But he was also an enormously talented songwriter, whose works and life—mythical or true—have aided organizing efforts. His songs were published in the IWW's *Little Red Songbook*, and several found their way into organized labor's permanent canon.

Suggested Reading

William D. Adler, *The Man Who Never Deid: The Life, Times, and Legacy of Joe Hill, American Labor Icon*, 2011; Joe Hill Project, http://www.joehill.org/, accessed December 7, 2010; Joyce Kornbluh, ed., *Rebel Voices: An I.W.W. Anthology*, 1988; Gibbs Smith, *Joe Hill*, 1984.

HILLMAN, SIDNEY

Sidney Hillman (March 23, 1887–July 10, 1946) was the president of the Amalgamated Clothing Workers of America (ACWA), a key leader in the early days of the **Congress of Industrial Organizations** (CIO), and an advisor to President Franklin Roosevelt.

Hillman was born into a Jewish family in Zagare, Lithuania, the son of Schmuel and Judith (Paikin) Hillman. As a child, he gained a reputation for possessing an acute memory and was able to recall long sections of the Talmud effortlessly. His parents hoped he would become a rabbi, but instead his studies in economics brought him into contact with a **Marxist** study group. This association led him into involvement with the Bund, a (secular and **socialist**) Jewish labor group in Russia. Hillman was involved with trade unions as a young man, and spent eight months in jail during 1904–1905 for taking part in a **May Day** protest. Upon his release he took part in an abortive 1905 revolution in Russia. When the czar launched pogroms and began jailing dissidents, Hillman fled to England in 1906.

The following year he immigrated to the United States. Hillman settled first in Chicago, where he worked in a warehouse and later as a retail clerk. Eventually, like many other Jewish immigrants, he gravitated toward the garment industry, where he **apprenticed** as a garment cutter. He was working for industry giant Hart, Schaffner, and Marx in 1910, when a strike broke out. Hillman was able to use his skills as an agitator and organizer to help bring order to the citywide walkout of more than 45,000 garment workers. The strike reached an ambiguous end, and Hillman was part of a group that split from the United Garment Workers (UGW), an overly cautious affiliate of the **American Federation of Labor** (AFL). Hillman became the **business agent** for a rival organization.

During the 1910 strike, Hillman met Bessie Aranowitz (1889–1971), an activist in the **International Ladies' Garment Workers' Union** (ILGWU). Hillman took a post with the ILGWU in 1914, and Aranowitz and Hillman married in 1916. The two were a good match, and each agreed that the UGW was an ineffective union. Later in 1914, Hillman's local garment cutters union merged with several others to create the ACWA; Hillman was elected its first president. Although the ACWA grew steadily and benefited greatly from capital/labor accords during World War I, the AFL did not recognize it until 1933. The ACWA often found itself not only battling employers, but also fending off **raiding** from both the AFL and the **Industrial Workers of the World** (IWW). In addition, organized crime groups active in the garment trades threatened ACWA locals in the 1920s, and the rise of the Communist Party of the United States (CPUSA) led to a new contender for the loyalty of garment workers.

To combat such challenges, the ACWA under Hillman actively promoted **social unionism**. The group set up union cooperatives, banks, and **cooperative** housing units. In an unusual move for the time, the ACWA even offered **unemployment** insurance for members and, in 1920, became the first national union to advocate a five day work week. Hillman, who was still a socialist at this juncture, also helped establish a short-lived ACWA factory in Russia. The latter experiment bought temporary peace between the ACWA and the CPUSA, but Hillman eventually tempered his youthful radicalism, and he utterly rejected revolutionary ideology. The experience of World War I deepened Hillman's beliefs that the interests of capital and labor could be reconciled. Also unusual for the 1920s was Hillman's willingness to accept modified **Taylorism** as a more efficient way of producing garments and textiles.

By the late 1920s, Hillman battled declining ACWA membership in the wake of an anti-union climate and the ACWA's battles against organized crime. The election of Franklin Roosevelt in 1932 and the passage of the National Industrial Recovery Act led to a revival of ACWA fortunes and to affiliation with the AFL in 1933, though the ACWA's **industrial unionism** and the AFL's control by **craft unionists** were an ill fit from the start. Hillman was, however, an enthusiastic supporter of the New Deal. By this time Hillman—once an advocate of a separate **labor party**—had further tempered his views and cast his lot with the Democratic Party. Roosevelt appointed him to the National Recovery Board in 1933, the first of several New Deal political posts he would hold. Hillman is often credited with helping craft such landmark bills as the **National Labor Relations Act** and the **Fair Labor Standards Act**.

Hillman's political clout exceeded the power he held within the AFL. He was an early ally of **John L. Lewis** and was one of the cofounders of the 1935 Committee for Industrial Organizing, the renegade faction within the AFL that eventually bolted and formed the rival CIO. In 1937, Hillman became vice president of the CIO. He used ACWA resources to set up union organizing committees for steel, rubber, retail, and autoworkers. Hillman was also influential in helping textile workers rebound from their loss in a 1934 nationwide strike. ACWA money helped underwrite the Textile Workers Organizing Committee, which, in 1939, became the Textile Workers Union of America (TWUA).

Hillman was an essential aide to President Roosevelt during the World War II era. He served on three wartime presidential commissions during World War II, and was co-chair of the Office of Production Management. His most lasting achievement came in 1943, when Hillman founded the CIO's political action committee (PAC) to support President Roosevelt's reelection bid. The CIO's PAC is widely considered the first such political fundraising organ of its ilk, though PACs are now a standard feature in American politics. Hillman became so associated with government/labor cooperation that he was sometimes criticized by more militant leaders for becoming too cautious. Hillman and Lewis became estranged when Lewis turned against Roosevelt and the New Deal. Hillman took flak in 1941, when he spoke out against **United Auto Workers of America** members striking a North American Aviation plant, and in 1943, when he opposed the **United Mine Workers'** refusal to abide by a wartime **no-strike pledge**. Hillman's 1945 role in setting up the World Federation of Trade Unions is sometimes cited as leading organized labor down an ill-advised path of **Cold War** unionism that made organized labor subservient to U.S. foreign policy objectives.

Political conservatives also attacked Hillman. Both he and the CIO's PAC were thoroughly investigated by the Federal Bureau of Investigation, though those investigations came long after he had repudiated radicalism and the TWUA operated according to conventional trade-union precepts. Hillman died suddenly at his home on Long Island in 1946. In 1950, the Sidney Hillman Foundation was created to grant annual prizes for those who gain distinction in public service and social justice. In 1992, Hillman was elected to the Labor Hall of Fame.

Suggested Reading

Melech Epstein, *Profiles of Eleven*, 1965; Steve Fraser, *Labor Will Rule*, 1991; Matthew Josephson, *Sidney Hillman: Statesman of American Labor*, 1952.

HOFFA, JAMES RIDDLE

James Riddle ("Jimmy") Hoffa (February 14, 1913–July (?) 1975/1982?) was the controversial president of the International Brotherhood of Teamsters (IBT; widely known as just the **Teamsters**) from 1957 to 1971. His very name continues to evoke the corruption that plagued parts of the union movement in the post-World War II period.

James Hoffa was the son of John C. and Viola (Riddle) Hoffa. His father was a coal driller who died of lung cancer when Hoffa was seven. The remnants of his family moved to Detroit, and Hoffa was forced to leave school at age 14 to help support his mother's meager laundress's income. He worked as a stock boy until 1930, and got fired when he and four coworkers tried to organize a warehouse laborers' union. In 1936, Hoffa married Josephine Poszywak, with whom he had two children, Barbara and James Hoffa, Jr.

In 1934, Hoffa joined the IBT. The Teamsters were then among the nation's more progressive unions, organizing warehouse workers and chauffeurs as well as truckers. The IBT was also among labor's more militant unions, with members in the upper Midwest often espousing **Trotskyist** views. Hoffa rose quickly in the IBT ranks, holding numerous offices within the organization. He was elected president of his local in 1937 and helped organize the Central States Drivers Council to coordinate regional policy and set rates for drivers and handlers. Hoffa also gained a reputation for his fiery temper and his willingness to resort to fisticuffs. In 1942, he became president of the Michigan Conference of Teamsters. In 1952, he became IBT vice president, at a time in which the Teamsters were being investigated for alleged links to organized crime and its president, Dave Beck, stood accused of looting more than $300,000 from the IBT treasury. Although Beck assumed the IBT presidency in 1952, Hoffa was the de facto head of the IBT for much of the time that Beck was under investigation. Despite the union's woes, Beck and Hoffa were spectacularly successful in building the Teamsters from a union that had around 420,000 members when World War II began, to one with more than 1 million members by the 1950s.

Hoffa himself was accused of bribing a U.S. Senate investigator in 1957. He was acquitted of the charge and became IBT president that same year, when Beck was jailed for corruption. The Teamsters were expelled from the **American Federation of Labor-Congress of Industrial Organizations** (AFL-CIO) in 1957, but Hoffa shrugged it off and continued to build the union. His tenure was marked by controversy from the start, with his detractors claiming he borrowed freely from union pension funds, further tied the IBT to organized crime, and cooperated with extortion schemes. But Hoffa also streamlined the IBT bureaucracy and skillfully negotiated a 1964 regional contract for freight haulers that was the IBT's first national agreement. With that contract, Hoffa had the ability to bring the trucking industry to a standstill—power he used to win **wage** increases and generous **fringe benefits** for the Teamsters' rank-and-file. The Teamsters grew to become the nation's largest union and was so powerful that even IBT members who believed that Hoffa was corrupt admired his acumen in improving conditions and wages for union members.

Hoffa's union activities were relentlessly investigated, especially by Democrats. He was pursued by U.S. Attorney General Robert Kennedy with such vigor that an unfounded rumor implicated Hoffa in the assassination of Kennedy's superior, his brother President John Kennedy. Hoffa, who flirted with Trotskyism in his youth, did switch allegiance to the Republican Party, and the IBT became one of the few unions in the nation to endorse GOP candidates. In 1964, Hoffa was convicted of jury tampering, fraud, and conspiracy and sentenced to 13 years in prison. After three years of appeals, he entered a federal penitentiary, although he refused to give up the presidency of the IBT until 1971. That year, President Richard Nixon pardoned Hoffa after Hoffa promised that he would not seek another IBT office until 1980.

Privately, Hoffa felt that his former protégé and acting president, Frank Fitzsimmons, was plotting to rid the IBT of his presence. Upon his release, Hoffa worked to rebuild his power base. On July 30, 1975, he attended a business luncheon in Bloomfield, Michigan, at which several alleged organized-crime figures were in attendance. Hoffa was never seen again. Allegations and rumors abounded, and the FBI investigated leads for seven years, but turned up nothing. Hoffa was declared legally dead in 1982. His disappearance remains an unresolved mystery; scores of theories have been proposed to explain his presumed demise, despite the fact that there is little tangible evidence to substantiate any of them.

Corruption and racketeering charges plagued the IBT for decades after Hoffa's disappearance. It was not until the 1990s that the IBT began to rehabilitate its image, though it no longer wields the power it did when Hoffa ran the organization. His children have tried to rehabilitate their father's image, and in 1998, James Hoffa, Jr., became IBT president.

Suggested Reading

Steven Brill, *The Teamsters*, 1978; Joseph Franco and Richard Hammer, *Hoffa's Man*, 1989; Robert Kennedy et al., *The Enemy Within*, 1982; Dan Moldea, *The Hoffa Wars: Teamsters, Rebels, Politicians, and the Mob*, 1993.

HOMESTEAD STEEL LOCKOUT AND STRIKE

The Homestead Steel strike of 1892 took place 11 miles from the center of Pittsburgh, Pennsylvania, and is among the most infamous strikes in American labor history. It pitted organized labor against Andrew Carnegie, reputedly the world's richest man at the time. Although Carnegie cultivated an image as a philanthropist and a friend of labor, Homestead revealed the limitations of his charity and further exposed the excesses to which unregulated business could fall prey. It was among the traumatic events of the 1890s that presaged **Progressive Era** reform.

Carnegie purchased the Homestead plant in 1888 and converted it into the showpiece for Carnegie Steel. The 1892 **lockout** and **strike** were precipitated by Carnegie's relentless drive to contain labor costs, though such penny-pinching was out of keeping with his well-publicized insistence that rich industrialists had a social obligation to disperse their wealth and to uplift the masses. Carnegie was traveling in Scotland when the strike began, and had left the Homestead works under the supervision of Henry Clay Frick, a man who had made his fortune converting coal into coke for the steel-making process. Carnegie's absence allowed him to disavow responsibility for the brutality that ensued, but he knew of and acceded to everything that took place.

In 1881, Carnegie and Frick formed a partnership and Frick served as general manager of many of Carnegie's manufacturing concerns. Unlike Carnegie, Frick seldom pretended to be a friend of labor; the events of 1892 would win him the sobriquet "America's most hated man." Skilled workers were represented by the Amalgamated Association of Iron and Steel Workers (AAISW), who had struck the works successfully in both 1882 and 1889. Frick was determined to deskill steel making and in so doing break the power of **craft unionism**. By 1892, the AAISW represented just 800 of Homestead's 3,800 employees, though it did possess a healthy treasury and commanded the respect on non-union workers. Frick baited the AAISW by negotiating with the union for five months before making an offer that included an 18 percent wage decrease. Workers naively believed that if they could only contact Carnegie, he would intervene on their behalf with Frick; they remained unaware that Carnegie had given his approval to Frick's plan to break the union. At the end of April Frick announced that if the AAISW did not settle within 29 days, he would consider the union illegitimate and cease future negotiations. He also began to plan for the eventuality of a strike, and soon the Homestead works was dubbed "Fort Frick" because of the barbed wire and guard emplacements that ringed it.

On the evening of June 28, 1892, Frick closed the plant and locked out the workers. An official strike vote was taken on June 30 and the AAISW enlisted support from other organizations in the region, including the **Knights of Labor** and four other Carnegie concerns, which launched **sympathy strikes** in support of the Homestead workers. Frick hired 300 armed **Pinkerton** detectives to guard the Homestead facility and as a prelude to bringing in **scabs** to resume steel production. Getting them to Homestead would prove the flaw in his plan. Workers determined to keep the plant closed had driven away previous strike-breakers, so Frick planned to bring them into the plant via the Monongahela River, which backed onto the plant. On July 5, Pinkertons were loaded onto two barges and were towed toward Homestead. As the Pinkertons arrived in the early morning, they were met by rowboats and a steamboat filled with workers intent upon preventing the Pinkertons from disembarking. There were also thousands of armed workers, friends, and families on the shore and, at one point, a cannon was commandeered to battle the Pinkertons. Residents also broke down Frick's barriers and surged onto the Homestead works to fire on Pinkertons from the intended landing site. Although tossed dynamite missed its mark and attempts to set the river afire failed, the day-long fight cost the lives of nine local residents and seven Pinkertons. Hired tugboats sailed off and left the Pinkertons adrift and, in the early afternoon, they surrendered upon receiving promise of safe passage out of town. They had to endure the indignities of marching through a gauntlet of angry townspeople and several were badly beaten, but they were allowed to withdraw.

For the next several days workers controlled the Homestead site. On July 12, Pennsylvania Governor Robert E. Pattison sent National Guardsmen to the town. At first the troops were greeted warmly as workers mistakenly hoped they had come to restore order. Instead, Pattison imposed martial law, displaced **pickets**, and allowed Frick and other company officials to reenter the plant. Frick proceeded with his plan to hire scabs and troops fought off worker attempts to reoccupy Homestead. Among the uglier incidents in the days to come was a July 22 race riot between displaced white workers and black strikebreakers. The strike and the AAISW were broken.

There was a final act to the Homestead fiasco. On July 23, **anarchist** Alexander Berkman, the paramour of **Emma Goldman**, attempted to assassinate Frick. He managed to shoot Frick three times, including in the neck, but Frick survived. Neither Berkman nor Goldman had any connection with the strike, but Homestead officials seized upon the attack to link the union movement with anarchy. Several union leaders were arrested and tried on a variety of charges; though all were acquitted, they were **blacklisted** by the steel industry. Homestead ended in a rout. The strike was not officially lifted until November 17, but it was effectively over by the end of July and it would be another 40 years before effective unionism came to the steel industry.

The state militia enters Homestead, Pennsylvania, after violence between steel workers and Pinkerton agents erupted when Andrew Carnegie and Henry C. Frick locked out workers rather than negotiate. (Library of Congress)

In 1901, Andrew Carnegie sold his company, which produced one-third of all American steel, to J. P. Morgan for $480 million. Carnegie devoted the rest of his life to giving away his money, much of it going to build public libraries for the self-improvement of working men and women. His critics never forgave him for his actions and insensitivity at Homestead. Many saw him as a **social Darwinist** posing as a philanthropist. In the immediate aftermath of the Homestead lockout and strike, Carnegie and Frick quarreled bitterly over business matters. When, toward the end of his life, Carnegie sought to mend relations, Frick reportedly replied, "Tell Mr. Carnegie I'll meet him in hell, where we are both going."

Suggested Reading

Jeremy Brecher, *Strike!*, 1999; David Brody, *Steelworkers in America: The Nonunion Era*, 1969; David P. Demarest, ed., *"The River Ran Red:" Homestead, 1898*, 1992; Paul Krause, *The Battle for Homestead, 1890–1892: Politics, Culture, and Steel*, 1992.

HOMEWORK

Homework, also known as the "putting-out" system, is a controversial labor practice in which contractors and subcontractors finish goods in a satellite location separate from the employer's factory. This step often takes place inside a private residence—hence the name. Those engaging in homework are often paid **piecework** rates rather than an hourly **wage**. Although workers engaged in homework have greater flexibility concerning work hours, child care, and other domestic responsibilities, critics decry the homework system as one that forces individuals to labor for long hours, often for less than **minimum wage**. Much of this criticism stems from the fact that, historically, homework has been integral to the **sweatshop** system, especially in the needletrades industries. Technically, a sweatshop is a substandard workplace in which numerous people work in a shop-like setting, whereas homework involves a single family inside a private dwelling. However, because the two were often intertwined and shared in common their exploitation of labor, they are often paired. For much of the 19th century and part of the 20th century, entire families—especially those of recent immigrants—toiled long hours for sustenance-level pay. Homework was among the most exploitative forms of **child labor** in the United States.

The takeoff phase of the **Industrial Revolution** built upon early expansion of the cotton textile and woolen industries. The expansion of **capitalism** in the post-**Civil War** period was accompanied by a massive influx of immigration. Although many gravitated to factories and to unskilled and semiskilled industrial jobs, some immigrants encountered intense nativism and found it difficult to secure factory employment. Homework was often the pursuit of workers with whom Caucasians refused to work, such as Chinese and African American workers. Among the numerous homework options were finishing garments, rolling cigars, sewing collars and sleeves onto shirts, laundering, making artificial flowers, adorning hats, taking sales orders, and packaging goods. Employers frequently encouraged the practice of homework, as it constituted a secondary labor pool upon which they could draw in times of high demand and the very existence of such a surplus helped contain labor costs.

Labor unions have long supported laws outlawing homework. Because homework depresses wage rates and because it often involved children, much of it was greatly curtailed by the **National Labor Relations Act**. The at act did not eliminate the practice, however, and many workers continue to toil under conditions that do not comply with safety codes outlined by the **Occupational Safety and Health Administration**. Homework has proved hard to control as new waves of immigrants have perpetuated it. In recent years, university and college students have launched protests when they learned that much of their school's logo-ware is produced in homework and sweatshop conditions where workers toil for a pittance. In 2010, for example, student protests led to increased pay for El Salvadoran immigrants working on logo goods in South Carolina. The campaign against homework and sweatshops is complicated by the fact that some home workers, especially in rural areas, complain that anti-homework and anti-sweatshop laws restrict their freedom of contract rights, and that they willingly take on sewing jobs and other homework. In addition, much homework takes place off the record and/or surreptitiously. Recent investigations of Chinese immigrant labor reveal that many continue to toil under 19th-century conditions. The biggest challenge is that homework is easily moved offshore, far from the reach of American labor law. The ubiquity of computers and electronic communications systems now makes it possible to do everything from taking phone orders to reading x-rays to offering technical support from any location. Industrial homework remains a fixture of North American production, despite efforts to eliminate it.

Suggested Reading

AFL-CIO Now Blog, http://blog.aflcio.org/tag/united-students-against-sweatshops/, accessed December 13, 2010; Hugh Hindman, *Child Labor: An American History*, 2002; Elizabeth Kolbert, "The Unfashionable Mr. Lam," *Mother Jones* (September/October 2001); Alan Kraut, *The Huddled Masses: The Immigrant in American Society 1880–1921*, 2001.

HORMEL STRIKE AND LOCKOUT

The Hormel strike and lockout was one of a series of defeats suffered by organized labor in the 1980s, though some observers feel this one was self-induced. It involved a struggle of meatpackers in Austin, Minnesota, that pitted them against the George A. Hormel Company, the state of Minnesota, and their own international union.

Meatpacking, like many industries in the late 1970s and early 1980s, was hit by employer demands for **concessions**. Aging plants closed, and some jobs were lost, but corporate claims that concessions were necessary to maintain competitiveness were seen as specious, given that corporations faced little threat from imports. Nonetheless, the **United Food and Commercial Workers Union** (UFCWU) cooperated in a wave of **wage** and **fringe benefits** cutting, in some cases breaking intact **pattern bargains** to grant them. The Department of Labor noted that average wages in the industry fell from $9.19 per hour in 1982 to $7.93 per hour in January 1985. The UFCWU justified this decline as a job-saving measure and it ignored other worker complaints, including on-the-line practices associated with repetitive strain injury.

The wisdom of UFCWU policy was sorely tested in Austin, Minnesota. Unlike aging Chicago and Kansas City facilities, the Hormel plant in Austin was a state-of-the-art facility, having just opened in 1982. Workers there were affiliated with UFCWU Local P-9 and were covered by three separate agreements, one of which included a **no-strike pledge**, though it also included a promise that wages would not be cut prior to the contract's expiration in August 1985. Workers adhered to contract provisions, despite the fact that the Austin plant employed a **speedup** and had a poor safety record. Nonetheless, Hormel began to demand concessions and in October 1984 slashed wages from $10.69 to $8.25 per hour, even though it had just declared a $29 million annual profit. Local P-9 president Jim Guyette spoke out against concessions, even as the UFCWU continued to negotiate wage cuts across the industry. A UFCWU-negotiated agreement with Hormel workers in Ottumwa, Iowa, further undercut P-9's efforts to restore cuts. P-9 continued to honor its no-strike pledge, but it also launched an aggressive pressure campaign against Hormel that involved organizing workers' wives, high school students, and retirees. The cornerstone of P-9's strategy was hiring a firm to engage in a **corporate campaign** against Hormel; Roy Rogers of Corporate Campaign Incorporated (CCI) came to Austin to direct these efforts.

The presence of CCI led to conflict with the UFCWU, with both president William Wynn and packinghouse division chief Lewie Anderson coming to see P-9 as comprising dangerous dissidents prone to **wildcat** actions. In the meantime, CCI targeted banks with ties to Hormel and helped P-9 with its public relations campaign. It also unearthed agreements between Hormel and the apartheid government of South Africa and was able to elicit support for the workers from the African National Congress.

On August 17, 1985, P-9 workers walked off the job after more than 90 percent of the rank-and-file approved the strike. Because it came at the end of the contract and was thus a legal strike, the UFCWU was constitutionally obligated to provide strike funds, though Anderson and Wynn worked to undermine P-9. In January 1986, the UFCWU openly denounced the strike and P-9 leader Guyette, going so far as to resort to red-baiting. To UFCWU officials, clashes between strikers and members of the Minnesota National Guard were further indications of a situation spiraling out of control. Anderson even denounced Guyette on network television. The net effect of the UFCWU's assault on its own local was to tear Austin apart internally. The strike's **solidarity** was broken, and some workers returned to their jobs. In some cases, families were torn asunder over the question of whether to return to work. P-9 offered to return to work if Hormel agreed to rehire workers based on seniority, but the company spurned its offer. It had begun to introduce **scabs** in late January 1986, whom it insisted were permanent replacement workers.

The clash between P-9 and the UFCWU came to a head on March 13, 1985, when the parent union withdrew official sanction of the strike as well as all strike funds. This maneuver turned the strike, at least technically, into a **lockout**. P-9 gamely continued, and it garnered tremendous support from other unions and from activists such as the Reverend Jesse Jackson. In June, however, the UFCWU seized P-9 offices and records in Austin and placed the union in trusteeship. It even diverted funds raised by P-9 to replenish its own coffers. Approximately 80 percent of the 1,500 strikers lost their jobs. In September 1986, the UFCWU negotiated a contract with Hormel that raised wages to $10.70 per hour, a mere penny higher than the rate obtained in 1979, before the 1984 cuts. Even then Austin workers suffered, as Hormel closed part of the plant and rented it to a firm that paid only $6.50 per hour. The UFCWU was able to use procedural moves to turn aside an attempt by former P-9 members to **decertify** the union.

Since the strike's bleak denouement, scholars and activists have debated its significance. Some argue that the UFCWU's actions were a shameful betrayal of the rank-and-file that highlights the moral bankruptcy of **business unionism**. Several believe that if CCI had not been undermined, its corporate campaign would have been as successful as that used by **Ravenswood** workers. Nearly all scholars interpret the UFCWU's actions as heavy-handed and autocratic.

Defenders of the UFCWU charge that Rogers was self-aggrandizing and the CCI campaign a chimera. They also interpret the actions of Guyette and P-9 as undisciplined, rash, and dangerous. According to this view, the UFCWU was correct to accept short-term losses to bring all packinghouses under a common wage structure. This step allowed the negotiation of a 1986 contract that again raised wages. As noted previously, relatively few scholars accept this position in total.

Still other observers believe that it would not have mattered how P-9 and the UFCWU conducted themselves, as Hormel would not negotiate. The company refused to rehire most of the strikers even though scabs never matched the efficiency of the pre-strike workforce. The decision to close part of the Austin plant is seen as proof that Hormel's real interests were profit maximization and workplace control. In the negative political and economic climate of the mid-1980s, the unions simply had no chance. The real issue, from this perspective, is that no existing labor law prevents the hiring of permanent strikebreakers.

The events in Austin were made into an Academy Award-winning documentary **film** by Barbara Kopple titled *American Dream*. It stands as a powerful testament to the pressures felt by organized labor in the 1980s.

Suggested Reading

Hardy Green, *On Strike at Hormel: The Struggle for a Democratic Labor Movement*, 1991; Kim Moody, *An Injury to All*, 1989; Peter Rachleff, *Hard-Pressed in the Heartland: The Hormel Strike and the Future of the Labor Movement*, 1993.

HOTEL EMPLOYEES AND RESTAURANT EMPLOYEES INTERNATIONAL UNION

The Hotel Employees and Restaurant Employees International Union (HERE) was chartered by the **American Federation of Labor** (AFL) on April 24, 1891. In 2004, it merged with the **Union of Needletrades, Industrial, and Textile Employees** (UNITE). The newly christened UNITE HERE claims to represent approximately 265,000 workers.

HERE was originally a **craft union** that represented bartenders, waiters, cooks, and waitresses. In 1973, the union was reorganized, and **locals** were merged to represent hospitality workers in a variety of settings and occupations. HERE represents hotel and food industry workers as diverse as cooks, servers, cafeteria workers, hotel porters, laundry workers, and employees in airline food service. (UNITE represents mostly textile and apparel workers.)

HERE kept a relatively low profile for much of its early history, in part because the hospitality industry tended to have a higher-than-average turnover, which retarded the development of an activist core. But HERE also has had many **minority workers** in its ranks. In 1960, it was one of the first labor unions to embrace the student sit-in civil rights demonstrators. Other high-profile campaigns included a successful attempt to organized Yale University support staff in 1984. HERE was also one of the first unions to tackle organizing efforts in casinos and, by 1998, had organized more than 40,000 workers in Las Vegas. It enjoyed similar success in Atlantic City casinos in 2005. More recently HERE has been at the fore of immigrant rights campaigns, especially in California and the Southwest, where it has a large number of Latino members. Today it claims to have organized more than 60,000 hotel workers. It is one of the most racially diverse unions in the United States and was the first labor union to endorse the 2008 presidential campaign of Barack Obama. As of 2012, John Wilhelm was president of UNITE HERE. In recent years it has been involved with acrimonious attempts to organize Hyatt Regency housecleaning staff.

UNITE HERE left the **American Federation of Labor-Congress of Industrial Organizations** (AFL-CIO) in 2005 and joined the **Change to Win Federation**, but in 2009 rejoined the AFL-CIO after a bruising **jurisdictional** battle with the **Service Employees International Union** (SEIU). An internal dispute badly weakened the union and left the fate of UNITE HERE's treasury in limbo for several years, though both the internal bickering and the dispute with SEIU were resolved in 2010. Whether UNITE HERE can rebuild its tarnished reputation and overcome its internal difficulties remains to be seen. It lost roughly 180,000 members between 2005 and 2010, and some observers suggest that it may eventually be absorbed by the SEIU.

Suggested Reading

Steven Greenhouse, "Service Unions Agree to End a Long Dispute," *New York Times*, July 26, 2010; Hotel Employees and Restaurant Employees International Union, http://www.unitehere.org/about/, accessed December 13, 2010.

HUERTA, DOLORES

Dolores Huerta (April 10, 1930–) was a cofounder of the **United Farm Workers of America** (UFWA) and is currently a vice president emeritus of that organization.

She was born Dolores Fernandez, one three children of Juan and Alicia (Chavez) Fernandez. Her parents divorced when she was three, and young Dolores moved with her mother and two brothers from New Mexico to Stockton, California. Her mother toiled both as a cannery worker and as a waitress to care for her three children. Huerta took piano, dance, and violin lessons, was a Girl Scout, and sang in her Catholic Church choir. In 1945, her mother remarried James Richards, a Stockton hotel and restaurant owner, with whom she had two more children. Alicia Richards then turned her attention to the business world, and Dolores gained a multicultural perspective through the hotel's numerous Chinese, Filipino, Jewish, and Mexican clients. She also observed numerous down-on-their-luck families, many of whom her mother allowed to lodge free in the hotel. Her labor union awakening came largely through her grandfather, a coal miner who also worked as an itinerant beet harvester.

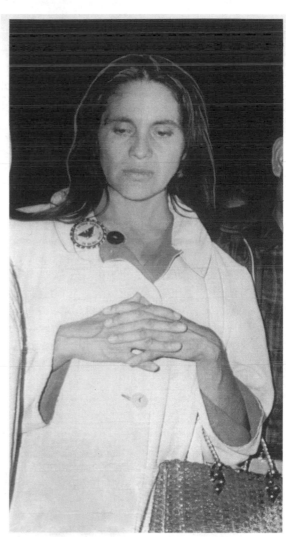

Dolores Huerta is a labor leader and civil rights activist who, along with César Chávez, cofounded United Farm Workers of America. Huerta has received numerous community service awards, including the Presidential Medal of Freedom in 2012. (UPI-Bettmann/Corbis)

A series of unsatisfying post-high school clerical posts led Huerta to enter Stockton College, where she took education courses before marrying. She divorced after the birth of her second daughter and returned to college for an associate's degree and a teaching certificate. In 1955, her concern for impoverished children and a deepening social awareness inspired her to join the Community Service Organization (CSO), a Mexican American social services agency, for which she taught citizenship classes and registered voters. The CSO sent her to Sacramento to lobby on behalf of Latino economic and social causes.

Huerta also concerned herself with the plight of migrant farm workers. She joined the Agricultural Workers Association, a community interest group, and met **César Chávez**, then director of the CSO in California and Arizona. In 1962, she and Chávez formed the National Farm Workers Association (NFWA), the direct progenitor of the UFWA. The NFWA launched the 1965 Delano table **grape boycott** that brought the plight of Latino migrant workers to the public eye. Huerta helped organize the **boycott** on the East Coast, where most of the distributors were located. In 1970, growers signed a contract with the NFWA. In 1968, Huerta helped coordinate the NFWA's entry into the **American Federation of Labor-Congress of Industrial Organizations** as the United Farm Workers of America.

Huerta served in numerous roles with the UFWA, but she also encountered intense sexism from both union members and allied groups such as the Roman Catholic Church. While living in New York City, she met Gloria Steinem and began to incorporate feminism into her labor activities. In the early 1970s, Huerta was also instrumental in organizing boycotts against Gallo wines and against lettuce growers. Her work led California to pass the 1975 **Agricultural Labor Relations Act**, which recognized the right of farm workers to organize and is the most sweeping farm worker legislation in the nation, as most agricultural labor is excluded from the coverage of the **National Labor Relations Act**.

Huerta's activism with the UFWA took a heavy personal toll. She has given birth to 11 children—including four to Richard Chávez, César's brother—but has divorced twice. In 1988, she suffered a ruptured spleen and several broken bones when she was clubbed by San Francisco police during a peaceful protest against presidential candidate George H. W. Bush. She is a **socialist** politically, and a member of Democratic Socialists of America, though she endorsed the failed presidential ambitions of Hillary Clinton during the 2007–2008 campaign. Huerta's devotion to community activism has garnered her several awards, including a Community of Christ International Peace Award. She also operates her own nonprofit foundation, which focuses on community organizing and welfare projects, especially those relating to women and children.

Suggested Reading

Julie Felner, "Dolores Huerta," *Ms.* 8, no. 4 (January/February 1998), 48–49; Mario Garcia, ed., *A Dolores Huerta Reader*, 2008; George Horowitz and Paul Fusco, *La Causa: The California Grape Strike*, 1970; Daniel Rothenberg, *With These Hands: The Hidden World of Migrant Farmworkers Today*, 1998.

IMMIGRANTS AND LABOR

The United States of America is perhaps the most heterogeneous nation-state on earth since the collapse of the Roman Empire. Strictly speaking, any resident whose ancestry is other than **Native American** is a product of immigrant stock, whether recent or not.

Of the various contributions of immigrants to American society there can be little doubt. This became abundantly true when the United States experienced the **Industrial Revolution** in the 19th and 20th centuries. Irish immigrants toiled as canal and railroad builders, often joined by the Chinese in the latter pursuit. The involuntary labor of African and African American **slaves** provided the raw materials for American factories and export trade before 1865, and African Americans after the **Civil War** worked under "Jim Crow" conditions until well into the 20th century. Hungarians and Poles labored in steel mills, Slavs in stockyards, Finns in timber fields, Russian Jews in the garment industry, and Mexican *vaqueros* on the cattle drives that brought animals to market, and immigrants of all sorts manned the factories, docks, farms, and shops that transformed the United States from a weak nation at the start of the 19th century into a world power by century's end. In more recent years, Latino and Asian laborers have been found in many of the **service industry** jobs shunned by other Americans.

Despite their myriad contributions, immigrants have historically experienced racist and nativist discrimination from those groups already entrenched in American society, including the labor movement. As labor historian Herbert Gutman observed, American heterogeneity has not translated into tolerance even though there has been remarkable consistency in the relative experiences of first-generation immigrants to the United States. This is partly because those experiences have been disconnected in time; that is, once a group becomes assimilated into American society, its members have a tendency either to forget or to romanticize their ancestral struggles. This has made labor history complex and hard to generalize. On the one hand, labor unions have often led the way in helping new arrivals adapt to their new homes; on the other hand, some have contributed to discriminatory practices that delayed assimilation.

Historians generally discuss three major "waves" of mass immigration into the United States. The first was a largely preindustrial influx that arrived before the Civil War, which was dominated by newcomers from the British Isles, northern Europe, and the various German states. Many of these individuals settled into independent **agrarian** production, the exceptions being slaves of African origin and the Irish; the latter were heavily concentrated in early industrial production and

German immigrants earn a living making cigars in a New York tenement in the late 1880s. (Photograph by Jacob Riis. Library of Congress)

infrastructure building. Slaves and the Irish also experienced the same sorts of prejudice and discrimination that "second wave" immigrants would suffer.

Between 1870 and 1920, more than 25 million immigrants came to the United States; they and their offspring helped swell the population of the nation from less than 40 million in 1870 to more than 105 million in just 50 years. Unlike earlier immigrants, the bulk of the second wave came from central and southern Europe and brought with them languages, religious beliefs, and cultural customs that the dominant English-speaking Protestant establishment found difficult to embrace. The majority of the new immigrants settled in urban areas and supplied the manpower for the takeoff phase of the Industrial Revolution. The labor of these groups was desired—many employers actively recruited immigrant workers—but the groups themselves faced fierce nativism. Some immigrants found that even the Irish discriminated against them. By the late 19th century the Irish had begun to assimilate into the broader culture and, in cities such as Boston, Chicago, Philadelphia, and New York, they had become part of the political establishment. Ironically, the Irish often joined the nativist chorus condemning new immigrant groups.

This attitude was also evidenced by **labor federations** such as the **Knights of Labor** (KOL) and the **American Federation of Labor** (AFL). Although the KOL membership was heavily Irish American, this federation engaged in vicious attacks on Chinese immigrants and lobbied for the **Chinese Exclusion Act**. Later in his life the KOL's top official **Terence Powderly** worked as an immigration commissioner and issued inflammatory nativist remarks the likes of which were once used against his Irish progenitors. In similar fashion, **Samuel Gompers**, the son of Dutch Jews, often countenanced discriminatory practices among AFL affiliates that he fought to overcome as a young cigar maker. By the same token, both the KOL and the AFL engaged in practices that were incredibly progressive for their time. The KOL's foray into anti-Chinese hysteria was a single blight on its overall campaign to universalize the **working class**. Nativist practices were forbidden among KOL **locals**, the federation's ritual book was translated into numerous languages, and the organization insisted that unskilled black and immigrant laborers be treated no differently than skilled, native-born workers. Inside the AFL, several constituent unions embraced immigrants far in advance of the rest of society.

By the middle of the second wave, several patterns emerged. First, the newest group to arrive generally met with the most derision, which had the ironic effect of improving the status of previously arrived groups. Second, in most cases immigrant groups took three generations to become fully assimilated. Third, as immigrants advanced toward assimilation, two distressing ancillary trends emerged. American assimilation very often entailed enormous amounts of amalgamation in which distinct cultural practices were abandoned or drastically altered to conform to patterns deemed "acceptable" by the elites who defined cultural norms. Related to this was the expectation that assimilating groups would embrace a nativist stance toward newer arrivals. This practice was not difficult to embrace in some cases, as immigrants often came to the United States bearing historic antipathy toward other groups. Many Greeks, for example, were predisposed to distrust Turks, as were Magyars to dislike Russian Jews.

Such nativism was often replicated in the workplace. In the building trades, for example, one often found all-Italian or all-Irish companies and crews. Employers often exploited divisions to deter unionization—a favorite ploy was to fill work crews with individuals who spoke different languages or with members of groups that had historically distrusted one another. The unease prevailing during the second-wave period is partially reflected by the amount of reverse immigration during the period; in some years, for instance, the number of Italians and Greeks leaving the United States outstripped the number of new arrivals. It is also reflected in the way the labor unions responded to new political ideals. Both the KOL and the AFL came to associate **anarchism** and **socialism** with foreign-born radicals and were wary of said views. This perception helps explain why, for instance, the KOL refused to endorse the May 1, 1886, **eight-hour** demonstrations, or to embrace the clemency movement geared toward freeing the **Haymarket bombing** anarchists. It also casts light on the AFL's decision to embrace the permanence of **capitalism** well in advance of other labor groups, and it helps explain the easy public acceptance of crude repression of the **Industrial Workers of the World** (IWW) in the early 20th century. The IWW was viewed by many as a repository of immigrant radicals, of foreign ideologies, and of dangerous antipatriotism when the organization refused to endorse U.S. entry into World War I.

World War I changed the immigration landscape of the United States. The devastation of postwar Europe largely stopped reverse immigration; there was simply little incentive to return to war-ravaged lands. The postwar period also saw a backlash against immigration that culminated in the Johnson-Reid Act of 1924, which dramatically curtailed the number of immigrants coming to the United States and imposed quotas heavily weighted toward northern and western Europe for those who were allowed to enter America. With the collapse of the American economy with the onset of the Great Depression, immigration slowed to a trickle by the 1930s. For organized labor, this trend created opportunities it might not have seized earlier. By the time that **industrial unionism** ideals gathered strength in the 1930s, most second-wave immigrant groups had been assimilated and the barriers erected by employers between these groups had been overcome. The **Congress of Industrial Organizations** (CIO) enjoyed great success with building **solidarity** across ethnic lines and did not have to resort to the great lengths—including the use of multilingual organizers and individual meetings for various language groups—that IWW activists had used just a generation earlier. There was even more acceptance of **communist** and socialist groups, which now appeared more "American." Heritage markers that had once been a barrier were now more easily embraced and compound identities (e.g., Italian American, Irish American, Polish American) became symbols of pride that could be used by clever labor organizers.

The rise of **Cold War** unionism in the postwar period worked against an overall greater acceptance of immigrants by either organized labor or the public at large. The outbreak of a new **Red Scare** returned ideological radicals to the fringes (and drove many underground) and overall immigration levels remained low, which further entrenched the "American" identity of in-place ethnic groups. In fact, it would not be until the 1970s that immigration totals returned to pre-1924 levels. When they did so, old discrimination patterns reemerged. Third-wave immigrants came from different heritages than members of either the first or second wave. The number of Asian immigrants nearly tripled from 1950 to 1960 as Chinese fleeing the communist revolution and Koreans displaced by war joined an already steady stream of Filipinos to America. Even more pronounced was an influx of Mexican immigrants, many of whom settled in the Southwest and West. Roughly 6 million Mexicans emigrated legally between 1961 and 1990, and untold millions more entered the United States illegally. Millions of other immigrants came from the Caribbean, Central America, South America, and southern Asia. The 1986 Simpson-Rodino Act largely reversed the discriminatory biases of the 1924 immigration bill, but it could not erase nativism.

Once again organized labor had to adjust to new demographic realities, and once again the transition was difficult. The response of many AFL-CIO affiliates to the new wave of workers was at first negative, though a few groups, such as the **United Auto Workers of America** (UAW) and the **Service Employees International Union** (SEIU), demonstrated prescience and sought to organize new workers as they would any other employees. The UAW was also among a handful of unions that gave early support to the **United Farm Workers of America** and its efforts to organize Latino field hands. As in the past, though, many workers believed that immigrants threatened their job security. That attitude became more pronounced when the U.S. economy soured in the 1970s and the first effects of **deindustrialization** and **globalism** began to take hold. The AFL-CIO's "Buy American" campaign during the 1970s and 1980s was mostly benign in intent, but many union members choose to interpret it in xenophobic terms. Moreover, the federation's initial response was to lobby for tighter immigration controls and job protection guarantees for established workers. The AFL-CIO was also slow to recognize the extent of the emerging global marketplace. By the end of the 20th century, however, it had largely corrected its course. The SEIU actively organized immigrant workers and showed impressive growth in doing so. By the 21st century, the AFL-CIO had become a strong advocate of immigrant rights and a supporter of hitherto unthinkable initiatives such as amnesty for illegal immigrants and human rights guarantees for non-unionized workers abroad. Among the many ironies of contemporary America is that the AFL-CIO now strands as among the most ardent advocates for immigrant rights in all of American society. That it has become so in the face of declining union membership must be seen as a testament to principle over self-interest.

Will the future entail a decline in nativism and a greater understanding of the American immigrant experience? Perhaps, but the past track record does not suggest that this will be the case. What Gutman observed of immigrants a century ago remains true: The struggles of new groups are discontinuous in time from those of assimilated ethnic groups. One factor that might change the equation is an ongoing demographic shift that will, sometime before mid-century, make those currently classified as minorities a numerical majority in American society.

Suggested Reading

James R. Green, *The World of the Worker*, 1980; Herbert Gutman, *Work and Culture in Industrializing America*, 1976; Immanuel Ness, *Immigrants, Unions, and the New U.S. Labor Market*, 2005.

INDENTURED SERVANT

An indentured servant is a person contracted to work for another for a specified period of time in exchange for services such as paying transportation costs to another country, room and board, land, or training. Indentured servitude was one of the earliest forms of labor exploitation in America. The term derives from the French *dent*, meaning "teeth." In the Anglo-American tradition, identical indenture contracts were written side by side (or top and bottom) and the agreement was torn in half in a ragged, tooth-like pattern. One half was given to the indentured servant and the other half to his or her master. Fitting the two pieces together could authenticate contracts. This was not usually the practice in American colonies, though, as indenture contracts became fairly standard.

Although most 17th-century European nations practiced some form of indentured servitude, the English model had the greatest impact on North American colonies. Many English colonies were established as joint-stock companies expected to earn profits for investors. Those English gentry and lesser nobility immigrating to North American colonies came with no expectation of laboring; that would be the job of servant classes and natives. When attempts to entice **Native Americans** to work or compel them to work as slaves failed, the colonies suffered a labor shortage. The joint-stock companies and landed elites turned to the English poor to meet their labor demands. Population pressures, land enclosure, and increased agricultural yields had created a large subclass of "sturdy beggars" in the British Isles, many of whom were reduced to casual and occasional day labor. A sizable portion of the population lived in dire poverty with few prospects of alleviating their plight. Many poor individuals were recruited to work in the American colonies. In many cases, individuals sold their perspective services to sea captains, who gave money to struggling family members who stayed behind in Britain. The captains, in turn, hoped to resell the contract at a higher price. Between 1620 and 1700, more than 100,000 poor English men and women came to the English colonies as indentured servants. Half of all white settlers outside of New England were either voluntary or involuntary servants. (A substantial number of individuals were forced into indentured servitude to pay off debts that would otherwise have led to imprisonment.)

Many servants faced deplorable conditions in the colonies, and a substantial number starved or died of complications related to poor nutrition and overwork. The situation was particularly dire in Chesapeake Bay colonies, where, until the 1640s, many servants died within a year of arrival. The headright system encouraged their exploitation. Land was reserved for servants who completed their term—usually four to seven years—but those benefits accrued to their sponsors if the servants expired before the contract ended. This knowledge encouraged some ruthless landowners to work servants to death and/or to use scarce food supplies as enticements to make indentured individuals work harder. Those who survived often ended up working as tenant farmers on plantations, as lands reserved as headrights were often of poor quality or remote from existing settlements. In like fashion, numerous indentured servants reached the end of their terms without ever having been taught promised and necessary skills for success. Many servants fled tyrannical masters, and colonial newspapers featured myriad notices of runaways. In rare instances, most notably **Bacon's Rebellion**, indentured servants joined military campaigns aimed at overthrowing colonial political establishments.

Indentured servitude began to decline in importance as colonial nutrition and health conditions improved. African **slavery** largely supplanted the indenture system. Although the first slaves came to Jamestown, Virginia, in 1619, and African slavery was well established in the Caribbean by the 1640s, fragmentary evidence suggests that early North American slaves in British colonies were few in number and were better treated than white indentured servants until the 1660s. It is important to recognize, however, that at least in theory indentured servants enjoyed far greater legal rights than slaves. They could marry whom they wished, travel freely, could not be resold without permission, and (again, in theory) could not be summarily punished or assaulted. By 1700, fewer indentured servants than slaves arrived in the colonies.

Indentured servitude in new guises increased again after 1808, when it became illegal to import new slaves from Africa. Landowners recruited laborers from as far away as India and China, a practice continued by 19th-century railroad contractors and manufacturers. Gang labor contracts made with a labor contractor, such as the Chinese coolie system or the Italian *padrone* network, could be viewed as forms of indentured servitude even though workers were paid **wages**.

An indentured servitude/slavery amalgam persists in contemporary America. In 2000, *Newsweek* and other news sources revealed that some wealthy Americans employ illegal immigrants as unpaid domestic servants. In addition, successful immigrants often use a form of indentured servitude to bring compatriots to the United States. The Southern Poverty Law Center charges that many of the 60,000 "guest workers" coming to the United States in 2004 were modern indentured servants. Other critics see parallels between indentured servitude and farm workers recruited by American labor providers from Asia, Mexico, and elsewhere. Many of these workers must pay upfront fees to recruiters as well as a percentage of their earnings.

Suggested Reading

John Bowe, "Bound for America," *Mother Jones* (May/June 2010); Gottlieb Mittelberger, *Gottlieb Mittelberger on the Misfortune of Indentured Servants*, 1754; Edmund Morgan, *American Slavery, American Freedom*, 1975; "The New Face of Slavery," *Newsweek* (December 11, 2000).

INDUSTRIAL DISCIPLINE. *See* Industrial Time.

INDUSTRIAL REVOLUTION

The Industrial Revolution is an imprecise term used to describe the shift from manual to factory-made, machine-driven labor. It also implies mass production, the use of machines to supplant handmade **artisan** goods, technological change, the expansion of transportation and communications infrastructure, the articulation of national and international markets, urbanization, and the development of a permanent **working class**. The Industrial Revolution required vast sums of money to transform the means of production and, therefore, was closely aligned with the rise of **capitalism** in Europe and the United States. Although the term "revolution" accurately describes the long-term effects of industrialization, the transformation was neither sudden nor even. In the United States, for example, industrial production dates to 1790, but the penetration of the factory system did not become widespread until the eve of the **Civil War** and many scholars do not identify an "Industrial Revolution" as occurring until the 1870s.

The Industrial Revolution first appeared in Great Britain as a consequence of British imperialism, which brought access to both raw materials and technological breakthroughs. Textiles was the first industry to shift to factory production on a large scale. James Kay's 1733 invention of the flying shuttle eventually led to the development of power looms to weave cloth. The power loom, first demonstrated by Edmund Cartwright in 1784, took full advantage of James Hargreaves's 1765 invention of the spinning jenny, a wheel that fed numerous spools simultaneously. James Watt's 1765 perfection of the Newcomen steam engine led to more efficient use of waterpower. By the late 18th century, these technological breakthroughs had begun to transform Britain, leading to dramatic changes in land use, the displacement of small farmers, and the rise of industrial cities. The first phase of the British Industrial Revolution is generally dated from 1790 to 1830, giving Britain a considerable head start vis-à-vis the new American republic.

American industrial production was not greeted with universal enthusiasm. Several of the Founding Fathers, most notably Thomas Jefferson, were aware of the social problems associated with British industrialism, championed **agrarianism** as the ideal for American society, and counseled against industrial development. Nonetheless, Samuel Slater and Moses Brown opened a textile mill in Pawtucket, Rhode Island, in 1790, which is generally considered the first American factory. Pawtucket and subsequent Slater factories were small-scale enterprises. Labor turnover was great, as land was still readily available, workers resented the pace of machine-driven work, and most Americans shared Jefferson's (and Benjamin Franklin's) view that working for **wages** for one's entire life was degrading.

Two developments destined to change American society were Eli Whitney's 1793 invention of the cotton gin and the introduction of the factory system in textiles. The cotton gin, which separated cotton fibers from the plant's husk, led to a dramatic increase in cotton production in the South and an equally dramatic expansion of **slavery** as a way to meet the labor-intensive needs of this crop. The first industry to capitalize upon slave labor was textiles. The "Waltham System" (soon to be redubbed the "Lowell System") replaced Slater's small-scale village-based production with large-scale industrial cities devoted to textile production. It was pioneered in Waltham, Massachusetts, but perfected in nearby **Lowell**, a planned industrial city incorporated in 1823 to honor the memory of investor James Francis Lowell. Lowell at first employed farm girls and women as a way to circumvent prejudices against wage labor by employing that part of the population deemed most expendable in an agrarian economy. After several strikes, including the Lowell textile strike of 1834, immigrants, especially the Irish, gradually supplanted women.

The profitability of the Lowell operation led its capitalist investors, Boston Associates, to build other textile enterprises throughout the Northeast. It also inspired other industries to emulate the factory model. Shoes began to be produced in factories rather than by individual cordwainers and cobblers, while mining of vast deposits of iron ore and coal stimulated the growth of the iron industry. Henry Bessemer's various patents in the 1850s gave rise to steel manufacturing and proved invaluable in producing rails for the emerging railroad industry.

By the Civil War, occupations that were once controlled by skilled craftsmen faced competition from factory-made goods. Some of the first labor unions emerged among **journeymen** craft workers whose pathways to upward mobility were blocked when independent master craftsmen/proprietors were supplanted by an emergent corporate ownership more interested in realizing profits than in preserving traditional work patterns. Some industrial workers began to complain that they were "wage slaves" who were treated as poorly as the black chattel working on southern plantations. This had the ironic effect of providing ammunition for southern slavery apologists who argued that slaves were treated better than northern workers. Those claims were overdrawn but in the North, journeymen's associations responded to deteriorating work conditions by mutating into prototypical **craft unions**.

Neither industrialization nor the labor movement was articulated fully when war fractured American society in the 1860s. Historians generally see the period following **Reconstruction**, roughly from 1870 to 1920, as the "takeoff" period for American industry. By the late 1870s, railroads crisscrossed the nation, bringing farm goods from the countryside to industrial cities and moving factory products to market. Edwin Drake's discovery of oil in Titusville, Pennsylvania, in 1859 eventually freed American factories from dependence upon waterpower and led to the expansion of "heavy" industries such as steel, rubber, and farm machinery. The expansion of the American economy, fueled by industry, led to demands for labor that were met in part by massive waves of **immigration** between 1870 and 1910. By the time of World War I, the United States was the world's leading industrial power. In the early 20th century, new applications of **assembly-line production** proved a boon to manufacturing of automobiles; indeed, by the end of the 1920s, as many as one of every three industrial jobs was somehow connected to the automotive industry.

Economic growth exacted high social costs. The development of a permanent wage-earning class and the closing of the frontier limited options for members of the working class. The pace of industrialization was uneven, and periodic recessions—the worst of which occurred between 1873 and 1878 and between 1893 and 1897—led to unemployment, labor strife, and misery. Machines made goods faster and cheaper, but they also displaced skilled workers, many of whom formed labor unions to protect their wage rates and privileges. **Samuel Gompers**, for example, was a skilled cigar roller who saw his craft destroyed by mechanization. Gompers would later head the **American Federation of Labor** (AFL), a consortium of trade unions seeking to make certain that pre-Civil War rhetoric of "wage slavery" did not become a social reality.

The Industrial Revolution magnified inequalities in American society that came into sharp focus during the Gilded Age. The late 19th century was a chaotic time in which **labor federations** such as the **Knights of Labor** and the AFL battled "robber barons" in numerous blood-soaked **strikes**, and **socialists** and **anarchists** questioned the very legitimacy of capitalism, as did thinkers such as **Henry George** and **Edward Bellamy**. Widespread poverty, long hours of toil, and social unrest associated with events such as the **railroad strike of 1877** and the **Great Upheaval** led even some members of the **middle class** to question industrialization's social cost.

Capitalism triumphed by the early 20th century, and American industry entered what economists dub its "mature" phase, though **child labor**, low wages, dangerous working conditions, and monopolies continued despite the efforts of **Progressive Era** reformers to curtail the abuses attendant with industrialization. America's global industrial might was challenged anew by the Great Depression that began in 1929 and stretched into 1940. A new labor federation, the **Congress of Industrial Organizations** (CIO), emerged to organize the **blue-collar workers** who were now an industrial reality, but had been under-represented within the AFL. Socialist and **communist** challenges also marked the 1930s. New Deal programs served to blunt radical challenges to capitalism, as well as to alter the relationship between workers and government.

Mobilization for World War II revitalized American industry, and the ravages of that conflict outside America left the United States virtually unrivaled in the battle for industrial supremacy at war's end. During the 1950s, American-made automobiles, consumer goods, electronics, glass, rubber, steel, and textiles dominated the global market. The postwar economic expansion also enabled increasing numbers of the working class to enjoy the fruits of prosperity and the external trappings of middle-class comfort. A marked decrease of labor militancy as directed at the legitimacy of the capitalist/industrial system was observed during this era; **Cold War** unionism conflicts centered largely on economic rather than ideological matters.

American industrial dominance continued into the 1960s, but eroded dramatically in the 1970s. What President Dwight Eisenhower dubbed the "military-industrial complex" was invaluable in war production that led to victory in World War II, but its continuation after the war shifted economic priorities away from technological innovation and toward military production. Thus, when European and Southeast Asian industries finally recovered from World War II, their state-of-the-art factories proved more competitive than aging American plants at satisfying consumer demand. Cold War conflicts such as Korea and Vietnam proved to be expensive drains on the United States' national resources. A bigger problem, though, was that the United States did not develop energy self-sufficiency. Boycotts by petroleum-exporting nations during the 1970s dealt American industry a huge blow. By that decade's end, economists spoke of the impact of **deindustrialization** in the United States. Many "smokestack industries," such as electronics, rubber, steel, and textile manufacturing, virtually disappeared from American shores in the latter part of the 20th century. Free trade policies associated with **globalism** also hurt American industries; during periods of high inflation, cheaper foreign-made goods destroyed markets for U.S.-manufactured products. Taxation policies from the 1980s onward also made it easier for American firms to relocate their factories outside U.S. borders.

As factories closed, new jobs emerged in what is now referred to as the "postindustrial" economy, but their creators have not adequately compensated, trained, or hired displaced blue-collar workers to fill them. This is especially true in the burgeoning **service industry**, which generally pays lower wages, has fewer benefits, and is mostly non-unionized. The industrial revolution transformed American society in a host of positive and negative ways; the full impact of postindustrialism has yet to be measured.

Suggested Reading

Eric J. Hobsbawm, *Industry and Empire: From 1750 to the Present Day*, 1999; David Hounshell, *From the American System to Mass Production, 1800–1932*, 1985; James S.

Olson, *Encyclopedia of the Industrial Revolution in America*, 2001; Josh Whitford, *New Old Economy: Networks, Institutions, and the Organization Transformation of American Manufacturing*, 2006.

INDUSTRIAL TIME

Industrial time refers to the unnatural pace of work associated with post-**agrarian** economies. Those working in agricultural production often worked long hours, but the rhythm of their work was determined by nature—that is, by the amount of light in the sky, weather conditions, seasonal cycles, the demands of livestock, and other natural factors. Similarly, independent **artisans** toiled long hours, but they were their own bosses and had control over the pace of their labor. Both artisan and farm labor are task oriented, such that the timing of most jobs does not depend upon strict and mechanical measurements of time. Factory production and other forms of **wage** work are altogether different. One of the most notable architectural features of early factories was the clock tower, as workers were expected to be at work at a specific time and were likewise dismissed at a set hour. In 1888, William Bundy, an Auburn, New York, jeweler, began marketing an employee time clock that required workers to "punch in" as they came to work. It eventually supplanted older systems in which supervisors monitored the entrance of workers into the factory.

Industrial time took advantage of technological advances in artificial lighting and power distribution that allowed factories to operate at any time in the day rather than on natural time. Inside the factory, the pace of machines set the production pace and output was measured. In many cases farmers and artisans actually toiled longer than factory workers, but their work patterns were marked by bursts of hard work followed by rest or more casual pacing; by comparison, factory workers had to adjust to the constant pace of machines and the demands of the managerial/supervisory class who monitored their output. Hourly production replaced the task orientation of preindustrial labor, and efficiency became a paramount concern. This is the origin of the phrase, "Time is money." Increasing output in profitable and efficient ways often entailed the imposition of forms of industrial "discipline" on the workforce. Early work rules not only enforced the specific times of labor, but also imposed moral regulations that mandated church attendance, set curfews, and regulated conduct at work. Old customs such as drinking alcoholic beverages while laboring also came under attack and were banned in most workplaces before the **Civil War**. Moral regulations of workers' free time mostly disappeared by the end of the 19th century, but by then industrial time and discipline had become the norm in American workplaces. According to the U.S. Census Bureau, the frontier had been claimed and settled by 1890, which meant that future Americans could not necessarily aspire to a life of independent yeomanry to achieve sustenance.

Once Americans adjusted to industrial time, permanent wage-earning, and the dominance of a cash-based consumer society, industrialists had an easier time imposing industrial discipline. Some of the methods were exploitative, with **speed-ups** and **stretch-outs** among the more resented work conditions. The early 20th century witnessed the full emergence of other types of industrial discipline, such as the widespread introduction of **assembly-line production** and the application of **Taylorism**, both of which aimed at making workplaces more cost-effective.

The implications of industrial time are among the more radical transformations of American society occasioned by the **Industrial Revolution**. It literally changed the ways Americans came to perceive time and had a spillover effect into such aspects of life as dividing the school day into "periods," the development of transportation timetables, and the very concept that social engagements "begin" at precise times. Non-Western cultures often marvel at the obsession that industrial (and postindustrial) societies have with time. The drive to turn time into money and to impose efficiency and industrial discipline on the workforce can also be seen in such American habits as relentless statistics keeping, the value placed on working hard, a willingness to tolerate substandard working conditions, the gradual diminution of work **stints**, and the endless clock-gazing in which American engage whether on the job, on break, or at leisure.

In the past several decades, the **computer revolution** has extended the artificiality of industrial time and discipline. Early machines separated workers from natural time; computers not only transcend the possible workday, but also break the association between time and space. Electronic communications make it possible, for instance, for an x-ray taken in Iowa to be read instantly in India. Although this is often referred to as a "real-time" interaction, there is nothing real or natural about it, given that there are 11 time zones between the two locations and a late-afternoon transmission from Des Moines arrives in the pre-dawn hours in New Delhi. Once time becomes money in a **capitalist** economy, nature is separated from work.

Suggested Reading

Daniel Nelson, *Managers and Workers: The Origins of the 20th-Century Factory System in the United States, 1880–1920*, 1995; E. P. Thompson, *Customs in Common*, 1993; David Zonderman, *Aspirations and Anxieties: New England Factory Workers and the Mechanized Factory System, 1815–1850*, 1992.

INDUSTRIAL UNIONISM

Industrial unionism is the strategy of organizing workers according to the general industry or occupation in which they are employed, rather than according to a specific skill set. An offshoot of the factory system that advanced alongside the **Industrial Revolution** during the 19th century was machines' supplanting of many skilled **artisan** jobs. The semiskilled and unskilled workers who tended those machines did not fit comfortably into traditional **craft unions**, and many such unions had little desire to organize nonskilled workers. The **American Federation of Labor** (AFL), for example, formed partly in reaction to the **Knights of Labor**'s (KOL) belief that **working-class** identity should transcend specific occupations. The AFL, by contrast, argued that shared skills created natural **solidarity** among members of a craft, and that a **labor federation** ought to be a collection of crafts rather than allegiance to abstract principles such as those espoused by the KOL.

Although the AFL criticized the KOL as naïve, it soon faced the problem that its foundations were antiquated. Mass production reduced many "crafts" to name only. The textile industry was the first to face the full impact of mechanization; by the 1820s, machines were doing the work once done by skilled spinners, fullers, and weavers. By the beginning of the **Civil War**, artisanal shoe production had given way to the same forces as textiles. By the time the AFL formed in 1886, many other mass-production industries were also in the process of deskilling their respective workforces. Skilled crafts remained central enough to the production of many goods to sustain AFL craft unions—in the meatpacking industry, for example, skilled **butchers** continued to play a crucial role in preparing mass-produced products for market—but traditional craft was increasingly endangered.

Several organizations anticipated this shift and pioneered in prototypical industrial unionism. The KOL, for example, successfully brought some Western railroad workers into a single organization that supplanted older brotherhoods in which engineers, firemen, brakemen, construction workers, and others were placed in separate organizations. When the KOL faded, the **American Railway Union** attempted to advance an industrial model for rail workers that largely collapsed in the wake of the **Pullman strike and lockout**. More enduring industrial union models emerged under the auspices of the **United Mine Workers of America** (UMWA), various **brewery workers** unions, and the **Industrial Workers of the World** (IWW). The IWW went so far as to ban craft unions altogether in favor of industrial unions. It also strongly criticized the AFL as a bastion of privilege whose values were not conducive to **class consciousness**.

The IWW held ideals deemed too radical by policymakers in the **Progressive Era** and World War I, and it went into decline during the postwar **Red Scare**. Nevertheless, this organization was correct in its understanding that mass industry was complex, included a wide array of nonspecialized labor that contributed to the final product, and often even entailed work done in different production facilities. The AFL responded to these changes in ways consistent with its founding principles, though its actions often made little sense. For example, rather than seeking to organize all autoworkers into a single union, AFL organizers dispersed them among various "crafts" that were more artificial than actual—wire installers became "electricians," those snapping in windows became "glassmakers," and individuals working with wooden trim became "carpenters." The artificiality of this classification was resented even by some of the AFL's most ardent craft unionism advocates. Highly skilled welders, for instance, saw themselves as a class apart from spot welders who spent their days on an auto **assembly line** applying a bead to the same fender on chasses passing by on the continuous work stream. By the late 1920s, many mass-assembly workers had also come to resent what they viewed as the haughty attitudes of old-style craft unionists. It did not help matters that the AFL placed some production workers into federal labor unions that were directly affiliated with the AFL. These bodies often lacked control over their internal affairs and were seen by the AFL as holding groups until the workers could be dispersed into appropriate craft bodies.

In 1935, industrial unionism advocates formed the Committee for Industrial Organization in 1935 to challenge the AFL to rethink its organization strategies. When the AFL failed to respond favorably, they eventually left the AFL and declared themselves the **Congress of Industrial Organizations** (CIO). The CIO was first headed by **John L. Lewis**, who led the UMWA out of the AFL, thereby robbing it of one of its largest affiliates. It would be the CIO that finally organized mass-production workers based on industries, such as the auto, rubber, textile, glass, electrical supplies, steel, and other heavy industries. The CIO model became the main union organizing strategy in the United States simply because semiskilled and unskilled labor was the reality for far more workers than craft production. By the time of the 1955 **American Federation of Labor-Congress of Industrial Organizations** (AFL-CIO) merger, even the AFL conceded the principle's soundness and set up an Industrial Unionism Department to advance that organizing style.

Industrial unionism remains a key organizational strategy for labor unions in the United States, though it, too, has waned in a postindustrial society. Today, craft and industrial union models coexist and both are focused more on economic issues than on debates over organizing principles. Some occupations such as auto, mine, and postal workers are devoted to the industrial unionism model, whereas others such as teachers and **white-collar** workers, if organized at all, tend toward craft unionism and see themselves as different from other workers within the same workplaces. The concept of industrial unionism, meanwhile, has migrated to offshore locations where production once done in the United States is now being carried out.

Suggested Reading

Philip Dray, *There Is Power in a Union: The Epic Struggle of Labor in America*, 2010; Simeon Larson and Bruce Nissen, eds., *Theories of the Labor Movement*, 1987; Frederic P. Miller, Agnes Vandome, and John McBrewster, eds., *Industrial Unionism*, 2010.

INDUSTRIAL WORKERS OF THE WORLD

The Industrial Workers of the World (IWW) was perhaps the most **class-conscious** of any **labor federation** in American history. It was founded in Chicago in 1905, and reached its apex on the eve of World War I. The IWW was the target of great repression before, during, and after the war, and it also lost members to the newly formed Communist Party during the 1920s. Although the IWW still exists, it no longer commands the power it did during the early 20th century.

At its founding, the IWW brought together numerous members of the Western Federation of Miners and prominent radicals such as **Eugene Debs**, **Daniel DeLeon**, **Mary "Mother" Jones**, and **Lucy Parsons**. It adopted a revolutionary constitution declaring that **capitalists** and the **working class** had "nothing in common" and called upon the latter to destroy the former. The IWW rejected the **wage** system, advocated the use of **general strikes** to disrupt society, and refused to sign contracts with employers, even if it won wage concessions. Many of its leaders, such as **William Haywood**, William Trautman, and **Elizabeth Gurley Flynn**, were influenced by a blend of **anarchism** sometimes dubbed **anarcho-syndicalism**, which postulated that society could be operated cooperatively on a not-for-profit basis by setting up various productive, distributive, and service units and linking them to one another like spokes on a wheel. The IWW organized its constituent assemblies as **industrial unions** and was contemptuous of the **American Federation of Labor**'s (AFL) exclusionary **craft union** mentality; IWW members routinely called the AFL the "American Separation of Labor." By contrast, the IWW promised to unite the entire working class into what it called the One Big Union.

The IWW's early years were marked by internal battles over organization and ideology. In 1908, Daniel DeLeon split the IWW when it appeared to him that the organization was abandoning **socialist** precepts and had been captured by Western anarchists whom he lambasted as "bummery." For a brief time DeLeon operated a rival IWW from Detroit, but it never supplanted the Chicago group. As DeLeon feared, the IWW came to reject ballot-box politics as a capitalist ploy and urged workers not to vote; Eugene Debs quietly let his membership lapse for this reason. The IWW was a small organization with approximately 5,000 members at the time of the split, but it did manage to unionize workers whom the AFL deemed unorganizable.

The IWW never completely reconciled the differences between its eastern industrial workers and the lumberjacks, agricultural workers, dock workers, and miners who made up the bulk of its western membership, nor did it clearly articulate its political views. Even so, its **direct action** tactics involved the group in numerous dramatic **strikes** that captured the imagination of many more workers than it actually organized, and earned the IWW the enmity of conservatives, who vowed to destroy it. Direct action—radical responses on the job—helped the IWW organize silver miners in Nevada, harvest workers across the Midwest, and timber workers in Washington and Oregon. Between 1909 and 1912, the IWW used acts of civil disobedience to overturn local ordinances that curtailed free speech and assembly. (Roger Baldwin, the founder of the American Civil Liberties Union, drew inspiration from these campaigns.) It was in the East, however, that the group made its biggest headlines. In 1906, IWW members at a Schenectady, New York, General Electric plant conducted what may have been the first **sit-down strike** in American history. The 1912 "Bread and Roses" textile strike in Lawrence, Massachusetts, was even more dramatic; the IWW organized 20,000 workers from approximately 40 different ethnic groups and won a strike against America's largest textile conglomerate.

Success and direct action strengthened the resolve of industrialists and conservative politicians to destroy the IWW. IWW members were nicknamed **Wobblies**, for reasons that are not entirely clear, and by 1912 "Wobblyism" had supplanted anarchism as a favored boogeyman in the mainstream press. Rumors floated that the IWW espoused violence and that it used **sabotage** to destroy private property. In these matters, the IWW was the victim of its own revolutionary rhetoric; more violence was done *to* rather than *by* Wobblies, and the IWW's attempt to parse the meaning of sabotage as a "systematic withdrawal of efficiency" was not convincing. Campaigns were launched to crack down on the IWW; in 1913, employers offered no quarter during strikes against Paterson, New Jersey, silk mills. Elsewhere, vigilante groups often took it upon themselves to harass, beat, and murder Wobblies.

The IWW's membership peaked at about 100,000 in 1917, the year when the United States entered World War I. The IWW opposed the war and ran afoul of espionage and sedition laws passed to outlaw criticism of war efforts or disrupt wartime production. Hundreds of Wobblies were brought to trial and jailed between 1917 and 1920, and violence against IWW members increased dramatically. The IWW never completely recovered from the government-led **Red Scare**, and key members, including Flynn, cast their lot with the **communists** during the 1920s. The IWW remained defiant despite its declining membership. It launched mostly unsuccessful organizing campaigns among construction, maritime, timber, and oil workers in the 1920s, but it did manage to lead two strikes in Colorado's coalfields in 1927 and with Boulder Dam construction workers in 1931. During the Great Depression, its main strength was derived from the auto and metal worker trades.

The IWW refused to comply with anticommunist provisos of the **Taft-Hartley Act**, which made it subject to further government scrutiny during the post-World War II Red Scare. It dwindled to near-oblivion in the 1950s, enjoyed a modest resurgence among the **counterculture** during the 1960s, and established a small presence among printers, musicians, agricultural workers, and social services agency employees in the 1980s and 1990s. Today the IWW has branches across the globe and in most U.S. states and Canadian provinces. Most of these operations are little more than clearinghouse chapters for those interested in the organization. The IWW has never used the **dues checkoff system** and depends upon voluntary payments. As a consequence, its membership fluctuates widely. It claims to have approximately 2,000 members, but probably fewer than half of them are members in good standing. Today's IWW appeals more to intellectuals and youthful radicals than to the industrial laborers and extractive industry workers who once made up its core. It has, however, been active in anti-**globalism** protests in the 21st century.

The IWW's heyday was brief, but influential. In an unintended twist, the IWW helped the AFL and other mainstream unions; some employers chose to negotiate with those organizations rather than face the possibility of dealing with the radical IWW. The IWW also called attention to issues that many Progressive Era reformers ignored, such as civil liberties, racial justice, and working-class poverty. Some commentators credit the IWW with indirect impact on future New Deal legislation; in essence, the IWW served as a warning that radical action lurked in waiting if reform waned. It also taught future union leaders that supposedly unorganizable groups such as immigrants and transients could be brought into the union fold. The IWW even made inroads culturally; IWW **music** written by **Joe Hill**, Ralph Chaplin, and others became working-class standards, including the union anthem "Solidarity Forever." Finally, despite its refusal to sign contracts, the IWW helped improve the material well-being of hundreds of thousands of workers before its decline.

Suggested Reading

Melvyn Dubofsky, *We Shall Be All: A History of the IWW*, 1969; "Industrial Workers of the World," www.iww.org/, accessed December 26, 2010; Joyce Kornbluh, ed., *Rebel Voices: An IWW Anthology*, 1998.

INJUNCTION

An injunction is a court order that either requires a party to do something or forbids them from acting in a given manner, such as engaging in a **strike**, employing **pickets**, or launching a **boycott**. It is a powerful legal tool that can both impose civil damages and result in criminal charges if it is violated. Injunctions have often been used against labor unions, which view them as egregious violations of free speech and free assembly, though legal opinion has generally disagreed with that perception. Technically, injunctions can be issued against employers and unions alike, but in practice nearly all have been used against organized labor. Many labor historians see cooperation between employers, courts, and government as a major reason why American labor unions have been weaker than those in other Western industrial democracies.

In the earliest days of the labor movement, employers seeking legal actions against worker organizations generally resorted to anti-conspiracy laws. As states slowly became loath to view unions as criminal conspiracies, organized capital turned to other means of controlling them. The first injunction against unions may have been during the **railroad strikes of 1877**, but they occurred in large numbers after the passage of the 1890 **Sherman Antitrust Act**, a bill ostensibly passed to regulate monopolies and cartels and ensure economic competition. The Sherman Act proved more potent as a weapon for labeling labor unions as engaging in illegal restraint of trade. One of the more dramatic uses of the injunction came during the **Pullman strike/lockout** crisis of 1894, when Attorney General Richard Olney—who was also a major railroad stockholder—convinced federal Judge Peter J. Grosscup to issue a "blanket injunction" against the **American Railway Union** (ARU). Because Pullman cars carried both interstate commerce and the U.S. Mail, Grosscup issued an order making it illegal for the ARU to refuse to handle *any* Pullman car anywhere on the grounds that it *might* be carrying commerce or mail. This order also made it illegal for the ARU to ask any other workers to refuse to service Pullman cars. The ARU had little choice but to defy the injunction, an action that led to the arrest and jailing of ARU head **Eugene Debs**. Debs later claimed that his six-month federal imprisonment led him to become a **socialist**.

After the Pullman strike, a torrent of injunctions were issued. By one estimate, at least 4,300 injunctions against unions were issued between 1880 and 1932, the bulk of which came during the **Progressive Era**. So many injunctions were issued that many labor historians see the term "Progressive Era" as problematic when applied to working people. In 1906, the **American Federation of Labor** (AFL) placed the Buck's Stove and Range Company of St. Louis on a "We Don't Patronize" boycott list. Buck's president J. W. Cleave, who was also president of the anti-union **National Association of Manufacturers**, sought and received an injunction against the AFL. AFL President **Samuel Gompers** was found in contempt and faced jail time before the courts overturned his conviction. A Danbury, Connecticut, hatters' union did not fare so well. When the Supreme Court upheld contempt charges in the case of *Loewe v. Lawlor*, both the union and individual workers were ordered to pay crippling damages to the company. Gompers sought anti-injunction laws and, also in 1906, issued to Congress a Bill of Grievances, but it was ignored. Although the AFL had traditionally been nonpartisan, it shifted support to the **Democratic Party** in 1908, when it adopted an anti-injunction plank. The presidency, however, went to Republican William Howard Taft, who had issued numerous injunctions as a federal judge. The AFL worked hard to defeat Taft in 1912 and threw its support behind Democrat Woodrow Wilson.

The 1914 **Clayton Antitrust Act** gave unions some relief from sweeping injunctions, albeit briefly. President Wilson viewed with alarm a wave of strikes that occurred in 1919 when employers sought to scrap capital/labor accords in effect during World War I. The emerging **Red Scare** made Wilson cautious; thus, when an injunction was issued against the **United Mine Workers of America** (UMWA) in 1919, Wilson allowed it to stand. Acting UMWA President **John L. Lewis** called off the strike despite the AFL's urging that he not do so. Lewis proved prescient regarding the shifting legal tides, however. The 1921 Supreme Court decision in *Duplex Printing v. Deering* ruled that the Clayton Act did not give labor the right to conduct secondary boycotts, and later that year the court struck down an Arizona law outlawing injunctions in the *Truax v. Corrigan* ruling. The **railroad strike of 1922** was severely hampered by a veritable gag law injunction that forbade unions from setting up pickets, holding strike meetings, making public remarks, using union funds to support the strike, or even publicly discussing the dispute.

The 1932 **Norris-LaGuardia Act** finally curtailed sweeping federal injunctions and restricted the use of injunctions in all but the most dire of circumstances. It, too, would prove a temporary measure. During World War II, the Smith-Connally Act was passed in response to the **coal miners strike of 1943**. Among other things, it allowed the government to seize industries critical to the war effort. Lewis and the UMWA defied the Smith-Connally Act in 1946 and were hit with a $3.5 million fine. The courts eventually reduced the fine to $700,000 but upheld the right to issue an injunction. The Smith-Connally Act expired at the end of 1946, but the **Taft-Hartley Act** strengthened injunction rights and allowed for the president to order an 80-day "cooling off" injunction during any labor dispute that (vaguely) threatened the health or safety of the nation. It would be used against the UMWA in 1950 and against the **United Steelworkers of America** (USW) in 1959, though the USW waited out the injunction and won most of its demands in early 1960.

Injunctions were often ignored during the 1960s and 1970s, especially when applied to public employees such as teachers and postal workers. Injunctions have seldom been used in the past four decades. Anti-union employers now have at their disposal more powerful ways of handcuffing labor, including the hiring of union-busting consulting forms and tying up grievances in slow and expensive court proceedings. Moreover, **deindustrialization** and assaults against organized labor in the

1980s sapped union strength. More significantly, favorable business **deregulation** and tax policy now make it easy for employers to move production and capital elsewhere when disputes arise. In the overall sweep of labor history, injunctions are part of the myriad strategies used by organized capital to oppose organized labor.

Suggested Reading

Foster Rhea Dulles and Melvyn Dubofsky, *Labor in America: A History*, 1984; William E. Forbath, *Law and the Shaping of the American Labor Movement*, 1991; Felix Frankfurter and Nathan Greene, *The Labor Injunction*, 1930.

INTERNATIONAL ASSOCIATION OF MACHINISTS AND AEROSPACE WORKERS

The International Association of Machinists and Aerospace Workers (IAM) represents more than 646,000 workers in more than 200 industries, with most of its membership in the United States and Canada. Machinists have historically been highly skilled craftsmen. They include those workers who use machines to craft parts, many of which have such fine tolerances that a measurement that is off by as much as 0.01 millimeter can cause the part to fail. Skilled machinists cut, grind, thread, ream, drill, and design the very pieces that make machines work, including those machines that make parts for precision goods such as automobiles and aircraft.

The forerunner of the IAM was the Machinists and Blacksmiths' Union, founded in 1859; this organization collapsed shortly after the Panic of 1873. In 1888, Thomas W. Talbott, an Atlanta railroad machinist, revived the union and dubbed it the IAM. The immediate object of the IAM was to raise **wages**, and its membership—like that of many top-tier **craft unions**—was restricted to white males. In 1895, the IAM joined the **American Federation of Labor** (AFL), two years after AFL President **Samuel Gompers** urged the IAM to drop its whites-only policy. The IAM refused to do so and joined the AFL during the one year in which Gompers was voted out as AFL leader. The IAM maintained racial segregation until 1947, arguing that it was necessary to retain southern members. Some critics charged that the IAM had ties with the Ku Klux Klan.

The IAM grew rapidly in the early 20th century. By 1915, many of its members had won an **eight-hour** workday, and by 1918, the IAM had more than 331,000 members. In the 1920s, the IAM even experimented with union-owned ship repair yards, print shops, machine shops, and a bank, but few of these ventures thrived. The IAM also lobbied for strong **child labor** laws.

Like many unions, the IAM was weakened during the Great Depression, its membership dropping to just 70,000 by 1935. The passage of the **National Labor Relations Act** revitalized the IAM, as did organization efforts in the burgeoning aircraft industry. For much of the 1930s and 1940s, however, the IAM competed for members with the **United Auto Workers of America** in the automotive industry and with the United Aerospace Workers for aircraft workers. In 1949, the IAM signed no-**raiding** agreements with both unions. These agreements became the model for other unions when the AFL and the **Congress of Industrial Organizations** (CIO) merged in 1955.

The IAM fought to maintain jobs during the reconversion of defense plants to civilian production after World War II. The 1950s were a period of rapid growth for the IAM, as production of jet engines perfected during the war led to expansion of the aircraft industry. By 1958, the IAM had more than 900,000 members. It also took tentative steps to atone for its racist past, and redressing this history is a major focus for the IAM today. In 1973, the IAM merged with the United Aerospace Workers. The IAM suffered a decline in membership during the 1980s as a result of downturns in the aircraft industry in the wake of the 1970s stagflation. It also suffered from a vitriolic dispute with Rhode Island manufacturer Brown & Sharpe, and from the anti-union policies that emerged during the **Ronald Reagan** administration. The introduction of computer-aided design, robotics, and numerically controlled machines has also affected the machine-tool industry. During the 1970s and 1980s many smaller machine-tool shops closed, and consolidation, mergers, and **outsourcing** have continued to erode the job market for machinists in the United States and Canada. IAM losses might have been even greater were it not for the union's militant spirit. At a time when many union heads sought to cut the best deals available, IAM President William Winpisinger resisted concessions. The IAM's 1991 battle against Eastern Airlines is regarded by some labor analysts as having saved airline unions from even greater losses.

Although the IAM has lost more than 80,000 members since the mid-1990s and a third of its membership since its peak membership year of 1973, it remains one of the most powerful **industrial unions** in North America and consistently maintains a high victory rate for union **certification** votes. Like other unions, however, it no longer exclusively represents just one category of workers. IAM members can be found in the transport, aerospace, railroad, shipbuilding, government employment, and woodworking industries. Also akin to other unions, the IAM is very concerned about job security and maintenance of **fringe benefits**. It has been embroiled in a controversy with Boeing since 2008 over issues such as resisting **concessions** and opposing the outsourcing of jobs. It is currently pressuring Boeing to close a plant in South Carolina, a **right-to-work** state whose workers rejected the IAM. The IAM has been a strong voice in opposition to **globalism** practices that encourage capital flight, and it has openly endorsed selective **protectionism**, which it believes is a necessary counterbalance to unfettered free trade. In 2010, its activism helped push the World Trade Organization to expose a pattern of illegal subsidies for European Airbus engines, a practice that placed American-made aircraft engines at a competitive disadvantage. The IAM also endorses automatic **cost-of-living adjustments** for workers, **pension** protection, and numerous other benefits that stand in opposition to existing trends to cut wages and benefits. It has lobbied for restoration of the National Aeronautics and Space Administration (NASA) as a government-funded agency and opposes the move toward privatization. The current IAM president is Tom Buffenbarger.

Suggested Reading

"History of the IAM," http://www.goiam.org/index.php/headquarters/history-of-the-iam, accessed December 27, 2010; Ernie Mailhot, Jack Barnes, and Judy Stranahan, *Eastern Airlines Strike: Accomplishments of Rank-and-File Machinists*, 1991.

INTERNATIONAL ASSOCIATION OF PAPERMAKERS.

See Papermakers.

INTERNATIONAL BROTHERHOOD OF TEAMSTERS. *See* Teamsters.

INTERNATIONAL LADIES' GARMENT WORKERS' UNION

The International Ladies' Garment Workers' Union (ILGWU) was one of the 20th century's most important voices representing needletrades workers, especially women and immigrants. The emergence of the ILGWU helped fill a void for women left by the decline of the **Knights of Labor** (KOL). Unlike the KOL, which was open to organizing women, many affiliates of the dominant **American Federation of Labor** (AFL) banned females from membership; in fact, numerous scholars credit the ILGWU with forcing the AFL to rethink its assumptions about the worthiness of women in the labor movement.

The ILGWU sprang to life on June 3, 1900, when 11 delegates from seven local unions representing about 2,000 members met in New York City. It received a charter from the AFL and began fighting for improved working conditions, higher **wages**, and an end to the requirement that workers purchase the equipment and materials they used. At the time, many of the needletrades relied heavily upon **homework**. Employers often required workers, the bulk of whom were women, to purchase their own sewing machines, needles, scissors, thread, and other materials. In some particularly abusive situations, unscrupulous employers provided sewing machines to women on a lease-to-own program that deducted costs from their earnings, but fired employees before the final payments were made, confiscated the machines, and released them to fresh hires. The ILGWU quickly established a reputation for militancy and for battling against both in-home and in-factory **sweatshop** conditions. It also operated educational and cultural programs for its members, an important benefit as the early ILGWU largely comprised Jewish and Italian immigrants working in urban sweatshops.

The ILGWU won public notice for an organized walkout of New York City shirtwaist makers in 1909, known as the **Uprising of the 20,000**. That **strike** paralyzed New York City's clothing industry and was followed by a successful strike of New York City cloak makers in 1910. These back-to-back successes secured the ILGWU's permanency. The ILGWU not only captured the public imagination, but also attracted considerable financial and logistical support from middle- and upper-class women. Among those inspired by the ILGWU was future labor

The International Ladies' Garment Workers' Union, shown here at a meeting in the 1940s, was a prime motivating force in the 1909–1910 strike known as the "Uprising of the 20,000." One consequence of the strike was an increase in the size and credibility of the labor group. (Library of Congress)

secretary **Frances Perkins**. Moreover, the two strikes suggested the potency of cross-gender organizing, as the cloak makers were primarily men whereas mostly women conducted the shirtwaist makers' strike. The two actions produced the first labor/management agreement in the American garment industry. Attributed to future Supreme Court Justice Louis Brandeis, this "protocol of peace" created an **arbitration** board to settle labor disputes, shortened the work week, created a sanitary commission to eliminate health and safety hazards, and won fixed rates for **piecework**.

The tragic **Triangle Factory fire of 1911** occurred in the firm that was a central target during the 1909 uprising. The ILGWU was among the shrillest voices in condemning the incident. It organized a protest funeral march of more than 100,000 people, and increased its membership dramatically in the tragedy's aftermath. But the Triangle fire also led to tension within the ILGWU, with activists such as **Rosie Schneiderman** calling into question the sincerity and reliability of ILGWU supporters who were not members of the **working class**. She called upon workers to build institutions of their own. In 1914, the ILGWU established a union health center to treat tuberculosis among garment workers. This measure occurred during a time in which textile and garment manufacturers rejected the idea that airborne fibers affected workers' health. Although strong suspicions of the link were present by the 1860s, it would take another hundred years before byssinosis—commonly called "brown lung disease"—would be universally accepted as an occupational ailment.

The ILGWU experienced internal upheaval in the 1920s. Many ILGWU members were **socialist** in political orientation and split over whether to support the emergent Communist Party of the United States of America (CPUSA). When Morris Sigman became ILGWU president in 1923, he sought to remove **communists** from the union—an attempt that led to revolt in New York City, where CPUSA support was strong. The dispute degenerated into factionalism that involved the intervention of organized crime figures and the calling of a hasty 1926 **general strike** that nearly bankrupted the ILGWU. It also marked the rise of David Dubinsky within the ILGWU; Dubinsky is often credited with helping the ILGWU survive. The upheaval lingered into 1932, when Dubinsky assumed the ILGWU presidency.

In 1935, the ILGWU was among eight **industrial unions** to form the Committee for Industrial Organization within the AFL. It was also among those expelled from the AFL in 1937, and was a charter founder of the **Congress of Industrial Organizations** (CIO). The ILGWU's Rose Pesotta was a key organizer among steel and rubber workers in the early CIO. Dubinsky, however, grew nervous about the tolerance for communists within the CIO, and the ILGWU withdrew from the CIO in 1940 and resumed its affiliation with the AFL. In the early 1940s, ILGWU contracts included **fringe benefits** such as paid vacations, employee health care, and **pension** plans. The ILGWU also commissioned housing developments for workers and opened a summer resort in the Pocono Mountains of Pennsylvania. The union thrived under Dubinsky's leadership. He is credited with increasing membership from approximately 40,000 in 1932 to 450,000 by the 1960s. Dubinsky also helped the ILGWU rid itself of divisive factions, though he had only partial success in cleaning up corruption in urban locals. The ILGWU eventually resumed its support for the **Democratic Party** after flirtations with in the American Labor Party in the 1940s and with the Liberal Party in New York State in the 1960s.

By the end of Dubinsky's tenure in 1966, both the garment industry and the ILGWU had changed dramatically. The Jewish and Italian workers who had dominated the ILGWU rank-and-file since its inception had given way to workers whose ethnic roots lay in Africa, Puerto Rico, Mexico, Central America, and southern Asia. Dubinsky's critics charged him and the ILGWU with being insensitive to changing demographics and with perpetuating racism. In addition, increasing clothing imports had begun to erode production within the United States. The ILGWU's membership began plummeting during the 1970s. By the 1990s, the union had lost approximately 300,000 members due to low-cost imports and the transfer of factories overseas, particularly to Latin America and Asia. The ILGWU officially came to an end in 1995, when its remaining 125,000 members merged with the Amalgamated Clothing and Textile Workers' Union to form the **Union of Needletrades, Industrial, and Textile Employees**.

Suggested Reading

Elaine Leeder, *The Gentle General: Rose Pesotta, Anarchist and Labor Organizer*, 1993; A. H. Raskin, *David Dubinsky: A Life with Labor*, 1977; Gus Tyler, *Look for the Union Label: A History of the International Ladies' Garment Workers' Union*, 1995.

INTERNATIONAL LONGSHORE AND WAREHOUSE UNION. *See* Longshoremen.

INTERNATIONAL LONGSHOREMENS'S ASSOCIATION. *See* Longshoremen.

INTERNATIONAL PAPER STRIKE

The 1987 International Paper strike was an ill-fated action that is now viewed as symptomatic of organized labor's troubles in the 1980s. It was centered in Maine, but ultimately involved all of the locals of the United Paperworkers' International Union (UPIU). In all, approximately 2,300 workers were involved, of whom 1,250 were in Maine.

Among the many troubling aspects of the UPIU **strike** was that it took place after the International Paper Company (IP) demanded **concessions** and givebacks from the UPIU immediately after recording record profits. This demand brought labor strife to a firm that had not experienced work stoppages in seven decades. International Paper, then the nation's largest and most profitable paper manufacturer, took large short-term losses to achieve what many observers see as a blatant attempt at union-busting.

The strike began as a **lockout**. **Paperworkers** were issued a series of untenable demands: pay cuts, a huge hike in medical insurance premiums, the elimination of all holiday pay, and an end to double pay for Sunday work. When the UPIU balked, IP locked out workers. The strike's epicenter was in Maine, especially the town of Jay. In retrospect, that may have been a strategic error on the part of the UPIU: Jay was a **company town** in which most residents had some tie or history with IP. Despite long-standing health concerns about the effect of the mill on worker health and local environmental quality, it had been 67 years since Jay had seen a strike. The lack of a militant tradition inside Jay's Local 14 of the UPIU placed it in a poor position to weather the 16-month struggle that began in June 1987. Nor was the **American Federation of Labor-Congress of Industrial Organizations** (AFL-CIO) prepared for the long battle. It sent organizer Peter Kellman to Jay. Kellman did a credible job of building a stronger union movement there and he launched a **corporate campaign** he deemed necessary to force IP to the bargaining table. Kellman and Local 14 cast attention on IP's poor safety, health, and environmental record, but they also encountered opposition from townspeople reluctant to take on the area's only major employer. Moreover, the AFL-CIO failed to provide resources for research that might have allowed for a stronger campaign.

International Paper responded by firing 1,200 workers in Jay and replacing them with **scabs**. Once this occurred, the AFL-CIO began to debate the wisdom of continuing the strike and began reducing support for it. The action lingered into October 1988, with Kellman and Local 14 waging a militant but unsuccessful fight. UPIU Local 14 was effectively **decertified** when workers were fired, though the official vote did not come until 1992. International Paper also suffered, however, as the corporate campaign revealed chemical spills and pollution practices that brought investigations by the Environmental Protection Agency and that led to the passage of local ordinances allowing the town to set environmental standards. The company was socked with heavy fines and was forced to make expensive alterations to its plants to reduce pollution. By the early 21st century, IP was being hailed for its ecological innovation. Such praise was premature, however, as the company was investigated for pollution in 2003 and was sued for violations of the Clean Water Act in 2005. Among the allegations was that the company was dumping 40,000,000 gallons of polluted water per day into the Androscoggin River.

International Paper made a large profit in 2002, but when revenues dipped in 2003, it sought to trim its workforce. In 2006, it sold all of its Maine operations to other firms. The former IP Androscoggin Mill was sold to Tennessee-based Verso, which employed approximately 980 non-union workers in 2010. Maine's paper industry remains profitable, but troubled. As of 2009, Maine had 47 operating mills, but just 7,500 paperworkers. Towns such as Jay have experienced the effects of **deindustrialization** and capital flight to overseas locations with less stringent environmental standards. In 2009, a mill owned by Wausau Paper closed. Moreover, current employment at Androscoggin Mill pales when compared to its peak of nearly 3,500 workers on the eve of the 1987 strike. It remains to be seen whether papermaking in Maine is a **sunset industry**.

Despite the loss of the 1987 strike, some observers detect notes of optimism from the result. First, Local 14 was able to craft remarkable **solidarity** within a community in which little had existed previously. Second, the strike demonstrated that union-breaking can entail a heavy cost for companies. International Paper remains a powerful corporation, but a less stable one than before the strike. Some investors have criticized company strategy and argue that resources diverted into the battle against the UPIU would have generated greater profits if put to constructive use. Finally, the strike demonstrated the linkages between economic issues and greater political and social concerns such as environmental quality.

The strike was also a costly one for organized labor. In 1999, UPIU merged with the Oil, Chemical, and Atomic Workers to form PACE, which in turn merged with the **United Steelworkers of America** in 2005. Although this union is affiliated with the AFL-CIO, not all paperworkers are happy with that situation. Fairly or not, the AFL-CIO was widely viewed as having sold out Local 14. Many union rank-and-file members, though loyal to their locals, hold negative views of the AFL-CIO.

Suggested Reading

Julius Getman, *The Betrayal of Local 14: Paperworkers, Politics, and Permanent Replacements*, 1998; Peter Kellman, *Divided We Fall: The Study of the Paperworkers' Union and the*

Future of Labor, 2004; Peter Kellman, ed., *Pain on Their Faces: Testimonies on the Paper Mill Strike, Jay, Maine, 1987–1988*, 1988.

INTERNATIONAL UNION

"International union" is an organizational term referring to a parent union that maintains **union locals** and affiliates outside the United States. Labor unions first applied the label to describe locals established in Canada, which remains the most common form of international union. Nevertheless, but in the wake of **globalism**, many unions now seek to create locals around the globe.

International **socialism** pioneered the idea of organizing workers across international borders. The **Marxist** International Workingmen's Association, better known as the "First International"—was established in Geneva in 1866. The **Knights of Labor** (KOL) was the first American-based **labor federation** to have a significant international presence, with locals as far flung as Australia, Belgium, England, France, New Zealand, Scotland, and South Africa. The **Industrial Workers of the World** (IWW) also sought to create affiliates abroad and had modest success in Australasia, Britain, and Mexico. Within the **American Federation of Labor** (AFL), the decision to form international unions was a matter left to individual affiliates. For the most part, those **crafts** in which international competition mattered—such as KOL glassmakers—the push for a strong international union took on urgency. That urgency was often lacking when the United States was in the throes of its **Industrial Revolution**, but its need in a post-industrial economy is self-evident.

An international union creates a federation that links isolated economic organizations (locals) and enables them to cooperate instead of competing with one another on issues of mutual importance such as **wages**, workplace safety, and health and environmental standards. International unions usually have a constitution and/or bylaws that govern the relationship of locals to the international union. In most cases, the international union maintains a bureaucratic staff who administer union affairs; hires researchers, organizers, lawyers, and lobbyists to service the locals; and assists in recruiting new members, building political pressure groups, and setting up worker education programs. In many cases, locals must also gain the approval of the international union before undertaking a work stoppage.

Today's international unions, such as the **United Steelworkers of America** and the **United Auto Workers of America**, may be affiliated with a larger labor federation like the **American Federation of Labor-Congress of Industrial Organizations**, but they are not governed by it and enjoy broad autonomy in accordance with the AFL's original stress on **voluntarism**. In an era of globalization, however, many international unions are looking beyond the United States and Canada, and seek to organize more powerful bodies in developing nations as a way to blunt the economic might of **runaway capital**. Locals of American-based unions have formed in Brazil, Japan, Mexico, the Philippines, and numerous European nations; they are particularly evident across Latin America and Asia. To date, gains have been modest and have not reversed the flight of American corporations abroad. Some observers question whether American-style unionism is exportable, particularly within a voluntarism system in which decision-making power remains in North America. To date, international unionism has been an export, but not an import; that is, an offshore international unionism has not taken hold inside North America.

The International Trade Union Confederation formed in 2006 and has representation in 151 countries. The AFL-CIO belongs to this Brussels-based organization, but thus far it has largely been a body in which policy is crafted rather than one that actively organizes workers. It does seek to become organized labor's center for maintaining pressure against global **capitalism** and for organizing protests at gatherings such as the World Trade Organization.

Suggested Reading

Robert Mathis and John Jackson, *Human Resource Management*, 2002; Kim Moody, *An Injury to All*, 1992; Michael Yates, *Why Unions Matter*, 2009.

INTERNATIONAL UNION OF ELECTRICAL, RADIO, AND MACHINE WORKERS OF AMERICA

The International Union of Electrical, Radio, and Machine Workers of America (IUE) organized workers producing electrical goods and consumer electronics. It is an example of **Cold War** unionism and organized labor's internecine struggles in the wake of the **Taft-Hartley Act**. The IUE received a charter from the **Congress of Industrial Organizations** (CIO) in 1949, and **James Carey** became its first international president. Carey, like many IUE leaders and members, had once been active in the **United Electrical, Radio, and Machine Workers of America** (UE), the CIO union that first organized electrical workers in the 1930s.

Carey was an ardent **Democrat** and supporter of the New Deal, but he grew nervous about the growing presence of **communist** organizers within the UE. He dutifully defended the UE from highly exaggerated outside allegations that it was controlled by communists, but he privately sought to marginalize the influence of ideological radicals within individual **union locals**. Carey was only partly successful in that endeavor, and his overzealousness contributed to his ouster as UE president in 1942. The passage of the Taft-Hartley Act in 1947 and the outbreak of the post-World War II **Red Scare** once again raised the specter of communist control of the UE, especially given that the Taft-Hartley Act required union leaders to sign affidavits that they were not members of the Communist Party. When UE members refused to do so, the UE became a target for union **raiding**. Between 1947 and the IUE's birth in 1949, the UE was raided more than 500 times and lost members and entire locals to unions such as the **United Auto Workers of America** (UAW) and the International Brotherhood of Electrical Workers.

CIO President **Philip Murray**, a Catholic, shared Carey's anticommunism and his belief that the CIO needed to distance itself from the UE. In 1949, Cary assembled a coalition of anticommunist liberals, Catholics, Democrats, and disgruntled UE members and launched the International Union of Electrical, Radio, and Machine Workers of America. The IUE both organized new locals in the electrical manufacturing industry and encouraged UE locals to leave their parent organization and join the IUE. In the supercharged political climate of the Cold War, the IUE flourished and the UE declined. By 1950, the IUE represented half of all organized General Electric and Westinghouse workers and the UE just 10 percent. At its peak in 1955, the IUE claimed approximately 325,000 members. By the early 1950s, the IUE's leadership core coalesced around Carey, secretary-treasurer Al Hartnett, and western states regional director James Click; all three were ardent anticommunists.

The IUE, though consistently anticommunist, was plagued by internal squabbling. Both Hartnett and Click were purged by Carey over policy differences, and in 1966 Carey was ousted from the presidency by Paul Jennings. By then, both the IUE and the electrical industry were in transition. In 1960, IUE leaders called an ill-considered industrywide **strike** against General Electric. Numerous IUE locals refused to honor the strike call, leaving the IUE in disarray. During this period, union membership in the electrical manufacturing industry tumbled. The strike's collapse did, however, lead the IUE to curtail adversarial relations with the UE. In 1969–1970, the two groups cooperated in a campaign against General Electric that secured higher wages for electrical workers and dealt a death blow to aggressive GE anti-union programs known as **Boulwarism**.

In many respects, though, the 1970 campaign was a swan song for the IUE. The recession of the 1970s hit the electrical and electronics industry hard. Foreign imports flooded U.S. markets, and by the 1980s the industry was beset by layoffs and plant closings that made it difficult for **industrial unions** to maintain membership services and benefits. Transitions involving unions mirrored the consolidation taking place within the electrical industry. In 2000, the IUE merged with the Communications Workers of America (CWA). Ironically, the UE survives and is among the more progressive unions in contemporary America.

Suggested Reading

Ronald Filippelli and M. D. McColloch, *Cold War in the Working Class: The Rise and Decline of the United Electrical Workers*, 1995; Ron Schatz, *The Electrical Workers: A History of Labor at General Electric and Westinghouse, 1923–60*, 1983; Judith Stepan-Norris and Maurice Zeitlin, *Left Out: Reds and America's Industrial Unions*, 2003.

INTERNATIONAL UNION OF MINE, MILL, AND SMELTER WORKERS

The International Union of Mine, Mill, and Smelter Workers was founded on May 15, 1893, as the Western Federation of Miners (WFM), a union of hard-rock miners with a reputation for feisty radicalism in the tough mining communities of the American West. The WFM changed its name in 1916 and was generally thereafter referred to as "Mine Mill." The WFM contained a host of colorful leaders, including **William Haywood**, a cofounder of the **Industrial Workers of the World** (IWW) in 1905.

The WFM formed in direct reaction to brutal conditions in Western copper mines, coal extraction, and rock-processing operations. At the time, company control in remote regions of the West was such that some mine barons operated as a law unto themselves. The WFM frequently compared mine owners to the Russian czar and it stood ready to use **direct action** to oppose their power. Its ability to do so was aided by the rough-and-tumble nature of hard-rock miners, who expected no quarter from management and offered little in return. The WFM was involved in some of the most brutal and dramatic **strikes** of the late 19th and early 20th centuries, including Cripple Creek, **Coeur d'Alene**, and the **Colorado Labor Wars**. The WFM affiliated with the **American Federation of Labor** (AFL) in 1896, but pulled out of that arrangement after one year when it became obvious that the WFM's brand of labor radicalism and **industrial unionism** were a poor fit. WFM strikes often turned violent. Although the WFM seldom initiated violence beyond beating up **scabs** and strikebreakers, miners had access to gunpowder and dynamite and sometimes responded to violence done against their members by blowing up mines. As a result, the WFM often stood accused of actions it did not commit. Most dramatically, Haywood and several other WFM officials went on trial in 1907 for the murder of former Idaho Governor Frank Steunenberg, but were acquitted of the crime and probably had no role in it whatsoever.

Haywood and other WFM members helped found the IWW and infused it with their militant spirit despite the fact that the WFM disaffiliated with the IWW after just two years. Ironically, the WFM grew more cautious in the wake of the Steunenberg trial. When the IWW moved toward **anarcho-syndicalism** and rejected ballot-box politics, the WFM quit the IWW in early 1908. In 1911, the WFM rejoined the IWW. Lost strikes in 1914, a business downturn, and competition from the IWW led to a decline in WFM membership. As part of a plan to revitalize the union, the WFM changed its name to the International Union of Mine, Mill, and Smelter Workers in 1916. Mine Mill did not thrive under the aegis of the AFL. Throughout the 1920s, the organization was infiltrated by labor spies and plagued by declining membership.

During the Great Depression, Mine Mill leaders led the organization in an abrupt turnabout that returned it to the militancy of its earlier days. This put it on a collision course with the AFL, and Mine Mill was among the founding affiliates of the **Congress of Industrial Organizations** (CIO). It was also one of the more progressive American unions on issues of race. Mine Mill greatly expanded its organization of Latinos, a practice begun during World War I. It also recruited African American and immigrant laborers. The **Taft-Hartley Act** hurt Mine Mill, however, as some of its leaders and members belonged to the Communist Party.

Even before the post-World War II **Red Scare** led the CIO to expel Mine Mill in 1950, the **United Auto Workers of America** and the **United Steelworkers of America** engaged in **raiding** Mine Mill. From 1950 through 1967, the organization maintained an independent identity, though it did enjoy friendly relations with what was left of the IWW.

In 1954, Mine Mill's long struggle to organize Latino zinc miners in New Mexico was dramatized in the now-classic **film** *Salt of the Earth*. Herbert Bieberman, who was on a Hollywood **blacklist**, directed it. Bieberman's presence and the controversial nature of the subject matter brought Mine Mill under intense government scrutiny. Several Mine Mill workers in the film were deported, and throughout the

1950s Mine Mill members were beaten by thugs, falsely arrested, and harassed by investigators. In 1959, Mine Mill vice president Asbury Howard was beaten and jailed for assisting with voter registration of African Americans in Alabama.

Mine Mill found it impossible to maintain its independence. In 1967, the union's remaining 37,000 members voted to merge with the United Steelworkers of America.

Suggested Reading

David Brundage, *The Making of Western Labor Radicalism: Denver's Organized Workers, 1878–1905*, 1974; J. Anthony Lukas, *Big Trouble: A Murder in a Small Western Town Sets off a Struggle for the Soul of America*, 1997; "Western Mining History," http://www.westernmininghistory.com/articles/7/page1/, accessed January 5, 2011.

INTERNATIONAL WORKINGMEN'S ASSOCIATION. *See* Labor Party; Marxism.

JACKSONIAN ERA AND LABOR

The years following the conclusion of the War of 1812 saw a dramatic move toward the establishment of universal white male suffrage within the United States. A wave of popular democracy ensued in which most states rewrote their constitutions and removed voting requirements such as property ownership, which had previously restricted the number of men eligible to vote. This expansion of the electorate would have profound influence on the nation's political practices. Among its consequences was the need for political candidates to make direct appeal to the farmers and working men who made up the bulk of the electorate.

The aftermath of the War of 1812 also saw a decline of the Federalist Party and the end of what is generally called the First Party System (roughly 1792 to 1820). It was followed by a period known as the Era of Good Feelings (1816–1824), a time of widespread political consensus in which the Democratic-Republican Party—the forerunners of the modern **Democratic Party**—enjoyed a near-monopoly over political power in the country. The disputed election of 1824, which saw John Quincy Adams take the presidency even though he received substantially fewer popular votes than war hero Andrew Jackson, ended the period of national consensus. It also ushered in both the Jacksonian Era (roughly 1824 to 1845) and the rise of the Second Party System (1828–1854), which are collectively called "the era of the common man" because of the appeals made by politicians for plebeian votes.

In 1828, Andrew Jackson exacted revenge for his loss in 1824 and soundly defeated John Quincy Adams, the sitting president. As part of its electoral strategy, the Jackson campaign made much of Jackson's "common" roots. The candidate was not college educated, was renowned as an Indian fighter and war hero, and was the first candidate who was from neither Virginia nor Massachusetts. His humble birth was emphasized, though at the time of his election Jackson was a prosperous slave owner who had enriched himself through land speculation. Nonetheless, Jackson was packaged as a "Great Commoner" and his unrefined ways were favorably contrasted to those of the patrician Adams. On Inauguration Day in 1829, Jackson threw open the White House lobby for all and provided cheese and drink to the general public.

Jackson laid the foundation of appealing to the "average" American in political campaigns. Few of his actions as president actually benefited the masses per se, though Jackson's veto of the Bank of the United States was couched in the rhetoric of assaulting autocracy. In like fashion, Jackson's policies of Indian removal and support for the concept of Manifest Destiny were sold as promoting opportunities for commoners, though the number who actually capitalized on these opportunities was limited.

Jackson and his successor, Martin Van Buren, served as president at a time when commoners were on the rise, both as settlers moving into new lands west of the Appalachian Mountains and as **wage**-earners in factories and laborers building canals and railroads during the early phase of the **Industrial Revolution**. Thus, when anti-Jacksonian sentiment eventually coalesced into the Whig Party, its candidates felt similarly compelled to direct their appeals to the common man.

Many of those targeted by party rhetoric came to question whether mainstream politicians truly had the best interests of commoners at heart. The building of factories coincided with early efforts to build a labor movement; in many cases old journeymen's associations mutated into unions. The late 1820s saw an outbreak of **strikes** and the creation of the **Workingmen's movement**, a loose array of third parties and reform groups that sought to place power directly in the hands of farmers, laborers, and their allies. The "Workies," as they were called, were not a unified movement, but various configurations of Workies contested political power, organized strikes, and founded newspapers aimed at ordinary Americans. The movement fizzled out when the economy soured in the 1830s, but it did well enough overall to reinforce the view of Democrats and Whigs alike that the masses could no longer be ignored by political candidates. This perspective was seen in great clarity during the election of 1840, when the Whig William Henry Harrison ran as "the workingman's friend." Helped in part by a slur that backfired on the Van Buren campaign, Harrison—also an Indian fighter and war hero—adopted a log cabin and hard cider jug as campaign symbols, though Harrison actually lived in comfort and came from a prominent political family.

The Jacksonian Era came to an end during the 1840s, its end hastened by the rise of a new **middle class,** the after-effects of the severe Panic of 1837, political turmoil following Harrison's premature death just 32 days into his presidency, and the emergence of new issues such abolitionism, temperance, and tensions with Mexico. The age of the common man continued, though references to it often represented a mere rhetorical ploy. Many working people thereafter continued to dream of a separate **labor party** that would match words to deeds.

Suggested Reading

James L. Bugg, Jr., *Jacksonian Democracy: Myth or Reality?*, 1952; Ronald P. Formisano, *The Birth of Mass Political Parties: Michigan, 1827–1861*, 1971; Lawrence Frederick Kohl, *The Politics of Individualism: Parties and the American Character in the Jacksonian Era*, 1989; Edward Pessen, *Most Uncommon Jacksonians*, 1967; Sean Wilentz, *Chants Democratic: New York City and the Rise of the American Working Class, 1788–1850*, 1984.

JONES, MARY HARRIS ("MOTHER")

Mary Harris "Mother" Jones (May 1, 1830/August 1, 1837?–November 30, 1930) was a colorful labor activist best known for her advocacy work on behalf of miners.

She was born in Cork, Ireland, the daughter of Richard and Helen Harris. Her date of birth is in dispute, with dates varying from as early as 1830 to as late as 1837. Moreover, May 1 was probably an invention chosen for its associations with **May Day**. The best available evidence suggests that she was born on November 1, 1837, and that Jones later exaggerated her age to drum up sympathy and dramatize the causes she took up.

The Harris family emigrated to Canada sometime around 1850 and eventually settled in Toronto, where Mary received both a public and convent school education. She briefly taught in a convent school in Monroe, Michigan, before relocating to Chicago, where she worked as a dressmaker. Sometime in the late 1850s, Mary moved to Memphis and resumed teaching. While there she met George Jones, an ironworker and a member of the Iron Molders' Union. In 1861, they wed, and Mary gave birth to four children in quick succession. George Jones introduced Mary to the labor movement and the social injustices that workers endured. Her domestic life was shattered in 1867, when her husband and children all died of yellow fever. Devastated, she returned to Chicago and opened a dressmaking shop, only to lose everything she had in the Great Chicago Fire of 1871. Destitute, she began attending **Knights of Labor** (KOL) meetings. Jones was inspired by the KOL's campaigns for better working conditions and the group's emphasis on mutual assistance. Several Chicago Knights aided Jones after the 1871 Chicago fire and she was able to resume work as a seamstress. Although Jones was not yet an activist, the KOL's willingness to organize women allowed her to deepen her understanding of labor issues and provided her with opportunities to speak and find her voice.

Although Jones witnessed the furor of the **railroad strikes of 1877**, it was the trauma of the **Great Upheaval** that launched Jones's career as an activist. She was particularly outraged by events in Chicago associated with the Haymarket riot. Jones blamed Chicago police for precipitating the violence that led to the **Haymarket bombing**, believed that the **anarchists** accused of the crime were innocent, and took part in clemency movements aimed at saving them.

The KOL declined rapidly in Chicago in the late 1880s and Jones, though in her fifties, transferred her energy and loyalty to the **United Mine Workers of America (UMW)** and, later, to the Socialist Party as well. She became a fixture on **picket lines** and workers dubbed the gray-haired crusader "Mother" Jones. Jones's fiery rhetoric and tenacious advocacy of workers' rights earned her other nicknames, such as "the grandmother of all agitators," "hell-raiser," and "the miners' angel." She became so engrossed in labor campaigns that she famously refused to endorse women's suffrage. Although she outwardly insisted that women's involvement in politics weakened their ability to be good mothers, Jones had long ago left the world of Victorian domesticity. Privately she held the view that the suffrage movement was trivial in comparison to labor's cause.

Jones enjoyed a reputation as a spellbinding speaker who easily mixed fieriness and folksiness. She was involved in a number of labor campaigns, but was best known for her work with the UMW, for which she occasionally worked as an official organizer, though she spent much of her life as an independent lecturer and

Labor leader Mary Harris Jones, known as Mother Jones, meets with President Calvin Coolidge in 1924. (Library of Congress)

freelance agitator. Grandmotherly in demeanor, but a fierce rabble-rouser, Jones referred to miners as her "boys," and thought of them as a surrogate family. Without a house or family of her own, Jones traveled wherever there "was a fight worth fighting" and lodged with **working-class** families. Her activities included organizing coal miners in West Virginia in 1902 and 1903, and those in Colorado in 1903 and 1904. In 1903, she drew public attention to the plight of textile workers by marching their impoverished children to Oyster Bay, New York, where she embarrassed President Theodore Roosevelt at his summer retreat. Roosevelt refused to meet with Jones, a pique that generated more publicity for Jones and the children than if he had.

Jones grew disenchanted with the conservatism of the UMW under the leadership of **John Mitchell** in the early 1900s and briefly quit the union. Although she was not an ideologue, Jones did embrace **socialism** in principle and attended both the founding conventions for the Social Democratic Party in 1898 and the **Industrial Workers of the World** (IWW) in 1905. Her time in the IWW was brief. Although she admired **Big Bill Haywood** and several other IWW leaders, Jones had no stomach for IWW factionalism and she soon drifted back to taking part in miner **strikes**.

In 1910, Jones agitated on behalf of Colorado copper miners and Union Pacific Railroad employees. She rejoined the UMW in 1911 and returned to the Colorado coalfields in 1913 and 1914, where she witnessed the **Ludlow Massacre**. She reached the height of her fame during the Colorado struggles, when she was deported from the area numerous times and then jailed for defying court orders to stay away from the area. She personally confronted Standard Oil's John D. Rockefeller, whose business interests owned Ludlow mines, after the massacre. Although the reforms Rockefeller put in place probably had more to do with his desire to counter the public outrage associated with the loss of life—and to stave off potential lawsuits and charges—Jones's intervention further cemented her reputation among miners.

Jones was imprisoned many times for her unionizing efforts and was even arrested for conspiracy to commit murder during the Paint Creek Cabin strike in West Virginia in 1913. Jones learned to exploit her advanced age and diminutive figure—she stood less than five feet tall—to avoid prolonged imprisonment, but her willingness to put her body on the line won her the unflagging admiration of workers. Her mere presence at a strike or rally bolstered morale, and she was much in demand. She was involved in New York City garment worker strikes in 1915 and 1916, and the **Steel Strike of 1919**. In the 1920s, Jones once again briefly quit the UMW, citing differences with **John L. Lewis**, but she was back in the fold by 1924, the year she lost a libel suit filed by the publisher of the *Chicago Times*. (It was a Pyrrhic victory as Jones had no assets, let alone the $350,000 assessed in damages.)

Despite advancing age and deteriorating health, Jones continued agitating well into her nineties. She held a 100th birthday party in May 1930, though it was probably just her 93rd. She died in Silver Spring, Maryland, on November 30, 1930. At her request, she was buried with her "boys" in the Union Miners Cemetery in Mount Olive, Illinois.

Mother Jones was among history's most determined and colorful labor leaders. Stubborn, defiant, and fearless, she inspired tens of thousands of workers during her lifetime, and she became a legendary figure in death. She has been the subject of numerous stories, tales, and plays, and the labor **music** repertoire contains several songs devoted to Jones. Her name adorns a crusading magazine and her aphorism, "Pray for the dead and fight like hell for the living," continues to show up on posters, bumper stickers, and T-shirts, and in the speeches of labor activists.

Suggested Reading

Linda Atkinson, *Mother Jones: The Most Dangerous Woman in America*, 1978; Elliot Gorn, *Mother Jones: The Most Dangerous Woman in America*, 2001; Mary Harris Jones, *Autobiography of Mother Jones*, 1925.

JOURNEYMAN

"Journeyman" is a term used to describe a person who successfully completes an apprenticeship and is qualified to work for **wages** in a given trade. Its origins lie in the medieval guild system, in which **apprentices** were taken in by a **master craftsman**, who taught them the trade. Apprentices were usually children and received no compensation other than room and board. Becoming a journeyman was the next step of one's vocation. The term derives from the French word for "day" (*journée*) and was so designated because such a worker was paid a daily wage, often with his original master, though according to guild rules he was now eligible to negotiate with whomever he wished.

The European-based guild system, though loosened from some of the strict rules of medieval society, formed the basis for **artisan**-based production in North America during the Colonial and early Republican periods. The guild system was, however, highly regulated and ill adapted to economic systems rooted in competition and free trade. It also depended upon a high degree of turnover within a given craft. When it functioned well, a journeyman could anticipate spending about seven years as a wage-earner. During this period he could save money and hone his craft until such time that his product was deemed of comparable quality to that of masters. The journeyman's expectation was that he, too, would be recognized as a master, and be able to take in his own apprentices and journeymen. The very idea of spending one's entire career working for wages was abhorrent to artisan culture and was viewed by individuals such as Benjamin Franklin as a dangerous form of dependency that threatened the very foundations of the social order.

By the early 19th century, the development of regional and national markets, cost competition, capital concentration, and the movement toward mass production had begun to erode the journeymen's prospects. Journeymen had long formed associations for fellowship and mutual support; these mutated into economic units organized to protect their tenuous status as free republican laborers. Journeymen's associations were the very foundation upon which **craft unions** were built. These entities emerged in Europe first, but several were present even in the late 18th century and they began to emerge in earnest in the late 1820s. Trade unions gathered in force during the **Workingmen**'s **movement** in the 1830s and, though most of the groups formed during that time failed to survive, they became as permanent a feature of American society as wage-earning.

Industrialization, mass production, and the decline of artisan-based production changed the very meaning of the word "journeyman." By the early 20th century, the term denoted a person who completed a trade union apprenticeship and was competent to work independently in that trade. It remains a distinct status among electricians, plumbers, carpenters, and others whose labor is not easily reduced to mass-production methods.

Suggested Reading

Bruce Laurie, *Artisans to Workers*, 1989; Laura Rigal, *The American Manufactory: Art, Labor, and the World of Things in the Early Republic*, 2001; Sean Wilentz, *Chants Democratic: New York City and the Rise of the American Working Class*, 1984.

JURISDICTION

In labor terms, jurisdiction refers to the boundaries that separate one union's territory and representation from another's. To a casual observer, such boundaries might appear obvious, but they are not. For instance, if a worker installs the girders on an office building, should that worker belong to an ironworkers union or a construction workers union? If labor unions in a metropolitan area form a **Central Labor Union** (CLU), how far into the suburbs can representation extend before it encroaches upon the jurisdiction of another CLU or labor council?

These are questions of great importance, as jurisdiction confers **collective bargaining** rights on the union that holds it. Union **contracts** often specify who can do certain jobs. They also protect employment for members. In construction organizing, for example, questions might arise as to whether a particular job should be done by a bricklayer or a carpenter. On a highway construction project, controversy could arise over whether traffic should be directed by off-duty police officers or by union personnel to whom the company would be obligated to offer **overtime** pay and provide **fringe benefits**.

Bitter jurisdiction debates raged when the **Industrial Revolution** introduced machines that deskilled work processes and made **artisan** labor less defined. **Craft unions** vied with one another to organize workers in mass-production industries, sometimes to absurd levels. **Assembly-line production** led to situations in which individuals installing wires were viewed as skilled electricians and those snapping in windshields were classified as artisanal glassworkers. The underlying assumption of **industrial unionism** is that such distinctions should be eliminated and that workers should be classified and organized according to products they create—in the aforementioned example, as autoworkers.

Rival **labor federations** also engaged in jurisdictional battles. This was particularly true during the late 19th century, when the **Knights of Labor** (KOL) vied for supremacy with the **American Federation of Labor** (AFL). The two groups' mutual antagonism was rooted in a fundamental disagreement over principles. The KOL believed in class **solidarity** and classified all workers as Knights, irrespective of occupation. By contrast, the AFL's **voluntarism** gave sovereignty to individual crafts and viewed shared skill as the only legitimate basis for organization. To the AFL, Knights practiced **dual unionism**. The squabble between the KOL and the AFL led to **raiding** on the part of each federation. The AFL also raided members from the **Industrial Workers of the World** (IWW) in the first several decades of the 20th century. In the 1930s, the AFL itself was raided when the newly formed **Congress of Industrial Organizations** (CIO) spirited away millions of AFL members who felt that industrial unionism was better able to serve them. The two federations engaged in numerous jurisdictional and raiding battles throughout the 1930s and 1940s, and a confusing array of unions emerged seeking to organize workers within the same industry.

The 1955 AFL-CIO merger established procedures to settle jurisdictional disputes, but they still occur nonetheless. Jurisdiction became less clear as shifts in work rendered older craft and industrial union models problematic. By the latter half of the 20th century, many labor unions sought to expand their base by organizing workers outside traditional skill and occupational boundaries. The **Teamsters**, for example, attempted to organize agricultural workers in the 1960s and 1970s, an effort that led to jurisdictional disputes with the **United Farm Workers of America**. Expanded bases became even more important from the

1980s onward as overall union strength declined, formerly separate organizations merged, and labor unions sought to replace workers lost in one occupation by picking up new ones in other fields. For example, the 390,000 members of the **United Auto Workers of America** include graduate students, farm implement assembly workers, teachers, casino employees, and health care workers as well as autoworkers. Disputes sometimes arise from these cloudy jurisdictional boundaries.

Suggested Reading

Philip S. Foner, *History of the Labor Movement in the United States. Vol. 3: The Policies and Practices of the American Federation of Labor, 1900–1909*, 1964; Grace Palladino, *Skilled Hands, Strong Spirits*, 2005; Lloyd Ulman, *The Rise of the National Trade Union*, 1968; "Where We Work," United Auto Workers, http://www.uaw.org/node/670, accessed January 21, 2011.

KIRKLAND, JOSEPH LANE

Lane Kirkland (March 12, 1922–August 14, 1999) served as president of the **American Federation of Labor-Congress of Industrial Organizations** (AFL-CIO) from 1979 to 1995. His defenders credit him with piloting the AFL-CIO through an extremely difficult period and securing the best deal for labor unions possible during a climate of severe economic challenge and virulent anti-union backlash. To his many critics, Kirkland was a career bureaucrat who embodied the weaknesses of **business unionism**, at a time when a more militant leader would have better served the AFL-CIO.

Kirkland was born into a well-regarded southern family in Camden, South Carolina. His father, Randolph Withers Kirkland, was a cotton buyer. Lane grew up in Newbury, South Carolina, a textile town, attended public schools, and counted millworker children among his friends. He also grew up with an air of what some saw as arrogance and racial insensitivity. His great-great-grandfather had been a secessionist, and Kirkland often referred to the **Civil War** as the "War of Northern Aggression." He also grew up as an ardent anticommunist.

During World War II, Kirkland served in the merchant marines. He graduated from the United States Merchant Marine Academy in 1942, served throughout the remainder of the war, and joined the Masters, Mates, and Pilots union. Subsequent critics often point to his military service as Kirkland's only brush with **blue-collar** labor. In 1944, Kirkland married the former Edith Draper Hollyday; the couple had five daughters before their divorce in 1972. After World War II, Kirkland entered Georgetown University and obtained a bachelor of science degree from the School of Foreign Service. Upon his graduation in 1948, Kirkland worked the Research Department of the **American Federation of Labor** (AFL), and, on assignment, wrote speeches for **Democratic Party** vice-presidential candidate Alben Barkley in 1948 and for presidential contender Adlai Stevenson in 1952 and 1956. He fully supported the precepts of **Cold War** unionism and shared the fears about **communism** that emerged during the second **Red Scare**.

Other than a brief stint as director of research and education for the International Union of Operating Engineers (1958–1960), Kirkland spent his entire working career as an AFL-CIO administrator. When he returned to the AFL-CIO in 1960, he became a key assistant to AFL-CIO President **George Meany**. Kirkland shared many of Meany's virtues and faults. He supported numerous Great Society programs, but was uncomfortable with the emerging **counterculture**, supported U.S. policy objectives related to the **Vietnam War**, and helped shape key racial legislation such as the 1964 Civil Rights Act, though he grew alarmed at rising black militancy during the 1960s. Many labor analysts credit Kirkland with deft maneuvering that helped settle an acrimonious transit workers strike in 1966. In 1969, Kirkland became the AFL-CIO's secretary-treasurer, a post second only to Meany's in influence and power. Although Kirkland spearheaded the AFL-CIO's refusal to endorse Democratic presidential and anti-Vietnam War candidate George McGovern in 1972, he still managed to secure a place on President Richard Nixon's infamous White House "enemies list." In 1973, Kirkland married Irena Neumann, who had been born in Czechoslovakia. When Meany retired in 1979, Kirkland was selected to head the AFL-CIO.

Controversy dogged Kirkland's tenure as AFL-CIO boss. Though it is by no means certain that anyone could prevented organized labor from the decline it experienced in the wake of the 1970s recession, the competitive pressures brought by **globalization**, and job losses associated with capital flight and **deindustrialization**, Kirkland's lack of public savvy did little to enhance his reputation. He was widely seen as Meany's right-hand man and was tarred by the perception that his own views were as out of touch as his predecessor's. Kirkland was often brusque (critics said arrogant), was prone to making cutting remarks, projected an air of contempt for the media, and refused most interview requests. In response, the media was loath to present Kirkland in a positive light, even when he did something admirable, such as bringing women and African Americans into leadership roles within the AFL-CIO.

Kirkland had the misfortune to head the AFL-CIO during the aggressively anti-union administration of **Ronald Reagan**. Thus Kirkland was the point man during such 1980s traumas as the **Professional Air Traffic Controllers Organization strike** in 1981, the failed **corporate campaign** of Hormel workers in Minnesota in 1985, and numerous **downsizing** assaults on the American workforce. Kirkland won kudos for his efforts in organizing the 1981 Solidarity Day rally against Reagan administration policies, but the praise faded as an air of futility settled over labor. He was similarly frustrated (and blamed) in 1994, when President Bill Clinton signed into law the **North American Free Trade Agreement**, which the AFL-CIO bitterly opposed. Insult was added to injury when Congress refused to support a federation-supported bill that would have outlawed the hiring of permanent "replacement workers" (**scabs**) during labor disputes.

Kirkland's greatest achievement as head of the AFL-CIO came in support of Eastern European freedom movements. Behind the scenes the AFL-CIO gave logistical and monetary support to the Polish trade union movement Solidarity, a key force in overthrowing communist rule in Poland in 1989. Kirkland would be posthumously awarded the Order of the White Eagle by the Polish government. In retirement, Kirkland asserted that his efforts in contributing to the rise of democracy in Eastern Europe and to the collapse of the Soviet Union were his greatest achievements. Yet even these efforts drew detractors; some among the rank-and-file charged that Kirkland spent too much time and money on foreign affairs and not enough on grassroots organizing. Among them, voices arose demanding a return to the militant spirit of the 1930s.

By 1995, Kirkland faced an open revolt against his leadership of the AFL-CIO, much of it coming from large constituent unions such as the **American**

Federation of State, County, and Municipal Employees; the Service Employees International Union, the Teamsters; and the United Mine Workers of America. Kirkland was forced to step down in August 1995; in October of that year, **John Sweeney** succeeded Kirkland as head of the federation. To date, Kirkland is the only AFL-CIO president to leave office involuntarily.

Unions commanded 25 percent of the workforce when Kirkland took office, but just 15.5 percent when he left. In recent years numerous observers have softened their criticism of Kirkland. The subsequent decline in union representation suggests that the roots of organized labor's problems reside more in political and economic structures and cannot be simplistically blamed on poor leadership. Kirkland received a Presidential Citizens Medal from President George H. W. Bush in 1989 and a Presidential Medal of Freedom from President Clinton in 1994. He was inducted into the U.S. **Department of Labor**'s Hall of Fame in 2002 and, in 2007 the National Labor College named its new research center after Kirkland. Whether these honors and subsequent research will rehabilitate Kirkland's reputation remains to be seen; at present Kirkland is generally perceived to have been a less-than-inspiring leader.

Suggested Reading

Paul Buhle, *Taking Care of Business: Samuel Gompers, George Meany, Lane Kirkland and the Tragedy of American Labor*, 1999; Arch Puddington, *Lane Kirkland: Champion of American Labor*, 2005; William Serrin, "Lane Kirkland, Former A.F.L. C.I.O. Head, Dies at 77," *New York Times*, August 15, 1999.

KNIGHTS OF LABOR

The Knights of Labor (KOL) was the largest **labor federation** of the 19th century. Its progressive views on gender and race were well ahead of its time, as were its efforts at international organizing, its political lobbying, and its anticipation of **industrial unionism**.

Uriah Stephens and six other members of a Philadelphia tailors' union in the throes of collapse founded the KOL in December 1869. The tailors, like numerous other **craft unions**, had found their power withering in the face of political repression and economic recession. When Stephens dissolved the tailors' union, he chose to pattern the KOL after a more successful form of voluntary association: fraternal orders. The new organization, officially dubbed the Noble and Holy Order of the Knights of Labor, operated in complete secrecy in accordance with a dense code of rituals loosely adapted from Freemasonry and defunct labor groups such as the Sovereigns of Industry. The secrecy and the complexity of KOL rituals meant that organization of the KOL proceeded slowly. The group did not expand beyond the greater Philadelphia region until 1874, and it did not write a constitution or statement of principles until 1878, at which time it contained about 10,000 members. The KOL gained momentum from the **railroad strike of 1877**. The KOL had not taken part of the 1877 strike, which ended in failure and led to the further decline of craft unions. In the aftermath, however, the KOL absorbed several severely weakened unions, including the Knights of St. Crispin.

In 1879, Stephens resigned as the KOL's grand master workman (president) to run for Congress. **Terence V. Powderly**, who held the post until late 1893, succeeded Stephens. Powderly, a Roman Catholic, lobbied the KOL to change its focus on ritual and secrecy to mollify Vatican bans on secret societies, and to insulate the KOL from hysteria over the **Molly Maguires**. In 1882, the KOL finally abandoned secrecy, although its ritual practices remained a closely guarded mystery, and at least one local assembly defied central authority and continued to operate in total secrecy.

The KOL embraced a multipronged reform agenda that embraced everything from land reform and the **eight-hour** workday to equal rights for women and the abolition of the **wage** system. It was not a trade union, but rather a federation of local assemblies that (in theory) rendered all craft and occupational identities secondary to the ideals of knighthood. Historians sometimes classify the KOL as a social-reform union, and many of its precepts inclined toward **utopianism**. In theory, the yearly General Assembly and the executive board it elected were the KOL's highest governing bodies. Local assemblies were an eclectic mix, with some being single-trade **union locals** and others mixed assemblies in which various trades comingled. In addition, some locals included workers of a single gender or race, while others had a heterogeneous membership. Contiguous local assemblies often combined into district assemblies to coordinate policy and tactics of mutual interests, and there were also state assemblies and a few national trade districts that represented the interests of specific trades. Each level of KOL bureaucracy had officers and labor courts to resolve internal disputes. On occasion, exact lines of authority were murky, and most efforts at centralization met with limited success. Knights also crossed ideological lines. All persons, including employers, were eligible for KOL membership as long as they were not lawyers, bankers, land speculators, gamblers, or liquor traders. (The KOL was officially in favor of temperance, though it organized **brewers**.)

The KOL's history was marked by frequent disconnect between its principles and practices. Officially, the KOL opposed **strikes**, believing that more was lost than was ever gained. Instead, it endorsed **boycotts** (both primary and secondary) as a way of bringing recalcitrant employers to their knees. Ultimately, the KOL hoped that a system of mandatory **arbitration** would settle all capital and labor disputes. The federation insisted that the interests of workers and employers were mutual, though it also yearned for a future in which the wage system and investment **capitalism** would collapse and be replaced by a network of productive and distributive **cooperatives**. The KOL attempted hundreds of cooperative experiments, most of which were short-lived and unsuccessful. In like fashion, the KOL conducted numerous strikes, official reluctance to endorse them notwithstanding. It won improved conditions for many workers, though it lost more strikes than it won.

As one of the first labor groups to organize mass-production industries, the KOL was the first labor federation to confront the full economic and political clout of organized capital. In 1885, it won a strike against the Southwest Railway conglomerate, which was controlled by Jay Gould, one of the most-hated robber barons of the entire 19th century. Membership soared from 110,000 in 1885 to more than

729,000 dues-paying members by July 1886, with hundreds of thousands more claiming affiliation with the organization. In all, the KOL may have had more than 1 million individuals claiming to be associated with the organization by late 1886. Knights were active during the **Great Upheaval** and KOL political candidates (or their allies) won local elections in at least 189 towns and cities. The KOL also claimed that a dozen members of Congress held KOL membership.

The year 1886 proved to be the KOL's high-water mark, and the organization quickly contracted from this artificial plateau. Fallout from the Haymarket riot weakened the KOL. Although the KOL had not endorsed the nationwide strike of May 1, 1886, and had repudiated **anarchism**, four the men arrested for the **Haymarket bombing**, including **Albert Parsons**, had at least tangential ties to the KOL. Moreover, the victory over Gould proved Pyrrhic on several levels. First, hundreds of thousands of new members flooded the KOL with little understanding of its principles, many joining in the hope that the KOL would coordinate their own strikes. Some of these new members did, in fact, lead the KOL to undertake a series of disastrous strikes after 1886. Each lost campaign caused the organization to shed members and provided employers with excuses to assault the KOL. A new strike against Gould in 1886 ended in failure, as did strikes in the Chicago stockyards, against New England textile manufacturers, and against the New York Central Railroad. By 1890, the KOL was a much smaller organization. It also faced competition from the **American Federation of Labor** (AFL), which formed in 1886, organized only skilled workers, and warred with the KOL. Conflict with the AFL led to ill-advised ideological and **jurisdictional** disputes with trade unions, and touched off internal conflict inside the KOL. On the electoral front, the **Republican Party** and the **Democratic Party** often cooperated to defeat KOL candidates.

Some scholars mistakenly write off the KOL after 1888. Caution is in order, however. The KOL maintained a membership of more than 200,000 for the remainder of the 1880s and more than 100,000 for at least the first part of the 1890s. By the 1890s, the AFL surpassed the KOL in urban America and became the dominant labor federation. In rural America, however, the situation was less certain and scholars have yet to investigate thoroughly the KOL's presence in the countryside during the 1890s. Suggestive evidence points to the likelihood that in many locales the KOL simply fused with the ascendant **populist** movement, which would extend the KOL's influence to the end of the 19th century. The KOL maintained a national office into 1917, and there was one operating local assembly as late as 1949. It is estimated that at least 2.5 million men and women passed through the KOL ranks and that more than 10,000 local assemblies were formed.

The KOL ultimately collapsed, and its promise and vision failed to materialize in their totality. Even so, one should not underestimate the Knights' considerable achievements. Terence Powderly, for instance, was a figure of international fame, and politicians, journalists, and clerics sought his advice on a variety of matters. The KOL also sent a paid labor lobbyist to Washington, D.C.—the first labor federation to do so. In this sense the KOL was the first major labor federation to recognize the importance of public relations and political access in advancing labor's agenda.

It was prescient on other matters as well. The KOL was the first labor federation to organize African Americans, women, and noncraft workers on an equal basis with skilled, white males. It organized more than 90,000 African Americans, more than 60,000 women, and untold thousands of unskilled workers—levels that would not be surpassed until the 1930s. The KOL also pioneered in international organization efforts, forming chapters in Australia, Belgium, Canada, England, France, Ireland, New Zealand, Scotland, and South Africa. It achieved its greatest success in New Zealand, where more than two dozen Knights were elected to Parliament, and where it enacted the bulk of its political and social platform. Despite practices that KOL critics found archaic, much of what the KOL attempted was far in advance of its time and many of its principles would be considered progressive even by modern standards.

Suggested Reading

Leon Fink, *Workingmen's Democracy: The Knights of Labor and American Politics*, 1983; Norman Ware, *The Labor Movement in the United States 1860–1895: A Study in Democracy*, 1959 (reprint of 1929 original); Robert E. Weir, *Beyond Labor's Veil*, 1996.

L

LABOR COLLEGES

Labor colleges were training and residential programs aimed at providing adult education and leadership instruction for individuals involved in the labor movement. Their heyday occurred in the years 1920 to 1940 and, at one time, there were labor colleges of some sort in most industrial cities. They ranged in complexity from campus-based degree-granting institutions to modest slates of classes that took place in borrowed or rented space. Unlike technical, vocational, and **apprentice** programs, however, labor colleges generally maintained a heavy focus on politics, sociology, and economics rather than vocational skills training. Many labor colleges were inspired by (or affiliated with) **socialist** or **communist** social movements, though others were more moderate in their outlook. Each was path breaking in the sense that adult education was novel. In 1940, barely 25 percent of all American men and women obtained a four-year high school diploma and just 5 percent of men and 3 percent of women earned a bachelor's degree. Numerous labor colleges were established in the country, including the following: Commonwealth College in Mena, Arkansas; Work People's College in Minnesota; **Marxist** labor colleges in San Francisco, Chicago, and Flint, Michigan; Brookwood College in Katohna, New York; and the Highlander Folk Center in Tennessee.

Several 19th-century schools, most notably Berea College in Kentucky, had a strong working-class focus and taught labor education curricula. Berea (founded in 1855) catered directly to students from low-income families and also admitted African Americans. Its focus on interracial cooperation became a standard for later schools such as Highlander. In 1921, the Workers' Education Bureau of America (WEB) formed with a major emphasis of creating labor colleges. Among the early WEB founders and supporters were James Maurer, a socialist and a leader of the Pennsylvania Federation of Labor; John Brophy of the **United Mine Workers of American** union; and Fannia Cohn, an activist with the **International Ladies' Garment Workers' Union** (ILGWU). The leftist bent of the WEB can be seen in such schools as Commonwealth College (1923–1940), which was originally an offshoot of Job Harriman's New Llano Cooperative Colony in Louisiana, a socialist utopian experiment. Among its founders and advisors were socialist firebrand Kate Richards O'Hare and Roger Baldwin, the founder of the American Civil Liberties Union. Commonwealth College would later help train leaders and have a close working relationship with both the **Congress of Industrial Organizations** (CIO) and the **Southern Tenant Farmers' Union** (STFU). The WEB would eventually become more associated with the **American Federation of Labor** (AFL) and promote its brand of **craft unionism**, but activist schools such as the Work People's

College (1903–1941) and various Marxist labor schools thrived during the Great Depression despite the use of **Red Scare** tactics by their critics. Both the Seattle and the Denver Labor College had strong radical roots.

Typical in this regard was the Brookwood Labor College located in Katonah, New York. It was launched as an experimental college by socialist and pacifist opponents of World War I. In 1921, Abraham J. Muste (1885–1967), a former clergyman turned socialist, joined other progressives to organize Brookwood, with Muste becoming its educational director. Unlike the formal educational system, Brookwood stressed working-class history and culture, and provided students—many of whom were also full-time workers—with tactical training on how to serve the labor movement. Roughly 40 to 50 liberal union members, mostly in their twenties and thirties, paid $500 per year for a two-year program that included history, English, sociology, economics, theories of labor organizing, speech and rhetoric, and labor history. Among its alumni were ILGWU organizer **Rose Pesotta**; Victor and Roy Reuther, the brothers of **Walter Reuther**; Merlin Bishop, the educational director of the **United Auto Workers of America** (UAW); and Frank Winn, the UAW's publicity director. Brookwood maintained a small student body, but it also held conferences that drew activists from around the country and provided a forum that helped legitimize the labor movement. Many labor leaders lectured there, and numerous Brookwood graduates were found among the leadership ranks in early CIO affiliates. This point led the AFL to withdraw its financial support for Brookwood, among the factors leading to its closure in 1937, though it was mostly the lingering effects of the Great Depression that contributed to its insolvency.

One of the enduring remnants of the labor college phenomenon is the Highlander Folk School, which has been an important center for social activists since 1932 and is now called the Highlander Research and Education Center. It was cofounded by Myles Horton and Don West, and was originally located in Monteagle, Tennessee. Highlander began life as a hybrid institution—one part labor college and one part "folk school." The folk school concept originated in Denmark and was associated with 18th- and 19th-century romantic and nationalist movements seeking to discover the unique "folk" cultures of emerging national states. Highlander was meant to be a school located in Appalachia for mountain people who otherwise had minimal educational opportunities. It combined adult education, labor organizing, and a cultural focus on activities such as traditional music and storytelling. It quickly mutated into a center for fomenting social and economic change, especially within the emerging southern organized labor movement.

Like Berea before it, Highlander embraced interracial and nonsegregationist practices that made it a better fit for CIO activists than for AFL craft unionists. During the 1930s and 1940s, Highlander provided logistical and leadership support for organizing drives and **strikes**, including singing and presenting labor plays on picket lines. Many Highlander staff members, including Horton, worked as CIO organizers. For a time, Highlander was the site for the CIO's Southern School, and it helped train organizers for the CIO's **Operation Dixie** campaign.

Highlander's relationship to the CIO waned in the wake of schisms within the federation in the late 1940s and early 1950s. The school's activism and its refusal to embrace the tenets of the post-World War II Red Scare put it at loggerheads with the CIO's central leadership at a time in which the latter expelled radical affiliates and embraced **Cold War** unionism. From 1951 to 1953, Horton ran an education program for the **United Packinghouse Workers of America**, a union that Horton respected for its commitment to interracial unionism. Highlander was, however, dropped from the CIO's list of preferred education providers in 1953. By then Highlander had turned its attention to the emerging civil rights movement. Throughout the 1950s and 1960s, it trained movement activists and leaders, as well as launching a successful effort to eradicate illiteracy in the South. The school's fierce commitment to social justice earned it powerful enemies, and it was often accused of harboring communists. In 1962, the state of Tennessee closed Highlander and seized and sold the school's buildings, library, and other physical assets. Undaunted, Highlander reincorporated as Highlander Research and Education Center and began operations in the city of Knoxville before moving to its current home in nearby New Market, Tennessee, in 1972. Shortly thereafter Highlander redirected its attention toward the problems confronting Appalachia, and it renewed its ties with organized labor. It has been among numerous voices in the South to engage in fights over occupational safety and health in the coalfields. Lately its focus has expanded to include training leaders and holding conferences that address issues such **globalism**, immigrant rights, **deindustrialization**, and capital flight and the rise of low-wage nonunion work in Mexico's *maquiladora* factories.

Highlander does not provide as much direct labor education as it once did, and the labor college concept has largely shifted to mainstream college campuses. The WEB was absorbed into the AFL's larger educational program in 1951 and, when the **American Federation of Labor-Congress of Industrial Organizations** (AFL-CIO) formed in 1955, it became the federation's Education Department. Many colleges now offer labor studies and education degrees and hold institutes and summer training programs, often in cooperation with the AFL-CIO. Among those institutions offering undergraduate and graduate degrees in labor studies are City University of New York, Cornell, Michigan State, Penn State, San Francisco State, the University of Massachusetts, the University of Rhode Island, and Wayne State University.

The most direct remnant of the labor college ideal is the National Labor College (NLC), which was created by the AFL-CIO in 1969. In 1971, the AFL-CIO purchased a former junior college campus in Silver Spring, Maryland, and gave the NLC a permanent home. Like labor colleges in the past, this institution operates labor conferences, trains union leaders, and offers academic courses. It offers a small residential program with six undergraduate majors in labor studies and has, since 1971, granted more than 1,100 bachelor's degrees. It also offers several certificate programs and training programs, though it is probably best known for educating labor union leaders in various summer institutes, conferences, and individual courses.

Suggested Reading

Frank Adams, with Myles Horton, *Unearthing Seeds of Fire: The Idea of Highlander*, 1975; Richard J. Altenbaugh, *Education for Struggle: American Labor Colleges in the 1920s and 1930s*, 1990; National Labor College, http://www.nlc.edu/, accessed December 19, 2010.

LABOR DAY

Labor Day is a holiday held the first Monday in September to commemorate the achievements of workers in the United States and Canada. Most nations celebrate a labor holiday of some sort, though **May Day** holds the distinction of being International Workers' Day. Although it is now an established fixture on the North American calendar, the first workers' holiday was born out of struggle and defiance. Parades and rallies were a staple of 19th-century **working-class** protests, and Labor Day emerged from those patterns.

There is dispute over when the first Labor Day was held, in part because the **American Federation of Labor** (AFL) engaged in some deliberate myth making. It was not unusual for workers to declare impromptu holidays during the 19th century, with Thomas Paine's birthday on February 9 being a favorite. Numerous rallies presaged the Tuesday, September 5, 1882, event in New York City that is widely regarded as the first Labor Day as the term has come to be understood. The U.S. **Department of Labor** notes an 1878 event in Boston as a Labor Day predecessor, though Canadian workers had rallied in Toronto six years earlier. In 1882, a smaller rally took place in Providence, Rhode Island, several weeks prior to the New York event.

The New York parade involved a scale seldom matched by other events of that era, however. Between 30,000 and 40,000 workers marched in New York City rather than report to their jobs, while tens of thousands more watched. The term "Labor Day" appears to have been coined by Robert Price, a **Knights of Labor** (KOL) member in Maryland. Price suggested an annual holiday in honor of KOL founder Uriah Stephens, whose birthday was on August 3, making the Rhode Island event closer to Price's vision. Sources often credit **Peter James McGuire**—a carpenter, KOL member, and future AFL cofounder—as the "Father of Labor Day." McGuire spoke at the Providence event and took part in the New York City parade, but he was not the main organizer of either rally. The planning of the New York City event was undertaken by the city's **Central Labor Union** (CLU), a cooperating consortium of local unions whose officers largely collaborated with those of the city's KOL local assemblies. A KOL machinist named Matthew Maguire was in charge of the Committee of Arrangements and was an important organizer of the day's festivities. Peter McGuire was an active CLU member, but the fact that Matthew Maguire was a committed **socialist** perhaps explains why AFL mythmakers preferred to credit McGuire for the Labor Day planning instead. Another factor was likely the AFL's reluctance to give credit to the KOL, its major **labor federation** rival in the late 1880s.

Origins aside, the size of the New York City event inspired workers elsewhere, and for the next several years, other cities held their own impromptu parades. New York was often held up as an exemplar, though it was not until 1884 that New Yorkers actually celebrated the event on a Monday, and not until

1886 that workers across the country rallied on that same day. In 1887, Oregon became the first state to recognize Labor Day as a legal holiday. In the same year, Massachusetts, New Jersey, and New York passed similar measures. Workers elsewhere simply took matters into their own hands and stayed away from work on the first Monday in September. By 1894, 23 states officially recognized Labor Day, which prompted Congress to take action. On June 28, 1894, Congress declared the first Monday in September to be a national holiday, Labor Day.

Large parades and speeches, followed by picnics and other forms of recreation, marked early Labor Day celebrations. The 1890s brought dampened enthusiasm for Labor Day, however. By then the KOL was in decline and the nation suffered from deep economic challenges and an organized capital backlash in the wake of the collapse of the **Great Upheaval**. By the 1910s, some labor leaders complained that workers had forgotten about the true intent of the day. Passions were rekindled during the Great Depression, a time in which public protest rose anew, and, after 1947, unions often organized protests against the **Taft-Hartley Act** on Labor Day. Since the mid-1950s, however, the holiday has largely moved from a day of protest to a more commemorative event, and today Labor Day is widely viewed as the symbolic end of summer. Media outlets generally pay lip service to American workers in early September, but in many communities "back-to-school" retail bargains and leisure opportunities are more in evidence than rallies or reflection upon American labor history. Ideologues hold that Labor Day wraps America's bloody labor history in a false cloak of respectability, while its defenders see it as an important affirmation of working-class heritage and culture. Both sides agree that the holiday needs to be revitalized.

Suggested Reading

Paul Buhle, Scott Molloy, and Gail Sainsbury, *A History of Rhode Island Working People*, 1983; Michael Kazin and Steven Ross, "America's Labor Day: The Dilemma of a Workers' Celebration," *Journal of American History* (March 1992): 1294–1323; Robert E. Weir, *Beyond Labor's Veil: The Culture of the Knights of Labor*, 1996.

LABOR FEDERATION

A labor federation is a collection of national and **international unions** that affiliate with one another in the hope of creating a larger, more powerful body that can secure rights for working people. A labor federation operates as an umbrella organization under which various unions find common cause. If one views the labor movement as a continuum from microcosm to macrocosm, workers in a given area or craft band together to form a **union local** that secures **collective bargaining** rights and negotiates **contracts** within a particular shop or business. Most local **craft unions** and **industrial unions** are, in turn, part of larger national or international unions that coordinate policy and lobby for the common interests of workers in a given craft or occupation. Various union locals might cooperate with other unions to create a central labor union (or council). The various national, international, and central labor unions often find that there are issues common to all workers, no matter what their occupation. For example, issues such as the **minimum wage**, curtailing **child labor**, health care reform, **protectionism**, and environmental standards affect all workers; they are also dependent upon legislative action on a state or national level rather than the success or failure of union efforts on a local scale. A labor federation seeks to unite unions on such issues to create a mass movement whose lobbying power is greater than that of the fragmented individual unions. The term "labor federation" generally connotes a national or international body, though it might also mean an organization of statewide or regional unions.

Dreams of a labor federation emerged in the early 19th century, but few went beyond the planning stage. The short-lived **National Labor Union** (1866–1873) is generally regarded as the first significant attempt at a labor federation, and the **Knights of Labor** (KOL; 1869–1917) as the first labor federation to enjoy success. The **American Federation of Labor** (AFL), founded in 1886, is the foundation of current labor federations. Whereas the KOL sought to bring together workers of all levels of skill, the AFL organized only skilled workers. It began to supplant the KOL in the 1890s, fended off a challenge from the **Industrial Workers of the World**—which insisted that **class consciousness** should be the basis of a labor federation—in the early 20th century, and enjoyed a brief monopoly until the 1930s, when the **Congress of Industrial Organizations** (CIO) formed to organize workers by occupation rather than skill. The AFL and the CIO merged in 1955 to create a federation that represented more than 15 million workers. As such, it could raise money for political candidates, exert pressure upon Congress, and become a countervailing force to organized business groups such as the Chamber of Commerce or the **National Association of Manufacturers**. One of the foundational ideas of labor federations is that unions must parallel business organizations in structure to secure their goals.

The AFL-CIO has faced other rival organizations, such as the Alliance for Labor Action (1968–1972) and the **Change to Win Federation**. The latter organization formed in 2005 and represents unions that believe the current AFL-CIO federation is too bureaucratic and does not attend sufficiently to grassroots organizing. Historically labor federations have exerted political pressure and have been at the forefront of progressive social change, but they seldom have clout, access, or resources equivalent to those possessed by organized **capital**. This does not mean that they are ineffective, however, and defenders of labor federations are no doubt correct in their assertion that individual unions unaffiliated with any federation are far more vulnerable than those inside such an umbrella organization.

Representation within a federation varies according to the organization in question. Most operated (or currently operate) under a representative democracy structure. Delegates from individual national and international unions are chosen to attend regular conventions, with each union's number of delegates generally determined by the union's size. The delegates then select federation officers and an executive board. They also debate and decide upon issues such as policy objectives and **dues**. The elected officers run the federation and administer its bureaucracy until the next convention. A written constitution usually dictates which decisions can be made by elected officials and which must be approved by the general membership. Federations seldom negotiate contracts; such matters are left to local unions. They might, however, administer **strike** funds that require federation approval for allocation. The AFL-CIO largely operates in accordance with the AFL's original principle of **voluntarism** and allows its affiliates to regulate all internal affairs that do not have a direct bearing on federation policies.

Richard Trumka is currently the president of the AFL-CIO. He heads an organization that also has an executive vice president, a secretary-treasurer, 43 vice presidents, six departments, seven constituency groups, three allied groups, and five special programs. The Change to Win Federation is chaired by Joseph Hansen. Its bureaucracy is far simpler than that of the AFL-CIO, as it devotes more of its resources to direct organizing.

Suggested Reading

"AFL-CIO. America's Union Movement," http://www.aflcio.org/, accessed February 7, 2011; "Change to Win: The American Dream for American Workers," http://www.changetowin.org/, accessed February 7, 2011; Philip S. Foner, *History of the Labor Movement in the United States*, 10 volumes, 1947–1994.

LABOR JOURNALISM

Labor journalism can refer either to publications produced by the labor movement or to reporters who specialize on labor issues but are employed by other media outlets.

Labor journals came of age with the union movement in early 19th-century America. Working people quickly noticed that the mainstream press did not represent **working-class** interests and, in many cases, were openly hostile toward unions. In the decades leading up to the **Civil War**, the early **Industrial Revolution** served to deepen class tensions. Those who felt that the mainstream press did not accurately represent workers established their own journals to tell their side of the class conflict. Two of the most prominent labor newspapers in antebellum America began publication in 1828: the *Mechanics Free Press*, founded by Philadelphia-based labor activist William Heighton, and the *Working Man's Advocate*, published by George Henry Evans. Both papers had ties to the **Workingmen's movement**. These early labor newspapers reflected the growing concerns of skilled male workers, known as "mechanics" or **journeymen**, who felt threatened by the growth of industrial capitalism and the introduction of machinery that threatened to deskill their professions. As increasing numbers of white women entered industrial labor, they, too, expressed their concerns with low **wages**, long hours, and the **paternalism** they encountered. This was especially true for women toiling in New England mills. Textile workers in Lowell, Massachusetts, responded to the corporation-sponsored *Lowell Offering* with the *Voice of Industry*, which both gave aggrieved workers an outlet and sought to educate the broader public about the conditions under which mill women worked. The leader of the **Lowell Female Labor Reform Association**, **Sarah Bagley**, edited this journal for a short time during the mid-1840s.

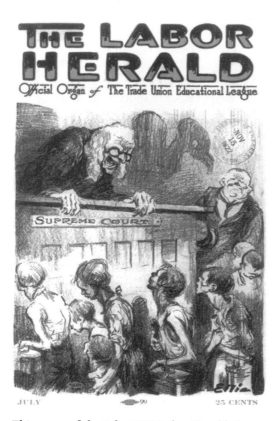

This cover of the July 1922 *Labor Herald* shows the Supreme Court looking down upon emaciated child laborers, referring to the court's ruling in *Bailey v. Drexel Furniture Company* (1922), which struck down child labor laws as unconstitutional. (Library of Congress)

After the Civil War, labor journals abounded, though many were under-capitalized and short-lived. Most national trade unions and employer brotherhoods had journals of some sort. In addition to dozens of papers published by affiliates, **labor federations** such as the **Knights of Labor** (KOL) and the **American Federation of Labor** (AFL) sponsored "official" journals. Workers could consult the *Journal of the Knights of Labor* or the *American Federationist* for information on struggles across the federation, their organization's official position on a variety of concerns, and decisions reached in conventions and by union officers. In addition, these papers sought to deliver political education to the rank-and-file. In the case of the KOL, many of its papers aspired to be alternatives to the mainstream press and also published fiction, poetry, world events, and general-interest stories.

Some quasi-independent newspapers were loosely connected or unconnected with specific unions, but were sympathetic to the cause of organized labor. *John Swinton's Paper*, which published between 1883 and 1887, so championed labor's cause and exposed social injustices that many workers viewed Swinton as heroic. Among the other important working-class newspapers of the late 19th century were the *National Labor Tribune* and the *Irish World and American Industrial Liberator*. Political radicals also published journals such as *The People*, *Appeal to Reason*, *Alarm*, and the German-language *Arbeiter-Zeitung*. The last of these was one of hundreds of foreign-language newspapers printed in the United States into the 1980s, many of which were labor journals. Several continue to publish today.

The early 20th century saw an expansion of labor journalism brought a further increase in the number of outlets for labor-oriented news. The AFL continued publishing the *American Federationist*, while the more radical **Industrial Workers of the World** (IWW) published numerous papers, including the *Industrial Worker*, *One Big Monthly*, the *Industrial Union Bulletin*, and *Solidarity*. The rise of **socialist** movements in the 20th century also led to a spate of papers sympathetic to organized labor, including the *International Socialist Review*, *Socialist Party Monthly Bulletin*, and the *Socialist Woman*. The *Daily Worker*, the official voice of the

American Communist Party, began publication in 1924. It published until 1958, briefly went out of business, resumed publication, and then merged with other papers. It proved difficult to maintain a daily journal devoted to **communism**, however; today the *Daily Worker* lives under the title the *People's World* and is a weekly.

The **Progressive Era** gave rise to crusading and muckraking journalism, and numerous mainstream newspapers increased their coverage of the labor movement. In addition, reform-minded magazines emerged. Some were associated with the political left, such as *The Masses* (1911–1917) and the *New Masses* (1926–1948), but journals such as *Harper's*, the *New Republic*, *McClure's Magazine*, and the *Nation* also spotlighted labor issues. From the Progressive Era and into the 1970s, city papers often employed reporters with expertise in the labor movement, including Harry Bernstein, Pat Owens, and Eddie Levinson. Among the best was Mary Heaton Vorse, whose accounts of **strikes** and the horrendous working conditions faced by some employees made their way into numerous papers and magazines. Vorse was one of several journalists to provide copy for the Federated Press, a progressive news agency founded by Carl Haessler in 1919 as a counterpart to the more conservative news services such as the Associated Press. Until it folded after World War II, the Federated Press supplied its subscribers with news that emphasized the concerns of labor. Labor journalism also took to the airwaves with the 1926 founding of WCFL, a radio station sponsored by the AFL's Chicago Federation of Labor, and WEVD in New York City, a station associated with the Socialist Party whose call letters honored **Eugene V. Debs**.

The period between 1880 and 1940 is generally viewed as the heyday of labor journalism. Even so, as late as 1956 the **Department of Labor** listed more than 800 separate labor newspapers. Many well-known individuals spent time either writing for union newspapers or reporting on labor issues, among them Daniel Bell and Betty Friedan. By the mid-1970s, however, mainstream journals, radio, and television were becoming more conservative, and labor coverage declined at roughly the same time labor unions began to contract. By the 1980s, many labor activists complained that labor reportage was being consolidated with economic and business reporting and that news of workplace issues and the concerns of working people reflected a business community bias.

At the end of the 20th century, labor journalism remained alive in some portions of the American press, and large international unions, such as the **United Auto Workers of America** (UAW), published monthly journals. These documents increasingly went online as the cost of publishing newspapers became prohibitive. One of the best sources for information about unions is *Labor Notes*, a publication founded in 1979 that seeks to "put the movement back into the labor movement." It publishes on a monthly basis and targets labor activists. The AFL-CIO has an online journal titled *Work in Progress* and most labor unions have similar news and information outlets. Since the early 21st century, most labor journalism has been produced by the public relations departments of unions and has been viewed as educational outreach.

A handful of liberal outlets such as *The Nation*, *In These Times*, and *Mother Jones* regularly print labor-related articles. National Public Radio also routinely reports on labor issues. Prominent individuals who have reported extensively on organized labor in recent years include Philip Dine, Kim Moody, and William Serrin. Many observers argue that revitalized labor reporting can play a key role in reenergizing the labor movement.

Suggested Reading

Jon Bekken, "A Paper for Those Who Toil: The Chicago Labor Press in Transition," *Journalism History* 32, no. 1 (Spring 1997); Joseph R. Conlin, ed., *The American Radical Press, 1880–1960*, 1974; Nathan Godfried, *WCFL: Chicago's Voice of Labor*, 1997; Labor Notes, http://labornotes.org/about, accessed January 31, 2011; Sam Pizzigati and Fred J. Solowey, eds., *The New Labor Press: Journalism for a Changing Labor Movement*, 1992; Rodger Streitmatter, "Origins of the American Labor Press," *Journalism History* 25, no. 3 (Autumn 1999); Work in Progress, http://www.aflcio.org/aboutus/thisistheaflcio/publications/wip//, accessed January 31, 2011.

LABOR PARTIES

The idea of forming a separate political party to represent the interests of working Americans has inspired and frustrated millions since **Workingmen's movement** parties contested offices in the late 1820s and early 1830s. These parties' agenda included abolition of debt imprisonment, worker's compensation, free public education, universal suffrage for men, and labor concerns such as shorter working hours and higher pay rates. Most of these parties disappeared in the wake of the Panic of 1837.

The premise behind most attempts to form labor parties is that major parties focus on the interests of elites and powerful business concerns and shortchange the needs of average Americans. Advocates have argued that because the American electorate overwhelmingly consists of non-elites, a well-organized labor party can be successful as it would have a far larger base than its rivals. The problems, historically, have come in marshaling the resources needed to organize and compete in the political arena, and in convincing the electorate to change its voting habits.

Unlike many other Western democracies, the United States does not have proportional representation in legislative bodies at any level of government. Its winner-takes-all system has made it very hard for third parties to contest national and statewide elections, though independents and third-party candidates have often won local offices. The current system, in which national politics is dominated by Democrats and Republicans, was formed when the latter party emerged after the controversial Kansas-Nebraska Act of 1854, though a two-party political system was thoroughly ingrained in American political life at least 20 years earlier when the Whigs formed in opposition to Andrew Jackson.

Jackson, like many politicians, was adroit at packaging himself as a friend of workers. The ability of major party candidates to co-opt working-class votes has been among the factors that deters the formation of labor-specific parties. The

Labor Reform Party is a prime example of this issue. It formed in 1872, attracted very few votes, and took down its parent body, the **National Labor Union**, when it collapsed. Another problem has been ideology. Various **socialist** parties formed in the United States during the 19th century. Some, such as the **Marxist** International Workingmen's Association—often called the Workingmen's Party of the United States (1876–1878), failed to appreciate indigenous forms of American radicalism and faltered because they were widely perceived to harbor foreign agitators. The same perception dogged the Socialist Labor Party (SLP), which formed in 1874 and is still extant. The SLP was an early advocate of **industrial unionism**, but its radical ideals made it an easy target for fear-mongers in the wake of dramatic labor uprisings such as the **railroad strike of 1877** and the **Haymarket bombing** of 1886. In the 1890s, **Daniel DeLeon**, a doctrinaire Marxist, headed the SLP and many American workers again perceived it as too radical and too foreign. By the 20th century the SLP was largely a fringe party of ideologues, though it did play a central role in cofounding the **Industrial Workers of the World** in 1905. (It was buoyed by several upticks in voting during 1930s and 1940s, but the highest aggregate vote total for national SLP candidates came in 1948, when the party got slightly more than 100,000 votes.)

Still another problem for labor-based parties has been a lack of unity. Parties on the left side of the political spectrum have tended to take ideology seriously and have been less willing to compromise than major parties. This has led to fragmentation and discord. The SLP has split numerous times, including a 1901 schism that resulted in the formation of the Socialist Party of America (SPA; 1901–1972), which has been the most successful socialist party in terms of winning more elected offices than its rivals. The SPA captured numerous city, county, and state offices during its pre-World War I heyday, and several members of Congress came from this part. Its perennial presidential candidate, **Eugene V. Debs** (1855–1926), was admired by millions of working Americans, even if they did not always vote for him. Typical of the fragmentation one sees in left parties, however, critics complained that the SPA was not a true working-class party and that it gained success by abandoning its core principles. This would especially be the charge leveled by various **communist** and **Trotskyist** organizations, though neither ever attracted a base as large as that enjoyed by the SLP. The Communist Party of the United States of America (CPUSA), formed after 1919, was active in community organizing during the Great Depression and some of its members played important roles in the early days of the **Congress of Industrial Organizations**, but it never did well at the ballot box. Moreover, although socialists and communists have generally been bitter political rivals, those actually holding political power seldom parsed the differences, and both groups have suffered from red-baiting. The SPA was devastated by the **Red Scare** following World War I, and the CPUSA was nearly eviscerated by the scare after World War II and subsequent repression during the height of the **Cold War**.

Labor parties have generally had their greatest success when responding to immediate conditions and perceived crises. Although it was overtly racist, California's Workingman's Party was strong enough by the late 1870s to pressure Congress into passing the 1882 Chinese Exclusion Act. On a more positive note, the monetary crisis of the late 19th century led to the formation of several third parties that appealed to **wage**-earners. In 1878, the Greenback Party became the Greenback Labor Party. It attracted many working-class votes and succeeded in electing numerous municipal and state officials, including **Terence Powderly** of the **Knights of Labor** (KOL), who became mayor of Scranton, Pennsylvania. It also fielded a few successful candidates for Congress before it morphed into the short-lived Union Labor Party in 1888. In addition, the KOL enjoyed electoral success during the **Great Upheaval**. Several hundred Knights won office as candidates of various impromptu third-party monikers, the most common of which was the United Labor Party. As KOL-linked parties declined, the **agrarian**-based People's Party rose in popularity. It, too, made appeals to urban workers, and a strand of labor **populism** emerged in the 1890s. Ultimately, however, the alliance between farmers longing for high commodity prices and wage-earners favoring lower ones proved fragile and was exploited by Republican William McKinley during both of his successful presidential campaigns (1896, 1900).

Aside from the SLP and the CPUSA, other 20th-century parties generally viewed as prototypical labor parties include the Minnesota Farm-Labor Party (MFLP; 1918–1944), the **Nonpartisan League** (NPL; 1915–1956), and two organizations called the Progressive Party (one in 1924 and the other in 1948). The MFLP and NPL drew their greatest strength from farmers, but also attracted industrial workers; both eventually merged with the Democratic Party. In 1924, Senator Robert La Follette, Sr., ran for president on the Progressive Party ticket. He received the endorsement of numerous labor organizations, including the **American Federation of Labor**. He won 17 percent of the popular vote and carried Wisconsin. In 1948, former Vice President Henry Wallace also ran on a Progressive Party ticket. Wallace was tarred as being an extremist and did not fare as well as La Follette. He did, however, win the endorsement of the New York-based American Labor Party (ALP; 1936–1956), a group founded in part because adherents believed that SPA head Norman Thomas was ineffectual. The ALP had numerous members who belonged to the **International Ladies' Garment Workers' Union** and the party very active in **Popular Front** politics. Its highest-profile success was the election of independent socialist Vito Marcantonio to Congress. For the most part, however, the ALP functioned more as a pressure group than as a conventional political party.

Since World War II, parties seeking a labor vote have fared badly in U.S. electoral politics. Numerous communist, socialist, and independent parties have continued to vie for local elections, but very few of their candidates have been elected to office. Several labor parties have been "labor" in name only, including the U.S. Labor Party (1972–1979), led by the quixotic Lyndon LaRouche. LaRouche's politics were a blend of libertarianism, Marxism, right-wing authoritarianism, anti-Semitism, and paranoia. Among LaRouche's targets was the **United Auto Workers of America**, a union whose progressive politics he abhorred. A more positive independent is Bernard Sanders of Vermont, who draws inspiration from Eugene Debs and the SPA. His Progressive Coalition of independent socialists, union activists, and reformers has been a force in Burlington, Vermont, politics since Sanders won the mayoralty there in 1981.

Ten years later Sanders became the first socialist to be elected to Congress since Vito Marcantonio. In 2007, Sanders was elected to the U.S. Senate.

There have been numerous calls for an independent labor party in post-World War II America, but few have come to fruition. Labor Party Advocates formed in the 1990s and, in 1996, held a convention to announce the formation of the Labor Party. Although it attracted the endorsement of numerous unions associated with the **American Federation of Labor-Congress of Industrial Organizations** and high-profile followers such as filmmaker Roger Moore, musician Patti Smith, and consumer advocate Ralph Nader, it remains an unrealized idea at present.

The lack of a labor party in the United States baffles many foreign observers. Independent labor parties evolved from trade unions and have been a staple of European politics for more than a hundred years. Most of them have advanced socialist ideals—such as universal health care coverage, government-funded pensions, public ownership of utility and transportation networks, and protection of worker rights—that are far in advance of what exists in the United States. In addition to the winner-takes-all schema of American electoral politics, several other explanations have been put forth to explain the lack of labor parties in the United States and the overall antipathy of voters toward measures that are even mildly socialist in nature. Advocates of American **exceptionalism** argue that the United States developed uniquely from other Western democracies in that basic rights were guaranteed earlier, an abundance of public lands acted as a safety valve that deterred radicalism, and their overall prosperity led citizens to link their personal interests with American **capitalism**. Still others have noted that the Democratic Party has, since the late 19th century, functioned as a de facto labor party in the United States, with organized labor making up its progressive wing. Several commentators have observed that much of the attraction of labor parties outside the United States is based as much in romance as in fact; many current labor parties now operate in the mainstream, very much akin to U.S. political parties. For their part, critics from the political left point to more sinister factors and argue that attempts to form left alternatives to the Republicans and Democrats are systematically sabotaged by the combined might of corporate power and compliant courts, media, and mainstream parties.

Still another consideration is that those calling for formation of a labor party often presume that it would have a progressive cast to it. This is not necessarily the case. As noted earlier, Denis Kearney's 19th-century anti-Chinese Workingman's Party was a reactionary movement. In 1998, Minnesotans elected former professional wrestler Jesse Ventura as governor; he tapped into a well of working-class discontent that was decidedly more conservative. Right-wing figures such as Patrick Buchanan often attract working class followers with anti-immigrant appeals and calls for **protectionism**. In like fashion, **Ronald Reagan** was quite popular among rank-and-file workers even though their unions opposed him.

A more dispassionate view is to separate the holding of elected office from the overall influence that third parties have had in reshaping American political discourse. Many things that are now standard features of American society—including an eight-hour workday, direct election of U.S. senators, free public education, and the secret ballot—originated among independent labor parties.

Suggested Reading

Theresa Amato, *Grand Illusion: The Myth of Voter Choice in a Two-Party Tyranny*, 2009; Vicki Cox, *The History of Third Parties*, 2007; Lisa Klobuchar, Alexa L. Sandmann, and Stephen Asperheim, *Third Parties: Influential Political Alternatives*, 2007.

LABOR PARTY ADVOCATES. *See* Labor Parties.

LABOR SPIES. *See* Agent Provocateur.

LABOR THEORY OF VALUE

The labor theory of value is the idea that the value of goods and services is determined by the amount of labor involved their production. From this logic, commodities, land, and goods have little or no intrinsic worth of their own; it is the labor that transforms them and imbues them with value.

Despite the surface simplicity of this concept, its implications are complex and its sources varied. The labor theory of value is often associated with **Marxist** economic theory, but it is deeply woven into **capitalist** theory. It derives in part from John Locke's influential essay "On Property" from *Two Treaties on Government* (1690) and is echoed in Adam Smith's *Wealth of Nations* (1776). English writer David Ricardo evoked it when developing his famed "iron law of wages theory," in which he argued that the profit motive and rents doomed workers to subsistence **wages**. Many of the underpinnings of the labor theory of value actually defended capitalism, if one interprets "labor" broadly to include groups such as bankers, land developers, importers, and retailers.

Working people and their advocates, however, derived a very different message from this theory. Thomas Paine drew upon it to champion the cause of the downtrodden, and the **Workingmen's movement** in post-Revolutionary America made it a central principle in battles against monopoly and class privilege. By the time of Ricardo's death in 1823, reinterpretations of his theories were under way, many of which used the labor theory of value as the centerpiece for envisioning noncapitalist economic systems. Both **Robert Owen** and his son **Robert Dale Owen** used the theory to justify **profit-sharing** schemes. The Quaker visionary Cornelius Blatchly employed the labor theory of value to develop utopian views of a workers' republic. Later writers such as Karl Marx and **Henry George** also drew upon this theory. Its refocused ideals were important for leaders of the **National Labor Union**, the **Knights of Labor** (KOL), and the **cooperative** movement.

From a **working-class** perspective, the labor theory of value divides the world into producers and nonproducers. "Production" was usually defined in a concrete, tangible manner—that is, by the goods one fashioned from toil. The KOL, for example, excluded bankers, lawyers, gamblers, and land speculators from membership, based on the grounds that they did not "produce" anything; therefore, they added no value to society.

The labor theory of value was such a powerful ideal in the 19th century that the morality of capitalism was frequently called into question. Some workers concluded that deriving profit from the labor of others was inherently evil and destabilizing to the health of society and the economy. The cooperative movement is largely rooted in the labor theory of value. Although many could not have clearly articulated the labor theory of value, 19th-century workers can be said to have had a producer ethos.

The labor theory of value was not the only challenge to capitalism that workers considered; they were also attracted to **anarchism, socialism**, Bellamyite nationalism, ballot-box politics, the single-tax movement, and other forms of resistance. In all likelihood, the majority of workers freely mixed popularly understood notions of the producer ethos with whatever other ideals they held. It was not until the triumph of **pure and simple unionism** in the early 20th century that the bulk of union workers could be said to have accepted the permanence of capitalism.

Suggested Reading

Karl Marx and David McLellan, *Capital: An Abridged Edition*, 2008; Edward Pessen, *Most Uncommon Jacksonians: The Radical Leaders of the Early Labor Movement*, 1967; Sean Wilentz, *Chants Democratic: New York City and the Rise of the American Working Class, 1788–1850*, 1984.

LA FOLLETTE COMMITTEE

The La Follette Committee—also called the La Follette Civil Liberties Committee—is the shorthand name given to Congressional hearings held between 1936 and 1940 that investigated allegations of brutal anti-union tactics used by U.S. employers. These hearings were chaired by Wisconsin Senator Robert La Follette, Jr., and were officially known as the Senate Subcommittee of the Committee on Education and Labor. The La Follette Committee's sensational findings did much to secure stronger **collective bargaining** rights for American workers.

The committee was created in response to concerns raised after the passage of the 1935 **National Labor Relations Act** (NLRA). Numerous labor unions and reform groups such as the American Civil Liberties Union (ACLU) complained that employers were ignoring the NLRA and that some were actually being more repressive than before the law was passed. The La Follette Committee investigated allegations of violations of free speech and assembly. It unearthed a mountain of **unfair labor practices** that made mockery of labor's right to collective bargaining. The investigation centered on four specific abuses: the use of labor spies, the use of **goons** in strikebreaking, the hiring of private guards who acted as paramilitary forces, and the stockpiling of munitions.

Investigative work began in 1936 and formal hearings started in 1937. The committee faced obstacles from the start and was forced to subpoena reluctant employers to ensure their testimony. Many employers resisted complying with the committee's demands in the hope that the NLRA, like the **National Industrial**

Recovery Act that it replaced, would be struck down by the courts. When the NLRA's constitutionality was upheld, the committee became more aggressive in demanding employer cooperation. La Follette and his colleagues discovered substantial evidence of employer disregard for the law. Among the committee's shocking revelations were those of southern sharecroppers beaten and killed as they tried to organize, and of the manner in which Harlan County, Kentucky, coal mine companies hired private armies, attacked and shot workers, and generally disregarded basic civil liberties.

As the committee prepared to draft legislation in the spring of 1937, the **United Steelworkers of America** union was embroiled in the "Little Steel" strike. Republic Steel President Tom Girdler recruited "citizens' committees" and the Chicago Police Department as veritable vigilante groups to intimidate striking workers. Company-induced violence spiraled out of control, and 10 workers were killed and dozens more were injured during the Memorial Day Massacre of 1937. Such gross injustices backfired and inspired the Senate to scrutinize industrial organizations such as the **National Association of Manufacturers** (NAM) and the International Metal Trades Association. Findings revealed that some industrial giants had stockpiled private arsenals. The committee found that from 1933 to 1937, some 2,500 corporations hired labor spies and that at least 3,800 **Pinkertons** and other detectives had infiltrated unions. These same firms spent more than $9.4 million on union-busting activities, with General Motors being the worst abuser. Strikers facing down Youngstown Sheet and Tube Co. in Ohio faced a company that had stockpiled eight machine guns, 369 rifles, 190 shotguns, 450 revolvers, 3,900 rounds of ammunition, and 109 gas guns. LaFollette also revealed the existence of the NAM-sponsored **Mohawk Valley Formula** for union-busting, which sought to tar labor leaders as **communists**, cultivate community support in the name of "law and order," use labor spies to infiltrate unions, and threaten to move businesses if civic leaders did not help put down **strikes**.

The La Follette Committee hearings in 1939 and 1940 revealed that migrant and agricultural workers suffered from similar brutality, especially in California. During these hearings the committee took testimony from luminaries such as author John Steinbeck and economist Paul Taylor. In late 1939, the committee introduced legislation to correct the worst of the abuses. Unfortunately, by the time the bills began to emerge in May 1940, government officials and the public were more focused on world conflict than on labor abuses. Interest in new labor laws dissipated due to the fear that such legislation would cripple defense production, as well as a belief that the NLRA, when properly enforced, already provided adequate protection.

The La Follette Committee left behind three important legacies. First, it called attention to the abuses of employers and reinforced organized labor's assertion that the NLRA was being ignored. Second, it bolstered the case that the federal government needed to play an active role in protecting civil rights. Third, the committee's work provided a foundation upon which African American civil rights activists could draw in the 1950s and 1960s.

Suggested Reading

Jerold Auerbach, *Labor and Liberty: The La Follette Committee and the New Deal*, 1966; Patrick J. Maney, *"Young Bob" La Follette: A Biography of Robert La Follete, Jr.*, 2002/1978; U.S. Congress, Senate, Subcommittee of the Committee on Education and Labor, *Hearings Pursuant to S. Res. 266, Violations of Free Speech and Rights of Labor*, 74th–76th Cong., 1936–1940.

LA FOLLETTE SEAMEN'S ACT

The Seamen's Act was passed in 1915 and was the culmination of a long effort to improve the working and living conditions for sailors. Although officially named the Act to Promote the Welfare of American Seamen in the Merchant Marine of the United States, it is generally called the La Follette Seamen's Act in honor of its sponsor, Senator Robert La Follette, Sr., of Wisconsin. When President Woodrow Wilson signed the bill on March 4, 1915, supporters lauded the measure as "the Emancipation Proclamation for seamen of the world."

Efforts to protect the legal rights of U.S. sailors date to 1798, but conditions for 19th-century sailors remained so poor that they often evoked comparisons to **slavery**. Moreover, changes in maritime technology led to demands for new laws more appropriate for highly skilled workmen. Bills such as the Maguire Act (1895) and the White Act (1898) protected certain categories of sailors, but abuses remained widespread. Under fugitive sailor laws, for instance, seamen attempting to quit their jobs were subject to arrest, and those who were allowed to leave had to forfeit all unpaid **wages** and reimburse advances. The latter provision highlighted a widespread pattern in which ship owners often paid advance wages to recruits, who were held in virtual peonage until the advance was repaid.

The 1915 bill was a collaborative effort between Senator La Follette and Andrew Furuseth, president of the Sailor's Union of the Pacific. Furuseth first sought passage of protective legislation in 1894, and he convinced La Follette to present bills to Congress during every session from 1910 to 1915. A competing but weaker bill passed Congress in 1912, but was pocket-vetoed by President William Taft. La Follette took up the fight anew in 1913, and added amendments for consumer protection to drum up public support for the bill. Ship safety was rightly a great public concern, as the record of large shipping companies in protecting their passengers was abysmal. La Follette added public safety measures to Furuseth's bill, including requirements that ships carry sufficient lifeboats for all passengers and that two skilled seamen be available for each lifeboat. La Follette noted that 13,000 deaths occurred from ocean disasters between 1900 and 1914, and that the April 1912 *Titanic* catastrophe highlighted the folly of carrying too few lifeboats and skilled seamen. Because he cleverly shifted the emphasis to the avarice and negligence of ship owners, the portions of La Follette's bill protecting seamen received relatively little public attention. Nonetheless, business associations so vigorously fought the bill that La Follette had to threaten a filibuster against appropriations bills to secure passage of the Seamen's Act, and it took personal appeals from La Follette and Furuseth to convince President Wilson to sign the measure.

The Seamen's Act resulted in a number of significant improvements for sailors. Among the most important changes were an end to imprisonment for seamen who left their ships before the finish of a contracted voyage; outlawing corporal punishment for offenses committed aboard ship; proscriptions against receiving or allotting advance pay; and regulations on those who preyed on sailors' wages in exchange for food, lodging, drinks, and clothing. The law also established a maximum nine-hour workday while in port; banned unnecessary Sunday and holiday work; mandated better quarters and food quality; prohibited employers from withholding pay for extended periods; instituted the right of a majority of crew members to demand inspections to determine a vessel's seaworthiness; required open access to washrooms and sickbays; and established the right of seamen to collect damages from negligent officers.

The shipping companies complained that the bill would drive them into bankruptcy and aggressively pressured the Secretary of Commerce to forestall enforcement of many of the act's provisions. Such practices came to a tragic end when the underequipped and understaffed Great Lakes sightseeing vessel *Eastland* capsized on July 24, 1915, killing more than 1,000 passengers. Public outcry forced the federal government to implement measures requiring stricter adherence to the Seamen's Act.

Suggested Reading

Jerold Auerbach, "Progressives at Sea: The La Follette Act of 1915," *Labor History* 2 (Fall 1961): 344–360; E. Kay Gibson, *Brutality on Trial: Hellfire Pedersen, Fighting Hansen, and the Seaman's Act of 1915*, 2006; Walther MacArthur, comp., *The Seaman's Contract, 1790–1918, A Complete Reprint of the Laws Relating to American Seamen*, 1919.

LANDRUM-GRIFFIN ACT

The Labor-Management Reporting and Disclosure Act is better known as the Landrum-Griffin Act, so-called because of the bill's sponsors: Representatives Phillip Landrum, a Georgia Democrat, and Robert P. Griffin, a Michigan Republican. The act places restrictions on how labor unions conduct their internal affairs and was passed in direct response to allegations of corruption among unions representing **Teamsters**, **longshoremen**, and others. Although the Landrum-Griffin Act was designed to curtail **racketeering** and protect rank-and-file union members, much of organized labor opposed it because it subjects labor unions to scrutiny not demanded of private industry. It was also seen as an extension of anti-union bills in the wake of the **Taft-Hartley Act**.

Momentum for the Landrum-Griffin Act came from the political climate of the 1950s and the findings of the Senate Select Committee on Improper Activities in the Labor or Management Field, informally known as the McClellan Committee, after its chairman, Senator John L. McClellan (Democrat-Arkansas). The committee initially investigated charges of corruption brought against both labor and management, but over time its focus shifted to allegations of corruption and auto-cratic leadership inside labor unions. The newly popular medium of television served to bring more attention to the McClellan Committee's work, and opponents of organized labor seized upon the publicity to launch allegations that corruption was widespread, that union offices were riddled with grafters, and that unions precipitated violence. They also raised the specter that unions were in collusion with organized crime and that the proliferation of corruption and the unwarranted use of secondary **boycotts** both endangered small employers and interfered with employee rights.

The Landrum-Griffin Act also caught labor leaders off-guard, because they mis-read the results of the 1958 congressional elections. Those contests had returned substantial **Democratic Party** majorities in both the House and the Senate, in part because of organized labor's active campaigning against **right-to-work** statutes and against antilabor candidates. After the election, however, conservatives raised fears of a Congress dominated by "labor bosses," and called on Congress to act "responsibly" by passing labor reform legislation. Conflict within the **American Federation of Labor-Congress of Industrial Organizations** (AFL-CIO) led organized labor to assume too much of their Congressional allies. Although the AFL-CIO expelled three of the unions identified as the most corrupt by the McClellan Committee—the Teamsters, the Bakery and Confectionery Workers Union, and the Laundry Workers Union—President Dwight Eisenhower and Congressional leaders insisted that reform legislation was necessary. The result was the Landrum-Griffin Act, the second major revision, after the Taft-Hartley Act, to the **National Labor Relations Act**.

The Landrum-Griffin Act provided for the regulation of union internal affairs, including how union funds were controlled and allocation. The legislation banned former members of the Communist Party of the United States of America (CPUSA) as well as former convicts from holding union office for a period of five years from either their resignation from the CPUSA or their release from prison. Both secondary boy-cotting and organizational and recognition **picketing** (picketing businesses that recognized a rival union) were greatly curtailed. A union "bill of rights" was put in place to protect union members' freedom of speech, provisions were established for periodic secret elections, and individual states were allowed greater freedom to regulate labor relations within their borders. Especially controversial was the creation of work categories cases that fell outside the jurisdiction of the National Labor Relations Board.

The effect of the act was to strengthen the antilabor provisions of the Taft-Hartley Act and to weaken labor's ability to unionize companies in the South, much of which remained unorganized. Very few of the provisions regulating unions under the Landrum-Griffin bill also apply to the business community. For example, many businesses place strict limits on the speech of employees and consider criticism of management to be a cause for dismissal. Recent years have also seen businesses freely move or even eliminate employee **pension** funds—maneuvers that are outlawed for labor unions. Critics argue that the Landrum-Griffin Act further tilts capital/labor relations in favor of management and that government has abrogated its role as a neutral mediator.

Suggested Reading

Janice R. Bellace, Alan D. Berkowitz, and Bruce Van Dusen, *The Landrum-Griffin Act: Twenty Years of Federal Protection of Union Members' Rights*, 1979; "The Complete Text of the LMRDA," http://www.uniondemocracy.com/Legal/lmrdatext.htm, accessed February 2, 2011; National Labor Relations Board, "1959 Landrum-Griffin Act," http://www.nlrb.gov/75th/1959landrumgriffinact.html, accessed February 2, 2011.

LASSALLEANISM

Lassalleanism, sometimes called social democracy—is a variety of **socialism** that was probably the dominant strain embraced by American workers in the late 19th century. It takes its name from the thought of Ferdinand Lassalle (1825–1864), a German law student and social theorist. Although he was a member of the Communist League, a veteran of the German social revolutions of 1848, and an admirer of Marx, Lassalle differed with Marx on several points and Marx considered him heretical to the socialist cause. His emphasis on a peaceful evolution to a socialist future was viewed by many Americans as both preferable and more likely than socialist ideals calling for violent revolution.

Marxism is often misunderstood in American **working-class** history. Although Karl Marx's critique of **capitalism** has inspired untold thousands, it is important to understand that those Americans who agreed with his economic analysis did not necessarily accept his social or political ideals. Several aspects of Marxist thought have deeply divided socialists. Three in particular were Marx's view of revolution, his emphasis on trade unions, and his opinion about the role of the state and government. Whereas Marxists saw government and the state as an evil to be destroyed, Lassalle believed that the state could and should be the protector of the working class. He argued that the right to vote was potentially the greatest weapon possessed by the masses. If exercised properly, workers could achieve a "people's state" at the ballot box, not the barricades. Although not as many people read Lassalle as Marx, Lassalle's ideas actually held greater sway during the Gilded Age, especially inside the **Knights of Labor** (KOL).

Marx argued that trade unions would be the building blocks of a post-revolutionary society. Given the collapse of **craft unions** following the **railroad strike of 1877**, many American workers found that a dubious claim. The KOL, in fact, was founded by members of a collapsed tailors' union who deliberately fashioned an organization that sought to avoid the weaknesses of trade unions, among them their lack of the very **class consciousness** that Marx asserted was a prerequisite for overthrowing capitalism. As the KOL and American Lassalleans saw it, craft unions tended to shatter working-class **solidarity** by encouraging loyalty to a single occupation rather than the larger working class. Lassalleans formed the Social Democratic Party of North America (SDP) in 1874, and some form of Lassallean party remained present throughout the Gilded Age.

Whereas doctrinaire Marxists placed their emphasis on a revolutionary surge from the masses, Lassalleans sought to rally them to cast votes for socialist candidates. Elected officials, Lassalleans hoped, would use the power of government to aid worker producer associations. Lassalle argued that strikes seldom did workers any good, an idea that profoundly affected the KOL. He agreed with Marx that the law of **wages** would drive down pay to its lowest level, even if workers won a strike. The ultimate solution was to eliminate wages altogether; workers needed to be owners, not employees. If workers formed and owned their own **cooperatives**, Lassalle noted, they would not have to share their income with capitalists.

The SDP underwent several name changes and mergers; in 1876 it became the Workingmen's Party, and in 1878 it was retitled the Socialist Labor Party (SLP). It tended to attract more English speakers—including its chair, Phillip Van Patten—than orthodox Marxist groups, many of whom labored to escape the perception that they were foreign imports whose ideas were ill adapted to American conditions. Lassalleans certainly did better politically. The SLP forged an alliance with rural **Greenbackers** and under the name Greenback Labor Party (GLP) elected state and local officials and as many as 21 Congressmen in 1878. **Terence V. Powderly**, the future head of the KOL, was elected mayor of Scranton, Pennsylvania, on the GLP ticket in 1878.

The SLP suffered a major split in 1881, when some of its members lost faith in both the ballot box and trade unions and became **anarchists**, but the SLP remained committed to reform and electoral politics. The SLP both supported other independent labor parties and was the beneficiary of a grassroots electoral surge during the **Great Upheaval**. Both **Henry George** and **Edward Bellamy** wove Lassallean themes into their own socialist thought. The SLP reached its height around 1890, at which time **Daniel DeLeon** headed it and moved the party back toward and overtly Marxist point of view. The SLP is still extant, but today is more Marxist than Lassallean.

DeLeon's transformation of the SLP signaled a shift in Lassalleanism's influence. In 1898, most Lassalleans shifted their allegiance to the newly formed Social Democratic Party, which merged with two other groups in 1901 to create the Socialist Party of America (SP). **Eugene V. Debs** became the leading light of the SP. Although Debs was neither a Lassallean nor a revolutionary Marxist, he retained Lassalle's faith in the ballot box, as did future socialist office-holders such as Victor Berger, Vito Marcantonio, and current U.S. Senator Bernard Sanders.

Ballot-box socialists raised the ire of anarchists, **communists**, and doctrinaire socialists. They were generally viewed as the "right wing" of the socialist movement, and elected city officials were often derisively called "sewer socialists." Marxism as a form of intellectual analysis has been so influential in the field of labor studies that it has been given prominence above that of Lassalleanism. The fact remains, however, that evolutionary socialist models have proved attractive to American workers. Students and scholars should approach terms such as "socialism" and "Marxism" with care, and should not confuse rhetoric with action or (necessarily) with deeply held convictions.

Suggested Reading

John R. Commons, *History of Labour in the United States, Vol. 1*, 2000 (reprint of 1918 original); Albert Fried, ed., *Socialism in America from the Shakers to the Third*

International: A Documentary History, 1992; Ira Kipnis, *The American Socialist Movement 1897–1912*, 2004 (reprint of 1952 original).

LATINO LABOR

The term "Latino" is a catchall category used to refer to individuals whose ethnic ancestry derives from the Spanish-speaking countries of Latin America, the Caribbean, the Iberian peninsula of Europe, and Spanish speakers in the United States. It is also sometimes improbably applied to Portuguese immigrants, especially those from Brazil and the Cape Verde Islands, and even to French or Creole speakers from the Caribbean. It is important to understand that the term mostly references individuals whose first language is not English and who are viewed as occupying **minority** status. It is neither a racial category nor a precise designation, and it joins terms such as "Hispanic," "Tejano," and "Chicano" in that it is often a self-selected designation rather than an anthropological category. Individuals tracing their ancestry to Mexico, for example, often favor the term "Hispanic," even though many Mexicans are, in fact, *mestizos*, and the product of centuries of European and **Native American** miscegenation.

Latino labor has long been present in North America. Spain was the first European nation to establish permanent colonies in North America, South America, and the Caribbean. As the United States expanded, it absorbed lands once colonized by Spain. The 1803 Louisiana Purchase transferred some Spanish speakers to U.S. control, and the 1819 purchase of Florida brought even more into the growing United states. The 1823 Monroe Doctrine was an audacious statement for a young, weak nation such as the United States, but it established the belief that the Caribbean, Central America, and South America were U.S. spheres of influence and implicitly opened the door for Latinos to come to the United States. The Mexican War (1846–1848) led to mass-scale absorption of Latino workers, and in the years leading up to the **Civil War** some apologists for **slavery** advocated the seizure of Mexico, Cuba, and parts of the Caribbean and the enslavement of parts of their populations. One such individual, William Walker, invaded Baja California in 1853 and controlled Nicaragua in 1857–1858.

The opening of the Great Plains to white ranchers led to increased contact between Anglos and Latinos. Many of the cowboys of American legend were, in fact, either **African American** cattle hands or Mexican *vaqueros*, the latter of whom taught many Anglo ranchers the skills necessary for survival. The American Southwest has long been a bicultural region shared by Anglo and Latino ranchers, herders, and farmers. That is not to say that relations between the groups have always been cordial. The El Paso Salt War of 1877, for instance, saw Texas Rangers engage in armed conflict with ethnic Mexicans living on both the U.S. and Mexican sides of the Rio Grande River, and at least 20 people died in the battles.

Borders between the United States and Mexico have been contentious and porous, with residents of the arid region treating boundaries as an irrelevant fiction. In the 19th century, political instability inside Mexico encouraged border crossing. Likewise, the U.S. government treated its southern borders cavalierly, as when military forces pursued the Apache war chief Geronimo deep inside Mexican territory several times in the 1880s, or Pancho Villa in 1916 and 1917. The upheaval resulting from the Mexican Revolution (1910–1920) also led some Mexicans to seek new homes in the United States.

In the late 19th century, the United States also became enmeshed in Caribbean affairs. The 1898 Spanish-American War brought the United States Puerto Rico as a spoil of war and Cuba as a U.S. protectorate. President Theodore Roosevelt added his famed corollary to the Monroe Doctrine in 1904, and in the next several decades the United States sent troops to Mexico, Central America, and the Caribbean on numerous occasions. In each case, population movement followed in the wake of that action; the same was true after the opening of the U.S.-owned and -financed Panama Canal in 1914. By the early 20th century, many Latino workers were located in Florida, the Southwest, New York, and California, where they worked in jobs as diverse as cigar making, agricultural labor, the garment trades, railroads, and the canning industry. More than 1 million Mexicans settled in the Southwest alone between 1900 and 1930. In 1933, President Franklin Roosevelt announced a "Good Neighbor Policy" and pledged to work with Latin American and Caribbean nations rather than invading them. Numerous Mexicans and Mexican Americans made their way north during the 1930s and 1940s to work in the automotive and aircraft industries.

During World War I and again in the 1940s and 1950s, the federal government supported the **Braceros** program to recruit contingency agricultural "guest" workers. Since the 1940s, Mexicans, Puerto Ricans, Jamaicans, and other Latinos have picked much of the American harvest. (Filipinos have also played a large role, as have other Asians in recent years.) The last *Braceros* program officially ended in 1964, but many growers had grown dependent upon cheaper Mexican labor and continued to hire those workers who made their way north. Lost in the current debate over illegal immigration is employer recruitment of and complicity in tolerating illegal migrant workers, whom employers paid low **wages** and worked hard. In fact, it was precisely the exploitation of Latino and Filipino agrarian laborers that led to the formation of the **United Farm Workers of America**.

Also lost in current immigration debates is the fact that President Roosevelt's Good Neighbor Policy ended with the emergence of the **Cold War**. As a consequence, Latin American politics often became entangled with U.S. foreign policy objectives. The United States frequently supported authoritarian regimes and military juntas in Latin America simply because they were useful allies in the ideological struggle against **communism**. These nations often had deplorable human rights records—a factor that encouraged large numbers of Hondurans, El Salvadorans, Dominicans, Chileans, Peruvians, and others to enter the United States illegally. Cubans, in contrast, were welcomed as refugees fleeing the communist regime of Fidel Castro.

In contemporary America, many Latinos are members of the **Service Employees International Union**, especially those involved in the hotel, restaurant, and building trades. Although Latinos work in all sectors of the American economy, they are disproportionately concentrated in the low-wage **service industry** sector.

Latinos join **blue-collar** unions at a higher rate than most Anglo workers and have been at the forefront in establishing reform groups such as Justice for Janitors. Latino workers have also been leaders in advancing the concept of international organizing and have been better attuned to the implications of **runaway shops**, movable capital, and economic **globalization** than many Anglos.

Latinos are likely to be a major factor in the U.S. labor force of the future as their numbers continue to grow. As of 2010, there were more than 50.4 million Latinos in the United States—three-fourths of whom are of Mexican heritage—and they have surpassed African Americans as the nation's largest ethnic minority group. They remain most heavily concentrated in the Southwest and West and now make up 44 percent on the population of New Mexico and more than one-third of the populations of both California and Texas. Nearly 16 percent of the overall U.S. population is now Latino. The boom in the Latino population has caused some social strains, as roughly one in five Latino Americans lives below the poverty level and members of this minority group suffer disproportionately higher levels of health-related problems. Increasing numbers of Latinos are moving into the **middle class**, especially in well-established Cuban American communities, but large numbers of poorly paid El Salvadorans can be found in the garment industry, Nicaraguans working in poultry processing, and Mexicans in domestic service, agriculture, and grounds keeping. Many Puerto Ricans, who are U.S. citizens, continue to engage in long-standing seasonal migration patterns in which they seek agricultural employment on the mainland (mostly the East Coast) during the planting, summer, and harvest seasons and return to the island during the winter. Puerto Rico remains underdeveloped and job opportunities are scarcer there. Latinos also have an ever-growing presence in the American South, where they often work in blue-collar and service sector jobs.

The **American Federation of Labor-Congress of Industrial Organizations** (AFL-CIO) has, since the 1970s, recognized the growing importance of Latino workers in the union movement. In 1973, the Labor Council for Latin American Advancement (LCAA) was created to advance unionization among Latino workers and to train Latino union leaders. It is an official constituency group inside the AFL-CIO and is also affiliated with the **Change to Win Federation**. The LCAA represents 1.7 million Latino workers.

Suggested Reading

Miguel A. De La Torre, *Encyclopedia of Hispanic American Religious Culture*, 2 volumes, 2009; Pierrette Hondagneu-Sotelo, *Doméstica: Immigrant Workers Cleaning and Caring in the Shadows of Affluence*, 2007; Labor Council for Latin American Advancement, http://www.lclaa.org/, accessed February 21, 2011; Elaine L. Odem, *Latino Immigrants and the Transformation of the U.S. South*, 2009; Pew Hispanic Center, http://pewhispanic.org/, accessed February 21, 2011.

LATTIMER MASSACRE

The Lattimer Massacre occurred on September 10, 1897, in Lattimer, Pennsylvania, a small coal patch near Hazleton. Sheriff's deputies working on behalf of a brutal employer killed 19 immigrant miners. This bloody event led Slavic immigrants to seek greater organization and strengthened their **solidarity** with the **United Mine Workers of America** (UMWA) in the anthracite region of northeastern Pennsylvania. It was also among the many horrific incidents occurring in the 1890s that led to reform during the **Progressive Era**, though the incident itself was quickly forgotten.

The Lattimer Massacre sprang from the UMWA's attempts to organize workers in anthracite coal-producing regions. The UMWA posed a serious challenge to the autocratic and semifeudal control that mine owners had imposed for decades. During the severe economic downturn that ensued during the Panic of 1893, coal barons imposed harsh cost-cutting measures upon miners who already lived in penury. By August 1897, thousands of immigrant miners had joined the UMWA and were determined to stop production until conditions and pay improved. **Strike** committees formed, and miners marched from colliery to colliery seeking to shut mines that were still shipping coal. In early September, the UMWA attempted to close A. Pardee and Company, a major Hazelton-area coal producer. The company's mostly Slavic, Polish, and Lithuanian immigrants formed a UMWA local at Pardee's operation in nearby Harwood and went on strike. They were joined by other Pardee miners, and the overall campaign of the UMWA led Italian immigrant miners at Lattimer to request assistance in closing the colliery there.

Many of the region's county sheriffs were politically allied with coal operators, and they published a proclamation on September 6 that outlawed parades and public demonstrations. Luzerne County Sheriff James L. Martin deputized around 100 men and armed them with Winchester rifles. On September 10, some 400 miners began a 10-mile march from Harwood to Lattimer, where they hoped to rally in support of the town's beleaguered workers. To signal their peaceful intentions, strike leaders counseled protestors to march unarmed, four abreast, behind two strikers carrying American flags. Deputies first confronted the march in West Hazleton. In the ensuing fray, one miner was injured and a deputy tore one American flag to pieces. This action embarrassed local officials and police were directed to allow the march to proceed in exchange for a promise to bypass Hazleton.

This instruction infuriated Sheriff Martin, who loaded his deputies on trolleys to Lattimer, with instructions to stop the march there. Word spread of an impending confrontation and additional company police and deputies rushed toward Lattimer. At the time, the town of Lattimer was a prototypical **company town** of just several short streets. Its mining operations lay at the end of Main Street, which was populated by a jumble of company-owned shanties occupied by newly arrived Italian immigrants. Martin deployed deputies along Main Street, and when marchers approached, Martin stepped forward with a drawn pistol and commanded them to disperse. The leading ranks heard Martin and stopped, however, those out of earshot pressed forward. The deputies opened fire—marchers later claimed that Martin gave the order—and several men were felled in their tracks, while others were shot in the back as they sought cover behind a thin row of trees. According to some witnesses, at least 150 shots were fired, and there were reports of deputies pursuing strikers before gunning them down. When the gunfire ceased, 19 miners were dead and 38 were wounded.

The Lattimer Massacre raised tensions rose in immigrant communities throughout the region. Governor Daniel Hastings feared reprisal against the Pardee Company and sent 3,000 soldiers of the Pennsylvania National Guard to Hazleton to patrol coal-company properties. The news of Lattimer paralyzed mining operations in the region, with thousands of miners who had been working walking off the job, joining the UMWA, and joining regional strikes. Immigrant organizations across the country condemned the killings and provided thousands of dollars to support the victims' families. Little of this response moved the hearts of Pennsylvania coal barons or their political allies. Sheriff Martin and 67 deputies were charged with just one murder and the case was heard before a jury stacked with nativists. The defense blamed the massacre on foreign and labor agitators and the trial included an anti-Slavic oration. On March 2, 1898, the jury returned a verdict of not guilty. Local authorities also took steps to quash discussion of the Lattimer Massacre.

Prior to 1950, so few historians had written about the Lattimer murders that the event was known as "labor's forgotten massacre." Few of the survivors spoke English and many of them left the area after 1898. Moreover, Lattimer was quickly overshadowed by the **anthracite coal strike of 1902**, which was more successful and which gained more national press coverage than Lattimer. The massacre actually received more notice in the foreign press, with labor activists in both Australia and New Zealand citing it as justification for passing mandatory **arbitration** laws. Scholars now cite the Lattimer event as illustrating the bloodiness of American labor history. Bloodshed was certainly on the minds of middle-class reformers in the early 20th century who sought industrial regulations aimed at reducing the chaos convulsing American society. Scholars also note the long-term effects of incidents such as the Lattimer Massacre in leading Slavic workers to cast their lot with the union movement. On the 75th anniversary of the massacre, the **American Federation of Labor–Congress of Industrial Organizations** and the UMWA honored the slain and wounded with a memorial, and in 1997, the Pennsylvania Historical and Museum Commission erected a marker at the site.

Suggested Reading

Perry K. Blatz, *Democratic Miners: Work and Labor Relations in the Anthracite Coal Industry, 1875–1925,* 1994; Michael Novak, *The Guns of Lattimer,* 1996; Edward Pinkowski, *Lattimer Massacre,* 1950; George Turner, "The Lattimer Tragedy of 1897," *Pennsylvania Heritage* 3 (1977): 10–13.

LAWRENCE TEXTILE STRIKE

The Lawrence textile strike of 1912 is one of the most famous labor protests in American history and one of the most dramatic protests led by the **Industrial Workers of the World** (IWW). The event was dubbed the "Bread and Roses strike" because of a 1911 poem written by James Oppenheim that was later set to music, though there is no evidence that the poem, song, or phrase was used during the strike. Upton Sinclair was the first writer to associate bread and roses with Lawrence, but he did so four years after the strike took place. Although the imagery of bread (higher wages) and roses (respect) certainly fit the profile of the walkout, its other name, the "Lawrence Nationalities strike," is even more apt, as more than 40 immigrant groups took part in the action, including Abyssinian, Belgian, Bohemian, English, French, German, Irish, Italian, Lithuanian, Portuguese, Spanish, and Turkish workers.

The strike began in earnest on January 12, 1912, when 20,000 woolen textile strikers left their posts to protest **wage** cuts and poor working conditions in Lawrence, Massachusetts. The immediate spark occurred one day earlier, when Polish women walked off their jobs to protest a pay cut instituted by the American Woolen Company. The cut came in response to newly enacted Massachusetts **protective labor legislation** that reduced women's weekly working hours from 56 to 54; American Woolen was one of several companies that violated the spirit of the new law by deducting two hours' pay from women's paychecks. Outraged Polish women yelling "short pay" walked out in protest. The walkouts were spontaneous **wildcat** responses and lacked direction at first, because the **American Federation of Labor** (AFL) was weak in Lawrence and had almost no presence among semiskilled immigrant laborers. The IWW filled the organizational void and set up organizing committees; by so doing, it demonstrated the possibility of bringing together diverse nationalities in labor action. It accomplished that task by sending organizers who were fluent in multiple languages, and by incorporating immigrant workers into decision-making roles. The IWW would also use its full panoply of **anarcho-syndicalist** tactics during the strike, including **direct action**, calling a **general strike**, and calling for acts of **sabotage** (broadly defined).

The organization sent many of its most capable organizers to Lawrence, including **Elizabeth Gurley Flynn**, **William Haywood**, Joseph Ettor, and Arturo Giovannitti; the latter two directed the strike's early days. The IWW would also have to contend with strikebreaking efforts led by the AFL's United Textile Workers union, which tried to position itself as a safer alternative to the IWW, though AFL organizer John Golden served mainly to discredit the AFL and make it appear guilty of union **scabbing**.

On January 29, striker Anna LoPizzo was killed by city police, but authorities used her death and an alleged dynamite plot (later revealed to be the effort of a local undertaker serving as a company-paid **agent provocateur**) as justification for requesting that the state militia take charge in Lawrence. Incredibly, Ettor and Giovannitti were jailed as accessories to LoPizzo's murder. This move backfired, as the arrest of the innocent men induced violent street clashes, a public outcry, and a public relations nightmare for textile firms and the city of Lawrence. American Woolen demonstrated tremendous ineptitude throughout the strike, and its public relations missteps probably played a bigger role in settling the dispute than any of the IWW's efforts.

The strike's most dramatic moments occurred when the IWW marched children to the local rail station to board trains that would take them to sympathetic **socialist** families in Barre, Vermont; New York; and elsewhere. Faced with eroding public support and a growing perception that children were starving in Lawrence, authorities foolishly tried to stop the children's exodus. On February 24, police confronted a march of women and children toward the station and used truncheons to beat them. This led to a nationwide outcry in which Lawrence officials were likened to the Russian czar and police to Cossacks. Outside money soon flowed into the strike fund. On March 12, 1912, American Woolen and other textile firms capitulated and more than 30,000 city workers received wage increases ranging from 5 percent to 20 percent. Employers also agreed to pay more for **overtime** work, reform their bonus systems, and refrain from retaliating against known strikers.

Lawrence demonstrated the potential of establishing the IWW as a major presence in eastern industrial cities. This did not happen, however, and less than 18 months after the strike the IWW had just several hundred members in Lawrence. The IWW proved to be far better at agitation than organization, and its loose structure based on voluntary payments of **dues** proved inadequate in a city as complex as Lawrence. Moreover, the IWW spent a lot of effort and money in winning acquittals for Ettor and Giovannitti. It probably also misunderstood the Lawrence rank-and-file and assumed that the anger associated with the strike translated into deeply held disregard for **capitalism**. In truth, IWW leaders were probably far more radical than the workers of Lawrence. Because the IWW refused to sign **contracts**, Lawrence manufacturers found it easy to roll back many of the gains made by workers on a piece-by-piece basis. The strike quickly became part of IWW mythology, though memories of the IWW's presence in Lawrence faded within a few years. Lawrence took on symbolic importance as an example of labor standing united against a common foe. As the strike's centennial approached, organized labor has seized on popular perceptions of the Lawrence uprising in hopes of rekindling interest in labor unions. The city of Lawrence holds periodic "Bread and Roses" festivals in its own efforts to draw tourists and investors to what is today one of the poorest cities in Massachusetts.

Suggested Reading

William Cahn, *Lawrence 1912*, 1977; Donald Cole, *Immigrant City: Lawrence, Massachusetts 1845–1921*, 1963; Melvyn Dubofsky, *We Shall Be All: A History of the IWW*, 1969; Bruce Watson, *Bread and Roses: Migrants, and the Struggle for the American Dream*, 2005.

LEWIS, JOHN LLEWELLYN

John L. Lewis (February 2, 1880–June 2, 1969) was one of the most important labor leaders of all time. He was the long-time president of the **United Mine Workers of America** (UMWA) and the first president of the **Congress of Industrial Organizations** (CIO). Few leaders have ever rivaled Lewis in influence, power, or determination. From the 1920s through the 1950s, he challenged corporate leaders, advised presidents, and battled with politicians. Lewis used his imposing size and bombastic style to his advantage and earned the reputation as a fierce and fearsome negotiator. Many observers charge that Lewis should have retired well in advance of

1960, when he officially stepped down as UMWA head, but at the height of his power one took on Lewis at one's own peril. Some observers argue that between 1936 and 1941, only President Franklin Roosevelt wielded more power in the United States than Lewis.

Lewis was born in Lucas, Iowa, the son of Thomas H. and Ann Watkins Lewis, Welsh immigrants. His father—not to be confused with Thomas L. Lewis, a UMWA cofounder—was a coal miner who held successive membership in the **Knights of Labor** (KOL) and the UMWA. After three years of high school, the 16-year-old John Lewis joined other family members in the coal pits. He joined the UMWA when John Mitchell led it. Lewis initially admired Mitchell, but came to feel he was too cautious and too conciliatory toward mine owners. He opposed Mitchell for the UMWA presidency when he was just 18, reconciled with him long enough to be appointed head of the international organizing staff in 1903, and split with him again in 1906, when Lewis blamed Mitchell for failing to maintain **wage** scales negotiated in 1903. After an abortive run for mayor of Lucas in 1907, Lewis regrouped. He married Myrta Edith Bell in 1907 and was elected UMWA secretary-treasurer in 1908, a position that gave him control over the union's newsletter, which he used as a personal forum. After a move to Panama City, Illinois, Lewis became president of his **union local** and, in 1917, became the UMWA's statistician, and shortly thereafter became a vice president. During World War I, Lewis served on the Federal Fuel Board.

In 1919, UMWA president Frank Hayes—plagued by ill health exacerbated by alcoholism—turned over many of his duties to Lewis and named him acting president. Lewis headed the UMWA during a 1919 walkout of more than 400,000 miners. He counseled miners to obey an **injunction** issued by President Woodrow Wilson, gauging correctly the atmosphere of the postwar **Red Scare** and the coming backlash against organized labor. In 1920, Lewis officially was elected to the UMWA presidency; he would hold that post until 1960. The decade of the 1920s was not an auspicious time to head a labor organization. Among miners, the overall political climate and overproduction during World War I led to falling wages and employer attempts to reverse wartime union gains. The UMWA was bloodied in postwar incidents such as **Matewan** and the **Battle for Blair Mountain**, and it had to contend with negative publicity following the **Herrin Massacre** in which UMWA strikers killed **scabs**. Lewis managed to guide the UMWA through a five-month **strike** in 1921 that delayed **concessions** from miners, but by 1922 the UMWA was suffering from layoffs and contraction. Lewis used the 1920s to streamline UMWA operations and consolidate his power. He did not hesitate to apply strong-armed tactics such as expelling rivals. Nonetheless, the UMWA was in freefall by 1933, having been reduced in size from approximately 500,000 members in 1922 to just 75,000 by the time Franklin Roosevelt took office.

The depression that began in 1929 caused Lewis, a lifelong Republican, to endorse Roosevelt in 1932. This relationship proved to be Lewis's avenue to national power. He advised Roosevelt on parts of the **National Industrial Recovery Act** (NIRA), including Section 7(a), which recognized labor's right to

collective bargaining; when the NIRA was struck down by the courts, he helped shape the subsequent **National Labor Relations Act**. Lewis also seized upon one of Roosevelt's off-the-cuff remarks to launch a UMWA organizing drive under the slogan, "The President Wants You to Join the Union." Lewis audaciously committed the UMWA treasury to the organizing drive and it paid off spectacularly; by the beginning of 1934 more than 90 percent of the nation's coal miners were enrolled in the UMWA and Lewis emerged as one of the most powerful union leaders in America. His reputation certainly dwarfed that of **William Green**, president of the **American Federation of Labor** (AFL).

Lewis and the UMWA were always an uncomfortable fit inside the **craft union**-controlled AFL. Although coal miners were highly skilled in their occupations, theirs was a backbreaking job that often involved as much brute force as artisanship. Moreover, the UMWA had few qualms about organizing black and immigrant workers. By the early 1930s, Lewis had become a full convert to the precepts of **industrial unionism** and began to press the AFL to give its full approval to organizing new unions built upon industrial union principles. His UMWA and several other AFL unions formed the Committee for Industrial Organization within the AFL to press for change in how heavy industry was organized. Old guard AFL leaders found industrial unionism to be a threat to craft prerogatives. Although they paid lip service to organizing mass-production industries, they consistently voted down calls to organize more industrial unions. In 1935, Lewis charged the AFL convention with blatantly ignoring the needs of industrial workers and of betraying its promise to them. After his initiative was voted down again, William Hutcheson of the carpenters' union swore at Lewis, who calmly decked him with an uppercut—the symbolic blow that led to the formation of the CIO. Although the CIO did not officially take shape until 1938, when the AFL expelled the UMWA and seven other unions, the Committee for Industrial Organization began operating independently of the AFL immediately after the 1935 convention and set up organizing committees to win workers to newly created industrial unions. The CIO organized more than 4 million workers by 1936 and Lewis was recognized as CIO president—though he was not formally elected as such until 1938—a position he would hold in addition to his presidency of the UMWA until the late fall of 1940.

Lewis supported Roosevelt again in 1936, by which time many political analysts considered Lewis to be the second most powerful leader in the nation. UMWA membership also rebounded by the mid-1930s, spurred by New Deal legislation, Lewis's hard-nosed bargaining, rank-and-file militancy, and the rising political influence of UMWA and CIO leaders. Successful industrial organizing drives in auto, glass, rubber, steel, and textiles enhanced Lewis's reputation.

By 1940, however, Lewis had grown disenchanted with Roosevelt, whom he suspected was rushing the United States into war. He was also angry that New Deal reforms had stalled, had personally quarreled with Roosevelt, and suspected the president of demagoguery, an ironic complaint coming from Lewis. He campaigned for Republican Wendell Wilkie and told CIO members he would quit the top post if Roosevelt was reelected. Roosevelt won easily. Lewis kept his promise, though he retained his presidency of the UMWA. In 1941, Lewis called a series of strikes for increased wages for miners, several of which were expressly designed to challenge the government's **Little Steel Formula**, a wage increase cap hammered out in the steel industry that became the model for settling other industrial disputes. In 1942, Lewis shocked the labor world by pulling the UMWA out of the CIO. It briefly rejoined the AFL in 1946, but withdrew in 1947 and remained independent for the rest of Lewis's tenure.

Under Lewis, the UMWA was one of the few unions to refuse to take a **no-strike pledge** during World War II. In 1943, Lewis demanded and won a captive mines provision in which miners automatically became UMWA members. Roosevelt was so angry with Lewis that he threatened to draft miners, but he was powerless to counter Lewis's cagey on-again-off-again responses to threats and **injunctions**. Although the Lewis won his point in 1943, many labor historians believe that the public outcry against Lewis contributed to the passage, over Roosevelt's veto, of the Smith-Connally Act, which gave the government the right to seize industries deemed vital to war production, and which also forbade unions from making direct political contributions. In like fashion, the UMWA's 1946 strike perhaps contributed to the passage of the hated **Taft-Hartley Act** in 1947. UMWA strikes in 1946 and again in 1948 did, however, gain UMWA members royalties for each ton of coal mined. Lewis used these funds to set up the union's Welfare and Retirement Fund, seen by some Lewis admirers as his greatest legacy. By the 1950s, the UMWA had the most extensive welfare and retirement program of any U.S. union, and funds were also used to fund hospitals and address miner health issues. Moreover, Lewis led the charge for mine-safety laws and for greater awareness of mining-related diseases. In 1951, he negotiated an agreement with bituminous-mine owners that led to several years of industrial peace, though critics charged it sapped rank-and-file militancy. In 1952, Lewis helped negotiate the Mine Safety Act, the first legislation to impose national standards on mine operators.

By the 1950s, John L. Lewis was indisputably the strongest labor leader in the nation, but debates raged (and continue to do so) about whether he was an unbowed champion of workers willing to defy written contracts, injunctions, fines, and threats of imprisonment, or whether he was an egoistic tyrant. Lewis was outspoken in his hatred of the Taft-Hartley Act, which he called a "slave labor" bill. His counseled unions to refuse to comply with its provisions, thereby making it a dead article. Lewis traded on his rebel image, even though the 1951 bituminous agreement blunted rank-and-file militancy. As the 1950s progressed, he came to support the same blend of capital/labor cooperation that he once criticized John Mitchell for holding. He retired as UMWA leader in 1960, though he maintained such influence over the group until his death nine years later that many union watchers felt he was still the de facto head of the union.

Lewis was awarded the Presidential Medal of Freedom by President John Kennedy in 1960 and was inducted into the Labor Hall of Fame in 1989. Lewis sired three children, including Katherine, who later held important UMWA posts. Her role in the UMWA added nepotism to the raft of charges Lewis detractors leveled against him. Among miners, however, the name "John L. Lewis" continues to evoke reverence and even his harshest critics admit that Lewis was, quite simply, one of the most powerful labor leaders that America has ever produced.

Suggested Reading

Saul Alinsky, *John L. Lewis: An Unauthorized Biography*, 2010; Melvyn Dubofsky and Warren Van Tine, *John L. Lewis: A Biography*, 1986; *John L. Lewis Papers* (State Historical Society of Wisconsin, microfilm, 1970); Robert Zieger, *John L. Lewis: Labor Leader*, 1988.

LITTLE STEEL FORMULA

The Little Steel Formula was an attempt to control **wage** and price increases during World War II. The **National War Labor Board** (NWLB) was created in January 1941 in hopes of fashioning a labor/management/public committee that would peacefully resolve labor disputes, control inflation, and ensure that war-time production would not be interrupted. NWLB decisions were considered binding.

In July 1942, employees at various "Little Steel" firms—those not working for industry giant U.S. Steel—complained to the NWLB that their wages were inadequate to cope with wartime inflation. They demanded a $1 per day increase. Upon deliberation, the NLWB granted a $0.44 increase (15 percent), based on the increase in steel prices since January 1, 1941. The NLWB was headed by George W. Taylor, a University of Pennsylvania industrial relations professor, who relied upon the Consumer Price Index (CPI), an instrument first developed by the **Bureau of Labor Statistics** in 1919 and adjusted periodically. The 15 percent increase granted to steelworkers in 1942 became known as the Little Steel Formula, as it became the standard applied to subsequent settlements imposed by the NWLB.

This formula proved unworkable, however, as inflation did not ease as NWLB mediators had hoped; using the CPI as a basis for the formula proved problematic because inflation was rising faster than data were being accumulated. Despite **no-strike pledges**, more than 2 million workers walked off their jobs in 1943 to protest the inadequacy of their wages. Most of these actions were **quickies** that were resolved without impeding war production. Several of the disputes were settled by increasing worker **fringe benefits**, an appeasement that technically did not violate the Little Steel Formula. The **International Association of Machinists** was among the unions that forced the WLB to surpass the Little Steel Formula.

Not as easily resolved, however, was a dispute involving the **United Mine Workers of America** (UMWA). In April 1943, UMWA President **John L. Lewis** demanded an increase of $2 per day and portal-to-portal pay to compensate miners for time spent being transported underground to the head of coal seams (which could be an hour away). Through a six-month campaign, the UMWA strike of 1943 smashed the Little Steel Formula. The UMWA victory proved problematic for labor, however. At one juncture, President Roosevelt considered seizing the nation's mines. An increasingly conservative Congress was inflamed by the UMWA's action and enacted the Smith-Connolly Act, which placed limits on labor's ability to strike in industries deemed essential to the national interest. Some historians believe that the UMWA's action also laid the groundwork for the **Taft-Hartley Act**.

Suggested Reading

James B. Atleson, *Labor and the Wartime State: Labor Relations and Law during World War II*, 1998; Ronald Donovan, *Administering the Taylor Law: Public Employee Relations in New York*, 1990; Robert G. Rodden, *Fighting Machinists: A Century of Struggle*, 1984.

LIVING WAGE

Much attention is given to the **minimum wage** in the United States, but few labor groups believe that it is an appropriate floor for worker compensation. In recent years attention has shifted to a living wage, the hourly rate necessary for a person to achieve a basic standard of living. The current federal minimum wage is $7.25 per hour, a rate that would yield $15,080 if extended over 52 weeks. Such a figure would barely place a two-member household over the official poverty threshold and would put a family of four $7,000 under the poverty line. Moreover, all such calculations are averages that fail to take into account differences in living costs within a region. For instance, a person making $35,000 in upstate Utica, New York, would need to earn $65,385 to maintain a similar standard of living in New York City. Conversely, the same worker moving to Columbus, Mississippi, would need just $31,210 to maintain his or her current lifestyle.

As these examples suggest and the **American Federation of Labor-Congress of Industrial Organizations** (AFL-CIO) insists, there is no one-size-fits-all answer to how high wages should be. Living wage campaigns take into account the relative cost of living and argue in favor of regional wage floors that would guarantee all full-time workers access to a lifestyle of adequate food, shelter, clothing, health care, recreation, and other necessities.

Living wage campaigns often differ from attempts to raise the minimum wage, in that they are local efforts rather than reforms that require Congressional action. These grassroots campaigns seek to create living wage ordinances on the municipal level. The first living wage ordinance was passed in Baltimore in 1994, which raised the city's minimum wage to $6.10 when the federal law at the time mandated just $4.25 per hour as a minimum. As of 2007, there were 140 local living wage ordinances and more than 100 additional campaigns under way.

The living wage movement was dealt a blow with the demise of the Association of Community Organizations for Reform Now (ACORN) in 2010. ACORN had been the largest community organization of low- and moderate-income families in the United States, with a membership of more than 175,000 families, organized into more than 1,200 neighborhood chapters in 85 cities. ACORN received considerable support from the labor movement and helped pass living wage laws in New York, Denver, Oakland, and Chicago. It became the target of conservative groups for its economic campaigns and for its role in voter registration drives that got out support for Barack Obama's 2008 presidential campaign. Right-wing groups produced a doctored video that purported to show illegal activities on the part of ACORN activists, which led to a cutoff of federal funds and the loss of the organization's tax-exempt status. Although courts subsequently ruled that ACORN was guiltless and that Congress had acted wrongly, ACORN chapters folded and the organization declared bankruptcy in 2010. Spinoff agencies have emerged but they have kept a lower profile.

The battle for a living wage is an uphill struggle, as local businesses—especially hotel and restaurant owners—have fought living wage ordinances in many municipalities. Opponents argue that these laws hurt their businesses and will necessitate job cuts, though this has not been the case in municipalities where such laws exist. Critics counter that living wage ordinances decrease opportunities for the lowest-skilled workers they are designed to help; faced with higher payrolls, employers simply reduce staff. The recession that (officially) began in 2007 also led numerous municipalities to insist that they could not sustain living wage costs during a period of cutbacks and declining tax revenues. Reaction against these ordinances also led some states, such as Arizona, Oregon, Colorado, Utah, Missouri, and Louisiana, to ban these initiatives.

Those who support living wage ordinances counter with research indicating that predictions of massive job loss are simply not true, though they concede that in some cases moderate job losses have occurred following these measures' adoption. They also offer evidence that increased wages have a salutary effect on many of the very businesses that most decry the living wage: hotels, restaurants, and retail outlets. They also argue that higher wages will, over time, benefit municipalities as better-paid workers will pay more in taxes and city governments will reduce their reliance upon government subsidies.

The AFL-CIO and most labor unions argue that a living wage is, simply, a matter of justice. The Working Poor Families Project reveals that roughly 30 percent of families falling beneath the federal poverty line are headed by full-time workers whose wages are inadequate to support their households. Far from being the "idle" welfare recipients of myth, these workers simply cannot support their families on the wages offered. Some advocates of the poor have turned the tables on conservatives by insisting upon moving individuals from welfare to "workfare" and have made the living wage a centerpiece of reform efforts. Living wage campaigns have become tools for union organizing and are likely to remain so in the near future.

Suggested Reading

Cost of Living Wizard, http://swz.salary.com/CostOfLivingWizard/LayoutScripts/Coll_Start.aspx, accessed February 16, 2011; Living Wage Campaign, http://www.livingwagecampaign.org, accessed February 16, 2011; Robert Pollin and Stephanie Luce, *The Living Wage: Building a Fair Economy*, 1998; Richard Troxell, *Looking Up at the Bottom Line: The Struggle for the Living Wage!*, 2010.

LOCHNER V. NEW YORK

Lochner v. New York, 198 U.S. 45, was a 1905 U.S. Supreme Court decision that had profound impact on American labor. The controversial *Lochner* decision gives ammunition to those who argue that the **Progressive Era** was often far less than "progressive" insofar as working people were concerned. The court, by a hotly contested 5–4 vote, ruled that a New York state law limiting the number of hours a man could work was unconstitutional.

The case stemmed from the Bakeshop Act, an 1895 bill in New York that forbade bakers from working more than 60 hours per week, or more than 10 hours per day. In 1901, Joseph Lochner, the owner of a Utica bakery, challenged the law after he was fined for the second time for exceeding the limit. His conviction was upheld twice by New York courts, each time by a single vote, and was eventually appealed before the Supreme Court. The court's ruling was an attempt to reconcile the Fifth Amendment, which guarantees both due process and property rights, with the Fourteenth Amendment, which conferred civil rights upon former slaves. The Fifth Amendment protected property, yet the Thirteenth and Fourteenth Amendments placed restrictions on it. The court made a distinction between personal rights and property rights that was, even more controversially, rooted partly in a reading of the 1857 *Dred Scott v. Sandford* ruling, which remained extant, despite the passage of the Thirteenth Amendment. According to the majority opinion, although human beings could no longer be considered property, an owner's Fifth Amendment right to dispose of his property appropriately remained in effect, and the Fourteenth Amendment strengthened it. The court drew upon the Fourteenth Amendment clause that forbade any state from depriving "any person of his life, liberty, or property, without due process of law." According to the court, Lochner had an inviolable right to dispose of his personal property—his labor—as he saw fit. It upheld individuals' "freedom of contract" right and ruled that an attempt to limit a person's right to work as many hours as he chooses was "unreasonable, unnecessary, and arbitrary interference" on the part of government. The *Lochner* decision, in effect, ruled that any attempt to limit the workday violated the U.S. Constitution.

The court was deeply divided by *Lochner*, with Justices John Marshall Harlan and Oliver Wendell Holmes, Jr., filing withering dissents from the majority opinion that accused colleagues of upholding **social Darwinism** and of sacrificing the general welfare, public health, and public safety in the bargain. Justice Holmes noted that freedom of contract was often a myth and cited numerous examples in which workers were forced to accept harsh conditions. The majority ruling, he argued, assumed that all workers had the power to decide on their hours of toil. He also argued that the courts routinely restricted working hours—such as enacting Sunday closing laws—and that the majority opinion rested on a peculiar reading of the Fourteenth Amendment.

Organized labor was stunned by the *Lochner* decision. The court, in effect, invalidated decades of efforts to limit the workday, including the entire **eight-hour movement**. The situation was muddied further by the 1908 **Muller v. Oregon** decision, in which the Supreme Court ruled that it *was* constitutional to limit the number of hours women could work. That ruling posed challenges to women's rights groups and organized labor alike. On the one hand, the *Muller* decision seemed to confirm Justice Holmes's assertion that working hours could be regulated and that freedom of contract was not absolute. On the other hand, the ruling in *Muller* was carefully couched in essentialism—the belief that the sexes were by nature different. *Muller* was a form of **protective legislation** that rested upon the argument that there was a social necessity to protect the more delicate health and weaker natures of women.

Reformers were left with a conundrum. On the one hand, *Muller* regulated the hours of labor. For women's rights advocates to argue against essentialism would mean they also advocated overturning the *Muller* ruling, which would place female employees under the logic of the *Lochner* decision. On the other hand, to accept *Muller* meant giving tacit approval to essentialism and opened the door for future discriminatory legislation.

The **American Federation of Labor** (AFL) faced a similar dilemma. The *Muller* ruling suggested that the workday could be shortened by Congressional action, but AFL officials were also aware that to make such a point entailed attacking the court's essentialist logic. Many AFL members agreed with essentialism, but there seemed no way to uphold the principle of shorter hours and the principle of essentialism simultaneously. In addition, although the AFL did not represent a large number of women, to argue against *Muller* would be to work against the interests of those women who were AFL members.

The *Lochner* decision's implications proved difficult to resolve. New Deal legislation would, in the 1930s, enshrine the eight-hour workday, but workers throughout the Progressive Era and through the 1920s struggled to fashion a response to the *Lochner* and *Muller* rulings. *Lochner* was one of numerous court setbacks for organized labor during the period; others included *Coppage v. Kansas*, **Loewe v. Lawlor**, and *Adkins v. Children's Hospital*. *Lochner* was never officially repudiated, but subsequent court rulings have tended to decouple personal from economic freedom and to entertain the notion that freedom of contract is not an all-or-nothing proposition.

Suggested Reading

Melvyn Dubofsky, *The State and Labor in Modern America*, 1994; Paul Kens, *Lochner v. New York: Economic Regulation on Trial*, 1998.

LOCKOUT

A lockout is sometimes nicknamed "an employer's strike." It occurs when an employer closes a facility and prevents employees from entering and working. Lockouts often precipitate a retaliatory **strike** on the part of employees, but the two terms are different and should not be confused. A lockout is an aggressive maneuver on the part of an employer aimed at forcing employees to accept management's work terms. It is often undertaken as a prelude to dealing with upcoming contentious issues such as layoffs or contract negotiations. A lockout seeks to intimidate, in the sense that it signals the employer's willingness to lose money in the short term in defense of what is seen as a management prerogative. In some cases it might be retaliatory in nature. Management might, for instance, respond to a perceived work slowdown or **stint** by locking out workers. Employers must be careful, however, as such an action in a unionized workplace might be interpreted as an **unfair labor practice** if a contract is in place, and it could result in heavy fines and an order to distribute back-pay to employees. As a result, most lockouts take place either at the end of a contract or as an attempt to dissuade workers in advance of a union recognition vote.

Many famed capital/labor clashes identified as strikes actually began when employers locked out workers. This list includes **Homestead steel lockout** in 1892, which was a deliberately provocative action taken by plant manager Henry Clay Frick with the approval of owner Andrew Carnegie aimed at breaking the plant's labor union. Other famous "strikes" that began as lockouts include the **Pullman** (1894), Paterson (1913), and **Ravenswood** (1991) actions. Lockouts have also occurred in professional sports and are often threatened. In 1990, for example, Major League Baseball owners locked out members of the **Major League Baseball Players Association**. Under federal law, employers can hire **scabs** ("replacement workers") during a strike. Baseball owners sought to do so, but a settlement was reached before the season opened. A strike that cancelled the 1994 World Series led to a threatened lockout and use of scabs, but this dispute was also resolved when replacement players proved a pale imitation of those players whom they sought to replace. National Football League owners called for a lockout in advance of the 2011 season, seeking to resolve a revenue-sharing dispute on management's terms; the dispute was settled without affecting any of the regular-season games. In the same year, a lockout by owners of the National Basketball Association delayed the opening of the season and necessitated shortening the schedule from 82 to 66 games.

Lockouts have occurred in other industries as well. In 2010, the **United Steelworkers of America** saw several of its **union locals** experience lockouts, including Kentucky and Illinois uranium workers employed by Honeywell, who were locked out during contract negotiations that stalled over health care benefits. Employers often prefer strikes to lockouts, however, as workers can draw **unemployment** benefits during a lockout, but not during a strike.

Suggested Reading

Millie Beik, ed., *Labor Relations: Major Issues in American History*, 2005; Robert M. Smith, *From Blackjacks to Briefcases*, 2002.

LOEWE V. LAWLOR

Loewe v. Lawlor is also known as the "Danbury hatters case." This U.S. Supreme Court decision dealt a blow to labor unions by ruling that secondary **boycotts** were illegal restraints of trade under the 1890 **Sherman Antitrust Act**. Even more troublesome, the Court agreed that employers could sue individual union members for damages incurred during illegal boycotts. In the case of *Loewe v. Lawlor*, the Supreme Court unanimously upheld triple damages in excess of $250,000 and attached worker assets.

The *Loewe* case had its genesis in what had been a series of victories for labor unions in the hat industry. By 1902, the United Hatters of North America (UHNA) had used boycotts to organize all but 12 of 190 hat manufacturers, including Roelef's, a Philadelphia-based firm recognized as an industry leader. The UHNA turned its attention to the C. H. Merritt and D. E. Loewe companies of Danbury, Connecticut, which were among the dozen holdouts. Rather than deal with the UHNA, Loewe sought advice from the American Anti-Boycott Association, an alliance of anti-union business officials, which pledged $20,000 pledge to help Loewe battle the UHNA. When strikers were replaced by **scabs**, the **American Federation of Labor** (AFL), with which the UHNA was affiliated, placed Loewe on its "We Don't Patronize" list. It also launched a secondary boycott and pressured wholesalers and retailers to stop carrying Loewe hats. Loewe lost approximately $33,000 during 1902 and 1903, but struck back. The firm argued that the UHNA boycott was an illegal restraint of trade under the Sherman Act. Loewe also took advantage of a Connecticut law that allowed property attachments for civil damages, and on September 12, 1903, attachments were placed on the assets of 248 UHNA members who held property and bank accounts. Loewe lawyers then pressed the courts to grant additional damages.

The immediate impact of Loewe's actions was to cripple the UHNA. Union membership declined, and numerous firms, including Roelef's, easily reneged on contract agreements at a time in which there was little statute law that required compliance. The UHNA saw a brief ray of hope in December 1907, when a U.S. circuit court dismissed Loewe's claims against the UHNA on the grounds that it was unclear whether the Sherman Act applied to labor unions. Upon appeal, however, the Supreme Court ruled the Sherman Act was applicable. The case was retried, and in early 1910 the UHNA and its members were held liable for losses incurred by the Loewe firm. A technicality voided that verdict, but a third trial in 1912 upheld the 1910 judgment. On January 5, 1915, the Supreme Court ruled that the hatters had to pay the company's costs and triple damages, a toll that amounted to $252,130. No hatters lost their homes or savings as a result of the *Loewe* decision; the AFL helped defray the costs, and rallies and contributions raised revenue to pay the judgment.

Nonetheless, the *Loewe* decision proved disastrous to organized labor in the short run, despite the 1914 **Clayton Antitrust Act** that exempted unions from precisely the liability under which UHNA members were sued. The *Loewe* decision, along with other antilabor decisions such as *Buck's Stove & Range Co. v. American Federation of Labor et al.*, *Adair v. The United States*, and *Hitchman Coal and Coke Company v. Mitchell* robbed labor unions of most of the weapons at their disposal. Anti-union court cases, the activities of groups such as the **National Association of Manufacturers**, the rise of the **open-shop** movement, and the suppression of radical groups such as the **Industrial Workers of the World** calls into question the legitimacy of the term **Progressive Era** insofar as reforms applied to **working-class** Americans during this period. Some labor historians regard the term "Progressive Era" as a romantic construction and charge that the period's reforms were designed mainly to stabilize the business community rather than to improve the lives of ordinary Americans.

Suggested Reading

David Bensman, *The Practice of Solidarity: American Hat Finishers in the 19th Century*, 1985; William Forbath, *Law and the Shaping of the American Labor Movement*, 1991; William Graebner, *Coal-Mining Safety in the Progressive Period*, 1985; Benjamin Taylor and Fred Witney, *U.S. Labor Relations Law: Historical Development*, 1992.

LONGSHOREMEN

Longshoremen—also called stevedores or dockworkers—are waterside workers who perform the often-difficult labor of loading and unloading cargo boats. Legend holds that the term derives from the Colonial practice of greeting ships from Europe with the call "Men long-shore," but that origin is by no means certain. In all likelihood, the term "long-shore" is simply a popular vulgarization of the adjective "alongshore."

In the days before mechanically powered wenches and cranes relieved some of the more backbreaking aspects of the job, longshoremen often moved every single item in and out of the cargo holds of ships. A steel "hook" used to grab boxes from the hold was a symbol of the profession, as were the presence of hand-operated block, tackle, and rope-riggings along the dock. The profession remains one that demands physical strength. Longshoremen have been essential in the economic life of North America from Colonial times on. In the "Age of Sail" from the 16th through the 19th centuries, most goods coming into or being exported out of North America involved ships. This was true also for much of the trade within the continent. Railroads eventually took over much of the domestic freight hauling in the 19th century, followed by motorized vehicles in the 20th century. In like fashion, after World War II many items that once moved by ship began to be transported by cargo planes. Nonetheless, a substantial number of goods still arrive and leave the United States by ship, and longshoremen remain important in ensuring that they are loaded and unloaded.

Before unionization came to the docks, waterside work was viewed as unskilled labor and was often done by recent immigrants; those who performed such duties were poorly paid and badly treated. The first attempt to unionize waterside workers came in 1864, when workers in New York City created the Longshoremen's Union Protection Association (LUPA). In 1877, dockworkers in Great Lakes ports formed an organization that was eventually named the International Longshoremen's Association (ILA), which received a charter from the **American Federation of Labor** (AFL) in 1892, and remains the largest longshoremen's union on the East Coast, the Great Lakes, Puerto Rico, and the Gulf of Mexico. Daniel Keefe, an Irish immigrant whose efforts responded both to the poor treatment of longshoremen and nativist prejudices against non-native-born workers, first organized the ILA. The **Knights of Labor** (KOL) also organized dockworkers in the late 19th century, especially in New York, New Jersey,

The 1901 emblem of the International Longshoremen's Association (ILA). Aggressive unionization of dock workers began after the Civil War. The ILA emerged from the National Longshoremen's Association during the 1890s, changing its name when Canadian workers joined the union. The ILA remains the principal union for longshoremen. (Library of Congress)

and the upper Midwest. Unionization efforts met with fierce resistance that precipitated more 30,000 **strikes** between 1881 and 1905. Neither the LUPA nor KOL dockworker **locals** survived, but the ILA was able to build an organization of around 100,000 by the dawn of the 20th century. Several smaller unions also formed along the Great Lakes, but most of these groups failed after a bitter three-year strike that broke out in 1909. By 1912, the ILA, which did not take part in the strike, was the only significant union left in the Midwest and East Coast.

The situation on the West Coast was different. Unions were slower to take hold there because employer opposition was even stronger and the **open-shop** system prevailed. Companies maintained tight control over hiring practices by operating employment halls. Particularly vexatious was the "blue book" system, which required workers to receive a blue **company union** card to secure employment. This card allowed companies to deduct part of a worker's **wages** as union **dues**, in effect paying the company for the privilege of working. Even more hated was the daily **shape-up**, which reduced longshoremen to day laborers and allowed bosses to engage in favoritism and graft by choosing who would get work on a given day. Both the **Industrial Workers of the World** (IWW) and the Communist Party sought to break the hold of employers over longshoremen. In the early 20th century the IWW used **direct action** tactics along the West Coast and engaged in numerous **quickie** strikes. IWW members along the West Coast also took part in worldwide waterside strikes in 1908 and 1913. Neither it nor the **communists** succeeded in breaking the power of employers, but they left behind a militant spirit that would later infuse the International Longshore and Warehouse Union (ILWU).

Developments in the West also impacted the ILA. The IWW tried to organize Great Lakes longshoremen and those in East Coast ports such as Philadelphia. Competition, employer backlashes in the 1920s, and the collapse of the economy with the onset of the Great Depression weakened the ILA, though Joseph Ryan, who was elected ILA president in 1927, kept the organization on sound financial footing. The arrival of the New Deal stimulated union growth across the nation, including the waterside. A key moment came in 1934, when a West Coast dispute led to a three-month work stoppage that crippled freight traffic from San Diego to Vancouver and evolved into a **general strike** in San Francisco. It was directed by the controversial **Harry Bridges**, an Australian immigrant, former IWW member, and suspected (though never proven) communist. The strike was won and Ryan was forced to recognize Bridges as the ILA's leader along the West Coast. Neither Bridges nor militant West Coast longshoremen were a good fit within the ILA, however, and both soon withdrew from it and joined the newly created ILWU. In 1937, the ILWU joined the **Congress of Industrial Organizations** (CIO), with Bridges rising to the post of director of the CIO's West Coast operations. Both the ILA and the ILWU honored **no-strike pledges** during World War II.

In 1945, the ILWU expanded its focus by organizing pineapple and sugar workers. The emerging **Cold War soon** offered new challenges to both the ILWU and the ILA. Because of allegations that Bridges was a communist, the CIO had moved to limit his power even before the passage of the **Taft-Hartley Act**. When the ILWU refused to endorse the post-World War II Marshall Plan, the CIO moved to expel it in 1950. Bridges and the ILWU actually gathered strength while banned from the CIO. In both 1946 and 1949, the ILWU directed successful strikes against autocratic employers in Hawaii. Dockworkers in that U.S. territory mostly looked beyond **Red Scare** tactics and the ILWU was able to consolidate gains there, including a 1954 **pension plan** that was the first of its kind for agricultural workers. When the FBI charged seven ILWU members with communist affiliations that violated the Smith Act and sought to force the **decertification** of the ILWU, it was rebuffed through a 1953 walkout. The ILWU not only weathered the storm, but it also played a role in negotiating Hawaii's statehood in 1960. On the mainland, the ILWU negotiated good contracts for its members. In 1960, it took the unprecedented action of agreeing to mechanization and the handling of containerized cargo, even though it meant job contraction. Bridges judged that these changes were inevitable and cut a deal that helped displaced workers and guaranteed the jobs of those who remained.

The ILA did not fare as well. By the 1950s, it stood accused of **racketeering** and connections to organized crime-allegations cemented in the public mind by Elia Kazan's 1954 Academy Award-winning **film** *On the Waterfront*. In New York City, a 1951 strike was viewed as having been called by organized crime. The AFL suspended the ILA in 1953, an act that led John Ryan to resign and inspired the creation of a new AFL dockworkers' union, the International Brotherhood of Longshoremen (IBL). The ILA and IBL soon clashed, and the ILA struck a deal with the **Teamsters** not to cross **picket lines** set up at IBL worksites. In the minds of some, this deal simply brought together the nation's two most corrupt unions. Thus, when the ILA won a **certification** election in 1953 to represent New York dockworkers, Governor Thomas Dewey moved to void it. For the next three years New York was convulsed by a series of **injunctions, wildcat strikes**, and clashes between rival labor unions. In 1956, the ILA finally secured certification. It was readmitted to the merged AFL-CIO in 1959, and the IBL was deactivated. By then, however, the ILA was weakened everywhere except in the Great Lakes. Its most significant rebuilding efforts took place after Teddy Gleason became ILA president in 1963. In 1965, Gleason negotiated a deal on containerization and mechanization akin to that signed by the ILWU five years earlier.

Both the ILA and the ILWU faced discontent among some rank-and-file workers who charged that the new work rules created a two-tier system in which new hires were treated as second-class workers. This issue was particularly troublesome for the ILWU, many of whose African American workers came in under new rules. By the 1960s, the two unions had laid aside many of their former differences. Bridges considered merging the ILWU with either the Teamsters or the ILA, but neither liaison occurred by the time he retired in 1977. In 1980, though, the ILWU absorbed a union consisting of inland waterway workers on tugs, barges, and ferries. An ILA/ILWU merger has not occurred, though the ILWU did join the AFL-CIO in 1988 after 37 years of operation as an independent union. This move effectively ended **jurisdiction** battles between the ILWU and the ILA.

Roughly speaking, the ILA and the ILWU continue to represent the same constituencies they always have, though each has expanded to include inland waterway workers, and the ILWU also includes chemical workers, warehouse employees, and Powell's Bookstore workers. The ILWU generally cooperates with the Pacific Maritime Association, an employers' consortium, but it called a slowdown in 2002, which ultimately yielded a six-year **contract**. It successfully negotiated a new six-year agreement in 2008. The ILWU contains vestiges of its old militancy and remains critical of U.S. foreign policy initiatives such as the Gulf War. As of 2011, Richard Hughes, Jr., was president of the 65,000-member ILA and Robert McElrath headed the 59,500-member ILWU.

Suggested Reading

"The ILWU Story," http://www.ilwu.org/?page_id=814, accessed January 14, 2011; Howard Kimeldorf, *Reds or Rackets? The Making of Radical and Conservative Unions on the Waterfront*, 1992; Mike Quinn, *The Big Strike*, 1996.

LORDSTOWN STRIKE

The Lordstown strike was a dramatic three-week **strike** against General Motors (GM) in Lordstown, Ohio, by Local 1112 of the **United Auto Workers of America (UAW)** union. It took place in February 1972. Many observers see this strike, coupled with a less-famous 174-day strike in Norwood, Ohio, also in 1972, as the swan song of **Taylorism**, **Fordism**, and many other dehumanizing aspects of **assembly-line production**. The Lordstown strike attracted widespread media coverage because much of the workforce was younger than the age of 25, and was apparently radicalized by the rise of the **counterculture** during the 1960s. The strike also took place against the backdrop of retooling auto production to adjust for changing tastes and consumer needs. At the time of the strike, the Lordstown Chevrolet Vega assembly facility was considered the most advanced in the auto industry.

By the mid-1960s, Detroit automakers were saddled with an oversized, gas-guzzling fleet. With more women entering the job market, many American families began purchasing second cars, especially more fuel-efficient foreign imports. American manufacturers sought to recoup their lost market shares by restyling their fleets and introducing their own economy cars. By the late 1960s, Ford was enjoying brisk sales of its Pinto line. In response, the Chevrolet division of GM developed the Vega, whose production began in Lordstown in 1968. Lordstown was a state-of-the-art facility that had opened less than two years earlier. Chevrolet managers hoped to produce 60 Vegas per hour from its assembly line and to sell more than 400,000 units annually. Unfortunately, the Vega proved to be a flawed vehicle. Chevrolet general manager John DeLorean warned GM officials of troublesome test results. The car was top-heavy, was noisy, and experienced engine problems. DeLorean suspected that the Vega was simply a bad car, but rather than redesign it, GM pressed for its production so that the company could compete with Ford and imports from Datsun, Toyota, and Volkswagen.

As DeLorean predicted, the Vega proved a troubled product. In 1971, GM was forced to recall more than 132,000 Vegas to correct potential fire hazards. Trouble was also brewing on the assembly line, where Vega workers complained of crushing boredom within a highly mechanized manufacturing process that reduced them to automatons. The plant had high levels of absenteeism, lax discipline, frequent confrontations between line workers and management, and allegations of alcohol and drug use among workers on the line. GM's response to the mounting crisis did little to address its root causes. On October 1, 1971, Chevrolet management was placed under the General Motors Assembly Division (GMAD), essentially ending Chevy's autonomy within GM's corporate structure. Important decisions were now made in the GM boardroom rather than by Chevrolet production officials. GMAD bureaucrats determined that the answer to Vega's woes was greater workplace discipline. Time-motion studies were ordered, with clipboard-carrying supervisors trawling Lordstown in classic Taylorist fashion. Some 700 "unproductive" workers were furloughed, special work arrangements between foremen and workers were eliminated, mandatory **overtime** was instituted, and **grievance** procedures were stonewalled.

GM's heavy-handed response was out of touch with contemporary social reality. The Lordstown workforce was young; even Local 1112 President Gary Bryner was not yet 30 years old. Most workers were disinclined to view the assembly line as much more than an immediate paycheck and were unmoved by appeals (or threats) to their careers. Many sported long hair, some were Vietnam veterans, and few were willing to accept arbitrary authority. Rock music, drugs, and alcohol were part of the culture for numerous Vega workers, as was anti-materialist rhetoric. These workers proved as big a challenge to the UAW as to GM. Rather than embrace the precepts of **pure and simple unionism**, Vega workers demanded that UAW officials negotiate items such as workplace rules, safety issues, and ways to relieve line-worker tedium. GM's most provocative act came when it set a new production target of 100 Vegas per hour. This entailed a **speedup** that left the average line worker with about 36 seconds to complete a task before another chassis appeared. The workers' response to the speedup was a mutually enforced **stint** that included slowdowns and, if deemed necessary, **sabotage**. Vega soon had poor customer-satisfaction ratings, and GM had acres of unmovable, mechanically unsound stock. Workers lampooned GMAD as "Got to Make Another Dollar," and filed more than 1,400 grievances against management in the four months preceding the strike.

Ninety-seven percent of Lordstown's workers voted to strike, though many had already declared a **wildcat strike** in advance of the vote. By early February, 7,500 workers were off the job, demanding a return to pre-1971 production standards. At the time, the strike was hailed by activists associated with the political left as the vanguard of social revolution that would deliver a hammer blow to inhumane **capitalism**. That assessment proved romantic and naïve. After three weeks and losses to GM estimated at $150 million, an inconclusive settlement was reached that involved vague promises of addressing workplace alienation. The speedup mostly remained in place, though GM also hastened the development of robots and computerized machinery that replaced human labor in some of the most tedious unskilled positions. Vega enjoyed strong sales thereafter, but it was constantly plagued by quality problems.

In the long run, the Lordstown strike was significant less for its revolutionary potential or the settlement reached than for its sociological and industrial impact. The field of industrial sociology received more attention during and after the strike, with scholars turning their attention to what was variously labeled as the "Lordstown syndrome" and the "**blue-collar** blues." Numerous studies appeared that further probed the phenomenon of worker alienation; many scholars concluded that the classic assembly line was a dehumanizing failure and that time-motion studies were more likely to breed resentment and strife than to increase production. The use of Fordist production and Taylorist management methods declined dramatically in the wake of the events at Lordstown. Automakers began to rethink production methods, particularly after foreign producers captured even larger segments of the U.S. market following the oil embargo of 1973 and reports of poor American car quality in the late 1970s and early 1980s. Although few automakers found it cost-effective to set up bumper-to-bumper production teams like those used by Sweden's Volvo, most sought ways to lessen reliability on human assembly-line workers. The UAW actively lobbied for more worker involvement in decision making, and some manufacturers grew enamored of Japanese production and management styles as practiced by corporations such as Honda and Toyota. Several experimented with **quality circles**, with mixed results.

American car manufacturers have been loath to scrap the assembly line altogether, but it has been steadily automated, a nod to the legitimacy of worker complaints. The Chevy Vega ceased production in 1977, for the most part unmourned by American consumers. The Lordstown facility made several other products for a time, and enjoyed brief resurgence with the Chevrolet Cavalier line, which it manufactured from 1998 to 2005. It also made the Pontiac Sunfire, which was essentially the Cavalier under a different name. Between 2005 and 2010, Lordstown made Chevrolet Cobalts, but in 2010 the firm declared bankruptcy, folded the Pontiac line altogether, and cut two of Lordstown's three shifts. In 2010, Lordstown began coproduction with Japanese carmaker Suzuki of a crossover sports utility/family sedan line called the Chevrolet Cruze. It sold fewer than 25,000 units in the United States in 2010 and the once state-of-the art facility in Lordstown faces an uncertain future.

Suggested Reading

Ruth Milkman, *Farewell to the Factory: Autoworkers in the Late 20th Century*, 1997; David Moberg, "No More Junk: Lordstown Workers and the Demand for Quality," *Critical Sociology*, 8 (October 1978), 63–69; Ken Weller, "1970–1972: The Lordstown Struggle and the Real Crisis in Production," http://libcom.org/library/lordstown-struggle-ken-weller, accessed February 11, 2011.

LOS ANGELES TIMES BOMBING

The *Los Angeles Times* bombing took place on October 1, 1910, and was an enormous setback for the cause of organized labor during the **Progressive Era**. It was the climactic event in the "Forty Years War," a struggle between Los Angeles labor and the virulently anti-union business community. At its center was a long-simmering dispute between publisher Harrison Gray Otis and the International Typographical Union (ITU). In 1890, Otis **locked out** union printers at the *Los Angeles Times*, hired **scabs** from Kansas City, and instituted a non-union policy destined to hold until the 1960s. Otis and the *Times* inspired the local **open-shop** movement, and Otis used his paper to smear the union movement in general. He was also influential in forming the Merchants and Manufacturers Association (MMA), a citywide open-shop consortium.

To the north, San Francisco was an organized labor stronghold, and the Union Labor Party was an important force in local politics. The events in Los Angeles alarmed San Francisco activists, who, by 1910, felt their own power threatened by gathering open-shop ideals emanating from the south. San Franciscans launched a concerted effort to organize Los Angelinos.

That effort would soon be complicated by events brewing far to the east in Indianapolis, where the International Association of Bridge and Structural Iron Workers (BSIW), led by union secretary-treasurer John J. McNamara, was also embroiled in open-shop struggles. The BSIW organizational efforts foundered, and only in Chicago and San Francisco was it successful in fending off the anti-union challenges of the **National Association of Manufacturers** and the Erectors of Structural Steel, a manufacturers' trade organization. As the disputes grew more intense, a series of dynamite explosions rocked several facilities connected with contractors with which the BSIW was in dispute. The bombings came at a time of already heightened tension in the wake of the assassination of President William McKinley in 1901. His killer, Leon Czolgosz, was an **anarchist**, and a series of anarchist assassinations and bombings plagued the United States and other industrial nations during the late 19th and early 20th centuries. Employers hired the Burns Detective Agency, a notorious union-breaking organization, to investigate the bombing of construction sites, and it linked the BSIW—not anarchists—to these bombings. The BSIW countered that the explosions were the work of **agent provocateurs** seeking to discredit the union movement.

In the early morning of October 1, a bomb exploded in an alley behind the offices of the *Los Angeles Times*. The explosion ruptured a gas line, setting off a catastrophic fire in which 21 men died and more than 100 individuals were injured. Unexploded bombs were discovered outside the Otis home, as well as the home of MMA secretary Felix Zeehandler. A nationwide investigation headed by detective William Burns narrowed its focus to James McNamara, brother of the BSIW secretary-treasurer, and to organized crime figures Ortie McManigal and David Kaplan, who were purportedly associated with the San Francisco labor movement. On Christmas Day, the Llewellyn Iron Works in Los Angeles suffered a bomb explosion. By then, McManigal and James McNamara were suspects in the *Times* bombing, but Burns withheld his accusations of them, as he hoped to link the pair to John McNamara and the BSIW. In April 1911, McManigal and James McNamara were taken into custody for allegedly attempting to blow up a Detroit railroad station. An interrogation of McManigal prompted the arrest of John McNamara as well, and all three were extradited to Los Angeles.

The impending trial came at an inopportune time for reformers. It was slated for December 1911, coinciding with a municipal election in which **Socialist** candidate Job Harriman, a labor attorney with a minor connection to the McNamara defense team, was favored to become the new mayor of Los Angeles. Organized labor, including the **American Federation of Labor** (AFL), threw its support to the McNamaras and insisted that they were being made the scapegoats in an elaborate plan to smear unions and to defeat reform candidate Harriman. Socialist leader **Eugene Debs** went so far as to blame Otis for planting the bomb himself. Business and political leaders responded by whipping up fear and equating votes for Harriman with support for the McNamaras. Needless to say, the *Los Angeles Times* took that position. The paper urged voters to throw their support to the incumbent Democratic mayor, George Alexander, and Los Angeles businesses gave considerable financial support to Alexander.

As the political maneuvering took place, lead defense attorney Clarence Darrow came to the shocking realization that his clients were guilty as charged. He sought a plea bargain in advance of the trial and enlisted the aid of muckraker journalist Lincoln Steffens. The AFL and Steffens quickly switched tactics and publicized the possibility that Otis had provoked the bombings through his vicious assaults on organized labor and his tyrannical behavior. This effort worked to some degree, as the *Times* found itself faced with bad publicity. Steffens was able to enlist the paper's tacit support for lighter sentences than might have been expected given the enormity of the crimes in question. On December 1, 1911, just four days before the municipal election, John McNamara pleaded guilty to conspiracy to bomb the Llewellyn plant and was sentenced to 15 years in prison. His brother James admitted guilt in the *Los Angeles Times* dynamiting and received a life sentence.

The McNamara case was a disaster for organized labor. It came at a time in which Progressive Era courts had already delivered stinging legal defeats. It also greatly damaged AFL efforts to pass itself off as a respectable alternative to the supposedly more radical **Industrial Workers of the World**. Although the McNamaras were promptly denounced as having betrayed organized labor, their crimes nonetheless deterred would-be support from numerous other reformers. Harriman lost his mayoral bid and, though the Socialist Party elected three assemblymen, it never regained its pre-bombing strength. Los Angeles remained an open-shop city until New Deal labor reforms were implemented in the 1930s, and union efforts were weakened in San Francisco.

Suggested Reading

Graham Adams, Jr., *Age of Industrial Violence, 1910–1913*. 1966; William Burns, *Masked War*, 1913; W. W. Robinson, *Bombs and Bribery: The Story of the McNamara and Darrow Trials Following the Dynamiting in 1910 of the Los Angeles Times Building*, 1969; Grace Stimson, *Rise of the Labor Movement in Los Angeles*, 1955.

LOWELL FEMALE LABOR REFORM ASSOCIATION

The Lowell Female Labor Reform Association (LFLRA) formed in 1844 and is often regarded as the first significant women's labor organization in U.S. history. Although women had organized in unions prior to the LFLRA and the group's lifespan was relatively brief, the LFLRA certainly organized women on a scale that surpassed earlier efforts. It also pioneered in what came to be called "women's organizing models"—that is, strategies for bringing women into labor unions that appealed directly to women's interests rather than asking women to subordinate their desires and issues to those of organizations controlled by men.

The LFLRA's guiding light was **Sarah Bagley**, who served as its first president, and the organization came to life in the wake of deteriorating conditions in Lowell, Massachusetts. The textile city began mill operations in 1826 and sought to merge the interests of investment **capitalists** with a vision of a utopian workplace. Lowell's main workforce consisted of single New England farm girls, who were targeted as employees because they were considered the least valuable laborers in the **agrarian**-based household economy that still dominated the region. To make Lowell acceptable within the **paternalist** culture of the day, the community's planners built an industrial city infused with educational and cultural enrichment opportunities and imposed strict regulations aimed at creating a moral environment. For example, boarding houses were constructed and headed by older matrons, who were expected to keep watch on the morals of residents and report any expected transgressions to company officials. In addition to workplace infractions, women could lose their jobs for offenses such as failure to attend church or suspicion of sexual impropriety. Lowell mill hands worked long hours for low **wages**, but the first decade of the Lowell experiment went fairly well. Lowell was an attractive city with wide streets, sylvan parks, and landscaped factories. It also provided social and cultural opportunities that would have been unthinkable for young women in their home villages. Lowell women even produced—with company backing—their own literary journal journals, the *Lowell Offering*.

Low wages and long hours remained a constant concern, however, and **strikes** in 1834 and again in 1836 took the sheen off Lowell's public image.

The 1836 strike by more than 1,500 Lowell women was particularly unpleasant, with workers complaining of wage slavery and much of the New England public agreeing that they were ill treated. The Panic of 1837 dealt a severe blow to Lowell's utopian pretensions. Faced with declining profit margins, Lowell Associates, the investment consortium that owned the mills, slashed wages and cut capital expenditures in the city. Mill owners also began hiring more Irish **immigrants**, who commanded lower wages than native-born women. Lowell women increased their complaints of **speedups, stretch-outs**, long hours, low wages, and workplace abuses. The atmosphere in Lowell was already seething when Massachusetts debated a 10-hour workday bill in 1844. Lowell officials responded to the bill by insisting they would dock workers' pay if the bill passed to make the pay rate reflect the loss of production involved in moving from a 12-hour to a 10-hour workday. Bagley and several other operatives formed the LFLRA in December 1844 to redress issues related to wages and to press for a 10-hour workday without wage cuts. Within a month, the LFLRA had more than 600 members. Bagley also started the Industrial Reform Lyceum to publicize grievances and expanded the LFLRA to other New England textile towns. Furthermore, she affiliated the LFLRA with the New England Workingmen's Association (NEWA), a regional expression of the **Workingmen's movement**.

Bagley's early efforts were impressive. Her testimony before the Massachusetts legislature did much to publicize conditions in Lowell, and Bagley and others also effectively used the NEWA's *Voice of Industry* newspaper to keep awareness of their plight alive. Bagley even briefly edited the paper. Lowell reduced its workday by half an hour, and New Hampshire enacted a 10-hour bill in 1847. Although the 10-hour bill failed in Massachusetts, LFLRA efforts did help unseat one of the bill's most ardent critics in 1845.

The LFLRA did not survive, however. The Workingmen's movement was already in the throes of dissolution by the time Bagley sought an alliance with the NEWA. Moreover, her strident personality and interest in politics were deemed inappropriate and perhaps ideologically dangerous during a period in which proscribed gender roles were the order of the day and women were thought to be endowed by nature to assume domestic, but not public, duties. Bagley clashed with *Voice of Industry* staff, was fired in 1846, and left Lowell. The LFLRA struggled through 1847 and dissolved in early 1848. It was not until 1853 that Lowell's workday shrank to 11 hours, by which time the city had become a typical industrial city stripped of social reform trappings and its workforce contained more immigrants than New England farm girls.

Suggested Reading

Mary H. Blewett, *We Will Rise in Our Might: Workingwomen's Voices from 19th-Century New England*, 1991; Thomas Dublin, *Women at Work: The Transformation of Work and Community in Lowell, Massachusetts, 1826–1860*, 1979; Tom Juravich, James Green, and William Hartford, *Commonwealth of Toil*, 1996.

LOWELL TEXTILE STRIKES. *See* Lowell Female Labor Reform Association.

LUDDITES. *See* Automation.

LUDLOW MASSACRE

The Ludlow Massacre occurred on April 20, 1914, and is generally regarded as one of the most egregious examples of raw violence directed at laboring people at the hands of organized **capitalism**. Workers at the Colorado Fuel and Iron Company (CF&I), a concern owned by the Rockefeller family, had been on **strike** since September 1913 in response to the company's **open-shop** efforts. Strikers were directed by the **United Mine Workers of America** (UMWA), which sought to make inroads in Colorado, a state notorious for resisting unionization efforts and one that was in the midst of events collectively known as the **Colorado labor wars**.

Ludlow was a **company town** in which miners lived in company-owned houses, were required to shop at the company store, were paid in scrip (a privately printed currency redeemable only at the company store), and were policed by a private company-controlled police force. Some 1,200 miners struck the CF&I in hopes of gaining union recognition and of bettering their lives. It was a risky move, as Ludlow was quite isolated. Many of the workers were promptly evicted from their company-owned homes and were forced to build hastily erected tent colonies on the outskirts of the town. The CF&I made a full display of force by hiring additional and heavily armed private deputies, and by convincing Colorado authorities to activate the state militia. Families forced to endure life in the tent colony and the ravages of a bitter Colorado winter faced constant harassment from guards and the militia, including threats to machine-gun the colony. Camp dwellers took precautions, including the digging of pits into which women and children could flee if gunfire erupted.

The threats became a horrifying reality immediately following Easter Sunday. On Monday morning, troops set fire to the occupied tents and sprayed machine-gun fire into the camp. Nineteen people, including 12 children, were killed in the resulting massacre. Four women and 11 children asphyxiated when burning tents trapped them in a pit dug to protect them. At least three captured miners were summarily executed by troops.

The outrage at Ludlow touched off 10 days of open warfare between strikers and the militia in which additional lives were lost, including those of three company guards and one Colorado National Guardsman. President Woodrow Wilson sent federal troops to restore order in the southern Colorado coalfield, but infuriated miners continued to attack and destroy mine properties long after the immediate crisis had passed. The UMWA soldiered on and violent conflict continued in the coal field through December, when the UMWA ran out of money and was forced to call off the strike. The exact number of deaths associated with the open warfare is unknown; estimates range from 69 to nearly 200. Approximately 400 miners would be arrested, many of them charged with murder raps that were later dismissed.

The Ludlow massacre attracted media attention. Newspapers of the day generally sided with organized capital, but the deaths of unarmed women and children led several to demand that John D. Rockefeller, Jr., be held accountable for the carnage. In the Congressional hearings that ensued, Rockefeller appeared defiant, unrepentant, and arrogant. He insisted that the CF&I was defending the essential rights of the American worker to freedom of contract just as surely as the patriots of the American Revolution had fought for liberty. Rockefeller even sought to deny that a massacre had occurred and claimed that two small squads of militia were merely defending themselves against a hostile tent colony. The regrettable loss of life, Rockefeller insisted, was due to outside union agitators seeking to deny workers their individual freedom, and was not the fault of the "defenders of property." Rockefeller's callous testimony shocked the nation almost as much as the massacre itself, and newspapers such as the *New York Times* printed lurid accounts of women and children dying "like trapped rats" in fire-scarred pits. In like fashion, photographs of the horrors of Ludlow repulsed the nation. Writer Upton Sinclair publicly announced his intention to see Rockefeller indicted for murder, and protests erupted throughout the nation in cities such as New York, Chicago, and San Francisco, where large immigrant populations sympathized with the largely Italian, Greek, and eastern European miners. The *New York World* revealed the treachery of the militia in the killing of Louis Tikas, a leader of the miners, who attempted to negotiate safety for women and children under the protection of a white flag. Tikas was lured to the militia line, then beaten and shot in cold blood.

Rockefeller was stung by the charges emanating from the usually compliant press and took steps to shore up his financial interests. He hired publicist Ivy L. Lee and former Canadian Prime Minister William Lyon McKenzie-King to rehabilitate the Rockefeller family image. From those efforts came the Colorado Plan of Industrial Representation, a system of **paternalist** benefits and a **company union**. These practices prevailed in the Colorado coalfields for many years following Ludlow, until the UMWA regained its strength and organized the state's coal miners.

Suggested Reading

Howard M. Gitelman, *Legacy of the Ludlow Massacre: A Chapter in American Industrial Relations*, 1988; Scott Martelle, *Blood Passion: The Ludlow Massacre and Class War in the American West*, 2007; Zeese Papanikolas, *Buried Unsung: Louis Tikas and the Ludlow Massacre*, 1982.

LYNN SHOE STRIKE OF 1860

The Lynn shoe strike of 1860 was an inter-gender work stoppage that ultimately collapsed, in part because its participants failed to retain their ideals. It reached an ambiguous conclusion that was in keeping with an industry that was in flux.

For much of the 19th century, Lynn, Massachusetts, led the nation in footwear production and was known as "Shoe City." By mid-century, however, many of its workers had become restive. This was especially so among **master craftsmen**, who observed the gradual but inexorable deskilling of shoemaking occasioned by the introduction of machinery and a shift toward factory production. The increased precision and output of the sewing machine created shoes that were more rapidly produced and whose overall quality was more uniform. In 1860, shoemakers found themselves in the midst of changes that would increase footwear production from 4,478,700 pairs in 1850 to more than 11 million pairs in 1870. The decline in artisanal production methods resulted in a loss of jobs for skilled workers in favor of semiskilled and unskilled machine tenders. Furthermore, the brutal 10-hour days the workers were forced to work created an atmosphere that was both uncomfortable and unjust. Coupled with recurrent repressions (1852, 1855, 1857, and 1859) that led to massive **wage** cuts, conditions were ripe for what would later be dubbed the Great Shoemaker's Strike.

The Panic of 1857 served as the immediate catalyst for the strike. The recession was brief, but more than 5,000 businesses failed, among them several Lynn shoe manufacturers. Moreover, as prices fell, wages were slashed and recovered far more slowly than shoe prices and profits. In 1859, Lynn workers formed the Journeymen Cordwainers' Mutual Benefit Society. The group issued a bill of wages and pledged to strike until their employers signed the bill. On February 22, 1860—the birthday of George Washington—thousands of shoemakers stayed away from work and marched for their rights. Within days the strike had spread to shoemakers in nearby towns such as Haverhill, Marblehead, Natick, and Newburyport. Between 20,000 and 25,000 workers eventually struck their employers.

Alonzo Draper of the newly christened Lynn Mechanics' Association led actions within Lynn. The strike committee sought, in vain, to maintain public order. During the very first march, strikers skirmished with expressmen, who transported materials to other locales to be finished. Lynn police were charged with preserving public decorum. Draper continually exhorted that strikers needed to conduct peaceful protests and engage in moral behavior lest they cripple the strike's effectiveness. To enhance the appearance of high moral principles, the Lynn strike committee debated the wisdom of enlisting support from women. After considerable debate, the Lynn strike committee agreed to bring women into the strike. It was not out of keeping to involve women in the strike, as many had long been involved in the shoemaking process. Many women took in **homework** related to finishing shoes. For the most part, though, Draper and the committee initially felt that women's presence would enhance the respectability of male workers by reinforcing widely held middle-class notions that women's primary social roles lay in maintaining order in their households and in supporting the ambitions of their husbands.

Draper soon discovered that not at all women agreed with those beliefs. Although women stitchers and shoebinders voted to strike, a faction of single women with fewer connections to **family wage** ideals touched off contentious debate over what women should demand. Led by Clara H. Brown, the workingwomen believed whole-heartedly that increasing the wages of women was equally important as increasing the wages of workingmen. Brown soon clashed with Mary Damon, who advocated that women should support their husbands and should expend their energies battling for an increase in male wages.

The constant infighting within the strike committee threatened women's participation in the movement. When women voted to enact a high wage list for workingwomen as well, they were threatened with banishment from a March 7 parade, and were finally allowed to participate only when they reversed course in favor of supporting male pay rates. The parade saw as many as 10,000 strike supporters parade through Lynn, with women holding banners with messages such as "American Ladies Will Not Be Slaves." The March 7 event proved to be the strike's zenith. Within weeks, workers began to return to their jobs with only vague promises of a wage increase. Moreover, police and militia roamed the streets to make certain there was no disruption of shipping, which made it easy for manufacturers to have shoes completed elsewhere. For their part, women failed to establish the principle that female wages deserved equal attention to those of men. They saw a continuation of the family wage and, therefore, remained subservient monetarily to their male counterparts.

By April, the strike was a spent force and workers quietly returned to their jobs. Most won small pay increases, but employers did not grant union recognition. Ultimately, the Lynn shoe strike of 1860 failed to address the concerns of artisan labor. The coming **Civil War** delayed faster implementation of machinery within the industry, but the war's end quickly transformed shoemakers into industrial workers. Soon few shoemakers could bargain based on their skills, and they found themselves subservient to employers with the ability to buy their labor.

Suggested Reading

Mary H. Blewett, *Men, Women, and Work: Class, Gender, and Protest in the New England Shoe Industry, 1780–1910*, 1988; Alan Dawley, *Class and Community: The Industrial Revolution in Lynn, Twenty-Fifth Anniversary Edition*, 2000; Paul G. Faler, *Mechanics and Manufacturers in the Early Industrial Revolution: Lynn Massachusetts, 1780–1860*, 1981.